by the same author
THE BROTHERS

BILLIONAIRE

The Life and Times of
Sir James Goldsmith

IVAN FALLON

ARROW

Arrow Books Limited
20 Vauxhall Bridge Road, London SW1V 2SA

An imprint of Random House UK Ltd

London Melbourne Sydney Auckland Johannesburg
and agencies throughout the world

First published by Hutchinson in 1991
This edition published in 1992 by Arrow Books

1 3 5 7 9 10 8 6 4 2

Printed and bound in Great Britain by
Cox & Wyman Ltd, Reading, Berkshire

ISBN 0 09 974640 9

Contents

List of Illustrations

Teddy and Jimmy with the major-domo of the Hotel de Paris *(Family album)*.
Teddy and Jimmy with their parents *(Family album)*.
Jimmy and his first wife, Isabel Patino *(Popperfoto)*.
Jimmy and Frank Goldsmith win custody of Isabel *(Planet News Ltd)*.
Jimmy, aged 21, during the custody battle *(Planet News Ltd)*.
Ginette Lery *(Topham)*.
Goldsmith with his third wife, Lady Annabel, and Lady Falkender *(Hulton Deutsch collection)*.
Goldsmith closes *Now!* magazine *(Times Newspapers)*.
With Annabel and their three children in Spain *(Family album)*.
Laure Boulay de la Meurthe and Jimmy Goldsmith *(Dafydd Jones)*.
Time magazine's portrait as 'The Lucky Gambler' *(Times Newspapers)*.
Goldsmith with Jacob Rothschild and Kerry Packer *(James Morgan)*.
Cuixmala *(Ivan Fallon)*.
Tycoon in retirement *(Ivan Fallon)*.

Acknowledgements

Before beginning this book, I wrote to Sir James Goldsmith saying I had
been commissioned by Hutchinson to write his biography. He had just
announced his £13 billion bid for BAT Industries, and was very much in
the news. To do the book properly, I needed access not only to him, but to
his family, his friends and his business associates. Few, if any of them,
would talk to me if Goldsmith pulled down the shutters. Sir James too had
a reputation as an active litigant, and I did not want to spend years fighting
my way through the courts towards an objective which, without some form
of co-operation from him, would be unsatisfactory anyway. I explained
that any book I would write would undoubtedly contain material and
comment that would be disagreeable to him. It would also be entirely my
book – it would not be an 'approved' biography. He would not be able to
alter a word. Would he assist me on that basis?

I had known Goldsmith for nearly twenty years, mostly in a professional
capacity. I had first interviewed him in 1971 at his home in Regent's Park
during his bid for Allied Suppliers; I had seen him irregularly during the
1970s at press conferences or over lunch, as he became a major figure on
the British and French financial stage. As a financial journalist I had
covered his takeovers, his move into Slater Walker, his attempts to
become a newspaper baron, the launch of *Now!* magazine, and much else.
We had our differences, acted out in the columns of the *Sunday Telegraph*
where I was City Editor. At the end of an acrimonious exchange of letters,
he sent me a note suggesting we have dinner next time he was in London.
In 1985 he sent me a copy of the first volume of his privately printed
Counter Culture, containing some of his speeches and articles. He had
hand-written a little note at the front: 'I enjoyed our exchange of letters
and hope we will meet again.' From then on I would occasionally ring him,

in New York or Mexico usually, to hear his views on the world stock markets, the state of the economy – or just for a chat. But I was still unsure how he would react to his life history being examined, without any control over the finished product.

Within minutes of receiving my letter, Goldsmith rang. 'You must see anyone you like, write what you like,' he said. He would set no conditions and put no obstacles in my path. Whenever I was ready to see him, he would be available. Over the next eighteen months, I spent many hours with him: in Mexico, at his amazing house on the coast; in Paris, either at his home in the Rue Monsieur or his restaurant, the Laurent; in London, either in St James's Place, or at his home in Richmond. During that time, I interviewed many of his friends, former colleagues and family – as well as some enemies, employees, business partners and disinterested observers. His brother Teddy unearthed for me the Goldsmith family scrapbooks, volumes of material carefully kept by the Goldsmith parents, Major Frank Goldsmith and his French wife Marcelle. Jimmy I believe did not know of their existence, and Teddy had never read them. 'Much of the early history is new to me,' Jimmy told me after I sent him an early draft.

Teddy had privately published a history of the Jewish families of Frankfurt, which included the Goldsmiths, and Jimmy some years ago commissioned a Mrs Gladstone to prepare a book, never published, on the family history. I liberally took material from both. Fortunately, there is abundant information available on the Jewish families of the Frankfurt ghetto, not least in the many books written on the Rothschilds.

At the end of two years I sent Goldsmith a draft manuscript which he read in a single long night. A few days later he sent me many pages of typewritten notes. 'As I said, I will comment on the facts,' he said. 'For the sake of accuracy, my comments will cover even trivial points of no significance.' He made no attempt to persuade me to change or alter any of the passages which he must have found offensive or painful. Only once or twice did he go beyond the facts, as at the end of the chapter on Isabel where he commented: 'There are moments, usually brief, in this rather squalid worldly existence, which have beauty and which are pure. At such times, there is a feeling of certainty – all is black and white and forever. Those who have never been fortunate enough to be touched by such emotions no doubt find them hard to understand or even resent their very existence. I think that this chapter reflects the views of such people.' I am still not sure whether this referred to the author, or to my sources. On the *Private Eye* affair, he simply remarked that he felt differently to me about it.

He also added a note towards the end pointing out what he obviously felt was a major difference of outlook:

'One of the difficulties is that, quite naturally, you see me through English eyes, as part of the English culture and as though I were an Englishman. In many respects I am. I am a deep admirer of the qualities that I perceive in British life – justice being the foremost. But in reality, when you dig a little deeper, you find that I am half Jew and half Auvergnat. So just as I expect you to judge me by British standards, you should expect me to react according to my own and different standards. I do not suggest that they are better, nor that they are worse – only that they are different.' He added a handwritten postscript to the typed note: 'I have never considered that I have ever lived in England in a permanent sense.'

Because Jimmy Goldsmith's life has been lived so much in the public domain, there are voluminous press cuttings on him, which are sometimes, because they are contemporary accounts, at least as useful as interviews. But this book is largely based on the many interviews I carried out, laboriously transcribed by my family and my researchers, on the hundreds of takeover documents and accounts Goldsmith has issued over the years, and on other documents.

I am particularly grateful to Sir James Goldsmith not just for his time, but for his courtesy. I am also grateful to Lady Annabel, to Madame Ginette Goldsmith, and to Isabel, Teddy, Manes and other members of the family. Claude Henry Leconte and Maurice Lignon were invaluable sources on the early business days in France, and John Aspinall and Digby Neave provided many anecdotes. Selim Zilkha, John Tigrett, Charles Hambro, Roland Franklin, Jim Slater, Lord Rothschild, Jim Wood, Madame Gilberte Beaux, Al Dunlap and many others helped me with the more mature business deals. Brian Crozier and Chapman Pincher told me about spies, and Communist infiltration. Geoffrey Wansell, who had written a previous biography of Goldsmith (which Goldsmith told me was a 'reliable' source) generously allowed me to quote from his interviews, including those with Marcelle Goldsmith whom he saw before she died. Without the assistance of my old book-writing partner and colleague, James Srodes, I could not have covered the ground in America.

I am deeply indebted to my own researchers and helpers: James Gray, who did much of the work on the historical background, my daughters Tania and Lara who transcribed many of the interviews, and my wife Sue who patiently organised them all.

Finally, a special note of thanks to my editors: to Richard Cohen who started me on this venture, to Paul Sidey with whom I finished, and to Gail Rebuck for her enthusiasm.

I

Almost a Rothschild

The Goldsmiths – or Goldschmidts as they then were – came out of the same ghetto in Frankfurt-am-Main as the Rothschilds, the Wertheims, the Bischoffsheims, the Oppenheimers, the Salomons and many of the other leading nineteenth-century European banking families. The Rothschilds were among the eleven Jewish families moved into the ghetto by the city fathers in 1460 as part of an exercise intended as separate development rather than human degradation, although it did not work that way for long. The forebears of Sir James Goldsmith arrived nearly 60 years later, driven from their native Nuremburg by the pogroms of the Holy Roman Empire and the confiscation of their property.

The genealogy of most families, other than the most ancient aristocratic ones, is difficult to trace. For some of the old Jewish families of Europe it is almost impossible. They were treated everywhere as foreigners, and given the name of the last town they lived in – for instance when the Goldschmidt family, along with all the other Jewish families, was expelled from Frankfurt in 1641, one branch of the family became Goldschmidt-Kassel, the other Goldschmidt-Hamel after the two Westphalian towns where they lived for a time. The use of patronymics only became established in the mid-eighteenth century, and it was only when Napoleon, who emancipated 15,000 German Jews in 1807, issued an edict, that Jews adopted hereditary surnames for the first time.

Nonetheless, the Frankfurt Jews kept detailed records of their dealings, their taxes and their ceremonies. It was also a tight, contained community, so it is possible to go back nearly 500 years in the Goldsmith history with some degree of certainty. There is indeed a surprisingly detailed record of the Frankfurt Jews. For the best part of four centuries the fortunes of the various families inside the ghetto, including the

I

Rothschilds and the Goldschmidts, would interweave and intertwine. The Rothschilds may now be the most famous family to emerge from the Frankfurt Jewish community, but for most of that time they were just another family, sometimes doing better than the Goldschmidts or the others, sometimes less well, depending on the energy and skill of that particular generation. The ascendancy of the Rothschilds only took place in the early nineteenth century with the extraordinary success of young Nathan in London and his brothers in Europe, and until then the history of the Rothschilds is not so very different from that of the Goldschmidts. The tie between the Goldschmidts and the Rothschilds still survives, and would display itself most spectacularly to the world in 1989 when Sir James Goldsmith and Jacob Rothschild, modern scions of those same Frankfurt ghetto forebears, launched the biggest takeover bid the world had ever seen.

The Goldsmith links with the ghetto, and with the Rothschilds, are important because even today, a hundred years after the foetid area of Frankfurt was dismantled and nearly 50 years since its remains were blasted away by American bombers, its influence, culture and ties go on, sometimes consciously, mostly subconsciously, playing no small part in shaping some of the largest corporate deals of recent years. Although the confident, worldly billionaire Jimmy Goldsmith, with his fine house, his private jets, yachts and his women may seem a million miles away, he is in fact only a generation away from Frankfurt. His father was born in that same tight Frankfurt Jewish community (although by that stage they had moved out of the ghetto to live in some style outside), his great-uncle married the last of the Frankfurt Rothschilds (and changed his name to Goldschmidt-Rothschild), and Jimmy Goldsmith himself learned early in life some of the pride and bitterness of that inheritance.

Let us start, therefore, the story of one of the most remarkable businessmen of the twentieth century in the ghetto in Frankfurt, which in its original conception had relatively modest overtones of the racial discrimination and prejudice which would later attach to it. There had, since medieval times, been segregated quarters of cities where Jews were compelled to live, but until the Lateran Council of 1179, which prohibited 'true believers' even from lodging amongst infidels, they had no legal force. Indeed, in many places the Jews welcomed their own areas, seeing them as a social expression of Jewish solidarity, although they equally represented the aversion of the Gentiles towards them. The segregated quarters were relatively open, where Jews and Gentiles were free to move around. Through much of the Middle Ages Jews were acceptable enough in many societies; they strictly observed their own Talmudic law, and were generally far better educated – and better behaved – than the largely illiterate populations among whom they lived. But acceptance was always fragile. In th fourteenth century Jews, in the absence of another scapegoat, were blamed for spreading the Black Death of 1348 and were massacred in their thousands. Those who survived fled mostly to Poland. Deprived of 'their' Jews, and therefore of a key commercial element, the towns and principalities invited them back – but with a difference. They were to be segregated in closed quarters, which were commonly known as 'ghettos' after the Italian word *borghetto* for the Jewish quarter in Venice beside the gunpowder magazine and arsenal. In Frankfurt the Jewish community fared better than in other cities. Although they were not precisely welcomed, their commercial and craft skills were seen as an asset to the prosperous city on the river Main.

The ghetto in Frankfurt, which contained the entire Jewish population of the area, was not at all an uncomfortable place, at least not at the beginning. The Jews built themselves broadfronted houses, were protected from the excesses meted out to other Jewish communities by the burghers, and got on with their lives in relative peace and prosperity. They had their own independent corporation, with their own officials, guilds, amusements and even courts. Jews were forbidden to own real estate, but they were protected from exploitation by Gentile landlords. They were enclosed behind walls and gates, locked at night and on church festivals – for instance, no Jews were allowed out over Holy Week. Outside, and sometimes inside, Jews wore distinctive badges. Frankfurt and Prague would develop as the most important Jewish ghettos in northern Europe, and Avignon, Rome and Venice in the south. In 1555 Pope Paul IV began to enforce, as a matter of formal law, the principles of the medieval segregation.

Some 30 or so years before that, however, the first Goldschmidt found his way to Frankfurt, attracted by the relative degree of freedom and independence in the community. Mosche (or Moses) was suddenly there in 1521, according to the records.

Where did he come from? And who was he? Before his appearance there is no record of the name in the Christian tax-lists, nor any mention in Jewish records, or on Jewish gravestones. Moses almost certainly came from Nuremburg, trekking south, along with many other Jews, down the Neckar valley, through towns such as Esslingen, Weinsberg and Bopfingen and eventually into the Rhine valley and Frankfurt. His house, along with those of all the other Jews, would have been confiscated around

1500, so the journey probably took 20 years, not unusual for a man who had nowhere in particular to go. It is possible, however, that he arrived in Frankfurt earlier: Moses almost certainly had the name Moses Itzig von Bopfingen, who lived at a house in the ghetto called the Weisse Rose (White Rose) in 1506, and this may also be the same Moses von Schaffhausen, whose sons were authorised to become goldsmith apprentices by the Nuremburg City Council in 1490, a time of relative peace in that city when there was a big increase in Jewish artisans.

At any rate, he was in Frankfurt in 1521, middle-aged, and obviously skilled in the art of goldsmithing, for he had an apparently prosperous business and a new name: Moses von Schaffhausen (or von Bopfingen) became Moses Goldschmidt. He moved into a house on the west side of the one large street in the ghetto, the Judengasse, and that same house, known as the Goldener Schwan (Golden Swan), remained in the Goldschmidt family until 1883.

Moses must have seen the ghetto as a welcome haven after Nuremburg; there were only 32 houses at the time, with fewer than 300 inhabitants, and he could do business outside in the city even if he could not live there. Jews could only enter Frankfurt on business; the city was closed to them entirely on Sundays, their wives and children forbidden altogether from the shops and parks. The city fathers when they created the ghetto may not have thought they were imposing a policy of *apartheid* out of prejudice, but the very separateness of the cultures and races began to create exactly that in the years after Moses' arrival.

Nevertheless, succeeding generations of Rothschilds and Goldschmidts who grew up, lived and died in the ghetto must have felt themselves better off than their more openly persecuted brethren in other European cities. As the centuries passed, however, the conditions in the ghetto deteriorated. The population, swollen by fresh arrivals, inevitably grew, and the area of the ghetto, finite and unexpandable, did not. There was no room to build laterally, so the houses grew vertically. By the middle of the eighteenth century the ghetto contained 3,000 people in only 200 houses, and the houses, including that of the Goldsmiths and the one with the Red Shield whose inhabitants were named Rothschild after it, had long been subdivided again and again, with every spare inch of space filled. In 1795 a foreign visitor, appalled by what he witnessed even in an age where there was much overcrowding and great poverty in cities all over Europe, noted: 'Up to the roof every nook and cranny was filled with narrow rooms whose inhabitants consider themselves lucky when they can leave their dingy hole and get a breath of fresh air out on their dirty and damp street.'

Around it the Gentile city of Frankfurt presented a greater and greater contrast. In the seventeenth and eighteenth centuries it prospered mightily, and its population grew. Soon its spacious residential quarters crept right up to the walls of the ghetto, and the outside world began to encroach on life in the ghetto very directly. New building regulations for Jews, passed in 1702, had decreed: 'So that it will be impossible to see the houses of Christians [the side windows of the Jews] shall be walled in and pasted over.' Their view therefore was limited to the Judengasse, consisting of cramped marketstalls, open sewers and a throng of women in their blue-black striped veils and men in the hats and kaftans prescribed by law. The street was closed at both ends, access strictly controlled both by the Rat (the city council) and by the Jews themselves who had long learned the need to protect their own inhabitants.

It was an existence that bred prejudice, never too far beneath the surface. The smell of the ghetto was pervasive and clung to the clothes of the Jews on their rare incursions into the rest of the city, marking them as still more different to the Frankfurt inhabitants. Originally prosperous enough, they at times appeared so poor and degraded that they seemed to confirm the belief of their Christian neighbours that they belonged to a lower form of animal existence. Just as crucially, they were debarred from membership by the restrictive practices of the craft guilds. But, by an odd irony, the medieval Roman Catholic church prohibited its own brethren from the ancient practice of usury, and so to money lending and trading the Jews turned increasingly as the principal outlet for their commercial acumen – and their only outlet from life in the ghetto. That of course simply reinforced the prejudice: if a Jew did manage, as many of them did, to prosper, it was simply seen as confirmation that he was in league with the devil, bleeding honest Christians who had to work hard for their cash.

From the earliest days of the ghetto, however, it *was* possible to prosper – and the Goldschmidts did. Moses died in 1531 and by that stage the family was already one of the better-off in the community. His son Isaak, already rich enough, married an even richer widow in 1553 and three years later Isaak's capital was estimated at 12,700 guilders, a considerable fortune in that day. Joseph Goldschmidt was, however, the most famous of the family. Probably Moses' grandson, he lived in the Golden Swan and was known from 1550 onwards as the 'modest Jew Joseph'. He was, according to the histories of the ghetto, the most eminent of the Jewish financiers of the sixteenth century, far more so than any of the Rothschilds. The city of Frankfurt was badly in debt, and Joseph Goldschmidt was one of the few financiers the senate trusted. His history is well documented and provides a picture of the role of the Jewish financiers at that time. Some of Frankfurt's most noble families entrusted him with large amounts of money, and he in turn lent money to the Archbishop of Cologne (who failed to repay it), among others. He had links with all the great financiers of the time, and acted as broker for a number of German princes, including the Landgrave of Hesse, Counts Johann and Ludwig of Nassau-Dillenberg and many others. A financial crash in the 1560s, plus the unwillingness of many of his aristocratic creditors to repay him, brought him down. In 1564 the Emperor Maximilian ordered the Frankfurt Council to close his business, and he was arrested in November the following year, charged with forgery and embezzlement. Questioned under torture, Joseph declared assets of 101,935 guilders and debts of 162,238 guilders, and the size of these figures is said to have come as a great shock to the people of Frankfurt. The accusations about and investigations into Joseph's tangled affairs went on until well after his death in 1572. Joseph's name is the only Jewish one to appear in the history of sixteenth-century finance, and the scandal and legal trials that surrounded him provide a picture of the importance and growth of Frankfurt as a money market at the time.

In 1641 all the Jews of Frankfurt were expelled and the Goldschmidts took on the additional names of the towns they settled in – Kassel (or Cassel) and Hamel. Later they drifted back again to Frankfurt when they were solemnly reinstated in all their previous privileges by imperial command, and given full compensation for their losses. Frankfurt would remain the main centre of the family until the end of the nineteenth century, but by the seventeenth century they had branched off into other parts of Germany, Holland and elsewhere, building a network of business connections across Europe. The spelling of the name varied from country to country: the Amsterdam branch, for instance, became Goldsmid. When Cromwell allowed Jews back into England, a Goldschmidt from Frankfurt soon arrived on the scene. There was also an Aaron Goldsmid, from Amsterdam, directly descended from the Frankfurt Goldschmidts, who moved to London in 1763 to found a finance business of that name. In Frankfurt the Goldschmidts and the Bischoffsheims intermarried to form one of the more significant of the banking houses, healthy, prosperous businesses run by men who every night went back to the miserable living conditions of the ghetto.

The records of the Frankfurt Jews record the assets of the family over the centuries: in 1585 the brothers and members of the firm of Moses and Lew from the houses of Korb and Wanne, 15,000 guilders; in 1620,

Beyfus from the Korb, 10,000 guilders, and so on over the centuries. In 1800 the combined assets of the leading Jewish families amounted to six million guilders, with the Speyer family owning 10 per cent, the Heis-Ellissons 5 per cent, the house of Haas, Kann and Stern 4.25 per cent and the Goldschmidts 4 per cent. At that stage they were richer than the Rothschilds who under Mayer Amschel Rothschild, who inherited a money changing and general trading business at 18, were already developing into an international merchant bank.

In 1789 came the event that was to alter dramatically the lives of the Jews of the Frankfurt ghetto: the French Revolution and the new law promulgated in Paris in 1791 which announced:

> The National Assembly, considering that the conditions requisite to be a French citizen . . . are fixed by the constitution, and that every man who, being duly qualified, takes the civic oath and engages to fulfil all the duties prescribed by the constitution, has a right to all the advantages it ensures; annuls all adjournments, restrictions, and exceptions, contained in the previous decrees, affecting individuals of the Jewish persuasion, who shall take the civic oath.

Of course, events in Paris in 1791 seemed a long way from the Judengasse in Frankfurt – until in April the following year Francis, the new Austrian emperor, allied with Prussia in an attempt to crush the upstart armies of the revolution and restore the divinely ordained Louis XVI to the throne. That prospect died on the fields of Valmy on 20 September when the republican army instead thrashed the advancing Prussians. Now it was the turn of the French armies to sweep south through Nice and Savoy, north to seize the Austrian Netherlands; under a brilliant general, Adam Philippe de Custine, a third army crossed the Rhine and captured Speyer, Worms, Mainz and, on 22 October, Frankfurt.

The French were thrown out again by Hessian and Prussian troops six weeks later, but for the Rothschilds, the Goldschmidts and other banking families the Napoleonic wars that followed were to provide a time of unprecedented opportunity. Life for them would never be the same again. Over the next 23 years of war, Frankfurt was to change hands – and sides – several times, the ghetto mostly an uninvolved observer of the armies marching in and out. Rothschild in particular had worked ceaselessly for 30 years to build up his contacts in the courts of Europe but, in times of peace, he had never succeeded in breaking through the barrier which separated the Jewish banker from the non-Jew. Kings and princes dealt with Jews, but only if they had no choice, and no Jew had succeeded in penetrating the inner circle of bankers who discounted bills and handled the business for the royal houses of Europe. Mayer Rothschild, however, had for years been on the threshold of it, offering more competitive terms, willing to take higher risks – and pressing, always pressing.

Now Rothschild's position was to change, with considerable significance for the future of the Goldschmidts and the other families. Mayer had gone to considerable pains to court, with only modest success, Prince William of Hanau, later William IX of Hesse-Kassel, one of the richest princes in the whole of Europe. William had bought coins and jewellery from Rothschild, but refused him full banking recognition. Now, as the French armies marched into central Europe, William desperately needed funds to raise and equip his armies, and found that his normal sources had dried up. Rothschild seized his chance, helping to raise a loan of 150,000 guilders in 1794. It was to be the first of many, not just for the Rothschilds but for the Goldschmidts and Bischoffsheims too. By the end of the Napoleonic wars the Rothschilds had become far and away the richest of the Frankfurt Jewish families, with Nathan, who only left the ghetto for London in 1798, already the most powerful banker in the world, richer even than the Barings described by the Duc de Richelieu in 1818 as one of the 'six great powers of Europe'.

The Goldschmidts would never again, at least until the present generation, match the power and glitter of the Rothschilds, but their links remained. Benedict Hayum Goldschmidt, Jimmy Goldsmith's great-grandfather, founded a bank in 1816 which prospered in the growing art of financing the industrial revolution taking place in every country in Europe, a bank not as powerful as the Rothschilds', but a significant one nonetheless. The freedom afforded to Jews in the City of London, which Nathan Rothschild made brilliant use of, also attracted Goldschmidts and Bischoffsheims: Solomon Goldschmidt was one of the more adventurous of the family which still had large numbers in the ghetto, joining his cousin Louis Bischoffsheim in 1846 to set up a bank off Throgmorton Street.

Nathan Mayer Rothschild, known henceforth as NM, was the first of his particular branch of the Rothschilds to leave Frankfurt. Asked 30 years later why he left, he replied, 'There was not room enough for all of us in Frankfurt', a disingenuous reply from an audacious raconteur who by that stage loved to embroider his own past. NM, of course, was one of five brothers, and only the third eldest at that. He was stifled by the narrow community and constantly at odds with his father and elder brothers whom he accused of having no imagination or sense of adventure, which was probably true enough but not altogether surprising in the circumstances. His elder brother Amschel, although later a very wealthy man who could have afforded to go anywhere, stayed in Frankfurt until he died aged 82. Although Goldschmidts had emigrated earlier, Jimmy Goldsmith's direct ancestors stayed on too, keeping close to the place they knew best and where again in the nineteenth century they were permitted a degree of freedom to carry on their businesses.

Just how wealthy some of the families had become as early as the end of the eighteenth century is shown by the fact that Nathan Rothschild set off with £20,000 capital and with introductions to the German-Jewish houses which had already established representatives in London. Frankfurt was the warehouse of free Europe, the centre for trade in everything from cotton and cloth to tea, sugar, coffee and all the other goods which flowed through the London markets and on into Europe. But during the Napoleonic wars Nathan Rothschild's efforts were so successful that the centre of power in the Rothschild family shifted to London, where it would remain despite the later success of Nathan's younger brother James in Paris. Although that shift had a lot to do with the benefits of doing business from London, it had more to do with the business acumen of Nathan. Amschel had built the family business from that of a modest trader and money lender business to the point where it had a declared capital of 800,000 guilders, but that, considerable though it was, was small in comparison with the achievements of his son. The transformation of the ghetto's leading family from wealthy banker into super-rich was accomplished in an astonishingly short time: in 1810 Nathan Rothschild was just one of London's successful entrepreneurs; five years later he was the principal financier to the British government, the man behind Wellington's successful Peninsular campaign, who financed Wellington's armies at the Battle of Waterloo. His history in those five years is one of the most extraordinary success stories in commercial history, unequalled by anything in the present day.

Until the rise of Nathan, the Goldschmidts saw themselves as a family at least as important as the Rothschilds. They had not been as assiduous as the Rothschilds in forming their contacts in the courts of Europe, but they were shrewd bankers with a network not all that inferior to the bigger house. But from the early nineteenth century on, the Goldschmidts became the poorer cousins, still welcome in Rothschild circles, never quite regarded as equals. A century and a half later, Jimmy Goldsmith found himself living with – and resenting – that gap, and set out to close it, in social as well as wealth terms. It would be one of the factors which drove him almost manically in his early and middle life, and caused him to seek friendship and partnership with more establishment cousins.

That, however, still lay some way ahead. The wealth of some of the Frankfurt families after the Napoleonic wars did not alter their social status. They were far from acceptable in the society of the German aristocracy and anti-Semitic riots were still regular events. In August 1819 a mob stormed through the Judengasse shouting their Jew-baiting cry of 'Hepp! Hepp!'. The militia intervened in time to stop the Rothschild bank being sacked – because of their famed wealth, the ghetto's first family were the principal subjects of the rioters, but the premises of other successful Jews were not ignored.

Prince Metternich's aide, Friedrich von Gentz, summed up the attitude of the ancient nobility at the time when he described the Rothschilds as 'vulgar, ignorant Jews, outwardly presentable, without the remotest inkling of any higher relationship'. But they were, he added, 'endowed with a remarkable instinct which causes them always to choose the right. Their enormous wealth (they are the richest people in Europe) is entirely the result of this instinct.' Yet wealth and financial power counted for something. Although Jews still did not have citizenship rights, Metternich in 1816 persuaded the Austrian Emperor to raise Nathan Rothschild's four brothers to the ranks of the minor nobility, entitling them to add 'von' to their names and to apply for a coat of arms: a hand grasping four arrows, symbolising Rothschild unity. Nathan, as an English national, was excluded (he would become the fifth arrow some twenty years later).

It was Metternich who gave Moritz Goldschmidt (later, when he became one of the most powerful bankers of the mid-nineteenth century, Moritz Ritter von Goldschmidt), a number of dispensations, without which the life of any Jew in Vienna was still unpleasant: Moritz's son later recounted how Metternich had arranged for him not to have to wear the still-compulsory yellow badge. Moritz, then only 17, left Frankfurt for Vienna in 1820 accompanied by his distant cousin Salomon Rothschild. For the next fifty years he was the senior associate of the Rothschild bank in Vienna, on good terms with the Rothschild family, and various histories of the Rothschilds show that many of Moritz's relatives worked for the different Rothschild banks around Europe. Through the house of Bleichroder, the Jewish bankers who became for many years the most powerful in Germany, Moritz became deeply enmeshed with the vast ambitions of Bismarck, around whom his fortunes were to revolve for many years. Fritz Stern, writing of Gerson Bleichroder's role in building the German empire, says that Goldschmidt and Bleichroder had been friends for years: 'both were *hommes du monde*, with entry to their respective courts and to Europe's international elite, and both were faithful Jews who regarded their Jewishness as a special bond between them.'

The branch of the large Goldschmidt family that Jimmy Goldsmith comes from returned to Frankfurt after a long stay in Kassel. Mayer Goldschmidt was a money changer who recorded a capital of 10,000 guilders in 1660 and, when he died in 1667, he was, according to the records of the community, a 'respected businessman'. This branch of the family became known as Goldschmidt-Kassel, and was probably the main branch of the family in the nineteenth century. His son, also called Mayer, dealt in cloth, laces and linens and went bankrupt in 1700, the year he died. The fortunes of the family seem to have varied considerably over the eighteenth century: one was a baker, there were silk dealers, and in the early part of the nineteenth century, Karl Leopold Goldschmidt became a lawyer; Jacob David Goldschmidt, born in 1783, taught languages and married the daughter of the banker Moses Amschel Rothschild on 7 March 1802 (one of his sons, Moritz Adolf, went to London).

All of these details are recorded in the official history of the Frankfurt Jewish families. They record the marriage of Hayum Solomon Goldschmidt to Gelchen Gans, the daughter of a wealthy businessman, in 1797. A year later she gave birth to Benedict Hayum Solomon, who is the first Goldschmidt of real interest to us: he was Jimmy's great-grandfather. He lived to be 75, dying in 1873, by which stage he had built up a very large fortune indeed. The bank he created, B. H. Goldschmidt, was a respectable rival to the Rothschilds in financing the industrial revolutions, as well as the wars, of the mid-nineteenth century. He opened branches in London, Paris and other cities in Europe, and travelled extensively between them, building up a wide network of clients and contacts. There were no nationalist barriers in the banking world in those days, and governments and businesses borrowed where they could get the best terms. Banking from Frankfurt was a truly international business, more so probably than it is today, even with the collapse of so many restrictions in recent years. For over half a century there was probably no country in Europe that Benedict didn't visit, no country where he didn't do business. Frankfurt remained his base and his home, but he seems to have been equally comfortable in other countries, probably speaking French as well as German and the Frankfurter Deutsch, the language of the ghetto that he spoke at home. For centuries, since the time of Joseph Goldschmidt, the family had looked out well beyond the walls of the ghetto or the surrounding country, and the conditions of the middle nineteenth century were ideally suited to them. The business throve, and moved into offices befitting its properity. These were in a fine, imposing five-storey building in the centre of Frankfurt, with the entrance on a corner in one of the more gracious squares. With prosperity came the offer of honours and official recognition: Benedict refused a baronetcy from Bismarck, proffered for his services in financing Germany's expansion (his cousin Moritz in Vienna, with whom the Frankfurt house did a great deal of business, accepted his).

But in the summer of 1866 Benedict retired to Paris. He was then 71, and had produced 14 children, to two of whom he left the bank. One, Maximilian Goldschmidt, was already regarded as one of the most able bankers in Europe, who had for some years been turning the bank into a pioneer of the joint stock bank in Europe, a larger and more flexible version of the old private bank. The other chosen son was Adolph, five years Maximilian's senior.

The official history of the Commerzbank, one of Germany's largest, lists the firm B. H. Goldschmidt, Frankfurt a/M, as one of its founding firms (they also include M. M. Warburg from Hamburg), in 1870. On behalf of this firm, the partner Adolph Benedict Hayum Goldschmidt participated, says the history, with 10,000 shares, mainly to be passed on to the Frankfurt stock exchange. Adolph was offered a seat on the board of supervisors. The founders of Commerzbank, mighty as it is today, were proud of the connection. 'Herewith the young bank established a relationship with a family which in the old banking town Frankfurt had a leading position,' says the Commerzbank history.

Adolph was Jimmy Goldsmith's grandfather, a partner in the firm B. H. Goldschmidt of 18 Mainzer Landstrasse in Frankfurt. In 1866 he married Alice Emma Moses from Birmingham, the daughter of one of Frankfurt's leading industrialists, Wilhelm Merton. Merton, founder of the Frankfurt firm Metallgesellschaft (today one of the largest engineering companies in Germany), was an intensely religious Jew who had moved to London where he changed his name to Moses. In that same year, Frankfurt sided with Austria against Prussia and on July 16 Prussian troops entered the town. Bismarck exacted a fine of six million florins, and ended its independence, making it part of his Zollverein. Its financial strength would remain however: it was the big Frankfurt banking houses which led the way to the restoration of Germany's economy after World War I.

Through the 1870s and 1880s, Adolph and Alice were very much a part of the Frankfurt social and business scenes, living in grand style as befitted their wealthy status, and also travelling around Europe extensively. They had four children: Carl, born the year after they were married, Edward in 1868, Nellie in 1871 and the youngest son, Frank – Jimmy's father – born in 1878.

The early 1880s were again a period of rising anti-Semitism in Eastern Europe, when more than a million Jews left their homes to move further west. Soon it spread into Germany, and many Jewish families left Frankfurt to seek their fortunes elsewhere – among them for instance Ernest Oppenheimer, the man who founded the huge Anglo-American Corporation in South Africa, who was born near Frankfurt in 1880. Adolph and his brother Maximilian stayed until 1893 when they were aged 55 and 50 respectively. Both had inherited wealth, they had both married wealthy wives, and their fortunes had prospered in the boom of the last 20 years.

They closed the family bank, and Adolph took Alice and the three younger children to Paris. Maximilian stayed for almost another half-century, one of the most forceful and interesting of the Goldsmith ancestors. The history of Maximilian, great-uncle of Jimmy, is an extraordinary one. In 1878 he married Minna Caroline Rothschild, the youngest daughter of Baron Willy Carl Rothschild, the head of the Frankfurt family. Fifteen years later he and Adolph disagreed on the direction of B. H. Goldschmidt, and they closed the bank down, each to go in his different direction. Maximilian had his eyes on even bigger things: the Rothschild empire. When Baron Willy Carl Rothschild died in 1901, Maximilian Goldschmidt might have been expected to take over as head of the Frankfurt house of Rothschild. By that stage he was 58 (he died in Frankfurt in 1940 aged 97) and one of the principal figures in the European banking community. Although he had grown up knowing the Rothschild tradition that only Rothschilds rule the house, there was no suitable family member left in Frankfurt, and unless the crown passed to Maximilian the house of Rothschild in Frankfurt would die, as the Frankfurt house of Goldschmidt had done eight years earlier.

The Rothschilds, however, remained determined to exclude outsiders, even fellow graduates of the ghetto – and relatives by marriage. Maximilian's desire to gain as much status and prestige as he could from the Rothschild connection is indicated by the name he had given his bank and by the fact that, in the wake of his father-in-law's death, he adopted the title Baron von Goldschmidt-Rothschild.

But it was not to be. After more than a century the house of M. A. Rothschild and Sons closed its doors for the last time, the waggons loaded with furniture and chests full of documents trundled away from the premises in Berkheimerstrasse, and an era had ended not only in the history of the ghetto families but in the commercial life of Europe. Maximilian, bitterly disappointed, had the consolation of inheriting huge estates near Frankfurt, where he eventually died. He was a lively man – in his nineties he still kept two mistresses, and when the Gestapo came to collect him in 1939 he ordered his butler: 'Tell them I did not send for them.' The men left and Maximilian died in his own home. There are still Goldschmidt-Rothschild bankers in Paris, Switzerland, Rome and Los Angeles – but none in Frankfurt – today, second and third cousins of the present generations of both families.

His older brother Adolph meanwhile had not stayed in Paris for long. Quite why he didn't like it is not clear. His wife of course was English, and may have been pressing to return to her home and family. But their stay in Paris also coincided with the beginning of the Dreyfus affair – on 22 December 1894 Captain Alfred Dreyfus was unanimously found guilty of betraying French secrets to the Germans and condemned to life imprisonment on Devil's Island. He was entirely innocent, but the battle to prove it, which did not end until July 1906, aroused a considerable degree of anti-Semitic feeling in Paris. It was enough to persuade Jimmy Rothschild to move from Paris to London, and may also have persuaded Adolph – although he left well before the height of the affair, which came in 1898 with the prosecution of Emil Zola for publication of his famous open letter *'J'Accuse'* to the president of the French Republic.

2

Frank Goldsmith, MP

It was 1895 when Adolph and Alice Goldschmidt with three of their four children arrived in England. Frank, Jimmy Goldsmith's father, was 17. There were plenty of relations and friends already living in London: Alice's sister Amelia was married to Sir George Jessel, the Solicitor General and later Master of the Rolls. There were Bischoffsheims and von Goldschmidts, Goldsmids, D'Avigdor-Goldsmids, Jessels, Mertons and Rothschilds, and many other rich Jewish families who had now settled in England. Adolph, like his father and brother, had travelled widely and had a number of business connections too.

They settled initially in London, buying a house at 16 South Street, in Mayfair. But Adolph and Alice also wanted something larger, in the country, and they bought a 2,500-acre estate at Cavenham in Suffolk, on which they then built their own brand-new Victorian house, with a large glass conservatory at one end, and elaborately landscaped lawns and Italianate gardens. Ownership of the local village of Cavenham came with the estate, as well as the responsibilities of squirearchy – which Adolph seems to have assumed without a second thought.

Although they continued to use the London house, their life revolved more and more around country living. Adolph was assiduous enough at fulfilling the duties of local squire, and biggest employer in the village, and Alice ran a busy and hospitable household. The family albums are full of photographs of the house: it was not huge, or even particularly handsome, but it was comfortable, with spacious lawns and gardens. A contemporary account describes it as 'well worth a visit – on a fine day' before going on to talk about 'its stately avenue and stretches of greensward, its lake and surroundings . . . lovely gardens and pleasure grounds around the well-kept lawns and a fine range of flowerbeds . . . kitchen garden and large glasshouses . . . many standards of rambler roses.' The family was clearly proud of it, and enjoyed it. It was a typical late-Victorian building, with a wide balcony at first-floor level over a large terrace where the family often sat looking out at the rose gardens, the lawns and the fields beyond. On the left was a large conservatory, and on the right the rooms had french windows onto the lawns. From the photographs everything looks to be in immaculate condition: the lawns perfectly kept, the pools and ponds clean, the house newly painted. There are servants in the background, by all accounts plenty of them: one picture shows Adolph's son Teddy, stepping out on the park in front of the house which is laid out as a cricket field. He and others are carrying cricket bats, and the caption reads 'Cricket: House *v* Estate'. The albums show garden parties, complete with brass bands, and groups of relatives and friends in clearly high good humour. There are pictures of golf being practised with obvious hilarity on the lawns, and one picture of a cloaked Adolph, wearing a cap and holding a golf club, standing over an ornamental pond. The caption reads: 'Fishing for Balls', written in his son Frank's hand.

Clearly Adolph and his family enjoyed the British way of life. There was shooting and riding, beautiful dogs around the house, and regular house parties. The albums that survive are Frank's – he was a keen and remarkably good photographer in the early years of the century – and from his pictures it is possible to get an idea of the guest list, at least that part of it which interested him: his cousins the Jessels; Alfred Wagg of the merchant bank Helbert Wagg (later Schroder Wagg), in which Adolph had become a sleeping partner; Goldsmid cousins, and also D'Avigdor Goldsmids – Sir Henry D'Avigdor Goldsmid was later a Conservative MP. There are pictures of the family playing tennis, playing croquet, of fine carriages drawing up to the hall door to deliver guests – and later one of the first electric cars (this is 1902).

Adolph at the time appears as a short, upright handsome man, with a beard – extraordinarily similar to his grandson Teddy Goldsmith today. One of 14 children himself, he clearly relished his family life. Most of the photographs show him smiling benignly, immaculately dressed in his tweeds. In one of Frank's old scrapbooks there is a picture entitled 'Papa at Ostend' which seems to have been taken about 1894. He wears a three-piece tweed suit, with the trousers slightly on the short side, a cap to match, a cravat and a winged collar. He carries an elegant walking cane, which he clearly does not need for support purposes. Another picture of him at Cavenham in 1902 shows him wearing almost exactly the same clothes.

Frank's elder brother Teddy by contrast appears as something of a dandy. He was taller than Frank, with an easy confidence and assurance that shines out of the pictures. He was a better shot, a better golfer, and clearly, from the poses in Frank's albums, fond of the ladies – and they of him. The main impression that comes out of these albums is of a rich, contented, active and close family, enjoying their life without any visible inhibition or concern. The eldest brother, Carl, stayed in Germany and later became one of the legendary gamblers in the casinos of Europe; he was held out as an object lesson to Jimmy years later. Nellie married Ernst von Marx, son of an old business friend of Adolph, who also features in Frank's albums, looking every bit the lawyer he was. He converted to Christianity from Judaism, but no one seems to have minded that. Later he became a civil servant in Hamburg, where Frank spent the summer of 1903, according to his scrap books.

Adolph did not abandon business altogether: besides his partnership at Helbert Wagg, he was an investor in some of the ventures of the day, for instance the Central Mining and Investment Corporation, founded in London in 1905, to acquire some of the successful diamond partnerships in South Africa. But essentially he was retired.

Other German Jews who had moved to England over the previous hundred years had been assimilated into its society without great difficulty, and Adolph was keen to be accepted too. Cavenham Hall was part of that process, and he and Alice furnished it elegantly and expensively. Their native language was Frankfurter Deutsch, but they had all been educated in other languages. They spoke French as well as English, albeit with an accent. Adolph and Alice did not go so far, as other Goldschmidts had, as to anglicise their names, but there was a long tradition of that among the Jewish community, and Teddy and Frank changed their name to Goldsmith from their earliest days in England. Within a couple of years they were, to all intents and purposes, young English gentlemen.

Frank had a lot to do in catching up with his education. He had first been in school in Germany, then in France, then at home in England. In 1894 he was sent to a crammer in Cheltenham – his scrapbook includes a photograph of the headmaster and his wife, whom presumably he was fond of – and in May 1897, aged 18, he was good enough to be offered a place at Magdalen College, Oxford. He was given rooms in the Chaplain's Quad No 2, and sent a little note which informed him that undergraduates were expected to provide for themselves sheets, pillow-cases, table-linen and so forth, but furniture would be provided.

'Gentlemen' were 'recommended' not to procure more articles than they might need: 'It will generally be found that Breakfast sets for half a dozen are amply sufficient; as, when large breakfasts or other entertainments are given, the necessary ware can be procured from the Junior Common Room, or elsewhere.'

At the beginning of term Frank Goldsmith was sent an inventory and valuation for the furniture he would take over from the previous occupant: he was asked to pay the sum of £45 8s for a set of walnut dining tables, a walnut sideboard, a set of oak bookshelves, and everything else needed down to 'painted washstand, roller blind, bottle and glass, watercan, wastepail'. Most undergraduates would have thrown these bits of paper away as soon as they had finished with them. Frank filed them carefully in his scrapbook.

Oxford (and Cambridge) had only accepted Jewish undergraduates since 1871, but by the time Frank went up, Jews had broken down most of the barriers against them, in the political as well as the academic field. In Frankfurt no Goldschmidt, Rothschild or any other Jew had ever been involved in politics. In England, Lionel Rothschild had become the first Jewish MP in 1858 and Nathan Rothschild's grand-daughter Hannah married the Earl of Rosebery in 1878. Rosebery was a political phenomenon, foreign secretary in his early forties, later prime minister. Nathan's son, Nattie, became Lord Rothschild in 1885, a rich and powerful friend to Queen Victoria and to many of the leading figures of the day. These were connections, going right back to the ghetto, which Frank, beginning to contemplate a career in politics, seems to have been fully aware of.

He was a handsome young undergraduate, his black hair parted in the middle in the style of the day, his accent increasingly British, his clothes and lifestyle elaborately so. He also had enough money to move in the richer circles of Oxford, inviting his friends to Cavenham for week-ends or the holidays, and seems to have been popular with both sexes.

He graduated with a second class honours degree in jurisprudence in 1900, and a BA. His cousin, Captain Herbert Jessel, was an MP and had also been elected Mayor of the City of Westminster, and this seems to have pushed Frank into becoming first a barrister, secondly a politician and thirdly a part-time soldier in one of the more social territorial regiments. He was called to the bar of the Inner Temple in 1903 and on 3 November the same year was elected a councillor of the City of Westminster's Conduit Ward, his local area in London which included his father's house in South Street. It was pretty small stuff, but he was only

25, and it gave him access to some of the leading politicians of the day. Jessel, who was chairman of the London Municipal Society and also MP for St Pancras (which he had inherited from his father-in-law, Sir Julian Goldsmid), seems to have regarded himself as something of a mentor for Frank, at least in these early years, and the two often appeared on platforms together. It was Jessel who suggested he should stand in the London County Council elections, running against the great George Bernard Shaw in the St Pancras division.

Jessel was presumably fully aware of Frank's German birth, but from some point in his life, perhaps even before he went up to Magdalen, Frank seems to have been at pains to hide it. It was probably done innocently enough, the desire of someone different to merge into his new social and political background. He was perfectly open, and proud, about being Jewish, but by the time he set his eyes on the political world, he seems to have gone to some trouble to shake off his German origins. Those who met him for the first time at Magdalen or in London in the early days of his political career simply assumed he was what he presented himself as: a young, rich, English gentleman, with a foreign father but an English mother.

A local North London paper, reviewing the St Pancras election, certainly took Frank at face value. He had, it said, 'all the advantages which youth, leisure, and good descent can confer, and in the last few months has been making friends in all directions.' He had, of course, 'good descent', but one can be fairly certain that was not what the reporter had in mind. By 1904 Frank was merging into the English landscape.

The same paper went on to describe his famous Irish opponent in rather less flattering terms. Bernard Shaw was 'full of quips and cranks and caprices' and 'far too brilliant a man to lose his time on the prosaic work of local government, which distinctly is not his line.'

Shaw's election manifesto makes amusing reading at this date: 'Many well-known authors seek election to Parliament; but there is no known instance on record of a man who, having attained a distinguished position in literature, has been found willing to devote six of the best years of his life to the homely work of Vestry and Borough Council merely from a sense of its importance to his neighbours,' said the great man. It passed straight over the heads of the St Pancras electorate who were unimpressed with this Socialist Irishman.

Frank won and *The Times* did an amusing little post mortem a few days later. Why had Shaw lost? Too late, the great playwright admitted he had been a 'quite extraordinarily unpopular candidate', attributing this to the 'paradoxical in politics' – by which he meant his looks. Frank was handsomer than he. This set off a curious debate in the press which ran for days. *The Times* took it up under the headline 'Beauty defeats Brain', adding 'a great proportion of the electors are women' who had been impressed not by the politics or the eloquence of the candidates but by their looks. Shaw's looks did not appeal, whereas 'the handsome features of the youthful Mr Goldsmith carried the day'. Goldsmith certainly went down well with the commentators as well as the women voters: another paper remarked that he was a man 'of imperturbable good humour, his countenance is invariably wreathed in smiles of huge dimensions and his affability unfailing under the most disadvantageous circumstances.'

In truth Shaw was pretty fed up with being a London county councillor. His diary records tedious hours spent on his municipal duties arguing over the appointment of sanitary inspectors, dustcarts and so on. 'Headache seems imminent, but I have ceased to notice that now. It's getting chronic.' Years later he wrote of his experience in local politics: 'The mornings I gave to it were followed by afternoons and evenings spent in the committee rooms ... fighting questions of drainage, paving, lighting, rates, clerks' salaries &c, &c, &c.' Shaw, however, was 50, young Goldsmith half his age, and local politics represented a springboard to better things.

By now Frank Goldsmith was fully in the social mainstream of the time. He joined his local army regiment, the Duke of York's Loyal Suffolk Hussars, which included many of the young aristocrats of the area, including Major the Hon Walter E. Guinness, who soon became a regular visitor to Cavenham. Frank's life was filled with social engagements, either for the council or the cavalry: 22 January 1904 Major Guinness invites him to the Yeoman Subscription Ball, tickets including supper – Gentlemen 10s 6d, Ladies 7s 6d, and 'God Save the King'. To the Mansion House at the invitation of the Lord Mayor of London, for dinner with the president and members of the Municipal Council of Paris; to a return bout in Paris, to the anniversary dinner of the Mutual Communications Society, to the Royal Dublin Horse Show, and much else. On 6 April 1906 he was at a dinner for 'The Pilgrims', a dining club of the great and the good, at the Savoy Hotel in London. The list of those present makes interesting reading: Mr Winston Churchill, MP, (on a table with Jimmy Rothschild), Sir Arthur Conan Doyle, Rider Haggard, Captain (later Admiral) Jellicoe, and any number of generals, admirals, dukes and earls, including a couple of German notables: Count Metternich and Major Count von der Schulenberg.

Frank pursued his political career with considerable energy. He actively sought more and more roles: he joined the board of the Royal Free Hospital, which was situated in his constituency, the council of the Passmore Edwards Settlement, became a vice-president of the King's Cross Philanthropic Society, and much else.

The publication *The Jewish World* congratulated him on his success and went on:

It is happy to note that he has already associated himself actively with Jewish institutions. He is a member of the Emigration Committee of the Jewish Board of Guardians and joint-hon. secretary of the newly-formed Jewish Emigrants' Information Board.

It added that 'if the fortune which has hitherto smiled upon Mr Goldsmith's public life continues he is destined to go far.'

Frank was certainly going far in the social world of England. It was still only a dozen years since he had arrived, speaking the language badly, poorly educated, a German Jew in a Britain which accepted but never liked either foreigners or Jews. None of his election material ever mentioned his German birth, although there were plenty of reports that he was the son of 'Mr Adolph B. H. Goldschmidt of South Street, Park Lane', a fact he could scarcely deny even if he had wanted to. He took every opportunity to enter the inner ranks of the English establishment. Unusually for a Jew in those years, he even became a Freemason, being invited to attend 'an installation meeting' at the London County Council Lodge on 21 March 1906 at 5.15 precisely. His formal invitation, again carefully pasted into his scrapbook, shows that he was proposed by Edward White and seconded by the Brother Secretary, Ambrose Pomeroy. There were six MPs in the lodge, and one peer – the Earl of Onslow.

In March 1907 Frank resigned from the Westminster Council and ran again for the St Pancras division in partnership with his friend George Alexander, the well-known actor-manager of the St James Theatre in King Street, who some years before had played with the great Sir Henry Irving. In the campaign Alexander made use of a new invention for electioneering: a gramophone which played one of his speeches, possibly the first time it was ever used.

Frank was allotted the task of escorting the new aldermen to sign in, be greeted by the chairman, and then taken to their seats. One paper referred to the 'handsome young Moderate Whip (Mr Frank Goldsmith) who is as exquisitely groomed as a best man at a Hanover Square wedding'. Frank's political career continued to prosper. He was made a whip for the Municipal Reform Party, which in turn supported the national Conservative Party – which is what he had his sights on. He seems to have served on an extraordinary variety of committees: chairman of the Building Acts Committee, which involved him in technical arguments over planning laws, education committees, the Blind and Deaf Children's After-Care Committee, and others. His scrapbooks are full of his speeches and debates – and his dinners, still dozens of those. He hosted regular 'smoking concerts' at the Unionist Club in South St Pancras, supported by Herbert Jessel, which according to the local paper 'enlivened the somewhat dull greyness of South St Pancras life during the winter season'. The *London Argus* reported that 'Mr Goldsmith, who as a debater on the Conservative side, pressed home the wholesome truth that even in summer the County Council's steamboats do not pay . . .'

But he was after bigger things. It was national politics that really interested him, and he began to work at getting his own seat. The Liberals had won Stowmarket, the local seat at Cavenham, in the election of 1906, forcing out Goldsmith's friend Walter E. Guinness. Guinness had moved to the nearby constituency of Bury St Edmunds, and Frank put himself forward as the Conservative and Unionist Party candidate for an election which at the end of 1909 was fast looming. The Liberals had only had a majority of 213 in the seat.

Asquith had become prime minister when Campbell-Bannerman retired, ill, in 1908, with Lloyd George as chancellor of the exchequer. He took over at an extraordinarily troubled time: there was a nasty mood of revolt in the labour world; the long struggle of the suffragettes had reached the point of violence; in Europe, Germany was busily building ships and armaments; and two other issues were reaching a head: reform of the House of Lords and Irish Home Rule. Yet Asquith would prove the longest-serving prime minister since Lord Liverpool, and only surpassed this century by Margaret Thatcher. But his budget of 1909, which dealt with taxation of land, was rejected by the House of Lords and in January 1910 Asquith went to the country on the issue of abolishing the veto of the Lords.

Frank set to with a will on the campaign trail. One report shows how he arrived in his motor car in the centre of Newmarket 'and was greeted by the huge crowd which awaited him in the High Street'. Newmarket was split into two constituencies and on this occasion the two prospective Conservative and Unionist party candidates were supporting each other. After Frank had been 'carried on the shoulders of his supporters to the committee rooms', he stood on a chair to make a speech 'which was punctuated by vociferous applause'. Whether the reporter was carried away or whether there really was this level of enthusiasm is difficult to assess, but the text of his speech is ordinary enough. There are also pictures among his cuttings of him being carried on planks placed on men's shoulders through the streets of Bury St Edmunds.

The speech by his fellow-candidate, Mr G. H. Verrall, is more significant, not because of any profound political oratory but because of what he had to say about Frank. Said Verrall:

> Surely Newmarket will not lie under the disgrace of having a Liberal Radical to represent it? (Cries of 'we won't'.) I take it that it is a disgrace. (Hear, Hear.) The Stowmarket Division of Suffolk had at one time a Portuguese Jew to represent it, and afterwards returned a London counter-jumper pretty nearly – (groans) – when it had the opportunity of returning country gentlemen like Mr Guinness and now Mr Goldsmith.

Now presumably Verrall, as an MP, was reasonably aware of what was going on in the area. It would have been impossible not to have been aware that Frank was a Jew, both because of his name and his activities for the Jewish community. Old Adolph was also an exotic character in Suffolk at that time. Clearly Verrall considered Frank a 'gentleman', which in his book would have been very important. Yet this speech suggests that he had no idea about Frank's background, and nor, from the recorded reactions, did his listeners – or the local reporter. The difference in Verrall's book between a 'Portuguese Jew' and a 'German Jew' might not have been great. Frank played the part of the English gentleman to such perfection that his fellow MPs believed it, his constituents believed it – and in effect, that is what he was, and would remain for the rest of his life.

Frank might have inwardly winced at Verrall's platitudes, but they seem to have gone down well enough with the crowd who carried him back to his car 'amid enthusiastic cheers'. His political platform also seems to have been popular enough: Frank was against Home Rule for Ireland, believed in the veto powers of the House of Lords, was in favour of reform of the tariff barriers and free trade, and also spoke up strongly in favour of old age pensions – an interesting mixture of views. Herbert Jessel also came up to speak for him, describing him as his cousin, 'universally beloved' by his constituents in St Pancras.

On polling day, Frank appeared on the balcony of the Athenaeum in Bury St Edmunds before what reporters called a 'huge concourse of people'. When the result was announced he had won – by a majority of 645. That evening he made a triumphant return to Cavenham. His car was stopped, and he was forcibly seated in a carriage to which his supporters tied ropes and dragged him through the village and up to the front door of the mansion. 'Mr Goldsmith said the reception had given him the greatest pleasure of all coming from the people he lived amongst, and with whom he always got on so well,' said the report in the local paper the next day.

His victory was a big event in the life of the village of Cavenham, seven miles away, and of the Goldschmidts, squires and owners of the village. Adolph invited everyone on the estate – about 200 of them – to the village hall where they were provided with a 'capital tea'. Adolph behaved very much as the squire should in these circumstances: he made a little speech in his heavy German accent, thanking everyone for the part they had played in his son's victory, and hoping they would all enjoy themselves. Edward also made a brief speech. The report in the local paper the next day said that 'some little disappointment was felt at the absence of the new member, Mr F. Goldsmith. It was however understood that after the strenuous political fight he had gone away to quietness, in which to recuperate.' No one seems to have worried about his absence for long:

> After ample justice had been done to the good things provided, the tables were cleared, the men were provided with cigars and tobacco, whilst the ladies and children were also well catered for. An exceedingly pleasant evening was spent, instrumental and vocal music adding to the enjoyment.

His election brought the number of Jewish MPs at the time to 16 – nine Liberal and seven Conservative (and 37 Jewish candidates in all), including Lionel de Rothschild, Sir Harry Samuel, Sir Philip Magnus and Alfred Strauss.

Frank was now in the House of Commons, and a new career began which he must have hoped would see him, at his present rate of progress, into the government within a few years and into the cabinet not very long after that. He was still only 31, with a widening circle of friends from his political activities in London and Suffolk, his contacts gained in the yeomanry, his membership of the Freemasons, and the many parties and dinners he went to. He was handsome, personable, articulate and rich, living still in his father's house in South Street, using Cavenham at the week-ends. His early months in the House, however, were ones of turmoil, not for him, but for the political world as a whole. Asquith had been returned in January 1910 only with the support of Labour and Irish members, and set about attempting to abolish the veto powers of the House of Lords. All through the summer he tried to persuade the other parties to support him in a compromise, but by the end of the year he had failed, and in December he went to the country again, this time with the voters, fed up with the blocking tactics of the Conservatives, more openly on his side. Once again Frank Goldsmith took to the hustings for a contest which this time would prove much tougher. His seat was a marginal one, and the Liberals sent a number of senior cabinet members to campaign in what they believed was a very winnable seat. He also faced a rather more formidable candidate, R. A. Barclay.

Barclay had only been selected a fortnight before polling day, but even so the newspaper accounts, and Frank's own records, suggest he put up a good fight. Frank, however, had worked hard in his constituency in the year he had been its MP. He persuaded his parents to open Cavenham Hall for a number of garden parties, including a fete for the Mildenhall and Icklingham Habitation of the Primrose League, which was, according to the local newspaper, a resounding success, Frank returning from yeomanry camp in Ipswich specially 'to entertain the guests'. Yet he only scraped home, his majority of 645 cut to 191.

The election was a resounding victory for Asquith, the Liberals winning an overall majority of 126, and the prime minister set about the huge tasks of reforming the Lords and bringing in an Irish Home Rule Bill, opposed most vehemently on both counts by the young member for Stowmarket.

At 32, Frank Goldsmith was still unmarried, a fact commented upon by some of his political opponents in the two elections. But he did not lack girlfriends. His scrapbook contains pictures of a very beautiful girl, with a tiny mole on her left cheek, on one occasion looking demure, almost nun-like, sitting in a garden that could be Cavenham, probably photographed by Frank; further on, the same girl appears, this time looking much more glamorous in a hat and fur collar. Against the two pictures, Frank has merely recorded the date: 1910. There are no private letters, no mentions in the gossip columns. Later on there are other girls, many of them, but quite who this particular girl in 1910 was, no one now remembers.

In the most extraordinary scenes ever seen in the House of Commons – at one stage, in what became known as the 'pothouse brawl', Asquith was unable to utter a single sentence in nearly an hour at the despatch box because of the roars from the opposition – the Liberals forced through the reform of the House of Lords by August 1911 and then turned to the Irish Home Rule Bill. Frank's speeches from the backbenches show how extraordinarily well he had fitted into his adopted country. In December he led the way in opposing a number of government amendments to its own Bill, which gave Asquith far more problems than he had encountered even with reforming the Lords. His speeches were thoughtful enough, well-researched, pointing out the inconsistencies between what was proposed and the systems under which, say, the judicial systems of other British colonies had been set up. 'It is, in my opinion, of the greatest importance, and it is essential, the Imperial Government should retain some sort of control over the appointment of the judges in Ireland,' he said in one speech. But they were also narrow. Frank in his immersion into the British political and social system seemed to accept the concepts of empire, which was already beginning to totter, the divisive class system, more marked in Britain than anywhere else in Europe, and the social inequality of the day. England – he never seems to have thought of it as Britain – was already changing with the rise of trade union power, the suffragettes, and the eclipse of the empire, the first serious crack in which was the issue of Irish Home Rule, but Frank hated that change, and channelled all his political energies into keeping the social order as he found it when he arrived from Germany, and as it existed around his father's estates at Cavenham.

Mostly he spoke in the same debates – and on the same side – as Sir Edward Carson, a brilliant but bigoted King's Counsel who was the leader of the Ulster Unionists (and the man who destroyed Oscar Wilde in the witness box). For the most part Frank's speeches now read as reasoned enough argument on a Bill which aroused an extraordinary degree of passion. But he sometimes became worked up too, particularly after hours of what *The Times* referred to as 'arduous' debate. At 9.25 pm, after a particularly acrimonious sitting, Frank rose to enter what *The Times* called 'an indignant protest' against the parliamentary procedures which had left only an hour to debate five clauses. It was reducing the proceedings to a farce, he said, 'lingering over the proceedings' according to *The Times*' reporter.

But he spoke on a range of other subjects too, mostly with a distinctly liberal bias: on the subject of the education of defective and epileptic children, for instance, when he asked why institutions which were supposed to have been provided under a bill passed a year before had not yet been provided. In July 1914, only a fortnight before the outbreak of war, he spoke again in the House on the Criminal Justice Administration Bill. It is a surprising little speech, basically moving an amendment whereby a person convicted of an offence should be allowed to keep whatever money he had left on him, after paying his fine. And again that week he seconded an unsuccessful amendment to prevent magistrates sending young people to Borstal. A young man, he pointed out, instead of getting a month's imprisonment for his offence, could be sent to Borstal for two years, which seemed to him a dangerous power to entrust to a bench of magistrates 'and one that ought not to be given'.

From 1912 on his scrapbooks take a more military tone. The build-up to the war had begun and Frank was taking his military career more and more seriously. His scrapbooks show pictures of camps from 1904 onwards, with Frank dashing in uniform, but now there are more of them. In January 1912 he took his War Office examinations for promotion to the rank of captain. He scored no more than average marks: 506 out of a maximum 800 (minimum pass mark 400), and a lowly 116 (16 above the pass mark) in cavalry training. But he was only a part-time soldier, in a regiment that did not take soldiering too seriously. By the spring of 1914 he was in command of a squadron of cavalry, replacing Walter Guinness (the Suffolk Hussars were almost certainly unique in the British forces in having two MPs among their officers) who was promoted to second-in-command of the regiment, and by the time war came in August he was a major.

For Frank the war began in some style. Until now, he had spent, with the rest of the regiment, some 15 days in camp each year, during which time training was never taken too seriously. The Loyal Suffolk Hussars, like other similar regiments in the Territorial Army, attracted rich young aristocrats who looked forward to their summer camp each year, who met socially for an annual ball and a number of dinners, but who were not serious soldiers as such. The war when it came was for them more of an exciting episode in their comfortable existence than it was the horrific event it soon became. Three days after the outbreak of war, Frank was pictured grandly leading his squadron on horseback through the streets of Bury St Edmunds to undergo four months of intensive training, designed to bring the regiment up to the standards of regulars. The *Bury St Edmunds Post* carried a contribution from 'a trooper' (a remarkably well-educated one, from the quality of the writing) from the camp remarking that the difference after training was 'as between the proverbial chalk and cheese', adding that when the Hussars went to the front – 'and we are going' – they would be well-trained enough 'to do their fair share towards exterminating the tyrannical militarist monster'.

The same paper carried a eulogy of its young soldier MP and the effect he had on the squadron. 'The whole Eastern Mounted Brigade may be searched through, and . . . there will not be found a squadron in which the work is carried out with more method and the drill with more smartness.'

There is no hint in this – or in any other newspaper article – of the true state of Frank's position at this time. Within weeks of the outbreak of war he discovered he had not shed his Frankfurt past all that easily. In 1914 Britain was swept by a blind wave of hatred for anything German – innocent shopkeepers with German-sounding names had their windows smashed, and dachshunds were kicked in the streets. There were rumours of spies in high places which became so rife when the German ships Goeben and Breslau slipped through a Royal Navy blockade and got to Turkey, that there were public demands that the First Sea Lord, Prince Louis Battenberg, born, like Frank, in Germany, should resign. At the Royal Naval College at Osborne, Battenberg's 14-year-old cadet son Dickie Mountbatten was, according to his biographer Philip Ziegler, even accused of being a German spy by his fellow cadets and temporarily ostracised. There are stories of him marching out to the flagstaff at Osborne, tears streaming down his face, determined he would one day take his father's place as First Sea Lord (which he did). The same feeling which drove Prince Louis from office and made the life of his son a misery affected in full measure Major Goldsmith.

He might have weathered it had it not been for a single, unfortunate, event. His brother-in-law, Ernst von Marx, whom he had liked to visit in Hamburg, was now a senior civil servant in Germany. In the early weeks of the war he sent a telegram to Frank, openly through the Post Office, asking 'How can you consider fighting for anyone other than your fatherland?' It was of course seen by everyone in the local post office, and within hours news of it spread through the constituency. In the mood of the time, it could not have been worse for Frank. Suddenly he found himself the cause of riots in the constituency, the marchers demanding he be stripped both of his commission and of his parliamentary seat. In the villages around Cavenham, there were clashes between his supporters and his opponents, ending in violence – Frank had to pay hospital bills for those who had tried to defend him. Some of his parliamentary friends, notably Winston Churchill and Lord Bessborough, stood by him, but even there he found himself shunned. People he had considered friends turned their backs on him in his London clubs. His father, very noticeably German, hid himself in his house, greatly shaken by this upheaval in his peaceful old age.

In those weeks, a great deal changed for Frank Goldsmith and his family. The days of country squire, of Cavenham and its estates, of aspiring politician and potential minister, even of enthusiastic (if not very brilliant) soldier – all ended overnight. The black mood that was descending on Europe with the war was magnified several-fold for Frank. When he left for camp shortly before Christmas, he left behind all he had known and enjoyed up to that time. He would never take up the reins of his old life again.

3

Soldier and Hotelier

Frank Goldsmith's scrapbooks, detailing his political speeches, his dinners, the ovations he received at Stowmarket, his political campaigns, even his girlfriends, become almost empty with the outbreak of war, as they are about the less agreeable events in his life. There are cuttings of the very early days, of the proud Major Goldsmith leading his squadron through the streets of Bury St Edmunds in August 1914, and there are 'Trooper's' reports from training camps. Then nothing, or almost nothing. They do not properly resume again for over 20 years, and then by another hand, his wife Marcelle. There is no record of the demonstrations against him, no word of the anti-German attacks, almost nothing of what he did in the war itself. Until 1914 Frank had been an open, goodnatured, ambitious and generous man, who had known little in the way of hardship or setback; the combination of the personal attacks on him, and then the war, was to have a profound effect on his life. August 1914 was to change everything for him.

In mid-December 1914 the Suffolk Yeoman Reserves were moved from their billets in Newmarket, and sent to Ely in Cambridgeshire. The yeomen were part of the centuries-old tradition of the landed gentry raising and maintaining, originally at their own cost, a local force to be put at the disposal of king and country in time of war. For the officers, membership of the yeomanry was as much a social duty (and pleasure, because on the whole it was fun) as it was serious soldiering. The tradition, still strong in 1914 in rural areas like Suffolk, was that the rich gentry were the officers and then provided, usually from their own estates, a number of other ranks. Frank, in keeping with the role he had chosen for himself as the landed aristocrat, had done precisely that. But none of them was ready for war.

After three months' intensive training, they were now being prepared for the front. Everyone assumed it would be France, where the war which was to have been over by Christmas was very visibly far from over, and this belief was further heightened when a few days before Christmas the order came through from headquarters: 'All leave stopped until further notice, and men on leave to be recalled.' The troops spent what was for most of them their first Christmas away from home, small hardship compared to what lay in front of them, but enough to bring another lengthy report from the erudite 'Trooper' to the local paper, the *Post*, in January 1915. This gives a detailed account of how Christmas was spent, mostly along the lines of 'no joyously ringing bells greeted us when we awoke on Christmas morning, but the plaintive note of the trumpet sounding reveille, and "stables" soon after.' It contains a reference to Frank, who was clearly making himself as popular as he could with the troops.

> The men of B Squadron came off particularly fortunate, and as an instance of the kindly thought of 'the Major', it may be just mentioned that each man in the Squadron received a useful and much appreciated gift, every one of which was personally addressed, and handed to the men by Major Goldsmith. If anyone is looking for a 'thick ear', and other minor decorations, the quickest way is to say anything about our Major to one of his men. It is much quicker than calling for cheers for the Kaiser.

Frank, still shocked by the anti-German feelings that had been roused against him, must have been grateful for this degree of appreciation (this piece is carefully pasted into his cuttings book). The feeling in the squadron towards Frank does seem to have been genuine enough, if no doubt exaggerated by 'Trooper' in his missives to the local paper. He was easygoing, clearly generous, and the same social skills which had been propelling him up the political ladder before the war must have helped in his relationship with the troops.

Until this time soldiering had been a purely social activity for Frank, who presumably had never thought seriously of having to fight. Now he was to fight for a country he loved but which he must have felt had turned its back on him, against the country of his birth. He was not sent to France, although that was probably the intended destination of the Suffolk in the early months of 1915, probably to be kept in reserve. Instead another front opened up thousands of miles away. The yeomen were destined to spend much of the war in Gallipoli and the Middle East, returning to Europe only in early 1918 when the German advances in Flanders deprived Allenby of his British units.

In March 1915, Frank Goldsmith and the Suffolk Yeomanry were at Woodbridge, near Ipswich, still untested in battle, still undergoing what must have seemed like interminable training. As the war wore on, it soon became apparent there was not going to be much of a role for cavalry, and the British army already had too many of them and not enough infantry. The Suffolk Yeomanry, like so many other yeomanry battalions, were dismounted and re-equipped and retrained as infantry, something which Frank and the other officers who very much enjoyed riding must have hated. They were, however, within reach of home, and for the yeomen the spring and summer of 1915 were tedious but not unpleasant. At least they were not in the trenches in France, or in the increasingly bloody fighting now going on in the Dardanelles. It was at Woodbridge that a letter found its way to Frank (which he did paste into his scrapbook). The secretary of Tattersalls Committee, the body which looks after 'the purity of the turf', settling disputes between bookmakers and the betting public, wrote to inform him that he had been elected a member of the Elective Committee, whose duties were to elect annually members of one of the most establishment groups in Britain. With it went membership of the Tattersalls Committee itself, only seven strong, which included the Earl of Suffolk and various other leading lights from the racing world. Frank had not been completely ostracised.

The letter was dated 11 March 1915, a week after he had been elected, and the secretary apologised for the delay. 'I did not write to you sooner as I was under the impression you were abroad.'

That spring Frank was given another appointment: he was made a Justice of the Peace, as his father had been too.

The fact that he was a Member of Parliament and had such a wide range of contacts and friends would no doubt have enabled him to secure a staff post in the War Office, or with some general of his acquaintance. Perhaps he would have done if it had not been for that extraordinary period of antagonism towards all things vaguely German. Perhaps, too, he now felt that no one would seriously trust him, that there would always be a nagging doubt about his patriotism and his commitment to the fight against the Kaiser, whose country he had often visited even since leaving it. The telegram from his brother-in-law had done him deep moral as well as public damage. Whatever his reasons, he clearly preferred to go with the Suffolks wherever fate and the War Office sent him. His friend Walter Guinness, a major and an MP, also stayed with the yeomanry, and that must have given him some comfort too.

In late summer they began preparations for moving at last, kitted out for the heat of the Mediterranean rather than for France. By that stage the Dardanelles campaign had already been lost, although the British war cabinet was reluctant to accept it. Throughout the summer, Sir Ian Hamilton, the commander-in-chief, had sent for more and more reinforcements, and in July and August a further five divisions arrived, only to find the Turks now had an equal number of troops on the peninsula. In August the Allies landed fresh troops on what became known as Anzac Cove – they were mostly Australian and New Zealand forces – and at Suvla Bay, further to the north, but none of the objectives was taken. It was the final reverse. The stalemate which had prevailed before the arrival of the new troops from England set in again, the troops facing each other from trenches similar to those in France.

The Suffolk Yeomanry eventually left their base at Leiston, in Suffolk, on 23 September 1915, by train for Liverpool where they boarded a ship called the *Olympic*. It was a distinguished regiment, even by the standards of the gentlemanly yeomanry: among the 25 officers and 474 other ranks, were Major Walter Guinness MP, third son of the Earl of Iveagh, the Earl of Cadogan and Viscount Duncannon, as well as Major Frank Goldsmith MP. The *Olympic*, crowded with nine yeomanry regiments, slipped her moorings early the next morning, and anchored in the Mersey all day, then, escorted by three torpedo boats, she set out for the island of Lemnos, at the mouth of the Dardanelles. There were German submarines about, as they discovered when, on the morning of 1 October, they picked up two boats containing 35 sailors off a French ship, sunk by a submarine. The regiment's war diary solemnly records that 'two shots were fired by the *Olympic*'s guns without effect. It is uncertain whether the submarine fired a torpedo.' But everyone stood to at their alarm posts in lifejackets for an hour.

They arrived at Mudros Bay in Lemnos after an eight-day voyage, and anchored there for nearly a week before they began transhipping into smaller craft for landing on the Anzac beaches. They arrived at nightfall, but a sudden squall made it impossible to get ashore and they had to anchor at Imbros, not before an orderly was killed by a stray bullet at Anzac, the regiment's first casualty in action. They spent their entire first day at anchor in one of the transports, an experience which the war diary records as 'exceedingly uncomfortable for all ranks, as ship not intended to hold such large numbers for so long a period'. They finally got ashore at midnight, marched for an hour, then spent the next day constructing dug-outs on the north slope of their allotted gully, 'the south slope being constantly hit by stray bullets'.

The regiment, a few days later, was attached to the 162nd Brigade of the newly created 54th Division, and spread around among the more seasoned troops 'for instruction', with every officer and man 'shadowing' a man of the same rank. Frank's B Squadron found themselves in trenches in an area which the troops called 'Brighton Road', and a day later they were involved in their first small action – a demonstration against the Turkish lines in which every man in the line had to fire a single round in order to establish the strength of the Turks. The demonstration, the war diary says mournfully, was unsuccessful 'as the enemy made no reply'.

That was one of the lighter moments in conditions which were grim, and getting worse. The trenches were spasmodically shelled, but dysentery and other illnesses presented a much bigger problem. By 24 October the regiment had 94 men in hospital with dysentery, and by the end of October the figure was 143, with another 30 excused, probably including Frank, who went down with dysentery but wisely refused to go to hospital. Walter Guinness took out a strong patrol in the hopes of cutting off a Turkish patrol, but they evaded him. They were now shelled every day and the diary also notes 'snipers very active'.

From Gallipoli Frank wrote regularly to his mother, often on scraps of notepad, usually in one of the squadron's brief breaks from the trenches. In one he says it's a 'lovely day, sun shining, aeroplanes flying over us being shelled by the Turks. They never seem to hit them.' He is continually asking her to send things: carbolic, tooth powder, newspapers (underlined), the throat lozenges 'I asked Edward for', vests and shirts 'if any remain'. As the campaign wore on, he was obviously feeling the strain of it. 'No one seems to know what is going to happen out here. The Turks will probably get more shells now that Bulgaria has come in.' He wrote from the brigade 'rest camp' where he had been sent for five days: 'The trenches are really no worse than this.' His post, he said, was 80 yards from the Turks – 'better than most trenches, where they are only 8 or 10 yards apart.' He wrote sometimes of the losses in the brigade – 'poor Montefiore was killed, the one who married a Samuel. He came out with us. Give my love to Papa.' As the weeks wore on, his letters become terser, written in pencil, sometimes no more than a few hastily scribbled sentences. 3 November 1915: 'Avery gave us some food (6 of us mess together) & we do ourselves a little better. For the first 3 weeks we lived on rations & I could not have stood it much longer.'

Two days later, early in the morning of 5 November, the regiment once again moved back into the trenches to find the Turks had been active in their absence. 'Many of their sandbag trenches have been concealed by brushwood, and new trenches have been constructed,' the diary records. The dysentery problem continued, and the numbers of casualties were still rising: they were now down to 19 officers, and 290 men, with 155 men in hospital. That day Frank could no longer hold out – he too was despatched to hospital suffering a particularly severe attack of dysentery. The reserve camp was no healthier than the trenches, and the weather, after an unusual cold spell – which should have reduced the dysentery problem – now became warm again. A quarter of a million troops were crowded onto a tiny parcel of rocky land, and the problems of disease were becoming greater with every passing day. By 10 November there were 186 officers and men of the Suffolk in hospital, and only 301 left in the field. Major Goldsmith, however, returned to duty that day, according to the diary, after five days in hospital. The diary continues to record the daily misery – shellings, disease, occasional forays, and even a court martial, of a Private Manning of A Squadron who was charged with self-maiming but acquitted. There were gales, and torrents of rain, which flooded the trenches and dug-outs.

On 22 November Walter Guinness, two years younger than Frank, was given temporary charge of 1/10 London Regiment to which Frank's squadron had been attached. The Yeomanry were now down to 15 officers and 217 men, less than half the original strength. The first few days of December brought blizzards which made the conditions in the exposed trenches even worse. Even the laconic war diary records: 'This period in the trenches was a trying one for all ranks. There is practically no shelter and very few places for resting in this trench.' Men were now going to hospital with severely frost-bitten feet. By 8 December the regiment's strength was so diminished that the squadron system had to be abandoned and the regiment split into two wings, Frank commanding the right. The 54th Division was now being withdrawn from the peninsula, and the yeomen were attached to the Australian and New Zealand Army Corps, tough, veteran soldiers who had been through the worst of the fighting.

However low his own morale may have been, Frank does seem to have been able to hide it from his troops. Years later one of the men who served with him, Charles Skivens, an ironmonger in the town of Beccles, wrote to him.

I have always hoped some opportunity would offer of ... thanking you personally for the very great kindness that we all received while serving under you. Towards myself you were particularly kind on Gallipoli and it is difficult to tell you how much I have always appreciated it and how much I have often thought of it . . . I am sure it helped me, as it did all of us, to carry on under circumstances which were to say the least of it, very trying.

On 12 December the order came through to the regiment to begin drawing on emergency rations until further notice – no more fresh meat or bread would be brought up because of the congestion on the beaches. The regiment did not know it, but the evacuation of the peninsula had begun. Food in the front line became a major source of complaint among the troops, used as they had become to poor fare. How Frank, who enjoyed his food and his good wine, coped with it can only be imagined. That same day's war diary records the Turks tunnelling within eight feet of the British trenches, and also records 24 men returned from hospital although 'the reason for this is not apparent as there are none of them fit for work.'

By the 15th it was clear to the regiment that the part of the peninsula they occupied was being evacuated, although they had not yet guessed the scale of the withdrawal. Each day, parts of each regiment were withdrawn and evacuated from the peninsula, while the others kept up a level of activity designed to fool the enemy. They were now ordered to destroy stores, bury ammunition in latrines and graves, and break up spare rifles. The parties leaving did so at night, with just a kitbag for each six men, one blanket per man, a waterproof sheet, a greatcoat, two iron rations and a landing ration.

Frank led one of the last parties of the regiment to leave for the beaches, abandoning the trenches at 6 p.m. on 19 December, with three other officers and 57 men. His colonel followed with another party three hours behind him, and the last party left the following night, leaving behind an ingenious arrangement of rifles to fire at various intervals to persuade the Turks they were still there. One of the Suffolk officers described how they had set up the rifles which would be fired by water dripping slowly from one tin to another which was attached to the trigger by a string running over a pulley. The troops had tested different methods in the days before evacuation and they seem to have worked, because they left without a casualty.

The Suffolk Yeomanry arrived in Alexandria on several different ships a few days before Christmas and marched through the town to Ramleh tram station before getting to their new camp at Sidi Bishr. Frank's letters suggest he may have had some leave, for he spent some time in

Alexandria, where he met a number of old friends. Years later, Frank used to talk about his time in Alexandria with some nostalgia. He related how, when he told his father he was being posted to the Middle East, Adolph told him: 'God, that's awful. I hope you don't end up going to Egypt. You might end up in Alexandria and lose a lot of money at the Mohammed Ali Club.'

'No, don't worry, Papa,' Frank replied. 'We're only going to Gallipoli.'

Adolph's travels as a banker had presumably taken him to Alexandria at some stage, and now his son was there – and according to his own account he did indeed lose money at the Mohammed Ali Club. He also managed to get to Cairo, and to the races. Every Saturday that winter the Gezira Sporting Club in Cairo had a race meeting for 'NCOs and Men in Uniform', and the various races were designated 'for Arabs' or 'for all horses the bona fide property of Officers serving in Egypt . . . Professional jockeys 10 lbs extra.' Frank, according to the racecards, didn't actually ride himself, nor was he a steward which, given his keen interest in the sport and his membership of Tattersalls, he might have been. But he participated with enthusiasm. There had not been much relaxation on Gallipoli.

By March he was in El Kubri, at the southern end of the Suez Canal, which was again threatened by the Turks. It was much better than Gallipoli, but scorchingly hot. 'I like this place very much,' he told his mother. 'It is 7 miles from Suez, right in the desert on the Sinai peninsula.' The heat he said was 'not unbearable. I wore shorts up to now, but have given them up, as my knees were caught by the sun and are very sore.' He complains that none of the things he asked to be sent out have arrived: 'Don't let Edward's servant send them as he is not very lucky. None of his parcels ever seem to reach here.'

He took a series of photographs of Alexandria and Cairo, most of them, as with his early pictures of Cavenham, of extraordinarily high quality. He found a group of Jewish refugees from Palestine in Cairo and sent home pictures of them, which he inquired anxiously about in later letters – had they been safely received? They were carefully pasted into a scrapbook, presumably by his mother or his brother Edward.

After the evacuation of Gallipoli there were over 400,000 British troops in Eygpt, recovering and reorganising after a campaign which had been gallant but ill-starred. The Turks too had been able to withdraw their divisions from the peninsula for use elsewhere, and were once again planning an attack on the Suez Canal. They had actually crossed it a year earlier before being thrown back with considerable losses, but for twelve months had been preparing another attempt. The British had built trenches along the whole length of the canal, which were incredibly wasteful in men and material. Men were needed for the front in France, and were now steadily being withdrawn. By attacking, the British would actually need fewer men to defend Egypt than they would by sitting along the length of the canal. In the spring of 1916 Sir Archibald Murray, who took command of all the forces in Egypt, decided to take the initiative. He would advance across the Sinai.

He set off in March with five divisions and four mounted brigades, with the object of cutting off the northern route across the desert and flanking the southern route. His intention was also to remove the defence of Egypt as far as possible from Cairo for fear of a sympathetic uprising. Accompanying the force, and travelling at roughly the same speed, he built a broad-gauge railway and a water pipeline. It was a well-organised and well-equipped operation: large numbers of camels had been collected to transport supplies, as wheeled transport could not travel through the desert. Special 'pedrails' were constructed for the guns. By the end of April they had reached the Qatiya oasis, 25 miles east of the canal.

Where was Frank during this time? The regiment, re-formed and regrouped, had now been amalgamated with a number of other regiments and were known as the 3rd Dismounted Brigade attached to the 42nd Division. Frank's letters provide a few clues. He was in El Kubri on 6 April 1916 and reports that the squadron is about to move, which it did, but only to a new camp at Suez where for two weeks it was given intensive training. On 10 May he wrote again to his mother to tell her about a trip he had just made to Alexandria, saying it 'was a great relief to get away from this beastly place'. He refers to a battle 'in which the Warwickshires were cut up. A bad job. Poor fellows!' But mostly he passes on details that he thinks will not worry her. 'Left Suez at 5 p.m. & got to Alex. at 5.30 a.m.' Typically Frank managed to see some friends on the way:

Had tea with Stradbroke [the Earl of Stradbroke owned a large estate near Cavenham] at Suez. He is very fit. Then met Vivian and travelled with him. He is going home, has got command of a regiment. Saw a lot of Evelyn R [presumably Rothschild] . . . Avery and all my Egyptian friends.

On 21 May 1916 he is back again at El Kubri, at the southern end of the canal, commenting that it is 'a much nicer and healthier place than our last beastly place.' This is the last of his surviving letters until 1917, and the war diaries for May and June are missing. But in early July, the brigade was at El Ferdan, halfway along the canal, where on 19 July a planned move to Alexandria was abruptly cancelled and they were put on general stand-to.

At this point the war in Egypt was going well for the British. The advance in Sinai reached Romani by July, when it met a force of 18,000 Turks under the command of the Bavarian, Kress von Kressenstein, a highly professional and intelligent soldier. Romani was held by 30,000 Allied troops, and when the Turks attacked on 4 August they were routed, losing half their force. They would have lost the other half if the intense heat and lack of water had not stopped the British pursuit. By September the defeated Turks had retreated along the northern part of the desert to El Arish, and the British force continued its slow and careful advance, bringing its railhead up to within 20 miles of the main Turkish force by December. There had been no fighting for two months, and now the advanced guard of the British force, known as the Desert Column, went forward. This consisted of the 42nd (to which Frank was attached) and 52nd Divisions. As they were about to attack, the Turks abruptly withdrew. There followed a number of smaller actions, one against a Turkish force of 1,600 infantry 20 miles south, and another at Rafah, which were regarded as some of the war's finest examples of the power of boldly handled mounted troops, and by the end of January 1917, the Turks had been removed entirely from Egypt's borders. Suez and Egypt were safe.

Little of the glory went to the Suffolk Yeomanry and Major Frank Goldsmith, however, who spent all those months on garrison duty at Dabaa, on the Arabian peninsula. They had now been reorganised yet again, this time as an infantry brigade, and were now known as the Suffolk Yeomanry Battalion of the Suffolk Regiment. The war diary suggests a tedious period for Frank, of training with Lewis guns, bomb throwing and drill – there seems to have been lots of drill.

While the regiment drilled, the war cabinet in London had become more ambitious: Murray was ordered to press on and capture Gaza, thus opening the way to Palestine. The British government wanted something more spectacular than simply chasing the Turks out of the Sinai desert, strategically important though that had been. But Murray was not given the troops he needed. The 42nd Division, without the Suffolk Yeomanry, was withdrawn to France, leaving him with three divisions rather than the five he requested. He also had the nucleus of a fourth, which was formed from dismounted yeomanry. This was Frank's new division – the 74th.

On 12 February 1917, the war diary of the Yeomanry simply records: 'A Company started their range practices but had to discontinue owing to heavy rain.' Frank wrote a long letter to his mother which contains no details at all of what is happening to him. But he does tell her about the rain, 'just a few showers', and comments on the tiny rainfall the desert gets – four inches a year. 'In England the lowest rainfall is 24 in (at Felixstowe) & the highest is something like 86 in,' he tells her with a degree of awe, as well as an unexpected knowledge. He goes on to talk about the Bedouin and the local Arabs who 'don't do very much ploughing. Only scrape the earth with a sort of biblical plough.' It comes across, particularly compared to his tense, pencil-written notes from Gallipoli, as relaxed and loquacious, almost as if he is on holiday.

Yet he cannot have been at all relaxed. Apart from the war itself, he was still brooding over his political career. At some stage out in the desert he had reached a momentous decision: he would not go back to Stowmarket. He had not been back in England now since he sailed for Gallipoli 18 months before, and had taken no part in politics since the outbreak of war. But he was still an MP. That February (1917), from his desert post at Dabaa, he wrote to Colonel Spencer Follett, the chairman of the local Conservative Party, saying he would not be seeking re-election. He would be leaving the world of politics, abandoning the only career that had ever interested him.

There was still a campaign to be fought – and survived – before he could think more about his future. Early in March the battalion, as it now was, was ordered to move back to Sidi Bishr, near the canal and some way from the front, where they spent another month refitting and re-equipping as an infantry battalion, and exercising field tactics. Yet even after all this they were clearly not seen at headquarters as crack front-line troops. They were still exercising at Sidi Bishr when, on 26 March, the Egyptian Expeditionary Force under Murray attacked Gaza. When Murray's first attack failed, he was ordered to try again, this time with five divisions, and some tanks, used for the first time in the desert. The battalion arrived in the area on 11 April and took up positions facing the Turks. It was the first time in over a year that they had seen action, and even now they were not to be part of the main attack, but held the line in support of the 54th Division which passed through them to attack again on 17 April. The tanks bogged down in the sand or were hit by the Turkish guns, and the attack was beaten off with 7,000 British casualties. The Suffolk battalion covered the retreat, digging in in old Turkish trenches. It was the end of the Sinai campaign.

There was now a long pause in the desert fighting. Murray was sacked, to be replaced by General Allenby, who came out from France in June, and began preparing an offensive which he proposed to launch in the autumn. Through the summer months the Suffolk, now dug in around Gaza, suffered a regular shelling of their positions, and spent a great deal of time digging, which the diaries plaintively record. On 30 June 'the Turk sent over about a dozen shrapnel shells – just a few minutes too late to miss a football match', and on 7 July, Major Goldsmith 'proceeded to new branch school of instruction at El Arish' for a course in trench warfare. Frank returned to put what he learned into effect: by the end of July a new firing range had been created for the troops and Frank took a party of 200 men there for practice. It is the last mention of him in the war diaries.

Allenby waited until October 1917 to launch his attack, and by the end of the year his army had run triumphantly all the way to Jerusalem in one of the more spectacular successes of the whole war.

Frank Goldsmith by that stage, however, had left the Middle East – and active service. His scrapbook contains a leave pass, written in the field, and dated 30 August 1917, from the headquarters of the 74th Division. He is given three weeks in the UK, starting from the date of embarkation, which is odd for a start: this was on the eve of the biggest assault yet in the Palestine campaign, and Frank was now a well-trained, experienced officer, part of a battalion which at last was deemed ready for front-line action. Only a month before he had been sent on a training course, hardly likely if his superiors believed he was about to leave the army. There is no record of him being ill, or wounded; nor do the war diaries record his departure, merely the fact that instead of 34 officers, there were now 33. Frank never went back to the desert, and took no part in Allenby's Palestine victory. In September 1917 he was back in London, after two years away, and on 17 October 1917, as Allenby was preparing to shell Gaza, he wrote to the War Office asking to be released from military service in order, he said, 'to return to his parliamentary duties'.

There are unexplained mysteries here. Frank was certainly under some pressure to represent his neglected constituents who had grumbled on and off at his absence, even while the local papers jingoistically rejoiced in his military achievements. But Walter Guinness, now in France as commander of the 10th Battalion of the London Regiment, was also an MP and stayed on the Western Front until the end of the war, winning a DSO in 1917 and a bar in 1918. Frank seems to have had no interest in or intention of returning to his parliamentary duties, even for the remainder of the war – and in October 1917 it seemed as if the war might go on for ever. In the first week of November the executive committee of the North West Suffolk Conservative and Unionist Association unanimously passed a resolution offering

> a cordial welcome to Major Goldsmith MP on his return from active service, and sincerely trusts that in view of the many requests and general desire in the constituency for immediate personal representation in Parliament he will look after the interests of the Division in the House of Commons until the next General Election.

There is at least a hint of reproof in that motion, even though an article in the local paper a few days later lauded him for refusing to come home despite a serious attack of dysentery, preferring to stay with his men.

Even more mysterious was the alacrity with which the War Office agreed to Frank's application to be released from military service. On 9 November 1917, it wrote back to say that his application had been approved, and he was to be transferred immediately to the Territorial Force Reserve. 'I am to take this opportunity of conveying to you an expression of thanks for your services to the Territorial Forces,' it ended. It was addressed to him at the House of Commons.

It is unlikely he would have been released simply to go back to parliament at this critical stage in the war, when casualties in France were enormous, and every trained officer was valuable. Presumably he had used his contacts to organise something else for himself, something which was acceptable to the War Office, and presumably to his own conscience. Far from showing any indication of attempting to avoid military service up to this point, he seems to have sought it as preferable to the rejection he had felt in the autumn of 1914.

In short succession Frank had now resigned both his military and his political careers. His military career of course meant nothing to him – he had entered the war as a major (admittedly only in the territorials) and three years later was still a major, although by now he was nearing 40. At a time of rapid promotion as the army expanded and when the rate of attrition among officers was high, he had either refused or been refused promotion.

But his political career before the war had been something else. He had been a very ambitious and successful politician, who could certainly have hoped to become a member of the next Conservative government even as a junior minister – which is what his short-term sights seemed to be set on. The anti-German feeling in 1914 and the riots in Stowmarket had hurt him, and devastated his father, who moved from Cavenham to London because of it. Later he told his son Teddy that his ambition had died with the anti-German riots which, he said, had shattered him, and that could be true. But was that enough, after three years of active war service, to persuade him to abandon an ambition he had held most of his adult life?

His scrapbooks provide only one clue: one of omission. Nowhere in them is there any reference to his German birth. In fact it seems to have been carefully removed. He remained until his death very sensitive indeed about his German origins, although in his old age he often told his children about his schooldays in a place he referred to as the 'gymnasium'. He could not deny the origins of his father – and he didn't try to – but from quite early days he does seem to have deliberately created the impression that his parents had arrived in England some years before he was born, rather than when he was 17. When his German birth became a political issue, he was deeply ashamed.

He told Teddy that after the events of 1914 he simply wanted to hide, get away from all his old life. Yet after the first flurry of anti-German feeling, there is little indication that his birth was held against him. In 1917 he was still an acceptable member of English society, as shown by his invitation to join Tattersalls, and by his reception among his fellow officers and men. Perhaps he now believed that the highest offices of government would be denied to him, and in that case there was little point in a political career.

There is no question of him leaving the army in any disgrace. For years afterwards he was assiduous in attending reunions of the Suffolk Yeomanry, bringing his sons Teddy and Jimmy on occasions to a band that grew fewer each year, but which contained many men who had served with him – and who held him in some obvious affection and respect. Had he simply decided he was wasted as a middle-ranking field officer, and might serve England (he never thought of it as Britain) better in some other capacity? Did he use some of his old contacts such as Churchill to get himself brought back, and arrange a more interesting job than sitting around in the desert – which is what he had done most of the time in Egypt, Sinai and Palestine?

At any rate he never did devote himself to his parliamentary duties or to his constituency. But neither did he leave war service. Instead, he got a job in Paris, transferred to the military branch of the Ministry of Munitions, where his task during most of 1918 was to run an airfield north of Paris.

This is a shadowy period in his career, unrecorded in his scrapbook, in war diaries or in letters home. The Suffolk Yeomanry who were in the thick of the advance on Jerusalem, were sent to France in April 1918, but Frank never rejoined them. Later he would relate how one of his first tasks in France was to set up a brothel for the airmen, and engage in a battle with the local council about the number of girls needed. Frank, according to his own version, insisted that to do it properly there had to be six girls, while the council wanted to restrict it to half that number.

Sometime during 1918 something else happened to Frank: he met a girl called Jacqueline Franc, probably the first real love of his life, with whom he was to share his life for the next ten years. Jacqueline, as the many pictures of her show, was exceptionally attractive. She came from a modest background: her father was a roadsweeper from the village of Choisy-au-Bac, about 50 miles north of Paris, and when Frank was introduced to her she was still grieving over the loss of her lover, a rich young Frenchman called Schneider, whose family were among the biggest industrialists in France. Schneider was killed on the front, and Frank appeared on the scene some time later to take his place.

Jacqueline was by no means the first girl in Frank's life, even if she was the most important to date. Before the war he had lived with a girl called Charlotte, who was also French, and his scrapbooks suggest he was anything but celibate. But he seems to have become obsessed with Jacqueline, photographing her and taking her with him everywhere. His scrapbook, silent for so long during Gallipoli and the Palestine campaigns, contains several pictures of her, and he had photographs of her near him for the rest of his life, even when he was married to someone else. There is one of the two of them together, taken in Paris in 1918, Frank in uniform looking grim and much older than the man who went cheerfully off to war in 1914, she looking adoringly at him. It also contains several pictures of her looking extremely glamorous, in a low-cut diaphanous dress.

After he met Jacqueline, he seems to have been in no hurry to leave the forces once war ended. On 11 December 1918 his commissioner in Paris wrote to him to say that he 'regretted that your services will, in all probability, not be required after January 31st 1919.' Why 'regretted'? Was Frank being demobilised against his wishes? Most people were only too delighted to be demobilised. In June 1919, seven months after the end of the war, he was attached to the Bureau de Contrôle in Paris, which was responsible for passports and immigration. His scrapbook contains a pass saying that Major F. Goldsmith was proceeding to London on duty and was officially attached to the Bureau – an odd office for him to work for.

By that stage his life had changed in other unexpected ways too. On 6 April 1918 Adolph died, aged 80, leaving, according to *The Times*, an estate worth £364,000, including £1,000 to his confidential clerk and £500 to his butler. It would have been considerably more but for Adolph's belief in Tsarist and Kaiser bonds, in which he had invested heavily before the war (and, presumably, but for losses in the Mohammed Ali Club in Alexandria). Alice, Frank's mother, had inherited a considerable fortune from her father, so Adolph's fortune went to his children. Cavenham, with its 2,500 acres and large house which Frank had once enjoyed so much, was now virtually unused.

It is difficult to work out why he decided to upend his life in such a dramatic manner. His mother, whom he adored, still lived in London, as did his brother Edward. His sister and eldest brother lived in Germany but he had little contact with them, although they would still get together for occasional family gatherings. He had become – and would remain all his life – an archetypal English gentleman, with an impeccable English accent, membership of the best clubs, and many English friends. Paris was not an unknown city to him, and he had spoken French all his life, which had gradually replaced Frankfurter Deutsch as the polite language spoken by the German Jewish community. But it was a foreign city to him, even though he had lived there for a few years, and often visited it before the war. He had put down roots in England, and had none in France. Was it love? If so, why did he not persuade Jacqueline to come to London and live with him? The Goldsmiths were not in the habit of letting their women dictate where they lived.

The scrapbooks give no clue. Frank himself in later life gave none either, other than to blame the events of 1914, which scarcely account for such a change. Prince Louis Battenberg was driven from office in October 1914, and never recovered his zest for life, but the tide of opinion and the period of abuse of everything German had passed within weeks. 'Prince Louis's resignation was a matter of sympathy, not rejoicing', said Philip Ziegler in his biography of his son, Mountbatten.

But the fact is that from the end of 1917 to the end of his life 50 years later Frank Goldsmith lived in France, mostly in Paris. He never involved himself even in local politics; and although he tried unsuccessfully to rejoin the British forces in 1940, and religiously attended the Suffolks' reunions, he never again had any military involvement.

His constituency at Stowmarket was divided into two, another reason perhaps for resigning, but scarcely a strong one. In December 1918 his old friend and army comrade Walter Guinness (later Lord Moyne), who had held the Stowmarket seat before Frank, took over one half of it again, without even a candidate put up by the Liberals. Frank did all the right things, wrote all the right letters of resignation and farewell, observed all the niceties, and left England on a note that left no ill will behind. A new life began for him in Paris.

In 1919 Frank Goldsmith had never been involved in business, never worked for a living in his life, and knew nothing about the industry in which over the next half century he would become a legend: hotels. He had money, he was an active, intelligent and energetic 41-year-old, and he had many friends and relations, including the Rothschilds and others, who were bustling with business plans of their own. His first significant investment in the early 1920s was in a cinema chain, a business which was clearly expanding at that stage, but which in his case seems to have been a dud. He got into the hotel business by accident. He himself later related that he had lent money to a friend who could not pay him back, but gave him shares in a hotel business instead. Involved with it was one of the best-known French hoteliers of the day, Henri Ruhl, who had founded and run some of the best hotels in France, including the Scribe in Paris. Ruhl, as Frank was soon to discover, was past his sell-by date; in his later years he had expanded the hotel group too rapidly, and because of losses in parts of it, including a casino in Cannes, had run it into severe financial problems. He built a hotel at Chantilly, 25 miles north of Paris, on the basis that the motorcar could not do more than 25 miles without stopping for refuelling – which was true when he planned it, not true by the time it was completed. Frank suddenly found that he had to invest more money to save his initial investment – and M. Ruhl. He had the money, paid up, and M. Ruhl, who later courted Frank's sister-in-law Suzanne, was retired on a pension.

Actually running anything, let alone a hotel group, seems to have been the last thing on Frank's mind when he first went to Paris. But having strayed into it, he discovered he enjoyed it, and was a success at it. By the mid-1920s the Hôtels Réunis, as he called the chain he built up, was to all intents and purposes his company – he ran it, he was the perceived proprietor, and it was rapidly building up into one of the leading hotel companies in France. He became almost a monopolist in the principality of Monaco where he ran the Hôtel de Paris, l'Hôtel Hermitage, the

New Beach Hotel and the Sporting Club, most of which had casinos. Within a dozen years he had become something of a legend in the business. Cuttings refer to him as the 'entertainment dictator of Monte Carlo', or 'roi des Palaces', or 'the leading figure in the French hotel world', but most of that was press exaggeration, created by the Fleet Street gossip columnists who liked to spend the season around his hotels in the south of France. Everyone, including those close to him, assumed he owned the hotels he ran, but in fact the Hôtels Réunis only owned a small number – the rest were managed personally by Frank under a separate contract.

Nor did he ever make much money out of it. The Hôtels Réunis had considerable prestige and some good hotels attached to it, but it was basically a management company. Most importantly, as far as Frank was concerned, it allowed him to lead a life of some comfort. By the standards of his son Jimmy he was a poor businessman, and never translated his management companies into shareholdings in the hotels themselves – which were the lasting and valuable assets. But on the other hand, from the time he started Hôtels Réunis until the Germans invaded France in 1940, Monsieur le Major Frank Goldsmith enjoyed his life. He never gave the slightest hint, either then or to his children in his old age, that he regretted leaving England. Nor did he show the slightest indication of resentment at the anti-German feeling of 1914. He simply changed one life and one country for another in middle age, and went on with the rest of his life in the same affable, charming way he had gone about the first.

In 1921 his mother Alice died aged 78, and he returned to London and Cavenham to help sort out her affairs. His brother Edward lived a much more leisured life, his chief claim to fame being that he became Commandant of the Metropolitan Special Constabulary Reserve. He died in 1951, aged 82, leaving an estate worth £106,000 – £6,000 and all his clothes to his butler of 20 years. Alice Goldschmidt left £135,000 to her children, enough to sustain Cavenham if either brother were interested. Edward was not, and Frank was living in Paris. Frank had his own house at 31 South Audley Street, which he still kept but seldom used (and which at one stage he had shared with Viscount Castlerosse, a newspaper columnist whom he found too rowdy for him). The brothers decided to sell both Cavenham and the family house at 14 South Street, just off Park Lane, and on 24 May 1922 the two houses, plus their contents, came under the auctioneer's hammer. It was a major sale: Messrs Christie, Manson and Woods offered 'French Decorative Furniture, Objects of Art, Porcelain and Tapestry'. It lasted two days and raised £13,000. It was followed by another sale, this time of Adolph Goldschmidt's picture collection, which raised almost as much. Cavenham Park Estate was advertised with 2,500 acres as one of the 'best residential, agricultural and sporting estates in the Eastern counties', with its own two miles of river, and the whole of the village of Cavenham plus part of the nearby Higham parish.

Frank meanwhile had bought an elegant apartment on the Rue de Pressbourg in Paris, which he put, together with the furniture, into Jacqueline's name. His headquarters in Paris was now the Hotel Scribe, which never became one of the great hotels of Paris. He got the management contract for the Carlton in Cannes, the hotels in Monte Carlo which were really an adjunct to the casinos, the Prince de Galles in Paris, the Hôtel des Roches Noires in Trouville, the Royal Hotels in Ostend and Dinard, and many others. By 1928 there were 48 of them, a few owned, most of them managed, forming a loose chain of luxury hotels under the direction of Major Frank Goldsmith.

With his success went a good deal of pomp and ceremony. He and Jacqueline travelled in style and with an enormous amount of baggage, from hotel suite to hotel suite – from the Scribe in April to the Carlton in the season, on to Monte Carlo and perhaps to London. In 1926 he persuaded the directors of the Savoy group of hotels in London, which owned Claridges, the Berkeley and the Connaught, to make him a director, and from then on he had the use of a hotel suite whenever he wanted (although he continued to give his address as North Audley Street). He went back to Palestine in 1925 to help encourage the Jewish establishments there, and was later a founder director of the King David Hotel, used by the British as its headquarters in 1945 and 1946.

He appeared occasionally in the gossip columns, usually in a flattering role, never again as the serious statesman he seemed set to become before the war. One London columnist wrote a glowing piece describing him as 'the Big Shot on the Riviera'. All the English sunning themselves in the south of France, he said, were only there for one reason: 'Major Frank Goldsmith enticed them there.' This columnist, unfortunately anonymous, seems to have known Frank for some years.

'Just after the war,' he wrote, 'Frank did not know one end of an hotel from the other.' Gradually, he added, he had seen Frank become more and more master of his business. 'Fools think he is easy. In fact, that whimsical manner hides a hard-headed mind for money-making.'

Later in life, his two sons Teddy and Jimmy – particularly Jimmy – viewed their father's efforts in business with a sort of affectionate disrespect. To them, he was affable, loving, patient and dignified but scarcely dynamic. Yet the creation of the Hôtels Réunis chain was entirely his; after the first few years there was no one else of any note involved, and the group grew at a more than respectable speed. He could not have obtained and kept the management contracts for expensive, prestige hotels without actually being good at it.

He was obviously bright; he was also personable; he was very interested in the comforts of life; he had a natural gift for – and some experience of – command; and he was, when he wanted to be, energetic. These characteristics may have been ideally suited to becoming a good hotelier. At any rate he took to it, and the clientele of these great hotels took to him with equal warmth. In the south of France, many of the best customers in the 1920s and 1930s were English, particularly in Cannes and Monte Carlo; but there were also a growing number of Americans and Germans too. Frank was perfectly at home with them.

Jacqueline went everywhere with him. Frank introduced her to his friends, one of whom, the novelist Ralph Nevill, became almost as obsessed with her as Frank was. Nevill wrote around thirty books, several of them about life in Montmartre in Paris, or Mayfair in London, which featured Jacqueline in one guise or another. Several of them actually contain pictures of her, which Frank bought and kept.

In 1927, however, tragedy entered his life. He was now in his late forties, slightly balding, with a bit of a stoop – still a distinguished-looking man, whom the gossip columns liked to describe as 'immensely charming . . . the type about whom women say to their husbands "Why haven't you got Frank's charm?" ' He had been living with Jacqueline for nearly ten years, but had not married her. He wanted children – the Goldsmiths always wanted lots of children, he explained to her. For several years she had been visiting specialists but with no success, until it was discovered she had a blockage in her fallopian tubes. An operation, relatively straightforward even in the 1920s, was recommended to clear it. Frank had the money and the contacts to ensure she had the best surgeon and went to the best clinic. But the operation, for reasons the surgeons could never satisfactorily explain, went wrong. Jacqueline died under the anaesthetic.

It was an extraordinary precursor to what would happen in the life of his younger son 30 years later. Frank took it very hard, burying himself in his work, seldom seen for the next six months even at the social engagements which were very much part of his business calendar. There was a sequel to Jacqueline Franc's death, which rankled with Frank to his dying day:

because the apartment and furniture were in Jacqueline's name, and because they were not married, her brother claimed – and got – everything, including a considerable amount of money. Frank actually had to move out and take a room in one of his own hotels. Frank had no liking for this brother in the first place – he was head of the Communist party in nearby Compiègne – and he disliked him even more when he erected, in her home town of Choisy-au-Bac, a mausoleum to her, complete with lapis lazuli and malachite. Frank was regarded by the villagers as an extremely wealthy man, and the rumours went around that Jacqueline had been buried wearing her jewellery. During the night, the mausoleum was broken into and rifled.

His scrapbooks suggest he found consolation among other women, most of them young, slim and beautiful, but it was in the autumn of that year that he finally met the woman he was to marry.

Jimmy Goldsmith's mother, Marcelle Mouiller, could scarcely have come from a more different background. She was born in Vichy in the Auvergne, in 1905, the daughter of a peasant farmer who at one stage owned some land near Macon, to the north of Lyon. He lost his farm sometime around the turn of the century and moved south to the town of Vichy. The Auvergne then was one of the most primitive areas of France, a land where three-quarters of the population were peasants, the only industry being clustered around Clermont-Ferrand. M. Mouiller seems to have been energetic and ambitious: in the town he got a job as a cook, and after some years started his own modest hotel called the Hôtel La Clôche; at one stage he seems to have had another hotel, called Hôtel Seville. He also went into local politics as a Socialist, becoming a member of the municipal council of Vichy, and might have made it to the head of the party had it not been for his wife. He was a Catholic in a largely Protestant area, and married a Catholic woman from Strasbourg called Brunner, who was known in the town as 'la Boche', and regarded with some distrust, even before World War I. She worked in the hotels and he ran them, and they had nine children, five boys and four girls. One of the brothers was drowned when he was eleven in the local river, another, Rico, was later shot by the Germans as a resistance fighter in World War II, and a third, George, became a wine salesman and later died from cirrhosis of the liver. The eldest son, Francis, was the black sheep of the family, and in later years the others would not even talk about him.

The women of the family, however, were more resourceful, and did much better with their lives. Around the outbreak of war in 1914, according to the family story, M. Mouiller went bankrupt basically because he guaranteed the debts of a friend. He sold the hotel and they moved to a house just above Cannes. Mouiller died just after the war, and his wife found it hard to cope with a growing family. It was Jeanne, the eldest girl, who effectively acted as a mother to four sisters, even after she married a Russian aristocrat and moved with him to Odessa. The Russian revolution drove them out again, and the marriage didn't last. A few years later she married a French Huguenot called Fort.

Jeanne Mouiller, as it happened, had been Jacqueline Franc's best friend for some years. Now she took it upon herself to find husbands for her sisters – and saw Frank, recovering from Jacqueline's death, as a possible prospect. In the summer of 1927 Frank planned a trip to Cannes to make some arrangements at the Carlton, and Jeanne arranged to go with him. If Frank was aware of the plot, he seems to have gone along with it unresistingly. They travelled, Jeanne without her husband, by train, to be met by the usual retinue of porters which greeted Monsieur le Major everywhere – and by Jeanne's younger sister, Marcelle. She was 23, 27 years younger than he.

The two sisters accompanied him everywhere in the week he spent in Cannes, and when Frank was ready to leave Marcelle insisted on accompanying them to the station in order, she explained, to see the inside of the famous Blue Train which ran between Paris and the south. Marcelle before she died told the rest of the story: she pretended to be fascinated by the luxury of the train with its oak panelling, and hand-stitched linen on the beds. Without apparently anyone noticing, the train began to move while she was still aboard, wearing only a summer dress over her swimming costume, and with no baggage. (Frank's version to his sons was that he grabbed her, and took her on to the train.) She resisted half-hearted attempts to put her off at the first station, insisting she would stay in Paris with her sister – which is what she did. Frank entertained her most evenings, taking her to all his favourite haunts: the Ritz in the Place Vendôme, the jewellery shops and the restaurants where he was well known. Within weeks she had taken the place of Jacqueline.

Marcelle never left him. By the following spring she was pregnant, and the first son, Edward, named after Frank's brother, was born in November 1928. Frank still lived in a hotel suite at the Scribe, where he had moved after Jacqueline's death, but now he bought an apartment, at 43 rue Emile-Meunier, in the Bois de Boulogne.

He and Marcelle were still not married, and Frank finally put that right, not in Paris or even Marcelle's home town of Cannes, but in London. In June 1929 a little item appeared in the British press saying that, 'A beautiful French girl, Mlle Marcelle Mouiller, who has been staying at the Hotel Splendide in Piccadilly since Sunday last, was married at the Princes-row Registry Office to Major Frank Goldsmith.' Frank gave his address as South Audley Street. One of the witnesses to the marriage was Sir Duncan Orr-Lewis, presumably a friend of Frank. (Teddy never discovered he had been born out of wedlock until many years later when his grandmother died, her estate to be divided between her legitimate descendants. Teddy was excluded, but his father gave him the money.)

Back in Paris the couple lived well: they had a nurse, a cook, a maid and later a governess, and Goldsmith had a chauffeur for the Rolls-Royce which took him from the *16ième arrondissement* to his office. It was into this comfortable, affluent scene that on 26 February 1933 Marcelle Goldsmith gave birth to her second son, whom they called James Michael.

4

The Gambler

Frank Goldsmith was 54 when his son Jimmy was born – by an odd coincidence the same age as Jimmy would be when his own son, Jethro (but also called Jimmy), was born in 1987. That age gap alone, and the fact that Frank had come late both to marriage and to parenthood, made his father a distant, but never aloof figure; his natural reticence, courteousness and busy life made him undemonstrative, but he was always warm; he came from a large family and enjoyed his own children. Jimmy Goldsmith in his late teens would have fights with him, but never to the point where they were not on speaking terms, and Frank for his part was remarkably indulgent even when the behaviour of his sons bordered on the outrageous.

Jimmy's mother Marcelle featured more prominently in his life in his early years, although in later life the reverse was true. Goldsmith may have been brought up to think of himself as one of the Goldschmidts of Frankfurt but he was only half Jew. The other half he would remark years later was 'Auvergne peasant', which was not strictly true. Marcelle was more *moyenne bourgeoise* than peasant, and grew up with no sense of inferiority towards her social betters. 'Marcelle would hate to have been called a peasant,' says an old family friend, 'and certainly she never gave me the impression of being a peasant. She was a beautiful creature who I don't think had ever seen a hoe or spade in her life.' Where Frank was low key emotionally, she was high key. 'She was very stimulating to Frank,' says a friend. The adult Jimmy Goldsmith was irritated by her – 'she could be very amusing, and some of her stories were very funny,' says one of the family, 'but somehow they rubbed each other up the wrong way.' Yet, later in life, Goldsmith would reckon he got as much from his mother's family as he did from his father's side – intellectually

53

he might have thought of himself as a Goldsmith, but emotionally he was much more Mouiller.

From the start Marcelle mixed with the friends and business acquaintances of her husband without apparent anxiety or effort, and fitted easily into his life at the hotels he ran. She was his hostess at the parties he gave, the opening of new restaurants or the refurbishment of old ones. She took as keen an interest as he did in the people who came to stay, and whom she had to entertain. The hotels were her home and she looked after them as such. She also played her role in fitting in to what remained of Frank's family. There is an early picture, taken in 1936, of a three-year-old Jimmy playing on her knee as she sits on the grass, surrounded by Frank's brothers and their wives, all of them (including Frank) formally suited and wearing hats. Frank's elder brother Edward is there with his wife Georgilia, and so is his sister Nellie and her husband Ernst von Marx, whom Frank never forgave, but tolerated for the sake of his sister. Marcelle was photographed for some of the magazines of the times, in golfing clothes, or posing in the gardens of one of the hotels in the south of France, entertaining important guests, in one described as '*la gracieuse et souriante Mme Frank Goldsmith*'. There is no trace of self-consciousness about her in any of these pictures, one of which shows her smilingly marching, arms swinging, out of the Carlton in Cannes, a confident, pretty young woman, in a knee-length military-style suit and shoes. She had jet black hair, worn long when Jimmy was born, later in a bob, and long, slender hands which Jimmy inherited. As he grew older and his remaining hair turned grey, Jimmy would come more and more to resemble his father, but he got his height and his piercing blue eyes from his mother. He also got his charged energy from her; his interest in business and money must have been in his genes, missing out Frank, who had little interest in it, and his elder brother Teddy who had no flair for it at all, magnifying itself in Jimmy. Teddy remembers his mother being absolutely obsessive about detail, something both her sons inherited. Goldsmith would later spend the first half of his business career consciously attempting to re-establish the Goldschmidt family wealth and catch up with his Rothschild cousins, but the blood of the Auvergne flowed equally through his veins.

Frank Goldsmith's life style in the late 1930s was extravagant and grand. It was also nomadic, another important element in the habits of Jimmy Goldsmith in later life. Although he retained his handsome apartment at 43 rue Emile-Meunier, in reality there was no fixed home. Frank and his entourage moved from hotel to wonderful hotel, the young boys Teddy and Jimmy often along with them, accompanied by baggage, servants and much pomp and ceremony. From the moment he was born, Jimmy Goldsmith enjoyed a quality of life perhaps only equalled by members of the royal families. There were always waiters, maids, valets, cooks, chauffeurs and doormen the press of a bell away; porters humped dozens of trunks onto trains and other porters picked them off at the other end. Hotel managers and staff stood formally in the foyers to welcome the proprietor, for all the world like a naval captain being piped aboard his ship. Jobs in post-depression France were much prized and Monsieur le Major, as he was always called, had the power to hire or fire hundreds of people in the hotels he managed.

An item in a gossip column gives an indication of the way they lived. It states that 'Mr Goldsmith is a very rich man', which of course everyone believed at the time but was never true, adding that the importance of his position

> may be gauged by the ceremony which accompanies his arrival and departure at any of his hotels. At the Paris at Monte Carlo, for instance, I saw him descend the steps between a row of bowing hotel officials and servants, his beautiful French wife stepped into his glittering car, Mr Goldsmith followed, a secretary hurried up to hear a final word of advice. Then the much-bemedalled negro porter arrived with a great black tin box full, I like to believe, of bank notes. The door was slammed, and Mr Goldsmith drove away.

Sir Hugh Wontner, now the president of the Savoy group, remembers visiting the cellars of the Hôtel de Paris in Monte Carlo and seeing row upon row of the finest wines, all marked for 'M. Major Goldsmith'. Frank took the young Wontner around his hotels, and Sir Hugh watched with a degree of awe the reception he received: 'He was a personality, a very polished and good-looking man, with astonishing grace. He was also, you would say today, laid back – he didn't give the impression he worked at all. He floated around his empire, and life was something that went on around him – that was the impression he gave. Yet you also felt there was much more behind him than he was letting on.'

The boys grew up used to subservience, to luxury and to getting what they wanted. Neither Frank Goldsmith nor his wife seems to have been a strict parent, particularly by the standards of the day. Nor were they always about. In Monte Carlo Teddy and Jimmy lived every winter in l'Hôtel Hermitage, an old-fashioned, rather faded hotel, while Frank and Marcelle lived in grander style at the Hôtel de Paris. There was an underground passage between the two, separated by many corridors, lifts and hallways. It bred in Jimmy Goldsmith an independence and love of a lifestyle he would never abandon, even in the days when 20 years later he could barely afford to eat. It would take him over 40 years and many millions of dollars to get back to the life he took for granted as a boy.

His playgrounds in these years were the terraces and suites of the best hotels in the world. The family travelled with the seasons, because that of course was what the best of the clientele did. Monsieur le Major wanted to be on hand when the Prince of Wales and his new girlfriend Wallis Simpson came to stay in Cannes, or the Aga Khan, the Rockefellers, the Mellons or the other wealthy families of the time booked suites in his hotels. He posed on the terrace of the Café de Paris with the Baron and Baronne de Bonstetten or the Comte Mittrowsky, or was pictured dining with Lady Stern. The Goldsmiths would spend spring in Paris, a couple of weeks in London staying at Claridges, then back to Paris, to Trouville, and to Cannes for the season on the Côte d'Azur.

The local papers in Suffolk recorded his occasional visits to his old home, mostly for reunions of the Yeomanry. He occasionally attended the races at Newmarket, staying with Anthony de Rothschild or one of his other old friends. But his visits were fleeting; his heart was now in France.

Jimmy Goldsmith's later love of gambling may have been, like his interest in business, in his genes. His father loved cards, but in a low-key formal sense, playing regularly in the Travellers Club in Paris, his favourite club in the world, and St James's in London. Frank's elder brother Carl was a much more ardent gambler, regularly seen at the casino in Ostend, highly fashionable in the 1930s. Frank often talked about him and of his addiction to roulette, which cost him not only his considerable inheritance from both his father and mother, but also his sanity – he ended his days in a Swiss sanitorium, blaming his ill-luck on a fellow-player, the King of the Belgians, with whom he had become obsessed. Jimmy himself discovered the joys of gambling early in life when, at the age of six, in the winter of 1939, he was staying with his parents in Monte Carlo. The Hôtel de Paris was one of the most elegant hotels in Europe, with large gracious foyers, and sweeping staircases. Jimmy was fascinated by a large slot machine installed in the bar, and his great joy as a small boy was to play there. People would give him coins and he would shove them in the machine, and watch for hours as others played. Marcelle decided this was no place for a boy of six, and forbade it, but he slipped back through the underground passageway from the Hermitage, and continued. One evening an old American woman kept feeding one-franc pieces into a one-armed bandit for no reward, watched in fascination by the young Goldsmith. When she finally gave up, she gave him a franc, which he inserted – and hit the jackpot. There was a search party already out for him, but he summoned a waiter to place the yield on a large silver tray, which he carried off in triumph to show his parents, who were in the dining room. Frank was less than pleased. His son could not have the money until he was older, he told him sternly. 'A boy of your age should not be gambling.' Jimmy had other thoughts however. He grabbed the tray, and ran off, whizzing up in the lift, then down again before diving down the passageway towards the Hermitage where his puffing parents finally caught him.

That same year, 1939, the threat of war loomed, even in far-off Monte Carlo. Teddy, now ten, was kept at school in Cannes, but the family was still moving about as freely as ever. Frank, as a former politician and soldier, must have been as aware as anyone of the threat of Hitler, and in particular of the anti-Semitism which went with it. When war came in September, the family was in Trouville, and Frank hurried them back to Paris. His immediate reaction, given his rejection of Britain, was an odd one: he wanted employment with the British Army. He wrote to an old friend, the Earl of Bessborough, and to Sir George Reeves-Smith, asking them if they could arrange it for him. They both took it personally to the top: to Leslie Hore-Belisha, the War Secretary (he resigned in January 1940, much to Winston Churchill's regret). On 14 October, Hore-Belisha's private secretary wrote to Bessborough, saying that the War Secretary had instructed him to let him know that 'Major Goldsmith's application for employment with the Army has been considered, but unfortunately he is ineligible for enrolment in the Army Officers' Emergency Reserve on account of age, the age limit for that Reserve being 60, while Major Goldsmith is 61.' A careful record, however, had been taken of his qualifications so that if the age limit was changed, he would be reconsidered.

Frank seems to have been very keen on getting back into the British Army in some role, and pursued it with a battery of letters. But in the meantime there was still a business to be run, even in wartime. Frank arranged a travel pass with the police in Paris (it is dated 6 December 1939), and the Goldsmith family moved back to the south of France just before Christmas. They spent the rest of the winter of the 'phoney war' there, with Teddy at school in Cannes. Frank made no plans to move to England, or anywhere else. This part of France had been untouched by

World War I, and he had probably no reason to believe it would be affected this time around, except financially – the hotel business was not good in France that year.

Then on 14 May came the breakthrough by the Germans in the north, the virtual collapse of the French army, and the hurried retreat of the British forces towards Dunkirk. Frank, suddenly concerned by the prospect of an invasion from Italy, now sent Marcelle with Teddy and Jimmy to the Pyrenees to stay with a friend of hers, but he himself stayed on in Cannes. It was early June, however, before the children departed – Teddy and Jimmy were issued with ration cards in Cannes dated 1 June. Shortly after they arrived in the Pyrenees, Frank must have realised that nowhere in France would be safe. He had to get the family out. The British consul was advising all British subjects to make their way to the port of Bayonne where arrangements were being made to evacuate them. He got word to Marcelle to travel north, and he would join her there.

In an interview a month later, Frank remarked on the lack of information on the course of the war. 'The most astonishing fact was the absolute and total ignorance of events among the French population.' English papers no longer reached Cannes, there was no news in the French papers, he said, and no one knew the French were already 'negotiating capitulation'. He certainly left his departure remarkably late. According to an interview he gave after the war, Frank left Monte Carlo '*sans bagage, sans rien*' on 23 June, and in another (earlier) one he said he left Cannes on 18 June. The earlier date sounds the more likely; even by that stage the country was in total chaos. On 10 June Italy, with 60 divisions, had entered the war, and had begun to attack the French from the east. On 14 June the Germans marched into Paris, and French resistance effectively disintegrated. Hundreds of thousands of refugees fled south in front of the rapidly advancing armies. By 14 June, the Germans were in Reims, and a day after that they took Verdun, the symbol of French fighting spirit in 1914. The French government moved first to Tours, then to Bordeaux and on 16 June, the 84-year-old Marshal Pétain took over and, with 'a broken heart', asked for honourable terms in an armistice. On 21 June Hitler presented his terms in the railway car at Compiègne.

Frank by that stage was at last on the road towards Bayonne, which Marcelle had already reached with Teddy and Jimmy. He was not quite travelling *sans bagage, sans rien*, except perhaps by his own pre-war standards. He left in the Rolls-Royce he had bought for Jacqueline years before, and which he used for formal occasions. At the wheel was his chauffeur Nelo, and Frank took with him another Jewish friend, Sydney Beer, a conductor, and Beer's Austrian wife Heidi. They skirted Marseilles, which was choked with refugees and got as far as Carcassonne before they were stopped. The town, like most others anywhere near the Spanish border, was filled with refugees and the French army had taken over. The armistice, which would give the Germans control of the entire west coast of France, including Bayonne, had not yet come into effect but there were plenty of rumours, and the roads were clogged – and blocked by troops who refused to let Frank and his Rolls-Royce any further. Frank's frame of mind at this point can only be guessed at: he and Beer were both Jewish, with all that meant. He was also English. Worse still, there was no way of getting word through to Marcelle who would be waiting for him, and who would probably go on waiting until it was too late. Would she have the sense to take the boys and get on the next boat out? He and Beer were stuck, and they were also hungry. They still had money, and found a restaurant in the town that would serve them a decent meal. It was there they found salvation. At the next table was a French officer and three soldiers who were expressing their disgust with Pétain. They talked about joining de Gaulle and the Free French forces, and Frank overheard. He too was trying to get to England, he explained, and what's more he had a car which with a bit of help could get them to Bayonne where he understood there were still ships evacuating people to England. The French soldiers, fully armed, joined them and at the first roadblock used their guns to force their way through the half-hearted attempt to stop them. The Rolls-Royce drove on, and finally reached Bayonne. The port by now was crammed to bursting.

Marcelle had already been there several days, and had managed to find one of the few hotel rooms in the town. But there were not enough ships, rumours were rife that the harbour was to be blockaded and bombed, precious little food was to be had, and everyone behaved as if the Germans were just down the road, although they were still hundreds of miles away. Typically Frank met an old friend, Claude Rollo, a member of the Travellers Club in Paris, who was also trying to flee. In the town also were the English Rothschilds including (now Sir) Evelyn and his two sisters Renée and Anne, a governess and their French mother, who had also left their flight to the last moment.

Teddy and Jimmy were sent out with a fistful of money to find food, but there was not even bread in the town. They came back with some nuts, which had to do the family that evening. On the docks the next morning there was pandemonium. There was a single Dutch freighter, requisitioned by the British and with a British crew, which steamed into the river Adour, and was now ready to take on passengers. The captain appeared at the side of the bridge and addressed the panicking crowd through a megaphone. The ship, he said, was designed to take 300, but he was proposing to take 3,000 – still only a fraction of the numbers on the dock. 'British-born subjects first,' he said. None of the Goldsmiths was British-born, but Frank had a British passport, and pushed his way through to present it, and explain that he was a former Member of Parliament, and also a major in the British army. They scrambled aboard, and a few hours later the heavily laden ship slipped downriver and out into the Bay of Biscay. It was the last ship to leave France.

As Jimmy remembers it, he shared a cabin with Evelyn de Rothschild, but Teddy recalls it differently: Jimmy was on the deck under a seat, while Teddy, who had become friendly with the Rothschild sister Anne, was invited to the Rothschild cabin. In any case Jimmy was marginally safer on deck than down below. The ship had to run the whole length of the Bay of Biscay, round the now hostile Brittany coast, and then sail up channel to Southampton – a journey of two and a half days in the elderly freighter. The German U-boats had not yet moved down to Brest and the other French Atlantic ports, but they were active, and a few hours out there was an alarm, followed by total panic as the captain ordered all his passengers on deck. There was no way they could all fit on deck, and no lifeboats for more than a fraction of them if the ship had been hit. Rumours went around that a torpedo had been fired at them but had missed, and the alarm subsided. Once they were at sea, the boys began to enjoy themselves, seeing it as an adventure rather than the dangerous voyage it was. The boys recall Frank and Marcelle being remarkably calm too, although inwardly they must have been deeply shaken by the events of the past few days.

The London they arrived in was wartime London, with blackouts and air-raid sirens and nightly bombings. The major took his family straight to Claridges where the austerity was muted, but the blitz was on and nowhere in London was safe, not even the cellars of Claridges where they adjourned nightly. With his business life abandoned in France, and no job for him in the British forces, the major had nothing to do, although he was well enough off; he had always kept money in London. Teddy remembers one little incident from this time: Marcelle one day turned up with a pot of jam. Where had she got it, Frank demanded? On the black market, she explained proudly. 'He made her take it back to where she had bought it,' says Teddy. 'My father was an unbelievably scrupulous man, who saw himself as an English patriot.'

Frank overcame his dislike for his brother-in-law Ernst von Marx sufficiently to attempt to persuade the Foreign Office to intervene on his behalf. A letter dated 8 July, replying to one from Frank a week earlier, from Lord Lloyd, minister at the Colonial Office and leader of the House of Lords, says he would 'do what I can about your Mr von Marx. The regulations are very strict, but I will find out what can be done.' This suggests that von Marx and Frank's sister Nellie had left Germany along with so many other Jews (von Marx's conversion to Christianity would not have saved him from the gas chambers), and were now interned. Ironically, the man who had condemned Frank for not fighting for his fatherland was now an exile from that land.

The Goldsmiths were not long in London. Frank, abandoning his efforts to get back into the forces – even his old colleague Winston Churchill could not help him – now went to the other extreme and organised a job for himself, as far away as he could get from the fighting. Within weeks of arriving in London, he took Marcelle and the boys to Liverpool and boarded another ship, this time bound for Halifax, where they arrived in July 1940. Aboard was a large group of children, shipped to Canada to escape the bombing; one of the Canadian papers pictured them arriving, with the caption 'sirens, blackouts and bombs are among the things least missed by young war guests in Canada'. The photographer has obviously told all the children to wave and Jimmy, in the forefront, listlessly lifts a hand, his gaze on something else, while Teddy, in the middle of the group, joins in more enthusiastically.

From Canada they travelled to New York and from there to the Bahamas, where Frank had arranged a job as manager of the Royal Victoria Hotel in Nassau. It was the first time in his life he had ever worked for someone else.

Four years slipped by uneventfully but enjoyably for the Goldsmith boys. The Goldsmiths had friends on the islands, other émigrés like themselves, or, on a different level, the new governor and his wife, the Duke and Duchess of Windsor – the Duchess greeted them effusively when she spotted them at an official reception, the first friendly faces she had seen in a hostile environment. Frank and Marcelle settled easily into a comfortable life of receptions, parties, endless conversation – and some work. The Bahamas in the early 1940s were as idyllic as any place in the world, barely troubled by the war in Europe. The islands were just emerging as the playground of the rich and idle, and the scrapbook kept by Marcelle is filled with the autographs of well-known actors, actresses and others who holidayed there: William Wyler, Simone Simon, Henry

Cotton the golfer, the actress Lilian Harvey and many others whose signatures now are mostly unreadable. The pace of life in wartime Bahamas was leisurely, without undue hardship – siestas in the afternoon, tropical weather, excellent food and wine. They bought a house in the Breezy Hill Estate, which Jimmy remembered as large until he returned to it 40 years later when it seemed much smaller.

Somehow, despite his uprooting from France, Frank had managed to recreate for himself and his family as near a perfect existence as was possible in wartime. There were invitations to dine with the Duke and Duchess at Government House, and frequent invitations to join them at receptions and cocktail parties. They were at Government House too that Christmas in 1940 when the Duke and Duchess gave a party for the children on the island, each brown paper label (both Teddy's and Jimmy's carefully preserved in Marcelle's scrapbook) signed 'Wallis Windsor and Edward'. Among the small population, every minor event was recorded in the local Nassau papers: 'Master Jimmy Goldsmith, son of Major Frank and Mrs Goldsmith, was a tonsillectomy patient at the hospital this week and is well on the road to recovery.' Another item related how Teddy and Jimmy had developed an interesting hobby: 'With some money they received at Christmas they bought three fowls and now have the very satisfactory number of 58, counting the little ones. All have pet names, and they spend every moment they can looking after them.'

On a couple of evenings a week Marcelle helped run a canteen for trainee air force pilots, organised by the Duchess, and Frank obtained a pass to travel during curfew hours as a 'watcher', although there was not much to watch out for. The boys were free to enjoy the sun and sand. Jimmy, young as he was, developed a love for games of dice, and he and Teddy gambled incessantly with the seashells they collected.

They did have to be educated, however, and in the case of Jimmy this was becoming something of a nightmare. From the start he hated school, the discipline and difficulty of it; and he hated sports too, despite considerable efforts to force him into them. Teddy's reports indicate that he was a model pupil, first at Belmont School, later at the Methodist Missionary Society, with lots of 'excellents' and 'very goods' against his name. Jimmy was a different matter. He was slow to read and even slower to write, and the more he fell behind the others the more rebellious he became. He was clearly bright, every bit as clever as his elder brother who steamed ahead without problems. But he could not apply himself.

Teddy recalls asking him, when he was seven, why he was not

interested in learning to read. The elder brother was genuinely puzzled, as were his teachers and parents. Jimmy, however, had an answer. 'Because when I grow up I'm going to be a millionaire and hire someone to read for me.' It became one of the family jokes, but Jimmy was deadly serious. His school reports showed him to be 'lazy' and 'uninterested', but there may have been another aspect to this which Goldsmith himself would only begin to suspect late in his adult life, when it manifested itself in his own son Manes. Many of the symptoms he exhibited in his early years are classical ones of dyslexia: his short attention span, his impatience, his slowness in reading (he read voraciously in later life, but still quite slowly), and an educational performance which fell well short of his intelligence and obvious abilities. By nature and upbringing both he and Teddy were misfits. But from these early days Jimmy Goldsmith was displaying an extra dimension which was to affect his whole life: the sense of having to prove to others that he was better than they were, to get his own back on those who jeered at him; he was already an outsider and would remain so always, drawn to other misfits like himself, always against the establishment, whatever that meant at the time.

None of this, of course, was understood by Frank or Marcelle, who just saw a wilful, unruly boy, with endless charm when he wanted to display it, a curiously grown-up manner, but an absolute refusal to get on at school. In 1942, when he was nine, they sent him and Teddy to boarding school in Toronto, hoping the austere English public-school-like atmosphere of St Andrew's College would do for him what the Belmont school in the Bahamas had signally failed to do. Again it was a dismal failure, but a more painful one. St Andrew's prided itself on its tough sporting tradition, and Jimmy Goldsmith, tall for his age, looked well capable of becoming a useful athlete. But he was uncoordinated – he never learned to drive a car well – and the more he was pushed into something he felt he was not particularly good at, the more he refused to do it. Competing in sports meant being beaten, and failure is something Jimmy Goldsmith never learned to accept gracefully. It mattered nothing to him that he was regularly punished, often severely. That was better than failing (another classic symptom of dyslexics). At the school's annual cross-country race, in which everyone was expected to take part, he deliberately strolled into the quadrangle 15 minutes after everyone else, a bag of toffee in one hand and the Toronto *Sporting Chronicle* in the other. Teddy, ill at the time, watched from the sickroom window as Jimmy appeared, in front of the whole school, apparently absorbed in the racing pages.

Both boys, particularly Jimmy, hated St Andrew's. For one thing it was incredibly cold, and they had never known cold before. Jimmy now recalls, probably exaggeratedly, that there was no heating, and he used to wear two sweaters on top of his pyjamas to go to bed. In the winter they had to heat the ink.

For a non-sporting boy, Jimmy at age nine developed an odd business. He began to trap animals, setting the traps at night and emptying them the next day. He recalls catching skunk, rabbit, and the odd wild mink, and selling the skins. At Christmas 1943, unable to go home to the Bahamas, he left school and went to New York, where he had been once before with his father. It would, he thought, be more fun than Toronto. He did not even tell Teddy, but caught a train to Grand Central Station, took a taxi to the Waldorf Astoria and checked in. It was some days before his angry parents arrived, but Goldsmith was having the time of his life, and still recalls the incident with huge amusement.

That summer the peaceful life of the Bahamas was ruptured by a murder which is still a mystery and cause of considerable speculation today, nearly 50 years later. When Frank Goldsmith prepared to leave England for the Bahamas, J. A. Noonan, the manager at the Royal Bank of Canada in Cockspur Street, London, gave him a letter of introduction to an acquaintance of his, Sir Harry Oakes, one of the richest men in the British Empire. Oakes was then 65, and had retired to Nassau after making a fortune from his Lake Shore Mines company in Canada, once the second richest gold source in the world. But in 1943 there were rumours that the Colonial Office was planning to levy taxes in the Bahamas to help meet the war costs. Oakes also felt he was being cheated by his partner, Harold Christie, who was heavily in his debt. Between midnight and dawn on 8 July 1943, Oakes was murdered in his bed in his huge house, Westbourne, where the Duke and Duchess had stayed in their early days on the island while they had Government House refurbished. There were allegations that the Duke was in partnership with Oakes in schemes to smuggle millions of dollars out of the Bahamas, which had become more and more of a money laundering centre as the war went on. The Duke took personal charge of the murder investigation, bypassed the local force, and called for help from the Miami police department where Captain Edward Melchen had been his bodyguard. The Miami policemen, to the astonishment of the local police, arrested and charged Oakes' son-in-law, Alfred de Marigny, who was tried in perhaps the most sensational court battle the Bahamas has ever seen. The jury was out only a short time and returned a verdict of 'not guilty', but recommended Marigny's deportation. The murder remains unsolved to this day, but the FBI had detailed files on the Duke's money laundering operations – including money taken from countries occupied by the Nazis. Years later de Marigny wrote a book in which he pointed the finger unequivocally at Harold Christie, as have others, with the suggestion that because of the Duke's involvement with Oakes, he had covered it up.

The Goldsmiths knew not only Oakes, but Christie, de Marigny and all the other people involved. They met Oakes on a number of occasions at Government House with the Windsors, and at the various functions Frank frequented. Marcelle's scrapbook records her fascination with the affair, the only topic on the island for months. Frank's letter of introduction to Oakes, unused, was pasted in his scrapbook.

There is another letter there too, pasted in for a similar reason. From the Bahamas Frank wrote to many of his old friends, including Walter Guinness, who had returned after the war to a glittering political career – financial secretary to the Treasury, minister of agriculture, and, from 1941 onwards, Churchill's secretary of state for the colonies and leader of the House of Lords. In November 1944 word reached the Bahamas that Guinness, now Lord Moyne, had been assassinated in Cairo by members of the Stern gang. Years later, in 1983, Israel's new prime minister, Itzhak Shamir, admitted that he had been one of the three people who ordered it. Guinness' last letter to Frank was also pasted in the scrapbook.

By 1944 Frank and Marcelle had reluctantly accepted that St Andrew's was not the place for their boys. The war was now being won by the allies, and although England was still under bombardment from V1s and V2s, the countryside away from the big cities was relatively safe. The school they chose could not have been better for Jimmy. Millfield, in Somerset, was then very new, the creation of the legendary R. J. O. 'Boss' Meyer, a man with ideas on education which would affect a generation, and who was among the first to recognise the special needs of children with a learning difficulty (Millfield today is probably the leading school in Britain for handling dyslexics). Frank had set his heart on either or both of his sons following his path to Oxford; Teddy, now 16, was to be crammed for university entrance, Jimmy for his common entrance and Eton.

The boys had been curiously removed from the war which was in its final stages when they arrived back. Both brothers have a vivid recollection of the announcement, over the ship's loudspeakers, of the death of President Franklin D. Roosevelt.

Until that moment Jimmy Goldsmith had never lived in England. He had been a regular visitor, and obviously spoke English, but his mother had always spoken French to him and if he thought of himself as anything, he thought of himself as French. Yet here he was in an English school for the first time at age eleven, tall and gangly, a slightly foreign figure with no desire to take part in either scholastic or sporting activities. No member of the Goldsmith family had ever gone to Eton, yet that was the school that some of Frank's old regimental friends, such as Walter Guinness, had attended, and the school he had set his heart on for Jimmy. A generation later he would never have made the academic standards needed for Eton, but Meyer, an inveterate gambler himself, recognised something special in this boy and worked hard on him. Jimmy actually did well academically at Millfield, certainly better than he had done before or would do again. He took what was known as 'upper fourth', the second best entry level to Eton (the best being 'remove'), and arrived there in the autumn of 1946. A year later Teddy went up to Magdalen College, Oxford, 50 years to the month after his father had done.

Jimmy Goldsmith never took to Eton, to some extent at least because from the outset he never liked his housemaster, Nigel Wykes, and Wykes never liked him. Wykes was both sporting – he had played cricket for Essex – and musical, and Goldsmith was neither. Contemporaries also remember Goldsmith being 'ten years older than his actual age', a precocious boy whose independence Wykes interpreted as rebelliousness. Where Boss Meyer had liked and encouraged him, Wykes did neither. Many years later, asked what he can remember about Goldsmith, Wykes says 'nothing good', and the feeling is mutual. The only subject Jimmy was even moderately good at was maths, and that was frowned on by the masters at Eton. When Wykes asked him what he wanted to specialise in, Goldsmith could only reply 'maths', to which the master remarked scathingly, 'I don't want any mechanics in my house.'

One should not be too hard on the housemaster, because Goldsmith already had a taste for activities which would inevitably bring him into conflict with the school authorities, notably his gambling. He had developed his nascent interest in gambling in the Bahamas, nurtured it at St Andrew's and Millfield, and at Eton allowed it full sway, betting endlessly on horses, dogs, cards and anything else he came across. He also had no interest in education, and would have needed something special to ignite him, which Wykes was not prepared to provide. If he had done well at Eton he would probably have followed Teddy to Oxford, and a career of an entirely different nature, but in adult life that thought horrifies him. Goldsmith would later develop an almost phobic hatred of the academic life, threatening to disown any of his children who dared set foot in university premises. Goldsmith all his life has also been against whatever he considers is the establishment, and that too was reinforced by his time at Eton. His academic record at the school also probably stoked the pent-up forces that he would later channel, with an almost frightening energy, into the serious business of making money.

His father was by now back in Paris, having taken up the reins of what remained of the Hôtels Réunis chain again. When he left in 1939 he had been forced to break his management contracts, and only three hotels remained in the group: the Scribe, the Carlton in Cannes, and the Mont d'Arbois in the ski resort of Megève. Frank went back to the Scribe, where his manager had managed to preserve his apartment as it was before the war, complete with his books, his objets d'art and everything else. He was now 67, an age when he could be expected to retire, but he resumed his life as a director of the Savoy in London, a role he took seriously, and as head of his hotel group. Marcelle's family had stayed in France through the war, and her brother Rico had been killed by the Germans. Before she left the Bahamas Marcelle received a letter from her sister in Cannes saying they were very worried about him as he had been 'taken by the Germans carrying arms'. Rico had been transferred to the prison at Fort Montluc, in the Auvergne, where 2,000 French Maquis were held. The allies liberated 1,000 of them but Rico was never found.

Frank's financial circumstances were no longer as comfortable as they had been before the war. But he could just about afford to pay for the boys' education, and sent Jimmy at Eton an allowance of £1 a week. It went no way towards the lifestyle young Jimmy had in mind for himself. He was already taking parties of his friends to the races at Windsor, holding dinner parties in the town, and betting on the track. He found the money from somewhere, never seeming to worry or care about it. At the end of the day, if the worst came to the worst, he reckoned his father would pay, but he doesn't seem to have had to go to him too often – at least at this early stage. If he had to be at school at all, Eton was not a bad choice for him, with its collection of what he called 'misfits, eccentrics and rebels', but he would have done better to have stayed at Millfield.

Contrary to the view that he himself would help propagate, he was not a complete academic failure at Eton. He attended as few classes as he possibly could, ignored as many rules as possible and passed the years between the ages of 13 and 16 in as enjoyable a manner as he could, actually doing moderately well in his school certificate exams.

He was 16 when he had an extraordinary stroke of luck, with a betting coup that still ranks as one of the most famous of the century. He bet £10 on three horses called Bartisan, Your Fancy and Merry Dance, at Lewes races, in an accumulator, where the winnings of the first go onto the second and then onto the third. All three horses won, and Goldsmith's £10 had become nearly £8,000. Legend has it he took his whole house to lunch in Eton, but the story is apocryphal, made up afterwards by people who barely knew him there. In reality, Goldsmith made little impact on Eton, or Eton on him.

Later, long after he had left, there would be much speculation as to the circumstances of his departure. His lifelong friends, such as John Aspinall, talk about him 'running away' from Eton. Others claimed he had been expelled, a view assiduously developed by *Private Eye* and its editor Richard Ingrams in their lengthy legal battle against him. The truth is slightly more complex. Goldsmith was certainly not sacked, but as he says himself, 'I could quite easily have been'. Wykes, although delighted to see the back of him, confirms this. 'He left Eton because I suggested to his father that it would be better if he went elsewhere. He was not suitable for my house.' Frank reluctantly agreed, and Jimmy, flush with his winnings, was only too happy at the move. 'I did not believe a man of such means should still be at school,' he joked a few years later.

He left with due ceremony, receiving the official book from the headmaster which today has become something of a symbol for him. It bears the inscription:

Hunc Librum, Jacobo Michaeli Goldsmith ab Etona discendenti dono dedit Claudis Aurelius Elliott magister Informator.

There was another ceremony observed by a departing boy at Eton – he was expected to give his housemaster a present. Goldsmith, knowing Wykes' love of music, bought him the nine symphonies of Beethoven, and solemnly presented them to a surprised and touched housemaster. When Wykes began to thank him, Goldsmith asked if he could have them back for a moment, then carefully extracted each record from its sleeve and smashed it over the housemaster's desk. Jimmy Goldsmith then departed Eton.

He was now six foot three, a striking-looking boy with penetrating blue eyes, lively smile, and bursting energy, who looked and behaved much older than his years. He had discovered girls long before most of his classmates, and stories of his more outrageous behaviour had filtered back to his parents in Paris. Frank still nurtured hopes that he would apply his brain to study and arranged for him to go to a crammer in Kent, but he hated that more than he hated Eton. He did sit his higher school certificate, and scraped through in three of the four subjects, failing the subject he should have been best at – French. The exams were of no significance to him, and he took them only because he was worried he might disappoint his father.

He was much more attracted to the life his brother Teddy was enjoying at Oxford. He never went to Oxford to study, yet it was at Oxford he had some of his most formative experiences – and made some of his most lasting friendships.

5

Aspers

Jimmy Goldsmith first met the man who would become his closest friend and soulmate when he was still 16. He had quit Eton and was in a sort of twilight period when he still had money left over from his famous bet, hated the crammer in Kent where Frank had insisted on sending him, and had not yet decided what he was going to do with himself. The one thing he knew he did like was gambling, and Teddy shared that interest.

John Aspinall was 23 when Goldsmith came into his life; he was a slim, blond, dandyish man, who at Rugby had called himself 'Jonas V. Aspinall', and had, like Goldsmith at Eton, come close to being expelled. At 17 he had joined the Royal Marines, in which he served for two years before a cousin persuaded him to pursue his theatrical interests at university. Aspinall was a showman, who at Oxford had set out to make an impact; obsessed by Oscar Wilde, he wore a salmon-pink suit and gold waistcoat, carried an ebony cane and snuffbox, and clutched a book of Lord Alfred's poems. His other obsession, which he caught from reading Rider Haggard when he was 13 (and never lost), was the Zulus, and in particular the great chief Shaka. The Zulus, as well as warriors, were wonderful raconteurs, and Aspinall was soon well known through the university as a story-teller, spinning tales which were wildly exaggerated and apocryphal but nonetheless entertaining.

Aspinall was just beginning to develop another interest which would become the dominant theme of his life: wild animals and their survival, a theme which would also have an important impact on Jimmy Goldsmith. He was also a cool, thoughtful, almost professional gambler, and by 1949, when Jimmy headed for Oxford to see his brother, Aspinall had been adopted as the mascot for one of the more outrageous gambling circles in Oxford.

In this circle was Teddy Goldsmith, a dreamer and thinker, who had not yet developed into the gloomy environmentalist he would become in middle age, but who was already expressing his doubts about the future of mankind. Teddy believed that unless the world controlled its population and industrial growth, the environment would rapidly become so polluted that the human race could not survive. He was bored by his academic studies at Oxford, unimpressed by his lecturers, and spent more and more of his time playing cards or at the races.

Teddy Goldsmith and John Aspinall first met at a party in Oxford given by a man called Michael Briggs and immediately hit it off. They were fellow spirits, both of them with their own odd obsessions, each seeing himself as a 'misfit' (a favourite word of both) even in the Oxford of the time which after the war was at its most varied. Aspinall also saw in Teddy another potential recruit for his card school, which he counted on to supplement his modest income. Teddy, he thought, was also 'amusing and engaging – he had such a charming face'.

As they left the party they agreed to meet again, Aspinall proposing they should have lunch. 'Yes,' agreed Teddy instantly. 'Let's have lunch tomorrow.' Aspinall arranged to meet at the Town and Gown in the High Street, and remembers looking forward to it, which was a mistake because Teddy never appeared.

They ran into each other again a week later at another party. 'So what happened to you?' Aspinall asked. 'You remember we were supposed to have lunch . . .' Teddy was full of apologies, exclaiming 'how terrible' and 'how awful' it was. 'I tell you what, lunch with me tomorrow.' The venue this time would be White's, also in the High Street. 'Don't forget to turn up this time,' said Aspinall as they were parting. 'One o'clock at White's, Aspers,' said Goldsmith, coining a nickname for Aspinall which would last the rest of his life. Promptly at one Aspinall was at White's, found there was a reservation in the name of Goldsmith, and again waited in vain.

Yet again they met a few days later. 'Oh my God, that lunch!' cried Goldsmith. 'Well, what happened, Teddy?' said Aspinall. 'I was walking along from Magdalen and I saw a friend on the other side of the road and I went over to talk to him, and he took me off to lunch and I forgot my lunch with you.' Instead of being offended, Aspinall laughed. 'Well, all right, now I know. From now on I know that any friendship we have, Teddy, is going to be based on this. I'm determined to remain a friend, but I'm not going to be disappointed if you don't turn up or if you forget appointments, because otherwise it's hopeless. From now it will be just sheer blind chance if we do meet.' It was the basis of a lifelong friendship.

Teddy joined Aspinall's little gambling clique which met at the digs of Milo Cripps, wealthy nephew of the chancellor of the exchequer, Stafford Cripps, and Jocelyn Baines, at 167 Walton Street, and it was there, in the winter of 1949, that Jimmy Goldsmith entered Aspinall's life. Baines was another clever misfit who went on to become a respected biographer of Conrad, before committing suicide; he had inherited a share in an antique bookshop in London, and was gambling it away (it was eventually bought by Cripps, now Lord Parmoor, who still runs it). Desmond Dunphy, with whom Aspinall had been in the marines, was another constant gambler. Also at the table was another Aspinall friend, Ian Maxwell-Scott, and John Pollock, the son of a judge, who had inherited £50,000 in his early days at Oxford and had already lost it all. Pollock, like most of the others at the table that night, was now living on credit and paying in IOUs, based on a collection of clocks left to him by a horologist uncle who had also been a judge. He showed the others a Sothebys catalogue with the item 'Judge Pollock's clocks for sale', promising to pay his debts when the clocks had been sold.

They were a mixed set, most of them from wealthy backgrounds. Cripps' mother had married the Duke of Westminster and she kept him supplied with cash; Pollock still had some credit, and so did Maxwell-Scott who had a rich mother. Teddy too had some money, not a huge amount, but Frank kept him comfortably off. The poorest player at the table was Aspinall, who needed to win to live and who therefore played very seriously. Most of the players drank heavily but Aspinall never did, knowing he could not afford to lose. Most of the players surrendered small amounts to Aspinall week after week without complaint. 'He gets a man to like him, looks him in the eye, plays his hand, takes money from him, and the man enjoys it,' one of the players later remarked. All of them were playing with some form of IOU, although these still had some reality to them; they had not yet reached the point which some games in Oxford in those days had when IOUs had been passed on so many times that they were completely uncashable. The players still believed in their own paper and, in varying degrees, in other people's paper too. Hard cash in the seventh week of term was unknown in the Aspinall school – none had been seen around the table for two weeks.

This was the scene the 16-year-old Jimmy Goldsmith entered that evening. At the back, behind Baines, sat his mistress, a dark girl with a trace of Sinhalese blood. Every so often Baines would throw a secretive glance to where she sat sullenly like a character out of Conrad, watching her master gamble. 'I was impressed as anything that anyone could have a mistress at that age,' says Aspinall. 'I had read about them in novels, but I had never actually met anyone with a mistress and she just looked the part. And there she was just waiting for him to finish the game, and being rather sulky.'

Aspinall was already adumbrating his future role as a casino-owner, gathering up the cards, controlling the stakes, handing out the chips, generally organising the game. While he was shuffling the pack, he was suddenly conscious that a young, striking-looking man in a long coat, smoking a cigar, had entered the room and was standing behind Teddy Goldsmith, who was sitting on his immediate left. Teddy made the introductions: 'This is my brother Jimmy,' and introduced the players around the table, Aspinall being the last. Aspinall had heard about him from Teddy, and knew he had recently left Eton, but word of his betting coup had not yet reached Oxford. (Later it would become so well-known – and exaggerated – that most of the people around the table could recite the names of Bartisan, Your Fancy and Merry Dance by heart. Twenty years later Aspinall gave him a present of a solid gold box with the names of his companies engraved on the outside and, on the inside, the names of the three horses.)

That night they were playing *chemin de fer* and the bank had got up to £150, which even for these hardened gamblers was a huge amount in 1949, even if most of it was in the form of IOUs. They were sitting around looking at this growing pile when suddenly the tall young man at the back said 'Banco'. With the lordly and condescending air of a 23-year-old to a 16-year-old, Aspinall said, 'Jimmy, this is a cash game.' Goldsmith did not give him a withering look, as he might have done, but produced from his pocket a wad of money. Aspinall, even by that stage of his life a skilled estimator of wads, decided there was £500 there. Goldsmith peeled off £150 and put it on the table, causing everyone to goggle – they had not seen cash like that for weeks.

Aspinall instantly moved his chair to one side, gestured to the spot between himself and Teddy, and said, 'Come and sit here, Jimmy.' Here was a nice little addition to the school who had to be good for a few pounds.

No one can quite remember who won that evening, although Goldsmith believes he lost and Aspinall believes he won. In any case Goldsmith was now part of the Walton Street school. Goldsmith remembers a girl, probably Baines' mistress, who sometimes wore a silk dressing gown around the house with holes cut in it to reveal her nipples. He settled into a life of parties, girls and gambling, living off his rapidly dwindling winnings from Eton. He had various runs of luck which replenished them, with continual betting on horses and dogs, but he was also living expensively. A few weeks after the Aspinall game, he had a big bet on a horse called High Stakes at Doncaster which was beaten by a short head. He went to hear the race commentary in a bookmaker's office where the laconic voice told him of his loss. He had about £500 on it – the equivalent of perhaps £20,000 now – to win at seven to four and it was narrowly beaten. It was a major financial setback, but he carried on.

Another member of the circle who was to feature through Jimmy Goldsmith's life was Digby Neave, brother of Airey Neave, one of the few people ever to escape from Colditz (and later, as one of Margaret Thatcher's closest friends and advisers, killed by the IRA). Neave was a family friend – his father had known Frank – and on Jimmy's first day in Oxford, Teddy took him to meet him at lunch. 'It was amazing, because he was terribly young, but he immediately became the centre of things,' says Neave. 'He was such a personality that one didn't forget him. You could always be sure that when Jimmy came into a party, he would make a difference.'

Aspinall was to see the strength of the Goldsmith personality a few months later. A group of the gamblers regularly went to Oxford dog racing together, and Goldsmith became so caught up in it that he bought himself a dog for £20 at what was called a 'flapper track', a kind of unauthorised, downmarket dog track. The dog was called Queenie, and he had it trained, although it never won anything.

One night he suddenly said to Aspinall, 'Let's go to the dogs.'

'It's the wrong night of the week, Jimmy,' said Aspinall.

'Nonsense,' snapped Goldsmith. 'There must be other dogs.' There were, but the nearest, explained Aspinall, was in Reading.

'So what's wrong with Reading?'

'Reading is 35 miles from here, and it will take an hour to get there,' explained Aspinall, laughing at the impatience and enthusiasm in his voice.

'Well, come on, what are we waiting for?' Aspinall tried to explain that even if they departed instantly they would miss three and possibly four races.

'So what's wrong with five races?' The others refused to go, but Aspinall was unable to resist Jimmy in full flow. Neither of them drove at that stage – Aspinall has never been behind the wheel of a car in his life and those who have driven with Goldsmith wish he had never learned – but they got hold of a driver and car and set off, Goldsmith still with a large wad of money in his pocket. They arrived at Reading with the lights at the track blazing and dashed onto the rails, opposite the winning post, just in time to see the dogs cross in a photo finish. From their vantage point they were convinced that the white dog, in their parlance number three dog, had just beaten the red dog, which in those days and under Greyhound Racing Association rules, was number one dog. Behind them was orange dog, which was number five. It took some time to develop the photograph in those days, so they had time to bet on the result.

'Three dog won,' Goldsmith exclaimed confidently and Aspinall agreed. 'Yes, definitely, three dog won.' They went in search of a bookmaker and found a large imposing man with a hawklike nose who went under the name Alf Eighteen. 'What price three dog?' asked Goldsmith. The bookmaker quickly sized them up: bright, young but clever punters. Instead of saying ten to one, as he might have done (in which case they would have smelt a rat), he snapped to his clerk, 'Take nine to four on', which meant that for every £9 bet, the punter stood to win £4. 'Take it once.'

Goldsmith pulled out his large wad and bet the lot – about £300. Aspinall, more cautious, bet half his smaller resources, and they found a bar overlooking the winning post to await the official result. They were sipping their drinks when the result of the photo-finish was announced: 'First number six, second number four.' It made no sense to them: the photo had been between their own highly fancied number three and number one. 'What's that?' snapped Goldsmith. 'Previous race?' An aficionado at the bar said, 'No, that was the last race – five minutes ago.' Goldsmith could not believe what he was hearing. 'But three dog won, I saw it.' 'No,' said the man, 'three dog was last.'

The truth was then explained. In Reading the dogs raced under a different – rival – set of rules to those Aspinall was used to. The saddlecloth colours, which denoted the dog numbers, were entirely different. Alf Eighteen had taken their money on a dog he had known was last.

Aspinall watched Goldsmith go white with anger. He said nothing but turned on his heel and stalked off. 'Jimmy, what are you going to do?' cried Aspinall, but Goldsmith didn't even seem to hear. Aspinall tried to follow him, and caught up with him as he stopped at the back of the pay-out queue at Alf Eighteen's stand. Aspinall stood behind him, and when Goldsmith got to the front he handed his ticket in to be paid. The bookmaker called out the number to his clerk: 'Four-six-four.' The clerk looked up his records: 'Four-six-four, Alf – he backed three dog in the photo. He wasn't even in the photo. Loser.'

Goldsmith stood his ground. 'I bet £300 at nine-to-four on the white dog – that's £433 you owe me.'

'Look, son, you backed a loser. Out of the way, there's people behind you want to be paid.' In fact Aspinall was behind him, and Alf Eighteen was well aware he hadn't won either. Goldsmith refused to move.

'I backed the white dog which won the race by this much' – he held up his hands to show the narrow gap. 'No, you backed three dog. You're in the book as backing three dog. That's what you said, son – you said three dog.' There was a chorus from the clerk and others who had heard. 'Yes, he said three dog.' Clearly they had been having something of a joke at these youngsters' expense.

Goldsmith still refused to move. The bookmaker, he insisted, had not just cheated a client, but also taken a bet from someone under age. Alf Eighteen looked at this tall, mature figure and said: 'What do you mean, under age?'

'I'm seventeen,' said Goldsmith. Aspinall chimed in to say he had just been to his seventeenth birthday party only a few weeks before (which was not entirely true), and Goldsmith produced his passport to prove it. But the bookmaker, who had faced down many angry clients in his time, refused to retreat. Eventually the two retired, 'furious, poorer and wiser'.

'What I noticed then was how he came across with such electricity and such anger,' says Aspinall. 'And there was another factor, which has also remained permanent with him: the moment he lost, it was as if nothing had happened. When we went to Reading dogs after that, he always bet with Eighteen.'

Goldsmith's Eton winnings, and whatever other money he had, were now running out. At cards one evening, he lost £5 to Digby Neave, and didn't have it. He offered instead to give Neave his car, which he reckoned was worth around that sum. Neave soon discovered that the car, a 1928 Singer, was not in Oxford but was still at the crammer near Tunbridge Wells which Goldsmith, it turned out, had left in something of a hurry. Neave never did discover exactly why, but Goldsmith indicated that he had had a disagreement with one of the teachers and had 'knocked him down'. He had left, abandoning the car which he had never learned to drive in any case.

Neave and Michael Briggs went down to Kent, and found the ancient car which had no brakes. They had no insurance, but got it going and drove it back, and Neave used it the rest of his time in Oxford.

As the weeks and months wore on, Jimmy Goldsmith's gambling was getting out of hand. His winning streak had deserted him, and now he was in financial trouble. Frank, now in his seventies and living in Paris, supported him up to the time he quit school at 17, but after that Jimmy was on his own. Marcelle sold an apartment Frank had acquired years before at Chantilly to pay Teddy's debts, but Jimmy's losses, and his behaviour, were going well past the point where they could be dismissed as a young man's wild fling.

'The gambling really was quite incredible in those days,' recalls Neave. 'He used to invite us down to the Carlton Hotel, and we would go for a long weekend, and gamble solidly. Once we arrived on a Friday and went to the casino, and I lost all the money I had and he lost all his. So the next day we borrowed some from the head waiter at the Carlton, and we lost that, and it was absolutely disastrous. On Sunday night at three in the morning the place was shutting, and then Jimmy had this unbelievable run of luck and got all the money back. We hadn't seen the sun, hadn't been outside the casino for three days.'

Goldsmith's lucky number was 23 in those days, and the others watched in amazement as it began to come up. 'I saw him bet on three tables at once and win on all three,' says Neave. 'It was the only time it ever happened.'

In Paris, these stories were getting back to Frank Goldsmith, who was becoming seriously worried by the behaviour of his younger son. In London, Frank had set Jimmy up with his own apartment in Pont Street where he took his pretty girlfriends, when he wasn't at Oxford with the others. It was a way of life that could not last, and Frank called a halt to it. He still had some control over his wayward son, and insisted he return to Paris. Even then, however, he displayed no anger to Jimmy, remaining, as Digby Neave recalls, remarkably equable. But he was also quite firm. Jimmy, he pointed out, had passed no exams, had not got to university and would never get a degree. Frank was semi-retired, much of his capital was gone, and he had Marcelle, much younger than he, to worry about. He still gave both his sons generous cash presents at Christmas and birthdays, but he was not in a position to do more than that. Jimmy, he insisted, must now learn a trade, and he had, he said, arranged for him to gain some experience in the hotel and restaurant business.

For a time Jimmy worked as a waiter and cook in the Luce Restaurant in Montmartre, but soon his father decided to move him away from the temptations of Paris and despatched him to the large and prestigious Palace Hotel in Madrid, well-known at the time because of its connection with Ernest Hemingway. Jimmy remained irrepressible. He might have loved his father, but he had no serious intention of working as a trainee in the Palace kitchens preparing hors d'oeuvres. He rented a spacious flat around the corner and immediately rang Digby Neave. 'Why don't you come down?' he boomed, proceeding to describe the delights of Spanish women and food (Goldsmith had never much interest in drink). Neave had no money either but he raised enough for his ticket, and arrived to discover Jimmy had quickly found a gambling circle, and had run out of money completely. 'The only thing to do is to cash in your return ticket,' he told Neave, who reluctantly agreed. The money they raised soon went too, but Goldsmith never worried. 'We'll be perfectly OK, because we can always eat at Horshers,' he told Neave. Horshers was probably the most expensive restaurant in Madrid; originally established in Germany, where members of the Goldsmith family (Jimmy knew from his father) had been clients, it had moved to Madrid some years before. Goldsmith soon re-established the family connection and obtained credit. ('Eventually poor old Frank had to pay,' recalls Neave, but the amount, Jimmy insists, was 'not very large'.)

The two of them spent a hilarious few months, living on credit and on their wits. Goldsmith had met a number of friends, and assiduously worked the cocktail party circuit, taking Neave with him. 'The food in England in 1950 was pretty awful, and here we were eating all this wonderful food in Madrid,' says Neave.

Goldsmith was still working at the Palace, but his attendances at work were far from regular. Nonetheless he did learn something of the catering trade – 'I do not suggest I was an exemplary apprentice, but an apprentice I was,' he says now. Neave only remembers him going a few times, however, one evening returning with an enormous pile of caviar. Miguel Primo de Rivera, son of the soldier and statesman, had been appointed ambassador to London and there was a dinner at the Palace to celebrate the event. Jimmy, in the odd life he lived in Madrid between the kitchens and the salons, had come to know Primo de Rivera, and upstairs that evening was there as a friend. Downstairs afterwards he helped himself. 'There was so much caviar left over that Jimmy returned with two buckets,' says Neave.

They threw a big party that night and the next day Jimmy decided he could not be bothered to go in to work. But he was worried about complaints to his father, and decided he needed a good excuse. 'I shall have to tell them I have broken my arm,' he said. He and Neave went down to the local chemist where they bought plaster and bandage and Neave plastered up his arm. They had spent the previous night in what Neave delicately refers to as a 'house of ill-repute', and Jimmy wanted to go back there and display his arm. 'It was a great surprise for the madame,' says Neave. 'And before the night was over – it was a very heavy and long night – we got into some difficulties, and Jimmy used his arm as a rather heavy instrument.'

According to Neave, the madame called the police, but Goldsmith persuaded the Guardia Civil to return to his flat for a drink. 'We were arrested,' says Neave, 'but we went home and the party went on all night.' Goldsmith says that part of the story is apocryphal.

Jimmy never seemed to tire of parties or women, but soon he did not have a job. Frank and Marcelle became worried about him when they had no word for weeks – except complaints from the Palace management. Then suddenly Goldsmith had gone from Madrid and Hugh Wontner, who had arranged the job in Madrid for him, next saw him at the races in Windsor. There were rumours he had bought a horse, but no one knew what with. Back in London Goldsmith fell in with Aspinall again, both of them penniless, and in the mornings they used to consider their next moves. One morning, they realised they had even run out of credit, a serious blow to their way of life. Gloomily, they sat around running through various options, until Goldsmith suddenly snapped his fingers.

'I know,' he said. 'My father's got a bank account at the Royal Bank of Canada.'

Aspinall was puzzled. How could that help them? Surely it wasn't possible to raid his father's bank account? With growing cheerfulness, Goldsmith insisted they set off for the bank. The Royal Bank of Canada was the principal bank in Nassau, with a branch right in the middle of Bay Street, and was the same bank which had given Frank Goldsmith his (unused) introduction to Sir Harry Oakes. Jimmy's connections with it therefore went back to his childhood. Aspinall, used to regarding banks with grave suspicion, waited outside while Goldsmith went in. When he re-emerged he had £100 in cash, around which Aspinall, in his more mischievous moments, built an elaborate tale of Jimmy's magical financial powers. In fact he had simply opened an overdraft.

But both men's luck was still out, and their losing streak continued. They owed money to bookmakers, to nightclubs and anyone else who would lend to them. By now Goldsmith's debts were £2,000, a large enough sum in the early 1950s. Some of the money was owed to bookmakers and they were pressing hard. He would have to ask his father for help, but Frank's patience had finally run out. And so had Jimmy's courage – he could not face his father.

He persuaded Digby Neave, regarded (wrongly, in Neave's own opinion) by Frank as Jimmy's most responsible friend, to act as a peacemaker. Frank had been indulgent up to that point, in fact probably far too indulgent. An excellent raconteur, he had kept his sons and their friends amused for hours with stories of some of his own gambling exploits, and those of his brothers. Carl was a legendary gambler, and Frank related how he and his brothers used to persuade Carl to go to the races because every time Adolph had to pay his debts, he was forced to give the other brothers an equal amount. Jimmy had taken advantage of his father's relaxed attitude to gambling, but Frank must now have feared he was taking after Carl, rather than after his own more controlled interest in betting.

A major family conference was organised. 'It was frightfully serious,' says Neave. 'We all wore ties and all that sort of thing.' There was even a family lawyer present, whom Neave found 'rather fearsome', and it was he who suggested a solution: Frank would pay Jimmy's debts if he would join the army. He would in any case have been called up at some stage, as National Service was compulsory both in Britain and in France. His father urged him to do it now.

The arrangements had already been made. Jimmy Goldsmith was taken by taxi to Victoria where he signed up.

Later Goldsmith would say that the army was the making of him. Given the life he had led up to that point, he could not have been expected to enjoy it, yet in a curious way he did. He was aware his life had no direction and that unless he found a role, he was headed for disaster. Those who knew him at this time remember his extraordinary, unchannelled energy, the only outlets for which seemed to be gambling and women. Money meant nothing to him, except when he didn't have any, but up to this time in his life he had shown no aptitude for anything: not for study, at which he was a conspicuous failure, not for sports, which he hated, and certainly not for any profession – he had barely done a day's work in his life. The gentle Frank was at times in despair over him, and came close at one point to adopting the suggestion of a lawyer friend, of sending Jimmy to Melbourne to become a fireman. 'The father recognised the brilliance of the son, but was nervous about the personality,' says one old family friend.

'He thought that Jimmy was going to shoot for everything and not make anything. If you have a son that gambles that way, and risks everything, you will worry a great deal. He thought that if Jimmy did make it he would make it in a very big way, and if he didn't – well it would be an equal sized disaster. He realised what Jimmy's character was.'

Teddy was too preoccupied with his thoughts and career to think too much about him, but Marcelle certainly worried greatly. His friends at that time were all misfits, gamblers, drinkers and rich ne'er-do-wells, mostly, like Aspinall, considerably older than he was.

In the army he was stationed in Towyn in North Wales, after training in Oswestry, and curiously he came to accept and understand the army discipline. As Lieutenant Goldsmith of the Royal Artillery he was put in charge of training a platoon of the most difficult young men in the regiment, and his natural authority, wit and physical appearance made him good at it. On leave with Aspinall he slotted straight back into his old life, but leave from the British Army in National Service days was strictly rationed and often he only had an overnight pass. His leaves were spent mostly in Paris, where the indulgent Frank would look after him, and where Jimmy had a number of girlfriends.

He finished his National Service early in 1953 to find that most of his Oxford friends were now embarked on careers. Just turned 20, he went back to Paris determined on doing the same. It was to be an eventful year for him. Not only would he launch into one of the most extraordinary business careers of the twentieth century. He would also get married in circumstances which were to make him front page headlines around the world.

6

The Runaway Heiress and the Playboy

When Jimmy Goldsmith left the army in April 1953, he was a 20-year-old, untrained, unskilled lad, some of the edge perhaps gone off his wildness and frustration, but his energy and restlessness as strong as ever. From as early as he could remember he had set himself the target of making money, getting on even terms with the Rothschilds and the other rich cousins he had so often stayed with, and of restoring the family name to where he felt it should be in the order of things – above the other great Jewish banking families. When anxious relatives asked him what he wanted to do with his life, he would reply, 'I'm going to be a millionaire', as much out of defensiveness as anything else. But he had nothing in mind, other than vague, unquantified thoughts that somewhere out there fortune awaited him. His old gambling friends were now moving up the career ladder, and the life in London no longer retained the excitement it held for him when he was 16.

He drifted back to Paris, partly because he felt more comfortable in France, partly because his father made him welcome and found a small room for him on the seventh floor of the Hotel Scribe. He had no other home. Teddy was there too, and more to the point, Teddy had a business.

It wasn't much of a business – and it was also fairly clear that Teddy was not very good at it. But at least he had a job. For some years Frank's only proposal for helping his sons into careers was to advise them to learn the hotel and restaurant business. It was his life, what he knew about, and he was now in his mid-seventies with his own money running short, and two grown sons who he still had to worry about. His attempts to train Jimmy up in the business had failed. 'I loved my father dearly,' says Jimmy now, 'but his ideas were that you sit down and listen.' Teddy had persevered more than Jimmy, but only marginally. After finishing at Oxford, Frank arranged for him to go to a hotel school in Lausanne. He never finished, although he did complete one of the courses, and he went on to work as a waiter at the Bellevue Palace Hotel in Berne. His heart was not in it, and he would soon have quit if, by total accident, something much more interesting had not come along.

Frank Goldsmith almost every evening went to the Travellers Club where he played cards, chatted, then went home for dinner. It was there that he met a man called Eddie Gross who was better known as the son-in-law of Sarah Bernhardt than as a budding businessman. Gross said he had met in London an exceptional doctor who had developed a cure for rheumatism. It was selling hugely in Britain and he wanted to launch it in France. Gross was looking for backers, and asked Frank if he might be interested. He already had five other people who had put in some money. Frank was more interested in the next part of Gross' proposal: to launch the product the group was looking for a young man with some energy who would work for very little but who would have a stake in the business. Frank, knowing how bored his son was with the hotel business, proposed Teddy.

Teddy jumped at the opportunity, and came back to Paris immediately. His salary was minute, but so was the company. The total invested was no more than a few thousand pounds. The product that Teddy now found himself with was Lloyd's Adrenalin Cream, developed by Dr Louis Moss, who in medical circles had something of a reputation as a quack. He lived in some style, with rooms off Harley Street, and developed a number of products which claimed to cure impotence, anaemia and of course rheumatism. He had developed his adrenalin cream several years before for which he made considerable and largely unprovable claims and which he had persuaded a company called Lloyd's, the creation of Ellis Stanning, to market for him. Stanning did so with some gusto, and Lloyd's Adrenalin Cream (which Teddy renamed Adremad) was quite fashionable in Britain in the early 1950s (and would remain so for some years afterwards). Now he wanted to open up the French market.

Teddy rather grandly called his new company Dagonal, named, he would joke to his friends, 'after the fish god of the Philistines', and started by test marketing the cream in the north of France where he thought rheumatism would be more prevalent. He had a tiny amount of money available for advertising, but knew a couple of young journalists, Herve and Gerard Mille, who ran the newspaper *France Dimanche*. Teddy explained that he couldn't afford to spend money on advertising, but how could he expound the virtues of his adrenalin cream?

They found inspiration on the horse track. One of the favourites for the 1952 Arc de Triomphe was a horse called Worden II, which only weeks before the race suddenly developed severe arthritis of the joints. Teddy had the idea of trying Adremad on it, and the brothers thought this was an excellent story. Dr Moss came over from London, and with much publicity the cream was dutifully rubbed in to the afflicted parts. The slightly bewildered owner and trainer were persuaded that at the very least it would do no harm – which was probably true – and if the claims made for it by its British proprietors were even fractionally true, it could do wonders.

Despite their best ministrations, Worden II did not win the Arc de Triomphe, but it did come second. It was enough to spark off a series of articles about how the distressed owner had appealed to the proprietors of Adremad, how Dr Moss had come to his rescue, and how the cream had magically cured the horse. Sales of Adremad took off, and Teddy suddenly had a potential success on his hands. He had arranged for it to be manufactured under licence in France, and now stepped up his orders considerably.

However, the agency for one product was never going to pay his bills, and as sales of Adremad began to fall off again he looked for other products to sell alongside it. One of his sidelines was a company called 'Lucifer' which made electrical plugs, which Teddy also thought had to be a great growth market with the electrification of rural France. There was nothing wrong with his reasoning, but accountancy was not his strong point – only later did he discover that the more plugs he sold, the more money he lost.

Teddy's infant business was struggling when his younger brother arrived back in Paris – and it might have died soon afterwards if fate, in the form of the French military authorities, had not intervened. Jimmy had now finished his National Service but Teddy had deferred it because of going to Oxford. Only a matter of weeks after Jimmy's return, it caught up with him. Both brothers could have opted to do their stint in either the French or British forces, but Teddy had done it in neither. His French papers had been sent to him, but to the wrong address, and he never received them. Suddenly, in the spring of 1953, the authorities arrested him and put him in jail as a deserter.

Teddy had been greatly enjoying his life in Paris, where he had lived well beyond his means. The thought of spending a couple of years in the Foreign Legion did not hold many attractions. Hastily he persuaded the French that his arrest had been a mistake, was allowed out, and hurried off to England to do his National Service there.

The upshot was that he had to abandon his business. There was no possibility of getting anyone from outside to run things. Total turnover was running at around £5,000 a year, which even in 1953 was a meagre amount. Nor was there anyone inside he could promote – it was virtually a one-man operation. But there was one hungry young would-be entrepreneur, available and ready to go. Teddy was not exactly bursting with confidence when he agreed to his brother's suggestion that he take over, but there was no choice.

As Teddy packed his bags and set off for London, neither brother had any idea of the consequences of what the French recruitment office had put in train. Jimmy Goldsmith's business career had begun. It would go through extraordinary ups and downs, taking him to the very brink of bankruptcy and disgrace on more than one occasion, bringing him huge success on others, and never for a second lacking interest, excitement and controversy. For the next 35 years he would devote himself to it with an energy and a passion which at times could be frightening; and in the end it would make him one of the best-known businessmen in the world – and one of the richest too.

Jimmy Goldsmith was three months into his career when an event occurred which was to make him front page headlines. From his mid-teens, even while he was still at Eton, he had been more than usually interested in women. There was always at least one pretty girl in his company, usually someone several years older than he. In those wild days at Oxford, girls were as much a part of his life as gambling. His hugely infectious laugh, his enormous zest and enthusiasm, his willingness to throw money around on high living, and of course his appearance attracted women of all ages to him, and he loved it. John Aspinall, who still professed to be a virgin when he was 25, was continually amazed at the procession of girls who accompanied his friend, and Digby Neave, particularly in the time they spent in Madrid, had been astonished by his easy success.

In the summer of 1953 Jimmy already had a girlfriend in Paris when he met the woman who was to change his life. It was 4 June 1953, the night of the Coronation of Queen Elizabeth II, when Jimmy Goldsmith first met Isabel Patino. He was 20, and she, that night, was 18. Later it became fashionable to describe her as 'exceptionally beautiful', and in some ways she was, but not in the classic sense. She was small, not even reaching Goldsmith's shoulder, with jet black hair worn fashionably short, and a slim figure. Her pictures show her as a darker-eyed, darker-skinned version of Princess Margaret of the same period – striking rather than beautiful. The *Daily Express* at the time described her as 'a brunette with an hour-glass figure' but that reporter had almost certainly never seen her.

She was also the daughter of Señor Don Antenor Patino, who had featured in the world press for years, not for anything he had done but for the fact that he had inherited one of the world's largest fortunes in 1947. His father, Simon Patino, was a shrewd half-breed Cholo Indian from Cochabamba in Bolivia, who became a bill-collector in La Paz. There are various conflicting stories of how he built his empire, but at the turn of the century tin came into demand for food containers, car bearings and solder, and Patino is said to have acquired an abandoned tin mine and a strip of land, 12,000 feet up in the Andes, for the equivalent of £25. Underneath it were some of the richest tin deposits in the world. Various estimates of his fortune in the 1920s put it at well over $100 million, and some ranged up to five times that. His annual income was said to have been greater than the Bolivian government's, which he basically controlled. He bought heavily into Malayan tin when it opened up, and dominated the world tin market for several decades. As his wealth and power grew, so he lived more and more like an emperor; he moved to France where he made himself Bolivian Minister to escape French taxes, and built his own legation, as well as huge houses in Nice and Biarritz. For the last 40 years of his life he lived outside Bolivia, but retained his citizenship. The house overlooking Nice was vast, and, according to one account 'hideous beyond belief; it included an amphitheatre for orchestral recitals, a Russian chalet, huge parks covered with palm trees, and a reconstruction of a Greek temple in ruins.' He had three palaces in Bolivia and much else besides. He married one of his daughters to a French count, another to the Marquis del Merito, chamberlain of King Alfonso of Spain, each with a dowry of $1m. For Antenor, his eldest son and heir, he arranged something grander still: marriage to Marie Christina de Bourbon y Bosch la Brus, the 16-year-old daughter of the Duke and Duchess of Durcal, and a relative of King Alfonso XIII of Spain.

Their marriage must have been one of the most extraordinary mismatches of the century. Antenor was a tiny, shy and rather ineffectual man, the Duchess of Durcal (as she later titled herself) was strong-willed, dominant – and hated him. She hit the headlines in the spring of 1940 when she was voted by the fashion designers of Paris as the world's best-dressed woman (the Duchess of Windsor was second), and Antenor pretended to be pleased. But he resented her extravagance, and her style of living. She bore him two daughters, but left him in 1944 to go to America, arranging a settlement of half a million dollars immediately, confirmed by a New York court, with another half million to be paid by 1951, or before then if Señor Patino was unfaithful. In 1945 Antenor started legal proceedings to cancel the agreement and arrange a divorce. For more than 20 years the actions would rage through the courts of France, the United States, Bolivia (where they were married), Spain and Mexico when Antenor moved there. Christina even arranged to have him arrested when he arrived in New York, alleging he was late with his maintenance payments. He was taken from his plane at Idlewild to spend a night in jail. Since 1947 Antenor had sought solace with the Countess Beatriz di Rovasenda, whom he would later marry when he thought he was legally divorced – only to find himself involved in another battery of legal actions from the Duchess, who slapped a writ on him, charging him 'with living in a state of concubinage in the marital home'. She insisted that divorce was impossible because she was Catholic, and would only become possible if she was given half his fortune. (She lost, but not until 1966, by which stage she had driven him from his magnificent homes in France, his fortune depleted by disastrous investments in Mexico and elsewhere.)

Antenor had inherited a reputed $200m in 1947 when Simon Patino died, and in 1952 a left-wing government took power in Bolivia, seizing what remaining assets he had there. The family fortune, however, had been based overseas for several decades and Antenor lived in a huge house on the Avenue Foch, one of half a dozen he owned.

In 1952 the Patinos suspended hostilities in the courts for a more pressing activity: they must find husbands for their two daughters, Christina and Isabel, who would inherit the Patino fortune. They could not be just any husbands: the Duchess insisted on both of the girls calling themselves 'Patino y Bourbon' to remind the world of their royal blood. The two girls were therefore rich, royal – and more than pretty. The search for a husband was given a particular urgency because Christina, the elder, had turned out to have ideas of her own in the way of romance. She had first fallen for a young American, and when her father refused permission to marry, she ran off with him to Madrid. But great wealth had great power, and Antenor managed to have her brought back to Paris. It was there, in his house on the Avenue Foch, that the younger daughter Isabel, then 17, joined them.

Even then the course of romance did not run smooth for the Patino girls. According to an account which Isabel gave to the *Daily Mirror* journalist Noel Whitcomb in the autumn of 1952, Prince Marc de Beauveau-Craon, whose family Antenor had known since before the war, proposed marriage. Prince Marc came from one of France's more aristocratic if impoverished families, with a large house, the Château d'Haroué, near Nancy, which was much in need of repair. He was a director of a small travel agency in Paris and manager of another firm, but he earned nowhere near enough to pay for the upkeep of his estate. Antenor disapproved, not because of his lineage but because of Isabel's age. When that became clear, Prince Marc shifted his attention to Christina, and they became engaged. They were married at the end of 1952 in a ceremony to which half the royal families of Europe were invited.

Antenor was a strict but fond father, and for Isabel's eighteenth birthday decided to give her a large party, not in Paris but in London where he had been Bolivian ambassador before the war. The girls, having spent so many years in America, spoke better English than they did French, and Isabel in particular had made a number of friends among the English living in Paris – including Teddy Goldsmith.

Frank Goldsmith knew them slightly as clients of his hotels, and Teddy had met them at a weekend party given by Prince Marc at the Château d'Haroué. Isabel, he says, struck him as a 'dynamic girl, full of go and great fun'.

The night of the Coronation also happened to be the eve of Isabel's eighteenth birthday, and her father had organised her party at Claridges. Teddy and his new wife Gill were both invited, as were some others of the Oxford set in which both Goldsmiths had moved several years before. Among them was Dominic Elwes, then 22, son of the society painter Simon Elwes , and a man who would feature in the Goldsmith story 20 years later. Elwes was well-connected, the cousin of Lady Annabel Vane-Tempest-Stuart (later Lady Annabel Birley), and a part-time painter himself, but more a full-time playboy. Another was Julian Plowden, nephew of Sir Edwin Plowden, chairman of Britain's Atomic Energy Authority. These two gave Isabel a nickname, 'Gypsy', which would later be adopted by the British press, creating the erroneous image of a flashing-eyed Carmen.

Elwes and Plowden were part of the smart young society set of the time, within whose ranks Teddy (and Jimmy) moved with ease. Plowden was among Isabel's many suitors, and later claimed it was he who suggested she accompany a group of them after the Claridges dinner to a party at Al Burnett's Stork Room around the corner. The party had been organised by Mark Birley, whom Goldsmith had known slightly at Eton. Teddy and his wife went, as did Elwes – and it was there that Jimmy Goldsmith joined them. He was in London by accident, pursuing some new licences for his little business, but also probably in search of some fun on the biggest social evening of the decade. Elwes and Plowden later said they rang him, suggesting he join the party at the Stork Room, but Goldsmith went because his brother and John Aspinall, with whom he would normally have expected to spend the evening, were there. Plowden remembers Goldsmith being 'very worried, because he had not got a dinner suit'. He turned up in a blue lounge suit, but, says Plowden, 'When he saw Gypsy he forgot all that. I was a bit piqued because he was with Gypsy all evening.'

Isabel's appearance in the Goldsmith story is so brief and so poignant that it is now difficult to sort out the myth from the reality. In the years that followed she took on an almost mystical aura. But that should not devalue this extraordinary love story, which would stay – and will stay for the rest of his life – fixed in Goldsmith's memory as an all too brief period of great passion and beauty. It is much more than an everyday tale of two young attractive people meeting and falling in love. How it might have turned out if they had been given the rest of their lives together is another matter, but this particular moment was for both of them at the time intense and unspoilt love. From the moment Isabel entered his life to the moment she left it was less than a year, yet in that year more drama, adventure, fun, joy and sadness were packed in than most people experience in a lifetime.

After the birthday night, Jimmy went back to Paris the next day, and Isabel followed soon afterwards. As the summer wore on they began to see more and more of each other, despite the growing disapproval of Antenor Patino who, whatever else he was not, was a watchful parent and learned soon enough whom she was seeing. Young as he was, Jimmy Goldsmith's reputation with women went before him. Goldsmith had no money, no royal connections, no title; and he was a Jew. Jimmy Goldsmith was not at all what he and Madame Patino had in mind for their second daughter.

Patino decided to put an end to it, as he had successfully done with some of Christina's less promising relationships. He may or may not have known that by that stage they were lovers, but he probably suspected it – or at the very least he must have feared it. His wife had been 16 when they married, but even so Isabel must have seemed terribly young to him. He asked Goldsmith to come and see him in his office.

Initially it had never occurred to Goldsmith that Don Antenor Patino would raise objections to his courtship. He had grown up curiously classless, aware enough of his own heritage and keen to restore it, but unimpressed with money or titles in others. He had never thought of himself either as socially acceptable, or socially unacceptable – it had simply never arisen. When it did, he was astonished, but determined to overcome it.

Señor Patino's confrontation with Jimmy Goldsmith did not go as planned. If he expected an overawed and nervous young man, he was unnerved by the tall, confident young man who now appeared before him in his study. For his part, Goldsmith assumed that Antenor's resistance to his relationship was token and, once convinced of his serious intentions, would vanish. If Isabel expected a fiercer resistance, she kept it to herself. Patino started by asking for an undertaking that Jimmy would not see his daughter again. If Goldsmith attempted to see her in the future, he warned, he would be forced to send her away to a convent where the young man would never find her. Goldsmith countered by saying he had every intention of seeing her, and in fact planned to marry her.

Patino, initially, was remarkably polite. 'I'm afraid that's quite impossible,' he said. Why? 'She's far too young.'

Goldsmith, still not suspecting the anger the Bolivian was hiding, easily countered each objection, until Patino, no verbal match, exploded.

'Young man,' he shouted, 'we come from an old Catholic family.'

'Perfect,' replied Goldsmith, 'I come from an old Jewish family.'

'It is not the habit of members of our family to marry Jews.'

'It is not our habit to marry Red Indians,' Goldsmith is said to have replied.

There are only two possible sources for this reported conversation, and one of them is dead. Goldsmith related this version (or one closely approximating to it) to his friends at the time and relates it still, as amused as ever at his own repartee. Whether he actually said it or wished later that he had, is now immaterial, but probably he did. It is a conversation that has become part of the Goldsmith legend.

Whatever the wit, this was an occasion when Goldsmith's persuasive powers failed completely. Patino would not contemplate his marriage to his daughter 'at any price'. Goldsmith had entered the office calmly and confidently. He now not only lost his equilibrium but to some extent his senses. Patino must have known that, in reality, if his daughter was determined to marry, then that was what was going to happen. He could delay it perhaps, but in the end he would have to give in.

Don Antenor's first action, however, was to remove Isabel from Paris. She was sent, with her chaperone, Princess Maria Windisch-Graetz, into the French countryside to stay at the Château d'Haroué, with Prince Marc and her married sister Christina, who Patino believed were very much on his side (possibly because a very large dowry was involved, with a handsome sum to restore the château to its former glory). She had, however, written to Jimmy, and he took the next train to Nancy. Goldsmith had known Prince Marc, ten years his elder and already taking on the mantle of family protector, for some years, but resisted the temptation to go to the house. Instead he stayed in Nancy, and Isabel secretly visited him there.

Isabel's sister was in the later stages of pregnancy, and the Patinos' concentration at the time was focused more on her than it was on Isabel. At the end of September Don Antenor brought Isabel back to Paris. She was able to slip out of the Avenue Foch house to see her lover, and did so on numerous occasions, despite the two chaperones designated to watch over her. Don Antenor threatened her with a convent somewhere abroad, although quite how he could have imposed that on a wilful 18-year-old is not clear. She certainly feared it, she confided to her friends.

In mid-October 1953, the journalist Noel Whitcomb passed through Paris, dropped in at the Hôtel Crillon for a pre-lunch glass of champagne and heard the gossip about Antenor's two daughters. The source was a man called Michael Mordaunt-Smith, a relative of Frank's old friend Lord Bessborough, who picked up odd bits of gossip and passed them to newspapers. Through Goldsmith, Mordaunt-Smith had met Isabel, who told him about her father's opposition to Jimmy, and went on to relate the problems her sister had had. This was now relayed to Whitcomb, with a few bits of embellishment and embroidery. Mordaunt-Smith thought there might be a story for Whitcomb about the young lovers, and the way in which the rich and autocratic father had intervened, but the *Daily Mirror* journalist was more interested in the story of her sister, of how, as Mordaunt-Smith related it, Don Antenor had showered trinkets worth £150,000 on Christina when she did the right thing by marrying Prince Marc. Patino, Whitcomb learned, was so obsessed by social status that he had spent 'unbelievable amounts' on the prince's château so that it was worthy of his daughter, and his heirs. Christina was about to go into the American Hospital at Neuilly to have her baby, with a room specially booked for Prince Marc over the confinement, and Whitcomb made much of this: he interpreted it as an old Indian custom for the father to be present at the birth and Prince Marc must be there, although that was the last thing in the world the poor fellow wanted.

At Mordaunt-Smith's suggestion, Whitcomb phoned Isabel to check some of the details. Goldsmith was in the room with her at the time, and roared with laughter as he learned the thrust of his story. He had no love for Don Antenor, nor for Prince Marc, and thus encouraged, Whitcomb wrote his column. He later claimed he checked the details with Goldsmith and Digby Neave over dinner that evening, but as Goldsmith remembers it he never met Whitcomb until much later.

Whitcomb later insisted that his story had been rewritten, with disastrous consequences, by the *Mirror*'s sub-editors, but whatever the truth, what appeared was a highly fanciful piece, part faction, part fiction, which ran under the heading:

THE CHRISTENING PRESENT WILL BE SEVENTEEN BEAUTIFUL GOLD MINES. HIS HIGHNESS MUST ATTEND THE CONFINEMENT

Don Antenor was described as 'the multi-millionaire son of a South American Indian' who with 'the incredible snobbishness born of the Indian greengrocer' refused to allow his two beautiful daughters to mix with anyone other than royalty. Papa, Whitcomb went on, 'doubtless through some fidelity to Indian custom', had basically bribed Prince Marc to be at the birth, and was so delighted when he agreed that he gave him seventeen gold mines in Canada. 'So everything ended happily after all . . .' Whitcomb's piece ended lamely (in fact Christina's marriage lasted no more than a few years and she went on to marry twice more).

Nothing could have annoyed Patino more. He took no pride whatsoever in his Indian blood, insisting that he was of 'Spanish ancestry', and in truth he was no more than a quarter Indian. Goldsmith knew this was a raw spot, and had joked about it to his friends, including Mordaunt-Smith, who had passed it on with reckless disregard for the consequences. Patino immediately issued a writ against Whitcomb and the *Mirror* and won the ensuing court case.

The courtship between Jimmy and Isabel continued in secret through the autumn, and in November Isabel realised she was pregnant. They kept it to themselves, but began to lay serious plans for getting married. Then, on 9 December, Don Antenor acted. He must have discovered that the couple were still meeting (although he had no idea about the pregnancy), because he abruptly sent Isabel and her elderly chaperone, Princess Windisch-Graetz, on a world tour in his private plane, the first leg taking them to North Africa. That same morning the Patino lawyers turned up at Goldsmith's apartment to threaten him with the French law of *détournement de jeunesse* or *détournement de mineur*, under which Goldsmith could have gone to jail – Isabel was still a minor under French law, and it was a criminal offence to take her away from her appointed guardian. The lawyers demanded an undertaking that Goldsmith would never see her again.

Goldsmith refused to give any undertaking of any kind, insisting instead that he would find her wherever she had been sent. According to the accounts of those who saw him that day and over the next few days, he went into a wild rage which would have frightened even Antenor Patino if he had witnessed it. It was not just the loss of Isabel and his unborn baby – although that was bad enough – but there was the added insult to his family as not being good enough for this 'Red Indian's son'. Also the Patinos, whom he had duped for months, had now outwitted him. He summoned his friends to a council of war. Digby Neave soon arrived, as did another old friend, John Train, and Mike Mordaunt-Smith. Whitcomb, in London at the *Daily Mirror* office, recorded that he was rung later that day by Mordaunt-Smith who told him the story. Jimmy, he reported, was 'frantic with rage and anxiety'. He also, according to Whitcomb, added the further news, 'strictly between ourselves, old boy', that Isabel was pregnant, but this is probably another of the many rewritings of this episode that were to take place: Goldsmith did not tell even his friends at the time, and certainly nothing appeared in the *Mirror* (or any other paper) until much later.

It was two days before Jimmy discovered where Isabel had been taken: Casablanca. After days of striding up and down his apartment, of hours on the telephone, of threats and counterthreats, of consultations with lawyers, family and friends, Goldsmith now had a course of action. A hotel in Casablanca was marginally better than the Spanish convent to which he thought she might have been despatched. How to get there before she was moved on again? And how to get her back? There were scheduled flights to Casablanca from Paris, but Goldsmith decided he would need a private aeroplane. After ringing round Paris fruitlessly, he found one at Croydon Airport in London. It was an eight-seat de Havilland Dove, somewhat ancient, but should be able to get there carrying Goldsmith and the couple of friends he might need if he were to carry out his rescue. He hired it for £1,000. The plane would be in Le Bourget that evening, and he would set off the instant it landed and refuelled. Digby Neave and John Train would accompany him.

The plan soon went awry; Antenor Patino was alerted, and immediately ordered Isabel back to Paris, taking the first commercial flight leaving Casablanca that day.

Goldsmith and his two friends were at Le Bourget that evening as their de Havilland landed. They stowed their luggage, and prepared to take off, but had to wait on the runway, engines revving, for a commercial flight to land. They watched, without realising, a Comet jet bearing Isabel taxi clear of the runway before they were cleared for take-off. She was already on the tarmac as they lifted off on a journey which all aboard still remember as the worst of their lifetimes. Goldsmith sat, chewing his handkerchief, while the plane flew laboriously south, stopping to refuel first in Bordeaux and then in Madrid in the middle of the night, and on again. The crew were exhausted and wanted a rest, but Goldsmith would have none of it. The day was well advanced by the time they arrived in Casablanca, miserable and tired, and began the job of finding Isabel. Neave and Train grumpily decided to investigate the casbah, leaving Goldsmith frantically phoning hotels, embassies and everyone he vaguely knew there.

It took him some hours to discover she had already gone. It had been evening the day before when Isabel arrived back at the Patino house. Early next morning, she crept downstairs and telephoned Goldsmith's apartment, to find him gone. What happened next owes much to a girl called Simonne, a god-daughter of Marcelle Goldsmith, whom Jimmy had taken on as his secretary at Dagonal. From a call-box in Morocco, Goldsmith told Simonne to go to the Patino house, ask for Isabel's maid, and tell her she was under instructions from Señor Patino to pick up Isabel's passport so that she could get some visas in it. Simonne, however, improved on this plan: she posed as a driving instructor, telling the Patino housekeeper that Isabel was taking driving lessons, and the passport was needed for stamping. Once Simonne had the passport, getting Isabel out of the house was relatively simple: Simonne booked her on a flight leaving Le Bourget for London, and sent round a car to pick her up. There was no difficulty: Don Antenor did not lock his daughter up, and she went out as if she were going to a cocktail party, wearing her young girl's pearl necklace and a short leopardskin coat.

While he waited for his two-man crew to have a few hours' sleep before setting off for London, Jimmy stayed on the phone. He rang a firm of London solicitors, Withers and Partners, and asked them to inquire into how he might get married: he had a vague notion about Gretna Green in Scotland, and wondered if that were still possible. He also rang his family and friends to bring them up to date, and to arrange for Isabel to be met in London. The *Mirror* journalist Noel Whitcomb, hearing the latest events from Mordaunt-Smith (whose journalistic role Jimmy knew nothing about), decided to involve himself, and it was he who picked Isabel up and brought her to his home, just as Jimmy was preparing to set off for London, a journey that would take him 24 hours. He had had no sleep since he left Paris, and not much in the days before that.

While they waited for Goldsmith to arrive, Whitcomb's wife took Isabel shopping. 'She hadn't even brought a toothbrush,' said Whitcomb. 'Later, walking with us down the local high street, she saw that there was a sale at the drapers. She went in and bought a skirt marked down to £3, and a blue woollen twin set for 45s 6d.' (A month later Isabel was married in that same skirt and twin set.) Shortly after they got back, one of the shops telephoned to say that the young lady who had been with Whitcomb had dropped a necklace, which they were keeping safely for her. It was Isabel's pearls.

Jimmy arrived at Croydon Airport that evening and went straight to Whitcomb's house, meeting the journalist for the first time. He was unshaven, tired, but triumphant. His lawyer, Iain Scott Smith turned up too, and they began to work on a more detailed plan. Smith formally reminded Isabel of the seriousness of the step she was taking, pointing out that her father would probably disinherit her. 'Isabel was astonished that he could consider a few million pounds of any consequence when happiness was at stake,' Whitcomb recorded at the time.

Until now nothing of this had appeared in the papers. For the Patinos, it was a scandal which they wanted to keep as private as possible. Goldsmith claims he had no inkling of the publicity the elopement would create, and using the press as a weapon against Don Antenor was something that had not occurred to him. 'I was only twenty and not yet understanding of that world. That is why the *Mirror* had an inside track.' Here he was, making his plans in the house of a columnist from Britain's biggest circulation paper with a readership of 14 million (one in three of the adult population of Britain), with Whitcomb merrily joining in the arrangements. Yet Whitcomb held off. The story of a beautiful 18-year-old Bolivian heiress eloping to Scotland with a 20-year-old Etonian with a reputation as a playboy was, he knew, 'a ticking timebomb'. Yet, he says, he also had 'an obligation towards my young friends to protect them as far as possible from the added difficulties that would arise for them if the press got hold of their story too soon.' Whitcomb's account, which he wrote in his autobiography published in 1990, differs markedly from Goldsmith's own account or Neave's recollections, and he does seem to have awarded himself a more important role in retrospect than others believed he had in the event. At this time, he was playing for bigger stakes, setting himself a private deadline: he would print the story the day Antenor Patino discovered where the couple were.

He also, he says, arranged to cover some of the costs of the couple in Scotland in return for the inside track on the story – a claim which Goldsmith indignantly repudiates. Mordaunt-Smith, he believes, was being paid by Whitcomb who may have assumed some of it was passing on to him. 'One of the few insults that has never been made against me is that I am a scrounger. All my life I have despised them. I cannot remember, going all the way back to my teens, the times when I have not been the host, other than eating at people's homes or with my parents. I have always been more comfortable being a host than a guest.' The *Mirror*, he acknowledges, did have the inside track – but only because he had known Mordaunt-Smith.

He paid for the trip by borrowing from Dagonal, and decided he would do it in the style to which Isabel at least was accustomed. They set off for Scotland in a chauffeur-driven Rolls-Royce, stopping near Chester to see Teddy Goldsmith, then in an officer cadet training school at Eaton Hall. 'Jimmy suddenly appeared in this massive car with Isabel,' says Teddy, 'and everybody saluted because they thought it was a general.' By the evening of 13 December they were in Edinburgh and formally recorded their residence there. Jimmy gave his address as 14 Drylaw Crescent, Blackhall, the home of one of the solicitors, and his occupation as 'hotelier', and Isabel registered hers as 14 Church Hill, Edinburgh. They now had to wait 15 days to establish residence before they could publish the banns, and then another seven days before the actual ceremony could take place.

In this brief lull, there was no question in anyone's mind that Patino would pursue his daughter. Everyone, from Whitcomb to the lawyers to Jimmy and Isabel, all took it for granted he would be searching, that he would find where his daughter was when the banns were published – and that he would come after her in person. Patino was neither an evil nor a nasty man, as Goldsmith himself would freely admit. 'I never blamed him. I would have felt as he did, if I had been in his position. I would have considered Isabel too young and me unsuited to be married at that time – my life had been too frivolous.' Nor was Patino a very forceful or strong personality, even if he was used to having his own way. In this case he was driven by love for his daughter – and fear of what might happen to her in the hands of a man he regarded as a ne'er-do-well.

Unbeknown to Jimmy or Isabel, Don Antenor called on Frank Goldsmith at his office in Paris two days before Christmas. He was civil, courteous, even humble. The only report of what was said between them came from Marcelle a few days later. 'My husband told Señor Patino that he was not against the wedding,' she said in a newspaper interview, 'but that he thought Isabel and Jimmy were too young and should wait. Señor Patino, too, said he was not opposed to the wedding providing his daughter went to him and told him that she was in love with Jimmy and wanted to marry him. Señor Patino told my husband, "If she says that I will make no difficulties".'

That message never reached the couple.

On 29 December 1953 the banns were duly published. In London, Whitcomb, who had a friend monitoring the notices of marriages published in Edinburgh, wrote a seven-page memo to his editor, detailing the story so far, insisting it should not be broken until he gave the go-ahead, and promising the *Mirror* 'the inside track'. He presented it to his editor personally. But it was not until the morning of Saturday, 2 January 1954, that Antenor Patino arrived in London. He did not stay, but booked himself on the night train to Scotland. The wedding was set to take place any time from Wednesday onwards, anywhere in Scotland, by any authorised registrar or minister. Patino had only a few days to stop it.

In Edinburgh, Patino took a floor at the Caledonian Hotel and immediately called together his lawyers, detectives and aides. In London, Whitcomb wrote his story, and that evening the presses of the *Daily Mirror* began running off its regular five million copies of the scoop. Some of the other papers had small items to the effect that a rich Bolivian millionaire Antenor Patino was on the way to Scotland in search of his runaway daughter – that much was now public knowledge. Only the *Daily Mirror* had the full story. It actually carried nothing in its first edition, which would be read and picked up by its rivals, but quickly replated to devote its full front and back pages to it. The headlines were: HEIRESS ELOPES – ALL-NIGHT DASH BY MILLIONAIRE FATHER.

'Lovely, slender, dark-eyed Maria Isabella Patino y Bourbon, heiress to millions, whose beauty and charm have captured Paris, has promised to wed Mr James Goldsmith, a handsome, tall ex-Etonian who is only twenty.'

Goldsmith, said Whitcomb with some exaggeration, was a 'director of seven French companies', and went on to set out the dramatic story of Jimmy's plane journey to Casablanca and the pursuit of the couple by the father. It was the signal for the press to descend on Edinburgh.

Looking back now, it is difficult to understand why the story should have become such an event for the press. Certainly, it was romantic and there was one of the world's richest men involved, but Jimmy Goldsmith was totally unknown, and the fact that he had eloped was hardly a matter of international importance. Today, the story would still make the tabloid papers, but the interest in it would be more subdued. In January 1954, however, it was a huge story, and not just for the popular press: even *The Times* kept its readers abreast of it on a daily basis. The *Daily Express* called it 'The elopement of the century', and elopements in the 1950s, just as they had been when Jessica Mitford eloped in the 1930s, were big news.

Whitcomb's story appeared on Monday, two days before the wedding could legally take place. Jimmy and Isabella had left Edinburgh on 30 December, in a modest Standard Vanguard driven, in his traditionally haphazard and precarious manner, by Jimmy himself, and were touring the Scottish Highlands, staying with friends of the solicitors who had put them up in Edinburgh, or registering in separate rooms under their own names, remarkably openly. They were now celebrities, welcome anywhere, although still ostensibly keeping their position secret. The journalists were on the trail, but never found them. Instead they laid siege to Señor Patino. Then his estranged wife turned up too. The two of them had to dodge in and out of his hotel by the back entrance. It was a total humiliation for him, particularly as, according to Whitcomb's reports, Goldsmith and his daughter were enjoying themselves hugely – which they were. Goldsmith was reported to have placed a bet on a horse called Sir d'Orient, owned by John Aspinall, which won at Newbury at five to one on New Year's Day, but he never did. 'That was not the mood.' He and Isabel were too wrapped up in each other to consider anything else. They arrived at the Golden Lion Hotel, Stirling, just before lunch on New Year's Eve, booked single rooms on the second floor, took no part in the Hogmanay celebrations, and left after lunch the next day. The press traced them to Dundee, then to the Drummond Arms, Crieff, in Perthshire, back to Stirling again (where Isabel had a cold), but always a day or two after they had moved on.

In Cannes that week Frank Goldsmith, presenting a medal to the manager of the Carlton, Jean Mero, who had done the job for 25 years, gave a little speech. 'I am a man in the news at the moment,' he said, 'not because I own hotels but because of my son Jimmy. My wife was worried because she says we have no news of Jimmy. I told her we have never had so much news about him as now. We hear something new every day.' The audience laughed appreciatively, but privately Frank and Marcelle were deeply worried about their younger son. Patino was a powerful man; where was this going to end?

For Don Antenor, stuck in Edinburgh in January, surrounded by the press, with a wife he hated, chasing a daughter who didn't want to know him, laughed at by half the world, it must have been torture. The hotel staff at the Caledonian were told that Señor Patino was 'ill and tired' after his fruitless search for his daughter. The hotel itself was in uproar, with the press ringing night and day, and chambermaids and waiters on constant duty down the hallway to attend to the Patinos' needs and keep strangers away. An elderly member of the staff was reported as saying: 'Never has the hotel seen such a situation as this. It's most unusual. We shall be very glad to settle down in peace again.' From that day on Patino acquired a notoriety and an image he would never shed to his dying day; he would never again be Don Antenor Patino, one of the world's richest men, but 'the man who chased that young couple around Scotland . . .' He didn't wholly deserve it, but everything he did, such as turning up in Edinburgh with a large retinue, made things worse.

Whitcomb, who arrived in Edinburgh on the day his story broke, described the scene there as 'the most astonishing media circus that I have ever witnessed in the whole of my career, and I have seen a fair few.' Reporters and photographers began pouring in from all over Europe, and even the United States. Soon there were hundreds of them, making up what one reporter called 'the most memorable army of pressmen ever to gather under one roof'. Because the *Mirror* had the full story and had clearly been in contact with the missing couple, other reporters watched the *Mirror* team, not knowing that only Whitcomb had any idea where the missing couple were – and he was no longer sure. One of the *Mirror* reporters kept an ironical diary of events, which gives a graphic description of the extraordinary atmosphere:

Martlew [the *Mirror* reporter] went to the register office in a big Humber. So did twenty other reporters. Mortars was casing a hotel exit. So were twenty other reporters. Craig cased another exit. Twenty reporters from other papers watched Craig. Mary Malone went to powder her nose and half the women reporters in Fleet Street followed her into the Ladies.

Reporters went to Paris to besiege Frank and Marcelle in case the couple turned up there. Frank laconically remarked that his son Teddy had not told him of his marriage until after the event and he didn't expect Jimmy would either.

On 5 January Antenor presented a petition to the Court of Session, and was given an 'interim interdict' preventing the issue of a marriage certificate to his daughter. Goldsmith's lawyers had anticipated that, and were ready, serving their own notice of appeal within minutes. The next day the interdict was lifted. None of that could have been a surprise to Patino: there was no precedent for stopping a marriage by legal process in Scottish law, and the large team of lawyers working with him must have advised him to that effect. The best he could hope for was a delay, and he achieved a single day. What then was he hoping for? Why had he brought his wife over too? Since Isabel was very fond of her mother, perhaps Antenor hoped that where he had failed, the duchess might succeed in persuading her not to go through with the marriage.

On the night before the wedding, Jimmy and Isabel moved back to Edinburgh to the old-fashioned Prestonfield House Hotel, four miles from the Caledonian and the centre of the city. Whitcomb and Mordaunt-Smith also joined them there. Isabel still wore the same clothes she had left London in three weeks before, and after dinner the four of them sat around, while the meticulous Whitcomb went on taking notes: Isabel read a book called *Désirée* by Annemarie Selinke while Goldsmith, he says, read *History of Western Philosophy* by Bertrand Russell (Goldsmith says he has never read Russell 'except to cast a glance at the writings of a man I believe to be unsound'.) Towards midnight Goldsmith's lawyers rang from the city. Patino was throwing in the towel. He would withdraw all objections to the marriage, stipulating only one condition: that Isabel would agree to meet her mother before the ceremony. Isabel was only too pleased. 'It has hurt me terribly to know how anxious and distressed Mummy must have been,' Whitcomb noted her as saying. However, she insisted that her mother should know beforehand that she had no intention of changing her mind. That message was passed back, and a meeting was arranged the next day.

That same night, in the early hours, Antenor Patino quietly crept out of the hotel without any of the reporters noticing, and headed back for London. And in Edinburgh early the next morning Isabel met her mother, who was not aware, until then, that she was pregnant. There was no question of an abortion in a Catholic family. Whatever hope Madame Patino might have had of dissuading her daughter was now abandoned. 'If that's what you want we won't do anything to stop you,' she told her daughter, according to Isabel later.

By now, however, the event had gained a momentum of its own, as much to avoid the press as the vanquished forces of the Patinos. Whitcomb and the *Daily Mirror* were organising an elaborate charade which the young couple were persuaded to go along with. At 9.30 in the Court of Session the next day, the Patino lawyers formally withdrew their objections, and Goldsmith's solicitors immediately collected the necessary licence, and brought it back to their office. It was then entrusted to a charlady who emerged, still with her mop and bucket, and slipped it in the window of a car, driven down the street by Whitcomb, who then took it to the Bank of Scotland premises in Kelso where the wedding party was to gather.

Goldsmith and his bride-to-be left Prestonfield House in even greater secrecy – and discomfort – in the back of a delivery van, pausing to be photographed by the ever-present *Daily Mirror* photographer, and arrived at the Bank of Scotland three hours before the documents. Whitcomb was making up for his earlier reticence by turning the event into a circus, with the young couple the increasingly uncomfortable performers.

The whole of Britain, and particularly the whole of Scotland, knew the marriage was to take place that day. Somehow word spread that, of the 200 registry offices available, the couple had chosen Kelso, and a crowd gathered outside the registry office. When Isabel walked from her hotel, in the same leopardskin coat she had worn since leaving Paris, the same pearls and the same twinset, but now carrying, according to one report, a 'bouquet of lily of the valley but wearing no hat', there were 50 people outside. When the married couple emerged there were even more. Everyone was on their side. Well-wishers pressed forward to shake hands and cry good luck, and the wife of the rector of Kelso gave the bride a present of a white elephant. They drove back to Edinburgh, all attempts at secrecy at last abandoned, while the Patinos, separately, went back to London, with Don Antenor making the reported, but unlikely, remark to his lawyer: 'Everything seems to have ended happily.' In Cannes Frank Goldsmith was genuinely pleased. Asked by a reporter for his comment, he remarked: 'It is a happy ending. It was the only possible end to the children's romance. Jimmy is very much in love and has the means to get married. I hope they will be very happy.'

Jimmy and Isabel moved into the honeymon suite in Prestonfield House that night. The next day they had a celebratory lunch at the George Hotel where they at last faced the press, Isabel still in the same clothes, still clutching her leopardskin coat around her against the January cold. The groom was in forgiving mood, remarking how pleased he was that 'an amicable solution had been reached' with his in-laws. They had, he said, been constantly travelling for weeks, covering 200 miles in Scotland. How much had the runaway romance cost, asked a reporter? Goldsmith just shook his head and smiled: 'We were extremely well received in Scotland and everyone was very nice.' His little company in France was doing well, but he had borrowed heavily these past few months.

That evening John Aspinall had a phone call from Goldsmith. 'Aspers, we're getting into King's Cross at four in the morning, and we're going to have a wedding breakfast at the Ritz. Will you come along?' Aspinall was delighted. Like other Goldsmith friends, he was basking in the newfound fame of his friend. 'I was saying to everybody, "Look, this is my friend, Jimmy Goldsmith, the man on the front pages." And I couldn't believe that my friend from Reading dog track was now an international hero.'

Even the arrival in King's Cross station before dawn was a colourful affair. 'Blazing arc lamps, microphones and newsreel cameras were waiting for the couple' wrote one newspaper the next day. Another had a picture of Isabel stepping off the train, still in that ubiquitous leopardskin, with the caption, 'Porters queued to get a close-up of Mr and Mrs James Goldsmith, the couple whose runaway marriage intrigued the whole nation.' The same papers carried pictures of a dispirited Señora Patino, heavily wrapped in mink coat, in a London street.

As Dominic Elwes and other old friends joined them for breakfast, the mood of the press reflected that of the party. The veteran *Daily Mirror* columnist Cassandra, often curmudgeonly, summed it up. In a column headed 'The Lovers', he wrote:

> It was wonderful while it lasted. As exciting as a fox-hunt with the hounds called off at the last moment. As romantic as a motorised version of Lorna Doone. As thrilling as a Western cowboy drama in which the singing cowboy wins the tempestuous but inevitably yielding cowgirl.
>
> At last, Mr J. Goldsmith has married Miss I. Patino.

7

Kidnap

In those early months of 1954 Jimmy Goldsmith seemed to be favoured by the gods. He was still not quite 21, but already had a business going which, although not a conspicuous success, had given his life the purpose and direction he needed. He had just married the girl he loved and she was expecting his first child, an event which he looked forward to hugely. He was intelligent, energetic, handsome and in good health. Life seemed full of hope.

There were a few blemishes. For one thing, Jimmy had no money. He had spent lavishly in the past couple of months, hiring aeroplanes, cars, lawyers and hotel rooms without stopping to think how he would pay for them. He had piled up debts of around £2,000, a figure he had reached once before, and which his father had paid for him. He did not want to ask his father again. He had no home other than his room in the Scribe, and had also neglected his fledgling business which needed constant attention.

But these were minor shadows on what was probably the brightest horizon he would ever enjoy. He returned with Isabel to Paris elated after the chase around Scotland, the outwitting of the Patino parents, and the extraordinary publicity which had attended its every move. Everyone now greeted him as a hero, the young playboy who had risked everything to win the hand of his runaway heiress, and had won in such a spectacular manner. He resented the term 'playboy' which he reckoned no longer applied to him, but overall Jimmy Goldsmith had never had so much goodwill, and probably never would again.

Back in Paris, the Goldsmith parents rallied around as he hoped and expected they would. The major was now more patriarchal and benign than ever, but the past few months had tried even his urbanity and serenity. Digby Neave, now living in Paris, found him unusually upset as he was hounded by journalists hunting for news of his son. He was not worried for himself, but was concerned that Jimmy had got himself into trouble he could not get out of.

The chase had ended well, however, and Jimmy was back in Paris with his bride. Frank gave them a suite at the Scribe, and Marcelle Goldsmith welcomed her new daughter-in-law with affection. She instantly took to this girl who had never received much affection from her own parents, and who had undergone a lifetime's experience in the past few months. Even the Patinos were friendly.

Yet Goldsmith's natural pessimism would not let the new euphoria last long. He was emotionally drained by the past few months, the adrenalin running down as he attempted to pick up his life in Paris again. An interesting insight into his state of mind at the time is provided by the American columnist Art Buchwald who visited them at the Scribe shortly after they got back. The Goldsmiths at the time were holding open house for journalists from all over the world who wanted to catch up on events at first hand. Buchwald's article is a whimsical one, revealing more in what it leaves unsaid. It started, 'We spent a pleasant two hours in Paris with the Goldsmith newlyweds', where Buchwald reported they were to spend a month before going on honeymoon either to Cannes or for winter sports. 'When we entered their suite at an hotel which Mr Goldsmith's father owns,' wrote Buchwald, 'we found the couple having trouble about the heating. The radiators weren't working properly, and there was some discussion about what could be done about it.' The conversation didn't get much above that level in their two hours, which sounds remarkably unlike Jimmy Goldsmith who, even in those early days, when his interest in politics and the wider world was embryonic, could say an awful lot in that time. When the Buchwalds asked Isabel if she had any clothes besides those she had taken to Scotland with her, she replied, 'I'm sorry, I don't make any statements. You'll have to ask Jimmy.' What did Jimmy have to say about her clothes? Only that she didn't have many clothes, and most of them were at the Patino house. How much had the little escapade in Scotland and Morocco cost? 'Someone said it cost somewhere around £2,000 and they weren't far wrong,' said Goldsmith. This desultory interview was at this stage interrupted by the appearance of a number of photographers, followed by several French newspapermen. The Buchwalds watched it all in some amazement. 'The reporters had him in a corner, the photographers were busy taking pictures of Mrs Goldsmith, and the plumbers were hard at work trying to get the radiators started,' said Buchwald. Goldsmith looked on grim-faced. 'I'm so fed up smiling,' he muttered.

After they had all filed out, Buchwald restarted his interview with an odd question, one that he had possibly been primed to ask by one of Frank Goldsmith's circle in Paris. Was Goldsmith's father happy about the turn of events?

'I wouldn't quote him as saying that,' replied Goldsmith tautly. But was he amused by it all?

'I wouldn't say that either,' said Goldsmith. 'Father knew nothing about the elopement until the press contacted him. My father is 75 years old and things like that don't amuse him any more.'

The Buchwald interview is a curiously tightlipped affair, possibly explained by the fact that Goldsmith had by then given so many interviews that he was just going through the motions. If he had to do it all over again, would he do it the same way? asked Buchwald. 'Yes, indeed. We're both very happy with the elopement.'

As Goldsmith politely showed them to the door, the Buchwalds had time for one final question:

'Are you sure you don't want to say anything further about your father-in-law?'

'Yes, sir,' said Goldsmith. 'Very sure.'

In fact the article does not quote him as saying anything about Señor Patino at all, but Buchwald had obviously tried to tempt him into an outburst against him. Goldsmith had learned some diplomacy by then – or else he did not want to wound his wife further. Patino had made one further attempt to have the marriage annulled, travelling yet again to Scotland to be rebuffed by the judges. Back in London, he found the usual group of reporters, whom he told: 'She can now look after herself, and her husband. They can expect no financial assistance from me.'

In Paris Goldsmith repeated that he didn't want any of the Patino money. If Isabel had hoped for reconciliation with her parents once she was married, she was disappointed. Jimmy, however, didn't want any more open warfare with his in-laws, and was clearly intent on not offending them any more than necessary. In his eyes, and those of the rest of the world, he was the wronged party, even if in the eyes of the Patinos he was the reckless, penniless, non-royal, Jewish playboy who had seduced their daughter, made her pregnant, and run off with her. For all his ability to hate, and to strike back at, those who have done him injury, Jimmy Goldsmith showed a tolerance towards the Patinos at this stage which he would go on doing for the rest of their lives, even though they were to do him still further injury in the not-too-distant future. (Many years later, when both their financial circumstances were very different, Antenor came to him for help, and Jimmy acted as if he were part of the family.)

For the moment, honeymoon and a separate home for the newlyweds had to be postponed while Goldsmith attended to his business, stretched to the limit because of the debts he had now added to it. Jimmy went back to Dagonal, selling Lloyd's cream 'with adrenalin', complete with the little human outline on the box featuring the approximate 'trigger spots' of some of the more common forms of rheumatism (neck, back, elbow, knees etc.). It was hard work, even in a France which was emerging from its post-war austerity into the sustained boom which was to make it once again one of the richest countries in the world; but he enjoyed it and the business was alive and active, even if it was also fragile.

The first five months of 1954 were for Jimmy Goldsmith an extraordinary interlude, which he would later try to recapture in his memories as a magical period between the excitement of winning and marrying Isabel and the subsequent tragedy that overtook her. He had married in the same mood of adventurous excitement he had applied to everything up to that time, treating the chase as something more than a merry jape, but not much more. Back in Paris there was the joy of planning a home together and looking forward to the baby. They were two very young people without a serious care in the world.

Isabel and marriage brought a profound change to the life of Jimmy Goldsmith. Long before he met her, Goldsmith had been fascinated by beautiful women – and his fascination was reciprocated. From his mid-teens he already looked 20, and was often mistaken for that. Digby Neave and John Aspinall remarked on the electricity he gave out which attracted women as it did men to his company. 'He was just enormous fun to be with,' says Neave. None of his friends knew when he had lost his virginity but it was at a young age, because by the time he arrived to stay with his brother at Oxford he was already an experienced lover, who made an immediate impact on the girlfriends of his new friends who were quite a few years older. Within days of arriving at Oxford he had a new girlfriend, later the first wife of Tony Crosland, much to the amazement of Teddy who knew little about this side of his brother's life. ('It was entirely platonic and of no significance, I believe, to her,' says Goldsmith now.) John Aspinall, too, watched in awe as Jimmy charmed young women.

In May 1954, this almost perfect time in his life came to an abrupt end. Until this time, Isabel's pregnancy had been a perfectly normal one; she was a healthy, fit girl and there was no history of any illness in the family. She and Jimmy had lived quietly together at the Scribe, with Jimmy throwing himself into his business, while Isabel slept late every morning. Then, one particularly lovely evening in May, they dined in Montmartre on the terrace of a restaurant looking down over Paris, and talked about their future together. The next morning, 12 May, Goldsmith woke early, and dressed without disturbing her. Isabel was sleeping deeply, more deeply than he remembered, but she was breathing regularly and, it seemed to him, normally. He let himself out of the suite and walked to his office at the Place de L'Opera, with no conscious presentiment that anything was wrong. Yet something bothered him because later in the morning, just before ten o'clock, he rang his mother. Would she mind looking in on Isabel? She was now seven months pregnant, and Goldsmith's concern was not untypical of a young husband encountering for the first time the mysteries and the physical change of prospective parenthood. Marcelle used her own key to let herself into the suite above her own, to find Isabel still asleep. She did not wake as Marcelle entered the room, and when she picked up the sleeping girl's hand, it was limp. She immediately called a doctor, and Isabel was rushed across Paris to the American Hospital at Neuilly. She had suffered a massive cerebral haemorrhage.

Goldsmith followed the ambulance in his car. Isabel, in a deep coma, was put on a life-support system, and soon surrounded by doctors. Goldsmith listened to the diagnosis, and then asked who were the best brain specialists. He rang his friends, his father, anyone he could think of who would know, and within hours he had a list of the best in the world. The American Hospital itself numbered several internationally renowned specialists, and that afternoon Goldsmith held an emergency council. The advice he received was not cheerful: the best hope, perhaps the only hope, was for Isabel to undergo a difficult operation to relieve the pressure on the brain. She should be moved to the nearby Hartmann Clinic, which specialised in such operations.

That evening the surgeons operated while Goldsmith paced the corridors, or sat helpless in the tiny waiting room of the Hartmann. Both Patino parents joined him there, as did his own parents. By a curious coincidence the Patinos were due in court the next day for the latest episode in their interminable divorce proceedings, but for the moment that was postponed. Antenor's hostility to Goldsmith was undiminished, but as Isabel lay dying, Jimmy and the Duchess of Durcal embraced.

In the early hours the surgeons informed the relatives that the news was neither good nor necessarily bad: the operation had relieved the pressure, but Isabel was still in a coma. The official bulletin from the hospital described her condition as 'satisfactory', but it wasn't. Later that day, Friday, 14 May, they began to warn him to expect the worst. They didn't think they could save her. But what about the child? The child, although more than two months premature, could still be saved by a Caesarean operation. Goldsmith told them to go ahead.

Just before noon the doctors delivered a five-and-a-half pound baby daughter to Goldsmith while Isabel remained unconscious. The doctors operated on her again, but without success. Just after eleven that evening a priest delivered the last rites, and before midnight Goldsmith agreed with the doctors that the life-support machines should be switched off. She died a few hours later, with Goldsmith, the Patinos and the Goldsmith parents present.

Goldsmith emerged from the hospital in a state of shock. A reporter keeping vigil outside the hospital described his appearance: 'His shoulders sagging in his dark suit, he stared straight ahead, not hearing his friends' attempts to console him. Finally they led him away down the gravel path of the flower garden outside the clinic.'

Digby Neave was one of those friends, and remembers well the depth of his friend's despair. Until that moment Goldsmith had always believed he could have anything in life he wanted – wealth, fame, women, nothing was out of his reach. Now something had happened to him which no amount of ingenuity, talk or energy could help him with. He had always given full rein to his emotions, his joy encompassing anyone who came within yards of it, his depression equally unchecked. Now he was in emotional territory he had never plumbed.

For years afterwards he would not speak of Isabel's death, and even today finds it difficult. Years later when Digby Neave's first wife died, Goldsmith rang him to console him and Neave asked: 'How long does it take to get over it?' 'I don't think you ever do,' replied Goldsmith.

According to Teddy, his brother 'just worked for about eight years. He never went out, he never went to a party, he never saw anybody. He just worked.' Aspinall, his closest friend, says much the same thing. It is not entirely true, but the substance is correct. There were women in his life during this time, there was a modest amount of gambling and the odd party, but essentially there were seven-day working weeks, total immersion in a business which would mushroom from a few employees into a substantial company almost overnight, and a devotion, brought about by the pressures of survival, to learning how to run it. The wild partying, the all-night gambling and the visits to the brothels were things of the past. In those months of marriage and tragedy, Goldsmith had grown up.

The next years of his life would in other senses be difficult too. Life up to that point had been almost absurdly easy for him. The only problems he had experienced had been at school and he didn't care about that; he knew – as did anyone else who met him – that his mind was at least as quick, and probably a great deal quicker, than most. He could absorb and retain large quantities of information, analyse situations much more quickly than anyone he knew, and persuade much older and more experienced people to do what he wanted them to. He had been spoilt by an easy-going and indulgent father who forgave him everything, and seldom reproved him, and by a mother who adored him. Now he encountered a harsher world.

The publicity which had attended the runaways and the chase in Scotland made Isabel's death an equally public affair. The fairytale which had cheered the readers had turned to tragedy. Over 600 people turned up for the funeral at L'Eglise St Honoré-d'Eylau, on Tuesday, 18 May, with an even larger crowd outside. 'Some 3,000 people, the majority of them women and young girls, pressed on to the pavements of the Place Victor Hugo outside, making it necessary to call the police,' reported *Le Figaro*. 'Society and the ordinary folk of Paris turned out for the funeral,' reported the *Daily Mirror*. 'Traffic stopped as elegantly dressed socialites rubbed shoulders with shoppers and shabby charwomen.' Inside the church the walls were hidden by immense black drapes with the initials P.G. – Patino Goldsmith – in stark white letters. The service lasted an hour. Goldsmith, according to reports, stood erect, choking with grief. After the service he remained with his family and the Patinos for another hour while the mourners filed past the catafalque bearing Isabel's embalmed body, and offered their condolences. *Le Figaro* reported that there were five duchesses, a princess, two marquesses, two counts and the ambassadors of most of the South American countries at the service – a tribute to the Patinos rather than to Goldsmith. But there were also a number of Rothschilds, Goldschmidts and other cousins. The coffin was taken to the vaults of St Pierre de Chaillot, after which Goldsmith went to visit his daughter, still in an incubator in the hospital.

Jimmy Goldsmith had met Isabel Patino in June 1953, married her in January 1954 and she was dead by May – all in less than a year. In that time he had passed his twenty-first birthday, and had become a father. He had discovered love and grief, life and death, all in this concentrated period. 'When you're twenty, a year is a very long time,' he said later, but that interlude in the middle with Isabel must have seemed desperately brief.

His father had experienced a similar tragedy with Jacqueline Franc whose portraits he still kept on his walls and whose photographs fill his albums. Jacqueline too had died in an operation attempting to have a child and it had taken Frank many years to recover. His father afterwards advised Jimmy to get out of Paris, and he agreed. As he began to think straight again he made plans. The first situation to be attended to was his baby daughter. He called the girl Isabel Marcella Olga, after her mother, his own mother, and his godmother, Olga Deterding. She soon emerged from her incubator, but how was a young man of 21 living in a hotel going to look after her? The Duchess of Durcal had returned to Paris for her daughter's funeral and had stayed on at the Ritz, where Goldsmith increasingly went in the evenings to dine with her. If Goldsmith had lost a wife, the Duchess had lost a daughter and they were able to console each other. The Patinos were living apart again, having resumed their divorce battle in the courts. Goldsmith found her difficult – as indeed had her husband and daughters (she now lives alone in a large house in Paris) – but he became fond of her, as she seemed to become fond of him. In that first month after Isabel's death, he felt an unexpected bond with the duchess (Antenor remained hostile) and was anxious to include her in the upbringing of her grandchild. Goldsmith refused to accept any Patino money for himself, but his daughter would one day inherit part of the Patino fortune, which was actually much less than commonly assumed, basically because Antenor was a disastrous manager of it.

The duchess was delighted with the arrangement. She proposed that as soon as the baby left hospital she should come to her, and she would move out of the centre of Paris to the Hôtel Trianon Palace in Versailles. She would enjoy looking after little Isabel through the summer. Goldsmith would provide – and pay for – a nanny, and when he returned would find an apartment into which baby and nanny could move.

It was June by the time he was ready to leave Paris. An English nanny, Deborah Cockbill, had been hired, little Isabel was with her grandmother, and Goldsmith was beginning to emerge from his black depression. He planned a trip to Africa, with his old friend Richard Reader-Harris, a former Tory MP. Another old friend, Geoffrey Bing QC, also a former Member of Parliament, was at that stage attorney-general of Ghana and they went to stay with him. Goldsmith enjoyed the hectic social life and seeing the country. Ostensibly he was there on business, but he didn't do much, although he did travel to Liberia where he found an outlet for his pharmaceuticals. From there he went to stay with other friends in Holland, and it was the end of July before he arrived back in Paris. Little Isabel was growing, although still requiring specialist care, and the nanny had proved a success. The duchess was pleased to see him, and Goldsmith agreed she should keep the baby for another few weeks while he found a place to live. His suite in the Scribe was unsuitable for a baby and a nanny, but Jimmy, still in debt, couldn't afford anything else. For the third (and last) time in his life, Frank came to the rescue, offering to pay the cost of setting him up in a home of his own. Through August Jimmy and Marcelle went apartment hunting, and by the first week in September he was ready to move in to the fifth floor of 23 rue Marbeau, overlooking the Bois de Boulogne.

On 11 September, little Isabel was christened at the Church of Notre Dame in Chantilly, and Goldsmith was ready to receive her in his new home. He told the duchess he wanted to arrange it for 14 September, and she agreed without hesitation.

The story at this stage should have been that of the grieving young widower moving into his first home with his baby daughter to rebuild his life. It did not work that way. There was one more remarkable twist which would, for the third time in a year, make Jimmy Goldsmith front page headlines, the struggling young father pitted against the financial power of his Patino in-laws.

The Duchess of Durcal would not give back her grand-daughter. She had originally agreed with Goldsmith to look after the child for two months which ended on 31 July. Then when he returned to find an apartment she persuaded him to postpone it for a further month. In early September she suggested he should first get everything ready at the apartment. 'She pleaded with me to keep my child until 15 September,' said Goldsmith. But two days before that deadline, on 13 September, Goldsmith received two registered letters, one from the baby's nanny, then another from Madame Patino, both saying his apartment was 'uninhabitable'. Goldsmith was astounded. He was delighted with the apartment, which was on two floors, with three large bedrooms and a terrace overlooking a private garden. One floor had a bedroom fitted out as a nursery, with a small room, with its own bathroom, next door for the nanny.

Clearly it was an excuse to keep the baby, but Madame Patino had brought along her own doctor to pronounce on the suitability of the apartment. She was advised that it was better for Isabel to stay with her maternal grandmother 'preferably in Spain' where it was warmer.

Madame Patino may have been moved by genuine concern for the child, who did require the care of specialists. She may also have been convinced that the centre of Paris was not the place for her to be and that she would be better off in Spain, or at the very least in Versailles. It is possible, given his quick temper and his speed to take offence, that Goldsmith misread the situation, but the evidence produced in court later suggests the duchess had carefully prepared the ground. She had lost a daughter, but she would keep her young grand-daughter, even if it meant a fight for custody in the courts (which she had been advised she would win).

Goldsmith was not yet aware that the trap was set, although he was becoming suspicious – and angry. He insisted he would have his baby back on the appointed day, but when he turned up Madame Patino raised further sets of objections. She demanded references of his servants; she insisted, Goldsmith said, that the nanny, if she were to look after the child properly, must have her own maid as she did now, and there was no room for one at the apartment. None of that was any of her business, Goldsmith told her furiously. He would give her until 5 p.m. that evening, and then he was going to take the child.

Madame Patino contacted Antenor, packed hastily, and took the baby and the nanny out of the Trianon. When Goldsmith arrived at Versailles, at 5 p.m., the door to her suite was locked. There was no reply. He knocked again, then hurled himself at the door, smashing it in, and burst into the suite. There was no sign of the baby, or of the nanny. The baby's little white cot and some of her clothes were still in her room, and suitcases were scattered over the floor where the duchess had not had time to finish packing. 'Even the baby's feeding bottle had gone,' he told his parents later.

Frantically Goldsmith went looking for her. The Patino house was barred and he could not even discover if Madame Patino was inside. He went to the Scribe to tell his parents and began calling friends in for help. His rage can still be rekindled 37 years later. His child had been 'stolen' from him; worse she had been 'abducted', indeed 'kidnapped'. Goldsmith concentrated on that word 'kidnap', which he was to repeat again and again over the next few days. Kidnapping was a criminal offence – well, Madame Patino must be charged with it. He summoned lawyers, and the police, insisting they file charges before the Paris courts alleging 'abduction of a minor', just as the Patinos had once threatened him with a similar offence. Goldsmith demanded the police alert every frontier guard, seaport and airport to stop the child being taken out of France. They must arrest the Duchess, he insisted over and over, before she got his baby to Spain.

Technically in France the charge of abduction, which was the charge Goldsmith formally insisted on, is brought against 'unknown persons'. He was very well aware that it wasn't 'unknown persons' who had abducted the child, and so were the police. The charge they filed was a lesser one of non-presentation of a child, but Goldsmith continued to talk about 'abduction' and 'kidnapping' – and still does. In France, the law on parental custody is quite clear, as Goldsmith's lawyers assured him, and if a child is taken away without the parents' consent, technically that is kidnapping.

Restlessly, he sought other means to apply pressure on the Patinos. He soon thought of the press, and the hatred the Patinos had for publicity. Goldsmith had discovered the press wholly by accident at the time of the runaway, and had watched in amazement as the packs pursued him and Isabel. It had worked very much to his advantage, but he had not planned it, or orchestrated it, except to some extent through Noel Whitcomb. The press, including Whitcomb, had turned up again in force when Isabel died, and again had been overwhelmingly sympathetic. Now for the first time he would seek their help, offer his story, use the press as a weapon to embarrass the Patinos. No one would relish being branded as kidnappers.

He began that evening, and continued all week, giving interview after interview. *Le Figaro* reported the 'kidnap' the next morning, setting in train the third Goldsmith story in a year to hit the front pages. The kidnap took place on Tuesday, 14 September 1954. *Figaro*'s report appeared on the 15th, and all that day Goldsmith was busily briefing the British papers with a blow by blow account of how he had gone to Versailles to fetch the baby. 'Little Isabel is terribly fragile,' he told more than one reporter. 'Any sudden movement or a long trip might kill her.' Doctors, he added, had told him she would not really be strong for three years. 'It is criminal, criminal.' He had, he added, been unable to contact his mother-in-law. 'I don't know where she is.'

That afternoon he met both Patino parents, reunited in their joint battle against Goldsmith, at the offices of their lawyer M. Pierre Lenard, who called it a 'family conference'. The Patino case, as set out by Lenard, was this: baby Isabel's health required the care of specialists. M. Goldsmith's apartment in the centre of Paris did not offer the same conditions as a house in the country. It was 'a case of life and death' for Isabel, and the Patinos were not going to stand by and see their grandchild, heir to millions, die because her father behaved irresponsibly. They appreciated that it was only under exceptional circumstances that a child should be taken from the care of its parents, but this was indeed an exceptional case. 'Madame Patino does not consider that it would be in the best interests of baby Isabel to leave her with her father,' said another Patino lawyer, Maître Gaston Bergery.

Antenor, who hated confrontation at the best of times, tried not to catch Goldsmith's eye, and watched with growing concern as his son-in-law's rage mounted. Later he said he thought Goldsmith was 'mad'. When Jimmy heard that, he became so angry even his friends began to fear Patino might have a point. 'Of course you can produce a house ten times the size of mine,' he told the Patinos, 'and put in fifty servants if you wish. But ask the hall porter downstairs if he would surrender HIS children if somebody offered them a palace. Of curse he wouldn't!'

Goldsmith stalked off, still ignorant of his daughter's whereabouts, still accusing his parents-in-law of being 'criminals' and 'kidnappers', and demanding their arrest. But the Patinos, buttressed by their bevy of lawyers, were committed to a course of action: Goldsmith was told that they intended to keep the baby. They would apply for adoption. In a brief statement later, M. Lenard said: 'The Patinos decided to institute summary proceedings at three o'clock next Friday before the chairman of the Seine Civil Court, President Ausset.'

President Ausset was about to have his day in the headlines. It was Marcelle Goldsmith, who knew much of the gossip in Paris, who told her son an open secret about the judge: he had a mistress of long standing called Reine. Eagerly, Goldsmith asked for her address, and every day that week he sent her a single rose, with his love. Ausset was one of the most distinguished judges in Paris, a weighty man both of body and intellect. A year later, when the case was long over, Goldsmith was to meet him at a dinner party, at which the mistress was also present. The judge solemnly thanked Goldsmith for the roses, and then added: 'Reine pestered me every day to side with you. I told her that was improper and that if she continued I would have to leave her.' Then, smiling at Reine across the table, he added: 'But then I felt it would be unfair to use you, M. Goldsmith, as an excuse for getting rid of her.'

By Thursday morning, two days after the disappearance, the British papers carried full and lengthy interviews with Goldsmith, complete with pictures of the empty nursery with teddy bears and a cot. Goldsmith was massaging the story for everything it was worth. With some journalists he was cautious about maligning the Patinos, with others he let his rage boil over. The child, he told one, had been 'abducted by professional kidnappers', before cooling down enough to tell the story in more elaborate detail. He seemed genuinely bemused by what he saw as the treachery of his mother-in-law. He was, he said, 'very fond of the duchess. This whole business has astounded me, but I will fight it to the death.' As he talked he paced up and down. 'It has been a terrible year for me and it seems everything is against me.' Up and down again, up and down. 'Even if I were rich I couldn't stand up against the wealth of the Patinos. They seem to believe they can buy everything' – up and down, arms waving – 'including my baby!' Finding little Isabel was impossible – the Patinos had half a dozen houses in Paris alone, he told reporters. A police officer who went to the Patino mansion had been refused admission. 'I'll search the house myself,' said Goldsmith.

The papers carried stories of Goldsmith's demands for the arrest of both Patinos and of the English nanny, who Goldsmith felt had betrayed him too. 'Arrest Papa Patino says Jimmy', read one headline that week, and there were others like it.

The Patinos, or at least Antenor, must by now have felt they had walked into a hurricane. Goldsmith had humiliated them before in Scotland, with the help of the press and the courts. But this time they were on home ground, had the best lawyers in France, and, above all, had possession of the child. This would be a battle they could properly fight in court where they assumed Goldsmith would be weakest. They began to hit back. A long statement from M. Lenard, acting for the duchess, said, 'The estrangement between M. Patino and the duchess is forgotten in the light of this terrible affair. We consider the baby is in such precarious health that her life hangs by a thread. She needs the best medical attention in the world.' The child, he added, suffered from a rare disease in which the blood lacks oxygen.

Goldsmith spent most of Thursday morning at the Prefecture of Police, angrily urging them to greater action. They were unmoved. A police commissioner issued a statement saying: 'The child appears to be in no danger, and we hope there will be an amicable arrangement between the families.'

On Friday, 17 September, three days after Jimmy had broken down the door, the battle moved into court, amid scenes which Noel Whitcomb, who had flown over to cover the event for the *Mirror*, described as 'the most fantastic I have ever witnessed'. Hundreds of lawyers, he said, joined crowds who 'swarmed all over the Palais de Justice' trying to catch glimpses of Jimmy and the Patinos. Marcelle was reported to have been so startled by the throng that she fled into the judge's room.

Goldsmith pushed his way through an hour before the hearing started, carrying in his pocket what he referred to as his 'certificate of sanity', signed by doctors. He intended to produce it if, as rumours suggested, the Patino side tried to make out he was insane or 'a dangerous maniac'. The Duchess of Durcal had hired probably the leading advocate in France, Maître René Floriot, who had defended the Nazi ambassador in Paris, Otto Abetz, and, in 1946, the mass murderer Dr Marcel Petiot who said he had not murdered 27 Jews and French Resisters, as accused, but 63 – and had done it all for France. Floriot was quoted in that morning's *Figaro* as saying: 'I will certainly not miss making the point that since the beginning of July Madame Patino has had care of the baby with the total accord of the father. One is thus surprised that he now suddenly wishes to take back little Isabel.' His client, he added, was not only claiming that Jimmy Goldsmith was unable to provide his daughter with the care she required, but also that he travelled a great deal.

In his opening address Floriot made all those points, and several more. 'Monsieur Goldsmith is convinced that we want to take away his child, and indeed, he believes we have already taken her to Spain. What a mistake. It was only when Madame Patino saw her son-in-law in a state of excitement, of which he later provided such abundant proof by forcing the door of her suite at the Hôtel Trianon, that she decided to put the little girl in security, fearing that her father would take her away at the risk of her already fragile life.'

When he came to give evidence, Goldsmith could not hide his agitation. He could not easily pace around the court, but he paced as far as he could round the tiny witness box. 'My child was taken to an unknown place without my permission,' he said. 'They have literally kidnapped her, which makes me very angry.' Judge Ausset kept asking him to calm down, to little effect.

Goldsmith in this mood is quite extraordinarily effective. As he gets angry, his speech becomes even more lucid, his sentences ordered, his grasp of facts and details quite exceptional. In his business life he could turn his onslaught on the opposing side with devastating effect. In the court he was obviously intemperate, but also lucid, as he explained that he had rented an apartment where Isabel would have her own bright room, her own nanny, and, at least in the early days, Jimmy's own mother who had agreed to move in 'to ensure that she receives proper attention'. However, he went too far for the judge when Ausset, asked by the Goldsmith side to determine who was actually looking after the child at that moment, turned to Maître Floriot and asked him if he would 'perhaps be kind enough to tell me her whereabouts'.

'I will, of course, your honour,' replied the Maître. 'But not in front of

Monsieur Goldsmith'. Goldsmith was in the witness box at the time, and cut in with a remark to the effect that 'my mother has led a blameless bourgeois existence for thirty years, which could hardly be said for Madame Patino who is, after all, currently suing her husband for divorce.' Judge Ausset asked for a little less invective and for rather more facts, and Goldsmith's advocate felt obliged to intervene. 'My client alone has the right to determine who should care for his child: and the excited state he is in, for which he is being reproached, in fact demonstrates his affection for his daughter.'

Since much of the argument seemed to centre on Goldsmith's flat, the judge finally decided he must see it for himself, and adjourned the court. Goldsmith and his parents dashed off to the rue Marbeau, where crowds had already begun to gather. The balconies in the street were filled with people, and by the time the judge turned up at 5.25 p.m. with the various lawyers a way had to be cleared. Three minutes later a black Cadillac drew up to deposit grandmother Patino who went in for another look. Ausset, the lawyers, court officials and Madame Patino (Antenor was nowhere to be seen) entered the building, and climbed to the second floor, to find the apartment immaculate, its balcony lined with flowers, its furnishings all in place. By any standards, except perhaps those of the Duchess of Durcal, it was an impressive place. Ausset spent half an hour inspecting it room by room, then announced he would give his decision the next day at two. The Goldsmiths were ecstatic. The judge had not exactly told them what he would say, but he had clearly not agreed with the Patino lawyers' view. 'In England a five-room luxury flat would be suitable even for a rich baby,' Major Goldsmith told the judge.

By early afternoon the next day the crowd outside the court had already grown to the point where it spilled into the nearby flower market, and the roads leading to the court were almost impassable. Patino versus Goldsmith was creating as much interest as any case in living memory. In the court Jimmy sat with his mother on one side, the duchess on the other side. The newspapers the next day would present this as the 'Battle of the Grandmothers'.

Promptly at two Ausset entered to begin his judgment. He had visited the apartment the previous day, he said, and found it 'comfortable, even luxurious', with all the necessary 'installations', it was airy and even had a terrace. Madame Goldsmith had promised to 'occupy herself maternally' with the baby Isabel, and she had represented 'substantial moral qualities to the court'.

The Patino lawyers had made various allegations about Goldsmith's financial state, but the judge was unimpressed by those too. The young man 'whose daughter is the subject of these custody proceedings,' he said, 'is clearly in a most enviable financial situation.' Any excitement he might have shown at the Hotel Trianon 'was clearly the result of his distress and anxiety to know the whereabouts of his daughter.'

It took 20 minutes for Ausset to arrive at his decision: the apartment, he concluded, had 'many health amenities', Goldsmith was 'wealthy enough to look after it' and the Goldsmith family was 'irreproachable'. Jimmy Goldsmith was to be given his daughter back by four o'clock the following afternoon.

Goldsmith whooped, hugged his mother, and emerged to declare, 'This is a great victory.'

Some idea of the interest the case had aroused is shown by some of the contemporary reports: here is the *Sunday Express* for instance. 'He (Goldsmith) left the judge's chambers with his mother to go down to the children's court. A crowd of 250 jammed the narrow staircases of the building congratulating him. Women grasped his hands and kissed him.' Others are in similar vein.

In the children's court Jimmy asked the police to start a search for the baby – he still had a nagging fear that the Patinos would spirit her away to Spain where he might never get her back. He insisted once again that the police on the Franco-Spanish border be alerted, and immediately began a search for her himself, visiting the Trianon, and insisting the police watch the Patino houses, a list of which he gave them.

That evening, as he still awaited the return of his daughter, Goldsmith's elation had evaporated. He had operated on a high for days, sleeping little, preparing himself for battle with Maître Floriot, and trying to anticipate the next moves of the Patinos. Now he was depressed and moody. A reporter who saw him that night emerged shaken by the depth of his anger. 'Tonight I met Jimmy Goldsmith, a young man in a cold passion,' he wrote. 'Those two words are the sparse truth about Jimmy Goldsmith.' The reporter, Terence Feeley of the *Sunday Graphic*, was a young man in his early twenties with an equally young wife who accompanied him to Goldsmith's apartment which Feeley described as 'lovely'. Out on the terrace, Goldsmith stopped to look at them enviously. 'So you're married. Perfect,' he said.

Feeley continued:

There is a terrible anger inside Jimmy Goldsmith now, and it poured out to us in a controlled torrent of clipped and biting words. He spoke quietly, almost casually, and the barbed words seemed harsher for it. 'This is my child, my blood,' he said. 'And for her I am prepared to fight hard with every weapon I can lay my hands to. Believe me there's plenty of mud to sling – and I am prepared to sling it now'.

The final event in this extraordinary chapter took place the next day, just 15 minutes short of the judge's deadline. The same black Cadillac drew up at Goldsmith's doorstep. Inside were the Marquise Ginori, Madame Patino's sister, the nanny, Deborah Cockbill (who would stay with Isabel for years) – and the baby Isabel. The rain poured down, and Goldsmith sheltered in the doorway. Fifteen police lined the pavement. No one spoke as the marquise, stoneyfaced, got out and elaborately unfolded a red umbrella, which she held over the nanny, who walked across to the doorway and placed the baby in her father's arms. The marquise then got back into the car and drove away. Goldsmith had his baby back.

8

To the Edge

When Teddy Goldsmith returned to Paris after his National Service he did not recognise the little company he had bequeathed to his younger brother. Where there had been only two employees, now there were a hundred. Sales when he left had been a few thousand pounds a year; now they were in the hundreds of thousands. In Teddy's time it had all been very amateurish, and low-key. Now it was a company driven by a man possessed, who worked 18-hour days, and who went himself to doctors to sell to them a widening range of pharmaceutical products. The original partners had set up Teddy in business believing, he says, 'they would make an instant fortune'. The operation was run on a shoestring. 'They hired the cheapest person they could find, who was me,' says Teddy.

When he left it was clear both to Jimmy and to the partners that the company was going to need a further injection of money to keep it going. And Jimmy, even then, had no ambition to work for other people. By the time his brother returned, Jimmy had bought out the other partners, and was in full control. But the company was still desperately short of capital, a problem which had been exacerbated by the speed of its expansion. It was to be a familiar pattern for the first half of Jimmy Goldsmith's business life: lots of growth but never enough capital.

Years later when Goldsmith ran one of the biggest corporations in the world he still yearned for the excitement of running his own small business, where he did everything himself: found products, organised licences, set up factories to make them, personally sold them, delivered them, sent out the bills, collected the money, did the accounts. He had never done anything like it before; he was on a learning curve which was almost vertical. He was living on his wits, taking risks which were calculated. With hard work and creative effort he could tilt the odds in his favour, which gave him some of the same thrill he got from gambling. 'I can't tell you how exciting it was,' he says wistfully now.

Later there would be much speculation about how Jimmy Goldsmith made his first fortune. There isn't much mystery about it. It was a simple affair of taking over a two-man business with licences for two fairly nondescript pharmaceutical products, and building it from there – but with an almost manic energy. 'I was the only salesman, the only director, the only anything – I was a quorum by myself!'

Although his relationship with Isabel was a genuine love match, there was also a hint – as spread by the Patinos – that he was a fortune hunter, interested only in her share of that fabulous wealth. He had continually stated that he wanted no part of it, and even the suggestion made him furious. Now it was no longer enough to become a millionaire – he had to make himself richer than the Patinos. That was the new goal. He also became aware in these years that his father, who had always seemed to have plenty of money, was not actually a wealthy man. Jimmy took upon himself the mantle of restoring the Goldsmith family fortunes. Why this bothered him is hard to explain; it certainly never bothered Teddy, or Frank for that matter.

Jimmy was also of course driven by the powerful need to forget. He no longer went out in the evenings, and he abandoned his old haunts, his clubs, his former girlfriends and his gambling partners.

And he was driven by the need to provide for a child, a nanny and a home which, despite the generous words of the judge, was actually rather expensive to run.

It was not long after the war and most of the big international pharmaceutical companies ignored the French market. Dozens of new drugs were being introduced to the more developed markets, and the medical profession in France had not kept up. As soon as he realised – which did not take him long – that there was little growth in the licences he inherited from Teddy, Goldsmith set off on an energetic search for new products. He travelled to Austria, to Italy, to Britain, to the United States. He emerged with a vaccine against colds which was to be his greatest success: Lantigen B, developed by the Australian group Beast & Gee. He also managed to secure the licence for a nasal spray called Rhinosterin.

Dagonal, when he started, simply owned a few trademarks and farmed out the sale of its products to a licensed pharmaceutical laboratory. Quite soon, Goldsmith formed his own manufacturing company, which he called Laboratoires Cassene, named vaguely after an aunt, Cassagne, and this too expanded rapidly. Goldsmith bought a series of licences for drugs and pharmaceuticals which Cassene was soon producing. He negotiated deals with Lepetit s.p.a., one of the largest pharmaceutical companies in Italy, with the big American group Smith Kline and French, and a number of others. He had ambitions to develop his own products from scratch, and also to get into derivative drugs, versions of existing products developed by other companies.

As the business took off, Goldsmith himself could not cope with selling the range. In the early days he was his own one-man sales force, literally going from doctor to doctor. He needed a sales force, but couldn't afford one on a country-wide basis. The solution was to plug into an existing sales force, and there was one available. Distriphar was the largest independent distributor of pharmaceuticals in France, with brands such as Alka-Seltzer and Vicks Inhalant, as well as Phillips' Milk of Magnesia and Murine Eye Drops. Early in 1955 Goldsmith suggested to its chairman, Elie Manthout, who also ran a large chemists' shop, the Pharmacie Anglaise, in the centre of Paris, that they form a joint company to distribute his drugs. The arrangement was a success from the start, so much so that Goldsmith bought the whole of Distriphar. He now had in place a basis for a successful, integrated business.

This was now growing at an almost unmanageable rate. He rented a warehouse in the Place Gabriel-Peri, which was soon filled to the ceiling with products, and which operated around the clock trying to keep up with demand. Goldsmith spent many hours there, unloading and repacking trucks.

Meanwhile Teddy spent his National Service first in England and then in Berlin. He returned to Paris in 1955 to gape in wonder at what was going on. Jimmy offered him a 30 per cent share of what had been his own company, and Teddy willingly accepted. 'I left him a tiny company and he had built it up and he wasn't going to hand it back to me,' says Teddy, with a hint of defensiveness. 'He had bought all the other partners out and it was now his company. I don't see that 30 per cent was an ungenerous offer.'

Teddy was put to running the distribution company, with disastrous results. 'I made a total mess of it, a complete hash. We had no building and had to run the whole thing from a warehouse without even a telephone – we had to use the café opposite to telephone. Life was really very difficult. Cash was short, and we had to do this 200 packets a day, sending off to wholesalers, and we were working three shifts. It was a *tour de force* getting the stuff out. We did it, but the accounts were a total mess, because I was hopeless at that, and really made a hash of it. We had to sleep there, practically, it was terrible.' Teddy moans at the distant memory. 'There was one man in the warehouse with us who had a nervous breakdown, collapsed, couldn't stand the strain. He was an ex-priest and he was in love with a girl called Simonne, who was also involved in the operation and was a god-daughter of my mother.' The young Goldsmith was already paying back some of his family's loyalty.

By now two other people who were to have a considerable effect on Goldsmith had joined Laboratoires Cassene. One was Claude Henry Leconte, a journalist and public relations man whom Jimmy had met several years before when he wanted some help on advertising. Leconte at the time was working for *Agence France Presse*, but freelanced as a consultant. He and Jimmy hit it off from the start. 'We broke completely new ground in advertising,' says Goldsmith now. 'We were the first people who really moved into advertising prescription drugs as opposed to proprietary products – which meant that the target was doctors. And we realised that when you speak to doctors you use funny words, but you basically use the same advertising as before. You still have to hit the same things' – he ticks them off on his fingers – 'affirmation, explanation, confirmation.'

Leconte and Goldsmith formed an enduring friendship. 'We loved each other,' says Goldsmith. For his part Leconte met a man who he remembers as 'very good looking with a great deal of hair'. He was, he adds, quick to anger 'and that was very, very terrible. But his anger had no gravity – he forgets his anger.'

Leconte placed dozens of articles about Cassene's products and its young whizzkid head, building up the little company's national profile. He also had another role: recruitment. Goldsmith did not have the time to interview all the people he needed to hire, and he found Leconte invaluable. 'He had great confidence in me,' says Leconte. 'Today I'm sure he would say I was rarely mistaken. And that is one of the reasons there was great affection between us.'

An even more important person joined with the takeover of Distriphar. Maurice Lignon was a handsome, energetic and experienced salesman, a generation older than Jimmy, who came to love the excitement and energy Goldsmith exuded. Teddy remembers him as 'very cool and very effective'. He came from near Montpelier, had a strong regional accent, and responded instantly to a basic incentive plan Goldsmith had started: the salesman who sold the most would get a handsome bonus. Lignon won three times in a row, doubling his salary each time, and winning a car the third time round. After that, Goldsmith took him more and more into his confidence, making him his second-in-command, and later managing director. Lignon brought a degree of professionalism to bear that neither Jimmy nor Teddy Goldsmith had, but even so, as 1956 wore on, it was clear the group was headed for trouble.

Apart from Teddy's efforts in the warehouse, Laboratoires Cassene had a more fundamental problem – the bulk of its products were for use in the winter only. In the cold months there was plenty of cash, as Vicks, Lantigen and the other products sold well. But in the summer turnover dropped alarmingly, and the liquidity problems became more acute. Goldsmith was a complete novice when it came to cash flow control, bank credit lines or anything else – he was, in those early days, absorbed in finding products and selling them for what he supposed was a profit. If the company had been properly capitalised to begin with, there would have been no problem. But what capital Jimmy had went on repaying his debts and on buying Teddy's old partners out. Expansion requires rather than provides capital.

But Goldsmith would not stop expanding. He wanted to acquire new lines but he also wanted to manufacture a range of his own, generic drugs. For that he needed chemists, doctors, research staff – and a factory. He found one, owned by a scrap merchant called Klein, half-finished and originally designed to make ski lifts (*téléphériques*). Goldsmith had met Klein's daughter, heard about the factory, and, although he had no money, went to see Klein. The place would need to be converted, but it was suitable. 'Can I buy your factory?' he asked Klein. He could, said Klein – and named a figure. 'I can't pay that,' said Goldsmith. But he proposed a deal involving part payment, and Klein agreed, taking a great deal on trust. 'I was very impressed with Mr Klein,' says Goldsmith.

Leconte found him a factory manager, and Goldsmith set about securing contractors, sub-contractors and everyone else he needed to finish it. 'It's a wonderful factory,' he says 37 years later. 'It's still there.'

By the autumn of 1957, his team of chemists had expanded its range of generics and was selling them to pharmacists at lower prices than were the international companies. They were essentially the same products – relatively unsophisticated pharmaceuticals but without the brand name. And the pharmacists loved them, since they could earn a 40 per cent margin on them as opposed to the 30 per cent offered by the big groups.

By now, instead of the 100 people he employed when Teddy returned, he was up to 400. The growth was explosive. The business he inherited just four years earlier had a turnover of £5,000 a year. Now it was £1.5 m, and more than doubling every year. Teddy left after a year, muttering that

'Jimmy needs some better staff, a better manager than me.' The two brothers would now go their own ways, continuing to see each other, but their interests would not coincide again for another 34 years.

The more Goldsmith grew, the more working capital he needed, and he had not yet learned that lesson. It wasn't that the business was unprofitable – it was simply that it was using up cash faster than it was generating it. He was spending money on his factory, on new offices – which were by no means grand – on the rue la Pépinière, on research and the development of his new range of drugs, on advertising and promotion to create a market for them. Every experienced businessman or banker knows that a company goes bust not because it makes a loss but because it cannot pay its bills. Goldsmith was desperately shuffling what money came in between suppliers, wages for his staff, electricity bills and everything else. When something unexpected came in, it was a major blow. Claude Henry Leconte was sitting in his office one day when Goldsmith rang him. The company faced a cash flow problem, he told him, which would last for the next three or four months – he had just received a demand for a large sum in back taxes, which he couldn't pay until the winter boom. Leconte had a good relationship with his own banker – could he go along and ask him to help? Goldsmith had not been able to secure any lines of credit himself. Leconte was only too well aware that a problem with the tax authorities in France is as serious as it is in any other country – there would be no mercy there. They would not wait, but would put the company into liquidation. He was highly nervous as he approached the bank, and the manager noticed immediately. 'What's wrong with you? Why do you look so worried?'

'I am not worried for myself,' replied Leconte. The manager listened to his story, then leaned forward across the desk. 'He told me to be at ease, and called his secretary in and proceeded to dictate to her, naming the sum that was necessary – which was hundreds of millions of francs.' Leconte sat stunned. 'You look surprised,' said the manager, and Leconte replied weakly that he was, 'just a little'. 'But,' said the manager, 'I know Jimmy Goldsmith. I know the man. Within ten years, Jimmy Goldsmith will be a new Rockefeller, a Dupont, a Rothschild. Be sure of that. That's the reason why it's a great pleasure to help out now, because I'm so sure of the future.'

That manager must have doubted his own far-sightedness in the months that followed. Besides over-expansion, there was another problem: some of the new products were dismal failures. For instance Goldsmith seized upon what he saw as a brilliant invention, a shaving cream in an aerosol can, which he called Rise. 'It never worked,' says Teddy. 'You pressed the button and either nothing came out at all or you got enveloped in foam.' Goldsmith promoted it heavily, however, but had to take it off the market when he discovered that the French patent, which he had bought, was not valid (it later became a major world product). 'It lost a fortune,' he says. There were other failures too: a rival to the Bristol Myers drug Bufferin, which his chemists developed, but which failed to gain a significant market share, and a pill which was an aspirin with antacids in it.

The hours he worked and his problems with money left little time for a private life, even if he had wanted one. As promised, his mother moved into his apartment after the court battle, to look after little Isabel. Maintaining her and the nanny was expensive, yet Goldsmith refused to economise. Goldsmiths always had butlers, and Jimmy insisted on having one too, even though sometimes he could not pay him. Maurice Lignon recalls how often either he or the butler had to lend Jimmy the money to pay his taxi fare. All his energies, all his resources and all his imagination were channelled into building his company.

But he did have one distraction, or rather a comfort. Ginette Lery was the pretty blonde daughter of a Paris Metro worker who joined the company in 1954 as an 18-year-old secretary, three years younger than her new boss. She had responded to an advertisement, and found herself working night and day along with the rest of the overstretched staff. 'He was very difficult,' she says, 'and very nervous.' But he was also, she says, an extraordinary enthusiast who inspired those around him who could stick the pace. It was more than a year after Isabel's death that they first met. Two years later they became lovers. By that stage Ginette was invaluable to the company and to Goldsmith, organising his diary, his letters, his papers and his meetings. He involved her, as he did Lignon, Leconte and some of the others, in his problems and his successes. 'He would be depressed for a few days when something big went wrong, or maybe just for two hours, then he would get on,' she says. At the same time, there was an atmosphere of fun and excitement in the office, even when Goldsmith's money problems were mounting perilously. Somehow the bills would be paid, a creditor persuaded to hold off for a little while longer, a bank talked into putting up a loan in time to pay off another bank – and all the time Goldsmith kept up the same extraordinary pace.

In the autumn of 1957 Goldsmith had learned enough to know that he would be in trouble by the following summer unless he could negotiate a substantial injection of new capital for the company. He had scraped through the bad months, and had made up his mind to take advantage of the better months of the year to work out a deal. He already had a good relationship with the Italian company Lepetit, and his plan was to offer it a third of the company in return for new money to recapitalise Laboratoires Cassene, and give him the breathing space to develop the dozens of plans he was working on. They reached agreement in principle for the Italians to buy 35 per cent of Cassene for new capital, but the details were still not settled by the spring. Lepetit then bargained themselves up to 50 per cent, but by the following June realised how parlous Goldsmith's position was. He had bills of exchange to be presented in the second week of July, and he had no money to pay them.

In the last week of June, the Italians came back with another offer: they wanted 80 per cent of the company. 'That's not what we agreed,' said Goldsmith, but he was very calm, knowing that his bargaining position was at its weakest. Lepetit were not necessarily being nasty: Cassene was a financial risk and they didn't want to take it on, and put in new capital, without full control, and without getting the benefit for themselves. He turned it down. 'They left politely and quietly, dazed that I had refused.' His own staff recall Goldsmith being furious with them.

Whatever the case, Lepetit was now out of the picture – and Goldsmith was in deep trouble. Teddy gave him all the money he had, but that was not much, and Jimmy was forced to tell his 400 workers how critical the situation had become. Goldsmith conceived one last daring plan, to which he committed every ounce of his energy. His idea was this: he would split France into a number of logical regions, appoint an exclusive distributor for each, and then offer him a broad range of generic drugs. The distributor would receive a higher profit margin than he would from selling rival drugs, so would the retail pharmacists, and the state health service would save large amounts because of the lower prices charged. From Goldsmith's point of view, he would benefit because he proposed to sell his stocks in advance, asking each distributor to place orders for £25,000, in return for bills of exchange which he would then discount in the money markets. It was a remarkably sophisticated operation for a 24-year-old to work out, let alone to put into operation.

By the time the plan was in place, he was only days away from bankruptcy. He and his ace salesman Maurice Lignon started on the telephone, working their way down a list of the big wholesalers. When he found they were not reacting fast enough, he decided he had to face them, and clinch the deals, not let things drag on for weeks. He did not have weeks. As he had done before with Isabel, he hired a small plane – a

Beechcraft – and he, Lignon and Ginette set off from Le Bourget on a frantic tour of the wholesalers. They flew all over France, landing at small airstrips on the edge of towns and dashing in to see their customers, all three of them hitting the telephones at every opportunity to set up new appointments, change others, re-book ones that had been moved or cancelled. Often the agents were not even expecting them, and Goldsmith would ring to say he was on the way and would be there in a few hours. In just three days they covered every region of France.

It worked. The three of them came back to Paris with £200,000 in bills of exchange, payment in advance for the drugs he would provide to his main wholesalers. The business was saved. All he had to do now was pack the orders, ship them out, and bank the money. He had weathered the storm.

Or so he thought. Not for the first or last time, Goldsmith wholly underestimated his competitors. He had just invented, on the hoof, an entirely different system of trading. The wholesalers were happy, because Goldsmith was offering them saleable products on which they could make a handsome margin. But he was destroying arrangements which had evolved over years, which the other pharmaceutical companies used profitably, and which they were determined to protect. They were not willingly about to surrender either market share or profit margins to a 24-year-old newcomer, who was rapidly beginning to pose a serious threat.

Goldsmith's new distributors, who were also wholesalers for the big pharmaceutical companies, were told that if they traded with him, their margins would be cut by the rest of the manufacturers, who might even stop supplying them with their best-selling brands. They must cancel the arrangement immediately or lose the franchises for some of the best-selling drugs.

Within weeks it was all over: the products were on their way back, the deals reneged on, the bills of exchange cancelled. Bankruptcy was now fast approaching, and Goldsmith's health was suffering. His head broke out in huge, ugly and very painful boils which caused his hair to start falling out. (Teddy still has a full head of hair at 61, and Frank lost his much later in life, but Jimmy, who had shown no signs of it before, suddenly went bald in his mid-twenties.) He was driving himself harder and harder, juggling bills and hopelessly inadequate incomings. He had no choice but to sell, although the thought of it was devastating for him – he had, he would say, created every brick, hired every worker, designed every package, written every bit of advertising, devoted every waking hour to it for four years. 'I loved that business – loved it as much as it was possible to love a business.'

In those last days, while negotiating with Lepetit and then in his final generic drug gamble, he tried everything, going from bank to bank, from friend to friend, staving off creditors, talking to his suppliers. But the business, successful as it had been, was insolvent. He was finished. And in France, bankruptcy was a far more serious matter than in Britain or some other countries: it meant in effect the end of a business career. 'At that time the dishonour was enormous – it was impossible to recover from it.' The Patinos would be delighted. His parents and Teddy, who had done everything to help, would be crushed, and he would have no way of providing for his daughter and for Ginette.

The bills of exchange were due for presentation on 10 July 1957, a Monday morning. Goldsmith's boils were causing him extreme discomfort, and that week-end he didn't bother to get up, lying miserable and depressed in bed where Ginette looked after him. On the Sunday evening, however, he bestirred himself sufficiently to take Ginette out to the cinema where they could forget their troubles for a few hours. He was almost suicidally depressed.

On the Grands Boulevards the film, *Around the World in Eighty Days*, starring David Niven, was running, and they went in. The story was extraordinarily apt: Phineas Fogg, believing he has failed, discovers he has gained a day in his circumnavigation – and wins his bet after all.

The French banks had not had a strike since the 1930s, but that week-end they started one that would run for six weeks. In his depressed, uncommunicative mood, Goldsmith knew nothing about it. It was only when he arose late the next day and made his way down towards the bank to hear the bad news that he saw the headlines. His bills could not be presented. He was still in with a chance.

He negotiated feverishly over the next few weeks, this time with his biggest competitor, Laboratoires Roussell. Cassene was still in trouble, of course, but Roussell wanted its licences and generic drugs. It was still a race between the negotiations with Roussell and the negotiations between the banks and the unions, and Goldsmith won only by a hair. He was at dinner with Teddy and their old chemist friend, Elie Manthout, when he was called to the phone. The others waited anxiously until Jimmy returned to announce it was done. Roussell had bailed them out.

The bank strike, Goldsmith says years later, 'was the most astounding and unexpected bit of luck I have ever had in my whole career.' The Roussell deal was a remarkably good one in the circumstances. They took over the whole of the company, debts and all, and left Goldsmith the royalties on the sales of Lantigen B, which were running at around £4,000 a month, a very reasonable income for a young man in 1957. In addition he received £110,000, which represented riches to him after what he had been through. Lignon would go with the company to Roussell, not the only time Goldsmith would sell him with one of his companies.

Laboratoires Cassene still exists as a company, a prosperous part of Roussell. There was never anything much wrong with it that an injection of capital and a more cautious manager could not have put right. It had lasted just over four years, which had taken Goldsmith through the death of Isabel, the kidnapping, and an extraordinary, if brief, corporate history. The lessons he learned would last him a lifetime. He would continue to take risks, but he would also consolidate whenever he could. The experience bred into him a degree of insecurity that he still retains, however rich he is today. As Madame Gilberte Beaux, a wise French banker who was to play a major role in his business life later, would remark: 'Jimmy thinks every morning that he has nothing. Every morning he thinks he is only rich up to a point: the point at which his company has the ability to make profits and to grow.'

9

Mothercare

In August 1957 Jimmy Goldsmith took himself and Ginette Lery on holiday to Spain, his first break in over a year. He was badly run-down, suffering from nervous exhaustion and the aftermath of his appalling attack of boils. For weeks he had barely slept, working with fiendish energy to save his fledgling business. He had avoided bankruptcy only by the most extraordinary stroke of luck, but he had lost his company, a considerable emotional, as well as financial, setback for him. He would smart for years over what might have been. He knew he had a good business – and so did the others who had worked closely with him. Maurice Lignon, older and more experienced, continued to view him with a respect and affection in no way diminished by the fact that Goldsmith had been obliged to sell him along with the company. Claude Henry Leconte stayed with him too, in expectation of a new beginning. Teddy, no businessman, understood better than anyone how much effort his brother had put into the business, and how near it had been to a major success. Disgrace had been avoided, and there was enough to begin again.

In 1957 Goldsmith was still only 24, and life had to go on. He had at least emerged with something from these four years: a capital sum which went to pay off his personal debts and still left a bit over, plus the Lantigen royalties. Once the holiday was over and his mood began to shift again, his interest in rebuilding his business returned. His name was now well known in the pharmaceutical industry, he had the contacts both in distribution and among the manufacturers who could supply products to him under licence.

Soon after he returned to Paris in September much of his old energy returned. His success and failure had received a considerable amount of publicity in the industry, and it was this that caused a certain Dr Laffort to seek him out that autumn. Laffort had a small laboratory and a factory on the Loire, where he manufactured pharmaceuticals, but he had little idea how to market them. He had observed from afar Goldsmith drive up his market share with a few decent products of his own, and it seemed to him that if he could harness that energy to his little factory it might be a good deal for both of them.

The deal he proposed to Goldsmith was a simple one: Goldsmith should take over the running of his laboratory, and pay Laffort a royalty on sales. It was not quite as generous a deal as it first appeared: Laffort was taking a view on the young Goldsmith's abilities, knowing that the harder he worked and the more he succeeded, the more Laffort would get for a laboratory and a business which would probably not have survived and which no one else would have bought from him.

Within weeks, Goldsmith was making a go of it. This was the business he knew and understood, which was still wide open, and where the opportunities to market new drugs and products in an innovative way were considerable.

Selim Zilkha was born in Baghdad into a prosperous Jewish family in 1928. It was a time of relative peace in a country basically run by the large Jewish population, the wealthiest and best educated community in Baghdad, as well as the largest – nearly half the 200,000 people living in Baghdad at the time were Jews. However Selim was only 40 days old when his father left, first for Lebanon where they stayed for eight years, and then for Egypt, before moving to the United States in 1941. He spent three years at college in America, did his spell in the army, then served his apprenticeship as a banker, first in New York, then in Paris and finally with Hambros Bank in London, working alongside the current chairman Charles Hambro (and Baron Claus von Bulow, the man later charged with, and acquitted of, trying to kill his rich wife). In 1954 his father sent him to Paris to open a branch of the family business, and then he moved back to London to run the branch there. By 1957, the Zilkha family bank, Banque d'Arbitrage et de Crédit, had branches in Geneva, London, New York and Paris, with a Zilkha brother responsible for each.

The Paris branch, still very new, had recently moved to new premises, which happened to be 23 rue de la Paix – where the Hôtel Réunis had its offices and where Goldsmith rented space. They opened for business that summer, on the ground floor – a small, discreet, private bank, run by bankers from the same type of old banking family as the Goldsmiths. The

Zilkhas were Sephardic Jews from an entirely different culture to the Ashkenazi Jews of Europe. In appearance Zilkha could not have been more unlike Jimmy Goldsmith – short, with jet-black hair, and a dark complexion, he was sober and conventional, but a keen golfer and passionate bridge and backgammon player.

The Zilkhas' new Paris premises opened just as Goldsmith's Cassene was hitting the rocks. As he scurried from creditor to creditor and bank to bank, Goldsmith never spared this new bank a thought, even though it was housed in his own premises. But on his return from Spain he found a circular, sent to everyone in the building, offering the bank's services. In the past it was Goldsmith who had sought out banks and asked them to handle his business. Here was a bank actually offering him something. The fact that the same offer had been made to everyone in the building did not matter.

The circular mentioned that the Zilkha bank was interested either in taking deposits or making loans. Goldsmith waited a few days, then asked the manager, a M. Ross, to come and see him. What, asked Goldsmith, did the banker think he could do to help him? He had, he said, plans for expansion. There was an enormous demand for new drugs, and the established companies were slow and behind the times. Drugs could be manufactured under licence at a fraction of what they were being sold at – some of the profit margins were disgraceful. There were companies which he had wanted to buy and which could have been revitalised, and they were still available. Pacing up and down his little office, he gave a compelling performance. He answered in detail every objection and question put forward by the banker – he had facts and figures at his fingertips. He knew what he wanted to do, he was convinced he could do it – but he needed money.

A few days later Selim Zilkha, chairman of the bank, arrived in Paris on one of his regular visits. Had the circulars pulled in any clients? he asked his manager. Yes, he was told, 'One, we've got Jimmy Goldsmith.'

Selim knew the name, but only from the social columns. He had no idea of Goldsmith's business expertise or his financial standing, but having listened to his manager's explanation of what he wanted, decided he must meet him.

Zilkha was a banker, half a dozen years Jimmy's senior, and had led an even more cosmopolitan life than Jimmy. This college-educated American citizen from a well-to-do family who had lived in half a dozen different countries, was confronted by a young, almost-failed business-man with a reputation as a socialite, a head taller than himself, who was asking for money. Although a successful entrepreneur, Zilkha by nature is essentially a cautious man, but Goldsmith's enthusiasm and his persuasiveness quickly infected him. His recollections of that meeting, and his own reaction to Goldsmith, are significant in that they echo those of others who met him in these early years. 'He was 24, but it was quite incredible what experience he had of life already,' he says. Goldsmith, he says, was ahead of him on everything: 'He was ahead on his gambling, ahead on his business – he just had amazing energy.

'That was the beginning,' says Zilkha over 30 years later. 'It was all through a circular – for me the best circular I ever sent.' The two talked not only of Goldsmith relaunching in France but of moving into Britain, where Goldsmith had never done any business, but which he regarded as almost as much his home country as France was. Zilkha's British connections would make it easier.

The royalties from Lantigen B, and his deal with Laffort, gave him his base. Now he wanted to get the licence for two new drugs developed by the American pharmaceutical company Schering: Prednisone and Prednisolone, both of them cortisone derivatives. If Cassene had specialised in anything, it had been rheumatic drugs, originating from Teddy's Adremad, and these were a new and apparently improved (anti-inflammatory) treatment for rheumatism. His plan was to continue where he had left off: manufacture them in France, using the Laffort laboratory, and probably in Britain too, and then market them as hard as he had done before. Unfortunately while he was still struggling with his first company, Schering had licensed the manufacture of the drugs to Lepetit, but no one was yet selling them in Britain. He flew to Italy and then back to Paris to see Roussell, which was doing well with Goldsmith's old company, putting his complex little deal together. Roussell's British subsidiary, another Schering licensee, would manufacture the drugs, and sell them to Goldsmith in Britain.

By the autumn of 1957 the focus of Goldsmith's business was beginning to switch to London, not because of any great desire to leave France or because he thought the opportunities were better there – simply because that was the only market he could obtain for the cortisone tablets. Uncertain about his own standing in Britain where the runaway episode and his playboy image had made the most impact, he decided to appoint a British chairman, and chose an old friend, Captain Julian Snow, a six-foot-six former Labour MP (for Lichfield and Tamworth), as his local chairman. The company would be called Ward Casson, after Snow's middle name Ward and because Casson was close to Cassene.

Since the kidnapping episode Goldsmith's name had dropped out of the gossip columns, and his business ventures had never been large enough to attract much interest. But odd little mentions from time to time give snapshots of aspects of his life. For instance on 14 November 1957 the *Daily Sketch* carried a modest item on the launch of his business in London. It appeared in a column called 'Inside Information', and was an interview with Julian Snow. It concentrated more on his playboy image and the Isabel runaway episode than it did on the business. Goldsmith didn't object at the time, but it would take him many years, after this type of piece, to be taken seriously – particularly in the pharmaceutical industry where image was deadly serious. The *Sketch* item noted that he and Snow had gone into business 'to try to find a cure for rheumatism', although as it elaborated on his plans, it was clear enough he wasn't making any claims as ambitious as that. 'He concentrates on highly specialised drugs,' said Snow. 'They're used for the treatment of rheumatism and for skin diseases.' That bit was true enough, if a little bit exaggerated – all Goldsmith was doing at the time was manufacturing and selling drugs and other pharmaceutical products under licence. The fact that most of them happened to be for the treatment of rheumatism was an accident rather than design. Goldsmith himself was not pretending to market anything that was not already available, he was simply selling it in a different way and at a different price.

The item went on to say that Goldsmith flew in 'quietly' once a month from his Paris home to talk things over with Snow, although from what Snow said it sounded anything but quiet. His last visit to the office in Victoria Street, he said, had only been a few days before. 'I never know when he'll arrive. But he's always full of ideas.' In fact, as those who knew him at the time all confirm, he was bubbling with ideas, some of them workable, some absurd, which he threw at Snow in London and Leconte in Paris, at Selim Zilkha when he saw him (or telephoned him as he often did), and at anyone else he came into contact with. He developed them with enormous excitement and enthusiasm, desperately impatient for his fledgling business to catch up with his racing mind.

But if the last months of Cassene were a struggle, the first months of the new company both in London and in Paris were equally so. Launching drugs into a new market with no organisation and precious few resources was an uphill task, even into a market hungry for new products, and even with techniques already tried and tested in France. Goldsmith was holding his own, but no more than that. 'It was survival: big activity, big launches, but that's all,' he recalls. Soon, however, he hit his stride, finding not just new products but new laboratories to take over. One of these was a Paris-based company called Neotherap, which he bought for nothing but the liabilities. It was run-down, with a range of declining products which he knew he would have to cut out. But it came with one or two potential winners too, notably an aerosol spray gargle called Collargent, which looked particularly promising.

By the spring of 1958 he was again employing hundreds of people, with an organisation which was already beginning to run out of control despite the 12- to 14-hour days he was putting in. He needed to consolidate it, so he merged Ward Casson with Laffort to create his first Anglo-French group. He called it SPHAL, and then tempted Maurice Lignon to come back to help him run it. Just over a year after he had lost Cassene, he had rebuilt an organisation with the same team, and rapidly building up to a similar size.

Lignon arrived back at the end of 1958 to find he was taking on an organisational mess. Neotherap needed urgent attention, and he set to work to 'clean it up' as he puts it. Orders were cancelled, unprofitable brands dropped, people made redundant and the business reduced to just a few products. He and Goldsmith put their marketing energies behind Collargent, and within months they were selling more than they could produce. They had all been in that position before, however, and knew the dangers of too rapid an expansion without the working capital to finance it. Zilkha's bank loan had got them over their initial financial problems, but growth, takeovers and new factories had more than taken care of that. Goldsmith was keenly aware that he was heading in the same direction as before, unless he was careful.

There was one vital difference this time around: the royalties from Lantigen B, which were rising rapidly to the point where if he had simply closed the rest of the business he could have lived more and more comfortably off them. Roussell was already regretting not being tougher with Goldsmith over his royalties, and was willing to buy him out. As the months passed, the sum they offered became more tempting – particularly because of the cash problems everywhere else.

With Lignon aboard and Neotherap cleaned up, they were launching new products by the month, some 30 in all over this period. The French, and to a lesser extent the British, markets for pharmaceuticals were mushrooming, and the big American drug companies were only just getting going in Europe. Goldsmith was able to offer them a marketing service for their products.

In London, after a slow start, sales had begun to pick up too. Goldsmith used the same radical, innovative approach he had used in France: manufacturing under licence and then selling his tablets aggressively with a new style of advertising, seriously undercutting the prices of the more established firms. His Roussell-manufactured derivative tablets could be sold for £12.50 a thousand, well below the £60 a thousand charged by rival groups, although they were exactly the same: made under the same licence and in the same factory.

But success brought problems too. Curiously he seems to have learned nothing from his French experience when the big groups turned on him once he became a serious challenger. It happens everywhere in business – the small airline that forces the big ones to break their cosy pricing arrangements, the oil company that supplies cut-price petrol, the bank that cuts rates – the outsider who breaks the cartel. Goldsmith had disturbed a well-established, comfortable and profitable pricing arrangement between the big laboratories and the wholesalers in France and had been surprised when they turned on him. Now he was doing it again, also without capital, and without an organisation which could withstand a serious counter-attack.

In Britain there was effectively only one customer for his steroid tablets: the National Health Service, which was required to be cost conscious. In reality, of course, doctors and hospitals prescribed whatever drugs they chose, so still had to be persuaded, irrespective of the savings, that Ward Casson's products were also as good as anybody else's. There seems to be no question that they were: the basic raw materials were imported into Britain from Switzerland, but the products manufactured by Roussell in Britain.

Goldsmith was blundering into a minefield which even the most politically adept pharmaceutical companies have never been able to avoid. The argument from the beginning – and it has not changed – of the big drug companies is that they spend many millions of pounds on research, most of which is non-productive. This is paid for by the drugs they successfully develop, and bring to market, the whole process often taking years. The price of that drug bears no resemblance to its cost of manufacture. The customer is in effect paying for the development cost, plus the research on all the drugs that fail. The company that sneaks in the back door, as they see it, and markets the same drug under sub-licence from overseas, is cheating. When some of the big teaching hospitals in London began taking his steroid tablets in November 1958, the establishment hit back.

In December the medical journal *The Lancet* carried a letter written by two academics from University College Hospital Medical School which was highly critical of Ward Casson's tablets. Professor Max Rosenheim and Dr Eric Ross solemnly warned of the dangers of 'substandard' cortisone tablets, adding that Ward Casson's products did not 'break up as quickly as they should'. This was followed by questions in the House of Commons about 'these cheap imported products'.

Goldsmith, now spending more and more time in London, protested as forcibly as he could. He might have been vulnerable if he had done the manufacturing himself, but because Roussell did it for him, he was safe on that score. He commissioned independent research tests on his tablets which he sent to the British Pharmacopoeia Commission, and also offered them for scrutiny by the Medical Research Council, making sure that the world knew about it. Julian Snow wrote a reply to *The Lancet*, largely dictated by Goldsmith, making the point that since Ward Casson started to force prices down 'it has been continuously slandered'. The attacks became 'almost hysterical', he said, 'once we secured the contract for London teaching hospitals'.

Goldsmith had one further weapon, which he had used before: the press. He rang Chapman Pincher, who had been involved in writing the advertising copy for Lloyd's adrenalin cream all those years before, and briefed him on the story. Chapman was interested, partly because of his knowledge of Goldsmith's pharmaceutical business, but also because of who Goldsmith was. On 27 January the *Daily Express* carried an article under Pincher's byline, whose first sentence again showed that press interest in Goldsmith at this time was inextricably bound up with the runaway incident:

'Mr Jimmy Goldsmith, the 25-year-old Paris financier, whose wife, Bolivian tin heiress Isabel Patino, died nearly five years ago, is in London to discuss legal action against British drug makers.'

Pincher pointed out that Ward Casson had forced down the price of drugs 'with enormous savings to the taxpayer, Goldsmith claims'. But the manufacturers, Goldsmith told him, were putting him out of business 'by taking advantage of unproved claims that his tablets are below standard'. The speed with which his price cuts had been followed, said Goldsmith, 'proves that their prices were originally high'.

Goldsmith had at least persuaded the minister of health, Derek Walker-Smith, of this. The day before Pincher's story appeared, Walker-Smith had answered a question in the House of Commons about the tablets, pointing out 'the sharp drop in prices was the result of increased competition'.

'I was breaking the club rules and they hated me for it,' says Goldsmith. Even at the low price he was charging he was still making a profit, and he was able, in the end, to win the intellectual battle, proving beyond argument that his tablets were neither substandard nor imported. But the club was exacting its revenge. The skirmish over the cortisone derivatives was followed by another over tetracycline. He was being presented around the industry as a young playboy trying to make a fast buck by peddling inferior 'imported' products at knock-down prices. Again he was driving himself harder and harder, spending most of his time away from Paris. Lignon, running the SPHAL business, saw him once every few weeks in Paris, but that was all.

As his business became more complex, so Goldsmith's financial skills, later his greatest strength, developed. He took his first tentative step into the stock market world when he bought control of a little public company, Clinical and General Services, into which he injected Ward Casson. But there wasn't much to inject. Money was desperately, chronically short. In fact, as Lignon recalls, 'there was none at all. We had no money, we were just juggling.' Goldsmith was used to it, but in the spring of 1959 it was Ginette who had to bear the burden of it. She was pregnant, and concerned about the bills that would arise when she had to go into hospital to have her baby. They were not married but had now lived together for five years, and she had come to accept – not without a fight – that Goldsmith's energy and appetite were not confined to business, and that there would always be other women in his life. In May she told Jimmy that she would go quietly into the state health service and have her baby. They could not afford private hospitals and private doctors – in fact they could not even afford the rent on the apartment. Goldsmith would not hear of it, insisting she had to have the best room in the best hospital. He was made all the more nervous because of what had happened to Isabel, so even if there was no money, somehow he would pay for it.

Goldsmith had attempted to separate the royalties from Lantigen B from the company so that if anything happened to him – and it was perilously close again – his daughter Isabel and his unborn child would be protected. As the problems mounted, however, he was no longer able to do that. 'I decided I had to give this new business a chance, get in some capital,' he says. He began to negotiate the sale of the Lantigen B royalties, and set up a meeting with Roussell for 9.30 in the morning to complete the deal. Ginette was now very heavily pregnant, due at any moment, and he said to her: 'For God's sake, don't have the baby tonight, because I've got to be *compos mentis* in the morning, and I can't spend all night in the hospital.'

No sooner had he said it than she went into labour, and Goldsmith did indeed spend all night at the hospital. Ginette produced a son, but it was not an easy birth, and it was a tired and haggard Goldsmith who arrived for the negotiations the next morning. Lignon complained that he sold the rights for half what he should have got for them, but he desperately needed the money, and Roussell, given the fact that it was manufacturing Lantigen B, was the best prospective buyer among the pharmaceutical companies.

It would be some time before the money for the rights actually came in and in the meantime Ginette and the baby were still in hospital. Within days of giving birth Ginette was up and about, ready to leave for her home at 41 rue Spontini. But there was a problem: French hospitals don't allow their patients to leave until their bills have been paid, and Goldsmith had no money. As the days turned into weeks, Ginette became more and more frantic. There was, she knew, no point in talking to Jimmy, so each day she rang Lignon at the office. 'Maurice, has any money come in today?' The answer was invariably the same: 'Maybe tomorrow.' The bill mounted each day, and all the time it became more embarrassing for her as she was clearly fit and well.

Finally, Goldsmith appeared, beaming. He had paid the bill, and he was taking her and their son home. Where had he got the money? She knew from Lignon that nothing had arrived at the office, where the juggling with money had become as bad as it ever had been in the days of Cassene. Goldsmith explained that he had won it. He went to the Travellers Club, got involved in a game of backgammon, and made enough money to pay the hospital bill. If she wondered what would have happened if he had lost, Ginette kept those thoughts to herself.

On the morning of 7 June 1959 Jimmy Goldsmith invited a small group of ten male friends and relatives to the 'Brith-milah', or circumcision, of his son Frank Manes Ernest Henry Benedict Hayum Goldsmith. Although Jimmy was only half Jewish, and his son only a quarter Jewish, it was a very Jewish ceremony, conducted by Rabbi Andre Zaoui and carried out by Dr David Levine. It was, as the invitation said, 'traditionnelle et masculine', followed by lunch. Frank and Teddy were there, as was a distant cousin, Gilbert de Goldschmidt Rotschild [sic]. Claude Henry Leconte was also invited, but the invitation list shows no Lerys, or other members of Ginette's family.

The sale of Lantigen B was nowhere near enough to solve the cash problems. It helped for a few months, but the all too familiar capital shortage was emerging in both Britain and France. Goldsmith employed several hundred people, with a wide range of products, and an increasingly complex corporate structure, based in two countries. He needed a new injection of capital and the only way he could get it was to sell something. There was nothing much worth selling in Britain, but his companies in France were doing rather better. The two businesses Laffort and Neotherap, run by Lignon, would go – and once again Lignon would be sold with them. Laboratoires Sarbach bought them, and with the money Jimmy launched a new company, Laboratoires Lanord.

Until this time, all of Goldsmith's seven years in business had been spent in the same industry. Shortly after Manes was born he developed a new thought. It came, again, largely by accident. In December 1959 he happened to be in the Chez Fred nightclub in rue de Ponthieu, in Paris, when he met Charles Clore, then regarded as one of the leading entrepreneurs in Britain. The son of a Jewish tailor from the East End of London, Clore had begun his business career by taking over the Prince of Wales theatre, and then expanding his interests into property, engineering and shipping. In the 1950s, 30 years before ever it was used on Wall Street, Clore became master of the hostile takeover bid. When Goldsmith met him, he had made an unsuccessful bid for the Watneys brewery group, with its five breweries and 3,670 pubs, his first defeat. Turned aside there, he took over instead the Mappin & Webb jewellery shop group which also owned a chemists chain called Lewis & Burrows.

Goldsmith got into conversation with him that evening, and ended up agreeing to buy the Lewis & Burrows chain in Britain. He knew about chemists shops, as he had spent a great deal of time in them trying to sell his products, so in a sense it was simply moving from manufacturing and distribution to the retailing end. He would, he reasoned, have captive outlets for his products, allowing him to stand up against the power of the big drugs companies who, with the exception of Boots, were not in retailing. He rang Selim Zilkha who loved the idea. 'As Jimmy was telling me about this I told him then and there that I'd join him, and that we could buy it together.'

'Oh yes, I'd like that,' said Goldsmith. Zilkha planned to spend Christmas in St Moritz, but, he said, he would delay his trip to complete the deal. It didn't run quite as rapidly as that, however, and a few days later Zilkha received a letter from Goldsmith, hand-delivered, saying the deal was going to take a little time to put together. Zilkha went to St Moritz, and the deal was finalised at the end of January. 'So we became partners in a chain of twenty-eight chemists shops,' he says. 'It was fifty-fifty.' Goldsmith bought his share through his little public company Clinical & General Industries, and Zilkha bought his with his brothers.

If retailing was a new experience for Goldsmith, it was equally new for Zilkha. 'I like to say that I've been to my shirtmaker, to my tailor and to my shoemaker – but that's all. Ever,' he used to quip. For both Goldsmith and Zilkha this new venture was to be a full-time, wholehearted commitment. Zilkha wanted to get out of the family banking business and do something on his own. 'I never liked lending money,' he says surprisingly. 'This was an ideal way of changing.'

For the first – and only – time in his life, Jimmy Goldsmith agreed to work jointly with someone else. Zilkha insisted that Goldsmith had to spend at least two full weeks of each month living and working in London, and Jimmy readily agreed. He had given up his battle against the drug companies, selling his business, and in France Lignon was concentrating on proprietary and dietetic products. Jimmy lived at the Ritz but began looking for something more permanent where he could bring Ginette and the two children. In April 1960 a *Daily Mail* reporter rang up Major Frank Goldsmith, now 81, to ask about Jimmy's move to London. 'He really prefers London to Paris,' said the old man. 'After all, he *is* British you know.'

That autumn he found the place he had been looking for: a large cream-painted house in Regent's Park with a graceful curved frontage (22 Sussex Place). It was as elegant as anything he had ever lived in, his first London home. He brought Ginette, who could barely speak English at the time (she later became fairly fluent), Isabel who was now six, and little Manes. A diary item quoted Isabel's nanny as giving a somewhat over-simplistic reason for the move: 'He wants Isabel to be brought up as English. That is why we have come to live here.'

It was during this time that Jimmy finally emerged from the dark cloud that had hung over him so oppressively since his wife's death. He had been fun to work with, even in the most difficult financial times, at Cassene, but he had also worked as a man driven to forget. In his second business, particularly after he opened up in Britain, he had raised his head and begun to look around him more. His horizons widened as he read voraciously, and talked to a wider and wider group of people. He developed a keen interest in the political life of France, and now of Britain which under Harold Macmillan was emerging from its postwar greyness. He had never lost touch with that same group of friends he had formed in his late teens, particularly John Aspinall, but now added others. He was gambling again, sometimes through the night, going straight to his office the next day, apparently none the worse for wear. There were plenty of women in his life too, and he was once again living his life with a zest which had gone out of it when Isabel died.

He and Zilkha got their new joint company under way in the early months of 1960, operating initially out of offices in Holborn, but then moving to the less salubrious area of Brixton, in south London, where they took a dingy office above a warehouse where they stored their stock. The office adjoined Brixton Prison, one of the toughest and largest in Britain, but neither man cared about the surroundings. From the moment they began, Goldsmith spent all day every day working in the tiny office with Zilkha. 'We had desks opposite each other in the same little room,' says Zilkha. They adjourned for lunch to a pub in nearby Lyham Road, an unlikely spot for Jimmy who had dined all his life in the very best hotels and restaurants in the world, but the West End was too far away. 'We were designing new shops and working on all sorts of ideas,' says Zilkha. 'And we were very happy just going to our pub.' They spent two years working like that, once again a hard slog for Goldsmith who was still pushing a large debt uphill.

He brought to the retail business the same intensity as he had to pharmaceuticals, continually throwing off new plans and ambitions. 'He had a new idea every day about what we could do with the business,' says Zilkha. Turning the chemists chain around was not proving easy. They redesigned the shops, changed the product lines, put in new management, advertised, did everything they could think of. But the losses still mounted.

He and Ginette took a house in Cannes for Christmas 1960 and invited the same old group of friends: John Aspinall, Teddy, Peter West, Digby Neave and others. The gossip columnists spotted Aspinall and Goldsmith in the casino, and the *Daily Express* carried what it presented as a scoop: a picture of Goldsmith and Ginette strolling along the seafront. 'Today I present the first picture of Mr Jimmy Goldsmith with the attractive, auburn-haired French girl who has become his close friend, Ginette Lery,' wrote the diarist. Until that moment Goldsmith had kept his relationship with Ginette out of the gossip columns, and confronted by the *Daily Express*, he refused to give much away: 'Jimmy is shy about his relationship with Ginette,' it reported. 'Neither he nor she will say whether they intend to marry – or whether they are even married already, as rumours suggest.'

The photograph is an interesting one: Goldsmith still had some of his hair but it was receding rapidly. Even for a stroll on the Cannes beach he wore a shirt and tie under a smart sports jacket, a white handkerchief as always in his breast pocket. He smiled relaxedly at the camera, although Ginette looked far more nervous.

Back in London, Goldsmith finally came up with the idea that would make Zilkha a fortune. 'One day he said we should open a different type of store, doing everything for the mother and her baby,' says Zilkha. 'I used to encourage him with all his ideas every day, and I loved that idea and I said, "Oh yes, we must do that." '

Goldsmith had seen the French chain Pre-Natal and was impressed by that. They had until then been selling mother-and-baby products in the stores, but Goldsmith was now proposing to go a crucial step further. Neither man was to know at the time that one of the most successful retailing ideas for the Britain of 1960s and 1970s had just been conceived. And like most Goldsmith ideas, it had a stuttering start. In March 1961 they added another 50 shops to their empire: the W. J. Harris chain of pram and nursery furniture outlets. They would use some of these for the new development. The plan they worked out in their Brixton office was to open six large chemists shops with departments devoted entirely to the mother and her baby. They began with two, one in Kingston, the other in Ealing, both prosperous suburbs of London. 'And they were big failures,' says Zilkha bluntly. Why? 'Because they were a confused proposition. You need to have a simple proposition in retailing to attract the public.'

Both men still believed in the concept, but were under different financial and time pressures. In the first year they had lost £140,000; in the second £180,000. Even to Zilkha this was a great deal of money, and it was a fortune for Goldsmith. 'He didn't really have any money, but somehow he did,' says Zilkha. 'I helped him a lot with that, with his French affairs financially, and just talking about it and analysing it – I had someone in Paris who was doing that so I don't think he was all that worried.'

The French business was fortunately going well. In 1960 Maurice Lignon had come to him with a proposition: there was a new American product which was claimed to provide a suntan without exposure to the sun. It was called Man Tan, and Lignon had been in touch with the manufacturers. The licence for Europe was available, and Lignon proposed that Goldsmith buy it and launch it in France under a new name: Night Tan. The potential in Europe was enormous, he told Goldsmith. It seemed a good idea to Goldsmith too, but he had no funds.

Everything was committed to the development of his retailing chain in Britain.

'We were talking about two million old French francs,' says Lignon (about £20,000). Goldsmith got the money from Zilkha who insisted on becoming a joint partner in Lanord, Lignon was hired back – for the third time – and they went to work. There was a degree of synergy between the different businesses in the sense that Lewis & Burrows, the Goldsmith/ Zilkha chemist chain, could buy the raw materials in England cheaply and ship them to France. Within three months Night Tan was on the market, but the operation had been organised in such a hurry that no one had checked the registry of names; Night Tan turned out to be owned by someone else, so hastily they changed it to Right Tan, and went on selling it. Lignon insisted on cash on delivery: he had had enough of living hand to mouth.

Right Tan was a success, and at last Lanord prospered. It had a good year in 1960 and an even better one in 1961 – possibly because Goldsmith stayed away from it, letting Lignon run it carefully and conventionally. It saw Goldsmith through those two years of losses in his partnership with Selim Zilkha, and paid for his time in London. The Goldsmith life style was as extravagant as it had ever been, and was brought to public notice in May 1961 when John Aspinall persuaded Jimmy to throw a party on Derby Day. Aspinall had always given a Derby Day party, but this year he wanted to make it something special: he ordered a Taj-Mahal-shaped marquee from Maples for £12,500, with a 70-foot high dome, and proposed setting up in the communal garden behind Goldsmith's house in Regent's Park. Goldsmith was delighted with the idea. He had to apply to the Crown, which owned the property, for permission to erect it, and, to the consternation of the residents of the other 14 houses (all of whom were invited to the party) which backed onto the gardens, it took twelve days to put up – and four to dismantle.

Aspinall, who paid for the party, and Goldsmith invited 150 'society guests' as the gossip columnists labelled them. Aspinall spared no expense: the marquee featured a small cabaret-type dance floor, surrounded by 40 tables; real carnations twined around the pillars, and the guests entered up a short flight of steps on thickly piled carpet to the strains of an eight-piece orchestra.

One resident was quoted the next day as saying: 'Goldsmith has certainly made the place sit up. Other residents have built marquees for wedding receptions and such like. We never expected this huge building. It's like a village.'

Goldsmith was loving his social life in London, but financially he was not making any headway. He and Zilkha dropped the pharmacy business from the two experimental stores in Kingston and Ealing, concentrating only on mother and baby under the name 'Mothercare'. It was working, but it would take time and Goldsmith was losing patience. 'I think Jimmy sees things very clearly,' says Zilkha, 'and he knew that what I was going to try to do in England was really a very hard job. It wasn't a thing that was going to happen overnight. I think he realised that it wasn't his way of doing things. It was going to be a hard slog, and that suited me, it's what I like, but he has a different sort of mentality.' Zilkha's family would support him, but a further injection of cash by him would mean the business would no longer be fifty-fifty. Goldsmith couldn't stand that. He had, he says, decided years before that he would never accept a partnership with anyone that was less than equal.

In the first weeks of 1962 he decided he had no alternative but to sell out. Zilkha of course would buy – there was never any question about it, neither was there the slightest ill will from either party. Zilkha in turn would sell Goldsmith his half share in the French Lanord business. It took less than two months to finalise the deal, except for the final amounts on either side. They argued about the figure, but there was no easy way of settling it – friends they might have been (and still are), but both were also hard, tough negotiators. In the end Goldsmith proposed they settle the final amount – both recall it was 'quite a bit' but won't now say how much – over a game of backgammon. Goldsmith had developed his game to the point where he was regarded as world class. It suited his quick mind and gambling instinct perfectly, and he would calculate the odds of throwing a particular number or combination in seconds. He had introduced Zilkha to his father's old club, the St James's Club, where they often played backgammon, but this particular game took place in Zilkha's home in Portland Place.

It was to be the best of three. Goldsmith won the first game, Zilkha the second. In the third game Zilkha was clearly ahead, and with only a few pieces left on the board, Goldsmith suddenly said: 'Well done, Selim, you've won.' The only possible combination that could stop Zilkha was a one on his next throw, followed by a double five or better for Goldsmith. On his next throw, Zilkha threw a one – and then Goldsmith threw a double five.

And so at the end of February 1962 Jimmy Goldsmith, now 29, returned to Paris with Ginette, Isabel and Manes. For his part Zilkha would stay with his developing mother-and-child company and was soon opening one on every High Street in Britain. When he sold the company in 1982 it was worth £120 million, and he received over £60 million in cash for his personal shareholding.

Goldsmith moved to a new apartment in the rue de Lubeck with Ginette, Isabel and her nanny. 'He left everything he had done in England,' Lignon recalls, 'and came back with me in Paris, in his father's office, where we were running Laboratoires Lanord.' As he had done with Zilkha, so he now moved into the same room as Lignon, with a desk opposite him. Lignon remembers him 'cogitating' on the next move. The company was making a healthy profit, but was small. For the first time in his career, however, Goldsmith had some money from the sale of his half stake in Lewis & Burrows. And he had a new idea which he had picked up from one of his visits to America, which he had not yet had the chance to develop. In the early 1960s the US fashion for slimming products had not yet hit Europe, where there had been food rationing in the immediate postwar years. Goldsmith was convinced the idea would soon catch on. One product in particular had caught his attention in America on one of his trips in search of new products and ideas: a powder called Metrecal. Mixed into a drink, it suppressed the appetite – that at least was the theory. Goldsmith was impressed with the promotion of Metrecal. Everyone he met in America seemed to be talking about it. The product itself was simple, and he reckoned he could copy it without any difficulty – he had no intention of paying for the licence.

After a long search through company records, he found a company called Laboratoires Milical. The name was close enough to Metrecal for his purposes. It was in fact an old-established French pharmaceutical company, which, very conveniently, happened to have a long-standing interest in slimming products. Goldsmith bought it cheaply, and was soon manufacturing a Metrecal equivalent under the name Milical – except, he reckoned, his version tasted better.

Metrecal was owned by the big American group, Mead Johnson, which soon spotted the rival and decided to take action. Goldsmith was ready for such a move. He argued in court that since Milical was an old French company which had been marketing slimming products for years, he was entitled to use the name. 'Milical has been in existence far longer than the new American product,' he submitted. For some reason, Mead Johnson sued him only over the use of the name, not for having copied their idea. Goldsmith launched a countersuit, alleging that Mead Johnson was actually copying his Milical name, and the American firm backed down.

Just as Mothercare was the key to Zilkha's large fortune, Milical was the launchpad for Goldsmith's. Twelve months after he developed it, he was selling it all over Europe. He opened subsidiaries in Holland, Germany, Scandinavia and Italy. He expanded back into Britain, rubbing off some of the hurt he still felt over having to back out of his partnership with his friend Selim. After nearly a decade of extraordinarily hard work, expansive ideas, launches, crashes and financial struggle, he had broken through. He was on the way to a considerable fortune. Or so he thought. Only Jimmy Goldsmith would be able to find himself back on the edge of ruin just a few years later.

10

The Takeover Game

'Cavenham Foods, the new bakery and confectionery group which will result from the merger of the James Goldsmith-controlled food companies, looks like becoming one of the most interesting shares on the Stock Exchange,' wrote the *Sunday Times* on 18 July 1965. It was a brief item on a small but clearly interesting company which had, as the paper mentioned, a turnover of £27m 'and no profits to speak of'. Goldsmith, however, had been expounding his hopes that profits, if all went according to plan, could exceed £900,000 in four years' time. 'Obviously everything depends on the management – and on past form, it has a pretty good chance of succeeding,' the *Sunday Times* concluded.

If the author had known the full story of Jimmy Goldsmith's business form up to that time he would have hesitated before writing that. On 'past form', if everything depended on Goldsmith's management, Cavenham Foods would expand its turnover with great rapidity, but it would also pile up debts in the process, and would probably, in the four years' profit projection the newspaper talked about, encounter a major cash squeeze and even, perhaps, come close to bankruptcy.

An earlier piece in the *Sunday Times* that year described Goldsmith as 'the slightly enigmatic figure who has surprised the Stock Exchange with a succession of bids and deals'. Few people connected this tall, immaculately dressed and energetic businessman with the playboy of a dozen years earlier. In the City, he was taken at face value, his reputation neither good nor bad, another bright man who might or might not make it into the big league, someone worth keeping an eye on. In the food industry, where Goldsmith had concentrated his burst of takeover activity, he had aroused a degree of unease, but the mid-1960s were a time of rapid change in Britain, and Goldsmith went with the flow.

For the past few years he had spent less time in Paris where Right Tan and Milical were still growing, and more and more in London, which again became the centre of his business life.

Since the end of 1961 there was another reason besides business for being in London. He had fallen in love again, this time with a tall, brown-eyed model, one of the most glamorous women in London. There had been other women, many of them, but even for Goldsmith this was something special.

By now he had moved Ginette and the children back to Paris. Until this time his sex life had been active but conventional enough. He would point out to anyone who asked that the Goldschmidts had always had mistresses, and it was a tradition he saw no reason to change (his father was the source of this information, and as he grew older, he confided to Teddy and Jimmy more and more tales of his own past life as well as that of his family). Ginette must have been all too aware from the earliest stages that theirs was an unequal relationship, and that Jimmy was going to be very difficult for her to hang on to. Goldsmith's friends never expected him to stay with her long, certainly not after he had recovered from the shock of Isabel's death and returned to his normal ways. Ginette was pretty, loved his friends, such as John Aspinall and Digby Neave, and was an excellent hostess. His daughter Isabel never accepted her, and there would be tension – and downright enmity – between them most of their lives, but she was a good mother to his son Manes, and provided the home in Paris he wanted.

Although he was deeply fond of Ginette, his relationship with her was very different to the romantic one he had had with Isabel. They had grown close as they worked side by side in his early business. Ginette had helped him through grief and money problems. She had also looked after little Isabel and had borne him his first son.

Each summer they rented a house in the south of France, where Goldsmith held open season, inviting his old friends, their wives and families, playing backgammon and gambling, talking and soaking up the sun, before returning to his increasingly complex businesses.

But his English model offered something different: she was exciting, sociable, bright, matched his own love of parties and late nights, knew most of the people he knew – and to be seen with her was good for his ego. He wanted to live with her, but like many a man in a similar position, he could not bear to leave Ginette.

And so from the early months of 1962 Goldsmith began another way of life which he has maintained to the present day: two households, in two different cities, each run by a mistress/wife. From the beginning, Goldsmith was frank about both relationships, each woman knowing about the other, a fact which may have made it easier for him but hard for Ginette, who was not married to him, and must have felt very vulnerable at the time.

He now decided to rectify that, in much the way his father had before him. His brother, Teddy, had been born out of wedlock, and so had Jimmy's own son, Manes. Goldsmith talked to both women openly about his plans: he had no intention of swapping one woman for the other, but wanted to keep both equally in his life. He would have, in effect, one wife in London and one in Paris, each with her own household, including children. His immediate proposal was to reassure Ginette by marrying her, thus making Manes legitimate, and then he would divorce her and marry his model. 'For me getting married is having children, not a piece of paper,' he insisted. By marrying Ginette, he told her, she would be his wife for ever, and even if they did legally divorce, that would not make any difference to his relationship with her.

To the outside world, particularly in England, Goldsmith's ability to carry on two relationships at once was a source of gossip, bafflement and jealousy. In truth it was probably never as comfortable as he might have made it out to be. Friends remember furious rows; and Ginette, for all her love and loyalty to him, must also have suffered considerably.

Early in 1963 he married Ginette in a quiet ceremony in Paris. His mother, disapproving of his widely known taste for other women, was delighted. But in a typically Goldsmith gesture he threw a party for his model at Maxim's in Paris, and invited all his friends, who assumed it was a kind of engagement party.

In the autumn Ginette discovered she was pregnant again, and the delicate balance swung. It meant that Goldsmith could not now divorce Ginette until after the baby was born. It ended his London relationship. She was not content to remain the mistress of a married man. After another row, she left him, although he believed he would be able to woo her back.

His daughter, Alix, was born on 3 January 1964, into considerably better style than her elder brother. There was no worry this time about paying the hospital bills, although Goldsmith's life style in two cities and his rapid advance on the takeover front were devouring his funds.

All this time, Goldsmith had been actively expanding his business empire.

He had decided, after his early ventures, to get the financial side right this time; he was also determined to short-cut the process of growing a business from scratch.

Goldsmith had seen Roussell take over his perfectly good little company, feed in some capital, and grow it again, without the sweat and torture he had experienced. He had become impatient with the slog required to get Mothercare off the ground. And so, in 1963 he discovered the activity for which he was to become best known in the United States 20 years later, and which was to make him his considerable fortune: the aggressive and, if necessary, hostile takeover bid. In the mid-1960s it was still a relatively new phenomenon in Britain. It was totally unknown in America, where the hostile bid only arrived in the 1980s, or in France, where the bulk of Goldsmith's business experience had been gained. The conditions for the hostile bid in Britain were ideal: there were at the time thousands of small family-run companies, which were too small and too unambitious to succeed in an increasingly competitive international business world dominated by large companies. Britain was unique in Europe in having a well-developed stock market, with many small and medium-sized quoted companies unprotected by controlling blocks of shares, as they were in France and Germany. Years of government-imposed restrictions on dividends had held down share prices, which often meant that asset – or 'break-up' – value far exceeded the price at which a company could be bought on the stock market.

The classic exponent of the aggressive bid was Charles Clore, whom Goldsmith often met and chatted to after their first encounter several years before when Clore had sold him Lewis & Burrows. Clore was a huge figure on the British financial scene in the late 1950s and early years of the 1960s, as he took control of the British footwear industry and of the Selfridges stores group in the most-publicised takeover contests ever seen. Clore's classic tactic was to buy shares in a target company over a period of months (and sometimes years), doing it gradually so as not to arouse suspicion. His buying remained secret because he hid it under nominee names, thus allowing him to accumulate a significant shareholding without pushing up the share price, and – more importantly – without the board being aware of it. By the time Clore made his bid, he was often in an impregnable position. Even if the bid failed, he still made money. Sometimes his offer would attract another bidder into the arena, giving him a hefty profit on the shares he already held. The mere announcement – or carefully planted rumour – that he was a shareholder would also drive up the share price, as would the efforts of the board to fight him off. It was a no-lose game. And, crucially for Goldsmith, you didn't even need cash to do it – a highly rated share, offered as a swap for the much lower-rated share of the target company, was good enough.

As Goldsmith was making his entry into the bid arena, the free-for-all of the Clore era was coming to an end. Clore's bid for the brewers Watney Mann, although it was beaten off, helped inspire the City's first tentative takeover code, 20 years after President Roosevelt had created the much more restrictive Securities and Exchange Commission in the United States. But it still left plenty of room for an imaginative young man to manoeuvre in.

For Goldsmith, business up to this time had been too much work for too little reward. He had not made the vital breakthrough to the point where he was seriously rich. Before his eyes men such as Clore, Sir Isaac Wolfson, who built the Great Universal Stores group, Hugh Fraser who bought Harrods, and others were putting together large corporate empires through financial engineering and manipulation rather than by the more traditional manufacturing route.

In the 1960s the morality of the hostile bid, which would become one of the most debated corporate themes of the 1980s, was only beginning to be discussed. Over the next five years in Britain the proponents of the takeover, including Goldsmith, were to argue that their efforts were galvanising all the inefficient and lazy companies in the country, forcing them to make more effective use of their assets, or make way for someone else who would do it for them.

The opponents of hostile takeover bids, including the trade unions, the Labour Party and a large section of industry and the City, insisted that a group of young and unscrupulous men were simply taking over perfectly good companies, stripping their valuable assets, and selling what was left to someone else. Factories which had provided jobs in a tight community were, the argument went, being closed and developed as office or shopping developments because there was more money in it. Companies would no longer spend on long-term research and development because the existing shareholders might not be around to see the results. 'Short-termism' was not then a current phrase, but that was the flavour of the criticism.

To an extent it was true. Few of the financial empires now being created would survive the recessions that lay ahead. Many were mere paper-shuffling exercises, which created no new jobs, no exports, no new products – just short-term gain for clever young City whizzkids, who had never run a real business.

*

The success of Right Tan and Milical plus the sale to Selim Zilkha had made Goldsmith reasonably well off, but the lessons of the early years had not been forgotten. He had to protect Ginette and the children, and when he returned to Paris in 1961 after his partnership with Zilkha broke up, one of the first actions he took was to sell one-third of his company. 'I wanted to consolidate so that if things fell off again, I would not be in danger of going broke,' he said.

The man he chose as his partner was a distant cousin, whose grandfather had married Adolph Goldschmidt's sister. Baron Alexis de Gunzberg was then aged 46, 14 years Goldsmith's senior, with a financial ambition which was said to match that of his new partner. He was a grandson of the founder of Shell Française, and a cousin of the Rothschilds, so his connections were many times better than Goldsmith's. With him as a partner, Jimmy Goldsmith would find few doors in France closed to him, as he had done in his early days. But Gunzberg, for all his contacts and background, probably had even less money than Goldsmith did.

He paid for his one-third holding in Goldsmith's company, now called Gustin-Milical, in an unusual way: with shares in Source Perrier, the French mineral water company. The rights to the source had originally been sold by the British newspaper baron Lord Harmsworth in 1951, and the new owners, Perrier, who had the French Coca-Cola franchise, rapidly built it up. De Gunzberg was a big shareholder in Source Perrier, a partner of the chairman; he was also a director of a number of French companies, and for his part Goldsmith was delighted at the swap: Perrier was highly profitable and still growing rapidly. It gave him both a useful income and excellent security.

Now he was ready for something more exciting. The slimming business was a growth area, and he began searching for new products he could add to what he already owned, preferably in Britain where many old and mature companies with good brand names could be bought cheaply.

Before he launched himself onto the takeover scene, he spent some months working out a strategy. It was not desperately profound, and basically came down to buying companies at less than they were worth. The trick was to be in a position to add value to them, either by managing them better or by selling off parts, or by a combination of the two. Goldsmith had considerable faith in his own energies and skills, so better management was not a problem, at least in his own mind. But the financial climate had to be right – there was no point in committing himself on the eve of a recession.

Clore and some of his followers had created conglomerates, buying up companies because of their asset value rather than the business they were in, but Goldsmith preferred to stick to what he knew, and perhaps expand into other industries later.

The economic boom of the 1950s was running down in Britain in 1963 as the Conservative government struggled through the Profumo crisis and towards an election after a dozen years in power. But the stock market remained healthy enough, and Goldsmith decided it was time to begin the first of his takeover runs.

His first investment owed little to Charles Clore tactics. Towards the end of 1963 he bought 60,000 shares in a company called Procea Products, which was a small public company making slimming products, notably a low-calorie bread called Slimcea. He made his acquisition openly, on the grounds that it was a logical expansion of his slimfood group in France. Procea was an old-fashioned group, with a factory at Slough, near Heathrow Airport. There was nothing hostile about his purchase, at least initially: he was welcomed onto the board, representing as he did 20 per cent of the company, and the *Financial Times*, remarking on the poor performance of Procea since its shares had been floated on the stock market four years before, commented: 'This 20 per cent holding, which ought to make Mr Goldsmith the principal shareholder, puts him in a strong position to inject some health and energy into the business.'

In many ways Goldsmith's involvement with Procea, at least in these early days, was not dissimilar to the shareholdings he would buy in his later years, such as in BAT in 1989 or in RHM the same year. It put him into a position where he could recommend improvements to the company, and if it didn't take his advice, then he could take control. For the moment, however, he did not have the money – or the shares – to go above 20 per cent, so Goldsmith concentrated instead on working his way into boardroom control without a full-scale bid.

In the meantime, however, Procea was producing a poor return on his investment, and Goldsmith needed money. He still had no close relationship with a bank, and no one to back him for the deals he had in mind. He talked to Charles Clore one evening, who suggested that he should visit a friend of his who specialised in financing just such young entrepreneurs as Goldsmith. It was on Clore's recommendation that Goldsmith first met Sir Isaac Wolfson, one of the richest men in Britain and the first man since Jesus Christ to have a college in both Oxford and Cambridge named after him (because of huge charitable gifts). Wolfson was in his early sixties, and had moved from retailing (including Burberrys and Scotch House) into banking with the purchase of a group called Drages, which had a half share in the minor bank Ralli Brothers. Wolfson, Clore warned him, often napped during the day, but barely slept at night, and had developed a habit, well known among those who dealt with him, of starting his working day at five in the morning. Because it was difficult to talk to anyone else at that time, he would invite eager borrowers to come and see him before breakfast. Clore laughingly briefed Jimmy on this habit, adding that those who were in the direst trouble had to be there at five, and those in the least financial trouble could be in his office at a more respectable hour. 'I was, of course, always there at five,' says Goldsmith, adding that as he came out 45 minutes later the publisher Roy Thomson, owner of the *Sunday Times*, but, until he found oil in the North Sea, short of money, was on the way in.

Wolfson's right-hand man was Harry Recanati, one of the toughest bankers in the City at the time. Wolfson and Recanati were not in the business of straightforward lending in competition with the big banks. They were in the business of taking risks, relying on their own wits and judgement, and charging high rates for their money with hefty penal clauses for default. There are still those in the City today who remember how Recanati's bank, Ralli Brothers, foreclosed on them, of the bailiffs arriving before dawn to batter down the door. Others, however, were grateful for the fact he backed them when no one else would.

Goldsmith came from a banking family which had survived for hundreds of years lending money under similar circumstances. He cheerfully accepted what others regarded as usurious rates. Wolfson and Recanati took extra risks, he reckoned, and were therefore entitled to charge extra interest. Ralli, as well as lending money, took a stake in his company, which Goldsmith and de Gunzberg had an option to buy back at a much higher price.

It was Wolfson's money which allowed Goldsmith to make his next move in putting together what was emerging as an increasingly complex jigsaw. In 1964 he created a new, private, company in Britain which he called Cavenham Foods, taking the name from his grandfather's estate in Suffolk which Frank talked about often. De Gunzberg owned one-third of Cavenham, Goldsmith owned another third, and Ralli owned the rest (which Goldsmith had an option to buy).

Cavenham's first deal was to buy control of a small public company called Carsons, a Yorkshire-based chocolate company. Carsons was a mess – the previous year it had lost more than £50,000, had not paid a dividend for two years, and had been going downhill for some time. But it had some property assets, a stock market quote, and was ideal for Goldsmith's purposes. He transferred his Procea stake into it, which he valued at £310,000, which gave him 55 per cent of Carsons, and he became chairman. In June, Carsons made a bid for the rest of Procea, and for the capital of another small confectionery company, Yeatman. The offer for the two companies amounted to £1.5m, and Goldsmith was able to tell the Carson shareholders that 'facilities to cover these liabilities have been arranged' – as indeed they had been, with Wolfson and Recanati. On 24 June 1964 he warned shareholders of rough times ahead:

> The food industry which your company is now planning to enter in a more general way, is dominated by extremely strong and well-managed groups, and is a highly competitive industry. Moreover, the reorganisation which will follow if the proposed offers are successful will inevitably be a lengthy and expensive operation. Whilst, therefore, we are very hopeful that the ultimate result of these mergers will be beneficial to your company, the material benefits are unlikely to be realised in the immediate future and it is impossible to forecast at this stage an early resumption of dividends.

That was polite enough. But in case any shareholders did object, the last paragraph was blunt: Carsons, he said, had become a subsidiary of Cavenham Foods, 'a recently formed private company of which I am chairman and in which I have a substantial interest.'

Thus within months of Goldsmith acquiring control, Carsons had made two acquisitions, more than trebling its size. That autumn Cavenham, still the private master company, made another bid, this time for a small biscuit company based in Carlisle, Carr & Co., an old-established firm with slowly declining profits but one useful asset: its biscuit factory.

That summer he bought control of yet another quoted company, J. & A. P. Holland, an old family confectionery group which had diversified into plastics and paper. If the other companies he bought were rundown, Holland was a ruin. In many ways it was typical of what was happening in Britain in this postwar period, when fragmented industries were being concentrated rapidly by mergers and takeovers, only for the bidder to become a target itself. Jack Holland, the son of the founder, had the idea of taking over many of the strategically placed wholesalers of confectionery in Britain, and as many manufacturing companies as he could buy. His plan was to create a group capable of taking on the big confectionery groups such as Rowntree or Cadbury. If he had the distribution already sewn up, he reckoned, he would have a captive market for his manufacturing side. He bought 250 wholesalers, and a dozen manufacturing companies, and then ran into major indigestion problems. 'The whole thing was a disaster,' says Martin Kram, whose family had sold its business, employing some 250 people, to Holland, and then watched the value of its shareholding halve in six months, and the board split over how to get out of its difficulties. The television and entertainments group Granada had a stake in Holland, and its chairman, Sidney Bernstein, was also adding to the pressure.

That summer its problems and the division on the board hit the financial pages, and to Goldsmith it looked like an excellent addition to his portfolio. 'Things got very bad,' says Kram, who was only 23, but on the board, 'and I think the Holland family were very concerned they were going to lose everything. They had tried to sell the company to several other organisations, and it had always fallen through. So everybody looked on Jimmy Goldsmith as a sort of saviour.'

It was Goldsmith's biggest, and most high risk, purchase yet.

As 1965 opened and the *Sunday Times* discovered him, Goldsmith was in control of a ragbag of confectionery companies, employing 6,000 people, with a turnover of £30m, net assets of about £7m, but no profits. The companies were run by different managements, were situated in different cities, and had no central control. But Goldsmith had a strategy: unwanted factories would be closed and sold, the money used to concentrate production into larger, more modern and efficient units, with a single headquarters, a unified sales force and a proper divisional structure. He would buy out the minority shareholdings, and sell off those subsidiaries which did not fit into his grand plan.

That at least was the theory, but when Goldsmith tried to put it into practice he discovered it was far from simple. The first stage – which his critics would call the asset-stripping stage – went well enough. The previous summer he had met the man who would work out the financial framework for him. Roland Franklin was a partner in the small City merchant banking firm, Keyser Ullmann, who had become chairman of a confectionery group called Mayfair several years before. He knew something about the confectionery industry as well as merchant banking. He was also, as it happened, the financial adviser to Yeatman when Goldsmith, through Carsons, mounted his bid for it. He first heard of Jimmy Goldsmith, who would have a major impact on his life, when the managing director of Yeatman came to see him.

'I have met a very strange fellow at the Ritz,' he began. 'He wouldn't sit down. He walked up and down behind the potted palms and he thought he wanted to buy my business. Actually, he wasn't clear whether he wanted to buy my business or to sell me *his* business.' Would Franklin come and meet him?

Franklin did, and found in Goldsmith a keen financial brain who was clearly after bigger things than the little Yeatman. Goldsmith explained how he intended to put together a number of old-fashioned confectionery and food companies, rationalise them, sell off old factories and other unwanted assets which should bring in some cash, and create a company with some well-known but underdeveloped brand names capable of holding their own in the food sector. Its foundations looked pretty shaky to Franklin at that moment but he could see the potential, and he was impressed with Goldsmith.

'He was a very overwhelming character,' says Franklin. 'He was outside the realm of normal experience, or at least outside the realm of my experience at that stage. I didn't know what to make him of at first. I didn't understand the world he moved in. I knew nothing about the gambling, the womanising, which were all very alien to me.' But he was deeply impressed with the thoroughness of Goldsmith's financial knowledge.

Goldsmith was impressed with Franklin too. He rang up a few days later with a proposal. Would Franklin act for him in his bid for Yeatman? It meant that Franklin would be acting for both sides, an unusual event in a takeover bid, and one that would be frowned on today, but Franklin was happy to accept. Keyser Ullmann now became Goldsmith's merchant bank, advising on the emerging strategy of one of the more complex and fastest-moving little companies in Britain.

Franklin was hard at work on his scheme for putting the various Goldsmith interests together in early 1965 when the *Sunday Times* article appeared. At this point, Cavenham had shareholdings in three publicly quoted companies, Carsons (having absorbed Procea and Yeatman, which had both originally been quoted on the stock market), Carr & Co. and Holland. 'Various techniques are being explored,' wrote the *Sunday Times* on 31 January, 'but the most probable solution would be to select one of the present companies as a vehicle to make share exchange offers for the others. Holland would seem to be the most likely choice.'

That article ended on an odd note, showing just how little the journalist had understood Goldsmith's psychology. 'The major framework of the group is now complete, and no more takeovers are to be expected from the Cavenham quarter. Future additions, if any, are likely to be small private concerns.'

Within months, he and Franklin were pushing through the next stage of their plan. Carr's factory in Carlisle was sold in June 1965 raising £600,000 cash, and leased back for £63,000 a year. Carr then used the money to buy Cavenham's controlling shareholding in Carsons, whose shares had begun to rise, giving Goldsmith a profit of £75,000.

Carr & Co., rather than Carsons, now emerged as the company at the top of the pyramid. It made an offer for Holland, which Goldsmith's private company Cavenham again accepted, thus transferring his shareholding into Carr's. And the name of Carr & Co. was changed to Cavenham Foods.

It was bewildering for anyone other a professional corporate banker to follow. Goldsmith was too small at the time for anyone to take too close an interest in what he was doing, but there were financial journalists who spent months reconstructing these early moves. Charles Raw of the *Sunday Times*, who devoted years to an exposé of Goldsmith in later years, reluctantly concluded: 'There was nothing illegal – in 1965 – about this type of incestuous share dealing.' But, he added, it was largely as a result of deals like these that the Stock Exchange changed the rules. Within a few years, Raw pointed out, it would have been impossible for Goldsmith to pay his own private company cash for its shares while offering paper to the other shareholders. That, however, was a technicality, and not worth the investigative efforts Raw put into it. More serious for Goldsmith was the fact that he was not meeting his forecasts, a factor for which the City was less forgiving. In 1964 he told shareholders that losses for Carsons would be down from £68,000 to £8,000, but in the event the company lost £120,000, and he was now making optimistic forecasts for Cavenham, causing the share price to rise, but which again he would miss.

By the summer of 1965, however, his first master plan was complete, his various acquisitions and shareholdings (or at least most of them) concentrated into a single company. He wrote to his band of shareholders to proclaim that:

> The future of Cavenham will depend on the effectiveness of its reorganisation and integration, from the benefits that concentration can bring to all parts of the group's activities, and from the ability of the group's management to carry out this reorganisation and then to build on the new basis thus created.

It was a fairly grand message for a company which organisationally and financially was in poor shape. Yet Goldsmith was confident, predicting profits of £215,000 for the first year, and forecasting that profits in the following year would be 'substantially greater'.

He also reorganised the board and management, getting rid of most of the old Holland, Carr and Carsons people, bringing in Roland Franklin as a director, and a series of bright young marketing men. He hired John Greenhalgh, a veteran marketing expert who had worked for Procter & Gamble, and others from Mars and Unilever, the best marketing training grounds of the time. And he threw himself into creating a modern, streamlined and logical group. Eleven food factories and six paper factories became seven food factories and four paper as he closed down some of the facilities, creating a considerable number of redundancies, and selling off what assets he could. Cavenham, he said, would have two divisions, manufacturing and wholesaling, and 'any activities which prove to be incompatible with total integration in these trades will . . . be sold.'

The merger was completed in July 1965 and Goldsmith took Ginette and the three children on holiday in Italy. He invited Roland Franklin to join them, and he found they had hired what he describes as 'an extraordinarily luxurious house' where Sophia Loren was reputed to have lived, filled with Jimmy's friends. Franklin felt out of things as he watched fit and bronzed young men and women do swallowdives into the pool until he saw the gangling Goldsmith walk gingerly out along the diving board, hold his nose, and jump in feet first. 'I thought, this is my kind of person.' Franklin, however, never much enjoyed the Goldsmith-style holiday. 'My wife and I were probably too square. Ginette we liked, we could handle her, but when it got too complicated we dropped out of the holiday entourage.'

Goldsmith was in excellent form. He seemed to have few doubts that he was at last on the edge of his breakthrough; he had the brands, the management and the organisation he wanted. All it required now was effort to make things work. Yet the truth is, up to this point what he had put together was an insubstantial empire, built more on smart paper transactions than on anything concrete. Cavenham was far from being a viable company that could survive in the tougher conditions which were now hitting Britain. The Conservatives had lost the election of October 1964, and in the budget of 1965 the new Labour government, under Harold Wilson, introduced a selective employment tax designed to support manufacturing industry at the expense of service industry. That had knocked a hole in Cavenham's profits because of its large distribution side, but little else was going well in the company either. Goldsmith had shown he could buy companies, but even in the eyes of his own managers the big question was: could he run them?

When he returned from holiday, he certainly tried. His head office, which he called Cavenham House, was at Slough, not far from Heathrow Airport, and Goldsmith put in longer and longer days in an attempt to bring some order to his creation. 'It was a terrible mess to begin with,' says one of his directors at the time. 'I couldn't see it succeeding, and of course it so nearly failed. I got disillusioned with all the comings and goings of the executives and I told Jimmy that it was all being run in the wrong way. People didn't seem to matter too much, and not enough thought was being given to the products and not enough thought was being given to personnel.' There was, he remembers, 'an awful lot of breaking up and selling off going on, and I told him I was disillusioned about everything and I should go.'

Goldsmith, recalls this former director, was very gracious about it. 'He said that was my prerogative, and if I didn't like it he certainly didn't want to keep me there, not if I didn't believe in him. "I can assure you it will be a great success one day", he told me.' The director left, selling the £50,000 worth of shares his father had given him.

But others were joining. The annual reports and the irregular issue of *Cavenham News*, a house journal Goldsmith introduced in a burst of enthusiasm to let everyone know what he was doing, chronicle an extraordinary period of comings and goings.

One of the comings was another acquisition, a tobacco wholesaler called Singleton & Cole. It would be no more successful than any of the others. But it was to prove significant for two factors: unknown to Goldsmith, it contained a hidden asset which was to save him from going bust; and it brought him into contact for the first time with a man who was to become for a time a far brighter star in British commercial life than Goldsmith, someone who was to have a major impact on his life and career: James Derrick Slater.

I I

Enter Jim Slater

Jim Slater in 1965, when Goldsmith met him, was just launching himself into a burst of perhaps the most frenzied takeover activity the City of London has ever witnessed. By the end of the decade it would make him the single most powerful influence on the business scene, and on the business morality of the day. Five years after that he would be gone, his business and his reputation in ruins, in the most spectacular rise and fall of the postwar period. At this point in their careers, Goldsmith and Slater were roughly level pegging in their embryonic business empires, but where Goldsmith was to find the Sixties hard going, Slater, using similar methods of buying companies below asset value, and selling off the unwanted assets, found it all terribly easy.

Four years older than Jimmy, he was the same height, with a similar gangling figure, but without the striking Goldsmith looks and charged energy. Slater in his private life was as conventional as Goldsmith was unconventional, an accountant from a middle-class family who married his secretary. Yet they shared similar quick mathematical minds, and the ability to detect in balance sheets what escaped even the best of bankers and accountants.

Slater's approach to building his company differed from Goldsmith's in one crucial respect: Jimmy, despite the ornate and complex financial structure he used, was attempting to put together a group based, however loosely, around a single industry. However badly, he was at least attempting to develop brands, make them in his own factories, and sell them through his own distribution network. Slater on the other hand had no interest in manufacturing anything. For him, the interest lay only in realising as much gain from each acquisition as he could, the profits to be used to make still bigger takeovers. One of Slater's favourite phrases was, 'a long-term policy is an excuse for a short-term mistake'.

Unlike Goldsmith, Slater was a great chaser (or setter) of the latest corporate fashion, sensing shifts in business trends, in stock markets and in individual industries before others did. In this early part of his career, he had picked up on a new style of company which was then making waves in the United States. In the early and mid-1960s there was a merger wave on Wall Street based on the management theory that a primary manufacturer should seek out some enterprise that provided counter-cyclical balance to its existing business. This was known as the 'conglomerate' bid, its arch-priest a Dallas-based entrepreneur called Jimmy Ling. Within a few years, while Goldsmith was still struggling to bring his food companies into line, Slater had combined the idea of the conglomerate with the hostile takeover to such effect that this period of British corporate history became known as 'the Slater era', and the Conservative government of Edward Heath, which won power in 1970, was labelled by many 'the Slater government'. Slater's growth and glamour were such that he bred an entire generation of followers and imitators, spreading his philosophy across Australia, Singapore, Hong Kong, South Africa and Canada. The flame would burn brightly for a few years, and then sputter out in the changed climate and deep recession of the mid-1970s.

Slater is important in the Goldsmith story, not just because he became – and remains – a close friend, but because some of the early Goldsmith business philosophy paralleled or was inspired by Slater. From his first appearance on the public stage in September 1963, some years behind Goldsmith, to his peak in 1972, Slater's career was so dramatic, he eclipsed men like Goldsmith, James Hanson (now Lord Hanson, chairman of one of the most successful conglomerates in the world), and Jeffrey Sterling (now Lord Sterling, chairman of P&O) who were regarded as mere followers of the guru. Goldsmith was never a copyist, but in these early years Slater was well ahead of him in stamping his own financial philosophy, such as it was, on the markets – and in making money.

Slater had originally been something of a star in Britain's motor industry; at 35, he was the youngest man on the board of Leyland Motors, considered by the then chairman, Donald Stokes, as a potential successor. A self-confessed hypochondriac, Slater quit the motor industry because of his health worries, and in 1963, as Goldsmith was taking his stake in Procea, he started a small investment advisory business.

He teamed up with Peter Walker, one of the brightest of the young Conservative politicians, to found Slater Walker which over the next seven years grew from an obscure little company with a market value of £1.5m into a group capitalised at over £200m.

When he was publicly pilloried as an asset-stripper, a word not much used in the mid-1960s but rapidly coming into vogue as the great pejorative description of the day, Slater spelled out his own philosophy, one conveniently developed retrospectively for activities which had very few altruistic motives at the time.

'The object of Slater Walker from the beginning was to inject better management into a range of existing companies,' he said. 'Clearly it must be of advantage to the economy to have dead assets liberated from basically hopeless ventures, and channelled instead into other enterprises that might be more successful.'

Even with Wilson's government, this was a perfectly respectable intellectual argument, and was one that Goldsmith would make his own, and develop in defence of his activities years later in the US. The Labour government was to introduce the state-sponsored Industrial Reorganisation Corporation in 1966 and fund it with £150m to encourage mergers in the hope of improving Britain's international competitive position. British industry was hopelessly fragmented. The IRC was designed to create large units in strategic areas such as electronics, cars, textiles and machine tools, and would, in Wilson's words, 'drag Britain kicking and screaming into the twentieth century'. Slater insisted he was doing the same thing, only in a different way.

'The financial predator acted as a catalyst in stimulating fear within the fat and lazy managements, thereby making them more active,' he said later in his book *Return to Go*. 'In some cases companies were bought by predators and then resold into stronger hands. In a sense, fear of the predator was an essential discipline for many boards, as without it they would have tended to rest upon the laurels of their predecessors.'

Whether Goldsmith or Slater developed this argument first is a moot point, but it was Goldsmith who even in these embryonic days thought on a wider plane to the more insular but better-known Slater. When they met for the first time in September 1965 neither Goldsmith nor Slater was yet thinking any such highflown thoughts. Slater happened to have some shares he wanted to sell, Goldsmith was in the market, and their discussions were largely limited to the price. The shares were in the aforesaid tobacco retailer Singleton & Cole. Slater had bought a 20 per cent stake but had decided against bidding for it himself. The holding represented what was known as a 'strategic stake', a term invented by Slater to describe a shareholding which basically delivered control of a company, and was therefore, he argued, worth a premium on the market price. Goldsmith did not disagree, and just a month after the merger of the Cavenham companies had been completed, he and his partner de Gunzberg bought 112,000 shares each from Slater at 13s a share. The deal was done through their private company, Cavenham Investments, but the two men gave the publicly quoted Cavenham Foods an option to purchase the shares at cost.

Towards the end of their negotiation, Slater casually asked Goldsmith what he thought about the stock market. He was unprepared for the response. Pacing up and down the room, Goldsmith told him:

'I think that next year there might be the last major bull market of our lifetime.'

While Slater was digesting that, he went on, 'However, the main problem is of course the ecological one.'

This left Slater even more bemused. He had never heard the word 'ecology' before, and had no idea what Goldsmith meant. 'As he said "of course" with such confidence I did not want to profess ignorance, so I thought I would keep my options open by saying something relatively neutral,' said Slater later.

'I quite agree that is the main problem,' he muttered.

Goldsmith soon explained what he did mean.

'Before long there will be a shortage of water; in America the crime rate is rising at over 30 per cent per annum; within five years you will not be able to get fish from the sea; there will be a shortage of food.'

As he went on, Slater ruefully recalled, 'I began to realise that "ecology" might be another word for "trouble".'

Singleton seemed to Goldsmith to fit well with his general scheme: its wholesaling interests, merged with his own, would create a major presence and give him economies of scale and selling power.

While forging on with the task of reorganising his existing businesses, just before Christmas 1965, Goldsmith opened negotiations with the Singleton board. He had encountered opposition before in his takeover bids – the much larger J. Lyons had tried to outbid him for Carr & Co. and the Holland family had not given in without a fight at J. & A. P. Holland – but, for the first time in his career, he now entered openly hostile territory. The management, led by the chairman George Waddington, had no intention of being taken over.

Goldsmith first tried peaceful negotiation. He drove up the M1 motorway to Birmingham to visit the company, but on the way his hire car broke down. In a blind fury he got out and kicked it. His discomfiture continued when he finally got there. Goldsmith had not been brought up in England, and outside London knew remarkably little about the country's culture. What, he wondered through lunch, was this Aston Villa everyone kept talking about? He returned without agreement, but determined to push ahead with his bid. His own colleagues, battling to reorganise the companies Goldsmith had already bought, tried to persuade him to stop, consolidate and leave Singleton for later, but Goldsmith was in no mood to listen. He had a momentum going which he was determined to maintain. He had to complete his group before someone else woke up to the cheap acquisitions still to be made. This would give him real leverage, and some useful assets, he believed.

In April the Singleton board appointed a merchant bank, S. G. Warburg, which was establishing itself as the great defender of takeovers in the City of London, and suddenly Goldsmith had a fight on his hands. The professionals at Warburgs could see instantly both Goldsmith's strategy and his weakness. He had no cash so he was offering shares, whose price was buoyed up on the prospect of Goldsmith's forecast of profits of £215,000, and a 'substantially greater' figure in the following year. That was not good enough for Warburgs who advised Waddington that he should turn the bid down.

Goldsmith reacted by insisting that he and de Gunzberg, holders of 20 per cent, should be appointed to the board. This was what had happened at Procea, enabling Goldsmith to gain control. Warburgs saw through that one too, and the Singleton chairman wrote to his shareholders again to say the merger talks had broken down 'because Cavenham wanted to get control of S. & C. without any cash payment.' Waddington had no intention of allowing them onto the board.

The battle had become a public one, and Goldsmith now fought it through the financial press, which on the whole took his side. 'It's a fine old company,' he told the *Observer*, 'but its recent profit record leaves much to be desired.' Singleton's shares had risen from 11s 9d when he first made his approach to 14s 9d now. The *Sunday Times* summed up the battle: 'Singletons argue that if Goldsmith wants the business he must pay for it – in cash or underwritten paper. Goldsmith in turn says he won't pay cash because the shares are too high, buoyed up by his own market dealings.'

In truth of course Goldsmith – or Cavenham – did not have the cash, and he was not in a position to offer underwritten paper. And the credibility of Cavenham was taking a knock from Warburgs which had examined his balance sheet and the company, and could see just how vulnerable Goldsmith was. Waddington, primed and directed by Warburgs, had now become highly critical. At the end of April 1966 he again wrote to shareholders. 'I think I can sum up your directors' views by saying that agreement to the Cavenham proposal would be equivalent to exchanging the substance of Singleton & Cole for the shadow of Cavenham,' he said. Goldsmith, he added, should 'come out into the open and make a realistic offer for the whole of the share capital.'

Within a week Goldsmith raised his offer. Cavenham's share price had risen from 5s 7½d in December 1965 when he opened negotiations to 7s 3d by early May. He increased his offer to two Cavenham shares, worth 14s 6d, for every Singleton share, valuing the company at £1.4m. Waddington, knowing that Singleton had hit tough times because of declining cigarette sales (they were affected by heavy duty increases in the budget) and by declining profit margins as a result of the shift to cheaper tipped cigarettes, gave in. He and Goldsmith later became friends, but in fact neither Slater nor Waddington had done Goldsmith a favour. To his group of troubled and problem companies, he had added another one.

On 13 May, Goldsmith once again confirmed the profit forecast of £215,000 for a financial period which had actually ended more than a month before on 2 April. He just made it, with a profit before interest of £216,749, a very slender margin indeed, and then only after including a 'special income' of £105,000 (after interest payments, taxes and other items, the net profit left to the group was only £33,000). But more importantly, he reaffirmed his target of profits 'substantially greater' for the following year which had now started. Within a few months he was forced to accept that he was not going to make it. He had hopelessly underestimated the cost and the difficulties of carrying out the huge reorganisation. Stock was overvalued or was not there, it was taking ages to get new machinery installed and working, much of the old management was hopeless, he had to find and train new people, and the economy, now in a tight financial squeeze as the Wilson government fought against the inevitable devaluation of sterling, was in a state of crisis. There had been a seven-week seamen's strike, followed by a major withdrawal of foreign money from Britain. On 14 July Bank Rate was raised from 6 to 7 per cent, a harbinger of the gathering economic storm. By the end of July Harold Wilson announced a package of measures which constituted the toughest deflation since 1949, including tight controls on hire purchase, a 10 per cent increase in indirect taxes (including tobacco), major cuts in government spending overseas, a travel allowance of £50 per person and, most controversially, a prices and incomes policy.

The effect on businesses everywhere was severe, but to Cavenham, vulnerable both to high interest rates and to higher indirect taxes, it was particularly harsh. That autumn Goldsmith warned shareholders that instead of profits being 'substantially' greater, they could be as much as £100,000 down. Even that was optimistic.

That autumn it became bitterly clear to Goldsmith that his reorganisation, far from saving the company, was going badly wrong. It was costing too much, taking too long, and not showing through in results. Two years after he started Cavenham, the company trembled on the edge of bankruptcy.

Goldsmith did everything he could to stave off financial collapse. His enthusiastic and immature plan, so confidently outlined in the *Cavenham News* of the autumn of 1966, was virtually abandoned. No matter what he did with the confectionery business, he could not get it right, and finally it was de Gunzberg who came up with an answer, or half an answer. Perrier by now had become Europe's largest manufacturer of soft drinks, controlling Vichy, Contrexeville, Pcshitt and Pepsi-Cola in France. It had 55 per cent of the total French soft drinks market, but had recently diversified into confectionery, buying up nine French confectionery companies, including Menier, Lindt (France) and other brands.

Perrier had not yet begun to reorganise them in a UK market which had been opened up to French competition with the prospect of joining the Common Market. On the other hand, Goldsmith's very expensive and painful reorganisation was just about complete, so his proposal was this: a fifty-fifty merger of the two businesses, each to keep their own profits for the first five years (or their losses in the first two), with Goldsmith to manage the joint venture. Perrier agreed, allowing Goldsmith to run the joint group which had sales of £15m in the two countries.

Goldsmith also announced a similar deal whereby Carr & Co. of Carlisle would manufacture Carr's Table Water Biscuits in the United States in partnership with the Harrell Corporation, but in the end that deal fell through.

There were a few bright spots: Slimcea and Procea were going well, increasing sales by 58 per cent in 1966/7 after a major advertising campaign. But in the overall context of the group, that was small stuff. The Singleton business was a major loss-maker, as was the confectionery wholesaling division.

As the months rolled by, an air of crisis not dissimilar to that which had hovered over his first little business in France now hung over the modern but unimpressive headquarters on the A4. The pressure on everyone was intense, with Goldsmith driving his team hard, but the figures continued to deteriorate as the cash flowed out. The group was heading for a loss of £1m, and something had to be sold.

Goldsmith found the answer in the most unexpected of places. The acquisition of Singleton & Cole, bought largely for its distribution business, was one of the principal causes of his problems. However, hidden away in the company were two small snuff businesses to which neither Slater, with his keenest eye, nor Waddington, who knew the business well, had paid much attention. Goldsmith had barely given them a thought, but to his amazement, as every other figure got worse, these snuff companies were rapidly increasing their profits. Margins on snuff, Goldsmith discovered, were enormous – it was made from waste tobacco, which could be bought for almost nothing, and sold for very high prices.

But there were no buyers for them in Britain and few in Europe, so he cast further afield. Conwood Corporation, based in Memphis, Tennessee, owned the American Snuff Company, formed after President Teddy Roosevelt broke up the tobacco monopoly. Barred from expanding in America, it responded with interest to a European acquisition.

The man Conwood chose to check out Singleton was John Tigrett, who was, like Jim Slater, to play an important role in the Goldsmith story from that point on. Tigrett is a remarkable man with an even more remarkable range of contacts around the world. He had built a fortune with his own toy business based in Tennessee, but then, aged 53, after the death of his two sons, had changed his life completely. He created a consultancy business advising some of the leading business figures of the day, notably Armand Hammer and Roy Thomson. He also knew Conwood whom he was advising on a major restructuring. The snuff business in America, like everywhere else, was in decline, but it had, Tigrett told them, 'an enormously long profit potential'.

Goldsmith had put the business into the hands of a broker who made contact with Conwood, who then called Tigrett. 'Look, there's some fellow in England who has got a snuff company,' and then proceeded to give him the figures. 'Those figures are no good,' said Tigrett instantly. He knew enough about the snuff business to know they were exaggerated. 'So what are we going to do about it?' asked the Conwood executive. 'You've advised us to watch out for a snuff company in Europe, and this is one.'

'Find out what the name of the fellow is and tell him I'll come over and see him in a couple of days,' replied Tigrett.

A few days later he flew to London and drove the few miles from the airport to Goldsmith's office. The place struck him as poor and shabby, and Tigrett was expecting the man who ran a snuff company out of offices like that to be of the same ilk. Goldsmith astonished him. He knew nothing about Tigrett's reputation as one of the shrewdest consultants on the international circuit, but quickly sensed a mind as clever as his own. Tigrett asked about the figures for the snuff companies, and Goldsmith went into them with a knowledge and depth that surprised even the American. 'He knew every figure for the industry, every name, every detail.' He initially assumed that Goldsmith had spent hours preparing himself for the meeting but as the conversation broadened, he realised this was not the case.

The following Sunday morning the two men met for breakfast at Goldsmith's house in Regent's Park. Goldsmith made no secret of his wish to sell. He wanted $2m, arguing that the companies were worth at least that, even to a forced seller. After breakfast they strolled out into the park, and Tigrett stopped.

'Jim, I'm not going to argue about the price,' he began, watching Goldsmith's face light up. 'But I'm only going to buy half.' Goldsmith's face fell through the floor. Half would only solve half his problems, and he desperately needed the whole.

If Tigrett agreed they were worth the price, why buy half? Why not the lot? he demanded. 'Because,' said Tigrett in his slow, southern drawl, 'I don't want to lose you.' According to Tigrett, he went on to say to a bemused and only half-flattered Goldsmith, 'You are the best financial brain I have ever come across, and I don't want to lose you.' He wanted a partnership.

That was all very well, remarked Goldsmith, but what was he going to do about the other half of the money he needed? Tigrett had thought of that. He would take Goldsmith to Switzerland, where he would arrange with some banks he knew to lend it. That way Goldsmith would get his $2m, but would also retain a half stake in the snuff businesses, with all the incentive he needed to make them perform. It was a far better deal than Goldsmith had expected.

A few days later Goldsmith and de Gunzberg accompanied their new American partner to Switzerland where Tigrett was as good as his word. They set up a new Swiss company, Conwood SA, which would be 50 per cent owned by Cavenham, 50 per cent by Conwood, into which the Goldsmith snuff companies were sold. This company then paid Cavenham the full price, £811,241, which it borrowed from the Swiss banks, another clever bit of financial juggling, which would add to the complexity but stave off the crisis. The value of the snuff companies on Cavenham's books was £76,100, so there was over £730,000 profit on the deal.

'That joint snuff company turned out to be the best company Jim Goldsmith ever had,' says Tigrett. 'Conwood made a lot of money out of it, and Cavenham made a lot of money out of it. In terms of the amount of money he put in, it was the best investment Jimmy Goldsmith ever made, the best deal he ever did in his whole life,' says Tigrett.

Yet even that was not enough. As the year wore on, so the cash continued to flow out, and Goldsmith was back in trouble. Yet his financial problems never seemed to affect his demeanour, at least not in front of the Cavenham executives. 'He always seemed very jovial, always laughing,' says a former executive. 'Most of us found it very difficult to assess him. He was such a different animal to anything we had seen before. He was very slim and had plenty of blond hair, ruddy complexion with piercing blue eyes, always immaculately dressed – beautifully tailored suits, looked very smart, a very attractive man.' The same executive also commented on Goldsmith's 'enormous grasp of reading balance sheets and figures – he could see things no one else could see. He was always leagues ahead of everyone and I was always impressed with him on that score. I was less impressed with what was actually happening to the companies.'

There is a curious and unexplained paradox here. Everyone he came into contact with, from the veteran international consultant Tigrett, to his own young directors and to bankers like Franklin, remarked on Goldsmith's exceptional financial skills, his ability to analyse and to act. In later years, when there was something to show for it, this would be a familiar theme. But at this time Cavenham, despite his stroke of luck with the snuff companies, was a financial disaster, weakest in the very areas where Tigrett perceived a financial genius. Was it just the power of his personality and his great presentational gifts which were so impressive, or was there substance as well?

There had been a great deal of share buying and stake swapping, but as far as the City was concerned, not a lot to show for it. On normal accounting methods, Goldsmith had missed several profit forecasts, and was, by any accounting standards, miles short of his latest one. He was acquiring a reputation as a wheeler-dealer, but not a very successful one, and laying the foundations for a degree of suspicion which he would later have difficulty in dispelling.

Why was there this gap between his obvious financial skills and his performance? The economic climate was bad, but others, notably Slater and a pair from Yorkshire, James Hanson and Gordon White, were thriving. Goldsmith was quick to criticise the quality of British management, but he was not doing much better. There was nothing particularly wrong with the industries he had selected: even in recession, the British public continued to eat sweets and biscuits, and to smoke. When he set up Cavenham, Goldsmith expressed his ideas for the company in the first issue of *Cavenham News*. Years later he would freely admit that 'almost every single idea I put down turned out to be wrong'. On the other hand what he could not show in his accounts, but what people like Tigrett and Franklin could glimpse, was the way in which he acknowledged his mistakes. He was now in the process of changing course to reflect both different circumstances and new ideas. He had done some good things, assembled a group of fine managers who were as enthusiastic about the direction of the company as he was, and who believed him when he said that, given a little time, the company would come right in a big way. From it all Goldsmith learned a profound lesson: 'How can you get it right first time? There are too many variables. It's only by changing that you discover what is right.'

The difficulty facing him that summer was: would Cavenham survive long enough to reach the promised land? Accounting tricks, the sale of assets and particularly the sale of the snuff companies had staved off a crash. But time and cash were running out.

The crisis finally broke at a dinner at Roland Franklin's home. The accountants that day delivered the latest profit figures, and it was only too clear that Cavenham was going to miss its profits forecast by a margin of at least £500,000. Franklin was with him as they read the accountants' report, and says he 'sort of turned the colour grey, and I was doing the same thing, except he couldn't see me doing it.'

'Jimmy, you know unless we have half a million pounds to put into this company, you're gone,' Franklin told him. Over dinner David Eastham, the senior partner of Cavenham's stockbrokers, Sebag & Company, delivered the same verdict. 'If a company misses its forecast by this much, it's customary in the City for the directors to make it up out of their own pockets,' he said. It was not at all customary, but Sebag had put its name to the forecast too, and would be severely embarrassed in the eyes of its clients when the figures were announced.

Eastham, his stockbroker, and Franklin, his merchant banker, were Goldsmith's principal City advisers. They were now delivering to him their joint advice: from somewhere, he must find £500,000 and 'gift' it to the company. Otherwise, Cavenham would fail.

Goldsmith's whole reputation hung on saving Cavenham. He had fought too many takeovers, made too many forecasts, sold too many shares to investors ever to recover if he lost them money now. Somehow he had to find the money, but as he flew to Paris the next day, he had only a vague idea of where he might get it from. As he says, not only did he not have £500,000, he didn't have £50,000. Yet at four that afternoon he rang Franklin in triumph. He and de Gunzberg would be putting £500,000 into Cavenham.

How had he found the money? In an ingenious way: his French company Gustin-Milical, run by the faithful Maurice Lignon, was profitable. De Gunzberg had a number of interests which he would pledge. Between them they produced enough security and enough guarantees to borrow from a number of French banks. They then lent it to Cavenham Investments, a private company which they jointly owned, and which had only one asset: over five million shares in the publicly quoted Cavenham Foods. If Cavenham had gone bust, these shares would have been worthless. But by injecting £500,000 into it, the shares would actually have a greater value.

So Cavenham Investments passed the £500,000 on to Cavenham Foods as a free gift 'to enhance that company's trading position' as it stated in the accounts.

It was a tricky, complex financial deal which would bemuse the City and the financial press for years afterwards. 'The press thought it was one of the most sinister things that had ever happened,' says Franklin. 'They couldn't understand it – a free gift of money to the company, not a loan or anything like that. It was cash.' It was, he adds, 'the best decision Jimmy ever made'.

Charles Raw and the *Sunday Times* as well as *Private Eye* later spent months trying to get to the bottom of this particular move, without finding anything other than financial juggling, again all perfectly legal, but so complex and so strange that they were convinced there had to be something wicked about it.

But once again Goldsmith had saved himself, albeit by a very fine margin, as the accounts at the end of that eventful year showed. The snuff companies and the £500,000 injection together were only £140,000 greater than the losses on factory closures, redundancies and trading. Without them, Cavenham for the year to 1 April 1967 would have lost £1m. More importantly, it would not have been able to pay its bills. Even with the injection and the snuff sale, there was no money for a dividend, and a net loss after all interest and other payments. The auditors, Price Waterhouse, were also not entirely happy with Goldsmith's methods of valuing goodwill in the balance sheet. Instead of giving Cavenham a clean bill of health, their report noted the amount of £950,000 attributed to goodwill by the directors who believed it was 'justified by the future prospects of the group. This is a question on which we do not feel able to express an opinion.'

This comment was more a 'reservation' than the dreaded 'auditors' qualification', but it was taken seriously enough by the City, and by the financial press. The black mark, however, was more than outweighed by relief at the fact that Cavenham was still there, and beginning to come right. Trading was looking up, but by now Goldsmith had learned caution. In December 1967 he told his shareholders that although the company was now trading profitably, and reorganisation costs had been accounted for, 'a firm forecast for the current year's trading is not yet possible.' But, he added, profits for 1968 'will demonstrate that the concept which led to the formation of Cavenham in August 1965 was soundly based.'

Frank Goldsmith never lived to see his younger son make the fortune he always believed he would. In the early months of 1967, as Jimmy Goldsmith battled for survival, Frank's health began to fail, and on 14 February he died, aged 88. *The Times* carried an obituary, briefly setting out his political career, his defeat of Bernard Shaw, his military record and his later career as a hotelier. ' "Monsieur le Major", as he was always called, was probably the leading figure in the French hotel industry in the interwar years and certainly the most popular. He was Chevalier of the Legion of Honour.'

Marcelle cut out *The Times* obituary and pasted it carefully into Frank's own scrapbook which recorded everything from his admission to Oxford to his political speeches, and now ended with his death. Underneath she wrote:

Nous nous sommes rencontrés en août 1927
Mariés juin 1929
40 ans de vie heureuse
J'aurais aimé celà pour nos fils
Hélas!

Ce sera peut-être pour nos petits enfants que
   nous aimons tellement.
       Marcelle

Jimmy, who had caused his father so much worry and concern, but had
also given him such secret amusement, was deeply upset. Although he
had only known him in his older years, and had had his battles and
disagreements, Frank had always been there to bail him out and to offer
advice and help. It was, he admitted years later, his need to impress Frank
as much as anything which had driven him on in business. 'A lot of what
I've done, I've done to satisfy my father, because it would have amused
him. I often wish he was alive today to see what I've accomplished.'

Their relationship when he was alive had been a strange one. Sir Hugh
Wontner, now president of the Savoy group, who knew Frank for more
than thirty years, said that Jimmy was always his main talking point, even
when he was at school. He remembers Frank flying to London every
Tuesday for a board meeting. 'He sat at our table for lunch, and then of
course the conversation was always about Jimmy – and Jimmy was always a
problem.' The stories were, Wontner recalls, always told with a hint of
pride and affection. Frank was neither censorious nor condemnatory, but
would tell him about a Jimmy escapade in a half-amused, half-scanda-
lised way. 'It was along the lines of "have you heard the latest. . . ?" '

Wontner and the other Savoy directors knew all about Jimmy's
gambling exploits, his troubles at Eton, how Jimmy knocked down his
tutor at his crammer in Kent, and much else. 'And yet,' says Wontner,
'Frank always used to say, "I know he will do very well one day." '
Wontner particularly remembers Frank's pleasure when Jimmy finally got
his little pharmaceutical business going. 'He was immensely proud of
that, absolutely delighted.'

A Tale of Two Women

While Jimmy Goldsmith was struggling with his embryonic empire, his old friend John Aspinall was also having his ups and downs. Although the two had seen less of each other while Goldsmith built his business in France, they remained the best of friends, talking regularly on the telephone, instantly settling back into their old relationship whenever they met. They had long recognised in each other similar qualities as misfits; they were two people who would always be apart from the rest of the world, but who shared an equal zest for living in it. They were very different people. Aspinall lacked the pulsing energy and intellectual power which Goldsmith brought to bear on any subject that caught his imagination, but he was more tolerant and forgiving than the excitable Jimmy. At this point – and for several years to come – Aspinall was the more dominant character in their close relationship. He had followed Goldsmith's every business move with great interest, listened to Teddy and Jimmy's wilder stories, and had invested what capital he could spare in Jimmy's ventures. They had from the beginning a relationship of complete trust, where neither held any secrets, and where each took genuine pleasure in the other's successes. But Goldsmith was part of Aspinall's circle rather than the other way round; Aspinall was the one who held forth in unstoppable flow from the top of the table. In his own zoological terminology, he was the dominant male of the grouping.

After Oxford, which he left without a degree, Aspinall continued in much the same way he always had, living off his wits, his gambling, his stepfather and his friends. He set up as an on-course bookmaker under the old nickname Teddy Goldsmith had given him, 'Aspers', only to be wiped out when eleven out of twelve favourites won at Kempton Park in two days. For seven months, with his friend Ian Maxwell-Scott, he rented a room in the Ritz where he ran a poker school. He was continually in debt, living far beyond his means, mixing with the big spenders of London society, dining in the best places, borrowing from one new friend to pay off another, lavishly entertaining whenever he was in funds. Regarded as one of the great raconteurs and storytellers in his time at Oxford, he had developed into a man with magnetic charm, his blond hair, blue eyes and infectious laugh making him the centre of any crowd.

His own story is almost as extraordinary as that of Goldsmith. He discovered he had Nordic blood by accident when he went to see his father, Robert Aspinall, who had by now retired from the Indian army. He had barely met Robert over the years, particularly since his mother had remarried Sir George Osborne, but Aspinall was going through one of his more desperate patches. He had debts of £2,000, he explained. Could his father see his way to lending it to him for a few months?

'I will do nothing of the sort,' replied Colonel Aspinall. 'You're nothing to do with me at all. I'm not your father, you see.'

Far from being shocked, Aspinall was intrigued. He persuaded his mother to confess all. She had, she told him, been lonely and unhappy in her marriage, and in India met a professional soldier (of Nordic descent) from Wick in Caithness, called George Bruce, with whom she had an affair. Her son had been conceived in India under a tamarisk tree after a dance. Aspinall tracked Bruce down to a flat in Campden Hill where he was greeted by a man in whom he instantly saw himself as a 63-year old, 'like Dorian Gray come to life'. Bruce had retired as a major-general after a distinguished army career, and eked out a very modest existence on the pension of a major which he supplemented by painting meticulously correct regimental portraits.

It was a story which Aspinall, instead of hiding, embroidered and developed over his dinner table, adding that when he had made a bit of money, he secretly supported his real father by tracking down the gallery where his paintings were sold. Posing as a Greek, he bought the lot, and asked for more. On the next occasion he saw Bruce, his father was in higher spirits. 'We've got something to celebrate today,' he said. 'Some Greek lunatic has bought all my pictures and wants more of the things.'

Aspinall visited Jimmy in Paris often, and joined him and Ginette in the south of France in the summer, where no matter how badly off he was, Jimmy always seemed to be able to rent a large house. Even at his lowest financial moments, he was invariably the host – from his earliest teens, Goldsmith had been uncomfortable accepting hospitality from anyone, and friends such as Digby Neave say they have never even been able to buy him dinner; he has always insisted on paying.

Neither Aspinall nor he had any money, but both managed to live well, never worrying about debts which they knew would somehow get paid (as they did), and spending hours debating the politics of the day, on which they were both increasingly out of sympathy with the rising level of socialism in Britain. In the evening, they would adjourn to the casino.

In 1955 Aspinall began to develop the system that was to make him one of the best-known and most successful gamblers in the world. He organised games of baccarat and roulette in a flat he rented behind Harrods, getting a friend, in return for half the profit, to provide the bank for the evening. Then he discovered a far more satisfactory way. He was invited to a *chemin de fer* party at which the organiser had installed a slot at the back of the table. Down this went 22 per cent of all the money staked. 'Very nice little game,' he explained to Aspinall. '£1,000 a week tax-free, thirty times a year, £30,000, can't complain.'

A century-old law forbade games of chance taking place in the same establishment on a regular basis, but there were ways around that. Aspinall rented a flat in Upper Brook Street in Mayfair, persuaded a gallery to lend him a Canaletto and a Pannini 'on approval', got his mother to provide the best food that could be found in London, and held his first solo party. He made £1,350 profit; the following week he made £3,250, and £5,000 the week after that. He shifted premises after every two games to remain within the law and his games soon became well known to all the big punters in London. It was wonderful money, but on the other hand a single bad night could wipe him out. At one game, someone lost £16,400 and when his cheque bounced Aspinall tracked him to the club Les Ambassadeurs, grabbed him by the hair and dragged him across the table. Convinced that a madman was beating up a fellow diner, the actor Robert Mitchum joined in, raining blows on Aspinall, who was finally extricated by his friends Mark and Lady Annabel Birley.

In 1956 he married a model, Jane Hastings, a brittle-looking beauty, whom he spotted at a fashion show at Fortnum & Masons. He took her to Sandown, gave her £100 to gamble, and was greatly impressed when she coolly came back and asked for more. When they married at Caxton Hall the bailiffs broke in. The Aspinalls slipped out the back way, and the writ was served on another blue-eyed blond man, Dominic Elwes.

But his gambling parties, despite the damaging losses, began to bring him a handsome income. Goldsmith was often there, as was Teddy, and they became familiar figures in a very particular London society. In June 1957 it was reported that the Duke of Devonshire had joined 'the group of rich men who support Mayfair gambler John Aspinall's all-night betting parties'. He had attended one at 27 Belgrave Square a few nights before and, after a few hours of *chemin de fer*, went home with losses of £3,000. But that was nothing in comparison to a young American millionaire, one Gerry Albertini, who was reported to have lost £24,000, a great deal of money in 1957, and was, according to the reports, 'consulting his lawyers about his losses'. Albertini was actually a good friend of both Aspinall and Goldsmith, and never did sue.

Later that year Aspinall organised what he boasted at the time was 'London's most fantastic gambling party since the war' in yet another flat in Upper Brook Street, which he had fully equipped as a casino with tables, scoops, rakes, card shoes and the rest of the equipment. He brought in two of the best croupiers from Ostend who would be well known to most of the gambling circle in London, laid on limitless quantities of free champagne and caviar, and sent out hundreds of invitations to an 'at home' party. Many of the so-called 'Princess Margaret set', the gay young blades of the time, were there, including the Marquis of Milford Haven, cousin of the Duke of Edinburgh, and Alan Clark, later a Tory minister. Lady Osborne, his mother, laid out her now famous game pie, the accepted staple diet at these parties, and was quoted as saying she thought the party was 'fun', adding that 'several people said they hoped we wouldn't be raided.'

This was almost a dare to the authorities, who were by now keeping Aspinall's games under surreptitious observation, although he was careful to stay within the rules which stated that it was an offence to assist in keeping a common gaming house, the latter in law being a house 'where a large number of persons habitually congregate for the purposes of gambling'. The police in Mayfair were more familiar with the law than the Paddington police, who raided Aspinall's premises when he moved into their bailiwick to be greeted by a butler in white tie and tails. They charged Aspinall and Lady Osborne with 'keeping a common gaming house', to which Aspinall's mother replied: 'Young man, there was nothing common here until you walked in.'

The next morning, to the delight of the press, 24 of the best-known names including several peers, a cousin of Prince Philip, and Lady Jane Willoughby, train-bearer to the Queen, appeared in Marylebone Magistrates Court. There was a commotion outside when the prostitutes, who normally came up before the magistrates first every morning, had to wait an extra hour. Aspinall appeared in the box in his sable-collared coat; his mother and most of the other women wore mink.

Aspinall was repentant, even indignant. Encouraged by Goldsmith, by

Mark Birley and his other friends, he fought and won his case, opening the floodgates for many other such games. It was too much for the authorities and within a year the government proposed to change the law. By 1960 a new Gaming Act, generally known as 'Aspinall's Law', was on the statute book, basically aimed at closing the loopholes which Aspinall had exploited. Although gambling was legalised, all the stakes had to be returned to the players, with no percentage down the *cagnotte*. The premises where gaming took place had to be an established club, not of a 'merely temporary nature'. The thrust of the Bill was summarised by one supporter in the House of Commons who said these clauses had been inserted 'to stop this country from becoming a casino country', adding that if people wanted to 'play these games, let them go to France'.

Aspinall's game by that stage was probably the biggest in Europe, with the chips ranging up to £500, and big-time gamblers from all over the world came to play. His own income was variously estimated at between £100,000 and £250,000 a year, and in one 18-month period he probably did clear £350,000. He lived well, spending in style, and ploughing back much of his profits into his game. Jane had learned to love the life of Royal Ascot and Goodwood, and soon replaced his mother as hostess at the gambling parties, where she was known among his friends as 'the Spirit of Park Lane'. By the late 1950s, when Goldsmith was slogging away with Selim Zilkha (but visiting Aspinall's parties at night), his friend was driving around London in a Rolls-Royce, had an expensive apartment, and was hunting for a large house in the country.

When the new gaming bill was announced it was greeted by those who resented his success – and there were many, particularly relatives of those who had lost money at his establishment – as 'spiking his guns'. Aspinall's reaction was typical. He organised the biggest party yet, in the flat of Claus von Bulow, at a cost of £10,000. He flew in an 18-piece orchestra from Monte Carlo, charged £35 a head for tickets (a monstrous price in 1959), and was greatly oversubscribed. 'There was no longer any question of his being accepted into the magic circle of the Top People,' wrote his biographer Brian Masters. 'Rather it was they who wished to be accepted onto Aspinall's guest list; you were not really a Top Person if you were unwelcome.' By now he had achieved such notoriety that he found himself the centre of a considerable public debate on the morality of gambling, and also on the inequities of class-ridden British society. Paul Johnson in the *New Statesman*, in a piece which quoted Disraeli's *Two Nations* (the rich and the poor), drew a graphic contrast between the life of the average working man and that of a property developer and the sybaritic circle which frequented Aspinall's parties. Aspinall, he said, who was reported to 'make' £50,000 a year tax-free, and the 'exotic creatures' who fed from his carcass, were symbols of the rottenness which was poisoning Britain.

The benefits Aspinall's friends derived from their activities, Johnson wrote, 'bear no relation to what they contribute, nor to the economic well-being of the nation. Their manner of life throws into a fearful perspective the moral criteria of a society which recently jailed a widow for concealing that she had supplemented her dole by taking in sewing.' Aspinall and his empty-headed guests, he concluded, were a 'squirming social scum' which would be swept into oblivion by time and history.

Aspinall made no attempt to rebut the accusation. Gambling was as old as the human race, he would point out, and if people wanted to do it, why shouldn't they? He had a low opinion of humans in general, increasingly preferring the company of animals. But he did enjoy gambling, and he did like gamblers, even when, as he was the first to admit, they were bores. He took an unapologetic stance over the morality of his business, writing some years later, 'I would happily separate any drunken youth from the maximum he could handle, or his family could handle, without the slightest compunction.' Indeed lack of compunction, as well as inability to hold a grudge, he regarded as two of the essential virtues for a professional gambler (he could never understand Goldsmith's lifelong grudges against those who had harmed him).

To the extent that Goldsmith was part of the Aspinall circle, what Johnson wrote was aimed at him too. He enjoyed a sybaritic life, frequented the gaming tables, had several women in tow, and in his business life was shuffling share stakes between his companies at bewildering speed. By Johnson's standards, he was a fairly 'exotic creature'. Yet Johnson's rhetoric rankled with him. He would argue that his wheeling and dealing (though he would never call it that) was vital to the process of restructuring the industries he had entered, and helped to keep his head above water until the results eventually came through. Goldsmith had never encountered in France anything approaching the type of class divide Johnson described, and was angry at it. He regarded himself as a serious businessman, working harder than any other businessman he knew. If he wanted to play hard too, that was his business.

When Aspinall began to make real money he moved with Jane into a basement apartment in Eaton Place, but that soon became overcrowded, not with people, but with animals. First he paid £20 for a Capuchin monkey (which is still alive), then he added a tigress, Tara (which has nearly 200 descendants today) and finally a pair of eight-month-old Himalayan bears. Taking the tigress and bears for a walk in the centre of London posed obvious problems, and in 1958, largely on the proceeds of a win on a horse called Prelone at Newmarket, he paid £6,000 for a house in Kent. Howletts, to which Jimmy Goldsmith would come many times in later years, was a deserted Palladian mansion near Canterbury in Kent. It was to be the base for one of the most extraordinary – and successful – private zoos in the world. Aspinall brought in the young architect Philip Jebb and perhaps the best-known interior decorator of the time, John Fowler, co-founder of the firm Colefax & Fowler, to renovate it for him. The restoration of house and gardens would take five years and cost £80,000.

If the 1960 Gaming Act had been designed to put an end to the Aspinall style of gaming, the opposite proved true; the Act ushered in a new era of betting shops, bingo halls and casinos, all unknown to Britain in the 1950s. More than 50 casinos opened in two years, many of them catering for tourists. Few of these were in direct competition with Aspinall's game, but when the lavishly appointed Crockford's opened, he began to feel the pinch. He decided to open a club himself.

In 44 Berkeley Square he found the perfect premises. Built by William Kent in 1740–2, Number 44 was regarded as a masterpiece of Palladian architecture. The house was also heavily conserved to the point where no commercial company would touch it. Inside it was shabby, but still grand, virtually unchanged since it was built. A wonderful staircase, described by Walpole as 'as beautiful a piece of scenery and, considering the space, of art as can be imagined', led up to a grand salon which was one of the finest rooms of its period in London.

Aspinall took a 21-year lease from Samuel Properties for £12,500 a year. Again he hired John Fowler to decorate it, with Jebb as consulting architect. They entered into the spirit of the house, turning it into the most beautiful gambling premises in Europe. Robert Harling, writing on the history of the club, said that if one 'had to lose a million, this is the place to do so in style'. At the back Aspinall created a small dining room looking out onto a small garden, a room that would become famous for something else in later years. He decided to call it the Clermont Club, after the first Earl of Clermont, who had lived there and who won the Derby in 1785. Membership would be limited to 600, each paying 20 guineas a year, and when it opened it included among its members five dukes, five marquesses, 19 earls, one royal (Prince William of Gloucester), an actor (Peter Sellers), two cabinet ministers, two Gettys, two Packers, two Arab princes and two Goldsmiths.

The Clermont Club was to be an important venue for Goldsmith. But so was the club that was created in the basement.

The man who rented Aspinall's basement was a 32-year-old Eton contemporary of Goldsmith's (although they had not known each other there), Mark Birley. Six foot five and very good-looking, he was the son of the painter Sir Oswald Birley. After Eton, he had gone to Oxford 'for a short time', before going to work for the JWT advertising agency. He had started the London branch of Hermes and now proposed opening his own special brand of nightclub, catering for much the same class of person as Aspinall upstairs.

If Birley was striking, his wife was even more so. Lady Annabel Vane-Tempest-Stewart before she married, she was the youngest daughter of the Marquess of Londonderry, who had inherited large estates in Cleveland, near Newcastle-upon-Tyne, and in Ireland before the war. Her grandmother, one of the most famous hostesses of the 1920s and 1930s, gave one of the grandest balls of the 1952 debutante season for Annabel, the first private function the young Queen Elizabeth II attended after her father's death. Daughters of marquesses were not expected to work for a living in those days, but at the age of 18 Annabel's father told her firmly: 'You've got two choices: either you go up to the estate and manage something, or you get a job in London. The one thing you're not going to do is sit there.' She happily opted for the job in London, and her father arranged for her to start work as a journalist on the *Daily Mail*. Before she started, however, she met Mark Birley, and they were married when she was 19. She was a tall, willowy brunette, with what the gossip columnists called 'sherry-coloured' eyes. Her face was too strong to be classically beautiful in the sense that Sally or even Jane Aspinall was, but in her different way, she was much more attractive than either of them, with a vitality which made her stand out in any company.

Birley's club was to be dark, mysterious and private, but with the same essential feeling of half country house, half private club which Aspinall's designers had created upstairs. It was a complex bit of construction, running from the area at the front, which was William Kent's work, then tunnelling under the house, the garden and the mews at the back. Birley had a clear vision of how the basement would look and work, but found it difficult to persuade anyone else of its merits. He struggled to find backers, envying the apparent ease with which Aspinall attracted investors for the Clermont. 'He really had to go cap in hand,' says Annabel. But, within a few months of opening, the club, which he called Annabel's (originally it was to be called Black's), was to become the most famous, chic nightspot not just in London but in the world. As Masters wrote in his Aspinall biography, 'Thus the two symbols of extravagant 1960s' hedonism, the Clermont Club and Annabel's, existed one above the other in the same building.'

Aspinall planned a grand opening for the Clermont, inviting 200 people to a gala ball, for 6 November 1962. But a month before the work was finished, he was faced with disaster. For some years he had befriended an American businessman called Eddie Gilbert, one of the whizzkids of Wall Street in the 1950s. Gilbert had bailed out Aspinall several times when he hit serious financial problems, but now it was the other way around. Aspinall had invested £150,000 in shares, 50 per cent of it paid up, in Gilbert's companies when in late 1962 Gilbert went spectacularly bust, the shares falling from $32 to zero in three days. Gilbert was charged with unauthorised withdrawal of funds from his companies – embezzlement in other words – and fled to Brazil, where Aspinall, although he had not only lost all his money but owed £75,000 to his stockbrokers on top, flew to see him. He and his wife Jane spent a week trying to cheer Gilbert up, borrowing money to pay for his hotel, hatching elaborate and far-fetched plans to help him recover his reputation and fortune. Gilbert eventually went to the famous Sing Sing prison in New York where Aspinall continued to see him, passing large-denomination dollar bills through the grille.

This disaster nearly killed the Clermont Club before it opened. Aspinall's stockbrokers pointed out that unless he paid his £75,000, they would be 'hammered', the old Stock Exchange practice of being put out of business. He borrowed the money from a merchant bank and paid it back over the next 14 months, and somehow scrambled together enough money to open as planned.

Jimmy Goldsmith, of course, was at the openings of both clubs. The party for Annabel's in March 1963, was the event of the season. Mark and Annabel had invited all their friends and prospective members, but there were so many gatecrashers (including, according to contemporary reports, Peter O'Toole) that the underground basement became a clammy smoke-ridden nightmare. It was nearly dawn before the crush thinned out, and at the very end of the party there were just two couples left on the small dance floor: Mark and Annabel Birley, and Jimmy Goldsmith and his model, a close friend of Annabel's, who knew all about their fiery relationship. She had attended an engagement party Jimmy gave for her, and was kept abreast of events which seemed to change by the week in what was a notoriously on-off affair. Like everyone else, Annabel was also aware that Ginette and the children were somewhere in the background, but Ginette never featured in this area of Goldsmith's life.

When the two clubs in Berkeley Square first opened, they were connected by a spiral staircase, so that Mark's members could slip upstairs to gamble and Aspinall's could go down to dance, mingle or dine. Annabel was often at the basement club, running the disco in the early days and generally helping out. She did not enjoy the place, simply because she was not a night person. For her it was work. It was work for Mark too, but he relished it, starting in the early evening, working until the early hours. Annabel had three young children (two sons and a daughter) by Mark, and that meant she had to be up early to see them off to school. They lived in one of the most exquisite little houses in London; Pelham Cottage was in the heart of South Kensington, yet was so hidden away that few knew of its existence. It had its own grounds, the only other house visible being that of Maxwell Joseph who occupied what was by common consent one of the best houses in central London. Mark Birley, with his perfect taste and style, had turned the cottage into a gem, and Annabel loved it.

Mark the night owl arrived home at breakfast time and slept through the day, Annabel, the early bird, was up and about before seven, but slumped in the evening. As the nightclub boomed, so Mark spent fewer and fewer waking hours at home, and as her children grew so Annabel spent more time with them. Without immediately noticing what was happening to them, their marriage was coming apart.

Shortly after their respective clubs opened, Aspinall and Mark Birley had a disagreement over the use of the wine-cellar. It seemed a minor matter, but it developed into a full-scale row. The two men stopped speaking (they have barely spoken since). The connecting staircase was closed, never to re-open. But Aspinall remained a friend and fan of Annabel's and to some extent it was he who pushed Jimmy Goldsmith in her direction. Annabel was sitting on her own at a table in the club one night in the autumn of 1963, waiting for Mark to return from sorting out a problem in the kitchen, when Jimmy Goldsmith's tall figure loomed over her. Could he join her?

*

Lady Annabel was now 29, an intelligent, thoughtful and strong-willed person. Mark had been her first serious boyfriend, and in their ten years of marriage there had been no one else in her life. She was not contemplating taking a lover, and certainly not Jimmy Goldsmith whom, if she thought about it at all, she viewed with a degree of disdain. Later she would say she found him 'jet-setty', using the word as pejorative, and in the 1950s sense: more 'café society', one of the faster, slicker, partying set of nouveau riche, not terribly acceptable in the drawing rooms of the English upper classes. She would use phrases such as, 'he was simply not my cup of tea' or, 'he was not part of my life'. 'To me he was very much Paris' – and very much on the periphery of her world. She had been aware of his existence for years, of course, but 'aware' only in the most uninterested sense. She read about his marriage and the death of Isabel when she came back from honeymoon with Mark, but it was several years later before she became conscious of him. It was at one of Aspinall's parties, with a baby tiger cub running around, when Jane Aspinall pointed at a figure sitting on the floor playing backgammon. 'That's Jimmy Goldsmith,' she said.

Later they would discover an odd little link between them. During the war, the Marquess of Londonderry's house had been requisitioned by the military, and the family moved around among a series of rented houses. One of them by chance was the Brown House in Worplesdon Hill, near Woking, owned by Frank Goldsmith's brother Edward. As a boy, Jimmy had sometimes spent school holidays there, and knew it well. His uncle often mentioned 'those dreadful Londonderry children' who had lived in the house during the war. Annabel's particular memory was of a portrait of a lady with a very low-cut dress, which they used for target practice with their bows and arrows. 'I was brought up hearing of those dreadful, uncontrollable children who showered arrows at my great-grandmother's tits!' Goldsmith told her.

That night in Annabel's Jimmy was at his most disarming, and soon Annabel was having her first affair. In the beginning – and for a year or two – she saw it as no more than a bit of excitement in a life which had been growing dull. Nevertheless, she did not tell Mark, who suspected nothing. When she first met Jimmy, her eldest son Rupert was seven and just going off to boarding school, but the other children were at home, and she would not leave them. So she would slip out in the evening, meet Jimmy at the Ritz, have dinner there in his room, and then return to Pelham Cottage well before Mark returned at four or five in the morning.

She found Goldsmith full of surprises. For a start he was not the playboy she imagined – he may have played hard but he was putting in a 12-to-14-hour working day. He was also passionate – and remarkably knowledgeable – about whatever he discussed, mostly the way in which Britain was declining as the role of the state advanced. Annabel had strong views of her own, and Goldsmith had never encountered this in a woman before. Ginette never argued or debated with him. In Annabel he had met a spiritual match.

She also discovered Goldsmith was as happy as she was to stay home in the evenings. Aspinall, still annoyed at Mark and fond of Annabel, encouraged the new relationship and gradually it became more open. Jimmy began taking her with him to Paris overnight, where Ginette knew nothing of it either. When she did finally tell Mark, her affair with Jimmy had continued for more than two years. Mark was desperately upset, as much because so many people in London knew about it as by Annabel's infidelity. He experienced a phase of considerable bitterness towards Goldsmith, but oddly enough Jimmy was the more jealous. He hated the idea of Annabel returning each evening to Mark's house and Mark's bed, and increasingly insisted it had to be all or nothing.

Mark and Annabel, however, went on living together in Pelham Cottage for several more years. Mark at first believed the relationship would burn itself out, and he was prepared to wait. He worried about the effect on the children, about what people would say, and he remained in love with Annabel. Jimmy on the other hand was not looking for another affair, but something more from Annabel.

There is an enduring myth about Jimmy's sex life at this time – and from this time onwards. There never were two wives (or even three in later years), or even two women with equal status in his life. Ginette had been at a great disadvantage once Goldsmith had emerged from his trauma in the years after Isabel's death. She was pretty, intelligent and devoted, but she was never a match for him, and their relationship was always an unequal one. That suited him perfectly during his years in France, but there was probably never a time when he was faithful to Ginette, and early in their relationship she had had to decide, if she wanted Jimmy, to accept that there would be other women in his life too.

Again there is a myth that she, and the other women in his life, would accept his polygamous nature with good-natured, or at least resigned, equanimity. It was never like that. Ginette had gone through an extremely difficult emotional time, and would continue to do so for years. Goldsmith assured her again and again that, whatever happened, he would never abandon her, that she was part of his life, and that, although he was in love with someone else, he loved her too. Her friends and family must have told her they had heard all that before. She was married to Jimmy, but in circumstances where she was expected to surrender her position as wife to someone in England she had never met. Ginette was not glamorous like his girlfriends in Paris and London, and she felt extraordinarily vulnerable. Goldsmith she knew had proposed marriage to Sally before he proposed marriage to her, and even when that fell through, rumours about the other women continued to reach her.

And yet, while his affair with Annabel was still relatively secret, Goldsmith decided to bring Ginette back to London. Ginette was more at home in Paris where on the whole she had Jimmy to herself. But at the end of 1965 Jimmy decided London was now his home, he wanted his children closer.

There were probably good reasons for this. Isabel was now eleven, and was not an easy child. Her childhood had been a strange, and by no means happy one. Nanny Cockbill was one of those very grand, snobby English nannies, who boasted of the great households she had previously worked in, and who attempted to bring Isabel up as a perfectly mannered English child. 'She even curled my hair in perfect little ringlets, a sort of Latino Shirley Temple,' says Isabel. Although Goldsmith had won custody, she was still half Patino, and her grandparents, her aunt Christina and her cousins featured as prominently in her life as the Goldsmiths did. From her earliest days, there was a considerable conflict between the two families over how she should be brought up, and she was aware she had to tread carefully for fear of offending one or the other. Jimmy was completely atheistic, and disparaging when she returned from a Patino visit with her prayer book and pictures of the Virgin. He didn't want her going to church, and even at age six she was subjected to a tirade against religion. It was 'stupid' and 'pathetic', designed to keep down the masses, he told her.

When she stayed with her maternal grandmother, she was subjected to a different kind of pressure. 'Where's your prayer book?' the duchess would demand. 'Why don't you know your prayers? How many times have you been to church?' Isabel remembers her visits as a nightmare, made worse by her return to her father's jibes.

She soon learned she had to keep her thoughts to herself, confiding neither to Patino nor to Goldsmith. 'Whenever I see children today, and I see how impulsive they are, I am always surprised because I never remember being like that.' No one told her the story of her mother's death – she was simply aware there was something deeply distressing, which neither her father nor either of her grandmothers would tell her about. Isabel never asked, sensing it was a forbidden subject, but she remembers wondering why, unlike everyone else, she had no mother. Was it, she wondered, a punishment? It was a difficult subject for Goldsmiths and Patinos alike, and they handled it by not talking about it. Eventually, she found a pile of yellow cuttings in one of Marcelle's trunks, and read for the first time the story of her own birth.

Isabel knew all about punishments. Because she was born two months prematurely and survived – a rare event in the 1950s – and then because of the court battle, she was regarded as delicate almost to the point of needing permanent hospitalisation. Nanny Cockbill exaggerated, for her own reasons, her fragility, determined to persuade her father and grandparents that only she, Nanny Cockbill, could care for her. When Isabel played up, her nanny threatened her with more medicine.

Marcelle was there at the beginning of her life but dropped more into the background when Ginette moved in. For the first five years, Isabel was on medication – pills to help her sleep, electroencephalogram checks for trauma. Eventually, Goldsmith snapped, 'There's nothing wrong with this little girl,' and fired the nanny. Isabel came off all medication, slept perfectly, and health-wise never looked back.

She was five when Manes was born, which was another shock for her. The nanny had kept her away from Ginette, and now Ginette had her own child. Isabel, already isolated, became a very lonely child. Her life continued to be full of rules that she knew she couldn't break but which were often difficult to fathom. In the house of the Duchess of Durcal there was a set of rules, conflicting with those of her father's house. When she was eight, she went skiing in Lech, Austria, with her aunt Christina and her cousins. She was cold and miserable and because of Jimmy's ferocity on the subject, she had not taken her prayer book, as the duchess insisted she always must. Her aunt chided her for her lack of prayer book, but insisted she accompany the others to church. When she got home, Jimmy accused her angrily of disobeying him. A few weeks later her grandmother Patino asked if she had brought her prayer book on holiday. Terrified of the formidable duchess, she answered 'yes'. The next time she stayed, the duchess confronted her. 'I spoke to the nanny, who said you didn't have your prayer book. You're a liar. Write down for me "I am a liar" a thousand times.' It was by no means the only time the duchess made her write out her lines.

On the other hand, the duchess, in different mood, could be delightful to her. Isabel, beautifully turned out and every hair in place, would turn up, nervously clutching her prayer book, and would be greeted with presents and love.

She adored Frank, whom she called 'Popski'. He was into his eighties, but she would join her Goldsmith cousins, Teddy's children Dido and Clio, at the Carlton in Cannes at Easter. The staff fussed over the third generation of Goldsmiths to stay at the hotel, where Frank escorted her into the dining room to sit beside him for lunch. She sang children's songs to him, which she had never done to Jimmy. One of her favourite memories of him is of how she used to massage cologne into his head.

Possibly because Isabel resented Manes, Ginette may have in turn resented her. Isabel felt that Manes was shown great favouritism by his mother and by Jimmy, while she was left out. Her Patino relatives at least made her welcome, part of the family, with the result that she grew up feeling much more of a Patino than a Goldsmith. As she grew older, she complained to her father that Manes could do no wrong, while she could do no right – and she blamed Ginette, who, she said, hated her. But Jimmy wasn't around very much, and when he was, she felt that he too favoured Manes and, later, Alix. Frank had been a gentle, affectionate father to Teddy and Jimmy, as Jimmy would be in later life to his younger children. But in his twenties, he was impatient, busy, and perhaps had too many other emotional commitments to get close to his eldest child. In later life, Isabel would sometimes say she wished the Patinos had won the custody battle after all – then she could have got to know her father as an adult, when her relationship with him became much better, rather than as a child.

Life was not easy for Ginette either, who had to cope with the money problems Jimmy ignored, with the children, with Isabel's resentment of her, and with continual moves from apartment to apartment. She also had to put up with the insults of the Duchess of Durcal, who couldn't be expected to like her – and didn't. 'She made Ginette's life very difficult,' says one family member. The duchess was highly critical of Ginette's family background, of her education, her manners, her appearance and much else. Once, when she was ten, Isabel sent her grandmother a Christmas card early in December. 'Both Ginette and Isabel were cursed by her – only tradespeople sent out cards so early, she said, and Ginette should have known better,' says the family member.

Isabel's first language as a child, because of her nanny, was English – which she spoke also to her father and grandfather. Then, when her first nanny left, and Ginette took over, she spoke French and forgot most of her English. Now, with the move to London, she was faced with learning English again.

This was the family that Jimmy brought to a new house he found in Chester Terrace, Regent's Park. Annabel arranged for Isabel to go to her old school in Lewes, which was probably unsuitable for her: it was a very English girls' boarding school, where most of the pupils were from the local Sussex area. Isabel stuck out as a foreigner, and she was miserable there. Her father, she believed, took no interest in her education.

Manes, a sweet-natured boy, had problems too. He was behind at school, and Ginette eventually took him to a specialist. He was diagnosed as severely dyslexic, and Jimmy recognised some of his own symptoms from his early days at school. Jimmy and Ginette took Manes out of his school in Brighton and put him into Millfield, where his father had begun his education in England, and which had grown remarkably over the years under Boss Meyer's leadership. Meyer remembered Jimmy very well. He asked Ginette how he was getting on, remarking that, when he had been a pupil there, 'he was very bright but unable to apply it'. Meyer was one of the few who had believed in him from the outset – he and Frank.

Ginette and the children were to stay in London for three and a half years, while Jimmy's relationship with Annabel became more and more public. He still had businesses in France, but now he took Annabel with him, leaving Ginette in London. He would spent many other week-ends with Annabel, and, since he worked late, or was out to dinners or to the Clermont, Ginette saw little of him.

In the summer of 1969 she persuaded him that it would be better if she went back to Paris. Isabel, now 15, and Alix would go with her while Manes stayed behind at Millfield. By now they had enough money to buy a house, she argued, and Jimmy readily agreed. While he battled on with Cavenham, she went househunting, and one day, in the rue Monsieur, behind Les Invalides, on the left bank, she found the perfect place: a large, completely private house, with its own large garden, hidden from the busy city. 'Monsieur', after whom the street was named, was Louis XIV's brother, known as 'Monsieur Frère du Roi', and the house had been built around what had at one stage been the royal stables. Cole Porter lived there in the 1930s and wrote some of his Paris songs in the room which Goldsmith adopted as his study.

The house had an extra feature which suited him well: it was already divided into two, each side totally self-contained, on two sides of a courtyard and garden. From the start Ginette lived in one side, and Jimmy had his own quarters, where he had his study and his books, in the other.

Goldsmith now had two households, in Regent's Park and in Paris. Annabel continued to live in her small house in Kensington with Mark

Birley and their children, but Mark was now seen around town with other women, and had rented a mews house nearby.

Annabel originally had told only a very few of her closest friends of her relationship with Jimmy. Men like John Aspinall and Dominic Elwes, who had staged his own runaway marriage with the heiress Tessa Kennedy, were hardly discreet, and the news spread. Goldsmith himself hated subterfuge, so once Mark had been told by Annabel, the barriers were down. The Londonderrys were not so happy with the situation, and for years Annabel had aunts who would not speak to her (although one of her aunts had actually married Lord Jessel, a cousin of Frank Goldsmith). Annabel, too, was desperately anxious not to embarrass or hurt Mark or the children, so the subterfuge dragged on. Goldsmith could distance himself from emotional problems. He had his business, his travel, his gambling or his growing interest in politics – which he hoped might be his long-term career, once he had made enough money to afford it.

13

Madame Beaux

Fathers can often be more important to their sons at the end of their lives, or even after their deaths, than before. When Sir Keith Murdoch died in 1951, he had only a modest shareholding in the *Melbourne Herald* and *Weekly Times* group, a company he had built but never owned. His son Rupert swore he would always retain a controlling shareholding in his own company, however big it grew – and however much he had to borrow. Similarly, Jimmy Goldsmith had always resented the fact that his father never actually owned the Société des Hôtels Réunis, even if the rest of the world believed he did. In Frank's old age, Jimmy, for the first time, began to take an interest in the hotel group. Monsieur le Major now had very few shares in it; in his declining years he had lived off capital, and gradually sold most of his shares to his fellow directors. Teddy had neither the interest nor the ability to attempt to do what Rupert Murdoch did (he eventually bought the *Melbourne Herald* group for A$2.5 billion), but Jimmy did.

The board of Hôtels Réunis was old-fashioned and aristocratic: Major Frank Goldsmith was the chairman, but there were also two cousins: Comte Jean Pastre, whose mother was a Goldschmit and who was said to have had a dubious war career (Jimmy was always told he had been a collaborator, but he found him a wonderfully cynical character) and Gilbert de Goldschmit-Rotschild. Then there was the Prince de Faucigny-Lucinge, an uncle of Valery Giscard d'Estaing. It was a very elderly board where everyone was an amateur and a gentleman. The company shrank with Frank's departure from France in 1940, and never had the money, the management or the drive to rebuild itself. It owned the Scribe and the Lotti in Paris and the Carlton in Cannes, but the management business of other hotels had been Frank's private business, quite separate from the Hôtels Réunis group, and entirely dependent on his ability to provide a service. As he became older and then retired, so it disappeared.

Even in the early 1950s the board viewed the young Jimmy with grave suspicion, and when Frank suggested making him a director, they gently informed him that they didn't think he would suit. The company did nothing other than run its three hotels, which it did properly and well, and there was no desire on anyone's part to do any more. Frank, who was not a man who relished unpleasantness or a fight, backed away. 'They all viewed me, not without reason, as a loose cannon,' says Jimmy.

When a vacancy did come up in the mid-1950s, instead of putting Jimmy on the board, they elected Marcelle. 'I was very fond of my mother, but she was not a businesswoman. She knew nothing about it whatsoever. So I rather resented that, because it was a bit of a family company.'

By 1965, when Frank's health was failing, Jimmy was making enough money to do something about the Hôtels Réunis. That same year the opportunity to buy the freehold of the Carlton Hotel in Cannes came up, and the board decided to take it. To raise the money it went to the Paris Bourse, and Jimmy seized the chance to increase his shareholding considerably. He arranged a credit line and began buying shares. He also took charge of Frank's remaining shareholding, and demanded a place on the board. When he heard, Frank was secretly delighted. 'He could hardly keep the smile off his face when my mother told him,' says Jimmy. The board, however, did not want to know. They had valued Major Goldsmith, they explained to Jimmy, as a colleague but they were happy to continue as they were. Among themselves there was said to be much muttering that if Jimmy were allowed anywhere near the place he would only cause difficulties.

But after a short fight they caved in, and Jimmy joined the board. He had been brought up when his father seemed to run half the hotels in France, and saw no reason why Hôtels Réunis should not regain that position. The Carlton was a wonderful flagship, the company's reputation still stood high, and although he had resisted every attempt to interest him in the hotel business, he was suddenly excited by it now. At board meetings he began urging the others to expand rapidly into a growing market, particularly in the south of France. 'The top item at every board meeting was whether or not the bar of the Carlton Hotel in Cannes should be repainted. I remember saying to them, "Why are we talking – look what's happening in the hotel world. For months we've been talking about redoing the bar, and all around us other groups are doing things, new hotels are being built." '

It was the last thing in the world this sedate board wanted to hear. After several months of making no progress whatever, Jimmy decided he would force the issue. At the next board meeting he told them: 'We're completely dead, and we'll continue to be dead as long as there is this board, and everybody has some shares and no one wants to do anything.' The current position, he added, was hopeless. 'Either you sell me your shares, or you buy my shares.'

Comte Pastre had died by this time, but Lucinge's stepson, François Ouvre, joined the board and Goldsmith arranged to meet him at the Hotel Lotti.

'Look,' he began, 'there's only one fair way out of this impasse, and that is the old Solomon's Judgment thing – one of us sets the price and the other decides to sell or buy at the price set. Would you agree to that?' Ouvre agreed. So Goldsmith proceeded to the next stage. 'What would you like to do: would you like to set the price, or would you like me to set the price?'

It was decided that Goldsmith should set the price, with three weeks to arrive at it. It never occurred to him that they might actually call his bluff and buy him out. 'I didn't have the slightest idea how I was going to finance it, but I was sure I'd find a way. I was already starting to move.' But when he did come back with his price, the Réunis board sat tight. He gave them eight days to decide, but the deadline came and went without any reaction.

It was now 1966, and Goldsmith had major problems in London, but he was still keen to take on this project, if for no other reason than to prove himself in the eyes of his father. With his keen sense of dynasty, the Hôtels Réunis was, more than anything in the world other than his name, his heritage. In his wilder moments he dreamed of restoring the Goldschmidt banking empire, of a huge company based on the Cavenham name which meant so much to his father – and of rebuilding the Hôtels Réunis.

When the board refused either to sell to him or buy his shares from him, Goldsmith took an entirely different course. He was now fairly desperate for cash, with Cavenham eating up everything he had and more. He could no longer afford to sit on an investment producing such little return with no prospect of doing anything about it. So he found a buyer for the whole company.

Maxwell Joseph was a hotelier and businessman almost as rich and well-known as Charles Clore (he later achieved what Clore had failed to do and took over the brewer Watney Mann). His Grand Metropolitan group which he had started with a few hundred pounds after the war was already one of the biggest hotel groups in Britain and had recently bought the Metropole in Monte Carlo. Joseph was also, by a complete coincidence, Annabel's sole neighbour at Pelham Cottage. Jimmy explained to him the situation with the board. 'Why don't you bid for it? A third party could break the deadlock.' Joseph could buy his shares and at the right price the rest of the board would have no excuse but to sell.

The negotiations were protracted, and Jimmy still hoped he might be able to rescue both Cavenham and Hôtels Réunis for himself. In August 1966 the *Daily Express* reported that 'there is speculation on the French Riviera' that Joseph was interested. A Carlton Hotel official confirmed that negotiations 'have been going on for some time,' adding that Joseph wanted to build on the tennis courts at the rear of the hotel 'but Cannes Town Council is refusing permission. That is why the deal has not yet gone through.' Jimmy was also quoted in the article as denying the tale. 'There is no suggestion we are selling the Carlton at Cannes. Contrary to selling we have just bought the freehold.' What he didn't say was that, although Hôtels Réunis was not selling the Carlton, the future of the entire company was up in the air.

Within three months of Frank's death, Hôtels Réunis, including the Carlton, became a subsidiary of Grand Metropolitan with Max Joseph its chairman. Jimmy stayed on the board until 1981, seldom attending meetings. 'Because my father was so loved in the company, I used to give gold medals and things like that, which I was happy to do.' But he regretted deeply what might have been.

His father's death bequeathed him another responsibility: he was now in sole charge of the family finances. Teddy was dependent on an income from what capital there was left and from his investment in his brother's companies. Marcelle had to be looked after. In Aspinall parlance, Jimmy was the dominant male, the silverback gorilla with responsibility for mother, wife, lover, three children, brother, brother's wife and children – plus about 6,000 employees. He inherited no money from his father (nor from his mother when she died more than 20 years later), but insisted that what there was went to Teddy and Marcelle, who willingly surrendered their precious capital to him to manage.

At the end of 1967, Jimmy's interests in France consisted of Gustin-Milical, and its subsidiary, Laboratoires Lanord. It was still run by Maurice Lignon, still making a profit, but expanding slowly. Now he decided to use it for doing in France what he had done in Britain – except that, instead of food, he would build a financial empire, which could complement his other interests. The House of Goldschmidt would once again rank among the financial institutions of the world. Alexis de Gunzberg began to look for companies they could buy.

The Union Financière de Paris was a financial group, not unlike Slater Walker in Britain, which had been created by a group of leading French civil servants for the purpose, their prospectus said rather grandiosely, 'of acquiring interests in various sectors of the economy in order to achieve regroupings on a national scale'. In March 1966 it hit cash problems, the banks appointed an administrator and it was agreed, in the best French style, to carry out an 'amicable liquidation'.

De Gunzberg picked through its assets and found one he thought might appeal to Jimmy: a shareholding in the Union de Transports et de Participations, a company which had once been an Algerian tramways operator. When its assets were nationalised in 1958, its compensation funds were used to build up property and investment interests. The bankrupt Union Financière de Paris owned 45 per cent of its shares, and that tranche was now being offered on the market.

The sale had been left in the hands of the managing partners of Union Financière: Count Thierry de Clermont-Tonnere, assisted on the financial side by a certain Madame Gilberte Beaux.

Goldsmith first met Gilberte Beaux at her office in December 1967. He was 34 at the time, a tall, handsome man with an extravagant life style, a wife and children in Paris, a mistress in London, an eventful past and an uncertain financial future. She was 37, short, plumpish, and married to a half-Russian 14 years her senior, by whom she had a daughter. Neither of them knew it then, but they were to form a partnership that would transform Goldsmith's financial fortunes, and last the rest of his business life.

She was born Gilberte Lovisi in Paris, on 29 July 1929, the daughter of a Corsican banker whose business crashed in the depression of the 1930s. He died when she was only nine, and his brother took possession of his shares in what remained of the business. It was to be a running wound in the family, which Gilberte resented all her life. In 1944 her mother took her, aged 15, and her two brothers to Marseilles, and it was there, two years later, that she joined a local bank as a *sténotypiste*. 'It was 1946 and it was a fantastic epoch when everything was possible,' she recalled later. 'The war had bled the banks white. In a physical sense too there were no more managers. That was when I began a fascinating career.'

By studying in her spare time she was promoted to the bank's foreign desk at the age of 20, and by age 25, by now back in Paris, she was appointed deputy manager of Seligman & Cie, a small but widely respected bank. She stayed ten years, and loved it. Edouard Beaux, whom she married in 1951, was a perfumier, and they had a daughter, Nathalie. But family did not interrupt a career that took her to the FIAT group, where for seven years she financed the export of Simca and FIAT cars, mostly to South America. 'It was really a bank which I practically re-created at the time,' she says. 'At that time it was more difficult to sell cars without credit, than credit without cars.'

From there she joined the Union Financière de Paris with de Clermont-Tonnere, to whom she was very close, and shortly afterwards found her banking skills turned in an entirely different direction: the liquidation of that company.

It says something for the circles in which Madame Beaux moved that she thought of Goldsmith's group at the time as 'a very little company'. She knew nothing of his problems in Britain, nor did she particularly care, except in so far as he could pay for what he was buying. Goldsmith and de Gunzberg however were very interested in her. Here was someone with all the contacts, and a job she was working herself out of. Gilberte knew more about banking than they ever would (although Goldsmith would only accept this latter statement several years later).

Union de Transports had some assets – around £800,000 of investments and properties. They could buy 45 per cent of it for £300,000 and, with a few additional shares, acquire control. As they continued to negotiate, Goldsmith became more and more interested in Gilberte and Clermont-Tonnere, who he began to feel would be major additions to his company.

As they were signing the deal, Goldsmith turned to Gilberte. He had, he said, nobody to manage the company he was buying. He was busy in London, and he had not yet worked out precisely what he would do with his French acquisition. 'Would you manage it for some months or weeks?' he asked Gilberte. 'Up to the time when I can think about what I will do with it?'

She agreed. Several months passed, however, before she entered the Goldsmith realm. She still had other businesses to sell for the Union Financière, and she and Clermont-Tonnere were working their way through their orderly liquidation when Goldsmith called again. He had been thinking about the business he had bought from her, and had big plans. He wanted to use it as the holding company for all his other interests, possibly with a bank at the centre. 'Why don't you join me and we could be associated in this venture?'

Gilberte was tempted, particularly at the prospect of running a bank, but she had a problem, she explained. 'It's a very good idea,' she told him. 'But I have other companies to sell, and in particular the financial companies, and if I don't sell them with my team and me in them, we will have great difficulty.' She preferred, she said, to 'keep myself for these companies'.

That was no problem, replied Goldsmith. He would buy them. 'What is the price?' When she told him, he had another question. Could she raise a loan to pay for them? 'Can it be done?'

Gilberte Beaux was witnessing, for the first time, the breathtaking cheek of Jimmy Goldsmith. His own resources were, as they had always been, stretched to the limit and beyond. The problems of Cavenham in Britain were deepening and he could not have found the money on his own. But Beaux, the banker, had contacts and standing in her own community. She took him to Switzerland and to Germany, found financial backers, and the deal was done. In the spring of 1968 Beaux took her companies, her team and herself to work for Jimmy Goldsmith. It was to be one of the most important decisions either of them was ever to take.

Clermont-Tonnere, to Goldsmith's delight, came with her. Although Gilberte was the technician, he was, certainly in these initial stages, more important. His credentials were perfect: he came from a very grand French family, and was also a product of the Ecoles Nationales d'Administration, which provided many of the mandarins of the French civil service, as well as the leaders of industry. He would be Goldsmith's ambassador to the court of '*les Enarques de France*'.

The first deal they did with Union de Participations (they dropped the 'Transports') was to buy Goldsmith's and de Gunzberg's shares in Gustin-Milical (80 per cent of that company) which in turn owned 15 per cent of Cavenham. The price paid was £535,000 or £20 a share – some 70 per cent up on the price of a year before, giving Goldsmith and de Gunzberg a handsome profit on paper. Union de Participations had thus now become the Goldsmith parent company in France, and its shares were rising rapidly.

But he still didn't have a bank, which Gilberte and Clermont-Tonnere were particularly keen on. When they found one, they also found an element of trouble.

This is what happened. Georges Schiff-Giordini was born in Pisa in 1899, and moved to France sometime between the wars where he put together a company called Société Générale Foncière, which owned a bank and some properties. In 1963, in failing health, he decided to sell his 30 per cent holding, but the price he asked was too high. He died two years later with his shares still unsold. The managing director, André Chevinesse, now 66, tried to encourage the two sons, Ellis and Guy, to take over, but they had no interest in the business, and insisted the shares be sold. Their administrators found an interested buyer, a property development company called Manera, but when Manera investigated the group it did not much like what it found. The non-property interests, it concluded, 'are either on the verge of liquidation or no longer do anything but manage a portfolio ... these subsidiaries are no longer effectively active.' However Manera was keen to acquire the property interests, and approached Goldsmith and Gilberte. Were they interested in buying the bank and financial side, leaving Manera just the property?

They were. But as usual they had no money. However, with Clermont-Tonnere and Madame Beaux aboard they were able to find it. The Goldsmith-controlled Union de Participations agreed to buy the Schiff-Giordini stake for £900,000, borrowing the money from two banks, Banque Rivaud and the Banque Française de Dépôts et de Titres. Part of the security for this loan was the share stake itself. In October 1968 the deal went through and Goldsmith instantly moved in to put himself, Clermont-Tonnere and Madame Beaux on the board of Générale Foncière in place of the existing (and rather ancient) directors. Then he sold the head office and other property to Manera for £2.4m, and moved the bank into his existing offices at 90 Champs Elysées, near the Arc de Triomphe.

So far, so simple, at least by Goldsmith standards. This was to reckon without a certain Michel Breton, however, a man who was to prove a thorn in their side for the next six years. In selling the property side, all the staff in that subsidiary were dismissed, and M. Breton, former assistant director of the banking division, resented it. He created the Association de Défense des Actionnaire de la Société Générale Foncière, or ASDAC, to oppose the redundancies and protect the staff. In other circumstances this would have been a minor irritation, and Goldsmith initially regarded it as such. Breton, however, knew how to cause the maximum embarrassment. He lodged a charge with the Procureur de la République (equivalent to the Director of Public Prosecutions in Britain), and then, in a registered letter to Manera, informed it of staff dissatisfaction with the 'shoddy' treatment they had received. He followed that up by contacting a number of major depositors, suggesting they ask the Governor of the Banque de France to hold an inquiry. Further complaints followed to the auditors, to the chairman of the Stock Exchange and to everyone who might have an interest. 'It seemed to me,' said Breton, 'that what M. Goldsmith was doing was quite wrong. Here was a respectable and well-established bank being bought by an outsider who was using the bank's own resources to finance the purchase.' He was, he admitted, 'angry about the way in which I and my colleagues had been summarily dismissed, but there was more to this than a personal grudge.'

Essentially what he and his fellow minority shareholders were alleging was that Goldsmith had bought control of the bank with its own money – which was illegal – and that he had 'pillaged' the assets, by selling the properties cheaply to Manera in return for a guarantee on the loan. As well as his complaints to the authorities, Breton decided to pursue the new owners through the courts. If he could prove his case, Goldsmith would face criminal prosecution.

The Brigade Financière, equivalent to the British fraud squad, was asked to investigate, and they did so very thoroughly. Goldsmith turned up at the office in the Champs Elysées one day to find the place full of people working for the police, who were sealing all the files. He had not known, until that moment, of the investigation, and he was shaken. Gilberte Beaux bore the brunt of it, painstakingly answering every query, but every director was interviewed, including General Pierre Koenig, one of France's greatest generals in the last war who was on the board when Goldsmith bought it.

None of this leaked into the press at the time except for one short and cryptic piece in *Canard Enchaîné*, placed by Breton. The Finance Squad finished its report in May 1969, and concluded that M. Breton was 'motivated by a clear intention to prejudice'. Breton, however, did not give up. He argued there was enough in the Finance Squad's report for further inquiry and he only finally dropped his battle in 1975.

The Générale Foncière problem, annoying as it was, did not impede the plan to create a French bank. After the first shock, they handled the investigation as if it were routine. As Breton pursued him with an almost messianic fervour, Jimmy and Gilberte Beaux, who increasingly became the closest business associate he ever had, continued their rapid series of deals. Until this time, all his share swaps and fancy financial deals had got him nowhere, although he would argue that without them he could neither have built Cavenham nor kept it alive through the bad years.

Under Gilberte's guidance, the frenzy actually did lead somewhere. She brought three companies with her, properly financed and organised, so that they were actually making more profit than Goldsmith was paying in interest. She arranged the finances for the deal, with people she knew and who were willing to trust her, and who were impressed with Jimmy when they met him. They were prepared to come in as partners, rather than merely lend money, giving Goldsmith an option to buy them out at a profit if things went well. They remain shareholders in his companies to the present day.

Everything was all in place by the spring of 1968. In the previous autumn they had bought Générale Foncière, which had a range of interests (even after they sold the property to Manera) and an ancient management. The sale of the property interests instantly changed the financial structure of the group, allowing Beaux to expand the bank – which is what Goldsmith had brought her in to do. In the first five months, the bank's funds increased by four million francs, and would have increased further but for M. Breton's effort. After a Breton letter, the Hotel Bristol asked for immediate repayment of a blocked account it held of 1.5m francs, but Gilberte Beaux more than replaced it with deposits from some of her overseas banking contacts. All the major clients stayed, although Breton asked them not to.

Beaux was both disciplined and industrious, creating in their new office in the Champs Elysées an order which Goldsmith quickly appreciated. She was also as tough with him as she was with anyone else. She had a high reputation in Paris banking circles and she had no intention of sacrificing it. She did not depend on Goldsmith for a job, and owed him nothing. But she enjoyed working with him, listening to the free flow of ideas, to his views on politics (which at that stage she had little interest in), and to his plans for how to create their *banque d'affaire*. It was she who re-ordered the companies they had taken over, selling off share stakes, closing down or reorganising some of the strange little businesses that came with Foncière (one made furfurol, an oil produced from distilling grain, at a cost twice as high as that of competitors, another had Tunisian mining interests which had been nationalised and still another had a sole activity: seeking compensation for its long-lost Polish and other East European loans), while concentrating the resources on the bank. Tigrett brought in new partners too: the Union Bank of Los Angeles and the Central National Bank of Cleveland were persuaded by him to invest in the man he told them was the 'finest financial brain he had ever met'.

However, even for the 'finest financial brain' the structure of the companies was becoming absurd, and Clermont-Tonnere and Gilberte persuaded Goldsmith to simplify things. Gilberte organised the merger of four companies into one holding company, into which all the other interests would be put, in much the same way as Goldsmith had consolidated his various food companies in Britain into a single entity. What to call it? None of the names was particularly memorable, and Goldsmith, Gilberte and Clermont-Tonnere kicked around a number of suggestions, until they finally came up with Générale Occidentale. 'It was just a short name, easy to remember,' says Gilberte, but it was the name that went up above the door of 44 Champs Elysées (and remains there still).

Goldsmith, prompted by Gilberte's open scepticism, soon learned that he had no taste for banking. He might have believed it was in his genes, but the ability to read balance sheets, do complicated sums in his head, and juggle the most complex of financial structures is not banking, which essentially is a dull, cautious business. All his life he had taken huge risks on the basis that there was a potential reward at least as big as the risk, if not greater. The business of banking he soon found was the opposite – you had to avoid risk. After tax and overheads, he complained, banking meant investing £100 to make a net profit of £1. 'If I take a £100 risk, I want at least £100 gain, not a £1 gain,' he complained.

'Jimmy is really everything *except* a banker,' says Gilberte. 'He has a wonderful mind, a kind of genius, but financial matters and banking are totally different.'

Goldsmith left her to run the bank, which she was more than happy to do. Gilberte discovered something else about Jimmy which others had noticed over the years. Despite the many women in his life, he didn't actually *like* women. Other friends of Goldsmith's noticed a similar thing over the years: Goldsmith and Aspinall shared the belief that in the animal kingdom the male was the dominant species, to be challenged by other males perhaps for leadership of the group, but never by a woman. 'I remember when he was only fifteen, there were always beautiful women about him,' says Digby Neave. 'Yet I always remember too that he never really *liked* women.' Gilberte Beaux, one of the few women of his acquaintance never to become one of his conquests, observed, 'There is something of the misogynist about him.' And yet the young Anglo-French tycoon and the woman banker would work together in a close and successful partnership that would often be stormy, but which built one of the largest companies of its kind in Europe.

In that first year with Madame Beaux, 1968, while the French interests were beginning to come together, Cavenham struggled past its low point. Profits were looking up. The days of struggle were not yet over, but Goldsmith was beginning, for the first time in his life, to look towards real security and real wealth.

14

Success at Last

If Jimmy Goldsmith had retired, died, been taken over or gone bankrupt before 1970, he would have been remembered – and then only in a limited circle – as an erratic and swashbuckling genius who promised a good deal but delivered little. 'I used to be able to talk convincingly to people on how we were going to do things – and practically without exception everything I said turned out to be wrong,' he admitted in an interview in January 1972 (to Ivan Rowan in the *Sunday Telegraph*).

The companies he put together as Cavenham had sales of £27m, which Goldsmith increased to £50m, then cut back to £11m. By 1970/1 sales were still only £35m, not much more than he had started with six years before. Profits before tax in his first year were £168,000, but instead of making the increased profits he forecast, Cavenham lost £618,000 in the year 1965/6. In the following year, when the snuff companies contributed a bonus of £700,000 and Goldsmith and de Gunzberg had 'gifted' the company £500,000, losses dived to £988,000; the next year it lost another £582,000, and for the year ended March 1969, Cavenham made only a tiny profit of £16,000. It paid no dividend for six years, and much of that time was so short of money that Goldsmith was not sure how he would pay his suppliers.

There were also some fairly dramatic changes of policy. Ownership of the confectionery business, as we shall see, was moved from Britain to Switzerland and then back again, and deals such as that with Perrier and Conwood SA in Switzerland were done and undone again. His deal with Harrell Corporation of the US was announced with a fanfare but never happened. There were strategies such as wholesaling in Britain, or making chocolate in Holland, which were launched and then abandoned. For two years running, the auditors were unhappy with his treatment of goodwill in the accounts, and entered reservations to that effect. Even when his hard work paid off and profits began to come through, Cavenham was scarcely a giant. Essentially it consisted of a lopsided mixture of slimming foods, confectionery, a minor presence in biscuits, a Dutch gin company, a tiny chain of confectionery and tobacconists' shops and two snuff companies. There was nothing in that to challenge the Unilevers of the world, which was what Goldsmith had set out to do.

Goldsmith's own reputation, after all the failed commitments, the tortuous – and profitless – paper chase, did not amount to much either. As *Management Today* noted a few years later: 'Views about Goldsmith both in the food trade and in the City ranged from (at best) the indulgent to the acutely sceptical – and almost certainly the sceptics were in the majority.'

Yet that, even before his breakthrough into the big time, was never the full story. Even at his low point in 1967, Goldsmith had been accorded a degree of respect far higher than his actual achievements merited, and well before he embarked on any of his major bids he carried with him a considerable reputation for financial acumen. In 1971 the *Sunday Times* felt obliged to examine, in all seriousness, the claim 'that Jimmy Goldsmith is a financial wizard', and concluded that if he wasn't, he was at least a 'combination of a financial Houdini and a commercial Master Builder'.

His belief in himself had survived the perils of these bleak years, and the respect in which seasoned bankers and businessmen such as Roland Franklin and John Tigrett (and in France, Clermont-Tonnere and Gilberte Beaux) held him had waxed rather than waned. Whatever scepticism existed in the City, Goldsmith was never dismissed as a minor figure going nowhere. Any thought of writing him off was always tempered by the nagging belief that here was a person who could make it big – and when he did, he would be someone you would want to be associated with.

Much of this, of course, had to do with his personality. His energy pervaded a room the moment he entered it, his booming voice and infectious laugh calling attention to him, even where his height and striking looks didn't. But there was something else. Goldsmith's odd string of deals may have raised eyebrows, but he had never stepped outside what was legal; and, more importantly, he had honoured his word with everyone he dealt with. There were no debts left unpaid, and Goldsmith, even where he had fallen out with people, left few genuine grudges behind. In the same way that, as a young man, he had somehow always managed to pay his debts (or get his father to pay them), so he retained that same code in his later life. Without it, he would probably not have survived the 1960s.

There were also, within the Cavenham picture, enough hints of what he could do once he found his touch and timing to encourage supporters and managers to retain their belief in him. Procea, for instance, made £50,000 when he bought it, lost money in 1966, bounced back to a profit of nearly £300,000 the following year and doubled profits to £620,000 the year after. It was visible proof that the Goldsmith style of management could work.

Head office expenses were slashed from a desperately top-heavy £217,000 in 1965 to £95,000 two years later and only £54,000 by 1969. The reorganisation of the various divisions took longer and cost more than Goldsmith ever expected, but from it had emerged a viable concern which had made money for anyone brave enough to stick with it.

The bright young managers whom he had persuaded to join him in the early years were now showing their paces. Jack Greenhalgh, the managing director, was a tough professional who had got on top of the chaotic machine Goldsmith had given him to run, and the team was champing for fresh acquisitions and fresh challenges. There was now in place a management organisation capable of running something far bigger. The system for taking over new companies had become much more sophisticated so that, as Greenhalgh says, acquisitions were processed 'through the sausage machine of a highly professional management'. They had steadily tackled the major problem areas, notably confectionery, which Goldsmith had stuck by through a horrendous trading period. Originally there had been 2,000 people employed in the Goldsmith-controlled confectionery factories; he closed a number of them, re-equipped and modernised others, merged the sales forces, and eventually arrived at a viable business. But it took six hard loss-making years, during which he had little to spend on marketing or developing new products. Confectionery losses of £650,000 in 1966 were halved the next year, cut to £206,000 by 1968 and became a profit by 1970, although it has to be said that if Procea was an example of successful Goldsmith management, confectionery has to be put down as an experience along the Goldsmith management learning curve. Finally, having nurtured a modest profit, Goldsmith injected it into the Swiss company Cavenham shared with Conwood.

The auditors' qualification in the accounts had gone by 1969, and even more importantly, although the company was making no great profit, it was generating cash to the extent that for the year ended March 1969

Cavenham's balance sheet showed nearly £500,000 cash in the bank. The shares had risen too: from 4s 6d (22½p) in 1967 to 6s 6d (32½p) in September 1969 and to twice that by the following February. Goldsmith and de Gunzberg owned eight million of them, so his wealth was increasing. 'It looks as if Cavenham Foods might see better days after a lengthy period of disappointing results,' commented the *Investors Chronicle*.

There is an important point to be drawn from this experience, which Goldsmith had certainly taken, and which would affect his behaviour for the rest of his life. Ask Jimmy Goldsmith if, looking back now, he would have preferred to have done well at school, gone on to Oxford where he would have met many of his lifelong friends, and even to the Harvard Business School, and he reacts as if one had kidnapped his son:

> No, I would have hated it at Oxford. I don't want my children to go there, and I would be very upset if they did. I've given them an apprenticeship and I've done everything I can to discourage my children from going to university. Apprenticeship is far more important. In business the biggest step is when you move from a small business into a big business. In a small business you do everything yourself: buying raw material, manufacturing it into products, selling it, writing the advertisements, talking to the banks, the accountants, the tax people; you hire everyone and you know everyone. A big business is totally different, and you have to find the right people to do these things for you. The big mutation from small business to big business took place for me quite late: it happened in 1965 when all of a sudden I had a business which was not rich and not prosperous, but it was a large business, with thousands of people instead of a handful of them. So I went out to get the best people I could find, and the best people were at Procter & Gamble and Mars and Unilever, and I managed to get them, really good people. And so I wrote our first issue of *Cavenham News*, rather nicely produced with an orange cover, and put all our ideas in it. And every one of those ideas was wrong! Every single one of the premises on which we ran the company was wrong: centralised marketing, massive centralisation of everything, massive specialisation – it was all nonsense.

'But I was *absolutely* convinced it was right,' Goldsmith goes on, beating his hand on his chair for emphasis, '*totally* convinced. I was absolutely throbbing with enthusiasm. And I managed to convince other people that it was right, when everything was wrong. The thing was falling apart, until we merged the confectionery business with others, and of course afterwards it was very easy to see the wrong theory put into practice.'

This is his point:

Practice in the hard light of reality shows things. What do you do when you realise the theory is wrong? You change or you go down the tubes. You change your ideas to make them realistic. But I've always thought to myself that if, instead of going into business, I had become a teacher in a business school and if I had run in there with those ideas, I would have taught them all my life. At no time would I have needed to change them. Now the possibility of someone knowing what's right and what's wrong without having tested and reacted, the chances of getting it right first time are trillions to one against. So the only way you can possibly work out a practical set of beliefs in business, principles or whatever you want to call them, is by the constant interaction of theory and practice. Theory in itself, the chances of it being right are obscure, so what you have to have is apprenticeship with a dose of theory. In other words, there must be a constant interaction of knowing theory, applying it and seeing the results, changing your ideas, reapplying them ... Therefore I have a fundamental disagreement with education which is based on theory as opposed to one which is constantly testing that theory in reality. So as far as my children are concerned, I would encourage them to become apprentices within the system. And when you look at the record of the business universities, they are not good. People come out with a number of ideas, and believe they are grander than they are, whereas they are less good than the people who have come up through the ranks.

The mid-1960s was the period when Goldsmith learned these lessons, and having absorbed them, he finally made the leap from struggle into the big time. It was not a Damascus-like conversion as much as an evolutionary process, and to the outside world little of this was immediately apparent. As the 1960s moved towards a close, it took a keen eye to spot the fact that within two years Goldsmith would not only make his breakthrough but do so in as spectacular a style as any entrepreneur of the time. Jimmy began the 1970s in confident style, with a flourish of deals. His companies both in France and Britain were doing well, but he wanted a tighter, clearer structure for them. In France, he was consolidating the companies he had bought from Madame Beaux, and then Générale Foncière, into Générale Occidentale. But at the same time, he was planning his most complex share swapping operation yet which would tighten his personal grip on Cavenham, and bring it under the control of his master company. He had made further acquisitions which needed to be accommodated in the whole: he had extended Cavenham's interests into continental Europe, first buying a Dutch chocolate company, Ringers, followed within a few weeks by the

£900,000 purchase of an even better known name, Melchers, a family-controlled company producing gin, Dutch brandy and crème de menthe under the Olifant label. When the *Financial Times* rang him in Paris to talk about his Dutch deals he willingly explained that his aim was to create a broadly-based Dutch food group, with, as the *FT* added, 'the finance coming in Eurocurrency through a Paris bank in which he and Baron Alexis de Gunzberg are partners'. Goldsmith added, 'It is obvious I have been very frustrated with Cavenham's for a while,' moving the *FT* to add its own comment: 'This was a noble understatement. For a man of Goldsmith's fiery and energetic temperament, it has taken a long time to pull the group . . . round to showing a profit.'

All of this was by way of prelude to his grand slam. In February 1970 Cavenham shares zipped up to 15s 3d (76p), valuing the company at £11.25m, on rumours that something big was afoot. It was. Goldsmith asked for his shares to be suspended while he put in place his new masterplan. 'Cavenham,' he announced boldly, 'is finally going forward to become the multinational company it has always wanted to be.'

The multinational strategy that he then unfolded and which he, Gilberte Beaux and Roland Franklin slotted into place, was for once something more than a reshuffle of his paper interests. It was basically a complete rearrangement of all his companies, French and British, to bring them into a single more logical structure. Cavenham would buy a controlling stake in the French dietary food business including Gustin-Milical and another company, Gremy-Longuet (maker of a popular French health product, Synthol). It would also buy back the 50 per cent stake in the Swiss group, Conwood SA, which it did not own, thus re-acquiring both the snuff companies and its confectionery interests (the latter had now been merged first with Perrier, then with Conwood SA and were finally back in Cavenham, and would soon move on again). Conwood, the Memphis company introduced to Goldsmith by John Tigrett, would accept shares in Cavenham for its holding, worth £1.87m.

The result of all this was that the French company, Unions de Participations (whose name was soon to be changed to Société Générale Occidentale), personally controlled by Goldsmith and de Gunzberg, now stood atop an extraordinary pyramid of companies in France, Britain and Holland. It owned 68 per cent of Cavenham Foods, the main operating company, which was quoted on the London Stock Exchange, 80 per cent of the Banque Occidentale (the bank run by Gilberte Beaux, acquired with Générale Foncière), and 80 per cent of a bank based in Holland. Cavenham in turn owned 65 per cent of the French dietary and pharmaceutical interests, now arranged under the umbrella of yet another company, Financière et Industrielle de Pétrole et de Pharmacie (or FIPP), and 100 per cent of Procea, Carr & Co. of Carlisle, the confectionery business and the old snuff businesses.

As the shares were suspended, Goldsmith went to some trouble to explain to the financial community what he was doing, and why he was doing it. He was conscious of the image he had built up in the past five years. He gave an interview to the experienced *Financial Times* journalist Kenneth Gooding, who began his piece, 'Energy and optimism are the two most obvious characteristics' of Goldsmith, adding that 'optimism has certainly helped him weather the five long years' since he had founded Cavenham. Goldsmith explained that when he started out he believed that simply by putting cash and good management behind some pretty lethargic businesses a successful major industrial and marketing group could be created. 'But it did not work out that way,' commented Gooding. 'Mr Goldsmith's optimism beamed out in each annual report', only to be confounded each time. Many lessons had been learned, and unlearned but at last, Goldsmith insisted with a degree of justifiable vehemence, the corner had been turned.

Goldsmith would later be accused, notably by Charles Raw of the *Sunday Times*, of obsessive secrecy in these and other deals, but there is no indication that he was trying to hide behind his complex structure at the time. If anything, Goldsmith seemed to be going out of his way to make himself understood, to put across his concept of his multinational food group, with its associated financial companies, of the bank at the centre providing finance, support and contacts, and of Cavenham as a manufacturer, wholesaler and retailer. The documents that went with the bid openly laid out the web of French interests without embarrassment (although omitting any mention of M. Breton and his activities).

As he talked about his banking business, Goldsmith could not forbear reiterating the boast he had made so often over the years. 'My family have been bankers for generations and I have always rather wanted to be a merchant banker myself.' The desire to rebuild the glory of the House of Goldschmidt still burned strong in 1970.

Events began to move at a gallop. Roland Franklin at Keyser Ullmann had bought control of a Scottish group of retailers, R. S. McColl, as part of a confectionery deal. In Scotland there were basically two rival confectionery chains: McColl's and Birrell's, the latter controlled by Cadbury's. Franklin didn't know what to do with his shops, but proposed to Cadbury's that either they should buy Keyser out, or he would buy them out. 'Every time we opened a shop, they did, so in the end I bought McColl,' he says. But having acquired it, Franklin realised it was too big for him. Goldsmith already had some shops, bought some years before with J. & A. P. Holland and with Singleton & Cole, and he had a man who was proving to be a star at managing them. Jim Wood was a former athlete, who perfectly fitted the Goldsmith management theory. He had joined Goldsmith from the modest background of a co-operative store in Liverpool. He was given the stores 'to play with' as Goldsmith later put it, and achieved profits of £25,000 on capital employed of £56,000, a return of 45 per cent. Goldsmith, bored to tears with the uphill struggle to make any money out of tobacco and confectionery wholesaling, was astonished. He sold out of wholesaling – 'There came a time when we simply had to admit that we did not understand the business,' he said with a frankness which surprised his interviewer – and decided to back Wood. In October 1969 he bought another 50 little shops selling confectionery, tobacco and newspapers (CTNs) from a receiver for £150,000. A year later Wood turned in profits of £135,000. 'About this time we began to realise we had a genius on our hands,' says Jack Greenhalgh. Wood, according to other colleagues at the time, had 'a sort of double vision – he can start by taking detailed accounts of stocks of individual shops, and emerge with a master plan for reorganising an entire chain.'

When Franklin offered his 422 shops for sale, Goldsmith was very much in the mood to buy them. He agreed on a price of £948,000, most of it paid in Cavenham shares which were then sold by Keyser Ullmann to Générale Occidentale in Paris, making it another fairly incestuous deal. Wood worked wonders on the new shops. McColl was losing £300,000 when it was bought. Wood closed 100 shops and a warehouse, reduced capital invested by £600,000, cut back sharply on theft ('things were literally walking out of the shops') and within months had a unit with profits running at £300,000 a year to add to the £135,000 he was already making.

This was to be an important development. Without it, the next planks of Goldsmith's expansion could never have been put in place. It was January 1971 when the McColl deal was completed, and already Goldsmith was stalking his biggest target yet.

The company in his sights was one of the best-known in the British food industry. Bovril had been born nearly a century before when a Scotsman, John Lawson Johnston, developed a beef extract, and subsequently created one of the most famous brand names of all time. Two of the founder's grandsons, the chairman Lord Luke and his brother the Hon Hugh Lawson Johnston, were still on the board of a company which had some wonderful assets and even better brands: Bovril itself of course, plus Marmite, Ambrosia Creamed Rice, Virol and Jaffajuice drinks. It also owned large estancias and meat works in Argentina. Inside also, a bit like the snuff companies in Singleton & Cole, was a dairy company which was to prove Goldsmith's key to unlocking it.

Goldsmith first focused on Bovril at the end of 1970 as he was emerging from what he calls the 'tunnel' of reorganising Cavenham. His own spirits had soared as the year progressed. Although he had almost voted for Harold Wilson's Labour Party in 1964 ('I felt that Macmillan's government was too class based, but in the end I couldn't bring myself to vote Labour and voted Conservative'), he had increasingly hated the Labour government of the 1960s. He caught the headlines briefly in March 1970 when in a speech at the Institute of Directors, the first major speech he had ever given, Goldsmith painted a picture of Britain in moral, industrial and spiritual decline, becoming a blinkered society which fed on envy and malice. But that was all in the past. In June 1970 the Conservatives, led by Edward Heath, had won, and, to Goldsmith's delight, Britain was committed to joining the Common Market, to encouraging private enterprise and to many of the other things he believed in.

He still nurtured the ambition that as soon as he had made enough money, he would go into politics. The only problem was that making money was taking more time then he expected. When Jeffrey Archer asked him for a contribution to help promote the 'European cause', Goldsmith gave him £100,000 from his own pocket, clear proof of his newfound prosperity.

In the spring of 1971, as Goldsmith was stalking Bovril, the Heath government cut taxes and began pumping money into the economy in an effort to prevent unemployment rising above a million, then regarded as a level above which Britain's social structure would break down in riots and chaos (under Margaret Thatcher it would go above three million with remarkably little public unrest). The economy was in a boom and Cavenham was going with it. The recent rise in the Cavenham share price meant the company was actually bigger than the much more establishment Bovril in terms of stock market value, but not in terms of assets. Bovril's profits had not risen since 1961. The company had barely moved in Europe, despite the fact that Britain would soon be joining the Common Market, and had done little to develop its brands.

John Tigrett delegated to himself the position of 'point man' as he called it. His international connections meant he could easily effect an introduction to almost any boardroom, particularly in the food industry, where he was seen as a representative of Conwood. He contacted the Bovril chairman, Lord Luke, and asked to see him. 'The story was I was thinking of investing a great deal of money in the company and wanted to ask some questions,' says Tigrett. 'He wasn't best pleased to see me, and I first asked him some questions about his balance sheet and Lord Luke said, "Wait a minute, I have someone who can answer that", so he called in this boy. So I said what about so-and-so; they had a big operation in Argentina and I wanted to know more about that. He had no idea what I was talking about so he called in another boy.

'So I took the train back to London and Jimmy said what had I found out? I said, forget what I found out, just start buying shares in Bovril. There's no question about it, it's a great company being run by somebody who doesn't know what he's doing and we can make a lot of money.'

Goldsmith began buying shares the next day, quietly at first so as to disturb the share price as little as possible. The shares were around 180p as they began, but by mid-summer the rumours of a potential bid began to circulate and Bovril zipped up to 250p. The London stock market was entering a bull phase, but the takeover boom had not started. Max Joseph had Express Dairies, and the Bovril bid would be the second substantial bid of this particular merger wave. Goldsmith realised that once he opened the bidding, it was going to be a race, with other far more powerful bidders ready to step in and Bovril unlikely to welcome him either. Although he was doing well, he had no resources for a contested bid, neither the cash, nor the City backing which Bovril would undoubtedly be able to muster once the alarm was raised. Keyser Ullmann, Cavenham's bank, was a second-rate merchant bank with a poor reputation compared to Warburgs, Morgan Grenfell, Rothschilds, Schroders or Lazards.

This was a time when outsiders were discovering how vulnerable the financial establishment was, and how nerve, quick reflexes and surprise could win the day against complacency. Jim Slater had sliced through the ranks of the City establishment with even smaller resources to topple some of the biggest names in British industry, and his disciples followed in his wake. James Hanson and Gordon White were developing their still-small conglomerate, backed by Slater, and Goldsmith was not deterred by the obstacles, simply determined to made the most of the strengths he had.

Fortunately his own share price was rising too: from 70p in April it rose to 86p on 1 June. The Heath boom was gathering momentum and so was

Goldsmith's now uncontainable excitement. 'In June 1971 I was 100 per cent certain that we were about to get back to a new cyclical boom in the market,' he says. He had missed the last boom of 1968 when Jim Slater had asserted his ascendancy because Cavenham was struggling for survival. But Goldsmith was determined not to be left behind this time.

The day before he launched his bid, Cavenham shares stood at 85p and Bovril at 247p. The terms of his offer, in Cavenham shares and loan stock, would be worth 310p a share, valuing Bovril at £9.7m. But if his share price continued to rise – as indeed it did to 95p – so his offer would become worth more.

On 27 June 1971, Goldsmith made his move, and immediately became embroiled in his first seriously contested takeover bid. Despite the elaborate planning, he was unprepared for the hostility he aroused – and which was to mark the beginnings of a long hate affair with the British press. If he had been a little more experienced in the takeover arena he might have been far less sensitive. Character assassinations and whispering campaigns are part and parcel of the takeover scene, the most reputable of merchant banks thinking nothing of repeating the most lurid details about the other side. To the bankers and the public relations men that get involved too it is a game, and without malice or serious ill will. They represent the case of their client in much the same way as a skilled barrister will defend his client by savaging the other side's witnesses.

There was a fair amount to be said about Goldsmith: he was a playboy, a gambler, with two women in his life, and a somewhat chequered company record, certainly not the sort to take over a good British company like Bovril.

Until that time, Goldsmith had always found the press on his side, a weapon to be used for his own purposes, as in the elopement and kidnapping incidents of his youth. Stories began to appear of a 'mystery buyer' for his shares, to explain their steady rise.

In fact there were other reasons to explain the strength of the share price. Four days after he launched the bid, Goldsmith was able to announce a deal which, with or without 'friendly' buyers for his shares, would have caused them to rise. It was one of two strokes of good fortune that were to swing the Bovril bid his way.

This one was due to Tigrett who was seeking ways to raise money for Jimmy, trying to repeat his success with the snuff companies. Cavenham's big success was its new retailing arm, and it occurred to him that he might either sell it or, preferably, bring in a partner in the same way as he had brought in Conwood. He found a potential investor in the Southland

Corporation of Dallas, Texas, which owned the 7-Eleven chain across America, and was looking to expand in Europe.

At the end of June Tigrett travelled to London with John Thompson of Southland and they met Goldsmith at his house in Chester Terrace. 'In no more than 45 minutes we'd made a deal and he agreed to give us thirteen million dollars, and we were saved again.' It wasn't of course quite as simple as that – Southland didn't actually put up that amount of money. But what the Americans did do was agree to buy a 50 per cent stake in the Cavenham retail operation for £3.3m, valuing a business which had cost Goldsmith less than £1m at nearly £7m – or $13m in those days. Tigrett had prepared the way, persuading Thompson to do a similar deal to Conwood: take this 'financial genius' Goldsmith in as a partner rather than buy him out.

The effect of the deal was to underwrite the value of Cavenham – and to persuade Goldsmith's shaky backers there was more to the company than they thought. It was enough for him to dive back into the market and continue buying Bovril shares.

Madame Beaux too played a crucial part; from the beginning she had worked full-time on the Bovril bid, spending most of the time in Goldsmith's house in Regent's Park which he used as his headquarters. He had to offer a cash alternative to his share offer, and that had to be underwritten – not an easy task for a company of Cavenham's provenance at that time. Roland Franklin had arranged a certain amount of underwriting but not enough, and in mid-July they were running into problems. Gilberte dashed back to Paris to talk to her banking contacts. 'At that time, it was rather unique,' she says. 'Underwriting like that in a hostile bid situation – it was one of the first done in France. And we had to do it just before Quatorze Juillet, which made it even harder. But we managed it.'

Then Goldsmith went on to the attack himself. On 16 July, he sent every Bovril shareholder a telegram telling them there was now a cash alternative of 310p a share. He followed this up with a formal offer document forecasting a 30–40 per cent increase in Cavenham's profits. He was continuing to buy Bovril shares in the market with every spare penny he could find, and now had 24 per cent, against 8 per cent held by the board. Rowntree Mackintosh owned 10 per cent.

Lord Luke had given way to his younger brother, Hugh Lawson Johnston, who was violently opposed to being taken over by Goldsmith. But Bovril was now 'in play', and even if he fought Goldsmith off, the chances were that Bovril would be taken over by someone else. Every acquisitive company in the food industry had looked at it at some point, but had been frightened off by the commitments in Argentina, and by the struggle they envisaged in remarketing its brands. 'We could never see what to do with it,' one food company chairman was quoted as saying at the time.

The Bovril board and its advisers scouted the industry for a bidder more acceptable than Goldsmith, and found one in the shape of Rowntree Mackintosh, many times bigger than Cavenham, which finally agreed to make a counter-offer. Its bid when it arrived in mid-July was worth £10.9m, £1m more than Goldsmith's original offer. The even bigger group Beecham started to take an active interest, but was deterred from bidding by the Argentinian business which no one wanted.

The Rowntree bid tilted the odds against Goldsmith, but he was far from finished. With the Southland deal in place, and the underwriting arranged, he could manoeuvre with more confidence. There was an extra incentive now in winning. Jim Slater, the guru of all takeover bidders at the time, told him bluntly that if he failed to get Bovril, 'You will never succeed in a bid in the City of London again.' That was not necessarily true, but it galvanised Goldsmith. To be classed as a loser was an unendurable prospect.

Yet Goldsmith, Gilberte, Franklin and the others were seriously beginning to think about pulling out, when Goldsmith was contacted by Annabel's neighbour, Maxwell Joseph, who had bought the Hôtels Réunis company. After buying Express Dairies, he found the milk business a source of useful assets and of cash flow. Would Goldsmith sell him the dairies owned by Bovril if the bid succeeded? The dairies were valued in the Bovril balance sheet at next to nothing, but Joseph indicated he was willing to pay between £5m and £7m. A bigger company such as Rowntree might not have sold to him, but shrewdly Joseph reckoned that Goldsmith would have little choice. Having been in the same position himself, he also knew how valuable an offer like this could be for a bidder. As with the Southland deal, Goldsmith could show the banks and underwriters Grand Metropolitan's offer, and raise more money.

It was a huge stroke of luck, wholly unforeseen. 'This story that we had spotted the dairies and the Argentina property is just a yarn,' says Tigrett. 'We had no idea they were there at the time of the bid. Jimmy was, even in those days, looking for badly run companies with a good core business and other hard assets, but we sure didn't know about Bovril's. That company was a brand name to us, a brand name and three products.'

The Southland deal and Max Joseph's offer, plus Jim Slater's cautionary warning, persuaded Goldsmith to raise his bid again. On 30 July he topped Rowntree with a bid worth £13m. When Rowntree in turn raised the stakes to £13.4m, Goldsmith again lifted his bid, this time to £14.5m. The price was now way beyond what the market reckoned Bovril was actually worth. Even Rowntree and Beecham were preparing to abandon the field to Jimmy.

By mid-August the bid was moving into its final stages when another event occurred, which to this day is a source of some bitterness and confusion. Jimmy was happily giving interviews to the key financial journalists, particularly from the Sunday papers who could have a powerful effect on the views of shareholders. A bad press can sway a bid one way or the other, and in the modern bid both sides have elaborate programmes for convincing journalists of the merits of their case. Goldsmith was approached by a journalist on the *Sunday Times* called Richard Milner, an experienced and able man with a good reputation, and a few days later Milner duly appeared at Chester Terrace. The Goldsmith style of conducting these interviews was to invite the journalist into his elegant drawing room on the first floor, where he would stand in front of the marble fireplace, cigar in hand, and hold forth on how terribly badly Bovril had been run, how much he could do for it, and how much he had already done for Cavenham once he had got it right.

But with Milner, Goldsmith found he had an unresponsive audience. Milner had his own agenda, a set of questions which Goldsmith at first parried and then became alarmed about. 'I suddenly realised he was incredibly hostile and only looking for bad news,' he says. Goldsmith later charged that Milner had already made up his mind before seeing him at Chester Terrace. 'It was clear he thought that I wasn't going to get Bovril, and that my group did not deserve to,' he said.

What Goldsmith didn't know was that the allegations Milner was making were not actually his own: they had been presented to him by a man who had never met Goldsmith, but hated him as much as ever Michel Breton did. By a strange coincidence the event is recorded, not by *Sunday Times* journalists, but by the playwright Arnold Wesker who in 1971 spent some months attached to the paper gathering background material for his play, *The Journalists*. Wesker took elaborate notes, which he shaped into a personal account of the workings of a large newspaper and of the journalists on it. He intended to publish his notes as a book, but because of a disagreement with the paper's editor Harold Evans and the Insight team over what he was allowed to report, the book, instead of appearing in 1972, finally appeared in 1977. Most of it has no relevance to the Goldsmith story. But when Wesker gets to the *Business News* office it becomes very relevant indeed.

Wesker's account starts: 'Someone from Insight comes down to *Business News* and reports: "I've just had an earbending fink on the telephone who says he's got damaging documents which will implicate Mr A." ' For legal reasons, Wesker couldn't give Goldsmith's name, but 'Mr A.' is unquestionably Jimmy Goldsmith, as the text makes plain, even down to 'there's this woman in high French financial circles who's also managing director of his French company'. The 'fink' was a man called Pinder, who had worked for Nestlé for about ten years, advising, he told Wesker, on reorganisation and investments 'while at the same time making a good deal of money from his own speculations'.

Wesker watched, fascinated, as the *Business News* team followed up this lead. Two journalists, Graham Sergeant and Milner, both of whom had written about Goldsmith in the past, were assigned to the story, and Wesker asked to sit in on the meeting, taking his copious notes.

> The basis of [the fink's] story [he wrote], which I listen to with total incredulity, my eyes growing wider and wider each moment . . . is this: he had discovered, after minute research, that Mr A.'s stated share price since 1967 was based on a false market and that Mr A. was able to achieve this through a complicated system of interlocking holdings which worked roughly in this way: the English company takes over a French company which is then able to buy shares in the subsidiary of the English company which then buys . . . and so on.

Graham Sergeant remembers sitting through that interview growing more embarrassed by the moment, because the central thrust of Pinder's accusation was not so much Goldsmith's financial manoeuvring, although that was part of it, but something much more sinister. 'The mafia in all this is snuff,' Pinder suddenly said. 'Oh, don't laugh, don't laugh.' He reached into his briefcase to produce cuttings from German magazines. Snuff, he explained, was the new narcotic. 'You can put your LSD in it and the kids in Germany and Sweden are all taking it up.' But this was only a start. Pinder had been listened to patiently and courteously, and, says Wesker, had 'been so praised for his research that his guard lowers and, his eyes agitated by a sinister intelligence, he confesses his passion.' This turns out to be his conviction that there is a Jewish conspiracy to take over the European food industry, with Goldsmith at the heart of it. 'You must see that they're trying to dominate the new and the most important areas of leisure and food,' he said.

Wesker is a Jew, but sat quietly in his corner telling himself, as he says, 'to sit still and not be so sensitive'. The weirder allegations were discarded. But Pinder's crowded sheets of figures and charts contained points which Milner felt should be put to Goldsmith – without of course disclosing the source.

Unwisely (and unprofessionally), as a condition of the interview, Milner had agreed to let Goldsmith see a copy of his article before it appeared in the paper. A few days later he sent around a page proof. On it were scrawled the corrections made by the lawyers. 'Goldsmith when he read it was absolutely wild,' says Peter Wilsher, then the editor of *Business News*, 'and came round demanding Richard's head. We spent an uncomfortable hour going through it, but in fact the piece would have been toned down anyway, both by the lawyers and by me. Richard had shown him the very raw version, which he had written in a rather full-blooded "this-is-the-man-you-love-to-hate" way, which would never have got into print. If the lawyers hadn't, I would have taken it all out.'

Goldsmith remained – and remains – unconvinced of that. He says he got the accountants Price Waterhouse to prepare detailed figures answering some of the allegations, but Milner refused to accept them. 'In those days I thought I could convince enemies, but I was wrong. They're not interested.' So he decided on more drastic action.

Wilsher was not aware that Goldsmith had first of all gone to Roy Thomson, the proprietor of the *Sunday Times*. Thomson was an old friend of John Tigrett, who had brought him together with Armand Hammer to form one of the most successful partnerships in finding oil in Britain's sector of the North Sea. At Goldsmith's request, Tigrett rang him to make an urgent appointment. Thomson and Goldsmith were also partners in an insurance broking firm, Wigham Poland, which was a further link. Naively, Goldsmith assumed that complaining to Thomson was the best way of bringing pressure to bear on a journalist. Thomson, in line with most proprietors, had a strict rule about never interfering in the editorial policy of his newspapers, and refused to do so now. 'He [Goldsmith] had asked Roy Thomson to tell me to stop,' wrote the editor Harold Evans in his book *Good Times, Bad Times*. 'I had seen Goldsmith and told him he was certainly entitled to have allegations fairly put to him, but not to expect an acquaintanceship with Thomson . . . or an incidental business connection in insurance and legal publishing to have any influence on the *Sunday Times*.'

'I did not,' Evans added ruefully, 'think I had bowled him over.'

Nonetheless, Goldsmith remains convinced that it was pressure from Thomson that forced the article to be changed, and over the next decade it was to become a practice of his which was to cause immense resentment among journalists, and at least partly explain the antagonism which a few years later would make Goldsmith the most written-about person in Britain. 'There were certain pieces of that article which were grotesquely libellous taken out, and certain pieces that were just nonsense. If Roy Thomson hadn't intervened we would have been forced to sue. Until then it hadn't even occurred to me I would ever sue a newspaper, because I had been treated very well by the press. And soon afterwards Milner came to a Bovril press conference and glared at me from the front row. And then it all calmed down, and when we've spoken since it's all been rather friendly.'

At one meeting with Milner he says the journalist looked at him and said: 'I'm no more than the instrument in this. I'm the silver bullet. But it's not my finger on the trigger.' So whose finger was it? Goldsmith didn't even know of Pinder's existence until a few days later at a Cavenham general meeting, he noticed a blond-haired man sitting in the second row 'who had exactly the same file Milner had. So I said to myself: if he's got the same file he may be the man who is the trigger for the silver bullet. So I immediately got someone to find a firm of detectives to follow this man and find out who the hell he was. And we discovered his name was Mr Pinder, that he had worked for the Food and Agricultural Organisation and that previously he had worked for Nestlé.' Goldsmith used his contacts in France to get a complete rundown from Nestlé. He also suspected Pinder had been used by one of the potential rivals in his battle for Bovril, although never by Bovril itself, and he eventually compiled a large dossier on him. John Davies, then the Secretary of State for Trade, also had a file on Pinder which he passed to Goldsmith, who finally decided he was a harmless eccentric, who either out of anti-Semitism or some other inexplicable motive had chosen to hate him. The final word on Pinder should go to Wesker who quotes one of the *Sunday Times* journalists saying to him: 'It must be very frustrating never having met the man?'

'Good lord no!' he replied. 'I don't ever want to meet him. I'm so dead against him that I'm frightened of being seduced by his charm.'

The much-worked-on article, now purged of most of its offensive material, appeared on Sunday, 15 August 1971. It was a lengthy analysis of Goldsmith's financial record, dwelling at some length on the missed forecasts at Cavenham, the early accounting tactics which Milner found distinctly dubious, the auditors' qualification and the more obvious mistakes that Goldsmith had made. But read at this distance, it seems innocuous enough, certainly in the context of a contested bid. It was partial, yes, but not savagely so. If Milner had really wanted to put the knife into Jimmy, he could, with a slight twist, have presented his information in a far more damaging way. It might perhaps have tilted a wavering shareholder away from Jimmy Goldsmith, but there is no evidence that it ever did.

In any case Goldsmith was now charging ahead, with or without the support of the *Sunday Times*. As the markets opened for business on Monday morning, he went straight in, and by the close had bought another 12 per cent of Bovril's shares to take his holding to 36 per cent. The next day his stockbrokers went into the market again, adding another 7 per cent. By Wednesday, 18 August, he was up to 47 per cent, and announced that the Prudential Assurance company and another group had promised him their holding, 'which will put us over the top'.

He had scraped up the money from wherever he could: Cavenham's cash resources plus what it could borrow from Keyser Ullmann, but in those last few frantic days he ran out. Fortunately the London Stock Exchange worked on a system of two-week accounts, which meant that shares could be bought in that period and only paid for a few days after the account closed. 'We were buying the stock without funds, to tell the truth,' says Tigrett. 'And we were getting right up to the ragged edge.' Goldsmith didn't disagree. 'Every penny in the world we had, and every penny of credit we could raise, was used to buy Bovril.' There was some controversy over the fact that some of the blocks of shares sold to him in the final days had not actually been owned by the sellers: on the London market it is possible to sell shares you have not got on the basis that you can then hope to buy them later at a lower price and make a profit. In subsequent years the takeover rules were tightened up to stop this, but it was a practice that was still common even in the Guinness affair in 1986.

The Bovril bid was classic, textbook material. Goldsmith sustained the initiative from beginning to end, anticipating and countering each move by the defence, and tipping the odds in his favour with his Southland and Joseph deals. The Southland and Maxwell Joseph deals had been strokes of good fortune, but after all the ill-luck of previous years, he was due a break. And he made the most of it. Financially, Goldsmith had also put himself into a no-lose situation: because he had bought so many shares at lower prices – his first purchases in February 1971 had been at 171p a share, one-third of the eventual price – even if Rowntree emerged the winner, he would still have come out with a profit.

'We made mistakes in other operations, but in this one – no!' says

Madame Beaux. 'It could not have been done better. From the beginning it was textbook. Every time I give a lecture in France on hostile takeovers I think of Bovril, because it really was fantastic.'

Just how fantastic, time would prove. Within months Goldsmith had sold the dairy interests plus a prestige farm to Joseph for £5.3m, reducing his net cost to £9m. Gilberte Beaux with her South American experience and knowledge of Spanish went off to Argentina where she did what Beecham and other large companies reckoned could not be done: she sold the meat works, and brought the money home. By the time Goldsmith had finished selling off the bits of Bovril he didn't want, he had recouped almost all his original purchase price, leaving him with the main brands. He cut overheads by £500,000, revamped the marketing and doubled profits to £2m a year. Some years later, when he decided to get out of food, he sold the brand names to Beecham for £36m.

'Bovril was the turning point in Jimmy Goldsmith's career,' says John Tigrett, and Goldsmith himself does not disagree. 'It was the most important deal of my life.'

Yet it was only the prelude to a string of others.

'Jimmy Goldsmith is now believed capable of everything,' wrote *Management Today*. 'Yet before the Bovril bid and, indeed, during much of the bid there were few people – least of all in the City – who believed he was capable of anything at all.'

15

Boom Years

In April 1971 Cavenham was still a small company, making less than £2m on sales of £35m – a 'commercial pigmy' as one observer described it. Nine months later sales were over £400m, eleven times higher. The share price had risen from 70p to 230p by January 1972 and to 350p later in the year. Goldsmith had, as he put it early in 1972, 'been sprinting rather hard recently'.

If the *Sunday Times* episode still niggled, Goldsmith could scarcely complain about the rest of the press coverage he received in the immediate aftermath of the bid. Bovril was generally seen as a brilliantly successful campaign won against the odds by better tactical skills and a high degree of courage. To the victor the spoils.

The spoils in this case were something more than the assets and business of Bovril, considerable though they were. Slater's warning that he would never win another bid if he lost that one had a corollary: now Goldsmith could win anything, or at least anything within reason. This was an odd time in Britain, a period which would later be seen as unhealthy for British business in the sense that the stars were the financial whizzkids, dominated by Jim Slater, rather than the manufacturers, who seemed to be in terminal decline. There was a boom in the financial sector and a raging bull market on the stock exchange, but not much of any enduring substance happening in the rest of the country. The Heath government, after early promise, had abandoned any serious attempt at tackling the more intractable problems of monopoly trade union power, disastrous industrial relations, creeping state control, and a climate, both political and social, which was anti-business. Slater's young acolytes were now testing his theories – and those of Goldsmith – to the extreme, pushing them to a limit where there could be no rationalisation, no industrial logic. They were taking over old companies, closing them down, selling their offices and factories into the biggest property boom Britain had ever witnessed, and using the proceeds to pursue the next deal. Few paid even a token obeisance to the philosophy that Goldsmith had expounded for years, that the takeover raider was essential for the health of industry as a whole. The raider picked off the companies which had grown lazy or fat, electrified others to look to their laurels and their profits, and kept the process of industrial evolution moving in the right direction. To many that was an essentially self-serving and flawed explanation for what they saw as the worst kind of corporate piracy and asset stripping. Even Slater paid less attention to his own justifications, shortening his horizons all the time, extending his stock market dealing philosophy (where his real skills lay) into buying and selling companies. In this new world, the young whizzkids vied with each other in a new skill: shuffling paper shares at ever higher prices between each other, and between their own increasingly complex businesses. Sentiment, whether for a product, a factory, or an employee, was a sign of weakness. If you didn't have the stomach for telling the workers in a Midlands factory that you were closing them down because their premises were worth more as a site for a new shopping centre, there were plenty of hired guns who would do it for you.

Goldsmith, even at his business nadir, had never been a pure asset stripper in the sense that he took over companies simply to pillage them. From his earliest days, he had actually been remarkably consistent: he was interested in 'core' businesses, and anything that was peripheral should be sold, the proceeds concentrated on strengthening the core. True, he had closed factories and caused redundancies, but there was at least an industrial rationale behind both his takeovers and his closures or asset sales. A close reading of his annual reports shows Goldsmith reiterating that point again and again, even if it also reveals a number of changes of mind in other areas. Nevertheless the excesses of a few dozen young men, many of them financed and encouraged by Slater, created a stigma which attached to him, as well as to James Hanson and to others active in the takeover arena. If he wasn't an asset-stripper, at the very least he was 'one of those smart City financiers', much more interested in making money than in building real businesses, with real jobs.

In 1971, with the boom beginning to run, the Slater stable paid little attention to the argument. There was money for everyone, and it was only when the music stopped at the end of 1973, that the pain began. Almost none of the Slater generation of whizzkids would survive the first onslaught of the crash. It was here that Goldsmith's harsh experience in his early twenties was invaluable. So was the inbuilt pessimism which had caused him to tell Slater, several years before, that this would be the 'last major bull market of our lifetime'. Time would prove him wrong in the long term, as markets enjoyed their greatest boom ever in the 1980s. But in the period ahead, it gave him a head start on everybody else. He knew that as sure as night followed day, the boom would be followed by a bust. He intended to be ready for it.

It would take Goldsmith's active young team a matter of weeks to transform the fortunes of Bovril. But even before they did, Goldsmith's sights were elsewhere. In gambling parlance, he was on a run and he wanted to keep it going. The Bovril battle finished on 18 August 1971 but by 10 September he had another acquisition to announce. By now, people were coming to him with deals, and just after Bovril, Willie Webster, chairman of a company called Wrights Biscuits, made an approach. Webster in his day had been one of the pioneers of multiple retail chains in Britain and in 1966, when Cavenham lost £1m, Webster's business, including Moore's Stores, was making £1m a year. Old age and a heart attack, however, had taken their toll on him, and the stores had lagged behind the changes on the high streets. His companies were now losing money at over £1m a year, and his wife had persuaded him to sell up and retire.

Between them, Webster and his wife owned 41 per cent of the company which they offered to Goldsmith, who happily accepted, before making a bid for outstanding shares at a total cost of £10m.

Now Goldsmith was really hitting his stride. A fortnight after the Wrights deal, he completed his sale of Bovril's milk business to Maxwell Joseph, then bought the South African Marmite company in the first week of December. By mid-December, he was paying £12.7m, a price which even a year ago would have seemed immense, for a French agricultural and pharmaceutical company, Sanders, with £35m of sales (Cavenham's total at the start of the year) and £2.4m profit.

Each of these deals made possible the next. Bovril had doubled Cavenham's size, and the Wrights and Sanders deals had doubled it again. Yet in the mood of supreme confidence that flowed through him, Goldsmith was already planning a deal which would double its size once more.

*

Under the nondescript name of Allied Suppliers, a group of some of the best-known names on Britain's High Streets had been assembled: Liptons, Home & Colonial, Maypole, Presto supermarkets, and many others, a total of 1,620 shops in all, but shops in a different league from Goldsmith's collection of little tobacco and sweet shops. These were the real thing, the very heartland of food retailing, shops such as Jim Wood had only dreamed of. The group also owned a tea business, operating mainly under the Lipton name. If Bovril had been an establishment company, Allied Suppliers was even more so, its shares included in the *Financial Times* 30-share index which, since the 1930s, was the equivalent of the Dow Jones Industrial Averages for measuring the level of the London stock market.

Like most companies at this stage, Allied had attracted more than its share of potential predators, but it was protected by the fact that Unilever held a key block of shares which, although only 12 per cent of the capital, gave it one-third of the votes (not uncommon in Britain in the 1960s and 1970s, before non-voting shares were scrapped). In 1970, Charles Clore, now an aging giant of the takeover scene, came close to buying Allied, but pulled out because the shares of his own Sears group were low, and the price Unilever asked was, he believed, too high. Charles Gordon, the man who brought him the deal, tried hard to make him change his mind. 'I told Clore he was making a big mistake and Clore told me he didn't know what I was talking about,' said Gordon. Later, he added, when Clore realised his error, 'he observed on many occasions at dinner tables in London that Goldsmith's good fortune had been created by a couple of proper Charlies, i.e. Charles Clore and Charles Gordon.'

Unilever had no interest in the retailing business, but what it did like was the Lipton tea business. A more aggressive company, or indeed the modern Unilever, would have taken over the whole of Allied Suppliers, stripped out the tea business, and sold the stores on to somebody else – possibly to Goldsmith. But in those days it didn't think that way – that kind of activity was for the financial wheeler-dealers only. It took no financial genius to work out where Unilever's interest lay, yet the simple deal that Goldsmith proposed does not seem to have occurred to any of the other bidders.

Goldsmith approached Cob Stenham, a bright, outgoing man who was finance director of Unilever at the time, and told him he wanted to buy his stake and make a bid for the company. But he had no interest in the tea business. If Unilever would sell him its shareholding, he would agree to sell back the tea business. Stenham was intrigued. Yes, Unilever would

Above: The beribboned major domo of the Hotel de Paris in Monte Carlo, where the young Teddy and Jimmy (in pram) spent many holidays.

Below: A brief period of happy marriage: Jimmy and his first wife Isabel Patino. Five months later she was dead.

Below: Teddy and Jimmy (left) with Frank and Marcelle Goldsmith, probably in the Bahamas where the Goldsmiths spent World War II.

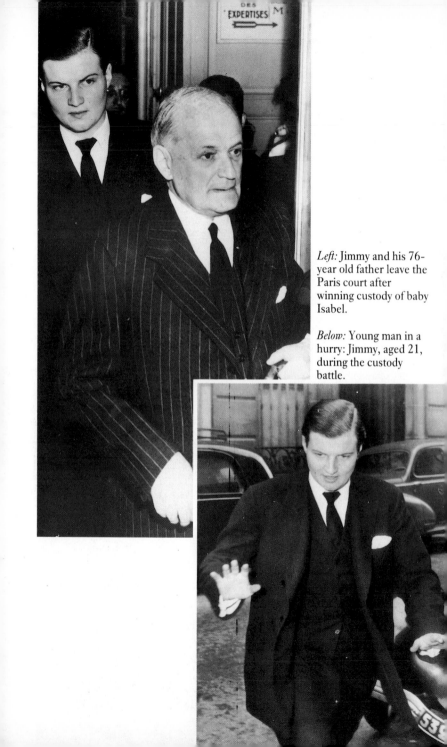

Left: Jimmy and his 76-year old father leave the Paris court after winning custody of baby Isabel.

Below: Young man in a hurry: Jimmy, aged 21, during the custody battle.

Left: January 1960. The new lady in his life: Ginette Lery, mother of his son Manes (and, later, daughter Alix).

Below: With his third wife, Lady Annabel, and Lady Falkender, at the launch of a book by his friend Henry Kissinger in 1979.

Above: May 1981: Goldsmith tells the staff of *Now!* magazine it has to close.

Above: From 1980 onwards, the main person in Goldsmith's life was Laure Boulay de la Meurthe, who has two children by him.

Left: With Annabel and their three children at their house in Spain.

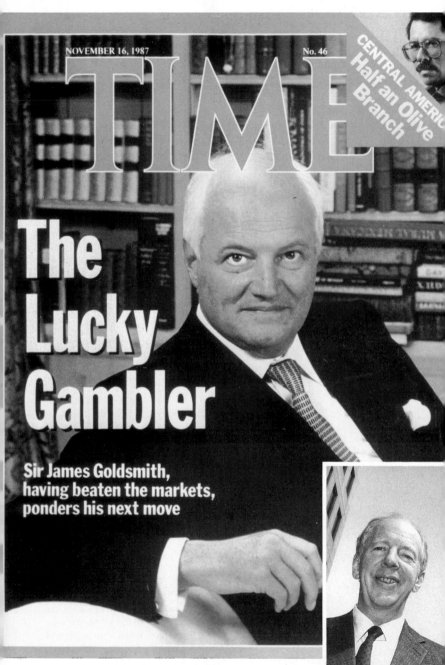

NOVEMBER 16, 1987

No. 46

TIME

CENTRAL AMERIC
Half an Olive
Branch

The Lucky Gambler

Sir James Goldsmith,
having beaten the markets,
ponders his next move

Above: Goldsmith's anticipation of the stock market crash of
October 1987 made him world news.

Above: Cuixmala, the Goldsmith house on the Mexican coast.

Below: The raiders: Jacob Rothschild and Kerry Packer join Goldsmith in a £13 billion bid for BAT.

Tycoon in retirement: Goldsmith at his Mexican hacienda.

sell its shares and were indeed interested, in principle, in buying the Lipton tea business. But they had to be very careful: Unilever, Allied Suppliers and Cavenham were all public companies, bound by strict rules. Unilever could not sell its Allied stake with the agreement that Cavenham would sell Lipton back to them – that would have constituted a 'special deal', or 'consideration' for the *de facto* controlling shareholder. Under any deal, there could be no suggestion that an unfair price had been set for Lipton in advance which would influence Unilever. They had to work out a delicate arrangement, which the Takeover Panel and the London Stock Exchange would accept, under which the price would be fixed independently, and after the event.

Goldsmith was taking something of a gamble: Unilever thought the tea business was worth perhaps £10m, £12m at the most, while Goldsmith wanted at least £15m. An independent arbitrator would decide who was right.

Early in the New Year, however, Stenham came back with a proposal: what about letting a leading accountant decide how much the tea business was worth? If Goldsmith would agree to the price set by him, then Unilever would too.

Goldsmith, who had done his calculations carefully, instantly accepted, paid Unilever £10.4m for its shares, and on 14 January bid for the rest. This was a big bid, one of the biggest ever done in Britain at the time: £82.5m, compared to the £65m market value of Cavenham. Bids by smaller companies for larger ones were almost unknown in 1972, but Goldsmith had started with 34 per cent of the votes and now went on a buying spree in the market to take his stake to 40 per cent. He was determined there would be no counter-bid this time.

But the Allied board could still fight, and he expected they would. The press that week-end was favourable, picking up the amazing series of deals he had put together in such a short time. The euphoria of the Bovril deal had not faded and the climate more than ever favoured the adventurous deal-maker. On Tuesday, 18 January 1972, Goldsmith met the Allied board in a private room in the Ritz. He came armed with both argument and a 'sweetener' – he proposed to increase his bid to £86m – and was prepared for a long, argumentative session. Whatever they may have been saying outside the room, the Allied board were remarkably timid faced with Goldsmith in full flow. He was the master of his facts and figures, seemed to know more about their business than they did, and easily dominated them. The Allied directors, unsure what to do before the meeting, tamely agreed to recommend his bid. There would be no battle this time.

In his bubbling, buoyant post-Bovril mood, Goldsmith was actually deflated. 'He was bitterly disappointed when Allied gave in,' an unnamed associate was quoted as saying at the time. 'He enjoyed a good fight.'

The *Financial Times* that week-end found him weary but triumphant. 'Even he seems surprised at the speed with which his openly expressed ambition to create a major, genuinely European food group is being realised,' it said. Just seven months before, the paper added with a touch of awe, Cavenham Foods 'was widely regarded as a nonentity in the food business, and at best a speculative stock.' After the Allied bid, Cavenham was in the same league as the biggest food companies in the land. Nevertheless, there were a few caveats which give a flavour of the City's view of Goldsmith at the time.

'Some people are still shaking their heads in disbelief,' commented the *Financial Times*. 'The argument runs thus: if the events of the past few months have materially increased Jimmy Goldsmith's reputation for financial wizardry – a reputation which has not always brought him universal approval – they have so far done little to prove that he can actually run the empire of his dreams.'

At that moment Goldsmith had temporarily given up running any empire, let alone the one of his dreams. Because of the Bovril bid he had missed his regular summer holiday, and had worked flat out for a year without a break. Now he was ready for one.

A number of issues remained to be resolved, however. John Tigrett's American friends Southland had an option to buy a half share of all his retailing interests, including Wrights and Allied shops. If they exercised it, it could bring in another welcome chunk of cash. The adjudicator had not yet sat to hear the arguments over the price of the Lipton tea business, and the reorganisation of Bovril was still in full spate.

Even as his business finally took off, Goldsmith continued to live his life on several different planes. In Paris, his office was run by Gilberte Beaux with an efficiency he himself could never have managed. The French operation was, at least before the Allied deal, as large as the British end. Maurice Lignon oversaw a profitable pharmaceutical and slim-food group. At the rue Monsieur, Ginette provided a home for his children (including Isabel when she was home) and for him when he was there. In London he lived a rather more bachelor-like and hectic social life, in which Annabel figured prominently – but so did the Clermont and John Aspinall. The gossip columns now talked openly about Annabel as his 'constant companion', but both of them had ceased to care. The William Hickey diary gave an impression of Goldsmith's social style at this time. After mentioning Annabel it observed that Goldsmith was often to be found in the Clermont. 'I have observed this balding, intrepid gambler play adventurously for four-figure stakes at *chemin de fer*. And in any backgammon competition his shrewd mathematical mind makes him an automatic favourite.' Goldsmith did indeed take backgammon very seriously at the time, entering whatever competitions were going, priding himself on being among the best players in the world.

Annabel's life had changed remarkably little. She had now been Jimmy's lover for seven years, and each year they saw more of each other, but she still lived in Pelham Cottage while he lived in Chester Terrace. She refused absolutely to go away with him during the school holidays or at half-term – these were reserved strictly for her children. But when the children went back to school, she and Jimmy usually went to the West Indies or somewhere warm in the winter, and France, Italy or Spain in the early summer. Her children were good-looking and very bright. Rupert, the eldest, got a scholarship to Eton (and later to Oxford). Robin was also ambitious and hard-working. She brought them up to show initiative, insisting they did holiday jobs, which Goldsmith admired. She was still officially married to Mark Birley, who had moved out of Pelham Cottage briefly at one stage, but she encouraged him to move back in again 'because he was so unhappy'. It was the summer of 1971 before he moved out permanently, buying a house in Pelham Street, with the garden adjoining that of Pelham Cottage.

Goldsmith was often in Paris at the week-ends, and she complained she found herself at a loose end. On one of these week-ends, in the winter of 1970, Annabel took up John Aspinall's long-standing invitation to bring the children down to his Howletts zoo in Kent to see the animals. Aspinall proudly showed them the chimpanzees first, and then took the family on to his favourite tigers.

For years Aspinall had expounded to all who would listen his absolute conviction that tigers were remarkably trustworthy animals if they were treated properly. Until that day he had been proved right. When they arrived at the tiger compound it was agreed that the younger children, including Annabel's daughter India Jane, would stay outside, but Annabel and her two older children plus Aspinall's two children and second wife, Min, went inside. He wanted them all to meet one of his favourite tigers, Zorra, which had been born at Howletts and had been reared by Min. Young Robin Birley, then twelve, stroked the animal which seemed listless and placid, until suddenly she turned, pushed the boy to the ground and gripped his head in her mouth. Aspinall prised the tiger's jaws apart by sheer strength while Min pulled her tail, whereupon the tiger wheeled on Min and knocked her over. Min screamed at her, and she finally backed off.

They rushed Robin to Canterbury hospital, his mangled head on Annabel's arm in the back of the car. He had a gaping hole where his mouth was and his bottom jaw hung by a thread. Annabel was certain he could not survive, but hours of emergency surgery saved his life. However, the bones on one side of his face were so crushed that they would never develop, and he grew to maturity with a lopsided face, but no other permanent damage.

On this occasion, Goldsmith could offer only comfort and support – Robin was Mark Birley's child, not his.

At the end of the Allied bid, Goldsmith flew to Corsica to join Ginette and the children for what should have been a holiday, though he had work to do. He and Unilever had chosen the most eminent accountant in Britain to settle the price for Lipton's tea business: Sir Ronald Leach, President of the Institute of Chartered Accountants. Goldsmith was determined to get the maximum price for it, and decided that, rather than leave it to anyone else, he would present his own case to the adjudicator. He called his accountants and financial advisers down to France to brief him, and for a week he rehearsed his arguments, committing to memory large numbers of figures, facts and forecasts. He then flew back to London, rested and ready. To Unilever, the biggest food company in the world, it was just another deal and Stenham's team had simply run through the papers a few days before. Goldsmith was at his best that day as he presented his case for three hours. Too late, the Unilever men began to realise they had paid the business too little attention, and they would have to pay the price.

At the end of the session, Goldsmith took the second part of his six-week break. He had left Ginette in Corsica. Now he took Annabel for a cruise on a yacht he had chartered in the Aegean; Aspinall and Min joined them there.

A great deal hung on the price Jimmy would receive from Unilever, both for his own ego and for the company's finances. On the yacht's radio-telephone he learned that Leach was about to deliver his binding judgment, but Aspinall had organised a run ashore to explore some of the historic sites and insisted he accompany him. Annabel stayed behind, and Goldsmith carefully instructed her about the telephone call he was expecting. 'Take a note of the exact amount the adjudicator has decided Unilever should pay,' he said, before climbing into the motorboat. Late that afternoon they returned. Had the call come through from London? It had. What was the figure? 'It was six million . . . or was it sixteen million, or maybe twenty-six million,' floundered Annabel. 'Oh, I knew I should have written it down.'

Hastily Goldsmith called London. The price Unilever had to pay was actually £18.5m. Even in his current, enhanced circumstances it was a great deal of money, more than any of the executives at Cavenham had ever seen. 'When the cheque came around we all touched it,' says one.

Still in the Aegean, Goldsmith rang Southland to determine what the Americans wanted to do about their option on the other retailing operations. To exercise it would cost £25m, and Southland decided it could not afford the outlay. That didn't matter – Goldsmith now had plenty of cash, and ways of realising even more with the property market continuing to boom.

However, he was quite unprepared for the acclaim. Goldsmith had moved with extraordinary speed from a City nobody into the big league, arousing interest far beyond the confines of the financial establishment. Ivan Rowan, a thoughtful, iconoclastic feature writer for the *Sunday Telegraph*, interviewed him and wrote a slightly quizzical piece which began: 'Someone remembers Jimmy Goldsmith competing for a taxi in the rush hour, standing out in the street and shouting, "Big tips, big tips".'

More interesting, perhaps, is Rowan's description, a first-time impression from a keen observer:

He is a very tall, spreading man . . . with an often amused face – high cheekbones, cleft chin, slightly small mouth – which stops being amused at his eyes: cold, turquoise, very watchful under slender eyebrows. There are good judges of men and business who believe that the City is going to have to accept Goldsmith as one of the shrewdest business empire-builders of recent times.

Rowan was not a financial journalist, but researched his subjects well, and would have talked to a number of City people to arrive at that view. Goldsmith was not to know that this was a honeymoon period before he and the press would be at each other's throats.

As the bull market continued in full flow, the rumours around Goldsmith were numerous. He was tipped to be about to buy every major food company in the country: Ranks Hovis McDougall, Reckitt and Colman, Unigate, Brooke Bond Liebig, Cadbury Schweppes, Rowntree Mackintosh . . . Nothing, in the view of the rumour-spreaders, seemed to be beyond his new magical reach.

Goldsmith himself, however, was turning his attentions in a new direction. His food company in Britain was large enough for the present, but the French and European arms were lagging. His Dutch acquisitions were not a success, and the company still fell some way short of his European ideal. Britain had agreed to join the Common Market the previous June, and Goldsmith wanted to be in the forefront.

He now began a series of moves in France. The first of these was an important recognition of Goldsmith's position in a circle that mattered to him considerably. The Rothschild family, his distant cousins, had always slightly looked down on Frank and his children. Through the Compagnie du Nord they were the biggest shareholders in one of France's largest food groups, Générale Alimentaire, but had no idea how to manage it. They had been forced to concede that their move outside the traditional style of banking had been disastrous, and now retreated, imposing a solution on each one of their problem expansions. Goldsmith was the solution for their food group.

In April, Cavenham bought one-fifth of Générale Alimentaire, and Générale Occidentale bought another 5 per cent, giving Goldsmith a 25 per cent stake – equal to the Rothschild interest. With this leverage, it was a simple matter to merge Générale Alimentaire with Cavenham's French subsidiary, FIPP, to produce a company with a turnover of £100m. Goldsmith did not actively get involved in the management of the new French company, but he did galvanise it. He found there was a man at Générale Alimentaire who, when he first met him, 'scared the pants off me'. Jacques Dumon was the same age as Goldsmith (39), a typical example of the modern French manager: ex-Harvard Business School, ex-Polaroid, ex-L'Express newspapers. But he had never been able to achieve much under the dead hand of the Rothschilds. Générale Alimentaire was the result of a merger of 51 family companies, and, before Goldsmith arrived, Dumon despondently reckoned it would take years to install the financial control systems and modern management it desperately needed. Within weeks Goldsmith changed all that. Dumon now reckoned he could move 'five times as fast as I otherwise would have been able to do', adding that all he had to do was pick up the phone and talk to Jack Greenhalgh or Goldsmith himself, 'and take an important decision. It's a dream come true.'

Goldsmith was still riding the stock market and property boom for all he was worth, although a great deal of hard work was going on to harmonise and restructure the acquisitions. He had proved himself in the acquisition field. But he had still to impress the financial community and the food industry that he was more than a shrewd financial operator. Many newspaper articles, even sympathetic ones, carried the reservation, 'He has yet to prove he can manage a group of this size.'

In fact Cavenham had for some years been a well-managed company, and Goldsmith was doing far more with his acquisitions than was realised. At Bovril, for instance, he concentrated all the management effort on the three main brands, Bovril, Marmite and Ambrosia, which had been starved of support. The vast bulk of the Bovril assets were not, he discovered, employed behind the successful brands at all – the farms and dairies for example had nothing to do with them. He kept a single farm to provide the milk for Ambrosia, but that particular brand had suffered badly at the hands of own-label canned milk puddings. 'We got to it just in time,' said Jack Greenhalgh, who went in himself to manage Ambrosia. The changes in Bovril were felt from top to bottom as the Greenhalgh team swept through. Eight of the ten main board directors had departed, and new marketing and finance people were installed.

Nevertheless, there was a great difference between the type of reorganisation Goldsmith had attempted in the 1960s and what he was doing now. The companies he originally bought for Cavenham were effectively dead, and he had neither money nor management to revive them. His purchases in the 1970s had top class brands and assets, and he had all the money he needed, plus a management team which had learned a great deal from the years of adversity. Within a short period, even his enemies had to admit that the Bovril brands, and the Allied stores, were better run, more successful (in every sense) and more profitable than they had been before. The management techniques which had once failed him had been changed, developed and honed – and they now worked.

If this amazing run of deals had been all he achieved in this period, Goldsmith would have more than earned himself the title one French magazine gave him in the middle of 1972 – *le sorcier de la City* – but in fact there was another whole stream of activities which almost added up to a deal a day. At the centre of this web of companies was a group, which was to become almost as important as Cavenham, called Anglo-Continental Investment and Finance Company. Such was Goldsmith's following at the time that within a year of his taking control, its shares had risen so steeply that, as Jim Slater remarked, they 'lost all touch with reality'.

When Goldsmith first came across it, Anglo-Continental was a tiny company. Founded in 1897, it provided a few financial services, owned a small bank and ran a unit trust. Total profits were less than £25,000 a year.

When he first bought into it, there was much speculation that this was to be his fun company, a group he would use to deal in shares, or as a purely financial vehicle for his more outrageous deals, leaving the staider deals for the now more respectable and solid Cavenham.

Goldsmith certainly was interested in using Anglo-Continental to make himself some real money. But he had another purpose in mind. At some point the fashion was going to turn, and Cavenham too would suffer. Goldsmith had taken over too many former highfliers to have any illusions about Cavenham's vulnerability. He was determined to have a financial arm ready to support it when the crash came. In the autumn of 1971 he took a controlling stake through Générale Occidentale, which would remain his master company, and brought de Clermont-Tonnere, Gilberte Beaux and John Tigrett on to the board. Tigrett in turn brought in the Union Bank of California as a major backer. And Goldsmith was off on a run which made his activities at Cavenham look staid. The strategy was simple. As Jim Slater explained, Jimmy 'was the first to realise that it made sense to Anglo-Continental shareholders for the company to issue its shares for hard assets, and that his company was in a very strong position to do this.' The shares were 37p in September 1971 when he first took an interest, 64p by November and 270p by the following June. He used his high-priced shares as currency, paying over the odds for companies on the basis that he was still boosting the underlying asset value. Jim Slater was more than happy to sell to him on those terms and Goldsmith became the almost automatic recipient of some very strange companies. In his hectic deal-making, Slater had acquired a vast battery of holdings, subsidiary companies, satellites and other bits and pieces. As 1972 wore on, with Slater approaching the peak of both his fame and his fortune, the two men became closer friends, dining together once a fortnight. At one of those dinners, early in July 1972, with the stock market at its highest ever level, they made their first deal of many: Goldsmith would buy Thomas Stevens, which owned a store in Cardiff and was run by Nicholas Berry, son of Lord Hartwell, the *Daily Telegraph* proprietor. Anglo would pay £9m for it. Slater also sold him Tanker Investment Trust for another £8m.

The two also agreed a deal which even the exceptionally clever Jim Slater found complicated: Anglo bought effective control of Slater's property satellite, Argyle Securities, with Slater retaining an interest. In later years, this company would become the centre of some controversy and investigation.

In the meantime Goldsmith did another deal with his old friend Harry Recanati, who had backed him at Cavenham all those years before: Anglo acquired 51 per cent of the Ralli Brothers bank in Switzerland. Recanati also sold him the Discount Bank in Paris, a one-third share in a firm of insurance brokers (Wigham Poland, in which Roy Thomson also had a stake) and some other assets injected by Générale Occidentale, including the Dutch banking subsidiary.

All this flamboyant wheeler-dealing revived some of the earlier criticism of Goldsmith. Yet he himself was fairly clear about what he was doing. In 1972 he gave a lunch in London for French journalists interested in Générale Occidentale. The venue was a private room in the Ritz, and over lunch one of the journalists asked him: 'Why Anglo-Continental?'

'Because,' replied Goldsmith, 'there's going to be a slump and when the slump comes the new companies, the ones run by entrepreneurs, will automatically become the most frail because they are the ones that have grown the fastest. They are the ones who are going to be in the most serious trouble, and their shares are going to be massively overvalued. And therefore I've got to be able to create another company which is going to be able to protect Cavenham when its shares fall and bolster our position.'

What he was trying to do, he went on, was to create in Anglo a vehicle which could do business on its own – insurance broking, financial services – which could do deals, but which would also be a 'cash point' for picking up Cavenham shares when they fell. 'Otherwise we will be bid for because our shares will drop more than the market averages.'

His habit of using one company to buy shares in another was to be at the centre of the investigations into the Goldsmith empire, but Goldsmith at the time made no secret of it. Years later, Goldsmith insists: 'It was a good prognosis. All my deals with Jim [Slater] were designed to build up Anglo's cash holdings. I bought investment trust after investment trust from him and liquidated the dross, and we built it up to seventy-five million pounds worth of capital, most of it in cash.' It was to save him, when almost every single one of the Slater generation of entrepreneurs disappeared in the mid-1970s.

Slater and Goldsmith got into the habit of meeting at Goldsmith's home in Chester Terrace, playing a few games of backgammon (which

Goldsmith usually won) and then driving to Wiltons in Bury Street, just off St James's. In years past Wiltons had been one of the haunts of Frank Goldsmith and the old proprietor, the great Mr Marks, remembered him well. On one occasion he stopped at Goldsmith's table and observed the two men sharing a small pot of caviar with some hot toast. 'Ah, Mr Goldsmith,' he exclaimed, 'nice to see you enjoying the caviar. Of course,' he added as he moved on to the next table, 'your father always used to have a large pot.' It was, Slater teased him, the only time he had ever seen Goldsmith rendered speechless.

Not for long however. They were soon discussing their biggest deal yet, like so many others, scribbled on a waitress' pad: Anglo would buy another package of Slater's cast-offs: a 44 per cent stake in the insurance broker Wigham Richardson, and stakes in two more investment trusts, Flag and Irish. They were to be paid for in a mixture of Anglo shares and loan stock, and the two men began to argue about the final price. Goldsmith offered £42m, but Slater wanted a small premium and asked for £43m. Finally, Goldsmith snapped:

'Let's not argue. I'll play you for the difference.' What game? asked Slater. They tossed a coin to see who should choose the game: Goldsmith would go for backgammon at which he knew he could beat Slater unless luck ran heavily against him, and Slater would choose chess where Goldsmith wouldn't stand a chance. Goldsmith won the toss, and they went back to his house to play backgammon. Slater lost his extra million, but even the £42m he received was a good price.

That deal marked the end of this particular phase. 'The effect on the underlying fundamental worth of Anglo-Continental was extremely beneficial to that company,' wrote Slater, 'but the share price never recovered from the weakening of the technical position occasioned by the issue of so many shares.'

The bull market was over, and with it the magic of Jim Slater began to fade. The deals he had done with Goldsmith strengthened his balance sheet but they would not be enough to save him as the young men he had backed began to be wiped out in their droves. Even though the property boom ran for a year after the stock market boom ended, it was still not enough to save a company which had made too many disastrous loans.

The case of Thomas Stevens is an interesting illustration of one of Slater and Goldsmith's deals. This was a small property company in which Jim Slater had bought a controlling interest. Typically he would produce one of his many young men from a back room, lend him the money to buy a large slice of shares in a little shell company, and feed him a number of acquisitions culled from the many other companies he owned and was breaking up. The share price would then rise, basically because Slater would spread the word it was the new favoured stock, allowing the company to make further acquisitions.

In this case the young man was Nicholas Berry, of a different quality to the others. As it happened Berry had, as a former financial journalist, written some critical pieces about Goldsmith before the Bovril bid. In one piece he called Goldsmith a 'backgammon-playing gambler', and an irritated Jimmy invited him over so he could explain what he was planning for Bovril. The two got on well enough, and Berry's next piece explained why he had called him a 'backgammon-playing gambler' before going on to give Goldsmith's defence.

Berry had a sceptical and original approach to many of the whizzkids of the day, but when he left journalism, he went to work with Slater and ended up running Thos. Stevens. Right on form, the share price rose, and Berry bought a hotel in Cardiff and then the largest store there, James Howell.

He was making progress with the company when, overnight, he found that he had been transferred from the Slater camp to Goldsmith's. 'Goldsmith was very decent about it to me,' says Berry. 'He behaved very well. What he got was in good shape, with no debt.' Goldsmith explained to Berry that he had bought Stevens basically to convert it into cash. Berry didn't object, 'and I helped him do it. It was done quite quickly, and he said he wanted to sell the department store, and we sold it to House of Fraser, and the hotel was also sold, and he raised quite a substantial amount of money.' Goldsmith paid around £7m for Stevens in his high-priced shares, and realised about the same amount in cash; Slater, meanwhile, had sold the Anglo shares in the market, so he too had his £7m. While the music lasted, it was a wonderful game. As for Berry, having worked himself out of a job, but considerably the wiser after his time with the two great financial wizards of the age, he left to start up his own company – which he still runs.

On 17 September 1972, a thoughtful article appeared in the *Investors Review* under the title 'Is the Game Over?' Another one came out on the same day in the *Investors Guardian* under the heading 'City turns against the highfliers', which concluded: 'As far as the stock market is concerned it is rapidly becoming bad news to have the tag "asset stripper" attached to a company and the frenzy that made investors think that almost any price was too low for these operations has disappeared.' That same week-end, a third magazine, the *Investors Chronicle*, wrote an article along the same lines, suggesting that financial shares which had led the market up were now leading it down.

Those three articles were enough to persuade Jim Slater of what he already suspected: 'The herd had begun to move, and I knew then for certain that the policy I had been following during the previous few months of liquidating major share positions had been the right one.'

Goldsmith felt the same (the two men often compared notes, of course, but one was a seller, the other a buyer), and a greater urgency was creeping into his drive for cash. By January he was as liquid as he could get. The boom was ending. Turbulent times lay ahead.

16

Top of the Boom

I would rather see finance less proud and industry more content.
Winston Churchill

'I believe the present government is the best government Britain has ever had,' said Jimmy Goldsmith in January 1972. That winter, as unemployment rose, the government of Edward Heath had slashed taxes, freed government expenditure from restraint and sparked the boom in which Goldsmith – and many others – was to make a fortune. But there was another factor that stoked the boom, particularly in property and secondary banking, and which was to have major consequences for Goldsmith. In September 1971, the Heath government introduced its new banking policy which it called Competition and Credit Control. It was the brainchild of the Bank of England rather than the Treasury or Department of Trade, and was designed essentially to replace the old 'ceilings' on the size of loans the commercial banks could make to private borrowers. Well before 'Thatcherism' had ever been invented, 'competition', or market forces, was to control the amount the banks would lend. From now on the price mechanism, or the level of interest rates, was to be the main restraint. 'What we have in mind,' said the Governor of the Bank of England, Leslie O'Brien, 'is a system under which the allocation of credit is primarily determined by its cost.'

The results of the policy were spectacular – and exactly the opposite to what was intended. Between December 1971 and December 1974 the total assets of British banks rose by £48 billion, or 131 per cent. Advances rose even more: 160 per cent. As one observer sourly remarked: 'More pounds sterling were created in these three years than in the whole twelve hundred years' history of the pound since King Offa.'

Where did this huge volume of new loans and advances go? Not to British manufacturing industry – it received £6 billion out of a total increase of £46 billion in advances. The government took some, but a major slice went direct to property companies, to 'other financial' companies and to personal borrowings. Only a fraction of this money was for genuine investment – the property industry cannot put up new buildings at that rate – so it financed 'speculation' in the true sense of the word, the buying of assets, not because the purchaser wanted to keep them, but because he hoped to make a profit through rising prices. The speculative boom was also encouraged by the emergence of a new type of bank, or financial enterprise. These 'secondary' banks could take deposits (usually Euro-dollar deposits where London led the world), but instead of using them for the tedious (as well as unprofitable) purposes of normal banking, they lent the money to buy shares and properties.

Slater Walker was not strictly a 'secondary' bank, because it owned a properly authorised one (Ralli, bought from Goldsmith's old friends Sir Isaac Wolfson and Harry Recanati). But nonetheless it was very much at the forefront of the movement, financing and supporting many of the little property companies and the new-fangled 'banks', and to a substantial degree epitomising the spirit of the movement.

In retrospect, it is extraordinary how few warning voices there were of the inevitable disaster. In many ways the circumstances were not dissimilar to the events leading up to the 1929 Wall Street crash and the previous Florida land booms. A huge amount of credit was being fed into the system, to be used not for investing in the production of new goods and services but to stoke a speculative boom that was already running far too fast. The normally cautious Bank of England, instead of demanding action to slow things down, was actually piling coals on the fire. And the Heath government was so concerned with unemployment rising again that it kept the accelerator hard down. House prices in a single year rose by 60 per cent, and office values often by more. A whole new breed of property entrepreneurs traded blocks of commercial property between each other at ever spiralling prices, often taking a profit of 50 per cent in a matter of months, trading on to someone else who in turn took a similar profit – much of it financed by the secondary banks, and by groups such as Slater Walker.

Goldsmith's judgement of the government in Britain at the time was essentially a blinkered and personal one, based to some extent on Heath's successful negotiation of Britain's entry into Europe. He and his friends were doing well, and there was no reason why he should get off the merry-go-round – at least not for a while yet.

242

Jim Slater revealed his famous market feel by beginning to dump shares early, but it never occurred to him until too late that property prices could crash, and that loans, considered perfectly safe in the conditions of late 1972, would be transformed into hopelessly bad debts 18 months later.

By the autumn of 1972 a few critical voices suggested that the economy was overheating, but they were muted, and the government vigorously rejected them as carping. Although the stock market had reached its peak the previous May, it was still high and many thought it would go higher still.

Goldsmith's vertiginous rise had given him a new status and standing in the world, not just in Britain and France but elsewhere. With British entry into the Common Market imminent, the new Europeans were the flavour of the day. In September 1972 he appeared on the cover of *Time* magazine. He was not on his own: there were seven other European bankers and industrialists, including Jim Slater, the eight 'new young Europeans who are making their influence felt from Iberia to Scandinavia ... Multinational in their attitudes, multi-lingual and young, they are quietly changing the style and stepping up the pace of European business.' Slater was delighted with it, and even more pleased when *Vogue* asked Cartier-Bresson to take some pictures of him for a series called 'Power People'. Slater by now had stormed the Far East, his influence dominating the stock markets of Hong Kong, Singapore and Malaysia. He had companies in Canada and was also feeling his way into the United States. Prompted by Goldsmith, the much more insular Slater began to open banks and satellites around Europe too, uneasily moving into areas where Goldsmith was at home.

Cavenham had become a genuinely European company, with subsidiaries in most countries. And Goldsmith held some strong, even quaint, ideas on how a European company should be run. Cavenham's subsidiaries, he said, 'should form part of the community in which they are based. National pride is a fact of life which can be a powerful asset in developing any major enterprise.' Cavenham's policy, he told its shareholders and employees, would be to participate in Europe 'as a major shareholder rather than as an outright owner', giving local management more or less total autonomy. He insisted that meetings be conducted in the local language, the reports then sent back to London. Fortunately, someone remarked, the Swedes preferred to use English for their meetings. Jack Greenhalgh liked the policy. 'It gave us an advantage over some other English companies, because we often found that other British companies had chosen a managing director for no other reason than he was the only one who could speak English.' It is a philosophy which had a brief vogue through the 1970s as a means of making the multinational corporation work. But as the concept of the multinational was replaced by the 'global' company, offering the same produce or service everywhere in the world with much stronger centralised control, it faded again. In time, it would probably have been another Goldsmith enthusiasm that was changed and adapted.

In January 1973 Goldsmith held a party at the Ritz in London. Organised by Aspinall's brother-in-law, Anthony Little, it was an extravagant affair, the event of the year. Little had been heralded as the new Aubrey Beardsley and was commissioned by Aspinall to recreate the Palace of Sinope at the Clermont for one of his parties, which took three months to prepare. Other Aspinall feasts were even more exotic: the Banquet of Montezuma, an Aztec party and so on. The basement of the Ritz with its huge mirrored rooms had been decorated with large quantities of orchids and palms, five jazz bands had been flown in from New Orleans and the overall effect, contrasting starkly with the cold January night outside, was of a hot Louisiana evening.

Annabel was Goldsmith's hostess, and he invited the great and the good: half the cabinet, bankers, leading editors, company chairmen, and all their old friends – 250 guests in all. It was half a fortieth birthday party – Goldsmith's birthday was six weeks off – but, when the press commented on it, Goldsmith converted it, retrospectively, into an eighteenth birthday party for Isabel. Goldsmith's eldest daughter, dressed in white, stood beside him in the receiving line, but she had invited none of the guests, and her name did not feature on the invitation. The fact that, unlike her sister Alix, she was never actually given an eighteenth birthday party but had to make do with this one rankled for years.

Goldsmith, however, was determined to enjoy the evening. It was the grandest, most extravagant party he had ever given. He was elated as he moved around the room, but beneath his high good humour he was conscious of something else. 'Enjoy it while you can,' he kept repeating. 'You won't see another party like this for some time.'

Later that month he set off on a long trip that was to mark a major change of direction in his life. He went first to New York, where as usual he took a suite in the Carlyle. From there he went on to Brazil and Venezuela, and by the third week in February he was in Acapulco where Annabel joined him for what was to be a long celebratory house party to mark his fortieth birthday.

It was from Acapulco that he gave the order to begin selling: shares, properties and companies which didn't fit. He had been mulling over how best to react to the economic downturn for some months. Goldsmith's moods swing violently, from enormous optimism to a deep feeling of foreboding. He is also a deeply superstitious man, to the point where he has always carried with him tokens of good luck. Once when he signed a deal he was wearing a particular pair of socks, and he insisted on signing all future deals in the same pair. For a long time, too, he had to wear the same pair of shoes on important days, and favoured certain ties for the same reason. He would, and still does, 'touch wood' – his head would do – to ward off bad luck, and would react furiously if someone said 'Good luck!' to him. 'Don't say that!' he would almost scream, fearing the reverse effect. Nothing annoyed him more than when his family or staff ignored his foibles. When a maid in Paris, finding this ancient and by now holey pair of socks, threw them out, Goldsmith went frantic and a great search of dustbins was initiated before they were recovered. When little Alix gave him a wicker basket, he used it for his papers, carrying it from private plane to Rolls-Royce as if it were a Gucci briefcase. All his life he has had talismans – a particular pair of cufflinks given to him by his father, a green stone frog Ginette bought him in South America, or a piece of amber which Aspinall gave him, which he continually plays with, squeezing, juggling, stroking it.

There is a deep melancholic streak in Goldsmith which, even at his high points, makes him distrust his good fortune and causes him to examine the hundred different ways he can lose it all again. Even in later years when he had the best part of a billion dollars in the bank, he would worry that a world banking crisis could wipe him out. In many ways this concern was what made him such a good businessman: the sense that he could never rest on his laurels, that the next decision might eclipse all the good ones taken, the feeling of vulnerability which contrasted so starkly with the complacency he found in so many of the companies he took over.

In 1971 and 1972 Goldsmith had enjoyed the boom, but all through it he fretted about what the downturn would bring. As he turned 40, he suddenly decided the bull market he had told Slater about was over. World commodity prices had doubled in 1972, a record increase which would inevitably push up prices everywhere and by themselves cause economic activity to fall sharply. The US was turning down, and Britain would too – even before the days of global stock markets, there was an adage which ran: 'If Wall Street sneezes, then London catches a cold.

And if Wall Street catches a cold, London gets pneumonia.' Already in Britain interest rates had risen from 5 per cent in the summer of 1972 to 9 per cent by the end of the year, and the Treasury was forecasting a slowdown from 6 per cent growth (absolutely breakneck by British standards where the long-term growth rate is less than 3 per cent) to 3.5 per cent for 1973. However, interest rates were coming down again as the government, still refusing to recognise the signs of overheating, tried to sustain the boom.

From Acapulco Goldsmith rang John Ritblat, one of the leading property men in London. Ritblat was both an estate agent, through his Conrad Ritblat business, and the chairman of one of the biggest property companies in Britain, British Land. He lived near Jimmy in Regent's Park and often dropped in to sip a glass of champagne in the evening while Goldsmith from his bath discussed the property market. He had, he told Ritblat, decided to sell all his property, the entire portfolio of surplus shops, buildings, head offices of the various companies he had taken over – the lot. He then rang Lionel Ross, Cavenham's finance director, to reinforce the instruction. The process of converting the investment portfolios and property companies Anglo-Continental had bought must be speeded up too – he wanted the whole portfolio in cash as soon as possible.

He was only just in time. Share prices in London were already dropping. Fortunately for Goldsmith, the property boom continued and would last for another year, deceiving many of the shrewder financial minds of the time. By April Goldsmith had sold two of the main Allied Suppliers' buildings in the City for £11.7m in cash (the buyer, Cavendish Land, later sold them on again to the Legal and General Insurance Company at an even more inflated price). He sold surplus shops to Guardian Properties (which went bust in the crash) for £17.5m, insisting that £8.75m be paid before September 1973 and the rest by the end of 1976. He sold some of his share portfolios, and the banking subsidiary of Anglo-Continental entered the turbulent period with a high degree of liquidity without which it could not have survived.

On 26 February 1973 Goldsmith spent his fortieth birthday in Acapulco with some of his oldest friends: Aspinall of course, Peter West whom he had known since he was 16, Dominic Elwes and another of the Clermont crowd, Lord Lucan; and, of course, Annabel.

During his extensive trip, he had been doing some long-term thinking

246

about his life. He now had the option to do whatever he liked: retire and live in some luxury, continue building his European multinational, become more of a financier and head of a *banque d'affaires* – or diversify further afield. He had never done much business in the United States, but that was the engine room of the world's business and it was a major market to be conquered. He had already taken the decision to go as liquid as possible before the pending crash, but that was a tactical rather than a strategic move. He was now looking beyond that. What did he really want to do with the rest of his life? Or at least the next decade? Where did he want to be when he was 50? Or 60? What country did he want to live in? And with whom?

In London he had never lived openly with Annabel, even though he made no secret of his relationship with her. She was, after all, a member of the Londonderry family, and there were certain proprieties to be kept up. He spent nights with her at Pelham Cottage and she stayed with him at Chester Terrace, but that was unsatisfactory for both.

For the past year he had been urging Annabel to accept a more prominent role in his life; in fact he wanted her to have his children. He loved Manes, his only son, but the boy, who had inherited his father's voice and looks, but neither his height nor personality, showed no great aptitude for business. Although he would later abandon it, Jimmy, up to this time, still thought in terms of the restoration of the Goldschmidt dynasty. That meant passing on what he had created to a son. He could love his daughters absolutely, but just as the Rothschilds never accepted daughters or sons-in-law into the partnership room, neither did the Goldschmidts. Goldsmith was hugely impressed with Annabel's children. If she could do that for Mark, he reasoned, perhaps she could do it for him. He wanted more children, a second family.

The break-up of her marriage had been bruising for Annabel and she hated the gossip that circulated about her and Goldsmith. Having a relationship with a married man was one thing, however; having a baby out of wedlock, for a person from Annabel's background, was something else. Even by the early 1970s in Britain it was simply not done, and Annabel, brave enough on most counts, shied away from it. On the other hand she had now been Jimmy's mistress for ten years, and at 39 was also keen to have more children. She remembers Aspinall walking her around the garden, explaining the importance to Jimmy, and urging her to defy the views of her peers and her family.

Now in Acapulco Jimmy became insistent. He wanted her to live with him openly; she could sell Pelham Cottage, they would buy a house together, and eventually they would both divorce and marry. For months she had been weakening; and now she relented. She would have his children.

Goldsmith was also thinking deeply about his business operation. Having seen something of America, he was not convinced he wanted to concentrate his efforts on Europe. He was also being encouraged by friends and business associates – Roland Franklin and John Tigrett, mainly – to exercise his talents in a bigger arena, where the rewards more closely matched the risks. America, even in modest recession, still throbbed with a vitality that suited him. It was also such a huge and prosperous market that Europe seemed second-rate.

As early as 1971, Goldsmith had tried several gambits, including an early run at trying to make use of his British retailing muscle by buying into an already positioned American brand name. Only a month before his fortieth birthday, he had looked briefly at Squibb Corporation's baby food business, second only to Gerber with 20 per cent of the market, but quickly dropped it. Madame Beaux had been working on potential American acquisitions for 18 months, but so far had been unable to bring anything to fruition.

The strategy for 1973 was to build up cash in Anglo-Continental, which would be used to make Cavenham as liquid as possible by selling properties and other unwanted assets, and to turn the focus onto America. In April Goldsmith had talks with Liggett & Myers, the tobacco and drinks corporation, with a view to buying a 20 per cent holding. Those talks broke down, but he now had the bit between his teeth and spent more and more time in New York. He sent Jim Wood as an advance party. As his thoughts crystallised, he decided that a retailing property was what they were seeking, and Wood clearly knew more about the inside workings of the various prospects. The acquisition had to be just right.

They say Columbus believed he had discovered India when he made his first Caribbean landfall in 1492. Since then most of the new arrivals to America have brought their dreams with them in their baggage. Goldsmith may be excused for thinking that he, too, had found a promised land of capitalism when he began to look beyond his Old World boundaries in that spring of 1973.

During his first 15 years' sojourn in the States Goldsmith reaped rewards that were beyond his dreams – about $2 billion for himself and his partners by best estimates, perhaps more. But he would ultimately move on to other pastures by the end of the 1980s. In part, he foresaw the economic hangover the United States later would suffer for its excesses. But more importantly, Goldsmith became frustrated and worn down by the repeated proofs that American-style government interference – at both state and federal levels – could be even more capricious and hobbling than the bureaucratic intrusions in Britain and France.

The myth of the American free-enterprise system is a potent one that finds its strongest supporters amongst the very capitalists and politicians who seek to restrain its forces. In the European parliamentary system there are real political divisions among the parties, the classes and the competing economic forces that encompass the entire nation. In America, both business and politics remain largely a power struggle between the various regions. Conservative and leftish politicians alike share a first loyalty to the economic interest of their region and view new arrivals – even those offering opportunity and stimulating change – with suspicion and often outright opposition. Time and again, Goldsmith would put together deals that appeared both profitable and attractive to all sides. Repeatedly the political and public outcry against what essentially was a free-market choice for the individual shareholders would put paid to his plans.

Still, at the start, America in 1973 looked a pretty good bet. Richard Nixon had just begun his second term with an overwhelming vote of confidence, largely due to his promise to wind down US involvement in Vietnam. The Watergate scandal was still more than a year from breaking and no one could foresee the world oil price shock that OPEC would spark later that winter.

'Despite all this talk today about him being an opportunist – and he was that too – he also had a pretty firm idea of what he wanted in a company by the time he came over to America,' says Roland Franklin who within a few months had left what remained of Keyser Ullmann to run Jimmy's office in New York. 'He bought badly run conglomerates. We improved things by moving companies to better locations.'

There was another key decision Goldsmith took that year. From the early days of Cavenham he had stuck with Keyser Ullmann as his adviser and merchant banker, largely out of friendship with and loyalty to Franklin. But Cavenham was now in the first rank of companies and needed a top bank. He had known Charles Hambro for years, not as a business acquaintance, but as a fellow gambler, meeting him often at the Clermont or in the south of France. They were not close friends, but when Hambro took over as chairman and chief executive of the family bank in 1972, it occurred to Jimmy that here was the banker he needed. He was under pressure from various quarters to move upmarket. Keyser had handled all his bids up to that point, and done the work perfectly competently. But they would not do for America. Goldsmith asked Charles Hambro if he would act for Cavenham, and Hambro was more than happy to gain one of the most active clients in the business. The move came as a severe blow to Keyser Ullmann, but not one that Roland Franklin could seriously argue about. Keyser had been founded by his great-grandfather in 1853, but now it was going bust. Goldsmith rescued him by taking him on full-time, and later that year sent him to New York where he was to head the operation for 13 years. The relationship with Hambros has lasted until the present day.

'We first kicked the tyres of something called First National chain of groceries,' Wood recounts. Then they discovered Grand Union.

It was Andre Meyer, the august head of Lazard Frères in New York, who first alerted Goldsmith to its possibilities. He had known Meyer, doyen of New York investment bankers and mentor to the equally respected Felix Rohatyn, for some years, and, using the Franco-American grapevine that Lazards represented, he asked him to look for acquisitions.

Based in Scranton, Pennsylvania, Grand Union had been started by the brothers Cyrus, Frank and Charles Jones in the 1860s, selling coffee, tea, spices and baking powder in their single shop. As they expanded and opened up other shops, they called it the Grand Union Tea Company; by the 1920s they owned more than 200 small stores, with 5,000 salesmen selling their produce, delivered in horse-drawn wagons. It became a quoted company just before the crash of 1929, weathered the depression and the war, and was an early entrant into supermarkets.

By the time Goldsmith heard of it, however, Grand Union was in trouble. Sales of $1.5 billion made it the tenth-largest supermarket chain in America, with 27,000 people in 600 shops, 531 of them supermarkets, in eleven states. But tenth place was a long way behind the giants of the industry, who were spending millions on bright new stores.

At this time, Goldsmith's finances in Britain were in good shape. Cavenham had some £90m in cash, and although the shares of Anglo-Continental had dropped sharply, Goldsmith had also converted much of its property, and that of its quoted property subsidiary Argyle, into cash.

His message to shareholders that autumn carried all the confidence of a man who believed his troubles lay behind him:

We started by acquiring and reorganising a group of small companies largely in confectionery which for the most part were run down to the point where they would have to be put into liquidation – and which in the process would have put some 2,000 people out of employment. We reconstructed this group of companies by strengthening management, closing and selling out-of-date factories, investing the proceeds to modernise other factories, develop new products, and put the companies back on the road to healthy organic growth. It sounds easy but it was not. We almost failed – but we also gained a great deal of experience.

A fortnight later, in early December 1973, with the financial world crashing around him, he announced he had bought a 51 per cent controlling interest in Grand Union for $62m. In some ways the story of Grand Union is almost a re-run of Cavenham. By Goldsmith's standards, it had grown away from its core business, selling television sets and electricals alongside food. 'It was almost impossible to buy your dinner there,' he complained. It would need drastic pruning, which would be both painful and expensive.

Grand Union may have been a legend among American retailing chains, older even than the venerable Great Atlantic and Pacific Tea Company (the present A & P stores which Wood now manages) but its profitability did not match its reputation. 'It is burned on my memory that Grand Union had $1.5 billion in sales that year but only made $1m in after-tax profits,' Wood remembers.

When we bought it, I was sitting in London as international head of Allied and Jimmy decided to keep me there and to keep on the chief executive of Grand Union at the time, Charlie Rudman. Now remember that just as we bought into Grand Union the OPEC oil crisis of 1973 hit and the markets went crazy. I really did have to stay in London and it fitted our thinking at the time to continue the management that we had. Jimmy always has operated that way. If he trusts a guy, he leaves him alone. If anything Jimmy over-delegates, but it was great to work for him for that reason. In other companies there are committees on everything, but you did not have that with Jimmy. He made you feel it was your company too.

But Rudman, who later would win kudos as the bankruptcy receiver for the W. T. Grant retailing chain, had a paternalistic attitude with respect for traditions and a reluctance to slash jobs. The Goldsmith mandate to cut away non-essential operations and to concentrate on improving the core business – in this case broad market grocery sales – clashed with the previous policy of adding new product lines (even lingerie and gardening tools), which had blurred the store's image as a dependable place to buy quality groceries.

'Charlie had his own style of doing things but we ran out of time. The oil price crisis turned things bad everywhere and sterling fell so badly that Jimmy was about to go broke again unless he sharply improved profits from the States. So I came over for just a year to play Visiting Limey to Charlie,' Wood says.

But the two soon clashed and Wood was left to run Grand Union singlehanded. At the time of purchase, Grand Union was a casebook study of the ills of the retail grocery business. One-stop convenience food stores were cutting into the low-price end of the business while speciality stores that stocked gourmet and high-priced items were competing at the other end. The company itself had a reputation for charging high prices for brand name products that could be obtained more cheaply elsewhere. There was also confusion in the consumer's mind as to whether Grand Union wasn't really a department store with food instead of a grocery chain with other items for sale. The only positive attitude consumer surveys did reveal was that Grand Union had a top rating for cleanliness.

'Jim Wood essentially began with Grand Union the way he began with the little CTN stores in Britain,' Tigrett notes. 'Of the 600 stores there were about 100 that weren't even grocery stores, they were discount stores, convenience outlets and so on. So $20 million was set aside to close them down as quickly as possible and Jim was then left with the stores that were making some money and all he had to do was concentrate on changing them so they made more money.'

Wood also was opening stores: bigger, brighter outlets, as fast as he closed the dingy little places. But he needed more, he needed to change consumer attitudes about where they shopped and what they purchased and then to generate real enthusiasm for shopping at Grand Union on a regular basis. But it was to be hard, unrewarding work for several years before the breakthrough came. Later Wood would say:

> Jimmy bought Grand Union for $19 a share at a time when it had been selling at $11, but had a book value of $27.50. That was before the big price increases of the Seventies. At that time it was a one per cent maximum business after taxes and was not much admired so he bought in at just the right time. But Jimmy got it for $125 million. He eventually sold it for about $1.3 billion; not bad. But what people do not acknowledge is that Jimmy did not just ride the price roller coaster up; we fundamentally changed the grocery store in America and we were able to do it because Jimmy was never satisfied with the

status quo. He was always willing to try a new idea and for each one that failed another would be a resounding success.

Back in London, the crash when it came was worse even than Goldsmith anticipated. The government's euphoria had survived a run on sterling in July 1973, even though the Bank of England had pushed up its minimum lending rate from 7½ per cent to a crisis 11 per cent. It survived even the outbreak of the Yom Kippur war on 6 October. But what it could not survive was the deliberate, politically inspired cutback in oil supplies by the Arab countries to the West at the end of October. Oil prices, $3 a barrel in September, rose to $12, spreading economic panic through the financial markets and bringing the West's economies to an instant halt. In Britain it coincided with a miners' go-slow (which developed into a full-scale strike) which within a matter of weeks forced Heath to announce a state of emergency, and a three-day working week. On 13 November, interest rates went up again, this time to 13 per cent. In the City of London, as everywhere else in the country, the lights went out when electricity supplies were rationed. During the course of 1973, share prices halved, and over the next year would halve again. The *Financial Times* share index, which still included Cavenham in it, fell from 544 in May 1972 to a low point of 146 by the first week in 1975, a fall, if inflation is taken into account, of 90 per cent – more than the London stock market had fallen in 1929–33. In those final weeks of 1973, the storm hit the property companies and the fringe banks with hurricane force. As property prices crashed, so depositors withdrew their funds from all the smaller banks, who in that situation could not repay them. On Friday, 21 December, the shares of most of the secondary banks and financial companies, including Slater Walker and Anglo-Continental, collapsed. On that day, the last working day before Christmas, the Governor of the Bank of England called a crisis meeting of the main City banks. He intended, he told them, to mount a rescue operation of the unprecedented order of £1 billion to prevent what looked all too likely that weekend: a panic run on the big clearing banks.

The bankers secretly put into place a 'lifeboat' operation, designed to prop up individual banks as they ran out of funds. In the event, some £1.3 billion was lent through the lifeboat to save threatened companies from collapse and default.

That Christmas, watching share prices plummet like a stone, Jim Slater forecast the closure of the London Stock Exchange. Others were talking about the end, not only of the financial system, but of capitalism in Britain.

253

The miners were winning their strike, the whole of Britain seemed paralysed, and in the first week in February Heath called an election – which he lost. The new Labour government, which instantly settled the miners' inflationary wage claim, was probably, at least in its first few years, the most anti-business one that Britain has ever seen. It certainly did not look like a government that would suit Jimmy Goldsmith.

For Jimmy Goldsmith, 1973 was marked by two significant events in his private life. The first was the marriage of Isabel. Her grandfather, Antenor Patino, had given her the eighteenth-birthday party that Jimmy hadn't, and it was there she met Baron Arnaud de Rosnay, a 26-year-old photographer. Isabel's teenage years had been no happier than her childhood. By nature, she was a solitary person, making few friends at school. She never felt part of Ginette's household, although Annabel had to some extent filled the gap in her late teens, urging her to go to parties, stay out late, and encouraging her to enjoy herself. Annabel had had a straitlaced youth, and became Isabel's accomplice and confidante in what she hoped would be the more carefree teenage years of Jimmy's eldest daughter. Her education had been poor, but she was still keen to go to art college. Goldsmith refused to allow it, telling her angrily that universities and art colleges were hotbeds of left-wing anarchists and worse, and no child of his would ever go to one. Goldsmith's mother, Marcelle, had given Isabel a taste for art, taking her to cities such as Florence and Amsterdam where they toured the museums. On one of these trips 'Mimi', as Isabel called Marcelle, decided they must see the red light district of Amsterdam, and they drove through it, the 16-year-old Isabel gazing fascinatedly at the prostitutes in the windows.

Over these years she had become closer to the Patinos, spending summer holidays with Antenor in his house in Portugal, where the old man liked to surround himself with his womenfolk. From his two marriages he had two daughters, each of whom in turn had two daughters, and each year they – and Isabel – joined him. To Antenor, men were for talking business, and he had little interest in business; he preferred to sit at his table, surrounded by his women. His father may have been famous for his lack of taste, but Antenor's houses were impeccable. He loved giving parties and presents, and every one of Isabel's birthdays was remembered with a special piece of jewellery.

By contrast, Isabel never spent a holiday with her Goldsmith cousins Dido and Clio, although she did spend occasional week-ends. She accused the Goldsmith family of treating her as a Patino child, never thinking of her as a Goldsmith. There may have been other reasons for that: Isabel, never gregarious, was not an easy house-guest. Hungry for affection herself, she found it difficult to show affection for others. She had grown into a beautiful young woman, but her strange racial mix was reflected in the complexity of her nature. Goldsmith, as he tried to fathom her, sometimes pondered her genetic make-up: of her four grandfathers, one was a Red Indian, one a king of Spain, one a German Jew and the fourth an Auvergnat peasant.

Rosnay's family were sugar planters in Mauritius, and Arnaud was a handsome, courteous man whom Goldsmith instantly took to. Perhaps to make up for his omission over her eighteenth birthday, Goldsmith announced he would give her an engagement party in a restaurant he sometimes used in Paris, the Laurent, set back off the Champs Elysées. It was another large and extravagant occasion; Annabel, Teddy and Aspinall plus various friends, including Annabel's cousin Dominic Elwes, came over from London, and Don Antenor Patino plus de Rosnay's parents were all there. There were 198 names on the guest list and more young people arrived later for the dancing. Towards midnight, wandering around the restaurant which has a number of rooms on the first floor, each with its own private little terrace, Goldsmith was suddenly struck by a thought and went in search of the manager. Who owned the restaurant? Would he sell? The manager at first thought he had drunk too much champagne (Goldsmith still barely drank at all, although he ate huge quantities), but arranged for him to meet the owners the next day. A month later Goldsmith was the owner of the Laurent.

At first Isabel thought he had bought it for her as a wedding present. Instead, he promised to build them a house on an island in the Mozambique Channel, which belonged to Rosnay's family. Rosnay had a development project for the island, but as the project fell through, so there was no house. Isabel never did get her present from Jimmy.

They were due to be married on 28 June at the Church of St Clothilde, near Goldsmith and Ginette's house on the rue Monsieur. Knowing Jimmy's hatred of churches, Isabel was not at all certain he would turn up. Most of the arrangements had been made by her grandfather Antenor, who had ordered her wedding dress, fussed over the jewellery she should wear, arranged her wedding gift list, and even her trousseau. But Goldsmith duly appeared to give her away, and that evening gave a dinner party for her at the Laurent.

In August, Annabel, approaching 40, discovered she was pregnant.

Although both she and Jimmy were delighted, her doctor was more concerned. She also faced the delicate task of telling her children, her family – and Mark, to whom she was still legally married. Annabel feared her husband would be desperately hurt by the news, and she worried greatly about how he would react. In the event, he took it well, generously offering her the chance to go back to him. But she had long made up her mind. For better or worse, she was going to stay with Jimmy, have his children, eventually become his wife. It never occurred to Jimmy that Annabel might have anything other than a boy, but in January 1974 at the Westminster Hospital in London she gave birth to a daughter, Jemima. Once he got over the shock, he was as pleased as she was – and even more pleased when a few months later she became pregnant again.

Goldsmith at first rode the economic storm well. He had prepared his companies for the crash, though not one of the order which now raged. The year that followed the oil price hike was a bad year everywhere, and for everyone. Jim Slater began a desperate juggling act to keep his head above water. He liquidated everything he could, dumping his companies in the Far East, his satellite companies and anything else he could realise, explaining to the world that in the new circumstances cash was king, and Slater Walker was going to be purely in cash. All the rhetoric about galavanising British industry by threatening inefficient companies with takeover had evaporated. As he said later, 'The social justification of a company like Slater Walker at this particular point was not readily apparent. We were liquidating investments simply to survive.'

Slater Walker as it happened was one of the very few shares that Goldsmith bought through 1974. He still believed in Slater, although he had no desire to work with him. But the huge number of share stakes Slater had built up offered a potential treasure trove when the markets turned. The two men talked seriously about merging, to form a different type of financial group which would take large investments in a small number of blue chip companies, offering them (or rather insisting they take) all their fee-earning services from the bank at the centre. Over the previous two years, Slater had come close to merging with Warburgs, Lazards and with Hill Samuel, and as Slater says, Goldsmith was the obvious person to turn to in his new crisis. As the fall steepened, however, Goldsmith became preoccupied with his own survival. 'The bear market had, of course, also affected his financial companies, and as a result he did not have enough energy to spare to be of real help with my problems at that time,' said Slater.

Goldsmith was also involved with the problems of a closer friend: John Aspinall. Aspinall had been a big investor in Goldsmith's companies from the beginning, and in the summer of 1972 his holdings were worth £2m to £3m. He had become less interested in the Clermont as his Howletts zoo grew and where once he had been famed for his gambling, now he was better known for his mission to save endangered species. He had become something of a character on the lecture circuit, where he spoke flamboyantly and eloquently, often on the theme that mankind's progress had been at the expense of the earth's capital resources and should more properly be known as 'regress' (not dissimilar to what Teddy Goldsmith was saying at the time, although from a different viewpoint).

His zoo cost him some £300,000 a year to run, but with Jimmy's shares riding high, he reckoned he had sufficient resources to keep it going without the Clermont. So he sold his club to Victor Lowndes of the Playboy Club. In the United States, Hugh Hefner, Lowndes' ultimate boss, could scarcely believe his good fortune. The price paid, £500,000, was an absurdly low one, as Lowndes proved when he made the money back in three days' trading.

Aspinall wasn't worried by the small sum he got for the club. He was 45, and had decided to retire from gambling, and devote himself to providing a sanctuary for 'beleaguered mammals and so enable them to survive the ecological blizzards of our epoch'. However he had not been long retired when he did something silly, for which Jimmy Goldsmith would get the blame. He had, he says, not only invested in Goldsmith's companies but also in Wall Street – on borrowed money. He had followed Goldsmith in, but not out again. 'I lost everything. My money melted away like snow in summer. I was bust.' He was without a club, without an income, without any capital and with hundreds of hungry animals to feed. He mortgaged his London house and other properties, and returned to the gaming tables, winning £160,000 at blackjack in a month, but that soon went. He sold his wine, his books and his pictures. His third wife, Lady Sarah, sold her jewellery.

Goldsmith bailed him out, guaranteed his debts to the banks (including Slater Walker), and arranged for his bank to lend him money – but not without strings. 'Goldsmith thought it would be helpful for Aspinall to understand the moral obloquy of financial suffering – that he must part with something to drive the message home,' wrote Brian Masters. According to Aspinall's account, he and his brother drove to London each week with a car-load of *objets d'art*, ornaments, books or prints, in return for which Goldsmith's bank would give him £3,000 in cash. Sometimes, instead of returning straight to Kent with the money, Aspinall claimed he gambled with it. The Goldsmith version is more prosaic: there were no monthly payments, no car-loads of antiques, though he does acknowledge, 'I was forced to keep things afloat (during a most difficult time for us all) and I did it in almost every way.'

It would be four years before Aspinall recovered his fortunes, and sent Goldsmith a book inscribed 'To Jimmy, who was the lifeboat on which we all clambered.'

As 1974 wore on, the British economy was in a terrible mess, and Grand Union had not yet responded to Goldsmith's tough medicine. Recession was everywhere, and interest rates, for those who had borrowings, were high. Despite his French and American interests, Goldsmith's greatest exposure was in Britain. In 1974 retail prices rose by 16.1 per cent, and the following year by 24 per cent. Companies went bankrupt at a startling rate and the stock market continued to fall. A huge volume of money switched into the hands of Arabs who didn't know what to do with it. Harold Wilson's Labour Party had no clear majority and it was clear that there would be another election soon, probably in the autumn.

That summer Peter Walker, Jim Slater's one-time partner in setting up Slater Walker and now one of the leading figures in Heath's Conservative Party, held a dinner in his house in Cowley Street, just behind Westminster. He invited Goldsmith who was surprised to find when he arrived that the principal guest was no less than Edward Heath, now leader of the opposition. The other guests were Selim Zilkha, whose Mothercare shops were weathering the storm, and Jim Slater who had known Heath for some years.

Walker opened the subject of the evening: what should the Tories be doing to win the next election? Discussions like this take place all the time, and on the whole they go nowhere. Most businessmen are as naive about the world of politics as politicians are about business, and often the only point is to flatter the ego of the rich in the hope they will contribute to party funds. Slater, for all his financial guile, was not a serious political or social thinker. Zilkha was no better, but Goldsmith, as Walker knew, was a different matter. He bubbled with ideas, solutions and advice, most of it impractical, all of it original, and now, not for the first time, he took over the conversation. Britain had to get back to fundamental planning, which meant it had to feed itself, to fuel its own industry, to avoid waste and live within its means. It had to become less dependent on the rest of the world for imports, and develop its agriculture as a matter of urgency – it was lucky in that it had efficient farmers and fertile land. Britain also had its own coal and 'was surrounded by a sea of oil'.

He was also highly critical of the way the Conservative Party was run. 'Your advertising is terrible, and your organisation is worse,' he said. If the Tories wanted to win the next election they had to reorganise at constituency level, where the real fight would be.

Goldsmith went home pleased with the way the evening had gone. He had been unprepared for it, but had responded to Heath, and Heath, in so far as he responded to anyone, had responded to him. In fact Heath suggested they meet again, and Goldsmith was delighted – although he reckoned nothing would come of it. Goldsmith had been fascinated by politics, or more accurately by the idea of becoming a politician, from a very early age – he himself says from age ten, when his plan was first to make himself a millionaire, and then a politician – 'I never thought of doing anything else.' By that he means his plan was to follow his father into parliament, but to continue where his father had quit. In his early business days in France Goldsmith barely had time to think about a private life, let alone a political career, and through the 1960s Cavenham had absorbed all his attention. He spoke to Edward Du Cann, then chairman of Keyser Ullmann and a leading figure in the Conservative Party, about the possibility of finding a constituency in the late 1960s, but then came the Bovril and Allied Suppliers deals in 1971 and 1972, followed by the crash and his move to America, and he never did any more about it. Some time later he spoke to Sir Keith Joseph, another leading Tory, adding: 'Keith, my personal life is not particularly suited to politics.'

'But there's no humbug, is there?' said Joseph.

'None whatever!' replied Goldsmith with feeling. Annabel had recently borne him a baby daughter, but all the world, including Ginette, knew about it.

'Then it won't matter,' said Joseph.

Walker knew of Goldsmith's interest in politics from Jim Slater, and reckoned here was a man who might be a useful addition to the party.

A few weeks later Goldsmith met Heath again, this time with Willie Whitelaw who had become chairman of the party in the spring. Nothing in either man persuaded Goldsmith that the Tories could win the next election, a view privately shared by Whitelaw himself, who spent that summer doing the rounds of the constituencies trying to restore battered morale. 'Our troops were in reasonably good heart,' said Whitelaw. 'Of course I did not allow myself to scratch below the surface, as that would have betrayed my inner anxieties. As a result I probably deluded myself.'

After four years as prime minister, Edward Heath was not used to blunt criticism, whatever the source, and cooled towards Goldsmith when he received it – as did Whitelaw. Goldsmith might have had some enterprising ideas, but they did not add up to an election-winning strategy. The two pillars of the Tory party struck him as weak and wet, while he struck them as a bull in a china shop.

Goldsmith's early high opinion of Heath gave way to one of gentle contempt. But while on holiday in August with Ginette and the children at Amalfi, where he had rented Carlo Ponti's house, Jim Slater rang. Apparently Whitelaw wanted him back to help with the campaign for the election which was clearly looming. Could he come? Goldsmith stayed on for a few days, then flew back from Italy.

On 18 September Harold Wilson brought to an end the shortest parliament of the century by calling an election for 10 October – only the second time there had been two general elections in the same year. The minority Labour government had been defeated 29 times in the two months before the summer recess, making it impossible to go on. The opinion polls gave Labour a big lead, Heath was unpopular everywhere, and Wilson believed he could increase his vote considerably.

Goldsmith was asked to help with fund raising, which was not how he hoped his talents would be used. He itched to take over the running and organisation of Central Office, and change it root and branch. It was an old-fashioned, archaic and largely amateur organisation. On the other hand, if Goldsmith ever had got near it, what delicate cohesion it had might well have disappeared. Goldsmith was not known for his subtlety.

It is a truism that the best people at raising money are those that have it to give in the first place. Goldsmith could ask without shame, on the basis that he had probably donated more than most – knowing also that most of those he asked did business with him, might do business with him in the future, or would at some stage be asking him for money for their favourite charities. He roped in Charles Hambro, and the two organised an American-style $1,000-a-plate dinner for their industrial friends who still had any money left after the past year.

Goldsmith longed to be included in the inner debates of the party where he felt he could make a contribution, but Whitelaw kept him at arm's length. At the height of the campaign the chancellor, Denis Healey, on the basis of a freak quarterly inflation figure of 2.1 per cent, announced that inflation was now down to an annual rate of 8.4 per cent. He said this tongue-in-cheek, and was surprised by the indignation aroused among the Tory ranks. Jimmy Goldsmith exploded. He knew all about the rise in food prices over the past year, he announced excitedly, and it was a great deal more than 8.4 per cent – for instance a ton of flour a year before cost £67, and now cost £138. He got his team at Cavenham to chart the rise in other food items, and to show how they were going to go on rising even more steeply. 'But it was never used. It was as if they were embarrassed by it.'

He himself used the figures in a speech he made before the election, and on 6 October, just four days before polling day, wrote an article in the *Sunday Express*. 'We are certainly facing the worst crisis we have ever faced,' he began. Capital investment over the next six months, he forecast, would be cut back 'more drastically than ever before in our economic history', and Britain could be facing unemployment on a scale never seen before. He did get close to an early version of Mrs Thatcher's monetarism, but shied away – that would work in normal times, he said, but not in the current, dismal financial climate.

A few days before the election Roland Franklin organised a dinner for some of his friends and contacts. Goldsmith was there, as were Slater, Tigrett, and another great tycoon, Tiny Rowland, chief executive of Lonrho. Rowland was very anti-Heath, who, in perhaps his most memorable phrase, had branded him an 'unacceptable face of capitalism'. Rowland hoped he would lose again. Although privately he agreed, Goldsmith bet Rowland £5,000 the Conservatives would win.

Labour were returned, but not by the convincing margin Wilson desired. Their vote actually fell by 200,000, but that decline was more than offset by the collapse of support for Heath and the Conservatives whose vote was the lowest since 1945. Labour now had a majority, but only a tiny one: 319 to 316. Wilson, however, was determined to govern with it, forecasting he would survive for two to three years before another election. In fact the Labour government survived for another four and a half years.

The election of October 1974 marked the end of Goldsmith's political ambition. He had nurtured hopes that if Heath emerged victorious, he might have invited Goldsmith to become a minister – there were precedents for non-politicians in the cabinet, as with Heath's appointment of the former Director General of the Confederation of British Industry, John Davies.

Would Goldsmith have lasted? Almost certainly not. Goldsmith has many talents but tact and diplomacy are not among them, at least not to the extent needed for a political career. He would have become furiously impatient with the Civil Service, angry with his cabinet colleagues, and would have chafed at the restraints of parliament. Goldsmith likes to tell things as he sees them. 'I have never been prepared to be a hypocrite. Hypocrisy is not one of my flaws.'

But when, in December 1974, he was invited to give the Lubbock lecture at Oxford University, he went to considerable trouble to get his speech right. Today, Goldsmith is an accomplished and much sought-after speaker, yet for a long time he was one of the most nervous. Curiously, for a man so clever in argument, he is a poor extempore speaker, particularly in French, and much envies the uniquely British skill of witty after-dinner speaking. Tigrett remembers briefing him for a speech to a grocers' association: 'I found him there outside in the hallway. He was so nervous and twisting his handkerchief as he walked up and down.'

The Lubbock lecture was long and highly critical of the state of Britain, where 'muddling through' was the pervasive attitude. The creaking financial system was in danger of collapse, he warned, and British democracy itself was under threat.

> It was once said that democracy can survive only for so long as the majority is willing to sacrifice the short-term for the long-term. When this is no longer the case, when the majority is more interested in the short-term, then the whole nation becomes a vast rotten borough. It chooses its leaders by the number of short-term inducements that are promised. To pander to this irresponsibility is evil. The government should make clear our changed circumstances and should explain the perils we face. It must preach civil duties not civil rights.

He concluded:

'The epitaph on the grave of our democracy would be "They sacrificed the long-term for the short-term, and the long-term arrived".'

Of course it never did, but the speech, which he distributed widely, was well quoted, along the lines 'Financial system could collapse warns Goldsmith'. Several papers reprinted extracts, and he was invited onto several television programmes to elaborate. He refused. His interest in British politics, except as an intelligent observer and sometimes commentator, flickered out.

17

The Fall of Jim Slater

Never, in my recollection, had any one person or company so dominated the
City of London as had Slater Walker in the early 1970s.

Jimmy Goldsmith, February 1988

Slater started as the great industrial renovator . . . but he quickly found his
true role to be that of an investment banker, someone who I think is cleverer
with money than anyone else in the world.

Patrick Hutber, Sunday Telegraph, March 1972

As abruptly as it had begun, the biggest share collapse in London's history
ended in the first week of 1975. For two months share prices rose
perpendicularly on occasion by up to 10 per cent a day. The shares of Jim
Slater's company had fallen from 260p to 35½p, but now they trebled in
two months. Both Slater and Goldsmith breathed a sigh of relief. Apart
from the effect on his own companies, Goldsmith with 5 per cent was by
now the biggest shareholder in Slater Walker.

Neither man, however, was emotionally in tune with the share price
recovery, both still anticipating greater disasters. 'It was one of those
market movements which caught most people, including myself, by
surprise,' wrote Slater afterwards. 'It was all over almost before it had
begun; each day one waited for a setback and buying opportunity, but
instead there was another significant rise.'

There is an important point here which Slater and Goldsmith
emphasised at the time and would emphasise again and again later. The
crucial skill lay not in knowing what property to buy or what company to
invest in, but in reading the business and stock market cycle correctly.
Hundreds of perfectly able young men had gone bust in the past year
because they believed the property market would go on rising. As Slater,
who did not always subscribe to his own principles, observed later, when

263

the market was going up it did not much matter whether you bought GKN or Tube Investments – 'the important point is to be fully invested in good quality stocks.' But when the market was going down, no stock would withstand it. In 1971 the London stock market had risen 40 per cent, but in 1973 it had fallen 30 per cent and by a further 50 per cent in 1974.

In the early 1970s it was almost impossible not to make money by investing either in shares or property – inflation and the booming markets carried everything up, regardless of quality. In the two years that followed the reverse was true – no one, however clever, made money in property, and only the very best survived. The brightest minds in the property sector, people like John Ritblat, Jeffrey Sterling, Gerald Ronson and Nigel Broackes, came through, but only by the skin of their teeth and often because the banks which lent them so much money did not dare put them into liquidation.

In 1975 the property market was still in ruins, littered with the corpses of whizzkids and overhung by huge portfolios now owned by the receivers. But perversely the share market, which tends to anticipate boom or bust by anything up to a year, replaced the biggest fall of all time with the longest and strongest period of rising share prices in Britain's history, only ending in October 1987 (and some would argue not even then).

If Goldsmith had previously had no claim to the reputation of 'financial genius' so assiduously accorded to him by John Tigrett and others, in the three years from 1971 to 1974 he made up for it, basically by getting his fundamental decisions on the cycles right.

Having ordered the sale of surplus property, he also gave instructions to the Banque Occidentale that it should make no more loans. Gilberte Beaux and Thierry de Clermont-Tonnere protested that they could not build a bank which would not lend money, but Goldsmith would not relent. He was however prepared to extend his interests in Générale Alimentaire when the Rothschilds, who had despaired of ever getting it right, offered him their stake. He also added another 30 per cent of Grand Union in the US, where Jim Wood was now busily at work, pruning back the unprofitable shops and adding new and bigger ones.

As the slump deepened, Goldsmith's fortunes and those of Jim Slater had become more and more interlinked. He acquired Slater's Far Eastern investment trust, again to be realised into cash, and he bought out Slater's stake in the French Compagnie Haussmann, which owned a valuable site in the centre of Paris.

Even before the slump, Slater had made up his mind to get out. He was a hypochondriac, continually worried about the effects of the stresses and strains of business life upon his health. A major kidney operation had left him weakened and depressed. His rise, and then his survival through the last two years, had depended entirely on his own intuitive reading of markets and hair-trigger reactions. He no longer believed he could keep it up. His attempts, which had come so close (Goldsmith later discovered an initialled press release announcing a merger with Lazards, which had been stopped overnight), at merging with one of the larger merchant banks, would have offered him a graceful exit, allowing him to inject his empire into a more respected establishment and take a back seat. Half a dozen other key decisions would also have saved him. If he had not rejected John Tigrett's proposal to back a North Sea oil consortium his £1m investment would have made him £100m.

Until 1973, Slater was the dominant force in their relationship (at least in business terms), even if Goldsmith was clearly the intellectual superior. Some time in 1974, the roles were reversed and half-way through that year Slater was looking to Goldsmith to bail him out. There were various plans discussed over their dinners at Wiltons and in more and more frequent telephone calls. Apart from the concept of full merger, there was another more complex scheme whereby each would buy 20 per cent in the other's main company and 'equity account' it, an accounting stratagem much practised by Slater whereby the whole of the profits of the company in which he held his stake could be shown in his own accounts. Goldsmith, through Madame Beaux, brought in the banking arm of Renault, the French state-owned car company, as his partner, and began buying Slater Walker shares at around 100p each. There was an understanding that Slater could, if he wished, require Goldsmith to buy his own shares in Slater Walker at well above that price. The asset value, Goldsmith believed (as did Slater), was well above this. Goldsmith would become deputy chairman of Slater Walker and, as Patrick Hutber, City Editor of the *Sunday Telegraph*, wrote after a chat with both men, become 'eventually its guiding spirit while Mr Jim Slater phased himself gently out'.

Goldsmith and Renault had acquired approaching 11 per cent of Slater Walker when a further collapse in the share price caused the operation to be suspended, leaving them locked in at well above the market price. They saw the shares fall all the way back to 27p.

In the early months of 1975, Slater almost agreed a merger with Tiny Rowland, but that too fell through. He also held talks with Adnan Khashoggi whom he had never heard of before. Within weeks of their negotiations opening, Khashoggi hit the headlines when the Watergate prosecutors in Washington named him as the major contributor to Nixon campaign funds, followed soon after by revelations of his enormous fees from Northrop, Lockheed and other defence contractors for supplying arms to the Middle East.

Goldsmith remained in pessimistic mood. As he watched the collapse of the fringe banks, so his fears grew of a run on his own banks. In August 1974 he had carried out a typically complex reorganisation at Anglo-Continental: he sold the 51 per cent stake he had bought in the Swiss end of the bank Ralli Brothers to the man he had bought it from two years before – the ubiquitous Harry Recanati who had financed Cavenham at its low point. That brought in £1m in cash, and removed a liability. Then Anglo swopped its other banking interests for shares in the Goldsmith Paris bank, Banque Occidentale, giving Anglo a 37 per cent state.

A few months later Goldsmith went a stage further: Banque Occidentale sold its bank in London to the International Bank of Luxembourg. But the most significant deal of all was the sale to the French Rothschilds of the Discount Bank in Paris, also originally bought from Recanati.

The Discount Bank was a minor French bank, with deposits of $200m, for which Goldsmith and Madame Beaux originally had big plans. The Rothschild bank had deposits of $1 billion, which put it squarely in the second rank of French banks.

The French side of the Rothschild family was going through a bad patch. Baron Guy and his two cousins, Elie and Alain, had reconstructed the bank at the end of the war and in 1956 brought in a new manager in the ample shape of one M. Pompidou, later to become one of the great statesmen of France. In 1962, de Gaulle appointed Pompidou as his prime minister, and the bank changed drastically over the next few years, becoming a trendy deposit bank with a drive-in counter on the ground floor. It became a small frog in a large pool, opening deposit branches all over the country in a hopeless attempt to compete with the state-owned French banks.

In 1973 the family began to reorganise their affairs. They pruned back their heavy shipping interests (then suffering the worst slump in 50 years), streamlined their credit and real estate companies, and, perhaps most important of all, sold their food interests to Jimmy Goldsmith. That was how Goldsmith had got hold of Générale Alimentaire, but now he was to get more. The Rothschilds paid him £5m cash for his 72 per cent stake in Discount Bank, plus loan stock which would give him a 7 per cent holding in Banque Rothschild, Paris. They also gave him a directorship of the bank. 'He can thus be said finally and indisputably to have arrived in

France,' wrote Patrick Hutber that week-end, adding that 'the infinitely ingenious Mr Goldsmith' had achieved successfully what Jim Slater had tried and failed to do when he sought his merger with Hill Samuel. Goldsmith, said Hutber who knew him well, had 'come in from what degree of cold his well-padded form may have felt'.

Hutber touched on a sensitive spot. As the journalist Sam White, who had known Frank Goldsmith well and had been a friend of Jimmy's since he was 20, put it: 'The achievement [entry into Rothschild dynasty] is not without its ironies as well as having about it a certain historical logic.' The irony was that 'up to recently he [Goldsmith] had been a distant cousin both literally and metaphorically', not just of the French Rothschilds but of the Lamberts of Brussels and the Oppenheims of Cologne, whom the family had held 'at something like a wary arm's length'. Now the Rothschilds had been forced by its financial problems to 'flex a knee-joint to the family upstart'.

Membership of the Rothschild bank was of enormous personal importance to Goldsmith. 'Until I was forty, my main preoccupation was to restore the family's shrunken fortune,' says Jimmy. He now had an extra reason for restoring the dynasty. Another son was born at the end of January 1975. Although this was his fifth child, he was more nervous than ever about it. The births of his children so far had not been simple, and although Annabel seemed to be strong and confident, Goldsmith paced his Leadenhall Street office, ringing the Westminster Hospital every few minutes, touching wood and carrying out all his other little rituals to ward off ill-luck. But all went well. They called him Zacharias, on the grounds that in both the Jewish and Christian faiths the name represented a child with a future.

That summer Jim Slater discovered a new hobby: salmon fishing. With his typically infectious enthusiasm, he attempted to engage Goldsmith's interest too. Slater Walker had acquired, among its hundreds of different assets, the Tulchan estate of over 20,000 acres in Scotland, with four salmon fishing beats on the River Spey. Slater had never been salmon fishing before, but on his first day caught an eleven-pound fish. For days he would talk of nothing else. He persuaded some friends to join him for a week: Selim Zilkha, Jacob Rothschild, Angus Ogilvy (married to Princess Alexandra) and Goldsmith. Apart from Ogilvy (and Slater), none of them had fished before, but Goldsmith joined in the fun, taking large bets on who would catch the first fish. Goldsmith enjoyed the male company and the fresh air, but, unlike Frank who in his youth loved to shoot and fish, had absolutely no interest in killing things.

Back in London, Goldsmith continued to think defensively. Jack Greenhalgh and his management team had completed their reorganisation of the Bovril and Allied Suppliers acquisitions, but Goldsmith was far from content. He insisted the business had to be continually reassessed, and that if something was no longer essential to Cavenham it should be sold. Where did the slimming foods side fit? The answer is that it didn't, but it had been the engine of his growth, the one business which had kept him going, both in France and Britain, through the 1960s. 'The main stream has changed,' Goldsmith told his managers. 'We must treat our own companies in precisely the same way we do companies we take over. If some of the elements are no longer central, we should sell them.'

In June 1975 he sold the French subsidiary Gremy-Longuet, which produced his original Milical, to SmithKline, the large American pharmaceutical group. And a month later Slimcea and Procea, the very first of his acquisitions in Britain, also went, to Spillers. It made Cavenham even more of a food retailer than a food manufacturer.

Jim Slater was able to use the better market to liquidate more stakes. He also employed his legendary market dealing skills to make handsome profits on the gold share boom. The fringe bank crisis had abated, the world recession had bottomed out, and it began to look as if Slater would scrape through, even if his company was considerably reduced in scale and importance.

His nemesis came from a most unexpected direction. In the early days of the property boom he had purchased a building in the City, Granite House, for £9m, acquired in four separate deals. At the height of the boom he put it on the market, and received a bid from the Singapore Monetary Authority, equivalent to its central bank, of what he called the 'staggering sum' of £22.4m. When the crash came, Lee Kuan Yew made no secret of his anger over this deal, which stoked his fury over other events taking place inside his small country. Slater had bought into Singapore's biggest company, Haw Par, several years before, sent out some of his bright young men, and proceeded to do what he had done to everywhere else: sell off assets, inject other companies, and generally wheel and deal merrily. It became the great game in town, with every other Singapore financial company trying to outdo Slater. The puritanical Lee hated Slater's 'freebooting style of capitalism'. There was no place for it in his tidy kingdom.

When his troubles came, Slater scrambled out of Singapore, but too late. Lee saw him as the epitome of all that was wrong with Singapore's finances, which in the mid-1970s suffered a series of scandals and crashes. When the management of Haw Par, without referring to Slater – who by that stage had nothing to do with it – decided to move their headquarters and domicile to the hated Malaysia to the north, Lee exploded. On 28 July the Singapore finance minister announced that there had been 'serious wrong-doing' at Haw Par, and two inspectors were appointed to investigate.

The centre of the investigation involved a little company called Spydar Securities which was designed as an executive incentive scheme to benefit half a dozen top people. Slater had never been a director of Haw Par, although Slater Walker controlled it – but he *was* a beneficiary in Spydar, which according to the Singapore authorities had benefited illegally from share dealings in other Slater companies in the Far East.

The press reports that reached Slater from Singapore made him all too aware of Lee's anger. There was much talk in Singapore government circles that Slater would spend years in Changi jail. The Slater management in Singapore hastily fled across the causeway to Malaysia and then further afield to avoid arrest. (To this day one of them is in Ireland, which has no extradition treaty with Singapore, and another is in the Middle East. A third, Jim Slater's deputy Dick Tarling, was successfully extradited, tried and sentenced to a year in Changi.)

The effect on Slater was catastrophic. Haw Par owed the Slater bank $29m which was now frozen, causing other banks nervously to begin withdrawing deposits. Slater Walker shares, which had risen to over 100p, slipped back to under 50p.

On Wednesday, 16 October 1975, Slater dined with Jimmy Goldsmith. He had been to see the Governor of the Bank of England and raised the subject of resigning from Slater Walker. The Singapore investigation and the threat of jail had wholly unnerved him. Goldsmith heard him out. 'As a large shareholder he had a vested interest, and as a good friend he was of course prepared to do all he could to help,' said Slater. But there was more to it than friendship. If Slater suddenly resigned, Goldsmith could see it would have a disastrous effect on the entire market, and on the financial sector in particular. All that he had done to protect his companies might again be threatened, with the close links between their two empires only too well broadcast. Cavenham, with its large cash holdings and its solid and profitable businesses, would not be seriously affected, but his financial companies would be. At one stage

Slater Walker owned a substantial shareholding in Générale Occidentale, and had also guaranteed a loan to another company, Haussman, before Goldsmith bought it. The links were close.

Goldsmith could not see how Slater, in his current nervous mood, could hang on. He had been trying to do a deal with the Singapore authorities, but emotions were running so high that he was getting nowhere. A new chairman and board would, Slater reckoned, stand a much better chance. Slater talked about going to South Africa where he thought Tiny Rowland might help set him up again. There he would be beyond the reach of Lee Kuan Yew. He then disclosed another problem: although his share stake in Slater Walker had once been worth £9m, he had borrowed heavily against it. The collapse in the price meant that his assets were now worth less than his borrowings. He was, in effect, a minus millionaire.

The main point of the dinner was for Goldsmith to help Slater make up his mind whether to go or stay – and to establish whether Goldsmith would be prepared to take over if Slater went. Jimmy, Slater pointed out, knew the Slater Walker business as well as anyone, had studied it carefully for months, and had the ability, the resources and the City connections to get it right.

At the end of the meal Slater indicated he had still not decided definitely if he would resign, but he thought he probably would. Would Goldsmith think about it, and he would let him know definitely over the week-end?

The week-end's news was bad. Patrick Sergeant, the *Daily Mail*'s City editor and doyen of the financial press, happened to be in Singapore and from there wrote a column critical of Slater and his style of operations. Up to that point Sergeant had been a Slater supporter. The fact that he had now turned was convincing proof for Slater that the rest of the press would soon follow.

On Monday morning, after reading the *Mail* City column, Slater rang Jimmy Goldsmith in Paris. He had definitely decided to go, and was now about to ring the Bank of England, and ask to see the governor urgently. He would suggest, if Jimmy agreed, that Goldsmith take his place, putting together, before any official announcement, a team of the best names in the City.

Goldsmith was not prepared to be stampeded. Slater Walker might have all sorts of nasties hidden away which Slater himself might not be aware of. He agreed that Slater had to resign. But he was not prepared simply to take over without some guarantees that his own carefully built empire would not be threatened.

At noon Slater was in the Bank of England to see George Blunden, the deputy governor and the man who personally oversaw the lifeboat operation protecting the fringe banks. Slater Walker was much more than a fringe bank. It was among the select group of banks fully authorised by the Bank of England to deal in foreign exchange. It also had a large position in the Eurocurrency market. It was not a member of the Accepting Houses Committee, the elite of the City's banks (as Hambros was), but its importance was considerable for all that, not least because in 1975 it was one of the best-known companies in Britain. It held hundreds of millions of deposits, and Richardson and Blunden were all too keenly aware of the dangers to the whole banking system if it failed.

Blunden consulted the governor, Gordon Richardson, who agreed that Goldsmith was acceptable, and the following day Goldsmith was called in. Was he prepared to take over as chairman of Slater Walker? asked Richardson. If so, what did he intend to do? How did he propose saving it?

Goldsmith indicated he was prepared to take the job in order to protect his investment – but only on certain conditions. The governor had to put the support of the government, as well as the Bank of England, behind him. 'First, I want to take a close look at it, and assess the true state of its balance sheet,' replied Goldsmith. 'I need to know how much support it needs.' He had sent for his own banking team from Paris who would be arriving in London that afternoon, and could evaluate the position within 48 hours. In the meantime, Goldsmith proposed approaching some senior figures in the City to persuade them to join the board with him. To avert a financial crisis, the announcement of Slater's departure and a rescue package for Slater Walker had to be made simultaneously, preferably at the beginning of a week-end when the banks were shut. The coming Friday seemed the right time. Richardson, impressed by Goldsmith's knowledge and confidence, agreed. The Bank would be behind him.

Goldsmith then rang Hambro. 'I must talk to you about something.' Hambro had never trusted Jim Slater. He had first met him when he was finance director at Leyland and disliked him, and nothing he had seen since had changed his mind. Hambro had further reasons for supporting Goldsmith's rescue operation: the bank was a major investor in Générale Occidentale and had taken up a rights issue of shares earlier in the year. If trouble for Slater meant trouble for Goldsmith then that in turn meant problems for Hambro. He would come aboard, and provide whatever Goldsmith needed in the way of banking expertise to save Slater Walker.

Gilberte Beaux and her team quietly entered the offices of Slater

Walker near St Paul's that afternoon and worked through the night, examining every loan, every asset, every investment. Charles Hambro sent some of his people to help her. By Thursday they reported to Goldsmith. The position at Slater Walker was far worse than anyone had imagined. Slater Walker needed £160m to pay depositors. The Bank of England would have to protect the Slater bank with its own and lifeboat money. If it took the bank off Goldsmith's hands, he would sort out the rest of Slater Walker. Otherwise, he could not manage it. (The Bank never disclosed how much it injected, but various estimates indicate it was in the region of £60–70m. Over the years, as the loan portfolio was managed by Hambros, it got it all back.)

The previous evening Goldsmith gave a little dinner party at the house he had now rented in Tregunter Road. Edward Heath, who had been replaced as leader of the Conservative Party by Margaret Thatcher earlier in the year, was there. So was the editor of the *Economist*, Andrew Knight, and Lord Rothschild, Jacob's father. Goldsmith took Rothschild aside to explain the situation; would he join him in the rescue operation? Rothschild, although he was the chairman of the bank N. M. Rothschild, for most of his career had resisted all attempts to make him into a banker. Victor Rothschild was generally regarded as the cleverest, the most entertaining and also the most unfathomable of all the Rothschilds. A *Sunday Times* portrait of him started like this: 'When asked about Victor Rothschild his friends variously describe him as a genius, an oaf, an academic recluse, a man of the world, a frustrated failure . . .' and so on, concluding that 'his name, his race, his money and his intelligence have made him one of the most complicated personalities in contemporary life.' He accompanied Churchill to Paris in 1944, but then became one of the hardest-working science dons at Cambridge. In 1970 Edward Heath asked him to head up his Think Tank, although he had been a lifelong Labour supporter, and it was only in his latter years that he finally joined the family bank. That evening he replied cautiously that he would let Goldsmith know the next day.

By Thursday Goldsmith had his new board ready to announce: Charles Hambro and Peter Hill-Wood, the man who personally looked after Goldsmith's business at Hambro; Lord Rothschild had accepted (to the irritation of his son whom he had not consulted, and who believed it was a mistake) and a more professional and respected banker from Rothschilds, Ivor Kennington; M. Dominique Leca, a member of his board at Générale Occidentale, and a senior executive of Union des Assurances in Paris. Sir Ronald Leach, the same eminent accountant who had acted as adjudicator in his dealings with Unilever, and head of the Accountants Standards Committee, became official adviser to the board, and Hambros Bank and N. M. Rothschild agreed to act as financial advisers to the company.

The news that something dramatic was about to happen leaked on the afternoon of Friday, 24 October, and the shares of Slater Walker plunged 12p to 34p, valuing the company at only £25m, against £170m at its peak. Hurriedly, the Bank of England agreed that the announcement had to be made that night.

That announcement shook the City as no event had for a generation. In the offices of the *Sunday Telegraph* Patrick Hutber at first refused to believe it. Then when the press release was handed to him, he went into his office, closed the door and put his hands over his head. He did not emerge again that evening. Slater's former staff stood shocked and confused in the churchyard south of St Paul's. The papers the next day contained almost nothing else, some devoting their entire front pages to it. Slater's collapse marked the end of what one paper called 'one of the most remarkable stories in the City's long history'. 'Only the abdication of the Queen . . . would command so many column inches,' commented another columnist.

Slater's statement attempted to put a braver face on it. He explained that during the past few years he had been advised to take things easier and would have resigned earlier had it had not been for the 1973–4 crash. Now, he went on, the Haw Par incident in Singapore had attracted adverse publicity which was damaging to the company, and a new board might have a better chance 'to resolve the outstanding problems'. He was, he added, pleased to be handing over to 'a man of proven ability with a long record of success in the companies in which he is interested'.

Jimmy Goldsmith was 42 when he became chairman of Slater Walker that autumn. It was to change his life in a way he could not have foreseen. The significance of what he had done, he says, only dawned on him several months later when he first met Harold Wilson, then 18 months into his second term as prime minister. To his surprise they got on well. Goldsmith found him 'a kind, loyal and pleasant man'. Wilson, as they were leaving, suddenly said that the task Goldsmith had undertaken at Slater Walker was more than 'just business'. His career from now on would assume a political dimension. He himself, he said, was a social democrat rather than a Marxist in that he believed in the mixed economy

273

with a vigorous private sector. But the hard left was agitating for a complete State takeover of the credit institutions of the City. Slater Walker, he went on (according to Goldsmith's account), would be the *cause célèbre*, which would offer them the chance to discredit the City and free enterprise.

Goldsmith, said Wilson, would be seen as the weak link, the only non-establishment director. 'If the hard left could destroy my reputation, then the salvage operation could fail and the Slater Walker group would go down,' says Goldsmith of that conversation. The ripple effect of the collapse of a company complete with a bank, an insurance company and a unit trust business would affect tens of thousands of people.

Goldsmith's arrival at Slater Walker certainly marked the point when the press, which until that time had either ignored him or been relatively favourable, turned nasty. Charles Raw of the *Sunday Times*, who had devoted two years to a major exposé of Jim Slater and his one-time partner Peter Walker, now switched his attention to Goldsmith, determined to expose him as a share manipulator, a liar and worse. From that moment on, the *Sunday Times* and Jimmy Goldsmith would be at war, a war which ended only when Rupert Murdoch bought the paper and Charles Raw left the paper.

18

Private Eye

'Have you seen this magazine *Private Eye*? It always seems to have a joke about you, mostly not very nice,' Annabel's sister-in-law remarked one week-end late in 1975. Goldsmith shrugged. '*Private Eye*? What is that?' She explained that it was a fortnightly, badly produced magazine, widely read by students, journalists, younger lawyers and City people. 'I'd never heard of it,' he says, 'I'd no idea what it was.'

In mid-December he flew to Singapore in his new capacity as chairman of Slater Walker. Haw Par, with a new chairman and a new board, owed Slater Walker, also now with a new chairman and a new board, some $29m, or £14.5m. Goldsmith wanted it back, and had arrived to negotiate terms. Jim Slater, wriggling to get off the hook in his last months, had offered to waive one-third of the loan, but Goldsmith was less conciliatory. He appointed lawyers, including the eminent Lord Goodman, to examine every detail of the loan and of the purchase by Haw Par of shares in Slater's subsidiary in Hong Kong. The criticisms by the Singapore authorities, they advised, were not justified. Legally, Haw Par was bound to repay the lot.

However, Haw Par was in financial trouble, partly due to the collapse of its investments in Slater companies, partly because the recession had also gripped Singapore and Malaysia, and partly because under its Slater-appointed management it had over-expanded. In many ways it was an Eastern replica of Slater Walker, with an insurance subsidiary, property and financial businesses. It had also taken a large shareholding in the world's largest tin producer, London Tin. In its fight to avoid repayment of the Slater loan, the company had mustered some powerful arguments. Only a week before, a Singapore Stock Exchange report claimed that Haw Par had paid £12m too much for its shares in

Slater Walker Securities (Hong Kong). They quoted a document from the former Haw Par chairman and Slater's deputy, Dick Tarling, saying the deal was 'ludicrous from Haw Par's point of view'. The loan, it alleged, had been made by Slater so that Haw Par could buy Slater's own company at an inflated price.

Goldsmith expected to be in Singapore for a week of tough talking and prepared himself meticulously. He had been there a day or so when Margaret Reid, a veteran journalist on the *Financial Times* who had covered Slater Walker for years, invited him to dinner at Raffles. She was covering his Haw Par negotiations and Goldsmith accepted. Before he set out for Raffles, he went through his post, brought out from London that day by his secretary. He stopped at a cutting from the latest issue of *Private Eye*. 'That's when I exploded. Up to then I'd been relatively calm. I'd reacted to the *Sunday Times* piece at the time of the Bovril bid, but that had been my only act.' This is not strictly true: Goldsmith had usually made a point of correcting stories he thought were inaccurate, and various letters and corrections had appeared over the years, but the general thrust is correct. He had a reputation for being prickly with the press, but no more so than a dozen other company heads.

The *Private Eye* article, which appeared in the issue dated 12 December 1975, was headed 'All's Well That Ends Elwes'. Its origins went back a year. It would run for another four years, indelibly changing the image of Jimmy Goldsmith – from that of a businessman with a clever financial mind and an immense capacity for making money, to that of an angry, obsessive right-winger determined to curb freedom of the press.

The Seventh Earl of Lucan was described variously as 'a man of enormous presence and beauty . . . who looked right, sounded better and had all the right ideas', to a man with a 'strange Crimean face, and views which appeared to be degenerating, under pressure, from paternalistic feudalism to the extreme Right wing'. John Aspinall, who claimed him as his 'fifth, sixth or seventh best friend', and in his whose club Lucan spent most of his waking hours, reckoned he was 'a figure like myself – born out of his time', with the qualities of loyalty, honesty and reliability. His parents had been strange left-wing political activists who sent him to Eton where he had an undistinguished record. He became a Coldstream Guardsman, was chosen for the Army bobsleigh team, joined a merchant bank earning £500 a year and then, after a £20,000 win at *chemin de fer* in 1960, took up serious gambling. Aspinall liked to have him around, almost as a house player, reckoning his good looks and charm brought in the big gamblers. He was not, according to those who knew him well, the aristocratic fool depicted by the press, but a secretive and tortured soul, a man of above-average intelligence who could not cope with his problems.

On the evening of 7 November 1974, Lucan booked a table at the Clermont for 10.30, but when his guests arrived he was not there and they started without him. Just as they were sitting down, a mile and a half away in Belgravia, a hysterical woman, blood pouring down her face, burst into the Plumbers Arms pub and shouted: 'He's in the house . . . the children are in the house . . . he's murdered the nanny.' She then collapsed. It was Lucan's wife, Veronica.

Downstairs in the basement of her house in Lower Belgrave Street police found signs of a struggle. There were teacups dropped on the bottom of the stairs, a lightbulb was lying on a chair – and the badly beaten body of Sandra Rivett, nanny to the Lucans' three children, had been pushed into a US mailbag. Nearby was the murder weapon, a piece of lead piping wrapped in tape. Veronica Lucan said she had heard a noise in the basement, gone down to investigate and been grabbed by the throat and beaten about the head. She had fought back, and when the intruder broke off, she had dashed to the pub next door for help.

Lucan and his wife were separated and they had been quarrelling savagely over custody of the children, at great expense and in open court. In the Clermont circle, Veronica Lucan was regarded as unstable, suspicious and resentful of Lucan's way of life. Lucan himself believed she was demented, and expected the judge to agree. When the judgment went against him, he never recovered, and over the next two years his friends watched him deteriorate.

Lucan had never been a close friend of Goldsmith's, but he was one of the Clermont set, and Goldsmith had included him in the invitation to his house party in Acapulco for his fortieth birthday in February 1973. Lucan was in deep emotional and financial trouble, and on the holiday was quiet, preferring to hang around Annabel and the children rather than join in the men's games. Annabel barely knew him, although she had seen him often enough at the Clermont or in Annabel's. 'I'd never actually spoken to him, but on that holiday he turned out to be so nice.' He would sit with her while she organised the meals, and play with the children, talking endlessly about his own.

Then in October Lucan turned up at Goldsmith's house in Paris. He needed a loan, he said, to 'buy' his children away from his wife, claiming that she was using the children to 'torture' him. 'He was absolutely devoted to the children,' says Goldsmith, 'and he thought he could get them away from her if he paid enough.' Would Goldsmith lend him £10,000?

Goldsmith has an almost morbid superstition about lending people money. He very seldom does, preferring to find some more complex arrangement, such as the one he had with Aspinall when he ran into trouble. Lucan, however, was in no need of the type of lesson Goldsmith had tried to impose on Aspinall. 'I'll give you the money,' he was told.

Lucan however would not accept a gift. They agreed that Goldsmith would guarantee a loan from the Midland Bank, and Lucan left for London. Goldsmith never saw him again.

The events of the night of 7 November and the next day have been the subject of exhaustive police and journalistic searches, but remain a mystery. Veronica told the police, and later the coroner, that her assailant was her husband. In the meantime Lucan himself rang his mother, the Dowager Countess, mumbling incoherently that there had been a 'terrible catastrophe' and there was 'blood and mess' all over the place at Belgrave Street. Could she go straight there? The police were in the house when the missing Lucan rang to talk to his mother after midnight. Then he drove to Uckfield in Sussex to the home of Ian Maxwell-Scott, one of those present at the original card school which Goldsmith joined in Oxford. Maxwell-Scott was not there, but his wife was. She gave Lucan whisky and tranquillisers and he drove off again at 1.30 am. He then wrote three letters, including one to his brother-in-law, Bill Shand-Kydd, carefully describing how Lucan had surprised an intruder in the house. 'The circumstantial evidence against me is strong, in that V will say it was all my doing and I will lie doggo for a while . . .'

The car Lucan was driving was found parked in Newhaven the next morning. In the boot was a piece of lead piping, also wrapped in tape, similar to the murder weapon. There was no sign of Lucan himself, but later that day a writ was issued for his arrest on suspicion of murder. The dead Sandra Rivett was similar in size and shape to Veronica Lucan; Thursday was normally her day off, a fact Lucan would have known. She had not gone out that evening, and the working theory was that the earl had let himself into the house, removed the light bulb at the bottom of the stairs, and waited for his wife to come down to make herself a cup of tea. Sandra Rivett had been murdered by mistake.

Jimmy Goldsmith had flown to Dublin the evening before to give a speech and knew nothing of this. Nor did he play any part in what happened next. That morning Aspinall decided to take charge, summoning those closest to Lucan to his house in Lyall Street. Charles Benson, racing tipster for the *Daily Express* who had known Lucan at Eton, came, as did Dominic Elwes, Bill Shand-Kydd, Stephen Raphael, a stockbroker and gambler, Dan Meinertzhagen, son of the chairman of Lazards bank and of the Royal Insurance Company, and a few others, all men. The meal had been organised at such short notice that everyone had to help themselves from the refrigerator.

This luncheon became the subject of interminable debate afterwards, with much speculation that this tight group of gambling chums of the missing earl had either arranged for him to be spirited away, or to cover up his escape. In fact all they did was air their opinions, some of which were bizarre, and discuss how best they could help Lucan if he did get in touch with any of them. In the meantime to the bafflement and irritation of the press, they refused to talk about him, thus actually fanning the suspicions that they knew more than they let on.

Goldsmith was still in Dublin and probably would never have been drawn into the affair, but for an article which appeared in the *Sunday Times* magazine in June 1975. Written by James Fox, a young old Etonian journalist, it was partly a reconstruction of that fateful night seven months before, and partly an examination of a group of people he presented as slightly sinister, and certainly unpleasant. It had been prepared with the help of Elwes, who had introduced Fox to Aspinall, telling him that the journalist was on their side, and would present the group, and their friend Lord Lucan, in a sympathetic light.

Both Elwes and Aspinall were widely quoted in the article, which if anything sided with Lady Lucan who emerged as a tragic victim. Aspinall had always despised Veronica Lucan and he made no bones about this to Fox. 'To be blunt, she had no money, she wasn't particularly pretty, and she had a shrewish temperament.' Fox presented the Clermont circle as a 'world united on foundations of class, privilege and wealth, whose traditions have always resisted the intrusions of a prying public.'

The article itself might have irritated Goldsmith, but what sent him into a storming rage was the picture on the cover of the magazine. It had been taken in Acapulco and showed Annabel with her arm draped affectionately over Lucan's shoulders, the two of them apparently sharing an intimate joke. They were actually sitting at a long table with more than a dozen other people, but the photograph had been cropped (with no sinister intent) to show just Annabel and Lucan. Apart from the fact that someone at his party – he did not yet know who but soon suspected (wrongly as it turned out) that it was Elwes – had taken a picture of this private gathering and then given it to the press, 'It suggested that Annabel was somehow romantically linked with Lucan which was, of course, perfect nonsense,' he says.

The article also stated that Goldsmith had been at the Aspinall lunch: and there was an oil painting, done by Elwes, for which the *Sunday Times* paid him £200, of the back-room at the Clermont, showing the gambling set: Lucan, Raphael, Goldsmith, Benson, the Earl of Suffolk, Aspinall, Peter West and Nicholas Soames.

When the *Sunday Times* article appeared, Goldsmith was in Sardinia with Annabel and her children. When he saw it, he was as angry as he had ever been in his life. Goldsmith was a jealous, possessive lover, and this was not only a slur on Annabel, but suggested he was a cuckold. Annabel tried to calm him, but he was uncontrollable. One eyewitness recalls him 'striding up and down in a towering fury. He was waving the *Sunday Times*, gesturing at it, and beginning to shout all over again.'

It also upset Mark Birley who had long accepted that he had lost Annabel to Goldsmith but was still married to her and concerned by the proprieties, and by the possible effect on their children.

It didn't take Goldsmith long to discover the details of how the article came to be written. He didn't blame Aspinall, or even the *Sunday Times* – he blamed Elwes. One of the group had seen Elwes doing the painting and had warned him that Goldsmith would not like it. Elwes is said to have replied that he didn't care.

As a result, Elwes was ostracised from the Goldsmith circle. Mark Birley banned him from Annabel's and he was shunned at the Clermont. Among the Clermont set, Elwes was sometimes referred to as the court jester, but that did him less than justice. He was clever, handsome, and above all witty. Even Aspinall, who liked to dominate conversation even when Goldsmith was at table, took second place to him. He was a quite exceptional story-teller and legendary raconteur, a brilliant mimic; even Peter Ustinov said that he was the only person he would defer to in conversation. Later his friend and contemporary Kenneth Tynan said of him that like the true alchemist 'he turned all our dross into gold ... People of quite remarkable ordinariness are permanently judged in my mind because of the skill with which they were sketched by this superb verbal cartoonist.' But he was also a wastrel and a scrounger, his life an aimless path from one rich man's door to another, dependent on patronage simply to eat. In 1958 he had eloped with the heiress Tessa Kennedy in an episode which was reminiscent of Goldsmith's elopement with Isabel. They had three children but the marriage broke up, and he remained, for all the fun he gave others, a deeply melancholy man. 'I look back on my life with nothing but unhappiness,' he wrote to John Aspinall in March 1975. 'Only the incredibly funny times, more often than not with you, have made it bearable.'

He painted a little, usually portraits of Britain's rich and famous, worked for a brief time as a journalist, but basically hung around the Clermont and Annabel's – and his rich friends.

Curiously, he cared enormously, even obsessively, about Goldsmith's rejection of him. Goldsmith obviously represented something he wanted and needed, and when Goldsmith shut him out of his life, Elwes took it almost as a death sentence. Like Lucan, he was an emotional wreck and this incident seems to have tipped him over. He wrote frantic letters, he apologised, he threatened to sue James Fox. He wrote in particular to Annabel and to her son Robin Birley. The columnist Nigel Dempster, for whom he had always been a good source, met him at the airport on his way to Nice a fortnight after the *Sunday Times* article. Elwes, he says, was almost incoherent, told him the story about being blamed for selling the photographs to the *Sunday Times*. According to Dempster, he burst into tears to the point where the *Daily Mail* journalist felt obliged to try to ring Goldsmith. He never got through. In fact Elwes did not sell the photograph to the *Sunday Times* – he had never taken a photograph in his life. It came from another source. But he had provided the painting, and he had been indiscreet in the article, but then so had Aspinall.

A friend who met him in the South of France found him weak and ill, trembling and stuttering. He had, he said, two topics of conversation: Lucan and Goldsmith. 'He blamed Lucan for what Goldsmith was doing to him.' Elwes, said the friend, was convinced that Lucan was still alive, and kept hoping he would reappear and somehow redeem his position with Goldsmith.

Goldsmith wrote angrily to the *Sunday Times*, pointing out that he had not been at the Aspinall lunch, and had played no part in whatever conspiracy they seemed to be alleging existed. When the William Hickey column in the *Daily Express* picked up the same story, simply lifting it out of the *Sunday Times'* columns, Goldsmith issued a writ. He also rang Jocelyn Stevens, then the managing director of Beaverbrook Newspapers, and insisted Stevens make sure it never happened again.

When Elwes returned to London at the end of August he found his father dying and his mother in a psychiatric home. Elwes had lost what little money he had in one of the fringe banks that went bust in the crash. On 5 September he took an overdose of barbiturates, leaving a suicide note which was said to curse both Mark Birley and Jimmy Goldsmith 'from beyond the grave'. But since the coroner never released it, this is speculation (but taken as gospel by *Private Eye*).

A memorial service was held at a church in Mayfair on 26 November 1975, over a year after Lucan's disappearance, and a month after Jimmy Goldsmith had taken over as chairman of Slater Walker. Kenneth Tynan, the leading critic of his day, delivered the first address. He was eloquent and biting, scathingly remarking that Elwes had loved the world of wealth far more than it deserved. 'Certain rich people elected him their court jester and he happily embraced the role. But they never really accepted him because in the final analysis he did not have quite enough money.'

Aspinall's address could not have been more different. Spontaneous and filled with quotations from his favourite Oscar Wilde, he described Elwes as a bard in an Anglo-Saxon court, entertaining the lords in wonderful fashion. Again and again he referred to 'genetic inheritance', saying that Elwes would have his fame in the immortality of the genes. His failure to make money was a 'genetic defect'. For all its orotundity, it was a brilliant speech, leaving the audience of Elwes' friends and family delighted.

However, one of the family, Tremayne Rodd, a godson of Elwes' mother, was less than entranced. As Aspinall emerged, the young man rushed up and punched him on the jaw. As he ran away he shouted back: 'That's what I think of your bloody speech, Aspinall.' The press photographers caught the moment perfectly, and Aspinall's unperturbed reply: 'I'm used to this sort of thing in dealing with wild animals.'

Reports of this particular incident in the next day's papers caught the attention of Richard Ingrams, the editor of *Private Eye*. He rang Dempster, who he knew had been a friend of Elwes, and should therefore know what was going on. Dempster did, and at Ingrams' request wrote him an eight-page memo. Ingrams had already asked one of his journalists, Patrick Marnham, to write a sequel to Fox's piece for *Private Eye*, but now he took a different tack. 'The reason,' he says, 'was the involvement of Jimmy Goldsmith. It struck me as rather extraordinary that the friend of Aspinall and Lucan, the hounder of Elwes, should be brought in to restore confidence as the saviour of Slater Walker along with the backing and blessing of the Bank of England.' For his part Goldsmith agrees that the reason he became of interest to Ingrams was because of Slater Walker, to which *Private Eye* had devoted hundreds of column inches over the years (from now on it contemptuously referred to Slater as 'Changi Jim' and its references to him dripped with venom and

Schadenfreude). 'It was suggested to Ingrams that the Bank of England's plan to save Slater Walker could be torpedoed if I were discredited.' Suggested by whom? This, of course, is an extension of his conversation with Wilson, and Goldsmith's attempt to rationalise behaviour he could not fathom. Ingrams and *Private Eye* were nothing to him, so why should he be anything to them?

Private Eye was not a stickler for accuracy, and the article was full of mistakes over perfectly checkable facts, but its thrust was clear enough. It started by saying that 'from the beginning the police have met obstruction and silence from the circle of gamblers and boneheads with whom Lord Lucan and Dominic Elwes associated'. It went on to mention the lunch at which, it said, Goldsmith was not only present but where he actually took the chair, and that it was he who ordered Elwes to go to the hospital to see Veronica Lucan, find out what happened, and more importantly, what she had told the police.

But there was more. The suggestion was that Goldsmith, as the leader of the 'Lucan Circle' (there never was a Lucan circle – Lucan was always a member of other people's circles), had orchestrated an organised obstruction of justice. Goldsmith, it said, was 'known for his ability in dressing up the balance sheets of his various companies with house deals whereby large sums are transferred from one company to another for purposes which are not altogether clear to outsiders.' It went on to mention his various battles with the *Sunday Times*, adding that Goldsmith 'has now taken to issuing solicitor's letters to unfriendly papers, and has instructed the *Sunday Times* not to mention his name again without first communicating with his solicitor.' This of course was another mistake – *Private Eye* had confused the *Sunday Times* with the *Daily Express*.

This was the full-page essay that Goldsmith read that December night in Singapore. In many ways it was far more wounding than the *Sunday Times* article, but although he was angry, he was less so than he had been in June. But as he fumed, he kept coming back again and again to Harold Wilson's warning: there must be a plot here. Why else would the *Sunday Times* start a campaign and *Private Eye* carry it on?

For the time being, Goldsmith took no action. For a week he pursued his argument in Singapore, then flew back to London late in December 1975. He stayed for just a day or so, saw Annabel and her children, then flew to Paris where he picked up Ginette, Manes and Alix and went to Gstaad where they spent Christmas and the New Year together. It was 3 January 1976 before he was back in London again.

Meanwhile Ingrams, by his own account, considered the *Private Eye* article a success. He was, however, much more interested in pursuing the Slater Walker angle. It is important to be clear about this. *Private Eye* had nothing personal against Goldsmith at this stage. But Ingrams took the view, as he had on other occasions, that Goldsmith could only have achieved his success by doing something crooked, nasty or shameful. He had no idea what it might be, but he would find out.

Ingrams now brought into the fray his financial investigative reporter, Michael Gillard. Gillard is an odd man: secretive, cynical, dedicated, he was well to the left in the political arena, and took genuine pleasure from exposing, often in the most tortuous detail, what he considered the misdeeds of the City under the anonymous byline 'City Slicker'. He had contacts in the Fraud Squad who used him as a conduit for material they knew they could never make stand up in court, and which was often uncheckable. Like many investigative reporters, the results of his work were uneven – sometimes brilliant, sometimes simply vicious. He saw little good in his fellow men, and certainly not in the world of capitalism and the City, which he knew well. Now he was to go after Goldsmith – and Goldsmith in turn would go after him.

On 9 January City Slicker (Gillard) reported that the links between Goldsmith and Slater were much closer than imagined. 'It is legitimate to query whether in view of the close personal involvement, Goldsmith is the most independent chairman,' wrote Gillard. To Ingrams' delight, Gillard had 'unearthed an additional item of interest' – one of Goldsmith's lawyers, Eric Levine, had also been the lawyer to T. Dan Smith, a corrupt public relations consultant who had bribed local councillors in the north-east of England, and whose links to senior Conservative politicians had originally been exposed by Gillard. The article referred to an 'intriguing link', i.e. between Levine, T. Dan Smith and Goldsmith.

Private Eye could get away with a great deal, because few people bothered to sue it – the publicity of a court case could be more damaging than the offending article. But this allegation went far beyond the bounds of journalistic licence. Goldsmith had never met T. Dan Smith in his life, had never had anything to do with him. He was barely keeping his corporate head above water when T. Dan Smith was charged and went to jail and the event barely registered with him.

The flavour of the City Slicker article can be gained by a reference to Goldsmith's recent holiday, where it said he was to be found in the Greengo nightclub 'with a variety of lissom young ladies of Ugandan extraction'. Ugandan extraction was a *Private Eye* code for kinky sex, and again hit Goldsmith where it hurt – Annabel, her family and others would now read that. In fact he had been to the Greengo only on a few occasions to collect Manes late in the evening.

Ingrams and Gillard had no conception of the pent-up anger they would unleash. They were making the mistake, as many others would, of judging Goldsmith by their own standards. Neither the Jews nor the Auvergnat believe in offering the other cheek, says Goldsmith. Nor do they see tolerance as a sign of virtue or of being civilised. 'In the case of serious aggression, attacking everything they cherish and more particularly their family, both races fight,' he says. 'For my part, in such circumstances, I consider tolerance to be degenerate.'

Three days after the issue was published, Goldsmith issued 63 separate writs for libel against *Private Eye* and another 37 against its distributors. He also, even more menacingly, applied to the High Court to bring proceedings for criminal libel in respect of the Elwes article.

One of the most famous libel cases in British legal history had begun.

19

Goldsmith v. *Private Eye*

The Earl of Lucan never did show up. In the weeks and months that followed his disappearance there were reported sightings of him everywhere. In January 1975 he was spotted in Melbourne, seen driving along the M1 motorway in England, buying flowers in Covent Garden, boarding a plane, catching a train . . . When he was 'definitely' found in Cherbourg, the press descended on the town, only to discover they should have been in St Malo. There were stories that Lucan had not driven to Newhaven at all, but had gone to Howletts where he begged John Aspinall to put an end to his misery by feeding him to his tigers. For three weeks the police watched the house of Digby Neave in Paris, and in New York detectives turned up at the home of Claus von Bulow to ask him if he was harbouring the fugitive.

By 1976 Lucky Lucan was in Bulawayo (where he did have a bank account), Capetown, Mozambique and, by 1977, Brazil where Lady Lucan urged him to give himself up. Clairvoyants, ESP specialists, journalists and conmen have all sought him. In 1979 the Australian police tracked him down and arrested him – or at least somebody who looked uncannily like him, including the scar on his neck and a 'smattering of German'. This Lord Lucan was disguised as a boilermaker under the name of Kenneth Charles Knight from Blackmore in Essex. Asked to identify him, Mrs Knight of Blackmore, Essex said: 'That's him – that's my Ken.' In 1982, John Miller, the man who kidnapped the Great Train Robber Ronald Biggs from Brazil, went around Fleet Street offering a new story: he could find Lord Lucan. He produced a man who looked amazingly like the tall ex-guardsman, but who on closer inspection proved to be an actor with a moustache pasted to his upper lip.

The story of Lucan's disappearance would be funny if it did not have its

286

tragic side. The missing earl left behind debts of £85,000 (which were paid off) and misery for his estranged wife and his children. Veronica Lucan, isolated and friendless, attempted suicide. She sold her story to the press for much-needed money, and complained to the Press Council about other reports. She still refuses to accept that her husband is dead.

The police pursued their inquiries, producing convincing evidence that the murder had been premeditated. Six weeks before the event Lucan told a friend that rather than face the bankruptcy court he would commit the perfect murder.

The police interviewed all the Clermont set, including Goldsmith. Chief Superintendent Roy Ranson did not much like them. 'We came up against the attitude of some of these people trying to put one over and to take us on and beat us.' Goldsmith, said Ranson, had come into the police station of his own volition to tell him what he knew – which was basically Lucan's money troubles and his visit to him in Paris. 'The man had enormous charisma. He looked like a bright star shining in the night. He had a beautiful overcoat with an astrakhan collar, a tailor's dummy. He was very polite, but it was very much, you know, 'Oh yes, my dear boy.'

So what did happen to Lucan? Goldsmith for one has no doubts. 'I'm convinced he's dead. He was so English the idea of him living anywhere else except England is absurd.' The belief that he's still alive is 'just as absurd', he adds. 'He was a murderer because he went mad under the pressure, and because he loved his children so much. But I don't think his code would have allowed him to do anything except fall on his sword once he realised what he had done.'

Aspinall too is convinced Lucan is dead. And James Fox, who began the whole *Private Eye* saga with that article in the *Sunday Times*, returned to the subject a decade later to interview as many of the same people, including the police, as he could. The detectives, he discovered, were sure Lucan was dead. Fox himself concluded: 'I believe that he got on the Newhaven ferry . . . and, dulled with whisky and pills, threw himself into the sea.' The fishermen at Newhaven, he added, pull up corpses in their nets with surprising frequency. But instead of telling the police, who impound the boat and the catch during their investigations, they drop the bodies back into the sea where within a matter of days they are eaten by crabs.

Jimmy Goldsmith, in deciding on a criminal libel case against *Private Eye*, made one of the biggest mistakes of his career. He committed himself to a level of public controversy and vitriol which eventually wore even him down. He lost months and even years when he could have concentrated his energies on more fruitful pastures. From being unusually open and transparent in his business life, he became secretive, obsessive, and even a little paranoid, seeing conspiracies where none existed.

Until his battle with *Private Eye*, he was building a broadly based public company in Cavenham, and, although his financial wheeling and dealing raised suspicions, Goldsmith had a justification and explanation: Cavenham was the flagship of his empire. The other companies were designed to provide it with resources, and to protect it from takeover. If it had not been for *Private Eye*, he would probably have gone on building Cavenham, in the same way as his friends James Hanson and Gordon White went on building the Hanson group until it became one of the biggest companies in the world. After *Private Eye* he craved privacy and anonymity, wished that he had kept Générale Occidentale at least as a private company, and began a long – and equally controversial – policy of withdrawal. In those years the hatred directed towards him from a widening circle of the press affected his family and his whole view of Britain. It raised his public profile to the point where his unorthodox private life, which had always been a subject of some comment, almost became a matter of public debate. Goldsmith could take no part in the rise of Thatcherism, even though it reflected many of his own political beliefs. He had, he now acknowledges, 'by mistake, got myself into a position in Britain where I could only damage anything I touched.' If it had not been for the image the *Private Eye* battle created, he says, 'I would undoubtedly have stayed.'

He has another rationalisation for it: he could not, he says, let his children's legacy be soiled by innuendo and smear. 'It would be throwing away everything I had achieved up to that point.' In the event, of course, his counter-attack on *Private Eye* would make matters worse. Goldsmith would win the battle – several of them in fact – but did he win the war? The best that can be said is that he didn't lose it.

When Goldsmith's battery of writs first arrived, Ingrams and his *Private Eye* team were unruffled. They were used to being sued, and had an adequate legal machine for coping with it. Writs arrived all the time, but very few came into court. *Private Eye* was adept at grudging apologies, and, occasionally, the payment of a small sum in damages. Goldsmith's legal threat, Ingrams thought, would be no different to a thousand others. His legal advice suggested that Goldsmith would be very unlikely to succeed in his criminal libel case.

No one realised Goldsmith's anger was so intense that he wanted something more than an out-of-court settlement. He was not after an apology or damages – he was after blood. In his angrier moments, although he would later deny it, he wanted to smash *Private Eye*, send its editor to jail, force the magazine to close. He had the resources, the energy and the determination to do it too, however long it took, and whatever the consequences. It became a personal crusade, with Goldsmith, as someone remarked later, as Don Quixote riding in to redress the wrongs of the world.

Criminal libel is notoriously difficult to prove. Dating back to the sixteeth century, it originally imposed the most severe penalties on offenders, but in recent times the law had fallen into disuse. There was the famous Oscar Wilde case, of course, when Wilde sued the Marquess of Queensberry and was outwitted in court by Frank Goldsmith's old friend, Edward Carson. Wilde ended up in Richmond jail. Winston Churchill had sued Lord Alfred Douglas for criminal libel when he was accused of deliberately losing the Battle of Jutland to make a profit on Wall Street, and Douglas was sentenced to six months imprisonment. But there have been very few cases since then. The difference between ordinary libel and criminal libel was traditionally that the latter had to be so serious as to be likely to provoke a breach of the peace, but that ruling had softened over the years, and the law was exceptionally vague. But, whereas Ingrams' legal advice was that Goldsmith would never get court approval to bring his libel case, Jimmy was receiving the opposite view.

Goldsmith was vulnerable too; he had a weak point, which was his family, or rather his two families. It was always said of Mrs Thatcher that she could stand any personal or political insult, but attack her son Mark and it went straight to the heart. In the days that followed, *Private Eye* began an investigation of Goldsmith's private life.

He was warned about it by his old friend Sam White, the *Evening Standard* journalist who had covered Paris for many years. White suggested a way to counter it: tell him the full details so that he could write it first. It is the old Fleet Street tradition of the 'spoiler' story, which one newspaper runs to take the shine off another's scoop. Goldsmith agreed, drafting a letter explaining his two families for the benefit of the *Standard* lawyers who otherwise might have been scared off by Goldsmith's fearsome reputation.

White wrote a widely read weekly column which had featured

Goldsmith as man and boy for more than 20 years, chronicling events from the Patino runaway and kidnapping to Goldsmith's elevation to the Rothschild board. On 30 January White's column was headlined, 'The Two-Family Man', and made public for the first time Goldsmith's marital position. 'It is a remarkable situation, made more so because there is no attempt at concealment', adding in parentheses what was the central point of the article – 'no "Tycoon's Secret Love-Nest Uncovered" here', although of course there was – as Goldsmith was more than aware. It was one thing for his women to know about each other, and Goldsmith made sure they did. His friends also knew, and had from the beginning. But knowing did not mean accepting. Annabel had relations who never in a million years could understand her situation. Both Annabel and Jimmy had children old enough to read about it, or hear it from school friends – how do you explain to them that their father had another wife, home and children in another city? Publicity was also embarrassing for Mark Birley who was still married to Annabel and whose children were at Eton. Goldsmith tried not to care what people thought about him; but he was forced to care because of the hurt any revelations could cause Annabel, Ginette and the children.

White did his best to defuse the situation. Both families, he said, were close: Manes was godfather to Annabel's son Zacharias, and Isabel was godmother to Jemima. 'Roughly speaking, of the twenty years Goldsmith has been married to Ginette, he has shared ten with Lady Annabel. The normal pattern of his life is that weekends are spent with his family in Paris . . . and weekdays with Lady Annabel.'

These details would certainly have come out eventually, and the White article was probably the best way they could be made public. They also probably took some of the sting out of *Private Eye*'s increasingly concentrated attack. It was Michael Gillard who invented the nickname 'Goldenballs' for Jimmy, a memorable play upon his name, his wealth and his sexual prowess.

But the floodgates had now opened. Over the next year Goldsmith probably attracted more column inches in the newspapers than anyone in the country, except perhaps for Harold Wilson. He later counted only 33 days out of eleven months when he did not make the front page of at least one national paper. 'The slightest rumour would become a major story. You can't imagine what it was like. Every morning I would wake up and there would be the most incredible stories. I started getting into this horrible situation of wondering what would be the next day's story. And it was sheer appalling nonsense. Fortunately after a time I began to get anaesthetised.'

In fact Goldsmith demonstrated again and again how sensitive he was as he angrily rang editors, wrote letters, issued further writs, and began to look for patterns in the stories, linking an unfriendly reference even in the *Financial Times* or *The Times* to a kind of imaginary central intelligence which somehow revolved around Ingrams and Gillard. There is no question that the press he received at this time was unfair and often malicious, but to some extent he had himself to blame. An often innocent remark by a journalist would be turned by Goldsmith into something sinister, and his counter-attack would be out of all proportion to the original slight. This in turn caused the journalist to retaliate, and within a matter of weeks Goldsmith had made another life-long enemy who would now see his (or her) objective as exposing this manic threat to press freedom. Goldsmith was probably right in that a number of journalists who disliked his attempts to crush *Private Eye* now began their own campaigns against him, but it was absurd to believe that Ingrams or Gillard (or anyone else) had organised them with a view to bringing Goldsmith down, along with Slater Walker and the whole capitalist system. Journalists are essentially poor organisers, the *Private Eye* journalists in particular. Gillard was a strange, lonely man with few friends on Fleet Street; Ingrams largely shunned society, preferring not to meet people his magazine might later attack. He neither smoked nor drank, and his only ambition was for *Private Eye* – which Goldsmith was now threatening to put out of business. On top of the dozens of writs, Goldsmith now announced he was setting up a fund of £250,000 which would be available for use by anyone who felt they were libelled by the magazine but hadn't the resources to fight it.

Private Eye was flavour of the month, the David versus Goliath, the freedom of the press versus right-wing censorship and worse; any young idealistic journalist had to take sides against Goldsmith, and the feeling ran so high that even the older hands kept their peace. There was nothing to be gained by supporting Goldsmith, but there was something to be lost.

As the spring advanced, the battle escalated on both sides in a way the British media world had never seen before and has not seen since. Goldsmith went on with his business and his busy family life. Cavenham bought a further 1.8m shares in Grand Union in the US to take its shareholding to 80 per cent. He also announced yet another complicated share swap between his various companies: Générale Occidentale, the master company in which Goldsmith personally had a one-third interest, made a bid for the outstanding shares of Générale Alimentaire (there was only 19 per cent left in public hands, the rest being controlled by either

GO or Cavenham). The entire 100 per cent holding in Générale Alimentaire, one of France's biggest food manufacturers, would then be transferred to Cavenham in return for shares. The overall effect was to tighten GO's grip on Cavenham.

Then Goldsmith went off to Barbados with John Aspinall. Annabel and their two children joined him there, along with Selim Zilkha and Jim Slater (who normally went no further than Bournemouth for his holidays). He returned to momentous events in Britain. On 11 March 1976 Harold Wilson announced he was resigning as prime minister. He had just passed his sixtieth birthday and the man who won the party election to succeed him, Jim Callaghan, was four years older. Speculation as to why he resigned would run almost as long as it did over the fate of Lord Lucan.

Although they had met for the first time only a month before, Goldsmith had become friendly with the Labour premier, unusual for a businessman who shared very few of Wilson's political views. In February 1976 David Frost held a dinner party to which he invited Jimmy and Annabel. Frost was attempting to persuade Harold Wilson to appear in a series of television interviews, and he also invited him, his wife Mary and Marcia Falkender, his personal and political secretary. Mary Wilson was the subject of a satirical diary in *Private Eye* each fortnight called 'Mrs Wilson's Diary', and she confessed to Goldsmith that she hated it.

Wilson was fascinated by Goldsmith. He symbolised everything that he had fought against all his political life: the jet-set buccaneering tycoon, from a rich, Old Etonian, Tory background, whose views were known to be to the right even of those of most of the Conservative Party. But Goldsmith, according to Marcia Falkender, also 'symbolised terrific success'. His Jewishness and half-French background made him classless, and this appealed to Wilson. Wilson knew about Goldsmith's efforts at Slater Walker, and far from resenting them, he told Goldsmith he was grateful for them. 'Harold was well aware that everything was so fragile that if Jimmy didn't pull that [Slater Walker] off it would have been very serious,' said Marcia Falkender later, 'for the government as well. A terrific panic in the City would have affected what the government was doing and we weren't in a very good position at that time either.'

Wilson invited Goldsmith to Downing Street for a chat one evening, and also included him in a lunch the Labour prime minister gave to discuss what Britain could learn from Europe. Despite his links with Heath, it was the first meal Goldsmith had ever eaten inside Number Ten.

It was not Wilson's actual resignation that was to affect Goldsmith. It was his resignation honours list. By long tradition a retiring prime minister awards those of his or her staff who have served them most loyally over the years: their particular friends in politics, their closest civil servants, loyal friends who have helped their political career, even their secretaries, cooks and drivers. It is the last spin of the wheel of patronage. Wilson had been thinking about his resignation honours for some time. According to Falkender, who had already been made a life peer several years before, Wilson used to write down names on scraps of paper and put them in his wallet. Then he transferred them to a card. 'What Harold wanted to do was to have a last honours list which represented the sort of things he'd been interested in, and the sort of things he'd like to see,' said Falkender. Wilson included Goldsmith's name; he also included James Hanson whom he was equally taken by. It would, however, be several months before the list became public. In the meantime, the first stage of Goldsmith's legal case against *Private Eye* was under way.

A few days before they came into court, the *Eye*'s lawyers sent a letter to Goldsmith's solicitor basically retracting the offending article. They were satisfied, they said, 'that there could be no truth in the suggestion that Mr Goldsmith was a party to an attempt to obstruct the police in investigating the murder'. The *Eye* now withdrew and apologised for this allegation. 'We leave it to you to decide how this apology and withdrawal can be made public.' It was, as Ingrams later acknowledged, a bad error: the *Eye*, in an attempt to influence the judge in its favour, had now admitted it had no defence to a charge of criminal libel. Mr Justice Wien was not easily persuaded. He began his summing-up on the morning of the second day, initially raising Ingrams' hopes as he seemed to side with him, then changing tack in his conclusion. At the end he paused, looked around the court, and declared: 'I have come to the conclusion that the public interest requires the institution of criminal proceedings.'

It was a dramatic moment, the first time in a hundred years that criminal proceedings had been brought against a publication. Normally, criminal libels were prosecuted by the police rather than by an individual. Ingrams now faced a potential jail sentence, and a burden of costs and other problems that his magazine could probably not survive. 'What no one had thought possible had come to pass,' he said. 'We had all been treating it almost as a joke.' His one consolation was that when he got back to the office he had a call from Tiny Rowland, who had fallen out with Goldsmith, offering him £5,000-worth of support.

As the Goldsmith lawyers began preparing their full case, which would come before the courts in the autumn, the next stage of the drama unfolded. On 2 May the *Sunday Times* carried an article that the Wilson honours list had run into difficulties with the Scrutiny Committee. Objections had been raised to a number of names, it said, particularly to three to whom Wilson wanted to give life peerages. The *Sunday Times*, although it knew the names, did not print them. But it gave some hints. 'One of the names is that of a City financier, another is a financier and impresario, and the third is a minor businessman.' It took no time at all for the rest of Fleet Street to unearth the names. On 19 May the *Daily Express* carried the front page headline:

'IT'S LORD GOLDSMITH'

'Wilson gives Slater chief a peerage'

The other two were Jarvis Astaire, the boxing promoter (who was on the board of Anglo-Continental when Goldsmith bought control, and stayed there) and Sir Joseph Kagan, maker of the Gannex raincoat worn by Wilson. Kagan was later sent to jail.

But was there ever to be a 'Lord' Goldsmith? When the list was eventually made public and Goldsmith emerged with a knighthood instead of a peerage, there was endless speculation that the furore over the *Private Eye* case had forced Wilson to retreat. Even today there are many who still believe that, and Ingrams publicly took credit for it. What happened was this. In his last few days at Downing Street, Wilson handed his various bits of paper and cards to Marcia Falkender, and asked her to put them together as a list. Normally she would have asked a civil servant where typing was required, but this was a personal matter, to be dealt with by his personal staff. Falkender wrote the names out on a single sheet of pink notepaper. The list was for evermore referred to, wrongly, as 'the lavender list', and was always deemed to be the work more of Lady Falkender than of Wilson himself. Wilson has never spoken about it, but Falkender is absolutely clear. Goldsmith, she insists, was never down for a peerage – and she definitely did not add his name. 'Everyone got the impression that I'd wanted Jimmy to go to the House of Lords, but that Harold had back-tracked and given him a knighthood instead. But why should I? I didn't know Jimmy very well then, and in any case there had never been any question of a peerage. Harold had always intended to give him a knighthood. That was what I wrote on the list.'

The speculation is forgivable. Goldsmith had been a friend and supporter of Edward Heath's; he was on the record as saying that the Heath government was the best Britain had had since the war; he had given money to the Tories, had offered to take over and reorganise

Central Office, had campaigned vigorously against the advance of socialism which he regarded as the world's great evil, and expressed views which at times would have embarrassed Mrs Thatcher. If Heath had chosen to give him an honour in his resignation list, eyebrows would have been raised, but at least it would have been understandable. The fact that the honour had come from a former Labour prime minister who had only known Goldsmith a matter of months was baffling. True, there were other industrialists on the list, several of them less conspicuously successful than Jimmy, but that was beside the point. Goldsmith was well to the political right, was a self-confessed adulterer, and was in the middle of the most celebrated libel case since Oscar Wilde. The list aroused as much fury in establishment Britain, which had never accepted Goldsmith, as it did among the Labour Party and its supporters, and considerably damaged Harold Wilson's waning reputation. 'Such a graceful exit,' remarked one Labour cabinet minister, 'and then he had to go and do this on the doorstep.'

Goldsmith himself can only guess at why he got his knighthood – 'I think he thought it would be useful for me in Slater Walker, because it showed the goverment's support.' But that, too, sounds unlikely. The official citation was: 'For services to exports and ecology', but Cavenham, as a retailer and food manufacturer, was not a great exporter, and Goldsmith's contribution to the ecology at that point was limited to financing the launch of his brother's Ecology Foundation, and a donation to Friends of the Earth in its campaign against the nuclear plant at Windscale. There were jokes that Wilson had got the wrong brother, and that it was Teddy who should have been knighted. Jimmy resented the sniping. He was proud of his honour, and would angrily insist that it was perfectly straightforward and no cause at all 'for public controversy'.

Oddly enough the knighthood had almost gone astray. Wilson's letter went to Goldsmith's house in Chester Terrace, but he had moved to Tregunter Road. He was woken up one night at Annabel's house, Pelham Cottage, to be told the *Daily Express* was leading its front page on his peerage. Was it true? 'I know nothing about it,' he said truthfully. A few days later he went to Paris, and he was sitting with Ginette in her large downstairs sitting room when the phone rang. It was Harold Wilson.

'Jimmy,' he said, 'you never answered my letter.'

Goldsmith apologised, but explained that he had never received his letter.

'I wrote you a letter asking you whether you would accept a knighthood,' said Wilson.

Another letter was duly despatched, with no mention of a peerage.

Early in May Goldsmith offered to settle with *Private Eye*, on tough conditions: damages of £15–20,000, an apology in open court, and an agreement not to mention either Goldsmith or Eric Levine for five years. After a week-end of bargaining, he dropped the damages and the five-year ban but insisted on a 48-hour vetting procedure before anything was published. Ingrams made a counter-offer of an apology, costs and a guarantee to check information in advance, so the difference between the two was very small. But the negotiations broke down.

Ingrams for one was pleased they had. 'To be honest,' he wrote afterwards, 'part of me was enjoying the excitement of the case and did not want it to end at this point.' A few weeks later he bumped into Teddy Goldsmith at a party, who remarked to him with a grin: 'You should be grateful to my brother, Mr Ingrams. He has made your life more interesting.' That was, Ingrams reflected, 'perfectly true'.

Goldsmith had not welcomed the attack from *Private Eye*, but he too was getting into the swing of it, his adrenalin flowing as he mounted his counter-offensive. The day after the negotiations ended, he launched his criminal libel case. A week later he added a battery of injunctions against other *Private Eye* writers, including Nigel Dempster, Auberon Waugh (who had never even written about him, and barely knew who he was) and Richard West, as well as Gillard and Marnham, the authors of the original offending piece. He now returned to the High Court to apply for a writ prohibiting 'words, pictures or visual images tending to disparage or cast doubt on the private or personal integrity of Mr Eric Levine'.

Private Eye, unable to explain the ferocity of Goldsmith's attack, decided that Levine must have been stirring Goldsmith up, and began to concentrate its attention on him. And the battle really turned nasty. In their pursuit of Levine, they talked to two men they believed would help them: John Addey, a financial public relations consultant, and Leslie Paisner, the head of a firm of solicitors where Levine had once been a partner. They were right – initially both did help, supplying the type of information they wanted on Levine. The *Eye* now prepared a major article on Levine which would make a series of damaging allegations. Goldsmith learned of this, put the allegations to Levine, who denied them, then called Paisner who visited him in his office in Leadenhall Street in the

City. Goldsmith confronted Paisner who repeated the allegations he had made to *Private Eye*. Goldsmith then asked Roland Franklin, now working for Goldsmith, to talk to Addey. Addey, a practising homosexual who kept that side of his life hidden from his clients, later rang Franklin to tell him he had lied, and it was he who had prompted Paisner into telling false stories about Levine. Why had he done it? 'He was reluctant to explain,' said Franklin in an affidavit, 'but finally said they were related to the fact that he had had a homosexual relationship with somebody and was being blackmailed on that account.' The man he claimed blackmailed him was the *Private Eye* journalist, Michael Gillard. Addey swore a statement to that effect, saying he was 'deeply ashamed' of his behaviour, and begging Levine's forgiveness. When he learned that Addey had lied to him, Paisner retracted his previous statement.

Goldsmith immediately rang the editors of a number of papers to tell them that the allegations against Levine might still be made, but the man responsible, Michael Gillard, had been blackmailing John Addey. 'I had every reason to believe,' he told a jury three years later when Gillard sued him for slander, 'that *Private Eye*, as part of their campaign, would try and publish these false allegations . . . and the trouble about these articles is that today it is possible to prove that they were all lies, but when they are made they do harm; and you have to be fairly strong to live through such lies.'

The British summer of 1976 was the hottest on record, but Goldsmith stayed on in London to oversee his fight. His case for an injunction to prevent *Private Eye* mentioning him was to be heard on 5 July 1976, and *Private Eye* prepared to question both Addey and Paisner closely. Ingrams says he approached the hearing with 'something approaching excitement'. His lawers had advised him he had a 'strong hand. And it would be fascinating to see how Paisner and Addey explained themselves.'

This was the first occasion Ingrams had had to observe Goldsmith at close quarters. His impressions give an interesting flavour of the man:

A tall, restless, nail-biting man, expensively dressed, he looked at least ten years older than 43. His face was tanned, his eyes a steely blue. In repose, his expression was curiously dead. But his face would frequently crinkle into a smile and – which was disconcerting – from time to time he looked across at me, nodding and grinning, as if trying to convey a message of some kind.

297

To *Private Eye*'s consternation, neither Addey nor Paisner appeared in court – Addey had gone to Italy before he could be served with a subpoena and Paisner's doctor testified that he was too ill to give evidence (he was indeed ill and died three years later, aged 70).

Goldsmith visibly enjoyed the cross-examination of the various witnesses. The battle had become one not unlike a contested takeover bid, to be won by clever tactics and stratagems, using the law, press and whatever other legal weapons came to hand – including private dectectives. When Gillard appeared in the box, his solicitor presented Goldsmith with a writ for slander, which Goldsmith opened, gave a mirthless smile, and passed to Eric Levine.

On this occasion Goldsmith lost. Mr Justice Donaldson refused to grant a general injunction, but Goldsmith announced he would appeal. He also announced he was issuing yet another writ about another *Private Eye* story on Haw Par, would be suing Gillard and Ingrams and that he would defend Gillard's slander action. 'He's gone right over the top,' commented Ingrams.

The committal proceedings for Goldsmith's case against the *Eye* began on 29 July 1976. The tiny, sweltering courtroom at Bow Street Magistrates Court was crammed with reporters, with photographers lining the pavement outside. When Goldsmith appeared he had Annabel on his arm, the first time they had been seen in public together. Goldsmith was aware of the speculation it would create, but he was telling the world that he had nothing to hide. One photographer got one of the most famous pictures ever taken of either them: Goldsmith glancing quizzically and rather grimly at the waiting throng, a half-chewed cigar in his left hand, his right hand clasping that of Annabel who wore a light dress, the skirt split to the waist, which flashed open to reveal the full length of a long elegant leg. The next morning, it would make every paper in Britain.

This day in court was merely a formality, but it was the only time in the dozens of hearings in different courts and before different judges that Goldsmith was to give evidence in person. All his life, Goldsmith has been unable to keep still as he speaks, and now he strode up and down the tiny witness box, banging the rail to emphasise a point, and waving his arms. At one point when *Private Eye*'s barrister, James Comyn, asked him, 'Isn't your aim to smash Private Eye?' Goldsmith leaned across and pointed at Ingrams. 'No,' he said, 'I only want them to be more TRUTHFUL!' Finally the bemused magistrate Kenneth Barraclough asked him if he would mind 'behaving a little less theatrically'.

Leaving his lawyers to continue the pursuit of *Private Eye*, Goldsmith went off on holiday to Corsica. Meanwhile, Ingrams was puzzled as to how the Goldsmith lawyers were able to produce photocopies of original *Eye* manuscripts, and in court in the middle of August his lawyers forced the admission that 'a highly reputable firm of private detectives' had been employed to go through the *Eye*'s dustbins. They didn't take the documents – that would have been theft – but made copies and put the originals back.

The original revelation that *Private Eye* had got its facts wrong lost it much sympathy in the early days of the battle. But public opinion swung as the implications became clear of successfully prosecuting a criminal libel case, particularly to journalists who were convinced it would become a common event. The disclosure about the private detectives added an element of farce, making Goldsmith something of a laughing stock. He justified his action by saying that *Private Eye* was attacking him with everything it had – which was true – and he had to hit back with everything he had. 'I also had to find out whether the campaign against me was really being co-ordinated, or whether it was my imagination.' His private detectives, he says, provided him with a list 'which confirmed what I had suspected'.

To fund its battle, *Private Eye* appealed for money from its readers, and each fortnight published the names of the contributors to the Goldenballs Fund. Money poured in, from names such as Anthony Sampson, the Earl of Lichfield, Sir Alec Guinness, Professor Hugh Trevor-Roper, as well as from taxi-drivers, lawyers, students and journalists. Goldsmith had managed to alienate not only most of the British press, but ordinary people too. He still had his friends and supporters, but they studiously avoided speaking up for him, reckoning their voices would be drowned in the howls of protest. Even the judges seemed to have turned against him: two contempt cases were lost that summer. The *Sunday Times* joined the attack with revelations about John Addey and Paisner which caused the latter to resign, and virtually drove the former out of business. And Goldsmith had not shut *Private Eye* up – it was back with further articles.

Goldsmith believed more strongly than ever that there was a conspiracy against him. There were, he reckoned, 40 to 50 journalists who had a 'symbiotic relationship' with the *Eye*, who were 'excellently co-ordinated' and who were using their columns 'to create an atmosphere around me'. He could not conceive that there might be another explanation, that in the world of journalism the resurrection of an old law with the penalty of jail was seen as posing a real threat to press freedom; nor could he see that most journalists felt a natural sympathy for the underdog. He was right that an 'atmosphere' existed which meant that to put in a good word for him was not dissimilar to defending Saddam Hussein during the Gulf War.

But this involvement with the press, which Goldsmith decided was pretty corrupt from top to bottom, triggered a new interest. The only way he could have a fair say would be to own his own newspaper.

20

Battle for Beaverbrook

The mid-1970s were bad times for Britain's newspaper industry. The recession had badly affected advertising, while costs had spiralled as inflation drove up wages and a falling pound pushed up the price of newsprint. Almost every newspaper in the land was in financial trouble. The business was notoriously inefficient, with absurd levels of over-manning and an appalling industrial relations records. Most groups were still controlled by hereditary press barons, who were running out of patience and money. Newspaper companies were shunned by the City banks who saw them as institutions largely owned by eccentrics for their own private indulgence. Ownership of a newspaper still carried great prestige, invariably a life peerage, and invitations to Chequers and Windsor Castle at the week-end. Although new electronic technology, which could have transformed the cost base of the industry (as indeed it eventually did) was available from the late-1960s onwards, no proprietor, not even Rupert Murdoch, had yet been able to replace systems which were now a century old. There had been little investment in re-equipping plants which dated from before the war.

This was a decade before Murdoch finally broke the strangehold of the print unions by moving his newspapers to a brand new plant in Wapping, and transformed the fortunes of the industry. The crisis in the mid-1970s was so severe that many of the proprietors, both old and new, were on the brink of panic. When the Labour government returned to power in 1974 it immediately set up a Royal Commission, the third such commission since World War II, not because it cared a hoot about the losses of the press barons (who were almost all Conservative Party supporters) but to examine what effect the plight of the industry might have on the public's choice of titles. The proprietors were at first highly suspicious, seeing it as

301

a prelude to socialist legislation and control of the industry. But by the end of 1975 the situation had become so serious that it was now the proprietors who were begging the government to intervene; they faced, they said in a collective letter to the commission, 'a crisis of unprecedented dimensions and dangers'. The commission agreed: its interim report, published in the spring of 1976, found that only four daily papers and one Sunday paper made a profit the previous year, and, even more ominously, 'the publishers of quality newspapers . . . made losses in 1975 totalling over £4m.'

All these factors made it a wonderful buyers' market – for someone with the courage and the money to enter it. Murdoch had analysed the situation clearly and was looking for more papers to add to the two he already owned. Robert Maxwell, Tiny Rowland and others were on the periphery, thinking about getting in; and Jimmy Goldsmith, for reasons which had little to do with the profitability of the industry, was contemplating buying up one of the newspapers which was clearly going to become available before long. In an interview in *The Times* a year later he set out his reasons for public consumption:

Firstly, I believe the industry is incredibly profitable, because no other industry could be so mismanaged and survive. Much more important than that, I believe it has a huge influence in the community and it is vital that it is run properly and constructively. I would not go into a mad, scatter-brained scheme on a structurally loss-making basis, I would only do it if the thing made sense as a whole, for the newspaper as well as ourselves.

This is a perfectly logical and even prescient analysis of the industry. But it was not his reason for wanting a newspaper. He freely admits that, at least as far as Britain was concerned (France was a different matter), he went into newspapers 'out of anger'.

The attacks on my children, the attacks on my family, the attacks on . . . These were things I couldn't believe could happen. I'd been brought up – not that I had very much English blood in me – in the English tradition of fairness, and I felt I had been treated unfairly to a degree that was impossible even for me to envisage. I became dangerous to them and I became dangerous to myself. Fortunately I controlled myself.

Goldsmith has always managed – as he says, sometimes 'only just' – to channel his extraordinary energy in a pre-set direction. He has mostly had around him a structure, in his case a company, which was driven by his booster power. When that energy was sidetracked, there were no longer any disciplines or tracks to run on.

In entering the media industry in both Britain and France, he says now that he 'betrayed' the business ethics on which he had based his career.

> The media for me was always an extraordinarily difficult thing to get involved in. I realised that if you are in business, and cease to run it like a business, you kill it and pay the penalty. And that is why for instance all my businesses were run as very tight ships, because I always worked on the principle that dividends could be paid and salaries could be paid, and then individuals could blow them on anything they liked – yachts or whatever, that was up to them. But if you started doing that in a business, in the same way a fish rots from the head down, it would rot everything beneath the top. So I had to be puritanical in business, even though I'm not naturally puritanical myself, and enjoy myself outside with what I pulled out. There had to be a complete dichotomy of point of view. Once I was in the business it was one way, once I was out of the business it was a completely different way. In my personal life I could do anything I liked, but in business you have to have a rational or economic reason for doing it.

He tried, he says, to apply that approach to newspapers. 'And I couldn't find a way of doing it rationally in a way that competed with the food industry, particularly in those days of Fleet Street and the high prices people paid for publications. So I had great difficulty in doing something which was contrary to my business ethic, but close to my heart.'

He was of course, as Rupert Murdoch proved, wrong about the newspaper business, and those same newspapers which seemed to Goldsmith expensive in 1977 were to become worth ten to twenty times that value ten years later. But despite that interview in *The Times*, Goldsmith says he really believed the industry could be transformed as Murdoch transformed it. He saw the problems, the unions, the need for reinvesting – never the commercial opportunities. But he did, he says, invent all sorts of rationalisations – that it was going to be a good business, produce a good return on capital and all the rest. However, he knew they were rationalisations, to persuade himself as much as others.

Goldsmith's hatred for the British press during this period trembled on the brink of paranoia. Even his friends feared his rage. 'The press can destroy even if it can't build,' he said in that same *Times* interview, 'and this is perhaps what we've seen most in the past few years – its destructive capacity.' Weakness, he added, had crept in at the top of the press, and that meant 'the top is frightened to exercise its authority and therefore its responsibility'.

Yet Goldsmith retained the ability to see what was happening to him, and was able to guide himself back on to the rails, to think rationally again. His great sense of fun reasserted itself – and his financial brain worked hard to make sense of this new direction. As opportunities presented themselves to become a press baron, he would also think more clearly about the practicalities. As a potential proprietor, he carried an enormous debt burden from the *Private Eye* case, which would be very difficult to shift.

His first attempt came about almost by accident. The *Observer*, self-appointed heir to the British liberal tradition, had suffered financially more even than other newspapers. The emergence of a third Sunday paper, the *Sunday Telegraph*, into the quality end of the market had hit its circulation hard, and although once competing head-on with the *Sunday Times*, between 1974 and 1976 the Observer lost 150,000 in circulation, falling to 670,000 – less than half that of the *Sunday Times*. For years the family of David Astor, the editor, had bailed the paper out when it got into trouble, but the *Observer* was now to be the first casualty of the crisis in the industry. Astor retired in 1975, and by early 1976 the paper's financial position was so perilous that Lord Goodman, chairman of the editorial board, sought assistance from Harold Wilson. Money was needed urgently for new plant. When Wilson resigned, Goodman pursued his case with Jim Callaghan but, by September 1976, as one of the paper's staff writers put it, 'a feeling of despair was settling on the trustees'. Astor wanted to sell. Goodman offered the paper to Rupert Murdoch, who instantly flew in from New York to start negotiations. All went well until the story leaked on 21 October. Clive James, the Australian-born television critic, protested that he had not come to London to have Murdoch catch up with him. A delegation of employees went off to see Goodman, and questions were asked in the House of Commons. Murdoch, furious at the leak and irritated by the opposition from the editor and staff, issued a statement from New York, saying that because of the leak and 'the deliberate and orchestrated attempt to build this into a controversy', he was no longer interested.

The thought of bidding for the *Observer* had not actually occurred to Jimmy Goldsmith until one morning, over breakfast at his house in Tregunter Road, when his eye caught an article about Murdoch's position. Half way down Goodman was quoted as saying that Goldsmith would 'never' get the *Observer* – he would be repelled. But Goldsmith had made no advances. How, he wondered, could he be repelled? Goodman, at this stage, was just past the peak of his once considerable powers. A man of immense presence and girth, he had acted as legal adviser to the leaders of all three main British political parties, particularly Harold Wilson who had been a close friend as well as a client. Goodman was the great go-between of the day, a wonderfully skilled 'fixer', brought in by companies, politicians and newspaper barons to sort out their differences. Recently he had semi-retired from his legal practice to become Master of University College, Oxford, but continued to be sought out for his counsel. Among the companies he advised was Slater Walker, and in that capacity he had actually helped Goldsmith over the Haw Par battle.

However, *Observer* journalists claimed they had heard Goodman say he would prefer the paper to fold than be sold to Goldsmith. And a government minister was quoted anonymously as saying something even stronger: 'He [Goodman] would rather go on a diet than do a deal with him [Goldsmith].'

Private Eye maintained it could explain why Goodman favoured Murdoch but was antagonistic to Goldsmith: Goodman was a great friend of Lord Rayne, married to Annabel's sister Jane, and the Raynes were said to resent the way Goldsmith refused to divorce Ginette and marry Annabel. Since Rayne and Goldsmith were close friends, this was not the case. Goldsmith had a different explanation: he understood that in the 'court of King Harold', Goodman jealously guarded his position as adviser, fixer and friend to Wilson. But he had fallen out with Marcia Falkender, and there was a considerable rivalry between the two. Goldsmith believed therefore that he found himself on the edge of a strange, internecine war. Later he discovered that Goodman saw him as a 'Marcia friend', and therefore a person who must not be allowed to gain power which would be used by Marcia. Goldsmith also came to believe that the leak of the 'Lord Goldsmith' story to the *Daily Express* had originated from Goodman in an effort to prevent it happening – although to this day Goldsmith insists he has no idea whether a peerage ever was intended for him.

Whatever his private feelings may have been toward Goldsmith, Goodman answered the phone to him early that morning. Goldsmith was irritated and came quickly to the point.

'Look here, what the devil is this nonsense in the newspapers? You know perfectly well that I'm not a candidate and haven't been trying to get this paper. So what is this aggressive act? You're just trying to suck up to the media.'

Goodman was immediately placatory.

'Not at all,' he said. 'I've been misquoted. It's not at all that. On the contrary we'd welcome you.' He was, he added, having breakfast that morning with David Astor, and the managing director Roger Harrison. 'Why don't you join us?'

Less than an hour later both Goodman and Astor actively tried to get him involved, possibly out of embarrassment on Goodman's part, but also because the more bidders there were in the arena the better. It was obvious to them that Goldsmith's interest, once kindled, would have another dimension than the purely commercial one, and he would pay a premium for his ambition to become a proprietor.

But would he, Astor was interested to know, guarantee the paper its much-prized editorial independence? The *Observer* saw itself as being on the left on many issues, while Goldsmith was on the right. Goldsmith was firm on that part. 'No. But I only intend to come in if I am invited by the editorial staff, by the management and by the shop floor representatives.'

This was a sensible approach – indeed probably the only approach. Ownership of newspapers in Britain had become a highly emotive and politically charged issue by the mid-1970s (and has become more so since), and Goldsmith's reputation as a right-wing reactionary whose ideas on freedom of the press differed from those of many journalists made him a particularly controversial figure. The Monopolies Commission has special rules for the transfer of newspaper titles, and if the public reaction was strong enough, they could block Goldsmith. So could the government, simply by referring a bid to the Commission. And even if Goldsmith bypassed those obstacles, the journalists and print unions could have combined to make his ownership both difficult and expensive. When the Thomson Organisation took on the print unions a few years later, both *The Times* and *Sunday Times* were closed for a year with such financially disastrous consequences that they were sold.

In Goldsmith's case, the *Private Eye* affair lay like a pall over the negotiations. It almost certainly would have influenced Goodman, and it affected the journalists, the politicians, the unions – everyone involved. At this point, Goldsmith was probably the least welcome newspaper proprietor any of them could imagine, although Murdoch ran him a close second. Editors and journalists on the whole prefer a placid non-intellectual type of proprietor whom they can dominate, or at least treat with a distant disdain. Roy Thomson, for this very reason, is still regarded as the perfect owner. Goldsmith's passion, combined with his interest in politics and business, frightened the *Observer* journalists, and his energies and his reputation as a hands-on manager made him positively terrifying.

That afternoon Harrison went through the figures for him. They were predictably dreadful. But the next evening Jimmy invited half a dozen senior *Observer* journalists, including the editor Donald Trelford and the political editor John Cole, to his home for dinner. He was courteous and polite, at his most charming. One of them posed the magic question: was he interested in editorial policy? 'Of course I am,' replied Goldsmith. 'If I'm going to invest in a newspaper, it will not be as a passive investor.' One of the journalists, the columnist Michael Davie, gave his version some time later: 'He claimed most persuasively – since he is nothing if not persuasive – that he would always attempt to get his views across by reasoned argument, not by diktat. He would never be another Beaverbrook or Northcliffe. He would never give orders about editorial content.'

The next day Goldsmith went through the figures in greater detail. 'I realised that old Roy Thomson had taken them for a ride. The *Observer* was a wonderful company as long as it didn't have its printing works. It was a publishing company, and not an industrial company.' When Thomson bought *The Times* in 1967, the *Observer* shared the building and the same print works, a relic of the ownership of both papers by the Astor family. Thomson, however, moved *The Times* to the larger and more modern print plant in Grays Inn Road where he printed the *Sunday Times*, and gave the old print works to the *Observer*.

> They'd had it valued and they said, 'Goody, goody, we've got it dirt cheap, Roy Thomson is going senile and has offered it to us at below market price', and they bought it and moved from being a publishing company to a printing company. And they were locked into the nightmare of Fleet Street, with a vast building, with all the union problems and also a one-day-a-week publication. And I could see no way of making it viable.

He told this to David Astor and Goodman. 'So I pulled out. And then I read article after article about how I'd been outmanoeuvred and been refused and all the rest. Complete nonsense!'

In the public eye, this was a conspicuous failure at a sensitive time, and *Private Eye* claimed it as a victory. Unknown to Goldsmith, Murdoch was back in the frame and on the verge of agreeing a deal when an *Observer* journalist, Kenneth Harris, in Aspen, Colorado for a conference, mentioned the *Observer*'s plight to Robert Anderson, the head of Atlantic Richfield, a major American oil company. In less than a week Anderson, interested in getting into Britain's North Sea oil concessions and reckoning the paper would give him the necessary political clout, had bought it. Murdoch was furious, 'partly at myself for getting sucked into the thing'.

Although Goldsmith had never actually mounted a bid, he had not retired from the game. Early in 1977, even as his struggle with *Private Eye* rumbled on, he took a more decisive step. For years Beaverbrook Newspapers had been seen as one of the more worthwhile prizes in Fleet Street, only retaining its independence because of the archaic share voting structure which kept in power the Aitken family. Under Sir Max Aitken, son of the founder Lord Beaverbrook, the circulation – and profits – of the *Daily Express* had declined rapidly. A succession of editors and changes of direction had made no difference. According to Simon Jenkins, then editor of the *Evening Standard* (a Beaverbrook newspaper), 'As with *The Times* ten years earlier, the proprietorial will to fight had gone.' Sir Max was recovering from a stroke, and Beaverbrook, which had property assets as well as newspapers, was high on the takeover list. Rupert Murdoch first bought a 20 per cent stake at 80p and in 1973, at Lord Goodman's prompting, sold it to Max Rayne for 125p a share. Goodman had at various times advised Rayne, Aitken and Murdoch, and was also chairman of the Newspapers Publishers Association at the time. His idea was that Rayne, a property developer, should take over the property portfolio which at that stage was included in the share price for nothing. The property crash spoiled what was actually a sensible plan, and in 1976 Rayne sold his shares back to Murdoch for 33p, one-quarter of the price he had originally paid.

That autumn, Murdoch and Goldsmith happened to meet for a drink in New York. Like Goldsmith, Murdoch was rapidly expanding his American operations, and needed all the capital he could find. Was Goldsmith interested in his Beaverbrook stake? He was. He bought them – 32 per cent of the non-voting shares – at 38p a share, or £1.566m. This stake gave him no formal power in the company, but he reckoned – rightly – that the Aitkens would soon put the group up for sale, and he had now bought himself a place at the top of the table when that happened. On the other hand if the company recovered he would still make a profit.

Highly sensitive to the atmosphere that had been aroused even when he didn't bid for the *Observer*, Goldsmith decided to proceed very cautiously. His plan was to join the board and act from inside, in much the same way as he had tried to do at Hôtels Réunis. Back in London he quietly acquired some more shares in the market to take his stake to 35 per cent and then, on 11 January 1977, went to a lunch at the annual Boat Show at Olympia sponsored by Beaverbrook Newspapers. This lunch, normally hosted by Sir Max Aitken, was a traditional feature of the show, and was designed as an event for the various editors to invite distinguished guests.

On this occasion it was hosted by John Junor, editor of the *Sunday Express*, and the main guest was Margaret Thatcher, now leader of the Conservative Party. That day however, even Mrs Thatcher had to take second place to Goldsmith when he calmly announced to the table that he was now the biggest shareholder in Beaverbrook.

He wrote politely to Sir Max Aitken, who had been too ill to attend the lunch, saying he hoped the Beaverbrook chairman would find Cavenham 'a useful' shareholder. 'My real interest was to become involved,' he said later (quoted in *The Fall of the House of Beaverbrook* by Lewis Chester and Jonathan Fenby). He also added, in a favourite phrase of his, that owning a national newspaper would be 'amusing'. Goldsmith was never down for long.

Once again Lord Goodman seemed to him to be an enemy in the camp. Sir Max Aitken, a weak and indecisive man himself, placed enormous faith in Goodman, and Goldsmith believed that Goodman turned Aitken forcibly against the new shareholder. Later Goldsmith would say that he reckoned Goodman was 'passively' opposed to him getting the *Observer*, but 'actively' against getting Beaverbrook Newspapers. The flamboyant managing director of Beaverbrook, Jocelyn Stevens, thought Goldsmith was excellent news and unwisely indicated as much, to find himself frozen out by his proprietor who made some acid remarks about him being 'Goldsmith's friend'. Three days after the Boat Show lunch, Sir Max told Stevens that, whatever he needed to do to save the company, it could not involve Sir James Goldsmith. Then Aitken departed for his house on the Cap d'Ail where the following day he had a serious stroke.

But he had given his instructions, and Stevens embarked on an energetic 'stop Goldsmith' campaign. He called in an American takeover expert, David Karr, who was based in Paris and reputed to know more about Goldsmith than Goldsmith himself. Stevens, along with Sir Max's son, Maxwell Aitken, flew to Paris to dine with him at the Plaza Athénée, and Karr later recounted that the Beaverbrook directors were 'scared of Goldsmith', reckoning he was going to make a hostile bid for the company which would be hard to resist. The best plan, he advised, was to seek an accommodation with Associated Newspapers, publishers of the rival *Daily Mail* and London *Evening News*.

Less than a fortnight after his deal with Murdoch, Charles Hambro hosted a dinner at the Hambro flat at 2 Wilton Terrace, Belgravia. He invited Jocelyn Stevens, young Maxwell Aitken, and the finance director Peter Hetherington. Hambro, an elaborately courteous old Etonian, expected a civilised discussion where differences could be aired. For his

309

part Goldsmith made an effort to be pleasant and conciliatory. But Stevens began by stating that Beaverbrook did not welcome Goldsmith's shareholding and regarded it as 'hostile'. Acording to Goldsmith, he then went on to say that if Goldsmith thought *Private Eye* had mounted a violent attack, he should wait and see what the Beaverbrook papers could do – and that would happen unless Goldsmith disposed of his shares. 'It was as though everybody had taken LSD,' Goldsmith remarked wonderingly of that dinner later.

Goldsmith hit back by remarking that at the first hint of any personal attack, he would launch his bid. He turned to Charles Hambro and to his partner Peter Hill-Wood, and told them that was a formal instruction. Later it emerged that Stevens had instructed the former head of the *Sunday Times* Insight team, Bruce Page, who had just joined the *Daily Express*, to prepare an exposé on the boss of Cavenham. Page, a left-wing journalist passionately opposed to Goldsmith, replied bluntly that he was not going to be a 'management hit-man'.

Nevertheless, that dinner marked the climax of Goldsmith's attempt to take over Beaverbrook. He went off on holiday with Annabel, while Goodman, on 3 February 1977, invited the senior directors of both Beaverbrook and Associated to join him at the Master's Lodge at University College. Stevens led for the Beaverbrook side, and Vere Harmsworth for Associated which in 1977, for the first time since the 1920s, was the larger and more prosperous of the two. The discussion focused on an immediate solution to both their problems: each had London evening newspapers, both of which were major loss-makers. The proposal that day was to merge them, thereby creating a single monopoly London evening which instead of losing nearly £10m a year between them, should make a profit. The basic plan was for Associated to buy the *Standard*, and give Beaverbrook a much-needed cash injection; Beaverbrook however would continue to print the London evening paper.

This meant in effect that the *Evening Standard* would be closed. As the editor, Simon Jenkins, began to search for an alternative bidder, 'My engagement diary became a *Who's Who* of actual and potential Fleet Street entrepreneurs: Tiny Rowland of Lonrho, Shell heiress Olga Deterding, Denis Hamilton of *The Times*, Sir James Goldsmith, Rupert Murdoch, Nigel Broackes of the Trafalgar House property and construction group.' All, Jenkins says, expressed varying degrees of interest; 'all wisely decided to await the anticipated crisis.'

*

By the time the crisis broke, Goldsmith was already a newspaper proprietor. *L'Express*, France's number one news magazine, had been founded by Jean-Jacques Servan-Schreiber, later author of the best-selling *Le Défi Américain* (forecasting the takeover of the world by American business), and two other liberals, Françoise Giroud and Pierre Viannson-Ponte. It was well to the left: anti-Gaullist under de Gaulle, anti-Pompidou under Pompidou, and strong critic of Giscard. Owned and written by intellectual left-wingers, it represented everything in French life Goldsmith hated. 'I thought it was the source of the intellectual sickness of France, because of its power,' he says. 'I bought it for no personal reason, in the way that later I started *Now!* magazine. It was a deep political conviction that it had been an evil cancer, not in intent but in result, in French philosophical thought. And I'd always thought to myself, the day I can afford it I'm going to buy it. And change it.'

That, he now acknowledges, 'was perhaps a bad reason for doing it', but his media strategy was multi-stranded, the common thread being that in neither country was he applying his normal commercial criteria.

If he proceeded with caution in pursuit of Beaverbrook in London, he moved much more confidently into *L'Express*. His first move was to bring in the writer and philosopher Raymond Aron as president of the editorial committee. Aron was a renowned but controversial philosopher and sociologist, and there was considerable resentment on the magazine when Goldsmith announced he would be writing a column.

Olivier Todd, a Cambridge-educated former BBC television presenter, who became managing editor, says that from the moment he arrived, 'Jimmy made it quite clear that he was not going to be a sleeping owner. But at the same time he wanted to show his liberal self. He wanted to give an ideological direction to the ship, but also wanted to recruit men like me to talk about the left wing – but you can't have your cake and eat it.' Years later, after he had been fired by Goldsmith, Todd concluded:

I see Jimmy as someone who probably never should have got into the newspaper business, because he didn't see that if you go into it you either do what the proprietors do and let your publications say exactly what they want regardless, or you become the editor yourself, especially if you buy an old liberal institution like *L'Express* with socialists everywhere.

Looking back now, Goldsmith would not violently disagree, although he does feel he achieved something.

I was very patient [almost as if that were a criticism], and I never fully changed it. Obviously I was not a formula for great friendships, or things of this kind, because I really went in to try and stem what I felt was a poison. And people forget how far I did change it, even though I didn't get all the way. When I appointed Raymond Aron – he came from *Figaro* – I had a strike because I was imposing a fascist! And when he died a few years later the whole of France, from left to right, turned out to bury a patron saint. That's how far things moved in that decade.

I bought *L'Express* out of a consuming political passion, but not a personal political passion. I wasn't seeking office and high profile in France – I had that without seeking it. I rationalised that I could make a decent profit, but the reality is I ran it not as a business. I ran it to pay anything I could to get rid of the people I didn't agree with ideologically, to try and bring in the people we wanted.

Started as a radical daily paper in 1953, by 1964 *L'Express* had adopted an American-style weekly magazine format, and by 1973 its circulation was 614,000. Servan-Schreiber's relationships with his journalists were often stormy, and in 1971 a group of his most senior people left the magazine after disagreeing with his policy. Several of them set up the competitor weekly, *Le Point*, owned by Hachette, and by the time Goldsmith bought out Servan-Schreiber's 45 per cent stake for £3.6m, circulation had dropped to a claimed 550,000 (but an actual 490,000).

In Britain, the *Private Eye* affair had given Goldsmith such a high profile that he could not go into a restaurant in London without every head turning, and it was several years since he had been able to walk down the street without being recognised. In France, although his interests there were almost as large, he was regarded as another successful businessman, not even particularly controversial. In Paris he could walk in the street, go to restaurants without anyone paying particular attention, and generally live a freer life.

However, when he bought into *L'Express*, *Le Monde* did a major but unbiased biographical article on him, while another national newspaper, *Le Matin*, commented that 'a paper which ceases to belong to its founder, journalists sold like part of the furniture – it is more than sad, it is serious.' On the other hand, *Le Nouvel Economiste* had hailed it: 'Après J-J Voici Jimmy.'

In London Goldsmith continued to expound his conviction that Britain was in terminal decline, run by unrepresentative government which was elected, not by the people, but by active minorities; the trade unions sponsored 120 Labour MPs, he pointed out, the House of Lords was 'another sad rotten borough', and the British people felt divorced from their leaders. In France, too, he reckoned there was a general drift to the left, led by *intellectuels gauchistes* such as those who wrote for *L'Express*. His old friend Claude Henry Leconte, who would play a significant part in his publishing venture in France, says that, before Goldsmith appeared at *L'Express*, there had been 'an evolution from pure Marxist-Leninism to something more dangerous and insidious, because they never could see how wrong they were about Communism, and they gave it an intellectual respectability.' They slowed, he insists, Europe's 'evolution towards the liberation that only happened in the past few years.' Goldsmith had learned that the previous owners of *L'Express* had sent a journalistic mission to Yugoslavia to learn about newspaper management. 'Can you imagine,' says Leconte, 'a country like France which boasts Montesquieu, de Tocqueville, Voltaire, Victor Hugo ... going to Yugoslavia to ask advice on the running of a newspaper? It is frankly incredible.'

Years later, Goldsmith could justify his investment in *L'Express* in financial terms. 'It didn't do too badly in that when we sold Générale Occidentale, *L'Express* was valued at 440m francs, and I paid about 70m francs for it. We'd injected about 180m francs over ten years. And the sales were much higher and it was a much bigger paper, and all the rest. But I have to admit I never ran it as a business.' By that stage the intellectual arguments in France had moved on, and so had Goldsmith. The left everywhere was in retreat.

By the spring of 1977 the Beaverbrook board was in turmoil, losses were mounting, the banks – and predators – were closing in. While Jocelyn Stevens was skiing in St Anton, Hetherington and young Maxwell Aitken tried to sack him. When he flew back on 5 April he was informed he should not return to the office. That evening he went to a dinner at the Mansion House where he happened to meet Goldsmith, among the hundreds of guests. Vere Harmsworth and Lord Goodman were also there. Stevens now seized upon Goldsmith as an ally again, and quietly told him what was going on. Goldsmith had heard rumours, but was 'utterly amazed' when he heard Stevens' story. But the Mansion House, in the presence of the Lord Mayor of the City of London, was too public a place for them to talk, and it was Jacob Rothschild who suggested they join him at a private party given by the socialite wife of a Persian diplomat, Hamayoun Mazandi, at her house in Chester Square. When they got there, they found an unoccupied room where the guests had piled their coats, and discussed Beaverbrook until well into the night.

Goldsmith had an added interest in bidding for Beaverbrook. He disliked the *Daily Express*'s rival, the *Daily Mail*, basically because of the diarist Nigel Dempster. That evening he pledged his support for Stevens, but insisted he could not intervene without some sign of support from Sir Max Aitken, who still controlled the family trusts, and therefore the company. The next day Stevens counter-attacked, persuading the sick Sir Max, in his hospital bed, to let him stay, then forcing Hetherington to resign.

It was Charles Wintour, the former editor of the *Evening Standard* and a central figure in the merger negotiations, who brought Goldsmith back into the fray. On Wednesday, 27 April 1977, he went to see him at his Leadenhall Street offices in the City for tea. Goldsmith, he recalled as if surprised at the civility of the man, poured from a silver teapot. Goldsmith said he liked the *Standard*, and if he was dealing with his own money he would happily buy it outright. It didn't much matter to him, he added, whether he made £43m or £45m a year, which was then the profitability of Cavenham. But there was no industrial logic to owning the *Standard* on its own, although the whole Beaverbrook group was another matter. He had a proposal for that, which involved a £5m guarantee for the Beaverbrook overdraft, and the underwriting by Cavenham of a rights issue which would inject another £5m. It was a recapitulation rather than a bid, innovative at the time, common practice in later years. How would Jocelyn Stevens react to that?

At dinner with Goldsmith that night, Stevens was most enthusiastic. But Goldsmith, he told him, would have to indicate a firm intention to bid by eleven the next morning to prevent the deal with the rival Associated Newspapers going through.

Goldsmith agreed, and the next morning his letter and proposals arrived just after eleven – in time for Stevens, with some glee, to make an announcement to the stunned Vere Harmsworth and Lord Goodman. It had the desired effect: the deal with Associated Newspapers was wrecked, and suddenly Goldsmith was the favourite. But later that day another runner entered the field: Tiny Rowland of Lonrho indicated he was interested in buying the *Standard*.

Once again, Goldsmith was front page news. *The Times* on Friday, 29 April 1977, led with the headline: 'Goldsmith plan halts merger deal by Fleet Street papers.' It also mentioned that Tiny Rowland had emerged as a contender for the *Standard*, quoting him as saying, 'there must be at least a dozen alternatives to the present plan, of which Lonrho might possibly be one.'

Rowland and Goldsmith had an uneasy relationship. Rowland's typically quirky donation of £5,000 to *Private Eye*'s Goldenballs Fund had irritated Jimmy, and they rowed over Ted Heath. Rowland still claimed Jim Slater and Goldsmith had not honoured their bets over the result of the 1974 election, and Goldsmith, who prides himself on having honoured every single debt of his life, dismissed it as mischief-making. Now they were to find themselves allies in the battle for Beaverbrook.

The next evening at eight o'clock Goldsmith met the print union leaders, along with Jocelyn Stevens and Maxwell Aitken, in Leadenhall Street, and told them he was not making a formal bid but was offering 'an intention, a plan, a hope' for the future. He wanted six weeks to look at the figures to see if he could keep the *Standard* alive. The unions, used to the layers of management with which the Aitkens surrounded themselves, were impressed with this tall, and elegant man, who offered them unlimited quantities of drink and cigars, and talked to them directly. 'He was a one-sheet-of-paper man,' said one approvingly afterwards. 'Three figures here. Four figures there. It will work or it won't.' Jimmy and Jocelyn Stevens then went to see Vere Harmsworth at his huge Eaton Square flat and after midnight, finally arrived at Annabel's.

Despite the long days and the apparent progress, Goldsmith was not actually getting anywhere. Although to the outside world and to the unions (and some of the management, notably Stevens and Charles Wintour) he was the front-runner, Sir Max Aitken became increasingly bitter towards him, especially when he saw the terms of the deal Goldsmith proposed. Essentially Goldsmith was offering a deal to keep the *Standard* alive, and to use his management skills on the loss-making *Daily Express*. In return, Aitken was asked to agree to enfranchise his non-voting shares, thus giving Goldsmith 35–40 per cent of the company, which amounted to effective control. Goldsmith's cash would go into the company, rather than to the Aitken family, and Max Aitken perceived it as an attempt to get him to sign away his family heritage for no reward.

'Sir Max's reservations about Goldsmith were shared by his son and other members of the family and close friends,' said Lewis Chester and Jonathan Fenby in *The Fall of the House of Beaverbrook*. Stevens was now regarded as Goldsmith's 'Trojan Horse', and Goodman remained implacably opposed.

Typically Goldsmith at this time was not simply pursuing one business opportunity – he was doing his apprenticeship on

L'Express in Paris, he was active in America, he was running Cavenham, and he was fighting his *Private Eye* case, which was due to begin at the Old Bailey in mid-May. He was also involved in something else, a move which would have more far-reaching repercussions than anything he had done for years.

Jimmy Goldsmith had decided to take Cavenham private. He was in the process of buying out all the outside shareholders, ending Cavenham's quotation on the London Stock Market, and removing it from the public gaze of financial journalists.

The *Private Eye* affair had not only damaged Goldsmith's chances of becoming a newspaper proprietor: it had also damaged his rating in the stock market. The big insurance companies and pension funds who control most of the investment money in the world's markets like their businessmen to be predictable. They pretend to welcome entrepreneurs, but only up to a point – usually the point when they move from being a medium-sized company into a large one which requires a different set of management rules. The City institutions which had backed Goldsmith in his early days had seen their investment multiply manyfold, but they had also seen it take a battering with the collapse of the financial community. They gave Goldsmith full marks for surviving, but they did not much approve of his involvement with Slater Walker, and they approved even less of his suit against *Private Eye*. Their objections were entirely different to those of the financial press: they just thought it was nothing to do with business, and therefore slightly nutty. It had become smart to be anti-Goldsmith, and even the big institutions followed the trend. They were now net sellers of the stock, which was languishing badly.

'Ingrams had been able to create an atmosphere which was against me, and which was there and had to be recognised,' Goldsmith says. 'I was out of fashion; shares in general were out of fashion. Business was fine. There was a slump out there, but Cavenham wasn't feeling it. And I sat back and said: "What shall I do? How do I benefit from this nasty situation?" And the obvious thing was to buy something that nobody wanted, which was my shares.'

Only a year before, Goldsmith had proposed a scheme whereby control of Cavenham passed into the hands of Générale Occidentale, which was of course in turn controlled by Goldsmith. He had, at the same time, given an assurance – which he meant at the time – that he had no intention of bidding for the 49 per cent of the shares still left in outside hands.

Cavenham shareholders approved the scheme almost without opposition. Early in 1977 when the shares stood at 100p compared to an asset value of 145p a share (much of it in cash or equivalent), Goldsmith had complained they were very seriously undervalued, which indeed they were.

Now he proposed that Générale Occidentale make a bid of 120p a share for the 49 per cent it did not own. The effect would be to end Cavenham's status as a public company, with all that entailed: no more published accounts, no annual meetings which the financial press could come to, no more outside shareholders to whom he had to be responsible. On the other hand, he would never again be able to use Cavenham shares as a currency to take over companies, but in any case their price was so low he would not have wished to issue more.

It was a momentous decision for a man who had used the stock market quotation medium with such skill over a sustained period. It was a retreat from everything he had been trying to achieve over the past 15 years – the abandonment of a major plank in his progression. He could explain it away by saying that *Private Eye* enabled him to become a very rich man by forcing him into buying his own shares, but that was never the point – although it was precisely what he was accused of. Later Goldsmith would remark that if it had not been for the *Private Eye* affair and the resulting stigma that attached to him, he would probably have followed 'the Hanson route', making bigger and bigger takeover bids, issuing more and more shares, and steadily diluting his own personal shareholding. (At that time Goldsmith was bigger than Hanson, which is now one of the largest companies in the world.)

From this moment on, Goldsmith's manner of conducting his businesses would alter. He had not yet taken the decision to withdraw totally from Britain, but that would follow inexorably from the moves he was now making. The events that were shaping at this time would take him on to America, and to a fortune to rival, or even surpass, any Rothschild in history. But his plans were conceived in bitterness and resentment – and even defeat. In effect Goldsmith was acknowledging that Ingrams and *Private Eye* had won, that although he might be awarded the victory, it was he who had to leave the field.

His bid for the minority shares of Cavenham went down badly in the financial press – and with a number of the big shareholders. The Prudential, with 6 per cent, said the price was too low – and it didn't like what Goldsmith was doing anyway. It would vote against, if he pursued the scheme. The bid would have cost Générale Occidentale £61m cash.

Anticipating some of the criticism that would inevitably arise, the independent directors of Cavenham, with Goldsmith's full approval, appointed Samuel Montagu as outside merchant bankers to advise them. Goldsmith was prepared to increase his offer to 140p, but when Samuel Montague indicated that was not enough, he dropped his bid on 8 March 1977, deciding the time was not right. He would evolve another tactic and bid again, this time clearing his lines properly.

In the meantime he was under greater and greater pressure to settle with *Private Eye*. The world – and even the protagonists – had almost forgotten what the original fight was all about. No one seriously believed Goldsmith knew anything about Lucan's disappearance, or had conspired in any way to pervert the course of justice. *Private Eye* had long acknowledged that Goldsmith was not at the Aspinall lunch, and it had offered to apologise for the 'conspiracy' allegation. The issue at stake for both parties was freedom of the press, or, as Goldsmith would have it, 'freedom of the press to abuse'.

By early May Goldsmith was under pressure from all sides to bring the case to an end. Even Madame Beaux, who normally stayed out of these things, argued that it was taking up too much of his time and energy, diverting his attention from more important events. In the atmosphere that reigned, every move he made was interpreted as Machiavellian even when it was perfectly innocent. It made it impossible to do business.

After I'd bought a third of Beaverbrook from Rupert [he says], I said to myself, 'If I bid for it, everyone's going to say that I bought a dud company on purpose to reduce the price of [Cavenham] shares so I could buy them in cheaply.' And that clearly was the feeling that was about the place. So I didn't buy Beaverbrook, and the reason was exactly that. All sorts of interpretations were put on it, but the reason I didn't buy was because I couldn't bid in Cavenham and buy Beaverbrook without being accused of reducing the value of Cavenham so I could bid again.

When Simon Jenkins approached him with a proposition early in May, the young *Evening Standard* editor – he was only 33 – found a not unsympathetic audience. Although he didn't know him well, Goldsmith liked the cerebral Jenkins and admired the paper he ran. To the outside world, Goldsmith seemed unperturbed by the *Private Eye* battle, seeming to relish the court duels, and the tactical battle of wits – and to some extent that was true. He had hated the personal attacks, but Goldsmith is a man who, even when he could not pay his bills, still throbbed with life, swinging wildly from elation to black depression and back again. 'At that time *Private Eye* had fantastic influence on the press, and in so far as I was concerned, it had created by brilliant PR this campaign against me – really fantastic,' he says. 'And I had a lot of admiration for Richard Ingrams. I think he's a sick man, but he's brilliant and he's got that Cromwellian streak that I admire.'

Nevertheless, he had not seriously considered settling the *Private Eye* dispute until Jenkins came to see him, to propose himself as mediator. Jenkins' motive was simple: Goldsmith, in his view, offered the best possibility of saving their precious *Evening Standard*.

> But it was abundantly apparent to me that Jimmy Goldsmith was anathema to the staff on the *Standard* because he was, as it seemed to them, persecuting the adored *Private Eye* [says Jenkins]. It did matter that the *Private Eye* affair be cleared up as soon as possible, so that problem wasn't on the books. I remember at this stage Charles Raw and Bruce Page took me out to lunch to warn me off Goldsmith, and they said if you think that's the only problem you'll have with Jimmy Goldsmith, you've got another think coming. And I remember saying, with a kind of a laugh, 'If I can clear this one out of the way, we will at least have the most public of all the blots on the Goldsmith escutcheon cleaned off.' There was no such thing as a proprietor with no blots on him.

Jenkins set about talking Goldsmith into a settlement. 'I kept telling him that this whole campaign was ridiculous. I said, "Why on earth are you continuing this – you're going to jeopardise the possibility of getting the *Standard* if you go on with this vendetta." '

Goldsmith replied that it was Ingrams who was pursuing the vendetta against him. 'He's accused me of being an accessory to a murder. It's outrageous.' Jenkins could see there was no way the two positions could ever be resolved. 'They were just implacably hostile to each other.'

But Jenkins observed a crucial difference in the manner in which the two men were facing up to the struggle.

> Goldsmith was smoothly in command of it all, but Ingrams was like a frightened rabbit. He was terrified of how his friends would regard him if he did a deal, he was terrified of going to prison, he was terrified of the lawyers – he was a wretched case, frankly. Whereas, Goldsmith seemed to me so self-confident and on top of it that I couldn't quite see why he was going on with it. He was very much in the driving seat; he was the man who was always taking the initiative.

Goldsmith, after 'a lot of soul-searching', agreed to let Jenkins mediate. He set three conditions: the first was that there should be a payment, nominal given the scale of the costs so far, of about £30,000, but which would be portrayed as 'substantial' for public reasons; the second was that there would be a full-page advertisement in the *Evening Standard*, to be paid for by *Private Eye*, admitting there was 'not a shred of truth' in any of the libels; the third condition, not to be made public, was that Ingrams should 'come and have lunch with me – or at least shake hands'. This latter, bizarre by most people's standards, was actually typical of Goldsmith. He had fought his fight with every weapon he could find, but having decided to settle, he wanted to meet the enemy face to face.

The criminal libel case was due to begin at the Old Bailey on 16 May 1977, but just eleven days before it Richard Ingrams and Jenkins arranged to meet for lunch. Ingrams was seeking information on the state of the *Standard*, and was unprepared for what Jenkins had in mind. When he heard the conditions, the *Private Eye* editor says he didn't even hesitate. 'Without waiting to consult my lawyers, I agreed,' he wrote in his book, *Goldenballs*. 'It seemed that the situation at the *Standard* was so fluid that Goldsmith's attitude could easily change overnight, especially if we began to haggle.' That, however, is not quite how Jenkins recalls it: 'I remember saying to Ingrams, whom I didn't take to at all, I must say, "These are the three conditions and he's insisting on them. But he will call off the race if you agree to them." And he found the third condition very difficult to swallow. He said, "He's going to charm me, I know he thinks he can charm me." ' Oddly enough, in his detailed account of his fight against Goldsmith, Ingrams never mentioned the third condition – on which he reneged. To this day he has never had lunch with Goldsmith. 'As far as I was concerned we could call it a day and move on,' says Goldsmith. 'He was not capable of that. I don't know why. Maybe he felt guilty, or maybe his hatred was becoming an important part of his life, or maybe it's some other quirk. I never could quite work out why he would rat on a commitment which was clearly undertaken there.'

When it was all over, Jenkins arranged a breakfast between Goldsmith and Ingrams, and Ingrams kept crying off. Angrily Jenkins rang him to point out this was a condition of the settlement, but Ingrams still refused. 'Oh, it's completely ridiculous,' he told him. 'Why does he want to meet me? We've settled it, we've taken out the ad, we've done all the things he wanted, and this is just pathetic.' Goldsmith, Jenkins told him, felt very strongly about it.

'But he simply wouldn't do it, and short of arresting him there was nothing I could do.' Later when Jenkins asked some of the *Private Eye* staff why Ingrams wouldn't meet Goldsmith, they told him that Ingrams' wife wouldn't let him, that she thought it would be 'final humiliation, having to shake the man by the hand'. Jenkins finally decided that Ingrams was in such a difficult psychological state that there was no way he could be pushed. To this day Ingrams has never shaken Goldsmith's hand.

But the deal was done, although there were still loose ends: there was no mention of Eric Levine, and Michael Gillard was still pursuing his case for slander against Goldsmith, But they could wait.

Private Eye made its apology, using all the required phrases such as 'not a shred of truth' and agreed that 'Sir James would have been entitled to very substantial damages for what *Private Eye* said about him.' Ingrams held a party to celebrate, Jenkins breathed a sigh of relief, and Goldsmith turned his attention to acquiring control of Beaverbrook Newspapers.

But it was, and he knew it, a Pyrrhic victory, an unsatisfactory and hasty compromise which haunts him still. He had made, he now agrees, a 'tactical error' in starting the fight, but having begun he reckons he should have finished it, laid the issues in front of the court, and forced *Private Eye* to acknowledge in a much more public way than a single advertisement its sins and inaccuracies. It had cost him £100,000, and preoccupied him for 18 valuable months, but money and time were irrelevant compared to what he considered the real cost. By settling he had allowed some of the mud to stick.

He never did win control of Beaverbrook – or even of the *Standard*. Goldsmith flung himself into the attempt, undergoing a crash course in the weird ways of the British print unions, much to the dismay of Jenkins who felt the unions would take advantage of him later. Encouraged by Jenkins and Wintour, the journalists were coming round. Goldsmith promised to leave the *Standard* alone, and to stop milking the profits of the *Sunday Express* to bail out the ailing *Daily Express*. As for the latter, wrote Charles Wintour in a letter to Michael Foot, the Labour minister whom he kept informed of events (Foot had once edited the *Standard*), Goldsmith would 'like to see it crusading again', adding in parentheses that Goldsmith 'has a great admiration' for Lord Beaverbrook, the apotheosis of all that was right and good at the group 13 years after his death.

When Goldsmith eventually did make his bid, it was in partnership with Tiny Rowland. They had a mutual friend in Edward Du Cann, the

Conservative politician who was also chairman of Keyser Ullmann (and now chairman of Lonrho). Both sides decided that, rather than fight each other, they would create a joint company between Cavenham and Lonrho (to be known as 'Cavrho'), which would buy Cavenham's shares in Beaverbrook, which would have to agree to enfranchise in return for much the same package Goldsmith had originally proposed: a rights issue of £5m and a guarantee for a loan of another £3m. Goldsmith would become chairman of Beaverbrook, Rowland would be deputy chairman, and Aitken would become life president. It was a complex and unwieldy bid which Sir Max Aitken continued to oppose, but which his board made him consider seriously. For weeks through the second half of May and into June, it remained the best bid on the table, until Rupert Murdoch, invited by Aitken to save his papers from Goldsmith, reappeared on the scene with a more tempting offer. That bid in turn was topped by another bid from Trafalgar House, owners of the QE2 and the London Ritz, which Aitken accepted. That gave Trafalgar 82 per cent of the voting shares, although only 12 per cent of the capital, and Goldsmith, offered a profit of £2m in a situation he was increasingly tired of (and in which he had lost in any case), bowed out.

He had other matters on his mind now, new worlds to conquer.

21

Marriage to Annabel

Ironically, at the time he began his corporate withdrawal from Britain, Jimmy Goldsmith had put down his deepest roots. Although seen more as an Englishman than a Frenchman, over his 45 years he had spent remarkably little time in Britain. He had hardly been there before 1944; between the ages of eleven and 17 he was at school in England but spent his holidays in France; his army days, 1951–3, were in England but again most leaves were in France; from 1953 to 1960 he was working in France; the first time he had worked in England was with Selim Zilkha, when they bought Lewis & Burrows, in 1960; from 1962 to the start of Cavenham in 1965 he was back in France, and Paris remained his main base and home until 1973, even when he brought Ginette and the family over. From 1973, London was his principal home, but even then he had a great deal of business activity in France, the United States and elsewhere, and spent every holiday abroad. He has never considered that he lived in England on a permanent basis.

This was reflected in the houses he occupied; during the 1960s, he had usually stayed in the Ritz. He bought a 96-year lease on an elegant Regency house in Chester Terrace, where he lived through most of the 1970s, but it had not been a real family house since Ginette went back to Paris.

When Annabel formally divorced Mark Birley in 1976, Goldsmith usually lived with her in Pelham Cottage, but Pelham, although unique in the heart of London, was tiny, and inconvenient, with most of the rooms opening into each other. He now had money in abundance, and the property crash had put plenty of large houses on the market. He began urging Annabel to find a place of their own. She was reluctant at first, loath to surrender her little home. But she now had five children, two of them by Jimmy. The cottage was getting crowded, particularly when the large and restless figure of Goldsmith stalked the small rooms.

Annabel and Jimmy had distinctly different ideas on styles. He preferred the large and majestic, she something much smaller and more intimate. Annabel had been brought up in large houses and didn't much care for them, but Jimmy still dreamed of castles in France and Rothschild-style mansions in Britain.

Annabel eventually found a compromise on the edge of Richmond Park, south-west of London. Ormeley Lodge stood close to the road, but behind high gates, its extensive gardens backing on to a golf course. Its origins were obscure but it was certainly early Georgian, and there were stories that Mrs Fitzherbert, a Roman Catholic widow who secretly married the Prince of Wales, later King George IV, in 1785, had lived there. The previous owner was Lord Howard de Walden, senior steward of the Jockey Club, who had maintained it in a plain country style. Annabel instantly loved it, but was far from certain it would appeal to Jimmy. He had dismissed, sometimes abruptly, too many of her suggestions.

Annabel was curiously unsure of Jimmy's moods. She, more than anyone else, could tease him out of his blacker humours, join in his amusement when he was cheerful, entertain his family and friends when that was required. But she still feared his rages, seldom directed at her but nonetheless frightening for all that. In his personal surroundings, everything had to be just right: his clothes, his lucky set of cufflinks, his cars, his papers and all the rest. Moving between homes and offices he had evolved a complex but highly efficient system which enabled him to produce a particular report or a piece of paper instantly wherever he was. Although he had his office in Leadenhall Street, and another, grander one in Paris, his office was really where he happened to be – which could be anywhere from the Carlyle Hotel in New York to his home in Paris where he looked out on to a large, completely enclosed garden. In truth, he had not worked in an office proper since the early days of Cavenham.

Annabel had first seen Ormeley Lodge with the sun shining and the deer grazing in the park. She was determined that Goldsmith's first glimpse should be equally perfect. It was, she told him laughingly, the best compromise she could find between Buckingham Palace, which he wanted, and Pelham Cottage, which she wanted. She chose a fine day in early summer, praying he would not be delayed at work, that there would not be a snarl-up in the traffic on the way out through south London, that the deer would be around. When he arrived in the quiet road by the huge park, Goldsmith was silent, brooding. Annabel watched his face anxiously, trying to interpret his reaction. She could see he wanted to be critical of it, because it was not the grand mansion he had in mind, but objections weren't that easy to make. Ormeley had large stables and staff quarters, views out onto the park, and spacious and bright rooms. It was a beautiful and most unusual house in a superb setting, ideal for children, with reception rooms grand enough to entertain anyone. To her intense relief, Annabel felt a 'wonderful quiet' come over Jimmy, which she had learned to recognise as a good sign.

They bought the house and Annabel set about transforming it, with a nursery for the young children and a large area in the basement where they could entertain 100 guests. Jimmy used the house in Tregunter Road as a base, both for himself and for his children (and even for Teddy, and Teddy's two daughters, Clio and Dido), but never properly lived there.

Although Jimmy still stayed with Ginette at the week-ends, there was no question of his dividing himself equally between the two women. He had been able to talk to Annabel during the *Private Eye* affair in a way he could not really talk to anyone else. The children had brought them closer, and now the first house of their own, furnished with the paintings and pieces of French and Chinese furniture that Jimmy had collected, brought them closer still.

In Paris he broke the news to Ginette which she must have long expected: he wanted to divorce her and marry Annabel. It would not, he insisted, in any way change their relationship: he would still return to her just as often, share her house, they would live as man and wife in Paris. Manes was now 18, and had been subjected to the *Private Eye* treatment in a manner which had turned Goldsmith's rage almost incandescent. Hurriedly, he had taken him out of England and sent him to Mexico where Manes, a good-natured but unworldly boy, soon settled down. Isabel was married, although not happily. And Alix, 13, was at school in England.

Ginette accepted Jimmy's assurance that 'marriage is not just a bit of paper – to me it's for life'. He would not give her up, even for Annabel, and Ginette, after a difficult time, decided she would settle for that. She was – and is – still an attractive woman, who gave Jimmy something that none of the other women in his life did. She had been through the bad times with him, known weeks and months when they could not pay the grocery bill, had roused him from his despondency over the death of Isabel, and seen him through his financial crises. Like many other successful men, Jimmy Goldsmith is something of a hypochondriac, becoming more so as he got older. He worried about the food he ate, and the city air he breathed; a cold for him was a minor crisis, and 'flu was almost a catastrophe. He would arrive home, either in Paris and London, and demand either of Ginette or Annabel: '*J'ai bonne mine?*', and wait intently for their answer. If Annabel casually said, 'You look marvellous' (as he often did after one of his holidays in the sun), he would say, 'You haven't even bothered to look,' and then insist she studied him closely. On the other hand, if she made an innocuous remark such as, 'You look a bit tired', he would fly into something of a panic. 'What – I look ill, you say? Where? What do you think is wrong?' His brother Teddy was worse, complaining, because of a head cold, that he was not long for this world – 'I'll soon be gone, my liver has packed in.' But Jimmy could be almost as bad, moaning, 'I've had it, I'll soon be in my grave', when there was actually very little the matter with him. A day or so later he would bounce back with all of his incredible vigour.

Ginette was more sympathetic than Annabel to this aspect of his nature, and, if Jimmy was ill, he went to her first, surrendering to her unquestioning care. He would never give her up, if he could possibly avoid it. Now however as quietly as they had been married, she gave him his divorce. Soon he would marry Annabel.

In the meantime, despite the *Private Eye* and Beaverbrook battles, there was a major business empire to run. Through 1977 and 1978 he was carrying through two plans: to complete his withdrawal from the public arena in Britain and concentrate his ownership in France, and build up his growing American interests.

At Grand Union, Jim Wood was opening stores – bigger, brighter outlets – as fast as he closed the dingy little places. But he and Goldsmith had accepted they needed more to compete with the giants in an industry where size counted: they needed to change consumer attitudes about where they shopped and what they purchased and then to generate real enthusiasm for shopping at Grand Union on a regular basis. It was in 1977 that Goldsmith introduced Wood to Milton Glaser and thus began one of the more remarkable partnerships in the annals of American retailing.

For more than 20 years Milton Glaser has been America's most respected graphic designer; his influence on the shape and look of the American scene during this time has been astonishing. When Goldsmith and Glaser first met in New York, the latter was the city's hottest graphics creator. He was teamed with another talented *wunderkind*, the publisher Clay Felker, and the two of them produced one of the most popular concepts of the age in *New York* magazine, a publishing triumph that has been copied but never quite duplicated by other 'city' magazines in every metropolis in North America.

At the time the duo were involved in a losing battle against Rupert Murdoch who was taking control both of *New York* and the other Felker flagship, the popular alternative newspaper, the *Village Voice*. Felker was a friend of Goldsmith and approached him to buy the magazines. Jimmy was tempted, but by the time he got involved Murdoch already had 51 per cent. 'It would have quite amused me,' says Goldsmith. 'I believed in *New York* at the time.'

Soon after Goldsmith bought *L'Express*, Felker came to Paris to look at it for him. The design, he said, was terrible, years out of date. 'You should meet my colleague, Milton,' he said, and soon afterwards Glaser was on his way to Paris. Several years before, Glaser had redesigned the French weekly news magazine *Paris Match*, and Goldsmith liked it.

From the beginning, Goldsmith and Glaser hit it off. Goldsmith was greatly taken by the bald, bespectacled New Yorker, who claimed that being born a Jew in New York helped give him his wide range of reference – it was much the same to him, he said, whether he was commissioned to design the jackets for the *Signet Shakespeare* or the poster for a Stevie Wonder concert. The two of them talked for hours about America, about New York, politics – and food. Glaser's feelings on American supermarkets was similar to Jimmy's: all the food was frozen, or canned, it was almost impossible to buy any fresh food. Glaser had become involved in designing restaurants, and was very interested in food. 'When I go to America, I find you can't live off a supermarket,' Goldsmith, who insisted his food was neither frozen nor canned, told him. As they worked on the French magazine, Goldsmith one day said to Glaser: 'Why don't you think about redesigning supermarkets?'

Before he went to work for Goldsmith in America, Glaser went back to New York where he created perhaps the most famous and potent advertising symbol in the history of graphic art: the 'I love New York' sign, with a small red heart representing the word 'love' that has been appropriated by every major town on the face of the earth. The irony is that Glaser created the design as a one-off job for a state tourism agency and never bothered to copyright it.

After that Goldsmith turned Milton Glaser loose on his Grand Union stores.

Milton was a superb idea of Jimmy's [says Wood]. I asked him to look at the stores with a fresh pair of eyes. I asked him to first redesign the house-brand labels but quickly added dozens of other things I thought might need changing or trying. I had always liked the old-style British delicatessen departments, the British notion of the clean white tiles and nice small lady behind the counter with good products.

You really have to think back to what the old American supermarket looked like in the seventies [he adds]. They had garish paint on the walls and the aisles were cluttered. Glaser put the word to it right away – he called it 'colour pollution' and we brightened up the stores at once.

But this was more than a cosmetic exercise. 'We began by changing the basic product and contour of the store itself. We started all kinds of programmes that are commonplace today, the amount of consumer information that is on cans and packages about how much fat, how much sodium and so on,' says Wood. They changed the use of space, introduced piazzas within the stores so that there was variable traffic, and pioneered producing food that had lower chemical content – natural beef, chemical-free vegetables and so on. Goldsmith one day had the eccentric idea of introducing live fish in tanks into the stores, in the way he had seen in Chinese restaurants. 'Children used to come in on Sundays and spend hours looking at these live things,' he says. They brought bakers from France, and introduced a range of in-store fresh baked bread. On another occasion, he took Annabel and the children to Tunisia and wandering around the souk, Goldsmith became fascinated by the range of spices offered by the merchants. He began to negotiate, and back in America put his staff to work on introducing a complete new spice centre in all the stores. 'Nobody else had it – no one knew where it came from,' he says.

The idea was basically a journalistic notion that we had developed in starting up new magazines [says Glaser]. First you have to get the reader or customer on your side. The customer had to feel that you are truly interested in their concerns. So we went to great lengths to provide information about how consumers could use the food, new recipes, demonstrations of new products. In doing that we changed the whole nature of the supermarket and the chain became – for a time – the pre-eminent grocery concern in America.

'Jimmy always had the larger view,' Glaser adds. 'He pushed Grand Union into the big league and he did things that other people copied.'

All this was an expensive proposition, however. At least $150m was spent in the first year of massive renovation. Many of Jimmy's ideas were

328

loss-makers, but he didn't care. 'They created an atmosphere in the store.'

The American retailing market, even in essential areas such as groceries, was slow to grow during the mid-seventies as the effects of higher energy costs worked their way through the economy and individual budgets. By 1979, just as Glaser was getting into full stride with his delicatessens, working bakeries and gourmet alcoves, OPEC struck with its second round of devastating world oil price increases. The United States once again responded by plunging into another round of stagflation, double-digit interest rates and inflation while economic growth remained virtually stagnant.

The timing could not have been worse for Goldsmith's burgeoning American store empire. In August 1978, Grand Union tried to grow its way to a heftier cash flow when Goldsmith purchased the Georgia-based Colonial group of groceries, another 359 supermarkets, for which he paid $133m. In the autumn of 1979, another 100 stores of the Texas-based Weingarten chain were added. In five years he had created a near-thousand-store empire that stretched from the Canadian border to the Gulf of Mexico.

The recession that sank Jimmy Carter's re-election bid in 1980 nearly sank Goldsmith's US grocery venture. Jim Wood, dispirited by the frustrations involved in welding such a far-flung operation into a coherent marketing organisation found he was closing stores almost as quickly as Goldsmith was adding them. Moreover, the inherited management team from Colonial stores was in open rebellion for the first few years after the takeover. The Tenglemann group approached Wood with an offer of an equity interest and a more manageable grocery chain, and he swapped ships.

'I had fifteen good years with Jimmy Goldsmith and they were very satisfying years,' he says now. 'He invested authority and he made you feel pretty good. Those were exciting years too. He was an entrepreneur and we bought and sold fifteen major companies on both sides of the Atlantic during that time. We bought companies the way I buy groceries today.'

Wood still likes to display a letter Goldsmith wrote to his wife Colleen in the early Seventies, which read:

Jim's doing a wonderful job and I know full well that this only would have been possible with your full support. As a gesture of our appreciation I would very much like you to do the following: pick anywhere you want to go in the world, reserve two first class seats and the best available accomodation on the spot.

Buy the clothes you need on your holiday and bill the whole thing to Cavenham. Yours sincerely, James M. Goldsmith.

Behind him, however, Wood left a supermarket group which, after the first flush of success, was running into major difficulties. It would be many years, and several hundred million dollars of investment, before Goldsmith would get it right.

Even while he worried about Grand Union, Goldsmith was preoccupied elsewhere. In Europe he was buying in all his British interests, and channelling control of them to Paris. The details of this operation are so complex that an entire book could be devoted to them (and there have been journalists who have tried). They are also, to this day, controversial and left behind a feeling that Goldsmith had outsmarted his own shareholders who had not been treated fairly. This was a time when it was unknown for companies quoted on the stock market to be taken private again. The natural progression was from private company to the privilege of full public company status, with a different and more rigorous set of accounting and disclosure rules, and all the advantages of being able to raise capital on the market. Goldsmith had been as good as anyone, indeed probably better, at using his shares to make or finance bids, but stock market sentiment had switched away from him, and since 1973 the Cavenham shares had underperformed the rest of the market. In the 1980s disillusionment with public company status would become more common when entrepreneurs, such as Richard Branson and Andrew Lloyd Webber decided that running a public company had more disadvantages than advantages, and bought back the shares they had originally sold. In the mid-1970s it was simply not done.

Even before *Private Eye*, Goldsmith had a reputation as a financial engineer who was just a bit too slick to be respectable. The fact that Cavenham was a substantial manufacturing and retailing company, employing some 60,000 people, with sales in 1977 of £1.6 billion should have proved beyond question that he was something more than the asset-strippers and would-be whizzkids with whom his name was often associated. Without the *Private Eye* affair, the criticisms and doubts would have faded and dropped away, as they had with many an entrepreneur in London and Wall Street. Within a few years Goldsmith would have been wooed by the establishment, Cavenham regarded as a blue chip company, its chairman heaped with honours. But the *Eye* case meant that even if he crossed the street someone would look for a deep and sinister motive.

The plan to return his extended empire into his own private hands began in May 1976 with the £100m quoted Cavenham bid for the outstanding minority of the shares in the French company Générale Alimentaire. The French government still nurtured the dream of creating its own home-grown Unilever or Nestlé, and for a time Perrier offered the best hopes. Then BSN-Gervais-Dannone was promoted as the great white hope, but in 1977 Goldsmith's business had become the favourite contender. Jimmy duly obliged with a complex series of moves, which ensured that the Paris-based Générale Occidentale increased its shareholding to slightly more than 50 per cent of Cavenham. In the formal document, Goldsmith indicated he had no intention of bidding for the rest, a statement which would come to haunt him. GO's stake in Cavenham was held part direct and part (16 per cent) through another Goldsmith quoted company, Anglo-Continental Investment and Finance. GO owned 67 per cent of Anglo-Continental which in turn owned 47 per cent of yet another quoted vehicle, a property company called Argyle Securities, a relic from the property boom which had tempted even the bearish Goldsmith into it. Anglo also owned 64 per cent of an unquoted insurance broking firm, Wigham Poland.

That was the general position in the summer of 1976, when Goldsmith embarked on the next stage of the strategy. GO bid for all the public holdings in both Anglo-Continental and Argyle, offering cash in each case. That cost GO £13.4m and left Cavenham as the only Goldsmith quoted company in Britain.

These moves were greeted with some opposition by the press, notably the *Investors Chronicle* which urged shareholders in the Goldsmith companies to reject them. Such articles never seriously threatened the plans, all of which were carefully worked out by Hambros and other merchant banks, and by some of the best brokers and lawyers in the land. But for months on end, Goldsmith's financial manoeuvrings dominated the financial pages of the papers.

In retrospect, it is interesting to compare Cavenham with the other major British food companies at the time. Sainsbury, now Britain's largest retailer, had sales of £535m, and Tesco, its major supermarket rival, had sales of £617m. Cavenham, with 37 per cent of its sales in America and another 35 per cent on the continent of Europe, was three times the size of either. It was the third-biggest food company in Europe, some way behind Unilever or Nestlé, but catching up. It was, in short, a seriously large, well-managed, well-financed and highly successful group.

In January 1977, Goldsmith proceeded to the next stage when

Générale Occidentale made its bid for the outstanding 49 per cent of Cavenham. Even by his standards this was a cheeky bid, particularly as only seven months before he had promised he wouldn't do it. The howls of protest were loud. 'This is a fantastic deal – for Sir James Goldsmith,' said the *Economist*. No excuses that he was fed up with twelve years of vilification in the British press, or that as chairman of a public company he was simply a 'target' could get him off the hook. 'If Sir James were right that the British press and stock market are uniformly hostile to entrepreneurial activity and that it is easier to do business through a private company than a public quoted one, then his complaints would carry more conviction. But his bundle of woes turns out, on further examination, to be a bundle of nonsense,' said the *Economist*, which had often been friendly to Goldsmith in the past.

The truth is that, until this point, Goldsmith's financial manoeuvrings, although they had attracted criticism, had never been properly studied either by the financial press or by the City. They were usually described as 'complex' and left at that, either because the writer could not explain them or because if he tried, his readers would not follow. The fact that Alexis de Gunzberg, Goldsmith's partner from the outset of Cavenham and Générale, had chosen this time to retire from the group raised further question marks. The announcement cited 'personal reasons of his own', which only added to the mystery. The truth is far more prosaic: de Gunzberg married a woman Goldsmith could not stand, and when the marriage ran into trouble he became seriously depressed and retired to live with his daughter in Florida.

It seemed to many of Goldsmith's outside shareholders that they had been used: used at Anglo-Continental to help finance the stake in Cavenham, and used in Cavenham to help finance GO and other companies (Cavenham was often a net lender to the rest of the group). Under no circumstances were they going to accept this offer, which was half the price Cavenham shares had reached at the top of the bull market four years before. 'Stop stamping your feet, Jimmy, and stump up your money,' ended the *Economist*.

A month later Goldsmith, in Barbados with Annabel and the children, rang Peter Hill-Wood at Hambros to tell him to drop the bid. Nevertheless he continued to negotiate over the next few months, offering to raise his bid to 140p a share if Samuel Montagu thought that might be acceptable (the shares had been 95p in the market before he made his bid). Samuel Montagu didn't. They valued the assets at 180p a share, and would recommend a discount on that – but not one of 40p.

The key to the offer was still the Prudential, whose investment chief, Ron Artus, was regarded as something of a guru in the City. Goldsmith went to see Artus, and offered him a deal: 150p a share, 100p of it in cash, for a full bid, or 155p a share for half its shares. The Prudential, resentfully, accepted the latter, and on 13 May, just two days after the end of the *Private Eye* case, Cavenham shares were suspended. The market eagerly anticipated a bid worth 160p a share in cash.

Goldsmith had one last surprise up his sleeve. Instead of his original bid of £60m for the whole of the 49 per cent not owned by GO, he now bid £40m for only 25 per cent. 'Cavenham minority shareholders seem to fall into two categories,' he explained. 'Those who very much want to sell and those who very much want to remain shareholders. This bid should satisfy both categories.' In a way this was a perfectly logical statement: there were some shareholders along for the ride, and others who resented the fact that, having supported him from the beginning, Goldsmith was now discarding them. This latter group, led by the Prudential, also suspected he could see greater value in the company's long-term prospects than the market did, and were happy to stay aboard.

'Sir James will make no new friends with this deal,' wrote *The Times*, 'but will deepen all the doubt and mistrust that have accumulated over the years.' Even Goldsmith's friend Patrick Hutber remarked that Goldsmith 'has his – in my view unfortunate – shareholders over a barrel', adding that Goldsmith was now 'totally indifferent to City opinion'.

The fact that one-quarter of Cavenham's shares would still be held by outsiders meant Jimmy would still remain chairman of a public company – on which his views were well-known.

In the event, his offer was oversubscribed by 17m shares, supporting Goldsmith's argument that he should have offered for the lot. He was not long in doing so. In August the remaining Cavenham shares sank back to 80p, and Hambros and Cazenove were besieged by complaints. The company was doing well, but life was uncomfortable for the neglected minority. It was Hill-Wood and his team at Hambros who worked out a scheme which they proposed to Goldsmith, on holiday on a yacht with Ginette and the children. He agreed, and from there announced his proposed offer for the final 25 per cent. He would not offer cash, or even ordinary shares: each Cavenham shareholder would receive four more preference shares for every three shares they held, which would then be cancelled. Générale Occidentale's 75 per cent stake would thus become 100 per cent.

By now the City, and even the financial press, was jaded with Goldsmith and the long-running saga of Cavenham. In the dog days of summer, the proposal went through with barely a murmur. A few dissidents pointed out that Goldsmith was using Cavenham's own capital to buy out its shareholders, but no one had the heart for the struggle.

From his yacht, Goldsmith also announced the final tidying up of Slater Walker, which was a substantial (and largely unsung) achievement. The Slater Walker banking business, containing £6om of outstanding loans, was swallowed into the Bank of England, leaving just the profitable unit trust company behind. An era had ended, not just for Goldsmith, but for the London stock market.

Later that autumn (1977) BBC Television's *Money Programme* decided to make an in-depth investigative report on Jimmy Goldsmith's business empire. The previous week the *Money Programme* had run an interview with Jim Slater, the first he had given since his fall, and now it was Goldsmith's turn.

The programme on Jimmy was a two-parter, the first episode a critical look at the rise of Goldsmith, which one of the linkmen, James Bellini, introduced with a remark that Goldsmith's move to France 'was just another controversial chapter in a colourful life and with Eton, the Guards and a few influential friends to help him, how could it be anything else?'

The programme then basically showed how Goldsmith had built up his company through a mixture of asset stripping, judicious borrowing and general ruthlessness. Cavenham didn't lavish money on new factories, 'it patched up old ones'; it had not introduced a single new product, and was not an originator or investor but 'an improver of other people's ideas'. It ended on this sombre note:

> There was to have been an annual general meeting today but Sir James has now bought out his British shareholders. The way he went about it caused bitter controversy. Has he used shareholders' money to pursue his own ends? Has he broken his word? Has he, at some stage, been guilty of financial sleight of hand?

These were legitimate enough questions. A great deal of public money was involved, important points of company law and disclosure needed to be discussed, and there was an unhealthily pervasive air of suspicion.

The following week Goldsmith himself was due to appear, to answer questions by the co-hosts of the programme, Bellini and Hugh

Stephenson, an intelligent, left-of-centre journalist who was editor of the business section of *The Times*. While Bellini, a minor academic, and Stephenson armed themselves with probing questions, Goldsmith diligently prepared his defence. Slater, who had been through the *Money Programme* mill, and his friend David Frost, then at the height of his television career, coached him in how to respond. He must insist the programme was live, so that he could not be cut when he said something they didn't like. He must set out with a clear number of points to make – and make them, regardless of what they were asking him. As long as he kept talking the cameras had to stay on him, so he must seize control of the programme and hold on to it. They put him through several dummy runs, with Slater insisting, 'Jimmy, you're answering a question – don't answer the question, make the points you want to make'.

The next week (4 November 1977) an unsuspecting Bellini began with a summary of the previous week's programme.

It's here, in the City of London, that you will find Sir James' strongest critics, among the people who look after British shareholders and among journalists, people like us, who write and talk about business. They say Sir James has pursued personal plans at the expense of British shareholders. His aim, critics say, is to keep control of his food empire through Générale Occidentale, his master company in France . . .

The cameras then focused on Goldsmith who sat poised, with a file on his knee, watching them like a large cat its prey. Stephenson's first question was innocuous enough: was there a grand design to Cavenham's growth in the past ten years, 'or have you operated in a more opportunistic way?' Goldsmith began by answering the question, but quickly switched into one of the most devastating attacks on an interviewer ever seen on television anywhere in the world.

You said Cavenham just patches up old factories – that is what you described as 'the Goldsmith style', and while you were saying this, it was interesting that your camera was on the old Colnbrook disused sheds and on the oldest part of the Bristol factory, our original factory, it was the Victorian part. And those two factories . . . are about as representative of Cavenham today as Henry Ford's original shed was of Ford Motor Company.

As he leaned forward to emphasise his points, he seemed to tower over the interviewers who were by now watching open-mouthed. 'We are currently engaged in a £237 million capital investment programme . . .

one of the largest in British industry.' How could they say, he demanded, 'that my style is to patch up factories?'

By now Stephenson and Bellini were actually stuttering, as Goldsmith insisted on an answer. 'I'm asking you how could you, how was it possible to say we patched up old factories', when he had built new ones, extended others, and was spending £237m (this figure was repeated at least a dozen times)?

While the interviewers vainly tried to interrupt, Goldsmith went on to his second point: they had accused him of buying and selling companies, of dealing in companies, keeping them if they were failures, selling them to raise cash if they succeeded. 'That's what you said, isn't it?' By now he was enjoying himself, in full control, far more familiar with his material than either of the two interviewers, who had not actually made the previous week's programme, and who were soon seeking to disavow parts of it. Cavenham, he said, now had sales of £1.8 billion a year, or about £7m per trading day. 'We have sold in all, since the beginning twelve years ago, companies whose overall sales correspond to nine per cent of that figure, so we have kept ninety-one per cent and sold nine per cent.'

Several times Bellini tried to get a word in, but Goldsmith was in full flow, battering them with fact after fact, statistic after statistic to which they had no answer. In 1972 he had announced he would consolidate, he said, and that meant concentrating on the mainstream activities, selling or closing all marginal activities. What he sold were largely diversifications made by previous managements: a plastic company and an underwear company in France had gone, so had Grand Union's engineering business, and a papermaking business which had come in with J. & A. P. Holland. They had no place in a food company. But, he said, stepping up the attack, the previous week the programme had said he had sold a Parisian publishing house. 'And you showed proof . . . We never owned that. You even exaggerated your own points by total misrepresentation of the facts. Why was that?'

BELLINI: That was an objective report by a reporter on this programme.

SIR JAMES: It was not an objective report.

BELLINI: It was a report by a reporter on this programme.

SIR JAMES: Are you responsible for him?

BELLINI: Personally no, I am a member of this programme team.

SIR JAMES: Will you stand by what your reporter said last week? Will you? I'm asking you a question?

STEPHENSON: Absolutely.

SIR JAMES: Good, well let's get on and analyse it.

Having pinned down the uncomfortable duo, he tormented them with growing relish, every so often prodding them with 'you even went so far, or your reporter did, as to purposely mislead people . . . why? I'm asking a question, are you going to tell me?' When Stephenson pleaded weakly that it was more conventional for them to ask questions, Goldsmith retorted, 'I don't mind about convention, I'm asking you why you distorted these facts.' When they couldn't recall the precise wording of the previous week's programme, he did it for them: 'I have a transcript here. Would you like me to take it out and read from it?'

The two besieged journalists were by now almost pleading with him: STEPHENSON: I don't want to start you off again – please, Sir James . . .

Goldsmith relented enough to let him ask a question, but soon returned to his pre-set theme. 'You made a number of shocking fundamental allegations about my company and I intend to take these and to understand why you did it . . .' They had claimed Cavenham produced no major new products. There weren't many major new products in the industry, he pointed out; maybe every decade or so something new came along. 'After the war there were frozen foods, then there were instant foods, then there were freeze-dried foods – these were great fundamental leaps forward in basic research in food. The remainder is development. And this is true for most industries, true for the motor car industry. What fundamental new product has there been in the motor car industry?'

He expounded the virtues of the Bovril cube, the result of five years' research and development. 'All I'm trying to show is that in every fundamental issue last week . . . you lied. That's what I'm trying to show, and what I intend to prove on this programme.' Stephenson and Bellini, however bemused, could not let that pass, and the studio by now was in uproar with all three talking at once. When Bellini finally restored order sufficiently to protest that the viewers were not being well served by this debate, Goldsmith retorted: 'My dear fellow, I am not here to serve anybody other than my employees . . .'

The truth is that around the country husbands were summoning wives to watch, phones were busy as businessmen rang their friends to tune in, and audience figures shot up as the programme continued. It was the best television in years.

Only once did either interviewer manage to halt Goldsmith – and that was at a point where, if they had not been so rattled, they might have let him damage himself. Two-thirds of the way through, Goldsmith began to get carried away. The amusement that had been in his eyes minutes before blinked out, and a disturbing, almost manic gleam appeared, familiar to those who had heard him on the subject of *Private Eye*. He moved from the attack on Cavenham to something much wider: the old theme of the infiltration by left-wing subversives.

Now what worries me, Mr Stephenson [he began], is that on a national scale, many of us feel uneasy about the fact we have been fed false information, that our political leaders are being attacked [there was a Labour government at the time]; that our political institutions are being attacked, that our national traditions are being eroded, that we have false information on immigration, on crime ... Cavenham is just a symbol. What worries me when I see a programme come through which is nothing but riddled with factual lies, lies of which you were apprised because you had the facts before, I wonder whether this is indicative of a far more malignant and general disease.

His friends, knowing the rage that could consume Goldsmith on this theme, willed him to stop. Men like Simon Jenkins and Patrick Hutber, greatly impressed by Goldsmith's analytical powers and his political knowledge, went cold whenever he launched into this type of tirade. Even to those who shared his political views, it bordered on the paranoid. Goldsmith, clinical and deadly a few minutes before, was now almost raving. A few minutes longer and Bellini and Stephenson might have snatched victory from the jaws of defeat, but at that precise moment Bellini managed to get a 'Can we stick to the facts?' question in, and Goldsmith visibly shook himself and pulled back from the brink.

Criticised for selling seven confectionery companies, he retorted that they had realised only £500,000 after redundancy payments, whereas he had invested £5.3m into the remaining facilities. The difficult question of why he had moved control of Cavenham he dealt with cleverly if disingenuously: 'The power of command has never moved from me. I founded the company from scratch. I had 78 per cent when it started, I still have that power of command and everybody in Cavenham realises and knows that, and it is not going to shift from me so long as I'm here.'

Stephenson did at one stage succeed in accusing him of lying when he told his shareholders he had no intention of bidding for the remaining 49 per cent of Cavenham. Goldsmith took the accusation calmly. 'I'd like you to cast your mind back over the past year. Interest rates have gone from fifteen per cent to five per cent, the stock market has changed, sterling has totally changed, the world has totally changed in this period. Now we said that we did not for one second believe that we would be able in a year to do an issue to raise sufficient funds to be able to bid for Cavenham.' By May, he said, his bankers were advising him he could raise the money, 'and that is what we did.'

The final moments of the programme were hilarious. The two interviewers were attempting to make the point that there were many unhappy former Cavenham shareholders around who felt that Goldsmith had used their own money to buy them out cheaply, when Goldsmith interrupted. From his portable filing system on his knee, Goldsmith produced his ace.

SIR JAMES: But you know perfectly well that's nonsense and so does Hugh Stephenson. He wrote it.

STEPHENSON: I wrote what?

SIR JAMES: My dear fellow, I'm delighted to quote it to you. I'm sure you haven't got much time, let me just quote it to you. This is on the fourth of August 1977.

He then read a *Times* clipping: 'The outcome . . . is that shareholders who were in Cavenham before the partial bid in May have effectively got a little over 155p for their entire holding. That is a price at which few would quibble.' Triumphantly, Goldsmith leaned forward, waving the clipping at Stephenson, who looked stunned. 'So what the devil are you quibbling about?'

STEPHENSON: The fourth of August I was on holiday in Ireland.

SIR JAMES: You *are* editor of *The Times* business paper, aren't you?

STEPHENSON: That's true, yes.

SIR JAMES: And this was signed by the Financial Editor of *The Times*, and are you responsible for that? I know he's not responsible for his . . .

nodding towards Bellini, who at that moment brought the programme to a close. Without waiting for the credits to fade, Goldsmith, still on camera, stood up, removed his microphone, and stalked off, leaving two bemused interviewers sitting forlornly on the couch, their dejection only too visible.

The programme was the most sensational the *Money Programme* ever made. It became a classic. Tapes circulated round like *samizdat*, used to train businessmen in the art of how to conduct television interviews, and in schools of journalism on how not to! Patrick Hutber called it 'as memorable a piece of television as is ever likely to be shown'.

But Cavenham was no more, at least in the public eye. It had begun its life at 20p a share and went out at 155p a share after twelve years, a less spectacular performance than once seemed likely, but still a major success. The name would linger on, but all around the City files labelled 'Cavenham' were consigned to the archives. It still employed thousands of people, earned a handsome profit and was ostensibly the same company it was before it left the public arena. But a light had gone out.

From the winter of 1977, Jimmy Goldsmith had another reason for preferring Paris to London: there was a third woman in his life. Laure Boulay de la Meurthe was a 26-year-old reporter for *Paris Match* when he met her. Slim, and blonde, she was also even more aristocratic than Isabel or Annabel: she was a Bourbon, niece of the Comte de Paris, direct descendant of King Louis Philippe and pretender to the French throne. Laure was – and is – an able and professional journalist, who lived quietly in Paris with her sister on the Left Bank. Even with Ginette playing a less prominent part in his life, Jimmy was involved with more women than most men could handle, but he was enchanted by Laure, and began a relationship which went far beyond a simple affair. As Ginette had before her, Annabel had to accept that Jimmy had lost none of his attraction for other women. Yet she must have hoped that she, with a little help from Ginette, could have kept him happy and busy enough not to need anyone else. It was a vain hope. In time, Laure was to become at least as important in his life as ever either Ginette or Annabel.

Yet he still went ahead with his promise to marry Annabel. It was to be a secret wedding, secret at least from the press. He chose, interestingly, to marry in Paris, with only a handful of his friends. A fortnight before the wedding, the *Daily Express* revealed the marriage would take place on 17 November. Goldsmith was furious.

Annabel wanted to get married quietly in the local registry office in Richmond where, she pointed out, famous pop stars had succeeded in evading press scrutiny. But Jimmy insisted it should be in Paris, where personal privacy was protected by law, and where they would be well away from rapacious British journalists. It did not work out that way. Annabel set off the night before with her sister Lady Jane Rayne, and her former sister-in-law (married to the pop star Georgie Fame), travelling under the name of Mrs Vane. They were followed by a *Daily Express* reporter who travelled on the plane, politely introduced himself to Annabel, then pursued them at the other end as they took a taxi from the airport to the Ritz. That evening Jimmy hosted a dinner party for ten, including Annabel's brother and Madame Beaux, at a Russian nightclub. The next morning Annabel set off for the ceremony by taxi, again followed by the *Express* reporter (who had sent her two dozen red roses at the hotel), but got caught up in traffic and ran the last few hundred yards in the rain to

Goldsmith's office. She was just getting into Goldsmith's car when Jimmy spotted the *Express* photographer, Bill Lovelace, and charged at him. Grabbing him in an armlock, and with the help of one of his staff, Goldsmith dragged him into the Générale Occidentale building shouting, 'Lock the doors'.

'Lovelace's camera was snatched from him, and damaged, the film was ripped out, Lovelace's glasses were broken, his knuckles scraped and ribs bruised,' said the *Express* report the next day.

Once again it was Jimmy's extraordinary over-reaction which embarrassed even Annabel, who had found both photographer and reporter perfectly civil. By manhandling the photographer, he transformed a minor item of gossip into a full-blown story. 'Perhaps he felt guilty about getting married in Paris because Ginette lived there,' says one of his close friends. Laure lived there too, and she can't have been any more delighted than Ginette.

Jimmy was still seething when he fired off a letter to *The Times* which appeared the next day. 'When a middle-aged couple who have shared their lives for fourteen years are able to marry it is appropriate that they should choose to do so with the dignity of silence,' he wrote. That, he said, was still possible in Paris – unless British journalists broke the law. 'Therefore I carried out a "citizen's arrest" of the journalist and disarmed his camera,' he wrote. He tried to end on a lighter note by thanking the *Daily Express* for a 'wonderful wedding present – the legal opportunity to manhandle a representative of its gossip column.'

It was a trivial incident but it marred the day for Annabel. It was also used as fodder for the 'Hate Goldsmith' campaign back in Britain. Patrick Marnham of *Private Eye* later wrote, 'Goldsmith, who had started adult life by being threatened with a horsewhip, had graduated to wielding one.' And the *Express* reporter wrote a dignified response to *The Times* pointing out that he had broken no law, that the so-called citizen's arrest was illegal, and that he had been scrupulous about not speaking to Annabel on French soil. 'There was no hole-in-the-corner subterfuge. The couple were aware of my presence in Paris. I deliberately kept out of their way so as not to ruin what should have been a happy day.'

Annabel felt there might have been better ways of embarking again on married life.

In December they held their wedding party at Ormeley Lodge, and Goldsmith stayed on for Christmas. Then, as he had done for years, he flew to Paris, picked up Ginette and the children, and took them to Gstaad for the New Year. Truly, as he had told Ginette, nothing had altered.

22

Guatemalan Oilman

Jimmy Goldsmith's disillusionment with Britain went deeper than his hatred of the press. Unable to explain the antipathy he had encountered he blamed the whole country, insisting in a speech in Florida on 2 October 1978 that it was 'an example of a society which has purposely reduced the scope for entrepreneurship'. Britain, he said, was caught up in class war, with a socialist government which believed that wealth was held only by the privileged class and that simply by appropriating this wealth, it 'could establish a welfare and egalitarian state'. Those few voices, such as his own, that attempted to alert public opinion to the situation, he said, were labelled as either extremist or cranky.

The late 1970s were indeed a bad time for Britain, which humiliatingly had to call in the IMF for help in 1976, and which endured some of the highest inflation and lowest growth rates in the industrialised world. The climate was starkly anti-business, turning sharply away from the world of enterprise. The City of London, still a major world financial centre, had been demoralised by the fringe bank and property crises from which it was making a halting recovery, and manufacturing industry was losing competitiveness almost by the hour as soaring wage rates, strikes and rising prices pushed up its costs. Output per man in Britain's nationalised steel industry was one-quarter that of an American steel worker, one-sixth that of a Japanese. Since the war Britain had lost its empire. Its place in Europe, once powerful, was now peripheral. It was poorer than Germany or France, and was no longer one of the world's three great powers. For all that, and for all Goldsmith's dire warnings, its political and social stability had survived the huge strains of the post-war adjustment, and although it had lost ground relative to its continental neighbours, it was still – astonishingly – more prosperous than ever.

Goldsmith had emerged as one of the most powerful voices against what he perceived as the decline of socialist Britain into penury and eventual social collapse. He made a number of major set-piece speeches, carefully researched and polished efforts delivered to large audiences, the text distributed to Fleet Street editors, politicians and others he hoped might be interested. He was a much sought-after speaker, not just because of what he had to say but because, having once got over his initial nerves, he was excellent at it. His name on a list of speakers was an instant draw.

In March 1979 he went to Florida again to address the congress of the International Chamber of Commerce, a large, prestige event, and again expounded his message about declining Britain, where the state was responsible for 60 per cent of gross national product, the highest levels of tax were 83 per cent on salaries and 98 per cent on income from savings, and Britain's share of world trade had fallen from 25 per cent to 8 per cent in 25 years. 'British industry has become a cripple and the British nation has been impoverished.'

He repeated the same message to a packed audience of directors at the Royal Albert Hall on 20 March 1979: 'Economically, in one generation we have been transformed from a rich country into a poor one.' The British people had become divorced from their leaders. 'Woe to a nation where the leaders no longer represent the led.'

In France he also made a number of major speeches, where the near accession of the Communists to power in the elections of 1978 had equally shaken his faith in that country. All his pronouncements were intelligent and thoughtful but because of their theme and the atmosphere that surrounded him, they generated no following wind. They were reported all right, often widely, but to many commentators it was just 'Goldsmith banging the old drum again'. However, a powerful antidote both to socialism and to Britain's crisis was taking shape in the takeover of the Conservative Party by the right under Margaret Thatcher. Deliverance from what Goldsmith hated was only a matter of months away. He was a witness to it, but played no part – probably wisely, since any support he gave to Thatcher at that time might have been damaging. Nor did he really believe she or any other politician could shift attitudes which he considered had become institutionalised. In his view, Britain was finished.

France, too, he believed, was in a perilous state. 'It seemed to me that both nations were set on paths which, unless radically changed, would lead to decline, poverty and unhappiness. And perhaps to subjugation,' he would write a few years later in his book, *Pour La Révolution Permanente*. At *L'Express* he allowed Olivier Todd to urge readers, in his own column, to vote for the Socialist–Communist coalition at the elections, although the magazine itself took the opposite view and Goldsmith kept muttering darkly that a left-wing government would be a 'catastrophe' for France. According to Todd, during the first two and a half years of his ownership, Goldsmith had only vetoed one article, and, he added, he was right to do so. *L'Express'* editor, Jean-François Revel, was a distinguished author and a man of sturdy intellectual independence, as was the columnist Raymond Aron. Goldsmith occasionally summoned them to a room upstairs in the Laurent for a fairly heated political chat, but on the whole he left them alone. *L'Express* might not have been perfect, but at least it was no longer injecting 'poison' into the system.

Goldsmith spent more and more time in the US, where Grand Union needed attention, and where increasingly he felt his future lay. He had taken a corner suite in the Carlyle as his New York home, and Annabel came over to decorate it.

Roland Franklin had been working for him in New York since 1975, acting as an advance party in search of acquisitions, and under his control the Générale Occidentale office on Fifth Avenue began to grow. Franklin had been more than happy to get out of London when Keyser collapsed. For a time he had been in serious personal financial trouble, and his son Vivian actually turned up in Amalfi, where Goldsmith had rented Carlo Ponti's house, to ask for help. Goldsmith rang Franklin, lent him money to pay off his debts, and was publicly attacked when this was revealed. For the proud Franklin, it was a bitter humiliation. 'You're better off going to America because there's so much animosity here,' Goldsmith told him, and Franklin thankfully packed his bags and departed.

But the heart of Jimmy's business empire was in Paris. When Générale Alimentaire had been transferred into Cavenham in 1976, the French authorities had agreed to it on condition that if Cavenham passed outside effective French control, it must reduce its stake in its major French subsidiary to below half. Goldsmith had agreed readily enough, but the political shift in France caused him to have second thoughts. He began to feel constrained, worried that he might not be able to move his capital about the world – and particularly to the US – as he wanted. From early 1978 Goldsmith began to plan yet another reshuffle which would have the effect of tightening his own control on his empire, which had substantial outside shareholders in Générale Occidentale, shifting the emphasis (if not the control) out of France, and making the whole operation more tax-efficient. He also wanted to secure a position where he could raise more capital to finance the modernisation and expansion of Grand Union – and make further acquisitions in the US.

In the middle of 1978 the *Financial Times* published an article which annoyed Goldsmith intensely by suggesting that control of Générale Occidentale, and therefore of his whole empire, had moved from Paris to Hong Kong.

On 17 April 1978, the shares of a little Hong Kong investment company called General Oriental were suspended pending an acquisition. It was then worth only £1.6m, but when it re-emerged on the stock market three months later, its capital had expanded thirteen-fold. It was now the effective owner of 31.3 per cent of Générale Occidentale, with an option on another 3.5 per cent. Typically, the chain by which it held those shares was not simple. The key was that same little British property company, Argyle Securities, which had run into trouble and which Goldsmith, with a 30 per cent stake, had bought in for Générale Occidentale. Argyle's property assets were sold to Cavenham for £18.8m in cash, and Argyle raised a loan to acquire 17 per cent of Occidentale 'by private treaty'. Argyle also bought a stake in another company, Trocadero, which at that stage was a private company owned by Jimmy himself. Trocadero's main asset was an 18 per cent stake in Occidentale. Between them, General Oriental, controlled by a private Goldsmith foundation, Bruneria, based in Panama, and Trocadero now had effective control of Occidentale.

Goldsmith had created a pyramid of companies, at the top of which was the Hong Kong-based General Oriental. At the bottom were the huge concerns of Cavenham, Générale Alimentaire, 98.5 per cent of the Banque Occidentale, a half share in *L'Express* and 63 per cent of the Lloyd's insurance broker Wigham Poland.

The principal of the 'pyramid' is as old as joint stock companies, and essentially works like this: a tiny company at the top can own controlling stakes in several companies beneath, which in turn own controlling stakes in several companies beneath them, so that by the time the base is reached, with dozens of minority holdings scattered throughout, the empire can be substantial – and controlled by whoever has the controlling shareholding in the top company. In this case, of course, it was Jimmy Goldsmith.

Goldsmith had constructed several pyramids in his career, but none as elaborate as this one. The documents ran to 50 densely packed pages, involving companies in Panama and Bermuda as well as France and Hong Kong. The *Financial Times* described them as 'staggeringly complicated' and the *Far Eastern Economic Review*, which was now to become the latest publication to invite Goldsmith's wrath, as 'of Byzantine complexity'. If anything, that was an understatement. As the *Economist* commented wryly, 'In Hong Kong Sir James has found one of the few major markets where honest punters love a paper mountain.'

These moves were of greater interest in French financial circles than in British. 'The authorities have for a long time been suggesting to M. Goldsmith that he should make his capital more French,' one official was quoted as saying. What was important to France, he added, was that there should be the equivalent of a Nestlé or a Unilever.

Goldsmith's life style and position in France were certainly comfortable enough. His office in the avenue de Friedland was the epitome of the private bank which Gilberte Beaux ran there: respectable and solid on the outside, discreet marble hallway and stairs inside. Goldsmith's own office was stunning. Reached through an unmarked door on the fifth floor, a single flight of stairs led up to an anteroom, which housed his secretary, and a small boardroom. One end of the room was entirely glass, and opened out on to a large terrace with a lawn as green as the centre court of Wimbledon – but bigger. The uninterrupted view was of the Arc de Triomphe and the Paris skyline. From the office it was a short walk to the Laurent restaurant, whose private rooms, also complete with their little terraces, he used as the office dining rooms.

His position as *directeur de la publication* of *L'Express* gave him considerable prominence. And Paris was his city even more than London; it was where he had been born, where his father had enjoyed a certain social status, and where he had many friends and relatives. It was also where he had an ex-wife and a mistress.

He would later deny that the French authorities played any part, but he did strengthen the Frenchness of both his capital and of his board. Typically, he did not do it by halves, but in a way which astonished even the French financial community.

On 15th March 1979 some sixty financial journalists, most of them French, were invited to the offices of Générale Occidentale for an announcement of some importance. Compagnie Générale d'Electricité, one of the largest and most powerful companies in France, was to invest

6om francs (about £7m) in Générale Occidentale. The deal, explained Goldsmith to the almost open-mouthed gathering, would give Occidentale a firmer 'anchorage' in France. Beside Goldsmith at the press conference was Ambroise Roux, the 58-year-old chairman of CGE, a major figure on the French industrial scene. Roux explained that from CGE's point of view, the stake was largely 'financial' rather than industrial – it would be made through a portfolio subsidiary.

Typically, the stake was a complicated one: CGE would be taking 60 per cent of a new holding company in which four other French institutions – Union des Assurances des Paris, Crédit Lyonnais, the French Lazard and Banque Rothschild – between them would invest 100m francs in new capital – not in Occidentale directly, but in Trocadero, which in turn would own 35 per cent of Occidentale. Roux, an old friend of Gilberte Beaux who had introduced him to Jimmy, would be joining the board, as would the 51-year-old Claude Pierre-Erosolette, son of a hero of the French resistance and chairman of Occidentale's principal banker, Crédit Lyonnais.

Roux was a prestigious addition to the Occidentale board. He was the epitome of the successful French businessman, the man who had risen rapidly through the French civil service to become *chef du cabinet* (head of the Private Office) of the minister of trade and industry in his early thirties, and had left in 1955 to join CGE, where he continued all the way to the top. He was described that week-end as 'without any doubt the most brilliant spirit, and most able tactician, among France's big employers'.

By this stage, the French financial press was abuzz with rumours about why Roux had teamed up with Jimmy. 'This is a situation most journalists would only have imagined taking place in a business novel,' wrote the *Journal de Finances*. *L'Expansion*, the business magazine, noted sarcastically that 'the industrial logic of a marriage between telephone exchanges and mustard is not obvious.'

There might have been little or no coverage in Britain, but for the fact that a *Financial Times* reporter from the Paris office, although not invited, had managed to talk his way in. Goldsmith was not best pleased: 'As long as the *Financial Times* prints only bad news about my companies, it will not be invited to my press conferences.'

Was there a link, the press wondered, between Roux's appointment and the anger of the French authorities over the Hong Kong companies? Goldsmith explains that his objective was simple enough: by moving back to France, he had removed his companies, and therefore himself, from the public gaze. He had been forced to dilute his own holding, and Générale Occidentale was vulnerable to a takeover bid. Now he had made it secure, and at the same time had brought in fresh capital which removed any doubts the authorities might have about the Frenchness of his company.

Goldsmith might have been forgiven if he had decided to rest on his laurels. He was only 46, wealthy, with his women, his children, his beautiful houses in London and Paris, a worldwide operation of which he personally controlled over 50 per cent, which revolved totally around him. No one could have blamed him if at that moment in his life he had settled for what he'd got.

But, repulsed by Beaverbrook, and inspired by what he felt he was achieving at *L'Express*, Goldsmith decided he would create his own magazine in Britain. In January 1979 he announced he had hired an editor, Anthony Shrimsley, former political editor of the *Daily Mail*, and over the next six months took on another 73 journalists, including some of the best names in the business: Patrick Hutber, the most distinguished financial writer in the country came from the *Sunday Telegraph*, Frank Johnson from the *Daily Telegraph* and others, such as the theatre critic, Clive Barnes, all joined. He set up a new company, Cavenham Publications, and announced he would spend £7m on his new magazine, £2.5m on advertising it to what he called 'the only major country in the free world without its own weekly news magazine'. It promised to be, commented Michael Davie in the *Observer*, 'the boldest publishing launch since the war'. Goldsmith threw himself into it, interviewing journalists, organising offices (in one of the old buildings in the City he had sold from Cavenham in 1973), talking to advertisers, holding meeting after meeting with his new editorial staff.

In the meantime, there was an unsettled bit of business. Goldsmith had named the *Sunday Times* journalist Phillip Knightley as a 'collaborator' of *Private Eye*'s. It was untrue, he apologised and paid him damages. He had also accused – orally so it was only slander as opposed to libel – the *Eye* journalist Michael Gillard of blackmailing John Addey, but later repeated this in a letter to the editor of the *Daily Telegraph*, Bill Deedes, which made it libel. Under the law, Gillard did not have to prove he was not a blackmailer, but Goldsmith had to prove he was. It was a five-day hearing, with Jimmy in the witness box for one and a half of them, giving what one journalist called 'one of the most remarkable performances in a courtroom I have ever seen'. He won the case (and later the appeal, despite the doubts of the judges themselves), and the *Private Eye* affair at last was over.

Or was it? Not quite. It would please the *Eye* journalists immensely to know that Goldsmith blames them, along with other journalists, for the failure of *Now!* magazine, which he launched in September 1979.

> The campaign worked. It was brilliantly done. They managed to make *Now!*, which was a new initiative, into something intensely personal [he says]. I remember Laure, who was a journalist herself, saying, 'Why are the press angry about a new paper coming out?' She couldn't understand how the press could be attacking a new paper. And it was very bitter, and then *Private Eye* did a brilliant job, because they would say the magazine wasn't selling and we would say we were, but they kept on saying it until we weren't. They managed to turn it into an un-smart thing to buy, because they were fashionable and we weren't, and in the advertising world, which is dominated by trendy little twerps, you can imagine to what degree they hated *Now!* They managed to do to *Now!* what has been done to Dan Quayle: they turned it into a non-trendy joke, which didn't matter to the readers but mattered terribly to the young people in the advertising agencies, who were frightened to discuss it with their clients. I thought the magazine itself was terribly good, but they turned it into a joke.

An article in the *Guardian* nine months after *Now!* was launched bears this out perfectly. 'I like *Now!* magazine and enjoy reading it each week,' it read. 'This is not a commonly shared opinion among journalists. You can only say it defiantly, certain it will bring the jeers and disbelief of your colleagues.'

This writer for one suggested that Goldsmith, accused by other journalists of being too actively involved, should interfere even more. 'Some writers say the peppier ideas frequently come from him, and if the majority are useless, enough are usable to make his interventions worthwhile.'

Yet *Now!* was good, sometimes very good – and would have been better if it had had time to develop. It suffered a number of early blows: Patrick Hutber, Goldsmith's star writer, had a hunting accident six months before the launch and never fully recovered. At Christmas 1979 he was in another accident, this time in his car, and this time fatal. He was mocked to the end by *Private Eye* which carried a piece by Auberon Waugh boasting that the magazine's curse had fallen on Hutber. Hutber's wife read it at his deathbed. *Now!* was launched during a television strike which meant it could not be properly promoted. And its brief life coincided with the low point of yet another recession which hit Britain in 1980.

Faced with losses of £12m a year (half that after tax), Goldsmith decided he could not justify it.

> I don't know what would have happened if we had lasted two or three years longer [he says]. A lot of people said, 'You went too early', and all the rest. All I know is that I went, as I usually did to Barbados, and I thought about it for a few days and thought it was just irresponsible, I couldn't justify it. So I came back to Paris, called poor old Shrimsley over. It was losing a million pounds a month and heading south, not north. It was one of the most painful decisions I have ever had to make in business.

As the 1980s opened, Goldsmith was preoccupied with a new problem which reared its head in the unlikely spot of the Guatemalan jungle. Much of the last three months of the *Now!* débâcle he had spent in Guatemala. This is one of the lesser-known episodes of Goldsmith's careers, yet one he is most proud of, since it pitted him as the defender of the small company against the might of the French state-owned Société Nationale Elf Aquitaine. Things began innocently enough when Gilberte Beaux was asked if the French bank would be interested in an investment in an oil exploration company which had found oil in Guatemala not far from the Mexican border, and needed to invest in a pipeline. It was run by a veteran oilman, John Park, who had originally worked for Standard Oil but in 1970 ploughed $6m of his own money into exploring a 4.5m acre area. Park's dream, which appealed to Jimmy Goldsmith when he met him, was that the great Mexican oilfields continued south, and that he would find fields as big as anything in America. He built an airstrip, and began a geological survey, eventually bringing two small wells into production.

When the oil price soared in the mid-1970s Park, for the first time, was taken seriously by the bigger oil companies. He acquired two partners, Shenandoah Oil from Texas and Saga from Norway, and found more oil. By now it was becoming a sizeable operation, and Park built camps for his workers, a network of roads and even a crude-oil processing plant. In 1978 Park's partners, with financial problems back home, pulled out, and he began looking for fresh investors who would finance a pipeline from his wells to Santo Tomas on the coast, 125 miles away. He also wanted to bring in an entire new oilfield, which he was convinced was there. It was a huge project for a small company, but Park was a tough and determined operator. In France he found Elf Aquitaine, and they agreed to set up a new company in which Park's company, Basic Resources International, would have 75 per cent and Elf would have 25 per cent. It was to be his biggest mistake.

When Jimmy heard about Park's approach to the bank, he was intrigued. He was interested in getting into the oil business, which in the 1970s had become the great fashionable industry, and this seemed a perfect opportunity. 'It was,' he says, 'just a high risk investment banking transaction', but he was interested enough to fly with Park to Guatemala. He brought Laure with him. It was an adventure, a break from the financial world, and a chance to see something different. In Guatemala City he immediately hired a helicopter, and with an astonished Park along, began examining the beaches, the mountains and the villages, fascinated by what he saw. He had never been to this part of the world, and he loved the wild jungle, dreaming of one day building himself a house with Laure right in the middle of it, well away from everybody. Finally, they landed at the oilfields, and Goldsmith stalked around, asking questions and doing rapid mental calculations. He was impressed by Park, and also reassured by the fact that Elf was involved. 'As bankers, that was a comfort as far as I was concerned,' he says. He decided he would invest; Générale Occidentale, he told Park, would back him for $5m, mostly for the pipeline.

Over the next few months, as he became more interested, and as Park needed more money, Goldsmith stepped up his investment to $30m.

But by the spring of 1980, Basic emerged as a serious problem. The military government suddenly woke up to the size of Basic's potential oil reserves, and commissioned a report which suggested its petroleum rights could be worth as much as $3.3 billion, against the $200m that Park had invested or proposed to invest. Basic was forced to begin the renegotiation of an agreement which its lawyers had assured it was legally binding under Guatemalan law.

No one in the oil industry would have been too surprised. It happened everywhere, and philosophically Park settled down to drive the best bargain he could. It was then he discovered that, without telling him, his partner Elf Aquitaine was quietly negotiating with the government to take over his field. The Guatemalans were unhappy that such a potentially important field was being developed by a tiny company like Basic. They preferred Elf, on the grounds that it was large, and government-backed.

Eventually a new arrangement was hammered out, whereby Basic and Elf would have a joint company, 80 per cent owned by Basic, 20 per cent by Elf, which would develop the field; and the government would take 55 per cent of the revenues. Park fought the deal to the point where, as he said, 'My name was becoming mud'. But the oil was there, and even on the basis of the new agreement he stood to make a fortune.

The Guatemalans, however, wanted even more concessions from Basic and with Park now extremely unpopular, Goldsmith decided to take over himself. He became chairman of Basic and flew to Guatemala to spend a full month, a long time for him, negotiating the deal with the government. Gilberte Beaux, as the only Spanish-speaker in the group, spent two months there, just as she had originally spent months in Argentina selling the Bovril subsidiaries. Jimmy also hired the American Vietnam war veteran Vernon Walters (later US ambassador to the United Nations), hoping he could bring some influence to bear on the generals who ran the country.

But although Basic hung on to its concessions, Park was forced to allow Elf to become the operating company. Basic was reduced to the role of financial partner, and although Park was upset, Jimmy was less unhappy. 'I thought they would be a good operating company, and I wasn't in the oil business, I was in the financial business. We were really just passive investors.' In August 1980 Elf became the operator and began drilling the first of six wells on which it had agreed to spend $42m over six years. By the end of 1980 they had spent $14m but were behind schedule. They produced a new budget for 1981: they planned to spend $50m, and a few months later increased that figure to $72m. Since Basic had to produce 80 per cent of the funding, Goldsmith and Park suddenly realised they were in for a great deal more money than they thought originally.

The only way they could raise the finance was to let Elf increase its shareholding, which it did, from 20 to 43 per cent. But a new idea was forming in Jimmy's mind, put there by Park, as report after report came in from the fields showing drilling going wrong, production going down, tools being dropped into wells, wells being lost, equipment breaking down. Park kept saying, 'They're sabotaging it', with Goldsmith insisting that was nonsense. Others were saying that Elf was merely inefficient, but Goldsmith didn't believe that either. 'For me, Elf was a great company, and it was like saying Shell is an inefficient driller – which everybody knows it's not.' When Elf started overspending, Goldsmith assumed that was the way state-owned oil companies behaved. 'Then I heard a rumour that they had decided to put pressure on Basic, so that they could pick up the concession.'

That infuriated Goldsmith.

Every fibre of my ideological being was offended – the nationalised company trying to kill the little private concern. And also self interest – the fact that they were so keen to get it – must mean there was something there. So it was a mixture of self-interest, fury, all these things put together. If I'd been logical, I'd have cut and run, and got whatever I could by selling out to Elf and forgotten it. I should never have risked all that money at a time I needed it elsewhere.

But he decided to fight. By now Occidentale's investment in Basic was up to $45m, and still rising. Through 1981 he had no choice but to continue stumping up, knowing that if Basic was in default, Elf would automatically receive the concession for nothing. Everything he had invested so far would be lost. By the end of 1981 the matter came to a head when Basic produced yet another revised budget, and Park refused to accept it. It was what the French had hoped to hear, and they immediately set about placing Basic in default with the Guatemalan government.

Goldsmith now launched himself into the fight in much the same way he had launched himself at *Private Eye*. The agreement with Elf contained an arbitration clause, and Goldsmith decided to sue the French oil group. First however he warned Park what to expect. 'As a state company they believe they're above the law,' he warned. They would, he told him, cut him out, and try to drag the battle on for ever. 'It's going to cost a fortune.' By now Goldsmith himself was in for $90m.

He started two independent cases, under two different items in the contract, one – the larger one – in the International Chamber of Commerce in Berne, and the other over royalties. 'Then we decided to get tough.' He also sued Elf in Guatemala, and he sued them in Houston where Elf had bought a major oil and fertiliser company. He claimed $294m in damages. He also hired a firm of private detectives to investigate the company and received a report which he claims showed years of 'corrupt practices'.

In Houston they had a black lady judge, a Carter appointee, who proved very firm. She asked for discovery, and the French, as a nationalised company, decided it was not going to produce any of its documents. The documents were to be destroyed, but Goldsmith's detectives were by that stage following them. The detectives watched as the documents were thrown into a pit, and then retrieved them.

At one point Goldsmith was told, by a source he will not reveal, that he should remember 'what happened to M. Mattei'. Mattei was the head of an Italian oil company which tried to compete with the French oil interests in Algeria. His plane was sabotaged and he was killed. When he was told this 'very formally', Goldsmith picked up the phone and in front of his informant telephoned a friend of his in the Senate, and told him the story.

'If anything happens to you, I'll make a speech,' said the senator.

'Yes,' said Goldsmith, 'but before, not afterwards!'

The legal battle escalated as Goldsmith took action against Elf in New York and Washington aimed at getting further documents and accounts. But in Houston, the Elf officials still refused to attend the court, insisting they were civil servants and therefore not involved in business. Goldsmith's detectives watched the big hotels, monitoring the bookings in particular at the Meridien hotel where the French usually stayed. It took six months, but eventually the detectives discovered Elf had made 76 reservations, including suites for the chairman, the managing director and the chief financial officer.

When the French oilmen arrived, they were accosted by dark-suited Texas lawyers who solemnly handed them subpoenas. And a photographer standing by produced visual proof of delivery. The judge ruled the Elf officials were there on business purposes, and that they had been properly served doing business in the state of Texas, and must appear at her Federal court. The judge said she would issue arrest warrants for the top six Elf officials in France if they didn't come.

In the meantime, two arbitration cases, in Berne and Paris, had finished, although the results had yet to be announced. The parties involved however had been told the result. 'We had won hands down,' says Goldsmith. 'They had tried to use all the influence in the world, but it hadn't helped them.'

It was at this stage that Elf decided to settle, and invited Goldsmith to meet the chairman, which he did in a hotel opposite his office in Paris. He had still not made up his mind if he would settle, although that was the sensible thing to do.

'Here I am,' he told the Elf chairman, 'representing commercial interests, which I have to negotiate for, including our own of course, as best I can. On the other hand, believe me or not, I'm so outraged by what Elf has been doing that I'm very tempted to tell you to get stuffed, and to see that all this gets out, no matter what your offer is.'

Goldsmith had never used *L'Express* to write about Elf. 'Don't think I wasn't tempted, but I managed to resist the temptation. Everybody in *L'Express* was very keen to do it.'

But he negotiated a settlement, agreed before the results from any of the arbitration cases were announced. Elf thus avoided the judgments coming out. The sum offered was probably the largest ever paid for damages in French history: $130m, plus a guarantee from Elf of 80 cents a barrel in royalties on every barrel produced over the next 20 years. Park paid off Basic's debts of $65m, distributed another $43m to shareholders, and went back into business, producing oil in Guatemala (he died a few years later). Goldsmith, having recovered all his money – and a bit more – remained a 10 per cent shareholder in Basic, and appointed Gilberte Beaux as chairman.

A few months later he met the Elf chairman at a dinner given by Jacques Chirac, who had just been made prime minister of France, in one of the splendid rooms in the Louvre which had been specially done up for the occasion. The whole of Paris seemed to be there, and Goldsmith found himself in the reception line beside his former adversary. 'By that time it was all over, and we laughed about it, and ended up on perfectly good terms.'

23

Brave New World

Although he didn't formally leave France until after François Mitterand came to power in 1981, Goldsmith had been preparing his departure for some time. During the summer and autumn of 1979 he ruminated over a business move which would be one of the biggest he had yet taken: his group, he decided, in its current form, no longer made sense. He had started Cavenham as a food manufacturer which had evolved into a retailer. Now retailing, because of the size of Grand Union, was over 90 per cent of turnover. In Britain he was still both manufacturer and retailer. Whereas that had once seemed perfectly logical, the trend in all the big retailing groups of the world was to get out of manufacturing. There was a fundamental conflict of interest: a retailer could buy from whomever it chose, and would do its best to squeeze the manufacturer. Goldsmith's retailing operations, which sold large quantities of what his factories produced, were not in the best bargaining position. Grand Union in the US had altered the balance, and Goldsmith, adding it all together, discovered that Cavenham was now the third-largest retailer in the world after Safeway and Kroger.

If he were an outsider bidding for Cavenham, without any of the hang-ups of having started the business, what would he do? Abruptly he made up his mind: he would sell all his food manufacturing businesses, allow someone else to take on the burden of creating the 'French Nestlé', and concentrate his efforts entirely on retailing. He did not realise it, but he had set in train a rather more fundamental move, which eventually would involve selling just about everything he owned in Europe. He was also thinking hard about the future of his banking and financial interests. In his new mood, they didn't seem to make much sense either, but they would wait. 'Jimmy decided to do to ourselves what he would do to a conglomerate,' says Madame Beaux. 'And everything was done very quickly. It is the way Jimmy works. Generally a plan is a long time maturing, but when he is sure it is the right thing, he moves very fast.'

It is of course possible to look at it another way. Picking up some of the *Money Programme* themes, for instance, it could be argued that because it was possible to sell the manufacturing companies at a profit, Goldsmith was simply taking that profit – dealing in companies; that he was an opportunist rather than a long-term businessman. He tried to shrug off such aspersions, pretending that he had enjoyed a good scrap, and that he was clinically applying his own philosophy of 'core business' strategy. To his friends he could claim that *Private Eye* had done him a great favour, depressing his shares and giving him the opportunity to buy them in for himself cheaply. 'It's made me a very rich man,' he would say.

But Goldsmith was tired of Britain and of France. In a couple of years he would be 50. In business terms he was now at his peak; he had accumulated in his 27 years in business an enormous breadth of experience and knowledge, and now fresh markets beckoned in which to apply that knowhow.

In short, Goldsmith was moving himself in emotional and personal terms – and his companies with him. If that made him an opportunist, well, that is what he was. Was that bad? It is difficult to find victims of his 'opportunism'. His employees certainly didn't suffer as a result; there were no shareholders other than big institutions, and they have never had any reason to complain (quite the opposite). The companies he sold are still around, managed by other people, mostly doing well – some might say better than ever.

Whatever the moral arguments, the break-up of Cavenham's food interests was among the most rapid deconglomeration in corporate history. It was November 1979 when he told Gilberte Beaux what he had decided, and by March 1980 it was done. Bovril, which had cost him £7m after the various sales, went to Beecham for £42m in cash. The French food manufacturing side went to BSN Gervais-Danone, A. B. Felix, the Swedish subsidiary, was sold, as was the company in Austria. These were followed by the manufacturing businesses in Spain and Belgium. The confectionery interests in Britain, including Famous Names Liqueur Chocolates, went to the management.

The whole lot realised around £100m, mostly in cash, a handsome sum in 1980. He would now deploy it where his sights were fixed: in the United States, where the biggest merger boom of all time would soon get

357

under way, with Goldsmith, an almost unknown name at the start, quickly moving to centre stage.

If the truth were told he had been searching almost from the start of his Grand Union takeover for yet another route for empire building in North America. The grocery business in Britain was not the same thing in the States where there were far too many competitors, the pricing was cut-throat and there was just so much anyone could do to improve management efficiency. The rest was hostage to the vagaries of the wildly fluctuating American economy, and that did not fit the Goldsmith formula of slimming down in order to concentrate on core businesses. Some other industry that offered harder underlying assets and where real economies of scale could be achieved – that was what was wanted.

Goldsmith had already begun his restless search for the big prize in almost every corner of the world of finance and in almost every industry or occupation. He was keen to find something that would lift him out of the ranks of being a curiosity in the US into the rarefied company of the major players on Wall Street. So, for example, there was a flirtation with the idea of buying Columbia Pictures in the late seventies, and the Basic Resources exploits in Guatemala in 1979.

But his real US adventure would begin modestly enough out of a shareholding in an ageing forest products company that appeared to be losing its way. Its name was Diamond International. In the secure files of the Générale Occidentale offices on Fifth Avenue in New York, a new project file had been opened as early as the spring of 1978 to follow the quiet purchases of small amounts of Diamond stock by Bovril (Canada) Ltd., the Cavenham pension fund and Banque Occidentale. The code name for the project: Operation New World.

According to Roland Franklin,

> It is easy with the benefit of hindsight to say that Diamond was attractive because of its timber holdings. But at that time, Diamond interested us because of our philosophy which pervaded everything we did in America: that the sum of the parts of most conglomerates was worth a great deal more than the whole. The attraction of Diamond was that it was a conglomerate and because it was particularly safe because of the timber.

Indeed the company was almost all parts and very little whole. Like Grand Union, the Diamond Match Corporation, as it had been named originally, had its roots in nineteenth-century American industry: the company had introduced the safety match to America in 1882. In the late 1970s its management sought to break out of dependency on consumer spending cycles by branching into product lines that were only tangentially related to lumber and paper prices. So the emphasis had been on added value products such as playing cards, paper plates for fast food service, and speciality papers with various coatings and glazes. As with Grand Union, the company also turned to a chain of speciality do-it-yourself shops. However, even though sales of $1.2 billion pushed Diamond International into the middle ranks of the *Fortune 500*, profits remained elusive while management continued to seek new acquisitions that might break the cycle.

It was Ira Harris of Salomon Brothers, then one of the leading investment bankers in America, who brought Diamond to Goldsmith. He had first suggested Goldsmith buy Columbia, but Diamond was a real proposition. 'We saw on the balance sheet that they owned 1.6m acres of land that was carried on the books at £27m,' says John Tigrett, who was to play a role in the early American acquisitions. 'We thought it was a mistake and asked Salomon to check, but they came back and said no mistake. Diamond had bought the land before 1900 and never had revalued it. I said to Jimmy, "This is like those dairies at Bovril – start buying that stock".' At first, Goldsmith responded with no more than a toehold investment of $15m that netted him less than the 5 per cent of Diamond's shares that require disclosure under US securities regulations. But in January 1979 he served notice on Diamond, and on Wall Street generally, that he had taken a stake in the company. Given what was happening in Europe at the time and the problems of Grand Union, outsiders could be excused for dismissing the purchase as a long-term investment that probably wasn't very smart.

Matters might have rested there if the Diamond chairman, William Koslo, had not continued with his acquisition policy by offering $100m for another Maine wood products company, Brooks-Scanlon Inc. This was on top of $400m in so-called productivity improvements which had failed to produce any real profits gains. Koslo's merger proposal angered Jimmy who had grown increasingly frustrated with Diamond's direction. It seemed to him that the Brooks-Scanlon bid was something more than a bad investment play. Since it would be financed by a large issue of 2.6m new shares, he suspected the underlying purpose was to dilute his modest holdings to insignificance. However, it would seem that Koslo's motives included a mix of both guile and genuine error.

The Brooks-Scanlon bid came only six months after the second OPEC oil price shock, and the US economy was about to plunge into its most painful round of recession and inflation. Japan's yen would begin a spectacular downward plunge and the export-dependent economies of Latin America and other Third World nations would be very nearly crushed. The old certainty that investments in raw resources would automatically offset inflationary price rises was no longer true; indeed, the opposite now applied and raw timberland holdings were among the hardest hit.

Goldsmith spelled out his objection to the Brooks-Scanlon deal:

Because they were buying the business on under-valued shares – their own paper – they were paying an over-valued price, which made it twice as bad. I thought it was, at least to some extent, designed to dilute our holding. I had to interpret it as an aggressive act. I need a stimulant before I can get going. When they came up with this load of nonsense about Brooks-Scanlon, that really triggered the fight.

Late in April 1980, Goldsmith offered to buy a 'substantial portion of Diamond stock at a significant premium' via Cavenham Holdings. Bowman Gray III, a Cavenham vice president, explained to Koslo in a letter that this was because Diamond had ignored his opposition to the Brooks-Scanlon merger. Yet there was more to it than that. Once again, Goldsmith was betting on his gift for looking beyond the economic conditions of the moment and spotting a change in market direction.

On 9 May 1980, Goldsmith followed up the Gray letter with another tactical gambit: a public offer of $45 for each Diamond share provided the shareholders rejected the Brooks-Scanlon deal, or at least postponed it. However, if the deal went through, Goldsmith's offer would only be $40 a share. In all, Goldsmith sought 4.5m shares which would boost his holding, which he had increased to nearly 6%, to roughly 35 per cent, depending on the number of shares tendered.

The offer caught Wall Street's still small arbitrage community by surprise and the rush pushed Diamond's share price from $32.65 to $38.20 in the first fortnight of May. Goldsmith followed that attack with another. He dispatched lawyers to the state of Delaware, where most companies are incorporated and where the state and the federal government maintain separate courts that deal only with complex financial questions. Delaware's court rulings on the raging takeover battle strategies that would develop in the decade of the Eighties were often used as laboratory proofs by the courts of the other 49 states as well. Cavenham sought to win a court injunction to block Diamond from having its annual general meeting on 14 May. Goldsmith would lose this as would Koslo when he countersued to block Cavenham's 'grossly inadequate offer' from going forward.

Diamond's other large-block shareholders gave neither side a clear victory at the shareholders' meeting. The final decision would have to depend on the proxies of smaller investors who had to mail in their choice between management and Goldsmith. But by 29 May, the *Wall Street Journal* reported that while it appeared that Koslo had won the necessary 51 per cent support, it was too close to call and the real outcome would be delayed until the Diamond shareholders reconvened their meeting in Bangor, Maine, on 5 June. The *Journal* article also noted that Goldsmith's dual offer was set to expire on 12 June, so time was slipping away.

Although Goldsmith was hardly a stranger to the USA or to Wall Street by this point, the novelty of his bid and the heated anger that Koslo had generated in response suddenly made the challenger a celebrity. Who was he? Where did he get his money? Indeed, did he have any? In some areas, Goldsmith's reputation had already crossed the Atlantic; *Private Eye* has a certain readership among New York and Washington journalists, and there are enough US-based British correspondents to pass on the word. The *Wall Street Journal* set out to answer the nagging question: does Goldsmith have the money? To its own surprise, it found that Générale Occidentale was 'a privately held company in France that had revenue in the year ended March 30 estimated at the current equivalent of $6 billion', which made it more than four times as big as Diamond. The *Journal* noted the controversy over Goldsmith's control of the company, and ended by concluding that: 'GO's controlling ownership is anchored in France through a company called Trocadero Participations, of which Sir James is president and in which he holds a 30 per cent stake.'

Koslo and Diamond suspected that if they dug deep enough they would find enough in Jimmy's background to expose him. Koslo hired a firm of private detectives which picked up the *Private Eye* material, but there was nothing in any of that which could be used to advantage. Goldsmith had a complex private life – they didn't know about Laure – but so what?

Private Eye was convinced – and probably remains convinced to this day – that there was something deeply rotten about Jimmy Goldsmith, that his business was at best suspect and at worst crooked. Despite years of investigation, nothing was proven. At this very moment Charles Raw was devoting large quantities of *Sunday Times* resources to preparing the most in-depth study of Goldsmith's business dealings yet; the paper, however, was on strike and when Rupert Murdoch bought it in 1981 the articles were quietly shelved, deemed to be unpublishable. Koslo's private detectives would not be the only ones to probe Jimmy's past either: other targets would hire other firms, who in turn raked over the voluminous material in Goldsmith's past. Nothing was ever found that could be usefully turned against him.

Jimmy had cared deeply when *Private Eye* began its campaign, basically because he saw it as a gross intrusion into his personal privacy. But, once the details of his two families had been revealed, he never worried again. He certainly didn't care about Koslo's detectives, regarding their probings as almost standard procedure in the takeover game. He had used detectives often enough. He took the view he had nothing to be ashamed of. People could look all they wanted.

A disappointed Koslo, whose hopes must have been raised when he first heard the rumours, soon came to the same conclusion and sued for peace. He telephoned Générale Occidentale's Paris office and asked for a meeting. On Friday, 6 June, Koslo and Goldsmith met at the latter's suite in the Carlyle hotel in New York and worked out a truce.

Goldsmith would hold 25 per cent of Diamond, and in return for a 'standstill' agreement not to raise it above 40 per cent of the company for five years, he also won the right to appoint three directors – himself, Franklin and Bowman Gray – to Diamond's board. Goldsmith also agreed to raise his offer to $42 a share even if the Brooks-Scanlon deal went through. Both sides would drop all litigation.

These were early days in the takeover era, and Wall Street's arbitrageurs mistakenly viewed the agreement as a solid rebuke for the foreign interloper, although it was nothing of the kind.

Diamond's shares, which had been bid up to $50 in anticipation of an old-fashioned proxy fight to the finish, plunged to $38.25. Goldsmith in fact was enjoying himself, sensing time and tide were with him. He was feeling the same great surge of optimism that affected him a decade before when he sensed the market upswing which sent him on a buying spree that had taken in Bovril and Allied Suppliers. He was utterly at home among the best investment bankers and corporate lawyers that America had, often way ahead of them in his tactical thinking. Even at this stage, Koslo had no serious inkling that the battle was already lost. Goldsmith was playing it long, determined that he would win his first major takeover battle in the US which he felt was just as important for his reputation as the Bovril bid had been in Britain. Lose this one and he would always be seen as a loser.

Goldsmith still went ahead with his offer for 4.5m shares at $42, while Koslo continued with his plans for the Brooks-Scanlon merger, which would involve issuing new stock. If Goldsmith got all the 4.5m shares he was tendering for, his holding would rise to 41 per cent. But the new shares issued by Diamond would dilute that again to 34 per cent. In the event, he got 2.5m acceptances – giving him 24 per cent of Diamond. Even that cost him $105m, but, to the market's surprise, Goldsmith seemed to be able to raise whatever sums he needed and word quickly spread that Citibank's London branch, plus the two Euro-powers, Crédit Lyonnais and Crédit Suisse, were backing his Diamond pursuit. In fact, Cavenham was flush with cash after its food manufacturing sales in Europe.

Goldsmith, like many successful men, has great confidence in his own personal charm, believing that once he shakes someone by the hand, meets him face to face, they will have a different opinion of him to the image nurtured by the press, opposition lawyers and advisers. To Koslo he had been presented as an ogre, an asset-stripper and a too-clever financier, instead of the serious long-term businessman he always saw himself to be. For his part, he developed a somewhat different opinion of Koslo as he watched him in action in the boardroom, and by September 1980, Goldsmith felt secure enough to make his own peace gesture by inviting Koslo to cross over and join the board of Cavenham. The personal *rapprochement* helped cool the antagonism between the two companies. The Diamond situation rested there for another fifteen months, while Goldsmith concentrated on Grand Union and on Basic. Then suddenly Diamond came to life again when, out of the blue, Conley Brooks, the former head of Brooks-Scanlon, offered Goldsmith 1.6m Diamond shares in September 1981 at the 1980 price of $42 a share; this in contrast to the current $29 a share price on the New York Stock Exchange.

What had happened in the intervening twelve months was one of the worst postwar recessions on record with the forest products industry particularly hard-hit. Diamond had been able to maintain sales turnover of $1.28 billion in 1979 and 1980 although profits had slid from $62m to $41m during that same period. Securities analysts on Wall Street were worried that 1981 would see a further plunge in sales and, worse, a lapse into loss unless something were done right away. Anyone willing to pay last year's price for the company must have a screw loose.

Goldsmith viewed Diamond still as a company that was terribly managed but possessed grossly undervalued assets and component operations that could be sold off to advantage. With the Brooks family shares under his belt he owned 5.5m of the 13.7m Diamond shares, about 40 per cent, and Koslo saw the writing on the wall.

In mid-October Générale Occidentale notified the Securities and Exchange Commission that it was taking a more active interest in Diamond's affairs. By 5 November, Koslo had agreed to talks with Goldsmith toward a takeover of Diamond and the New York Stock Exchange routinely suspended the shares.

Goldsmith's first offer of $21 in cash and $21 in debentures was later raised to a $44.50 all-cash offer for the 7m shares remaining.

Once again, Goldsmith injected funds of his own plus solid loan backing from Citibank and other major international banks. The remaining 60 per cent of Diamond would cost $378m with one-third coming from Générale Occidentale. In all, Cavenham had to raise $660m at a time when the US prime bank rate was trending toward 20 per cent for far more favoured customers. It meant more than $180m in debt service obligations for Goldsmith to own a company that was by now losing money.

This then was the extent of Goldsmith's faith in the prospect of a sudden flood-tide of prosperity sweeping back into America. In his own words, he 'bet double or quits for the last time. If my view was wrong, even by a year, I was blown away, bye-bye.'

By the time of the Diamond bid, Goldsmith's private life had changed considerably. In July 1980 he resigned as chairman of Cavenham in Britain, explaining, 'As I am domiciled in France, it is wisest that I should concentrate my efforts on my job as chairman of Générale Occidentale.' It was an odd statement, since he had been domiciled in France most of his life. It was actually a formal recognition that he was quitting Britain.

He set John Aspinall up in a second club, which opened in the elegant premises of the old Curzon House in Curzon Street; his investment was modest, some $625,000 in 1978, done through General Oriental, but when Aspinall floated it on the stock market, Goldsmith found he had 40 per cent of a company valued at £60m. He was seeing more of Laure, less of Ginette, and living less and less in Ormeley Lodge. On 28 October 1980 he became a father yet again, when Annabel, at the age of 45, gave birth to a son, Benjamin. It was the sixth child for each of them.

Goldsmith's energy during this period was extraordinary. He now had three women in his life, each of them fully aware of the others, but each of them – not without reservations or complaints – prepared to accept the role he set for her. He was deeply involved in *Now!* and *L'Express*, he was battling with the Guatemalan government and with Elf Aquitaine, trying to revitalise, for the second time, the Grand Union chain, take over Diamond, run his businesses in France, and more. In many ways this was probably his peak period, the time when everything came together, when he seemed to be able to take on anything and anybody. Substantial traces remained of the paranoia which had gripped him at the time of the *Private Eye* affair, but he had shaken off the worst of that mood, and was relieved to be quit of Britain even though the political climate was already changing under the new Conservative government.

In France a presidential election loomed in April 1981, and it began to look as if François Mitterand would win. 'Jimmy became convinced that if Mitterand won, it would only be a matter of time before the Russian tanks started rolling down the Champs Elysées,' said Olivier Todd.

'The socialists who came into France in 1981 are nothing to do with the socialists who are there today,' Goldsmith explained later. 'They were a radical bunch and their ideas were the sort of ideas that had come in with the most rabid of the socialists at that time. They only stayed that way for a few years and then they learned better and became social democrats.' Nevertheless, his analysis made him look westward where the land was bright.

But there were other reasons. Laure had gone to New York to live and work, and she had become the most important person in his life. Grand Union was at a particularly exciting stage, and needed more of his time – and he loved it. He wanted the freedom to do what excited him, which was to get in on the takeover game just beginning in America, and translate the concept he had for Grand Union into a profitable reality.

Well before the French elections, Goldsmith made up his mind to leave France, although he told only very few people. At the end of November 1980, just five weeks after her son was born, Annabel went to stay with him in New York. He had been in London for Benjamin's birth, pacing his office, ringing every few minutes, finally receiving the news late in the evening at Aspinall's new club where he had gone to wait. But shortly afterwards, he set off on his travels again.

Annabel was aware that Laure was around, but Goldsmith was careful not to embarrass her. On their first night together in New York, he took her to dinner to tell her something very serious.

He had, he began, decided to move the emphasis of his business to the US. Under US immigration and tax laws, he could only stay there for 122 days a year, but he would be spending more time in Mexico, Guatemala and other countries in Central America. He was leaving Europe.

Where did that leave her, and the children? Annabel wanted to know.

Goldsmith was absolutely clear on that. 'You've got to make up your mind,' he told her. 'I feel very, very anti-Britain, and I'm not going to have anything to do with it again. It's knocked me about too much. So if you want to live a proper married life, you must up and take the children and move to America, because this is where I'm going to live.'

Annabel, normally the most resilient of people, burst into tears and cried all through dinner, and most of that night. Laure, in a way, she understood – Annabel had been in that same position 18 years before. But if she moved, Annabel would have to take the children out of school. Jemima was seven and Zacharias a year younger, and she preferred that they went to school in England. She would also have to sell her beloved Ormeley Lodge, leave her family, her older children by Mark, her sister and her sister-in-law, to whom she was very close and who lived in a small flat over the stables at Ormeley. She thought of herself as very English, with deep roots, and didn't much care for the US. Even if she did make the huge effort and uproot, how would it work out? She had always felt sorry for Ginette, and could not stand the thought of finding herself in a similar position.

In the morning she told him she would not move. She would stay in Richmond, create her own life there; she would welcome him when he did visit London, continue as his wife whenever he wanted her to, and join him for holidays, but essentially she would adjust to living without him.

When she boarded the plane to fly home, she knew her life had fundamentally changed. In the years ahead she would sometimes wonder if she should have gone to America at that point, but equally often concluded she had made the right decision. She did not belong in the new world that Jimmy was building for himself, and would not have been happy there.

Goldsmith, however, was buoyant. He was accelerating the plans to move not just himself but his capital and his companies out of Europe. But it would not be an uncontroversial exit.

In the opening weeks of 1981 it was clear that the presidency of Valery Giscard d'Estaing was in trouble, his political prestige damaged by scandals, the mysterious deaths of three veteran cabinet ministers, deepening rifts in the government coalition and an economy which was in recession. *L'Express'* own opinion polls put Mitterand well ahead. A few weeks later, *L'Express* enraged Goldsmith by publishing an issue with a cover showing Giscard looking old and tired, staring disconsolately at a television screen out of which a much younger and more vigorous Mitterand stared back. Ironically, *Now!* had done something similar earlier in the year with an article he saw as antagonistic to Giscard, and Goldsmith had demanded the whole issue be pulped (he compromised by stopping the French sales that week).

The cover had been prepared innocently enough by *L'Express'* graphics people, Mitterand only being added at the last moment when it was known the two men would have a debate. But there was a clear editorial message: Giscard is finished, so vote for this thrusting young (at least he appeared young) socialist. It was too much for Goldsmith, who waited until the election was over and Mitterand had won before taking his private plane from London to Le Bourget. He then sent for Olivier Todd, brandished the magazine cover at him, and told him he was fired. The editor, Jean François Revel, resigned the next day, and the rest of the staff went into instant revolt. Goldsmith, more angry than perturbed, decided to face them.

He had given considerable thought to the method of controlling an antagonistic meeting since he had found himself at the wrong end of one a few months before. He had been invited to address the annual dinner of a large publishing group, Haymarket Press, in London and agreed, knowing the advertising industry would be there and *Now!* needed advertising.

I got booed and heckled, and that had never happened to me before. I didn't know how to handle it so I plodded on with my speech – about Europe or something – and reached the end and finally sat down. And for days afterwards, I thought, how could I have controlled that? What should I have done? And I worked it out in my mind, you know what the French call *l'ésprit d'escaliers*, as you walk down the stairs you think all the way down what you should have done. I re-enacted it in my mind and I realised exactly what I should have done. But thank God it happened, because the next time it happened was with the *L'Express* people. And when they started heckling I had no problem at all.

He was blunt and to the point that day. They had a simple choice, he told them: accept him in his new role as editor-in-chief or resign. If there was any trouble, he would shut the magazine. There was uproar in the French press and among the chattering classes in Paris, particularly as it was still less than a week since the election of the new socialist government. Todd described Goldsmith as 'an ultra-eccentric' in the Socialist daily *Le Matin*, and accused him of smashing what was, for him, 'only a plaything, the only fragment of a press empire he could conquer'. Goldsmith, however, didn't care. Twenty journalists left, and he appointed a new editor, Yves Cuau, who steered the magazine back from crisis. (Todd, oddly enough, was later far from bitter, reckoning Goldsmith was well within his rights, and felt the compensation was generous.)

Despite the row, *L'Express* remained one of the few assets Goldsmith would keep in France (the other was the Laurent restaurant which he still owns). Selling it, he says now, would have been 'an act of betrayal for the ideas that I tried to support and those I had supported'. But he would sell everything else, even Gilberte Beaux's precious private bank.

Gilberte was furious. They had often fought in the years they had been together, but this was different. 'First of all, I built the bank from nothing,' she says, 'to what was considered a very good and solid French bank. I did not want to make it too large, but kept it to more or less one thousand customers. And they were mostly companies. We had very good merchant banking activities, and a commercial department, and we also had a very good money centre. We were really among the best.'

'Yes,' she adds, 'I regretted the sale of the bank.'

Jimmy, says Beaux, had never liked banks in the first place. 'That's for sure. He is anything but a banker. He will tell you what he likes is investment banks, but when you are a banker you need also to have some commercial banking activities, trade activities and so on. And that is what we are doing.'

The French bank had never made any money – Goldsmith argued that commercial banks never do, since they take a risk of £100 just to make £1 profit ('too difficult for me, or most others, as we see every day') – but it had been invaluable for opening contacts, providing finance and services, and generally giving the Paris operation a heart that it otherwise lacked. The new government had drawn up a list of banks it intended to nationalise but although the Banque Occidentale's deposits were over $350m, twice the minimum set for nationalisation, it was not on the list. This was probably explained by the fact that the government knew about Goldsmith's negotiations with Crédit Lyonnais, which already owned a 22 per cent stake, and was the intended buyer. The price was a single French franc, but Crédit Lyonnais took on all the liabilities.

Suddenly Goldsmith was free, and loving it.

I was forty-seven, and discovered this wonderfully exciting new world. I remember an absolutely fantastic sense of excitement. I was starting with someone I was very fond of and arriving in New York to begin with the immense luxury of total anonymity . . . There was free enterprise, conservatives in power, and it was a new world to conquer.

For the first time in his life he went out on the street without a jacket and tie.

The first Reagan administration was the most exciting time because the first four years Reagan was president – he was a flag more than a president – he was the symbol for a lot of things that I believed were absolutely right and he was surrounded by fervent, radical, devoted people who believed in the same things. And those first four years for me were incredible. America is a country that is so adapted to newcomers and immediately I was absorbed by them. I loved it, it was one of the really good moments.

24

A Half Billion Profit

Fortune magazine, not given to hyperbole, stated that, in complexity and risk, the Diamond deal ranked 'as one of the financial events of the 1980s'. It also ranked as one of the most profitable: *Fortune* estimated that by the time he had finished with it, Jimmy made a profit of $500m. If Cavenham had remained a public company in Britain, a large chunk of that would have gone to his British and French shareholders, with a dramatic impact on the share price. But because of the buy-in, most of it now went directly to Goldsmith himself.

Goldsmith borrowed $660m on which he was paying interest at between 16 and 18 per cent. That meant interest payments running at $120m to $130m a year. Diamond's net income in 1980 had been only one-third of that – $40.6m – and in 1981 it was actually losing money, so in effect he was having to find some $180m a year just to keep it going. Grand Union, too, was losing money, and the fight with Elf in Guatemala, where his investment was now up to $90m, seemed to have no end.

Ambroise Roux, gazing at these operations in astonishment from the comfort of his chair at CGE, would comment that 'Jimmy was taking risks that were practically the dimension of the empire', but that was understatement. In ten years since the Bovril deal, Goldsmith had transformed himself from near-failure to hugely successful businessman.

'When he proposed to buy out the last 60 per cent of Diamond in December 1981,' wrote *Fortune* later, 'Goldsmith was a lonely leveraged bull pawing the ground for a stock market rally. He needed a sharp run up in stock market values if he was to sell off Diamond's divisions at a profit.'

Goldsmith probably worried less than anyone around him about the risk involved. All his life he had been a contra-theorist, betting against the general view. He would argue that doing what he does – and will probably continue doing for the rest of his life – actually requires less courage than doing the same as everyone else. 'If everybody agrees that you should increase capacity in ball bearings, for example, you can be absolutely sure that there's going to be a glut of ball bearings, and you'll end up losing money.' He himself, he says, never invested even in the stock market without first ringing half a dozen 'experts' and discovering whether they agreed with each other. 'When 90 per cent of people are thinking the same thing, you can be certain that if you do exactly the opposite you'll make a fortune.' This theory is not unique to Goldsmith: Joe Kennedy made a fortune in the crash of 1929 simply by selling when everyone else, including his shoeshine boy, was buying. 'Structurally if you can find unanimity and do the opposite you can be certain to be successful,' is how Goldsmith defines his personal market philosophy.

But having a theory and backing it with everything you possess are two different matters. Goldsmith believed in this particular deal to the point where he did not even want to bring in partners, or hedge in any way. He did his sums meticulously, researched Diamond until he almost knew every tree it owned, and Citibank had raised the money for him. After that everything rested on what happened to the markets.

He could, and did, still raise money from his existing operations – not to help pay for Diamond but to pay for the investment needed for Grand Union. The Allied Suppliers chain in Britain had been expanded and improved, and had emerged from the recession in Britain in good shape. Against the 1,650 grocery shops and supermarkets he had paid £86.3m for a decade ago, there were now only 900 shops, 128 of them now operating as modern Presto supermarkets. All Goldsmith's retailing interest had switched to the US and Grand Union, so it made sense in his current mood to switch his resources from one country to the other. Hambros sought a buyer for Allied, and found one in one of Britain's retailers of the day, James Gulliver, then building up a group which five years later would set in motion the great Guinness scandal by making Britain's biggest bid yet, £2.7 billion for the Distillers group. Gulliver paid £101m for Allied, the proceeds of which didn't cover the £120m a year Goldsmith was now investing in Grand Union.

With that sale, Goldsmith's last major link with Britain was gone. He still had a house, a wife and a family, plus a 40 per cent stake in Aspinall's casino. But he was now completely committed to the US financially and emotionally, his empire and fortune were on the line. Raising the money to pay for the rest of Diamond was a long, arduous and delicate affair, which he was forced to intersperse with flights to Guatemala City, or back to Paris as the battle with Elf hotted up.

Goldsmith had originally gone to Drexel Burnham Lambert because Baron Leon Lambert was a distant relation, another of the Frankfurt Jews who had popped up somewhere in the banking world. The original firm of Drexel was a genteel, old-fashioned Wall Street investment house which merged in 1973 with the brash bucketshop Burnham and Company. Under the leadership of Fred Joseph, it began to emerge as a major force in the corporate finance field in the late 1970s. In 1976 it merged again, this time with William D. Witter, a research boutique in which Bruxelles Lambert, headed by Goldsmith's relative Lambert, was a shareholder. In the late 1970s Joseph discovered he had a 'bright guy down on the trading floor doing deep-discount bonds'. He turned out to be the now notorious Michael Milken. 'Deep-discount' bonds is simply another name for 'junk' bonds, but they were only 'junk' in the sense that they were low-rated by the markets. In the capital markets of America, companies with low ratings found it difficult to raise money, and it was Milken who developed a new financial instrument, offering them long-term debt with few restrictions but at a very high interest rate. The high-yield, or junk bond, was, as Drexel would later say, 'a financial instrument whose time has come'. During the 1980s Milken and Drexel became the most powerful force in the takeover game, rivalled only by Ivan Boesky whose business was to take positions in takeover stocks. Milken and Boesky often operated together, sometimes illegally, to determine the course of a takeover bid, Milken so that he could finance it with his high-yielding bonds, Boesky so he could make a profit on the shares. Both made enormous fortunes, Milken earning over $500m in salary and performance fees in 1986. Both ended their careers in jail.

Drexel sought close links with all the major players in the takeover game. In March 1982, as it was putting together the financing for his Diamond bid, Goldsmith was asked to talk at one of its big conferences to which Drexel invited most of the big fund managers in America. Goldsmith was happy to accept, knowing that these were the very people he would need to support him. The Dow Jones was just coming off the bottom of 700 at the time, and Goldsmith told the meeting of his enormous confidence in its continued rise. It would go all the way to between 2,000 and 3,000, he forecast. 'Everybody looked at each other as though I was a complete lunatic,' he said later.

Drexel was enthusiastically behind him, but finding the money was not easy. There was the problem of how properly to value the Diamond timberlands in the depths of a bear market in raw materials resources. There was no market and no income. The banks would not accept the forests as collateral for any amount.

It was Drexel's Chris Anderson who found a way to establish a value, and so be able to borrow from the banks. The Travellers Insurance company, for a fee of $12.5m, agreed to pay him $250m for them, if and when he ever got control of them, and if he wanted to sell (which he didn't – at least not at that price). Goldsmith had now established a minimum value for the forest lands, and the deal became bankable – and on fine terms. He was able to borrow from Citibank at a rate reflecting the credit rating of Travellers.

The Diamond board helped matters along by selling its packaging outfit to one of Ireland's leading entrepreneurs, Michael Smurfit, for $80m and its playing card operations for another $45m. Some $44m of that was used to reduce Diamond's corporate debt, making it, from the point of view of the banks, a more attractive proposition.

Thus assured, Goldsmith's team of banks, assembled by Drexel and Goldsmith, came up with $440m out of the $660m he needed – then hung on like grim death as a new crisis developed. The stock market boom did arrive as Goldsmith had forecast, right after the summer holidays. By Labour Day in September 1982, the Dow Jones 30-share industrial composite was rapidly climbing back towards 1,000 and beyond. Would Diamond's shareholders suddenly regain their courage and renege on the deal?

As it turned out the shareholders had greater faith in Goldsmith's ability to put money in their pocket than in Wall Street's. On 1 November Bill Koslo recommended the remaining shareholders to accept the Goldsmith offer, and at the annual general meeting of Diamond on 1 December, 89.6 per cent of the shares, including Goldsmith's own holdings, were voted in favour of the merger. He had made it.

What happened next is largely forgotten or confused or lumped in with the rest of the mad takeover Decade of Greed, as the Eighties is now called. Quite wrongly, Goldsmith is put in the class of greenmailers such as Saul Steinberg, T. Boone Pickens and Carl Icahn (all major clients of Drexel's) who alternated between making formal takeover offers for conglomerates and buying just enough shares to be paid off by frightened managements to go away.

This variation of the old asset-stripping game drew an unexpected but understandable outcry from shareholders who watched the raiders pirate huge sums of wealth from their long-term shareholdings. The protestations expanded and became political as cities and states saw their traditional industrial base being destroyed and jobs being lost because the assets that remained to plundered companies could no longer function economically.

No less an authority than *Fortune* magazine charted the history of some of the Diamond International properties that Goldsmith sold off to pay off his debts. Those components sold off, the magazine noted, 'not only survived but flourished without conglomerate oversight'.

'When you take over a company you're viewed with a great deal of suspicion,' said Roland Franklin at the time. 'But when you get out to the plants in the field, you're hailed as a hero. It's like going to a pet shop and opening the bird cages and letting out the birds. People – managers, workers, everybody – have waited to be released.' A case in point was United States Playing Card Company, which Goldsmith sold to its management in 1983. Diamond had used the card company as a cash cow, milking it and reinvesting nothing for a dozen years. The new management-owners, however, began to raise new capital to invest in an automated production line and to take over other competitors in Europe and America. The company worked out a new labour union pact and moved operations to the lower-cost locale of Nevada. The result: the company's $3.5m loss in 1985 had turned into a $700,000 profit in 1986.

The *Fortune* survey had other proofs. William Simon, the former US Treasury Secretary and founder of the Wesray investment group, bought Diamond's Heekin Can company almost before the takeover deal with Goldsmith was completed in 1982. It quickly boosted sales by 40 per cent and profits by 50 per cent, in part by exchanging fat salary contracts for equity interests for its managers. Diamond Fiber, an egg carton maker which was slated to be closed down by the parent, also was sold to its existing management team who cut out three layers of bureaucracy, reduced the work force of 300 by 25 and revived both sales and profits in a single year.

In all, Goldsmith sold off six of Diamond's divisions and raised more than $334m of the $440m he owed directly to the banks. By the end of 1983, he had sold another three divisions for a further $353m – $149m from James River Corp. for the pulp and paper business and $129m for the retail lumber and do-it-yourself stores.

With the sale of Allied Suppliers in Britain, Goldsmith was free of cash worries again. Not only had he paid off the $440m he had borrowed from the banks, but he had also liquidated Diamond's own $162m residue of debts.

Now Goldsmith was ready to demonstrate to cynical Wall Street eyes what observers from Paris and London had learned years earlier: he was not merely a liquidator and asset-stripper, but could provide competent management for the properties he ended up keeping after a takeover and he could make them grow.

He had no intention of taking the $250m offer from Travellers for the timberlands: they were worth far more. As he had done with Grand Union, he set to work managing them, building new sawmills, using state-of-the-art computerised machinery, which would dramatically increase productivity and cut costs. Managing timberlands is actually a highly skilled task, involving delicate judgements concerning the level of harvest so that new growth and the 'cut' roughly balance. There must be careful management of the age profile of the trees so that they do not all mature at the same time, and a considerable knowledge of the market-place, particularly new markets such as Japan which demanded different quality and sizes of lumber to the home market.

In the summer of 1983, when he had barely embarked on his investment programme, timber analysts were already reckoning his forests were worth $723m. In other words, if he repaid everything he had borrowed, Goldsmith's profit was running at $500m.

He had no intention of selling. Once again, his acute sense of timing was spot on. By the early days of 1984 several coincidental events had occurred to transform the US economic scene. Reagan was well into his first term and had deftly steered through a demoralised Democratic-controlled Congress a series of laws that freed up billions of dollars in capital and changed the way corporations viewed and treated their capital assets.

The most immediate impact was felt from the 1981 Economic Recovery Tax Act, which was designed to spur economic growth by allowing companies to take speeded-up depreciation. An unintended side effect of the law was that it made the cash flow grow faster than reported earnings. But this growth was not reflected in stock prices and the consequence was that corporate assets in the early 1980s began to look more attractive than earnings prospects. Indeed, it was just a short step from there to the realisation that fast-growing corporate assets could be more easily collateralised by lenders who financed takeover credit lines.

Then too, the Reagan administration, by regulation and by policy directive, not only deregulated the US banking industry from its old lending constraint, but also signalled a much more relaxed anti-monopoly stance than any recent presidency had followed. 'Deregulation' was an article of Reaganomic faith. The American economy needed a good shaking up.

The conglomerations of widely different corporate enterprises that marked the 1960s had actually been the third in a series of takeover-merger waves that had transformed US industry. The first, at the turn of the century, had seen the formation of the huge monopolies and trusts such as US Steel and Standard Oil. The second, marked by the Roaring Twenties, had seen the big manufacturing groups like General Motors buy up suppliers – the cry then had been 'vertical integration'. The sixties brought 'synergy' and the ability to offset the slowing of one part of the business cycle with growth in another. In reality, companies 30 years ago merely sought to bury their gains from the stock price boom of that decade by buying other companies, rather than passing those profits on to the shareholders.

Now came the fourth wave of mergers as sharp-eyed financiers began to pry those assets apart to liquidate them. A reason not acknowledged at the time was that those assets had become vastly more valuable if only because of a decade of hyperinflation which had made fixed capital goods worth more and the earnings from profitable operations harder to come by. With share prices themselves suffering from an even greater undervaluing than the earnings, small wonder that corporate America suddenly became one big asset play.

By 1984 this combination of forces exploded. Not only were banks scrambling to lend money, but there were new competitors in the lending market: like Drexel, where Milken invented what became known as the 'blind pool'. He would raise a billion dollars for a company, then ring up and say, 'Here's a billion dollars: let us help you buy a company'. Then there were the investment hustlers like Morgan Stanley, First Boston, and later, spin-offs of the original players who went on to form firms like Kohlberg, Kravis & Roberts and Wasserstein, Perella.

For Goldsmith, the timing was perfect. Ira Harris of Salomon Brothers in Chicago and John Tigrett had convinced him that if he could multiply his raw timber land holdings from Diamond's 1.6m acres to 10m acres, he could be a major market force, perhaps even the dominant force, in a crucial industrial raw ingredient. Home building, even today, remains one of the three key manufacturing pillars – along with machine tools and motor cars – that underpin the American economy. In addition to lumber for homes and other construction, Americans consume more paper products for newsprint, packaging, and other uses than anyone in the world.

The Diamond deal made Goldsmith something of a celebrity. On Wall Street, he was now put among the major players who had the flair and the backing to take over large chunks of corporate USA. On 8 March 1985 the *New York Times* ran an editorial on the raiders which ran: 'T. Boone Pickens ... Carl Icahn ... Saul Steinberg ... Irwin Jacobs ... Sir James Goldsmith. Their names are spoken with a shudder in boardrooms from Pittsburgh to Bartlesville. They are the buccaneers of capitalism, making millions by taking over, or just threatening to take over, America's largest corporations.'

Goldsmith was in his element, developing the theme which he and Slater had argued for years in Britain but for which there was a far more receptive audience in America. Corporations, according to Goldsmith, belonged to shareholders, not managements who 'believe that the business that employs them has become an institution and they are the trustees of that institution'. Some managements, he said in an article in the *Wall Street Journal*, 'believe they have developed proprietorial rights. Shareholders then become no more than an inconvenience.' Over the next half dozen years, Goldsmith developed his intellectual case in favour of the takeover bid, particularly for what he called 'the failed conglomerates – the debris of the 1960s'. The role of takeovers through the market place, he insisted, 'should not be to change satisfactory companies. It is to improve unsatisfactory companies and to allow healthy companies to grow strategically by acquisitions.' In this comparatively early stage of the takeover boom, he received a sympathetic enough reception.

He still remembers an occasion when he flew in to Kennedy Airport. It was the day after Christmas, which he had spent in Ormeley Lodge, and he was now returning to Laure (having spent a few days with Ginette in Paris). The customs man stopped him. 'Are you the fellow that made $500 million on that Diamond deal?' When Goldsmith confessed he was, the man insisted on shaking his hand warmly, exclaiming, 'Any guy that can do that has to be something.' He ended up surrounded by half the customs men, all of whom wanted to press the flesh. It is perhaps a trivial incident, but for Goldsmith it epitomised the difference in attitude between London and New York. 'I had become something like a star football-player.'

By that stage he also had new targets in his sights. The first candidate, which was brought to him by Aymery Langlois-Meurinne of Paribas' New York subsidiary A. G. Becker, was St Regis Corporation. It was a $2.8 billion sales timber company that had strayed into oil pipelines and insurance holdings with the result that its profits stagnated. But it owned 3.2m acres of timberland that it carried on its books at $223m, a fraction of their worth. For this venture, Goldsmith decided to bring in some outsiders to help finance the deal. All his life he seemed to be betting 'double or quits', and with Diamond he reckoned he had done it for the last time. The figures were getting bigger, the competition getting tougher, and the defences more difficult to crack as lawyers invented ever more ingenious schemes to block the raiders. With capital pooled by Jacob Rothschild, Kerry Packer and Gianni Agnelli, in February 1984 Goldsmith formally announced he had acquired slightly more than three million St Regis shares – about 8.6 per cent of the total – 'for investment purposes'.

Before Goldsmith's disclosure, St Regis shares had been trading around the $33.5 to $38 range, but now the arbitrageurs, Wall Street dealers led by Ivan Boesky who bet on takeover stocks, smelled the profits of a takeover battle and the price rose as high as $40.12 during the buy-up that ended on 14 February. The arbitrageur community jumped on the bandwagon and St Regis management, predictably, went into its repel-boarders mode.

The next day Goldsmith met the St Regis chairman, William R. Haselton, and found him very nervous. 'They were panicking all over the place. I couldn't understand it. I remember saying to myself, "Why are these fellows so scared? They've got a big company."' Haselton wanted to deal, and Goldsmith told him: 'OK, I'll do a deal with you. I'll buy 25 per cent of the company. I'll come on the board and I'll stay with you. We'll build this company into a major business.'

The terms hammered out during the two-hour meeting were simplicity itself. Goldsmith would invest enough capital ($300m) to hold 25 per cent of St Regis, and would obtain a 'pocket veto' on any new investment.

'I had one problem,' said Goldsmith later. 'They had a deputy chairman who had caught the disease. He didn't like the core business of St Regis. He wanted to build a financial conglomerate and that was the last thing in the world St Regis was able to manage.'

St Regis was a fine old paper and forest products company, which, in Goldsmith's view, if it had concentrated on that business could have been a great success. 'But when it got into financial services and insurance companies it was a babe in arms; it was pathetic.'

He agreed to back the management, but for any transaction of an exceptional kind – of $100m or more – he insisted on unanimous approval of the board or a shareholder vote. 'The reason was obvious: I did not want to be on a roller-coaster where the management wanted to make St Regis into a conglomerate. This deputy chairman, who really thought of himself as the chairman-in-waiting, disagreed and the talks fell apart.'

This led to counter-offers by both sides to buy the other out. Goldsmith went so far as to have Robert Pirie, head of the Rothschild office in New York, arrange for Drexel Burnham to raise financing to back a bid for more than $1.8 billion, or $52 a share, for St Regis. Haselton and his group offered Goldsmith the same price for his shares.

'I warned Haselton that this would only bring down the wolves on them. Indeed as soon as I did step out of the door, Larry Tisch went in, Rupert Murdoch went in and they finally got taken over by a white knight, Champion International, who started off by firing the management,' Goldsmith notes.

Goldsmith had set out with the full intention of buying all of St Regis, in the same way he had bought Diamond, but in this case the odds were against him. To the thunderous cry of 'greenmail', he backed off, accepting the St Regis offer of $52 a share against an average purchase price of $35.50. He had made a profit of $51m for a month's investment for himself and partners, but that was poor consolation.

Goldsmith was withering in his contempt for the criticism and for St Regis management. 'I warned them that if they went around looking for a white knight to save them and then finally settled on one, the next morning when they woke up he would be black. Besides, I told them, if you're looking for a white knight, I'm white and I'm a knight.' Apparently, no one got the joke.

If anything the joke was on Haselton and his managers who paid millions more to the other raiders and lost their jobs into the bargain. By then Goldsmith had sought out a new prospective merger partner that offered everything St Regis had and more.

This time it was Rothschild's Bob Pirie who produced 'the book' on Continental Group, a Connecticut-based conglomerate that had been built on the old Continental Can Corporation. By now Continental had sales of $5 billion a year and a dog's breakfast of subsidiaries including insurance, oil and gas as well as its core can-making and packaging business. It also had 1.4m acres of undervalued timberland and 9m barrels of estimated oil reserves.

'Actually, I think Drexel first suggested Continental to Jimmy, but they had done their usual sloppy jobs on the research book, and he turned it down,' Pirie recalls.

'Jimmy never used junk bonds, not from Drexel, not from anyone,'

Pirie continues. 'He had Drexel set up fallback financing through his regular group of investors, "the Fan Club" they were called, and the banks, particularly Citibank. In fact, Michael Milken once called me at home on a weekend and cursed me for being an idiot because Jimmy had done a deal that hadn't used a Drexel credit line, so there was no fee for them.'

Indeed the high cash component that was the trademark of the Goldsmith takeover bids so frustrated Drexel that by the time of his attempt to buy Goodyear in 1986, Milken had taken his troops over to the other side. On more than one occasion, when a Goldsmith offer was bluntly refused by a besieged management, the question would come up: just who was raiding whom?

In Continental's case the bid announced on 5 June 1984 was classic Goldsmith: $50 a share to each shareholder or $2.12 billion for the whole company; the conversion of all Continental's convertible shares would add another $300m to that price. It was a big offer even by the standards of those days of the takeover wars. Indeed, the $2.4 billion potential total was the largest non-oil tender made to that date.

Goldsmith's bid was treated by the financial press and the arbitrageurs as yet another example of the shark-feeding frenzy that was developing. Remember that the time, June 1984, was less than a year after T. Boone Pickens had rocked the nation by stampeding the mammoth Gulf Oil Corp. into the arms of Chevron Oil with nearly half of the $13.3 billion purchase price being diverted to the investors – $400m of it into the pockets of Pickens' Mesa Partners.

Now Pickens was on the prowl again in the oil patch. Mobil was a rumoured target, although he would finally settle on Phillips Petroleum. The success of other raiders such as Carl Icahn, Ron Perelman, Saul Steinberg and Irwin Jacobs had drawn in some unlikely rivals, political figures who were in charge of the giant pools of investment cash that backed the pension trust funds of the state and local governments of the 50 states and thousands of communities across the United States.

These pension funds held scores of millions of shares in all the leading US manufacturing corporations. Inflation had hit them too and the governments and universities whose employees they protected wanted their payments indexed to the rising cost of life in America. Led by such activists as Jesse Unruh of the California state employees fund, and Harrison Goldin, the chief financial officer for the City of New York, the raiders were actually encouraged to take as much cash as they could out of the corporate asset pile.

Faced with a rebellion amongst the largest block of their shareholders, it is small wonder today that many corporate chief executives and their boards went slightly mad as they tried to protect what they felt was a necessary capital buffer against the vagaries of the business cycle. They also wanted to protect a corporate lifestyle that bordered on imperial opulence. Many corporations also diverted substantial profits into programmes whose pay-off was problematical, or at best years away.

Faced with Goldsmith's $50 a share offer, Continental's chief executive officer S. Bruce Smart, did the right thing – he stalled while he searched for a way to evade the unwanted embrace. Bruce was one of the few American executives to have done his sums correctly at the beginning of the decade. Since 1981, he had put Continental on a slimming regime aimed at redeploying assets towards greater profitability. In three years he sold off subsidiaries that had added $1 billion to his annual sales total, but which improved the overall financial strength of the company.

It was because Smart was making the right decisions that Goldsmith was attracted. 'The market has undervalued Continental because some of its strategic decisions won't pay off quickly. I think they have made the right moves and I'm willing to wait for profits,' he told financial journalists at the time.

Goldsmith and Smart met in the offices of Continental's bankers, Morgan Stanley. 'Why do you want to buy my company?' Smart asked bluntly. Goldsmith answered in detail: he wanted to sell the diversifications, which he listed, and concentrate on the core business, which was Continental Can, the leader in its field. Confronted with accepting Goldsmith's terms, or as Wall Street expected, by selling off enough parts of the company to drive him away, Smart chose a third course: he put the company up for auction. In an interview he gave later, Smart, by that stage undersecretary at the Department of Commerce in the Reagan administration, confessed that he had agreed with Goldsmith's plan, but he could not carry it through. He had been elected by his colleagues who would lose their jobs in a reorganisation of the scale Goldsmith proposed. He therefore, he said, felt it best to sell the company. Goldsmith, when he read the interview, commented that he was 'an extremely honourable man'. Goldsmith countered jibes that he lacked the money by producing a certified cheque for $1 billion and demonstrated he had guarantees of at least $1.4 billion more. Then he raised his tender offer to $55 a share bringing the total bid to $2.6 billion. Later he would raise it to $58 a share.

But in the meantime Smart sought a white knight and found two: Peter

Kiewit, a mining and construction company, and a Californian financier named David Murdock. Kiewit had been an early partner in the Goldsmith bid for Continental but had dropped out to pursue his own line. The partners' bid was $58.50 a share or $3.5 billion, 50 cents a share more than Goldsmith was willing to pay. He knew when he was not wanted. In leaving Continental, he took $10m in profits and another $25m in private compensation payments – not what he wanted but better than a poke in the eye any day.

The buy-out was treated as another rebuff for Goldsmith and a victory for Continental. Smart threw a luncheon celebration for his new partners at Stamford, Connecticut's yacht club, the social centre of this whitest of white collar communities. Officials of Kiewit flew in from the construction firm's Omaha, Nebraska, head office, and the minority partner David Murdock, normally reclusive at the best of times, also made a point of appearing at the head table. Smart's welcoming toast included the rather pointed aside that Continental actually was three times the size of its parent.

'I don't think we're going to find people coming in here from Omaha and telling us what to do,' Smart exulted.

A year later, Smart's management team was gone from Continental and the new Kiewit-installed managers quickly did what Goldsmith had urged from the start. Out went $1.6 billion worth of the insurance, paper products, gas pipeline and petroleum reserves and before the year was out another $1 billion worth of none-core industry operations were on the auction block.

By quickly paying off its debt, Kiewit ended up with a slimmed-down can and packaging company and, no surprise, 1.44m acres of timberland, all for the paltry cost of $200m.

By then Goldsmith was far down the road on other bids and had forgotten his disappointment. Even if it had been in his nature, there was no time to gloat over Continental's fate. His search continued through that summer of 1984. There was a brief fling with Colgate-Palmolive but he was more interested in core businesses that remained tied to forest products.

Crown Zellerbach was the next item on the list that autumn of 1984 that whetted Goldsmith's appetite. Why Crown Zellerbach? For one thing, William T. Creson, the company's chairman and CEO had made a serious mistake. He had made Jimmy Goldsmith very angry.

25

Reds in the Beds

Perhaps the most extraordinary characteristic of Jimmy Goldsmith is his ability to live his life on different levels, in different countries, with different people. Guatemala and Wall Street, with all the legal, financial and intellectual challenges involved, might have been expected to occupy even the peripatetic Goldsmith to the exclusion of everything else – or almost everything else. Yet still there was *L'Express* in Paris, the never-ending hangover from the *Private Eye* fight, and the continued battle against a British press which Goldsmith, even from a distance, saw as one of the more malign forces of his world.

In September 1981 Jimmy announced the creation of a new £50,000 prize, to be awarded to a journalist for 'the best investigative journalism into subversion in the media'. He remained convinced that 'the threat to our freedoms . . . is far more serious than even the British and European secret services, with all their knowledge, are prepared to accept'. He also set up a fund, which he insisted was not political, which would support individuals against institutions. He had come to understand, he said, that 'defending one's reputation, particularly in Britain, is a rich man's privilege'. The libel fund would also support anyone wrongly attacked by *Private Eye* or the media, journalists sued for libel and employees defamed by their employers (it is still very much alive, and has backed a wide variety of cases – personally vetted by Goldsmith).

However he would have preferred to have put *Private Eye* behind him – if *Private Eye* would do the same. Years after it had begun the battle, *Private Eye* went on – and on. Ingrams himself might have been prepared to throw in the towel but not everyone who worked for him was. When *Private Eye*, in August 1981, in a piece of pure fantasy, linked him with the murder of the Italian banker Roberto Calvi of Banco Ambrosiano, found hanging under Blackfriars Bridge in London, he sued and settled out of court for damages of £85,000 and an apology. He had never met Calvi in his life, never dealt with Banco Ambrosiano, and was astounded that the Eye could suggest such a link. He took his victory as a good sign: the atmosphere, he hoped, might be changing. But on 27 June 1982 Michael Gillard was at it again, this time in the *Observer*, again linking him with Calvi, and following up the next week with another story, connecting Goldsmith to another financial scandal, the crash of Imperial Commodities. The *Observer* for good measure added a third slighting reference, this time to John DeLorean, the Detroit carmaker who at that stage was busily losing the British government some £84m in an ill-fated venture in Belfast. This reference suggested that, just as Rupert Murdoch had once held out a story on DeLorean (which he did for libel reasons), so Murdoch was now refusing to publish Charles Raw's impenetrable articles for the *Sunday Times* because of his friendship for Goldsmith. By that stage, DeLorean had been arrested for cocaine smuggling, and was awaiting trial.

Goldsmith hit the *Observer* and Gillard with a ferocious blast in February 1983, complaining to the Press Council, a self-regulating body which handled complaints against the British press, that Gillard had now managed to link him with just about every scandal in a decade: 'with fraud, suspected murder, bankruptcies, dealing in cocaine and corruption of public servants'. In all those cases, he did not know the individuals, had no dealings with them, and played no part whatsoever in their lives.

The *Observer* was forced to admit that the facts of the articles were untrue, and the Press Council upheld Goldsmith's complaint, which the paper duly published. But that was not enough for him. He had discovered that one of the members of the Press Council, a Mrs Beryl Huffinley, was 'a prominent Communist party activist' (she was certainly a communist), and Goldsmith insisted he had a wider purpose: 'to improve the workings of the Press Council, which I believed to be incapable of acting in a sound, unbiased and effective manner'. The council's adjudication, he said, although in his favour, 'was the usual nauseous blend of perfidy, sanctimony and humbug'. He wanted its members sacked – particularly Mrs Huffinley – and 'the whole infected contraption' dismantled.

His campaign against the Press Council and the remnants of the *Private Eye* brigade, however, was only the tip of the iceberg. For many years he had been convinced that the infiltration of the media in Britain, France and other countries was an organised effort – orchestrated from Moscow, for the purpose of destabilising the western democracies. It was a familiar theme, one which caused his listeners' eyes to glaze over. He never went so far as to accuse – or to believe – that the *Private Eye* 'conspiracy' was organised from Moscow, but he certainly suspected that Moscow had a hand in some of the coverage that appeared on leading political figures – and perhaps had something to do with himself. In his mind, he had developed Harold Wilson's remarks after the Slater Walker takeover to the point where they now struck him as deeply significant – and sinister. For the most part, he reckoned the left-wing bias of British journalists was one of unfortunate fashion rather than of organisation, but that was beside the point. Organised or unorganised, the effect was the same: the commanding heights of the media were deeply infiltrated by left-wingers set on destroying free enterprise and the capitalist world.

He had seen confirmation of this view in that curious Arnold Wesker book on the *Sunday Times* (*Journey into Journalism*) where the left-wing playwright described his visit to the Business section, and his interviews with the journalists there.

'Far from being pillars of capitalist society,' wrote Wesker, '[the business staff] seem to me to be an army of very bright urban saboteurs.'

Wesker went on to quote one of the senior staff:

'You see,' this unnamed journalist told him, 'it's a question of the credibility of the *Sunday Times* which, as an old conservative newspaper, commands more respect than, say, the *Observer*, which is known for its liberal policies, and therefore we're a better journal through which to infiltrate radical views – more people will believe us.'

Goldsmith had almost leapt from his chair when he read that Wesker interview, and could not restrain his delight when, years later, the new editor of the paper, Andrew Neil, was quoted as saying:

'There was a group (of staff) who thought they owned the paper. They were bitter when they realised cosy collectivism was out. They were responsible, in my view, for a hard-left newspaper which they hid under the *Sunday Times* label.'

In December 1990 Germany's most influential news magazine, *Der Spiegel*, carried an extraordinary confession. The journalistic community had been gossiping for weeks about it, but here it was at last, spelt out in black and white: the magazine sheepishly admitted that its East German bureau chief was actually a Stasi agent, charged with disseminating disinformation through the columns of the magazine.

Even in that particular issue, the name of Dietholm Schröder still stood in the list of correspondents, although he was now described as being 'on leave'. Schröder, it emerged, had been called in for questioning by the German authorities and accused of passing military information to the East Germans.

'Only now, three months after unification,' wrote the magazine, 'is it becoming clear that the long arm of the Stasi reached not only into the offices of ministries, but into almost all social circles of the Federal Republic of Germany.'

For years *Der Spiegel* (the Mirror) in particular had resisted any such idea, and was prepared to go to court when it was alleged. The magazine was set up by the allies just after the war as an investigative weekly magazine, designed to spot and to expose corruption in postwar Germany. Headed by Rudolf Augstein, a brilliant young journalist (he was only 24 at the time), it gained a reputation for exclusive revelations, many of them involving Marckus Wolf, the head of East German Intelligence from the early 1950s. Wolf had long boasted that he had 'someone sitting in *Der Spiegel*', a claim which the magazine, and the West German authorities, were at pains to deny. But the rumours persisted, and all correspondents sent to East Berlin were carefully vetted to ensure they were bona fide. Yet what now emerged was that Schröder had actually been infiltrated, on Wolf's orders, into the West in the 1950s with instructions to make his way in the journalistic world, and had for years been beavering away inside *Der Spiegel* on behalf of the Communist bloc.

With Stasi files now available to the West, Schröder, of course, was not the only Stasi agent exposed in Germany: another prominent journalist, working for the radio station Sender Freies Berlin, had been dismissed from his post in the same week, after it was revealed that he too had been a long-time agent for the East. Suddenly, the concept of organised infiltration by the Soviet bloc of the western media, which had seemed to many to be paranoid fantasy, appeared to have genuine substance.

The *Spiegel* admission was of particular interest to Jimmy Goldsmith, who had long held that the magazine had been used, probably unknowingly, by Soviet agents. What is more he had gone to immense trouble, and the expense of about £1m, to prove it. Even as he was dealing with lawyers, investment bankers, taking business decisions in half a dozen different countries, Goldsmith was also meeting secretly with every leading Soviet defector he could get his hands on, including the famous Oleg Bitov who turned out not to be a defector at all, and who fooled Goldsmith just as he fooled the CIA and his other interrogators.

Goldsmith's involvement did not come about as a part of his self-appointed role of defender of the West and of the world of free enterprise and culture. It was, in its way, a re-run of the *Private Eye* affair, a case where Goldsmith's attacker expected the equivalent of a conventional arms response and found itself hit with a nuclear weapon instead.

The *casus belli* of this little episode lay in a country for which Goldsmith ancestrally had little affection, and where he had only modest business interests. Franz Josef Strauss was the leader of the Bavarian-based Christian Social Union (CSU), the junior partners to Chancellor Adenauer's CDU party in the coalition government. A thickset man whose fleshy features seemed to merge into his shoulders without benefit of a neck, he looked what he was: the son of a master butcher. But he was also remarkably clever, a gifted politician with a huge capacity for work, and a subtle, educated mind. When he had an audience with Pope John-Paul II, they chose Latin as their common tongue. With the Cold War at its height in the late 1950s and early 1960s, and with Adenauer then well into his eighties, so Strauss, then West Germany's defence minister, was the favourite to succeed. But he had no lack of enemies: he was a tough right-winger, the leading advocate in Europe for a pre-emptive Nato nuclear strike capability, a view which *Der Spiegel*, along with the army chiefs (and the Kennedy administration) opposed, preferring a build-up of conventional forces.

He never did replace Adenauer. In October 1962 *Der Spiegel*, under the heading 'Limited Defence Readiness', published the details of a secret Nato exercise staged in Western Europe the previous month. It was no ordinary exercise, but the first one of its kind, based on the scenario that the Soviet forces had launched a nuclear attack, with 15m casualties in West Germany and Britain. Besides the details of the exercise, *Der Spiegel*, even more damagingly, published the secret Nato analysis.

The next day the German federal police raided the magazine's offices in Hamburg and Bonn, arrested the publisher Augstein and several others, and imprisoned them awaiting charges of treason and other counts. The storm that followed was predictably violent, but was not directed at the magazine and its editors: it was aimed at Strauss who stood accused, as minister in charge, of having behaved as the Nazis did (in fact he was on holiday and had little to do with it). Augstein, from his cell, wrote an article accusing Strauss of all sorts of malpractices, under the heading, 'Shall the State go to ruin for one man?' Rumours spread of damaging revelations about the defence minister, showing him to be a neo-Nazi, of having profaned synagogues and Jewish graveyards (which later turned out, in part, to have been carried out by Soviet bloc agents in a deliberate attempt to blacken him).

Adenauer's three-party coalition government was shaky, and with the row boiling, he finally decided he had to jettison Strauss, who was forced to resign. The charges against the journalists were dropped, and the campaign against Strauss, seen as the most anti-communist of all the potential German leaders, escalated. Strauss re-emerged as a very successful finance minister in Chancellor Kurt Kiesinger's Grand Coalition government of 1966–9, before Willi Brandt won the 1969 elections, but he was tainted by the affair.

Strauss' best chance of getting the top job came in 1980, but during the Federal elections the *Spiegel* affair continually haunted him. He was beaten by the Social Democrat leader, Helmut Schmidt.

During the election campaign of 1980 *Now!* magazine had carried an interview with Strauss, detailing the smear campaign, and particularly mentioning the role of *Der Spiegel*. Goldsmith liked the article, remarking later that 'my sympathy for Strauss was triggered by the amazing similarity between the methods used against him and those that I had had to face.'

He remembered this particular article when, a year later, he was asked to give a speech to the Media Group of Conservative MPs in the House of Commons. Jimmy drafted his speech while he was in America working on the Diamond bid, but back in London rang the author of the Strauss interview, Brian Crozier, to ask for further information. The subject of his speech, he explained, was 'subversion of the media' and he was particularly interested in a reference by Crozier to the KGB's role in the *Spiegel* affair. 'Are you sure that's true? Can you give me further details?'

Crozier was one of those unfashionable journalists widely attacked in 1970s Britain as extremist as he preached the dangers of left-wing infiltration even more fervently than Goldsmith. Several of his books, most of which had a strong anti-communist flavour, had been critically praised, but they had also aroused a degree of wrath on the left. A biography of Franco, a hate figure of the 1960s and 1970s, written with the help of the Spanish authorities, made him even more of a target although the Spanish themselves didn't much like it (the Spanish translation, a best-seller in Spain and Latin America, was peppered with footnotes critical of the author). Born in 1918, he had worked for the *Economist* and for the BBC, and then founded the Institute for the Study of Conflict, a right-wing think tank.

In 1979, when *Now!* magazine started, Crozier became a regular columnist, continuing his crusade to highlight the organised infiltration of the West.

Goldsmith's speech was a typically detailed and well-researched account of the KGB apparatus for infiltrating the media, listing all the various front organisations used, and the manner in which it worked. Goldsmith drew on his own CIA sources in Washington, and accumulated all sorts of examples from different parts of the world, to make his point. In the light of the flood of admissions since from Moscow and the East, it all sounds tame now, but it was explosive – and unpopular – stuff at the time.

Crozier's contribution was a single sentence which read:

'General Sejna, the high-ranking Czech intelligence defector, admitted that the campaign by the German news magazine *Der Spiegel* to discredit Franz Josef Strauss was orchestrated by the KGB.'

It was not exactly new material: William Buckley, editor of the New York magazine *National Review*, had written about Sejna and *Der Spiegel* in much the same words, as had a defence quarterly called *Strategic Review*. *Now!* carried Goldsmith's text in its issue of 30 January 1981, and a month later Augstein and *Der Spiegel* sued. Goldsmith, after again checking with Crozier, decided to fight. The battle that followed took three and a half years.

In London Crozier pulled together a team of researchers and helpers to begin building the evidence they would need to go into court. Crozier himself set out to track down the man who was the source of the original quote, Jan Sejna (pronounced Shayna) himself. There was no doubt Sejna had said it (to Walter Hahn of *Strategic Review* among others), but that was scarcely evidence. Crozier made several trips to America where Sejna had been given a new name and a new identity, but the CIA kept him well hidden. Crozier had known Bill Casey, head of the CIA, for years, and asked to see him. He put his request directly to him, and the following day received a phone call. 'The director asked me to give you the unlisted number of the man you want to see,' said a voice. He then gave the number, and the name the Czech defector now lived under. Crozier, back in London by then, passed on the news to a delighted Goldsmith in Paris, who urged him to get back to New York as quickly as he could. 'Take Concorde. You'll feel much fresher.'

Crozier finally met Sejna, 'a thin little man with a high forehead and blond hair, looking like a minor businessman from the backwoods', in the lobby of the Madison hotel in New York. The Czech defector co-operated willingly enough, confirming what they wanted to know: as chief of staff to the Czech defence minister, he had seen instructions from the KGB relating to obtaining secret Nato documents with the object of using them to create a public scandal to discredit Strauss. He signed an affidavit to that effect. But he had no knowledge as to whether the same documents had been used by *Der Spiegel*.

This, however, was only one small part of the material Goldsmith was now gathering. In addition to a research team under Crozier plus a team of lawyers in London, he had also hired intelligence experts in the US and in France. He was becoming more and more intrigued with the Pandora's box he had opened, and determined to prove an allegation that had been widely sneered at. He had always believed this was so, but now proof positive, proof the doubting world would have to accept, was within his grasp. Half-way through the research, Goldsmith told Crozier he was prepared to spend up to £18m on launching a new daily newspaper which he would print in London and distribute around the world, carrying a verbatim account of the court proceedings.

If *Spiegel* had realised how seriously he was taking it – and how much information he was accumulating – it would probably have dropped its writ. By now there was a team working in Germany as well as in London and Washington. Crozier gathered testimonies and papers on the Soviet secret agencies, written by people regarded as the leading specialists in the world; he had papers and advice from ex-KGB officers, including Yuri Bezmenov and Stanislav Levchenko, and from the Czech former State Secret Security officers, Josef Frolik and Ladislaw Bittman. He used former Soviet journalists, and Czech anti-communists, Harvard academics, former advisers to the American National Security Council, ex-CIA men, former MI5 and MI6 spooks, and many others. Goldsmith himself was moving freely in Washington political circles, and had a wide circle of friends and contacts. He had been to White House dinners on several occasions and made sure he got to know the Soviet experts, who added further names to the list. He was also becoming more and more friendly with Bill Casey.

The evidence piled up, more impressive in quantity than quality. Other than Sejna's important but circumstantial evidence, there was little to prove the link between the KGB and *Der Spiegel*. A leading German professor was hired to tackle the huge task of analysing *Der Spiegel*'s news coverage and presentation over the years and just before Goldsmith's fiftieth birthday in February 1983, two large volumes of statistical notes and graphs arrived. They proved remarkably little. But a complementary report showed that in 1962, the fateful year, *Der Spiegel* devoted 385 pages to Strauss, an average of seven an issue, the overwhelming majority of them hostile.

They even compared quotations from *Pravda* and *Izvestia* with quotes from *Der Spiegel* showing what a jubilant Crozier told Goldsmith were 'similarities so striking that it would have been straining the laws of chance to attribute them to coincidence'.

None of this was proof enough for a court; it was obvious to anyone that *Der Spiegel* did not like Strauss, but that was its perfect right – Goldsmith as publisher of *L'Express* did not much care for Mitterand. To prove their case beyond doubt they had to have something more than Sejna had given them, showing how *Der Spiegel*'s coverage had actually been *orchestrated* from the East. There was any amount of supporting evidence, but very little that was conclusive. To go to court and lose would be a disaster for Goldsmith's whole *raison d'être*. He would spare no effort, and spend whatever it needed, to prove what he passionately believed to be true. By late 1983 and early 1984, with the libel case moving towards the courts, Goldsmith stepped up his own involvement, running the case almost as he would run another takeover bid. Sejna had lost the $100,000 the CIA had given him in an ill-judged restaurant venture in Chicago ('They saw him coming,' one CIA man remarked sourly.) Goldsmith sent his plane to Washington to fly him and his wife to New York for dinner. He personally sought out and interviewed most of the defectors, even though his team had been over the ground already. On 7 September 1983 he interviewed the ex-KGB man Stanislav Levchenko, who he discovered was number one on the KGB hit list. 'He was probably under some form of sedation,' he reported back to Crozier. 'On a normal day he would make an excellent witness', but Levchenko, he added, 'has not yet definitely decided to trust us but I think he is on the way.' The Russian, he said, was still considering 'whether or not he wants to participate in what he calls the "potential destruction of Der Spiegel"'.

The reason for this latter doubt became clear when Levchenko, with CIA approval, gave an interview to *Der Spiegel* a few weeks later, organised by the CIA to counter what the Americans considered the magazine's pro-Soviet line.

All this time Goldsmith was fighting for and winning Diamond, so money, tight in the early days, was no object. He now had resources – or his companies did – for other things. Laure at the end of 1982 discovered she was pregnant with her first child and Jimmy's seventh. They were still living in his generous suite at the Carlyle which Goldsmith, who had lived in hotels most of his life, enjoyed but which was not right for family life.

For some time Laure had been looking for a house, and early in 1983 they found what they wanted: two large brownstones together, just off Park Avenue. It was a large, brick town house on East 80th Street, marked outside only by a discreet number, but stretching back almost a block. Laure found a brilliant young French designer, Robert Couturier, to transform it into what they wanted. Couturier added a three-storey atrium at the back, spanning the two houses, which became the centrepiece, and a splendid curved stairway leading up to Jimmy's large drawing room. Jimmy and Laure became regular visitors to the salerooms, and the house was furnished with marble busts in the hallway, Oriental rugs, large sofas, leather-bound French classics (and Churchill's histories). For years Jimmy had done most of his work from one of his homes: a beautiful room in Paris looking out on a garden that seemed to be in the country, a room in Richmond with a view of the park, and now a spacious room in New York that was grander than any of them. It was there that Jimmy and Laure moved, with their new child, Charlotte, when the house was finally finished. And it was there that many of the East European defectors were brought to confess what they knew about *Der Spiegel* and the campaign against Strauss.

Word had spread in Washington circles of Goldsmith's expertise on the subject of Soviet disinformation, and in May 1984 he addressed the Defense Strategy Forum of the National Strategy Information Center in Washington, developing the theme he had taken up in the House of Commons four years before. He was able to add some of the information he had gathered in the intervening years. In front of a large audience, which included Casey himself and many of the leading American intelligence experts of the day, he set out some of the details of the *Spiegel* affair, adding that many of the most influential KGB agents were journalists.

But the collection of evidence was proving an uphill task. The problem was that not many of the defectors knew very much about the *Spiegel* affair, although they had much to say about other aspects of infiltration. They could offer opinions, and information on the way the KGB operated, but none of them had been actively involved in destabilising Strauss. Sejna was still the best witness, but he was not enough to convince a jury.

The defection of Oleg Bitov, a staff translator on the Moscow *Literaturnaya Gazeta*, seemed to offer the best evidence to date. Crozier and his team had to wait until he had been debriefed by counter-intelligence before getting to him, but he seemed worth it. He told the team that his paper (*Literary Gazette*) had briefed a special correspondent to prepare five articles which had then appeared in a condensed version in *Der Spiegel*. The author of the articles, according to Bitov, was a colonel in the KGB. Goldsmith heard the news with glee. It was, he told his team, 'game, set and match if we can prove that in reality it was written by a KGB colonel'. On 26 June 1984, Crozier invited Bitov to his offices in Regent Street to ask him to translate the original Russian articles so that the texts could be compared. Bitov added further details to his original story and worked with Crozier for a couple of weeks. Then abruptly he vanished from view.

He surfaced again in Moscow in September to say he had been kidnapped by British agents in Venice, taken to London and drugged, bribed and blackmailed. Bitov later wrote an account, published in the Moscow *Literary Gazette*, which gives a hilarious account of his meeting with Goldsmith on 25 May 1984, at his house in New York.

And there he was himself [wrote Bitov], looking like a character from Marshak. The owner of factories, newspapers, and steamships or, in real life, the owner of private aircraft and limousines a mile long . . . He sat with his legs crossed picturesquely, chewing a cigar . . . made as fat as a factory chimney. He looked down on his visitor from the height of his millions as though they were a throne.

The surroundings of the throne were nothing if not appropriate – real Louis XV furniture, sculptures by Benvenuto Cellini, paintings by old Dutch masters. Only the bookshelves were rather empty, apart from a lonely couple of thrillers and a Stock Exchange handbook. Probably the Old World's second-hand book dealers have not yet collected a sufficient number of antique volumes with gold-embossed spines.

When he read Bitov's article Jimmy hooted with laughter, and was so amused he published it in his first book of his own speeches and articles, *Counter Culture*, in 1985.

Instead of Bitov came a genuine defector: Ilya Dzhirkvelov, a senior KGB man, who defected to Britain from Geneva. Dzhirkvelov actually did have some knowledge about the *Spiegel* affair. He had joined the KGB in 1944 and until his defection in 1980 was involved in disinformation. MI5 was loth to let any of Goldsmith's team near him, but Crozier made contact, and the Russian provided details of a key meeting in 1960 at the Central Committee's International Department chaired by Boris Ponomarev, a Comintern veteran. The theme, according to Dzhirkvelov, was that more must be done to prevent politicians who were undesirable to the Soviet Union from coming to power. In particular, said Dzhirkvelov, Ponomarev mentioned Franz Josef Strauss. The defector then went on to tell the delighted Goldsmith team just what had been done: West German journalists, Social Democrats and others were to be invited to the USSR, and told that Strauss was linked with American intelligence. He himself was instructed to tell them quietly that the Americans were paying Strauss large sums. Ponomarev, said Dzhirkvelov, later told him that 'we successfully used *Der Spiegel* to undermine Strauss.' He was told the same thing by others, he added, who he named.

Dzhirkvelov said he himself had no doubt at all that the anti-Strauss campaign in *Der Spiegel* was based on material provided by the KGB. But he added a caveat, which Goldsmith had always accepted:

'This, of course, does not imply any collaboration between the KGB and *Der Spiegel*: many respectable and politically impeccable publications fell victim to the KGB's "active measures" without knowing by whom they were used,' said the Russian.

To Goldsmith and Crozier that made sense: the type of campaign they were talking about was far more effective if the magazine was not aware it was being used. 'I never suggested that *Spiegel* was *knowingly* used,' said Goldsmith later. 'I said it had been used. So have most other newspapers, including, on occasion, my own.' He did not know about Herr Schröder then.

The case was finally scheduled for October 1984, but in September, *Der Spiegel* gave in (it later insisted it was the other way about, and that it was Goldsmith who settled). Goldsmith was hugely disappointed, but he was the defendant, not the plaintiff, and therefore had no control of the case. But he took full-page advertisements in the leading newspapers in Britain as well as the *New York Times* and the *Wall Street Journal* to repeat the statements read out in court and his own personal declaration, headed, 'A victory for the West'. For its part *Der Spiegel* said it fully accepted 'that broadly speaking Soviet intelligence seeks to operate' in the way Goldsmith claimed but denied that the magazine itself was 'conscious of having been used in the manner mentioned by Sir James Goldsmith.'

Goldsmith then read out his carefully prepared statement on the court steps. Some of the papers, carefully collated by Crozier, were later passed to the writer Chapman Pincher, who published them in a book *The Secret Offensive*. Pincher corroborated much of it from his own intelligence sources, quoting a former director-general of MI5, the British counter-espionage and security service, saying that the KGB, and the Soviet bloc intelligence services, were 'very active in the press world in Fleet Street'.

In collecting his material Goldsmith unearthed some surprising material to support his broader case about infiltration. He was specifically interested only in *Der Spiegel*, but collected a large number of names of journalists said to be in receipt of material, wittingly or unwittingly. He has kept that information to himself, but claims that there had been, some years before, several on the *Sunday Times*.

Later he quietly awarded his £50,000 prize for 'best investigative journalism into subversion of the media' to a Greek journalist, Paul Anastasi, who had waged a lonely battle to expose Soviet agents operating in Greece (Goldsmith carried his story in *L'Express*) which led to him to be imprisoned; and to John Barron of the *Reader's Digest*. And then, as he wrote a year later:

'I have now retired from this arena and returned to the privacy that I would have enjoyed, had I not been provoked by such a nauseous campaign. I have neither desire nor intention to return from my retirement. Only another major personal provocation would force me back.'

26

Crowning Glories

If a company or an individual buys shares of a company with the specific purpose of frightening management so as to put management into using corporate funds to protect their position by buying out that block at unusually favourable terms, then I would call that person a greenmailer . . .

Sir James Goldsmith in deposition to the US District Court, Southern District of New York, 3 February 1988

In America, Goldsmith truly believed that he had found a country where he could not only win success for doing his best for himself but also for others. He treasured his friendships with, as he called them, 'the number ones', political superstars such as Henry Kissinger and major bankers such as William E. Simon, the former Treasury secretary under both Nixon and Ford; they had all made him feel welcome on the far side of the Atlantic and he found his opinions viewed with gravity.

But after his early welcome there came a rising tide of resentment and criticism that began to dog his dealings. He was being lumped in with the buccaneer crew of corporate raiders and asset takers, the Pickens–Icahn –Boesky crowd, and he didn't like it. The financial press was always eager to promote the drama of yet another old-line corporate name being taken down; the fact that Goldsmith had saved Grand Union and expanded it was conveniently forgotten. His bids for Diamond, St Regis and Continental were all treated as break-up raids.

Almost to prove them wrong, Goldsmith took a $100m stake in Colgate-Palmolive as a prelude to a bid, but ultimately let the prey escape. His private excuse was that he had come to like the soap-maker's chief executive, Reuben Mark, who actually went ahead and did all the things Goldsmith would have done: trimmed back to the core business, sold off the diversifications.

Crown Zellerbach was something else. Like Grand Union and Diamond before it, Crown Zellerbach had been one of the old brand-name legends of America – a 115-year-old aristocrat of the San Francisco business community, with widespread packaging and container operations. And, like the previous Goldsmith targets, the company had taken the conglomerate route during the 1970s with the predictable result that by 1982, the year William T. Creson took over, the company was running a $100m loss. Once again, Crown's operations, its logging mills and paper factories, were ageing and its more than 2m acres of timberland were undervalued.

In fairness, Creson had been trying to slim down the company considerably, but the management strategy was still anathema to the Goldsmith doctrine of sticking to core operations. Crown, among other things, had taken on a computer company that made printers and other hardware fixtures, none of which matched the computers that the company's various operations used. Thanks to more aggressive marketing of its paper towel and toilet tissues and a one-third reduction of its 28,000 work force, Crown's annual sales had climbed back to $3 billion in 1984 and the company was just back into the black in terms of earnings.

While this was hardly a triumph of management skills, Creson and his team understandably thought they deserved the time and support to put their programme fully into place. So it was that he objected strongly, on 12 December 1984, when Goldsmith filed public notice with the SEC of his intention to buy between 15 and 20 per cent of Crown Zellerbach shares which were then trading at $28.

Creson snapped that the Goldsmith bid was 'unsolicited' and 'not in the best interests of the company'. To Creson they were blunt words and nothing more than an accurate description of the situation. To Goldsmith they smacked of the kind of sneer he had come to associate with entrenched management which regarded itself as a class above the actual owners of the company. This was America after all – who was Creson to say what was in the best interests of the company? Wasn't that the role of the shareholders themselves?

During the early spring of 1985, Goldsmith and his now usual group of backers (including Jacob Rothschild and Bruxelles Lambert Group of Belgium) had begun to buy quietly. Even though the arbitrageurs smelled a fight brewing, the price of Crown Zellerbach shares moved up only fractionally, so that by 12 March 1985, Goldsmith owned 2.4m of its 27.2m shares (about 8.6 per cent) at an average price of $33.25 – an $80m investment.

At a meeting on 19 March in San Francisco between Goldsmith and Creson, the two made their enmity a personal affair.

Goldsmith recalls:

> I told him I felt their company was badly managed, and that its capacity to compete in the US market and in the world market had been severely impaired by that bad management. I said the company needed restructuring and refocusing, and that I would be happy to do it jointly with those members of management who agreed with the general strategy and wanted to work with that strategy. I also said that if people did not like that strategy they should be free to leave, and they would leave under the most appropriate and indeed generous circumstances ... and all those details were put into public documents.

Creson, not surprisingly, was not having any of it.

Nevertheless, Goldsmith pressed on.

> I also told him we were not going to go away and that he had four choices. He could sell by tender as Continental had done; he could work with us and let us build up our stake to 25 per cent as we had wanted to do with Regis; he could search for a white knight to save him; or he could bluff himself into thinking we would go away – which we wouldn't. And we then put all of that plus a flat statement from me that we would not accept any kind of greenmail. We put all of that into a public document which we filed with the SEC.

Creson did not take Goldsmith's frankness seriously. In part, he thought he could afford to ignore this suitor because six months before, in the summer of 1984, he and his board of directors had taken steps to make Crown Zellerbach takeover-proof.

In the opening years of the takeover frenzy it soon became apparent that the raiders were not dissuaded either by the threat or the reality of a target management breaking up its company to avoid being taken over. Indeed anything that boosted the price of even an unsuccessful tender offer was profit to the raider; only Carl Icahn would get stuck having to operate one of his surrendered properties – as head of the struggling former airline giant TWA, he has been accorded a kind of rough justice for his tactics, something that neither Pickens nor Boesky were ever careless enough to allow to happen to themselves.

By the summer of 1984, corporate executive suites throughout America sounded more like hen-houses on fox-alert. The attorneys and merchant bankers, who earned big fees by advising these frightened businessmen, frantically sought a foolproof way of making asset-rich corporate treasure ships look unattractive to the raider's eye. To Martin Lipton, senior partner of the New York law firm of Wachtell, Lipton, Rosen and Katz, goes credit for what was quickly dubbed 'the poison pill'.

At its simplest, a poison pill was a booby-trap for the unwanted suitor. Once triggered, the device usually allowed management and allied shareholders to put out a new issue of stock at a concessionary price, usually with the proviso that outsiders had to pay as much as double for those same shares. What this did was to take surplus capital from the company and put it to the benefit of management and its allies while making any further investment in the company prohibitively expensive.

In Crown Zellerbach's case, the poison pill was latent until someone acquired 20 per cent. Then it 'exploded', which meant it could no longer be redeemed by the company. Theoretically it became irreversible. If an outsider sought to acquire 100 per cent, the management and its supporters were then allowed to buy a new issue of shares at $50 a share which the outsider had to pay $100 apiece to acquire.

On 1 April 1985, Goldsmith challenged the poison pill by telling Creson and his board that if they withdrew their opposition, he was prepared to offer $41.625 a share, or $1.14 billion for the company. If they refused, he would not seek the full 100 per cent ownership, but would buy enough shares to force representation on the board at the annual meeting scheduled for 9 May.

Lawsuits and counter-suits filled the courts from California to Delaware. Creson even lobbied the US Senate finance committee in Washington which was holding hearings because of the public uproar over the takeover rampage going on in America.

Goldsmith, he told the senators, was akin to 'the men who pillaged England and Ireland in the ninth and tenth centuries'. Instead of helping to create wealth, raiders – and Goldsmith was included – destroyed the companies 'that built our nation's long-term wealth'. Goldsmith stored that criticism away for another time; this was not the moment to lose his temper.

A week later, the combatants were involved in an episode that, among other things, underscored Goldsmith's wisdom in not getting too much involved with the Drexel Burnham Lambert firm under Milken and Dennis Levine, by then Drexel's director of mergers and acquisitions. Levine at the time was in his late twenties, a podgy, bespectacled man driven by an overpowering desire to make money, and not too fussy about how he did it. Levine is now a legend as 'Mr Insider Trader', the man who, under the pseudonym Mr Diamond, dealt through a Swiss bank account in the Bahamas on privileged information gained through his job at Drexel. He created an elaborate network among the accounting, legal and investment banking young professionals on Wall Street, from whom he bought information, dealt on it, and then sold it on to someone else, usually the arbitrageur Ivan Boesky. It was his arrest that brought down Boesky, who then fingered Guinness and Ernest Saunders in Britain – and finally led to the demise of Drexel itself.

Goldsmith had taken the precaution of negotiating with Levine to set up a line of junk-bond credit should the bidding for Crown Zellerbach exceed the limits of the bank and investor commitments.

Blaine (always known as 'Fin') Fogg, an attorney from Skadden, Arps, Meagher & Flom, and Joseph Flom, Skadden's legendary senior partner, were among the most prominent attorneys one could have in a takeover battle in those days. Goldsmith first met Flom – he was introduced to him by Andre Meyer – in 1972 when Skadden was a small firm and Flom an unknown lawyer. In the years since, Flom had built Skadden into the dominant firm in the merger business, only rivalled by Wachtell, Lipton, Rosen and Katz. Either Fogg or Flom was always within Goldsmith's reach when a deal was on. Fogg recalls the strange events of 25–26 April.

'Goldsmith had a call the night before from Joe Flom that Mead Corporation wanted to talk to both of us and Crown's board in the morning. I went over to his East Eightieth Street house first thing next morning and we met with their lawyers who said they wanted to take over Crown at $50 a share,' Fogg says.

This was a high tension morning. Goldsmith and his lawyers, advisers (including Levine) and various members of his staff all met in his house, some sitting downstairs, a select few invited to his study upstairs. Mead's lawyer was George Lowy, a partner in the New York law firm Cravath Swaine & Moore, who was included, along with Roland Franklin and Fin Fogg, in the exclusive upstairs gathering. Lowy, acting for Mead, explained that his client and Crown had agreed on a friendly merger at $50 a share, and the company wanted to do a deal with Sir James about buying his Crown stock. Goldsmith replied that he wanted control of Crown, but not at $50 a share – 'that's too rich for me' – but if someone else wanted to squeeze him out with a $30m to $40m quick profit, well, he could go look elsewhere for his timber.

During the morning, several Goldsmith aides noticed the odd behaviour of Levine.

'At that point, I don't even think Levine was working for us yet. But I do remember that at mid-morning he said he had a meeting elsewhere and left. We went on with the meeting and it went well,' said Fogg.

In fact there was little to discuss at the meeting in the study after the Mead lawyer outlined his offer. 'I didn't welcome it,' said Goldsmith afterwards. 'It wasn't my original purpose. But I had no choice. You had to face the facts. They'll pay $50. I'm not going to pay $50. The deal took about ten minutes. And the charming man stayed to lunch.'

Lowy, the lawyer, had worked in Paris and over lunch Goldsmith warmed to him. 'He and Jimmy talked French politics and had a lovely time,' says Fogg.

At the same time as the discussions were going on in Goldsmith's house, the same terms were being presented to the Mead board in Dayton, Ohio. Ivan Boesky had bought 7.4 per cent of Crown, and would also accept $50 a share which, with Goldsmith's stake, would give Mead a hefty stake. What everyone underestimated, including Boesky with his hair-trigger reactions and his nose for every detail of a deal, was the opposition of the Mead directors. The company was having a bad time, and the board decided they did not want to take on the extra debt involved with buying Crown. They rejected the deal.

At Goldsmith's house the party was well into lunch when Lowy excused himself to tell the Mead management he had been successful in his negotiation with Goldsmith – Crown Zellerbach was theirs. It was then he learned that his client would not go through with it. His first thought, he says, was to get out of the town house without anyone noticing, but he thought better of it and returned to the table.

'You're not going to give me dessert,' he told Goldsmith. 'The board didn't approve the deal.'

Goldsmith in his own home is an impeccable host, with all the manners – and mannerisms – of his father, Frank. He is elaborately, almost old-worldly, polite, addressing his own staff in terms of, 'I wonder would you be so kind as to close the door as you go out', and insists on accompanying a guest out on to the pavement, closing the door of their car, waving as they drive off. It is not done for effect – it is second nature, the way he was brought up, inherited from Frank who in turn inherited it from his father; he could not change it if he tried. In New York the investment banking community, used to snatching sandwich lunches over their desks, were amazed at his courtesy – not least Lowy that day. He was just taking $40m away from Goldsmith, but Goldsmith almost apologised to him.

In fact, Goldsmith was delighted with the news. He wanted Crown Zellerbach badly. Mead had appeared unsolicited and made an offer higher than he was willing to pay. But now Mead was gone again, and Crown was within his reach.

Dennis Levine, still at the lunch table, did not take it calmly. Franklin later recalled him going 'a shade of grey'. He muttered something about another unexpected meeting across town and left hurriedly.

It was so obvious that everyone at the table noticed. 'He was anxious to get to his broker as quickly as possible,' Goldsmith joked. But he was annoyed. 'I don't want that man at any more of our meetings,' he told Joe Flom, and his own house counsel, Jane von der Heyde.

Levine, it later emerged, dashed from the town house to a pay telephone where he rang his banker in the Bahamas. He sold, through his secret Bahamas account, 100,000 Crown Zellerbach shares at a profit of $80,000 before the news broke.

But the day's strange events were not over yet. That afternoon Creson called Goldsmith from California and proposed a standstill agreement; Crown would cancel the poison pill, and in return Goldsmith would not buy more than 19.5 per cent of its shares for the next three years. Goldsmith countered by demanding to own one-third of the stock, and his standard proviso that his directorships be buttressed by a rule that would refer any crucial management decisions about sales or acquisitions to the shareholders if there was less than unanimous approval by the board. This time Creson hung up.

Almost at once Crown Zellerbach announced it would split itself into three corporate units, one consisting of the 1.6m acres of timber, a second composed of the plastics and packaging business, and a third to own the rest of the corporation which would be left with a sales turnover of $2.25 billion. How this would work with the poison pill in place, no one explained. Goldsmith thought the plan was badly flawed, but Wall Street pushed the Crown Zellerbach shares up to $44.

The bankers and advisers, who had at first arrived for breakfast, were still at Goldsmith's house at dinner time as they debated what to do. 'Jimmy was getting a little upset,' says Fogg. Joe Flom and Bob Pirie of Rothschilds had now joined them, and they all sat around trying to work out what to do. Why had Mead pulled out? 'We began to wonder if they had found out something about Crown that we didn't know,' says one of the team. 'Perhaps we were overpaying. The thing was getting very confusing, and we weren't sure the company was worth it.'

Over dinner Goldsmith and Franklin suggested they drop their tender offer for Crown, let the share price fall, and then decide on the next step. The next day Jimmy left New York to spend Easter in Richmond with

Annabel and the children, but was back in the first week in May, with a clear strategy. Again his greater experience of the hostile bid put him a step ahead even of his own advisers. Goldsmith had won Bovril by going into the market and buying shares, a strategy that was inconceivable to the New York lawyers who were working on the most elaborate of plans. Now he bought Crown shares from anyone who would sell, including Boesky's block – Boesky may well have felt as uneasy about the stock's uncertainty as Dennis Levine. By the first week of May 1985, Goldsmith owned 5.3m of the 27.2m shares, or 19.6 per cent; on the eve of Crown Zellerbach's annual meeting, he was about to explode the poison pill in Creson's face.

At the annual meeting, Goldsmith was elected to the board by the shareholders, but lost his proxy fight – and Creson further angered Goldsmith by accusing him of demanding greenmail.

'They had been trying to push greenmail down my throat and I'd been refusing it and three days after that meeting the Crown directors offered me $100m again in greenmail to leave them alone. But I turned them down. By this time I was boiling,' he recalls.

It took a little while for Goldsmith's strategy to dawn on Creson, but when it did he was horrified. By buying more than 20 per cent of its shares, yet stopping short of trying to buy 100 per cent, Goldsmith had landed Crown Zellerbach's management in the worst of all possible worlds. The terms of the poison-pill defence had allowed Crown to let it lie dormant and to sell off bits of the company to buyers as long as no one bought more than 20 per cent of the shares. Once that barrier was broken, however, the company could not cancel the device and any other white knight who came along had effectively to pay twice the going rate for his shares. Creson had cut himself off from outside rescue. By the end of May, Goldsmith owned more than one-quarter of the shares, and by early June the two sides were negotiating a joint restructuring agreement. Creson invited Jimmy to join the board, and all litigation was to cease.

It would not end so easily, however. Crown wanted to sell 1.6m acres of its timberlands to a partnership, and Goldsmith was absolutely against this move, on the grounds it would create a $180m tax bill. On 1 July he attended a board meeting which he remarked afterwards was the 'harshest' he had ever been at, but he finally felt his view had prevailed. 'They would spin off the assets I wanted – the forest lands – and we would exchange our stock. I would get out of Crown, which would continue,' he explained.

It did not work that way, and in retrospect Goldsmith is delighted it didn't. He left San Francisco for New York, and went on for a month-long cruise along the coast of Turkey, leaving Roland Franklin behind to iron out the details.

Again Creson and his directors went into full-court defence, stalling on the agreement and playing to the press while they waited for the courts in Delaware to rule on the various challenges to the poison-pill defence; they won in the courts, but lost to Goldsmith in the end.

Both sides would later accuse the other of breaking the deal, but Goldsmith's yacht rapidly became a war-room as he shouted instructions down the telephone. Creson told him the deal to swap the forest lands for his shares was off, blaming Goldsmith's lawyers, while Goldsmith insisted the deal was on. The battle became so rough that Goldsmith even participated in a board meeting down the satellite telephone, his words broadcast to the boardroom.

Goldsmith again reverted to his well-tried tactic of going into the market. By the end of July, he had bought enough shares – at less than the $42.50 he had offered in April – to control 51 per cent of the company. On 21 July, a Sunday night, Creson surrendered. The formula for agreement suited Goldsmith very well: the company was split into two, and shareholders, advised by Merrill Lynch, had the opportunity of either joining Goldsmith and his team in the forest and oil company, Cavenham Forest Industries, or of joining James River, who bid, mainly in their shares, for the Crown Zellerbach paper and pulp business. Forests were very much out fashion, so most shareholders opted for James River, one of the largest paper groups in America.

This meant that Goldsmith and his Cavenham Forest Products ended up with what they wanted all along: 1.9m acres of timberland at less than $100 an acre, plus $90m in cash, other assets worth $330m, and a computer company. The cost to Goldsmith of the entire deal had been $550m, all of it from his bank and backers, none of it from junk bonds. By the end of the year Wall Street was estimating that he had scored a paper profit of $340m to $440m just in those few months.

But Goldsmith was not about to cash in so quickly, even though everyone expected he would. He now had nearly 4m of the 10m acres of prime timberland that he had sought, in high growth stands from Maine to Oregon. He also owned one of the top three grocery chains in America, as well as a complex network of forest-products manufacturing plant and oil and gas production facilities spread from Louisiana to the West Coast. He needed management help quickly.

*

Of all the people he recruited in his career, Floyd Hall was arguably the most inspired. He came at the right time, saw instantly what Goldsmith was trying to do with his US retail operations, and made it work. He also made a great deal of money, both for himself, and for the man who hired him.

When Jim Wood had left Grand Union four years earlier, its troubles seemed to worsen. Wood had hand-picked his successor, and Goldsmith, busy elsewhere, gave him his head, and in Goldsmith's view he had made a mistake. Grand Union embarked on a major change of strategy, as Jimmy finally – and belatedly – discovered its 'core' business, and began trimming it back, selling or closing the small stores, and concentrating the business on its strong geographic regions. Grand Union, he reckoned, had major structural problems: it was too scattered over the country, and it had no single strategy, as other groups had. In America, a food retailer sells on price, on quality or on service, and the successful groups have a single, identifiable image right across the country. Grand Union in one area was a cheap food business selling on price, in another, particularly where Goldsmith's fresh food drive had arrived, it sold on quality, and in others its outlets were convenience stores. 'Our stores were dull, and our prices were too high,' said Goldsmith. Every time one of the major competitors opened up nearby, the Grand Union store immediately lost a large volume of business. The group, he reckoned, without a major shift was simply going to die as so many others had done.

Milton Glaser and Wood had completed one experimental store in the town of Wyckoff in New Jersey which Goldsmith wanted to use as the model for the rest. It contained all the Glaser innovations, with many promptings from Jimmy: fresh bread baked by French-trained chefs, live fish swimming in tanks, a range of spices bought from the souks of Tunisia, fresh fruit, free range chickens, eggs, beef from a ranch that used no hormones. Goldsmith kept telling them he wanted 'real food', and they gave it to him. Glaser even created a European-style delicatessen.

It was expensive, with perhaps as much as 20 per cent of the merchandise sold at a loss, but it drew the customers in. By 1980 Goldsmith reckoned it a success, but it was only one store and he had 800. 'I was convinced we had the right formula,' he says. He reckoned that only 300 of the stores could be converted to the new concept – the others would be sold or closed. In the summer of 1980, with the world still only slowly coming out of recession, he began what American retailers call a major 'retrofit' – taking existing stores and putting them into the new model, after it has been tested.

Financially, it was a perilous move. When the process wasn't going fast enough, he took personal charge himself, dismissing Wood's successor. The rest of the food retail industry stood back and watched sceptically as he wielded the axe, and his numbers dived. Between 1981 and 1983 sales fell from $4 billion to $3.5 billion and then dropped another $100m. With the closure of the Weingarten chain and half of the Colonial Stores, the company started losing money to the tune of $115m in one year.

'I was pretty certain we were right, but I was losing $10 million a month, and the trade press were making a joke of me,' he says. 'One said I was putting the company on the table like a gambling chip. And it was a huge loss. It was a great worry to me – both an exhilaration, and a worry.'

It took 18 months before Grand Union began to respond and the figures turned upwards. By that stage he had his new chief executive officer in place – and Grand Union would never look back.

Goldsmith chose Floyd Hall with great care. He ruled out anyone already in the food retailing business – the business was too clogged with tradition, full of people, he says, who 'thought of themselves almost as a utility, so you'd have tuna next to TV sets because it was the next item on the list'. He wanted someone who could think creatively, who would understand – and agree with – what he was doing with Grand Union, and who had shown he was a good retailer in an area other than food. But he also wanted something else: his new man must come from a humble background, must have left school early, and must still want to make big money.

Floyd Hall fitted all these. He was 45, had left school at 15, came from an underprivileged family, started work with the Singer sewing machine company, and then moved into book retailing. By the time Goldsmith heard of him he was one of the leading retailers in America. He had become the chief executive of Target Stores, the principal subsidiary of Dayton Hudson, which was perhaps the best general merchandise retailer in America – the Marks and Spencer of the US. Hall was earning $1 million a year, and had no thought of moving again. 'He was the best in the country in my view,' says Goldsmith.

Hall was in Minneapolis when Goldsmith called him. Would he be interested in talking about taking over Grand Union? Hall was intrigued enough to agree, and Goldsmith sent his private plane to pick him up. Goldsmith then outlined his proposed package.

'You've made a brilliant success, and when you retire in 15 years, you'll be the president of a great company, you can go to Florida and live on a good pension. What I'm offering you is your last chance to become a capitalist. If you look at my stores, you'll see the figures are terrible, but you'll see that it's in the process of turning round, because we've got the strategy right. The figures are now booming.

'I will give you an option,' he went on. 'I'll pay you a million dollars a year, and five per cent of the company at our cost, and you will make $30 million in five years.'

In fact, Hall made $60m in three years.

In less than a year, Hall had Grand Union back in the black – by only a $5m profit, but something of a miracle at that. Turning the corner was painful enough: the group was down to just 379 outlets by the end of 1985 and total sales were $2.6 billion, dropping it from eighth to tenth place in the US supermarket league.

Profits crept back up to $60m after taxes, and Goldsmith had clear reason to breathe more easily. Over the years he would become very close to Hall, who in turn came to respect the way in which Goldsmith could control a large business. Hall inherited a company battered and bruised by two years of closures and losses but which had found a viable strategy and which was on the mend. Hall accelerated that process, to the point where by 1986 the stores were all modern, well-positioned and profitable. Hall was by then beginning to open more stores than he was closing, and the Grand Union concept had been widely copied across America.

Goldsmith could easily have sold Grand Union during those years, but was determined it would not go out as a failure. 'I have been a grocer for almost thirty-five years,' he said in 1986. 'I intend to remain one.'

Al Dunlap was Goldsmith's next major recruit; he would come to refer to the brash American manufacturing executive as 'my Rambo in pinstripes'. Dunlap is one of those brash, wonder-workers that make the American corporate executive often seem larger than life. A West Point graduate, he had served as the executive officer of a nuclear missile base before going into business. By the time he was 44, his reputation for efficiency was such that he was called in to save the famous Lily-Tulip paper cup business from near bankruptcy. The company had been bought from its parent Owen-Illinois as an early purchase by the Kohlberg, Kravis and Roberts team of leveraged buy-out specialists (raiders in another guise). The trouble was that KKR found it couldn't turn its property around fast enough as it slid into loss with dismaying swiftness.

'People try to make management into an esoteric science like putting a man on the moon or transplanting hearts,' says Dunlap now. 'But it is basically about doing fundamental things: reducing costs, concentrating on your core business, investing in your core businesses and getting the right people to do the right things.'

Within three years, Dunlap found himself out of a job. He had turned Lily-Tulip around so quickly that KKR was able to take it public at $9.50 a share and sell it off at $18.50 in 1986. The deal left Dunlap with $5m in profits, but without a challenge. Goldsmith named him president of GOSL Acquisition Corporation, his American holding company, and set him to marrying Diamond and Crown Zellerbach's properties into a prosperous combine.

Along the way Dunlap, who now runs his own investment banking operation from his home on Hilton Head Island, South Carolina, became a big fan of Sir James Goldsmith and a vocal defender of the Goldsmith style of corporate governance versus both the raiders and the entrenched managers.

Look, I handled it all, the Crown Zellerbach and the Diamond holdings, and we had fantastic successes. People who know him from financial dealings miss a whole other side of him; I can tell you that he is no greenmailer, no junk bond issuer, no assets stripper. None of that.

What Jimmy wanted when he hired me was someone with American manufacturing experience. He had Grand Union as a separate entity but GOSL had all the Diamond and all the Crown Zellerbach properties together because he saw great opportunity in the timber and both companies had been exceptionally poorly managed.

His theory is that if you acquire the hard assets, you protect yourself on the downside. Then if you improve the operating assets they can really ring the bell on the upside. You can generate enough cash with the improved earnings to reinvest. And you can reduce your debt and make more efficiencies by selling off whatever is not essential to improving that focus.

Dunlap and Hall acknowledge another factor about Goldsmith which is not part of the mythology: his ability to attract loyalty among his senior staff. Gilberte Beaux, now basically presiding over a holding company with no operations in Paris (as well as Basic), stayed with him, as did Roland Franklin, well after the point there was no role for them. Says Dunlap:

Anything we went after was with the absolute objective of getting the company because the biggest reward lay in controlling and running it well. That's the way to make money. What the outsiders failed to appreciate was that in the years since Crown Zellerbach, we were involved in putting a lot back into what he bought. Jimmy is willing to spend capital.

The operating earnings of the Crown Zellerbach properties we took in 1985 went up six-fold from $25 million to $130 million through 1990, and cash flow rose from $22 million to $105 million on an annualised basis. We had a tremendous increase in operating earnings and in cash flow and we had more than $100 million in profit improvement during that time. Under Goldsmith, the earnings of the Crown properties grew at 56 per cent annual compounded earnings growth. That's not bad for a company that Fortune said was dead.

One key is that we out-invested Crown Zellerbach. We spent more capital on those properties than they did before us. We got six sawmills, 1.9 million acres of land, seven incompatible computer systems, two competing headquarters. We put in a new computer system, one of the sawmills became state of the art. We moved the oil operations to Houston where they became a success. We had an operation up in Omak, Washington, that was surrounded by an Indian reservation and Crown was going to shut it down and ruin the community. We fixed it up and had the employees buy us out in the second-largest employee buyout in history.

'And all you hear about,' Dunlap adds, 'is the rape, plunder and pillage stuff.'

27

The Battle for Goodyear

While Goldsmith had heard plenty of criticism about the alleged rape and pillage of corporate America, he was not ready to concede the point, especially not in the case of his own corporate ventures. In the summer of 1985 he had taken his turn before the same Senate Finance Committee hearings where, some months earlier, Creson had lambasted him as a raider and destroyer. The hearings were covering proposed legislation which might be used to limit takeover bids, either by allowing target companies more time to marshall their defences, or by putting regulatory handicaps on the attackers. Goldsmith found himself upstaged at first by the other two witnesses who had agreed to appear – T. Boone Pickens, who had just finished a particularly bloody raid against Unocal, the Californian oil giant, and Fred Hartley, Unocal's crusty chief executive.

Most of the day, the two men had slashed at each other all round the high-ceilinged Senate hearing room. Hartley, in ill health and nearing 70, made up in irascibility what he lacked in precision. At one point he charged that Pickens would have caused Unocal to vanish totally as a corporate entity if he had gained control. Pickens retorted by mocking Hartley's mannerisms. Finally, pleading the need to catch a plane to London, Hartley left the hearing.

In his prepared statement, Goldsmith brought the senators back to the main issues before them. 'Who would have believed a few years ago that conglomerates, created at the time by freewheeling entrepreneurs, today are described by some as sacrosanct institutions which would be protected from the marketplace by special legislation?' he asked. 'All that has changed in many of those companies is that the flame of the founder has been replaced by the complacency of the bureaucrat. And because the members of such bureaucracies control the disposition of vast amounts of

410

other people's money and the power and patronage that accompany it, they feel they are part of the establishment and therefore deserve special privileges,' he argued.

Speaking with an eloquence sparked off by his own emotional experience with the business environment in Europe, Goldsmith made sure the senators understood the perils of interference in the market-place. He said:

> During the past few months in the United States, there has been a national debate about hostile takeovers. It seems to me that this debate is really about your new entrepreneurial revolution and the freedoms that have engendered it. The question really being asked is whether or not large corporations should be treated like institutions and should be granted special protection from the marketplace.

Senator Chris Hecht was moved to ask, at the end of Goldsmith's testimony, 'How come you stayed in Europe and did not come to America many, many years ago?'

'A good question, Senator Hecht. Stupidity actually,' he answered and the chamber rocked with laughter. People were not aware of lack of freedom, he went on, until they tasted freedom, 'and I was never aware of the inhibitions in Europe until I fully tasted America.' Within a year, having discovered that America was as protective as any other market when it wanted to be, he would change his mind, but on this day Goldsmith was determined not to let some of Hartley's challenges to takeovers go unanswered.

> Mr Hartley talks about mergers and raids, mergers being good and raids being bad . . . the difference in his definition between a merger and a raid is whether it is hostile. I'd like to analyse that word. Hostile to whom, senator? Hostile to the entrenched management, not hostile to the shareholders. Who's calling it hostile? The owners of the business? They should decide. It's only hostile because those who mistakenly have come to believe they own the business don't want to give it up. There's nothing hostile about a hostile bid. There's no difference between a raid and a merger except that the established bureaucrat loses his job, not the owners of the business.

This was a familiar and consistent theme of Goldsmith's, one that he had developed since the mid-1960s in Britain, but which had now emerged at the heart of an argument that was just beginning to divide corporate America. Every business school in the country was now

411

carrying out studies into the long-term effects of so-called 'hostile' takeovers on the health of the nation's industry. Every business magazine carried endless articles on the subject, most of them anti-raider, the *Wall Street Journal* letters columns were full of it, and the subject was debated in golf-club locker rooms from Akron to Dallas, and from Wall Street to San Francisco. The men giving evidence to the Senate that day, the most persuasive of whom was Goldsmith, were the leading exponents of the art of the takeover. At this particular moment, there was a lull in Goldsmith's pursuit of Crown – he had just lost his proxy fight, but gained his seat on the board and was now negotiating his aborted plan for the restructuring. But what interested the senators and the business community was the ease with which he had destroyed the fearsome potion of the Crown poison pill, simply by crossing the 20 per cent threshold but stopping short of 100 per cent. In the offices of the big legal firms, lawyers were working through the night devising antidotes to the 'Goldsmith loophole', as it was instantly dubbed, in the thousands of pills which had been designed to be poison, but as one lawyer remarked sourly, turned out to be 'candy for the aggressor'.

The public mood at this moment was that 'takeover madness' had gripped America, and was threatening the foundations of the nation's economy. Something had to be done. T. Boone Pickens, Carl Icahn, Ivan Boesky and now Sir James Goldsmith had become household names in America, admired by a few, feared by many. No company in the land seemed immune from threat. And there was another element too: for most of the last century, Americans had circled the world, investing in overseas ventures, and exporting their culture. Abruptly, in this period, this process reversed. Foreign investors were buying heavily into America and, by the mid-1980s, they owned 16 per cent of US bank assets; they also owned investment houses, skyscrapers, stores and publishing houses; four of America's top ten chemical companies were foreign-owned. Supporters of the trend pointed out that foreign investment had created 3m jobs in America in a decade, boosted the stock market, paid for the American government's budget deficit, and had been of enormous benefit to the economy. But foreigners were being regarded with growing suspicion. Goldsmith was both foreign and a raider, although it was in the latter role that he was now defending himself to the senators.

That doesn't mean there are no abuses in takeovers [he told the committee]. That doesn't mean there are not going to be bankruptcies. That doesn't mean that people are not going to take on too much debt. Of course that does not

412

mean raiders are doing it for any other reason than personal gain. Raiders shouldn't put on a halo. They *are* doing it for personal gain. The important thing is whether their action is generally beneficial or generally detrimental, not why are they doing it ... The dead hand of the bureaucrat does not produce growth. It does not produce innovation. It produces complacency, ossification and decline.

Many of the conservative Republican senators hooted with delight. At last here was an antidote to the steady stream of carping and complaining from the other witnesses, each of whom stopped considerably short of actually recommending what they wanted the Congress to do. 'Hey, Boone, this guy does a better job of talking than you do,' cried Senator Hecht, adding:

'Sir James, personally I would like to invite you to be an American citizen and to join the Republican party. You could be one of our top spokesmen.'

Senator Phil Gramm, an even more senior Republican from Texas, and one of the most respected men on either side of the aisle, added his endorsement:

Sir James ... you've done a great service to this country today, whatever money you've made here. I hope you make a lot more since we'll get a hefty share of it. You have more than paid us back by what you have done today in bringing an outside perspective on the problem ... what a great tragedy it is in the great economic system that capitalism has built when we hear business people argue about everything except the job of management, which is to earn profits. We hear arguments made on behalf of the national interest for exports and job protection and investment and research and development, but it's obviously considered in this great capitalistic nation somehow a weak argument to say that we're trying to make money ... money that is the fuel that moves the hinges that built this country and that promises it a bright future.

Goldsmith was flattered and surprised by his treatment at the hands of the senators. 'It was one of the most remarkable days of my life. On the whole they thought like me and I've never had people so nice to me in my life. I'm not used to it.'

He was, at this time, busier than ever, and although he resisted it, the pace was beginning to affect him. He tried to hide it even from those close to him, but he was conscious of a slackening in his energy, a feeling that he was not entirely well – something more than his habitual hypochondria. Before arriving in Washington for the Senate hearings, he chaired a series

413

of meetings at the New Jersey headquarters of Grand Union, now in better shape than it had ever been; his day in Washington was followed by a trip to San Francisco for a Crown Zellerbach meeting, then a flight back to New York city, and on to Paris. 'I have almost lost track of time and exhaustion,' he said tiredly to a *Washington Times* reporter who travelled on one leg of the trip with him. When the reporter asked if he could check some of the facts with him in Paris, he said, 'Well, yes. Only I don't know when I'll be in Paris. As you can see, I never know where I'm going next.'

He was by this stage worth a minimum of $900m personally, and probably more. Fortune might estimate that the Diamond deal had made him $500m, but Crown Zellerbach was to prove even better. Besides that there was Grand Union, worth another $1 billion, a 10 per cent stake in Basic Resources in Guatemala, his publishing interests in Paris and his stake in Aspinall's casino. There were his houses and his investments, properties and share stakes, his restaurants and all sorts of other assets. He was 52, and probably at the height of his powers. He had his own Hawker Siddeley private jet, which he used continually around America, Concording to Paris and London for speed and freshness. He was careful always to take his long holidays, and even as he was preparing for the Senate hearings he was also discussing hiring Adnan Khashoggi's huge yacht, *Nabila*, to cruise in the Baltic, new territory for him (he never went through with it).

That July he went instead to the coast of Turkey where his holiday was interrupted by his final battles with the Crown Zellerbach board. Through the autumn there was the enormous task of getting to grips with his new acquisition, and the hugely tricky business of completing the break-up in the face of the elaborate defences the company had erected.

Although he had neatly circumvented the Crown poison pill, it was still there, and somehow a way had to be found to get rid of it. 'If you did a merger of Crown with James River or anybody, the pill's "flip-over" would take effect, and rights holders could buy Crown's stock two for the price of one,' explained his lawyer Fin Fogg. 'So you couldn't do a merger. It had to be an exchange offer.' The challenge, he adds, 'was to design a solution that would convince the courts it was not just a clever disguise for a merger, but something distinctly different ... We all wanted a transaction that would not be declared illegal.'

Goldsmith had first revealed his stake in Crown in December 1984, but it was July 1985 before he went past the 50 per cent level. By December 1985, a year after he launched his assault, Goldsmith and a sizeable battery of lawyers were still trying to find a way around the pill, with the James River sale conditional on settlement of a couple of lawsuits in a federal court in Chicago. It was well into the spring of 1986 before Fogg and his colleagues finally got everything tidied up. 'We consolidated the lawsuits, banged out a settlement which bought back each and every pill and paid pillholders $20 million, and extinguished the pill,' says Fogg. 'We achieved *total eradication*.'

It was an event of as much significance to the Wall Street legal firms – and to other raiders and target companies – as it was to Goldsmith. The balance, which had been tipping towards the defence, now swung back to the bidder. The raiders again built up to a frenzy of activity. The 43-year-old Ron Perelman, victor of a $1.8 billion battle for the cosmetics company Revlon, made a run on Transworld, owners of Hilton Hotels; Carl Icahn offered $5 billion for USX, the United States steel complex, once the biggest corporation in the world, and there were rumours about Lockheed, Borg-Warner and just about every other company in America.

In May 1986, after some 18 months of nerve-racking concentrated work to complete the Crown deal, Roland Franklin threw a party at the Water Club in New York for the team which had worked on it during that time – with the exception of Dennis Levine who was by now awaiting trial, and fingering everyone he could in the hope of reducing his prison sentence. Fogg gave Franklin a T-shirt with a 'Pill-Busters' logo, but it was not until August 1986, by now freed from all constraints, that the boards of Crown Zellerbach and James River were at last able to announce their deal, whereby Goldsmith sold Crown's paper division.

By that stage there was much speculation along Wall Street about where Goldsmith might strike next. He had developed a habit of buying stakes in three or four companies just to create a smokescreen, because the arbitrageurs, still led by Boesky, seemed to know just about everthing. Security had to be very tight. For Goldsmith had indeed identified his next target in the US: the mammoth Goodyear Tire and Rubber Company, thirty-fifth largest in the country and a $10-billion-a-year behemoth that produced everything from the full range of tyres and rubber products to lighter-than-air dirigibles and consumer products; it had oil and gas operations, real estate and advertising ventures.

Goodyear was a blatant example of a company which was very good at what it did originally but which had diversified into areas it knew nothing about. It had moved into the aerospace business in the 1950s, and made its first major petroleum industry acquisition in 1983 when it bought Celeron Oil for $850m. In the week Goodyear bought Celeron, their share price fell 15 per cent, knocking $350m off its value, a measure of its own stockholders' view of this particular transaction.

'They had put in an oil pipeline from Texas to California which went way over budget and it hadn't pumped a drop of oil yet,' says Al Dunlap. 'After we had straightened things out with Diamond and Crown, it looked a pretty good objective. Goodyear would be a roaring success today if Jimmy had gotten control of it, I remain convinced of that.'

Goldsmith had promised Dunlap the job of chief executive of Goodyear, and was in the process of making some other changes among his personal staff too. Dunlap was allowed to lop off nearly 50 jobs from Roland Franklin's deal-making and research office. Franklin, always bubbling with some new deal or other, was a skilled in-house merchant banker, but was less good at administration, and Goldsmith had transferred all that side of the business to Dunlap. At the same time, Goldsmith had dumped Drexel Burnham Lambert as his back-up banker, in part because of the Levine attempt at insider trading on Crown Zellerbach, but also because he resented the firm's irritation at not being allowed to charge the huge management fees for junk bond deals that were never activated. He had never actually borrowed any money from Drexel, retaining them only as a backstop, which he never had to use. By the standards of the time, his deals were capitalised strongly enough for him to be able to use more traditional forms of borrowing.

Merrill Lynch was chosen as the new team, in part because their reputation in the takeover market was spotless, but more important to Goldsmith, they were willing to invest their own cash in Goldsmith's deals to the tune of as much as $1.9 billion on the Goodyear bid.

Goodyear was on a different scale and in a different league to anything Goldsmith had attempted so far, but was still within his now considerable reach. He and Dunlap worked out their strategy in detail, analysing the management and the component parts, doing the sums a dozen different ways. 'Sure, we would have gotten rid of their top management because they're not doing the job anyway,' Dunlap admits readily.

But the employees further down the ladder, the ones with talent, they would have done well because they would have been promoted. It would have been good for the companies we sold off because they would get managements that knew what to do with them. It would have been good for the country.

416

So logic says, if you have a track record and these are your objectives, why shouldn't everyone agree that this is a good thing? But what happened was the management, who were not doing the job and who didn't have their own wealth tied to the company, these guys fought like hell to keep their shareholders from getting any benefit.

Jimmy at one point told the Senate that the top Goodyear management had about £2 million of their own holdings in Goodyear shares and here he was willing to invest billions; so why was he suspected of trying to ruin Goodyear? Go figure.

Goodyear was too big to manage properly; it had 133,000 workers in 28 countries, and dominated Akron, home of the headquarters of all the major US tyre makers: Firestone, Goodrich, Kelly and others. Goodyear also dominated Ohio politics and had enormous clout in Washington. For much of the Seventies, the Akron giants had been able to prevent their French rival Michelin from marketing its steel-belted radial tyres for all but the very smallest cars sold in the United States. The tactic had been simple: using tyre testing data provided by their own studies, the tyre industry had argued to federal safety officials that Michelin products would generate too much heat in the larger sizes. Only when Ford started using Michelin radials as standard equipment on its luxury model cars was the dam broken.

Still Goodyear looked like a capital trap closed to outsiders who did not know how to push beneath the surface of a balance sheet the way Goldsmith and Franklin did. Goodyear's shares had remained almost motionless in recent years despite the bull market rally which had nearly doubled most other Dow Jones Industrial Index components. Despite Merrill Lynch's orders and the rush by arbitrageurs, Goodyear stock traded no higher than $37 well into October.

Goldsmith that summer and autumn was feeling worse and worse. He had as usual taken a long holiday, but continued to feel low. He went to doctors and specialists in Paris and New York, who could not diagnose his problems. He was torpid, sweating easily, feeling slightly sick much of the time.

The previous year Annabel had persuaded him to buy a place in Spain, and he joined her there to think about Goodyear and recover his health. He had become fond of this house, after initial misgivings. Annabel had discovered it, and she took him to see it, again experiencing the same trepidation as when she first showed him Ormeley Lodge. It was a long drive from Marbella airport, up into the mountains, along a bumpy track, to a farmhouse, which had been extended, with a lovely terrace and a stunning view. It had previously been owned by a leading Spanish decorator who had converted it, while his wife had created a beautiful garden.

Until he saw it, Jimmy was more interested in buying an old monastery in France, but Annabel persisted with the house in Spain. Jimmy had at first rejected it, then someone else bought it, only to put it back on the market again. This time Annabel was determined to get it. It was a perfect day when they finally arrived, and Jimmy sat out on the terrace looking over the hills and valleys. It was immensely peaceful and as he had done when he first saw Ormeley, he went very quiet. She knew he liked it.

They had rooms built out the back for the children, and retained a Spanish couple to look after the place for them.

As he thought about Goodyear, Jimmy spent hours with his children, constructing as he always did difficult games of 'animal, vegetable or mineral' or other word games, and wandering around the farm with little Benjamin who was by now six. Each of the children was assigned a particular job by Annabel, with Zach, who was twelve, put in charge of the vegetables. Goldsmith wanted everything grown organically, and he explained to the children the evils of modern, processed food. He played tennis with them, and should have been fully fit, but if anything he was worse.

Franklin flew from New York with the analyses on Goodyear and several other companies, and out on the terrace, as he read them, Goldsmith made up his mind. Without telling his advisers which company he had decided on, he called a meeting in Paris. Merrill Lynch was to present a study of possible takeover prospects that had been commissioned by Franklin. Goldsmith, still unwell, flew from Spain and assembled at the meeting the charter members of his 'fan club', seasoned investment participants in past deals: Ted Field, an heir to the Marshall Field retailing fortune, who was determined to build his own stake; Johnny Pigozzi, heir to the French Simca fortune, who had become one of Jimmy's closest friends; and the two Fischer brothers, reclusive New Yorkers known for making big takeover plays.

Goodyear was not the top of the target list that day: the original purpose of the meeting was to look over another company, one with large real estate and timber holdings. But as the meeting progressed, Goldsmith became more and more convinced he was right. Goodyear was the one.

I saw all the elements of a company that needed a new strategy and a refocusing [he said later]. What I saw was a company that had a great core business in the tyre business, which had fallen into the trap of expanding for size rather than quality and value, that had diversified into a large number of areas of which it was now ignorant. They had spent most of its capital investment in fields like the oil and gas business, or the pipeline business, instead of spending that capital in its core business to get its factories into a state-of-the-art situation. As a result it had to go to Congress with other tyre manufacturers to seek protection from certain imports of tyres. Goodyear's diversification had failed, and its shares had dropped in value between 1982 and 1986 by more than 20 per cent whereas the general stock market had risen by well over 230 per cent in that same time. I saw a company which had lost its way but still had great strength.

There would be different views on that over the coming months, ferociously argued at all levels, but looking back now, most objective observers would accept that Goldsmith was right – or at least that he had a point.

'These are symptoms that are so common to major companies that have lost their way and where management wants to create empires,' Goldsmith later argued. 'I thought that there was a role to be played by major investors in refocusing the company which would improve its efficiency, its world competitiveness and its value.'

At the Paris meeting he told the Merrill Lynch team and his investment prospects that he believed that the company would fetch a considerable premium over its $3.3 billion market value, but that there was profit to be had. He was especially keen to have Merrill Lynch's full support. Even then, Goldsmith was growing suspicious of the ability of Wall Street to continue to float aloft those huge hot air balloons known as junk bonds and to leverage raiders into the treasuries of target companies without a thought of how those bonds would be serviced later.

'My sense was that the scene was changing in America. And I thought that the big investment banks would, in due course, want to use their balance sheets to help the financing of transactions. Therefore one needed a major banking partner,' he said.

Goldsmith kicked off on Thursday, 25 September 1986 when Merrill Lynch bought 1.7m Goodyear shares for $56.3m, about $33 each on average. Until then, most of the takeover raids of the previous three years had been concentrated in the petroleum and retailing sectors where cash was long and shares were depressed. Until Goldsmith's campaign against Goodyear there was a consensus among Wall Street analysts that some American corporations were just too big to tackle. The days of $21-

billion RJR-Nabisco sieges – or his own bid for BAT which would have been even larger – were beyond imagination.

By 25 October, Goldsmith's identity as a purchaser of shares had been established and published. The Goodyear chairman Robert Mercer flatly refused to countenance a takeover bid from anyone and the prospect of an all-out battle pushed the share price up to $48. In the meantime, Mercer sent senior aides to the company's apartment at United Nations Plaza in New York for secret meetings with Goldsmith. On the strength of those talks, Goldsmith invited Mercer to come to New York for lunch at the 80th Street house. He did so at the request of Joe Flom, the Skadden Arps takeover guru who, given the odd alliances of the corporate-legal community, was representing Mercer and Goodyear even though he retained his friendship with Goldsmith.

The lunch was not a success. Mercer got lost trying to enter Goldsmith's townhouse and was discovered wandering alone in the basement kitchen. Finally the two sat down together in the library over soft drinks while they waited for the food to be served.

Goldsmith would recreate the scene later.

We talked about generalities at first. One of Mercer's predecessors had just been appointed ambassador to Mexico and so we talked about that, trying to assess each other. Then we went to lunch and he asked me whether we had shares and how many . . . and I told him. I told him I thought Goodyear was a very good tyre company with great technology, able to compete worldwide. I felt, rightly or wrongly, that the diversification programme had not been a success. More importantly it had diverted management time and substantial capital away from the core business and into areas in which the company was not knowledgeable and which had not been a great success; and that this had been reflected in their share price.

And then I told him I would like to participate in the refocusing of the company. I believe he thought me rather ignorant because he went through all the points I made and tried to show me why all the diversifications had been very good. He then asked me about greenmail. I made it all quite clear that it was not our intention to sell the shares to the company for greenmail and that we wanted to participate in the company. He agreed that greenmail was not his intention either.

This would become an important point later when Goldsmith, not for the first time, stood accused of taking greenmail. He resolutely insisted that it was never his intention – what he wanted was the company, but not at any price.

Mercer also gave his version of this lunch, and as a measure of how two worldly, intelligent men can have entirely different views of the same meeting, it is worth recording here:

'The day after we found Goldsmith was after us,' he told his friend Lee Iacocca (reproduced in *Talking Straight*), 'I called him and suggested we talk.' Goldsmith, he says, invited him to the 80th Street townhouse for lunch – 'the most expensive lunch I've ever had.' They were not far into the meal, he says, when Goldsmith made it clear he wanted to take over the whole company 'for its break-up value'.

'In five minutes of discussion, I was able to determine how little he knew. For instance, he thought that our aerospace division was a recent diversification. But we'd been in that business since 1911. He didn't understand what we were doing in chemicals. Yet the chemicals business supplies synthetic rubber and other chemicals so that we can manufacture rubber products across a vast spectrum of product lines.' Goldsmith, said Mercer, then questioned Goodyear's involvement in the energy business, 'not realising that there are seven gallons of oil in each passenger tyre we produce'.

Iacocca, one of America's great management heroes for his turn-round of Chrysler and his forthright stance against Japanese and foreign attacks on American industry, was appalled. 'Can you imagine Goodyear being run by somebody that ignorant of what he was buying?' Mercer's argument is patent nonsense. Oil is a commodity, available to everyone at the same price. There is not the slightest advantage in a tyre company having its own – in fact, quite the opposite. Goodyear might technically have been in the aerospace industry since 1911, but its real investment came much later. Similarly, it is probably better to buy synthetic rubber and chemicals from a group which specialises in producing them – why produce your own?

In the weeks ahead, Iacocca became one of the more outspoken critics of Goldsmith. Jimmy, he said, had 'trotted over here from England' and assured everybody 'that he was doing a wonderful deed', making it sound as 'if he were the Red Cross or something' because Goodyear was badly managed. 'That's always the line these raiders take. They play on this myth that guys can rise to the head of big publicly held companies by being fat, happy, and stupid; that they're busy studying their golf scores and ignoring the poor stockholders.'

Goldsmith could easily dismiss Iacocca's argument, and Iacocca had his own problems as Chrysler's recovery faltered, but the antagonism caught him off guard.

On 31 October, he announced he had acquired 11.5 per cent of Goodyear's shares, paying $530m. What was not known until later was that he had recruited some heavyweight backers for this fight, including his old British friends James Hanson and Gordon White, who had just completed their own takeover and break-up, a classic of its kind, of SCM, the old Smith-Corona typewriter company which had also become a conglomerate.

The next week, on 5 November, Goldsmith called Mercer and told him he would make him a tender offer for the 88.5 per cent of Goodyear shares remaining and the price would be $49 a share, $4.7 billion in all. Mercer asked him to delay the public announcement until Goodyear's board of directors had met that very day. He promised to meet Goldsmith at the UN Plaza apartment that evening. When they met, Mercer informed Goldsmith the board had agreed to a restructuring plan that would surely boost Goodyear's shares above the $49 level the suitor wanted to pay.

The key to it was the sale of Goodyear's Celeron oil and gas firm and its aerospace division which included the company's trademark fleet of dirigibles – which is precisely what Goldsmith would have done, and what he was urging Mercer to do. In addition Mercer was prepared to buy back up to 20m Goodyear shares, including Goldsmith's, to insure against future takeovers.

'We went out into the hall and talked. There were three aspects: should we go ahead? Two, should we give them time? And three, what was the approximate value of their existing plan? I thought about $50 a share,' Goldsmith reports.

'I still thought our deal might have a shot in a showdown contest with the shareholders only if we faced the original Goodyear management plan, the $50 offer. But I felt we would lose if that offer were improved and I did not want to incur the costs and lose the goodwill that I thought I had built with Mercer,' Goldsmith adds.

Goldsmith held back on the tender, arguing to Mercer that he wanted to participate in just such a venture. An informal two-week standstill agreement was agreed to. It was one of the most costly mistakes Goldsmith ever made.

Events moved smartly against him. While Goldsmith and his partners cooled their heels in New York, Mercer and his team were mounting one of the most amazing public opinion campaigns in the history of America's circus-like public relations industry. Goldsmith was the man who was going to destroy not just the tyre company, but Ohio as well. Indeed, the docile press of the state roused itself to portray Goldsmith as a man who would wreck the small-town blue-collar way of life just to line his pockets. Worse than that, he was a 'foreign invader', his name appearing on bumper stickers and at football rallies as the whole of Akron seemed to mobilise to repel him. 'Who is to say he will not move the rest of our jobs overseas?' a Goodyear worker was quoted as saying in a remark typical of the hysteria. Move to where? Why would Goldsmith want to move the jobs anywhere?

It got worse. Mercer announced his raid amounted to 'economic terrorism' and that the massive restructuring he and others like him were forcing on corporate America was damaging long-term competitiveness as companies sold off profitable units and accumulated enormous debts to fight off takeovers.

'Within days we had an astonishing whip-up of emotion and hatred,' says Goldsmith. 'We had Ohio schoolchildren chanting anti-Goldsmith songs and making anti-Goldsmith masks and sending me hate mail. The Legislature responded to corporate pressure and the Ohio House was going to enact specific legislation aimed at preventing me from taking control of Goodyear. The situation was impossible.'

Not only was Goodyear stacking the deck in the Ohio state capital of Columbus, but it extended its reach to Washington. Congressman John Seiberling, a grandson of the Goodyear founder and himself a company legal counsel before he was elected to office, used his influence to win a hearing on the Goodyear–Goldsmith battle before a House panel governing monopolies. The meeting was scheduled for 18 November, a Tuesday. In Columbus, the anti-Goldsmith legislation was being rushed through the procedural maze and quite probably would be enacted a few days later. Such was the frenzy in the state at the prospect of the Anglo-French invader, the governor had promised to sign the bill into law minutes later. Even the unions, long at odds with Mercer and Goodyear, rallied to the company's side and the state's two powerful US Senators, ex-astronaut John Glenn, and Howard Metzenbaum, were quick to jump on the anti-Goldsmith bandwagon.

Then on Friday, 14 November 1986, came another hammer blow. The week had already been one of the heaviest of the whole takeover boom, which after a pause in the summer had erupted at yet new record levels. As dealers on Wall Street wearily tidied their desks before going home for the week-end, the bombshell that would effectively end the boom – and Goldsmith's chances of getting Goodyear – burst with a discreet announcement put out after the markets had closed. Ivan Boesky, king of the arbitrageurs and the man at the centre of every takeover bid in the past five years, had been arrested. In return for leniency, he had agreed to co-operate with the SEC's investigators, and over the week-end it became known that for six weeks Boesky had been walking into meetings wired up with a hidden tape recorder; all his thousands of telephone calls had been recorded, and the tapes were in the hands of the investigators.

The shock of it almost literally shook Wall Street. As Boesky's evidence led the way to further arrests the scale and depth of the insider trading network that revolved around the bid scene, and the junk-bond-financed bids in particular, became all too clear. The talk that week-end was of legislation to outlaw hostile bids, junk bonds – and of further protection for companies such as Goodyear.

Washington was flooded with bus-loads of Goodyear union members, old-age pensioners and schoolchildren; the crowd gathered to wave signs and demonstrate their case before an all-too-sensitive Congress. Goldsmith could scarcely believe what was happening to him. No one wanted to hear what he had planned for Goodyear, what his restructuring would mean for the company, its profits, its people and their job prospects. He was booed as he got out of his taxi outside the House building where the hearings were, but, characteristically, he plunged into the crowd and tried to sway them with his arguments. The boos grew louder and aides pulled him inside.

The reception that greeted him there was even worse. The two senators from the state made the unusual move of coming over to the House side to lend their testimony and weight to Seiberling's crusade. Goldsmith was 'the greatest shock to Ohio since Pearl Harbor', they charged. Akron's mayor, Tom Sawyer, a Democrat recently elected to Congress, also gave evidence, labelling Goldsmith a 'villain' and telling the senators that Goodyear was 'under siege and our communities and citizens are caught in the crossfire'. The lawmakers were presented with ample evidence that the voting public simply did not want Goldsmith to take over a corporation that was more than a corporation, a symbol of their culture.

Once again, Goldsmith tried reasoned argument. He had spent days making his speech as telling as possible. He carefully elaborated the case against the current Goodyear management: great managers of its past had defined the company's job clearly: 'to build better tyres, cheaper, and sell them harder'. The current management had forgotten that, and instead had made every mistake in the book. When the Celeron oil company was bought in February 1983, he said, the price of oil was $29.16 a barrel; now it was $13 a barrel. The pipeline, originally scheduled to cost $600 million, had ended up costing $1 billion – 'and we don't know if there is enough oil for the pipeline to operate profitably for years'. In December

1985 the company plunged even deeper into the oil business with a $480m bid, only weeks before the price of oil collapsed. In all it had wasted $2 billion in the oil and gas industry, instead of investing in tyres where imports had risen from 12 per cent in 1982 to 24 per cent in 1985. He contrasted his own record, and how he had 'liberated' companies out of 'tired conglomerates'. 'Up and down the country, hundreds of erstwhile stagnant divisions of large bureaucratic corporations have been freed.'

He ended by quoting Reagan's deputy secretary of the Treasury, Richard G. Darman. 'Mr Darman said that federal budget deficits are the cause most often cited for the economy's sluggishness. But he added, "I believe we have deeper cultural problems that demand our attention. High on the list one would find a problem that is sometimes captured with the term 'corpocracy', a reference to large-scale corporate America's tendency to be like the government bureaucracy." '

It was not a popular message in that room on that day. Goldsmith was largely ignored while he talked, and few questions were asked except at the end when Seiberling played to the crowds of Goodyear fans at the back of the room. 'My question is: who the hell are you?' he asked Goldsmith as the mob clapped and cheered.

'I was sitting behind Jimmy when that guy yelled, "who the hell are you",' says Al Dunlap. 'Jimmy had been fiddling with this paper clip and it just sprang out of his hand and he started, "I'll tell you who I am, Congressman" – and he proceeded to outline his record and he went on for ten, twelve minutes about how he would streamline the company, incentivise the management and build the company's share value back up. And Seiberling just went on to the next question as if Jimmy had never spoken. Jimmy kept saying, "Look at our company. I'll put our cash flow, our capital spending up against anybody." But they weren't listening.'

Even by Goldsmith's standards this was a full 24 hours. After the Senate hearings, he had lunch with Mercer at the Hay Adams Hotel where the Goldsmith aides had set up base camp. Goldsmith had not given up, and that morning had paid a fee of $22m to ensure he had the money he needed. Now he told Mercer to expect a tender offer by the next day. That was the only way he could get in under the barrier the Ohio legislature might put in place on Thursday. It was either Wednesday or not at all.

Mercer and Goldsmith's old chum Joe Flom put up a counter-offer to buy out Goldsmith's holdings right then and there. For $620m, Goodyear would buy back Goldsmith's holdings at $49.50 a share and net the investor partnership $93m profit. The company also planned to buy 40m of its own shares at $50 each, the offer extended to all shareholders – Goodyear's way of anticipating the cries of 'greenmail' it knew would follow.

Jimmy said he would think about it and went back to his suite to meet his lawyers. He had arranged to have his evidence to Congress taped, and in an interlude that afternoon he and his friend Johnny Pigozzi watched the tape. Goldsmith could scarcely believe what he saw. On the screen he saw he was sweating and red-faced, looking at times positively demonic as he made a particularly vehement point, all of it exaggerated by the television cameras.

'He kept exclaiming, "Is that really me? I don't believe I was so nasty",' says Pigozzi. 'And he was roaring with laughter, and striding up and down. He would stop and look at it and say "I can't believe how nasty I look on this thing. I look like a monster. It's incredible!" And he was sweating and going crazy on the screen, with his arguments – and he was fabulous, but he couldn't believe what he looked like.'

Late in the afternoon, Goldsmith broke off from his meetings to change into black tie. That evening he was host to President Reagan at a dinner to mark the tenth anniversary of a conservative think-tank in Washington, the Ethics and Public Policy centre. He returned to continue the negotiations with Goodyear, which went on right through the night. At dawn, he had to break again for a quick shower and shave before taking part, at seven in the morning, in a debate on the future of Nato with Mrs Jeanne Kirkpatrick, the noted American conservative and former US Ambassador to the United Nations, and Don Rumsfeld.

These were events he could enjoy, and were the compensations of life in America. He would not toss them away lightly.

But by the time he returned to the Goodyear negotiations, he had had enough. 'One thing I had to consider was the political and general environment,' he said later. 'I had been through that Congressional meeting where I had heard the greatest bunch of buffoons ask the greatest bunch of idiotic questions I had ever heard. This had become an emotional, a political, but not a logical argument. When I saw that, on top of what was happening in Ohio, and on top of that ghastly affair with Boesky in New York, it was clear to me that we were not living in the real world.'

The climate he reckoned had changed drastically. 'We have now entered the post-Reagan period with the triple alliance of big business, big government and big unions fighting back,' he said that week.

'He realised it was the end of this particular era, and they were going to use him as a symbol of all they didn't like about foreigners and about hostile bids,' says a friend. 'And he thought it was time to make a nice clean little retreat, and then he would come back again.'

He finally accepted the Goodyear offer, emerging with a straight profit for himself and his backers of $93m. Mercer responded to accusations of 'greenmail' by pointing out that other shareholders had received more than Goldsmith. Jimmy was even more direct. 'From our point of view, we failed even though we made some money ... I consider it a failure.' During the lengthy depositions taken from Goldsmith a year later he repeated that answer when he was asked whether he was proud of the profit he had made on the deal. 'The answer is, No. It was a defeat as far as I'm concerned. I would have liked to have been able to carry out the restructuring fully. I believe the values there were substantial. I would have been happy to carry my shares. But we lost. So the idea that we went in there for a small profit is totally grotesque.'

Goldsmith lost the battle, but not the intellectual argument. A year later he was able to show that the actions Mercer had taken were almost exactly what he had indicated he intended for the company – and what he told Congress he would do. Mercer announced that Goodyear would fulfil the definition coined by its former chairman, Paul W. Litchfield, in the 1920s – 'building better tyres, cheaper, and selling them harder.' Mercer had sold most of the diversifications, and paid back to shareholders $2.7 billion by buying back shares. 'In August 1986, when I was looking at the company, the total market value of the equity was about $3.5 billion,' he said in a speech to the Garn Institute of Finance in Washington in September 1987. 'So shareholders have received 80 per cent of the value of the company as it stood in August 1986. What do shareholders have now have for their residual 20 per cent? They have shares that now have a market price of $70 instead of $32, and they have earnings per share estimated to be in excess of $6.65. In 1986, the earnings had been $1.68.'

But for several years he continued to be stung by comments 'from the corpocrats', such as Iacocca, that his raid had left Goodyear awash with debt which he forced it to assume in order to pay its shareholders their $2.7 billion. The reality, Goldsmith argues, is very different. Goodyear received $1.6 billion for asset sales, and refused to accept an offer of $700m for the pipeline. 'I was not responsible for their debt, even though I have to read over and over that I was. I am proud of what I did to Goodyear. From the US economy's point of view, instead of a company that had to go cap in hand to Congress they are able to open a state-of-the-art factory which, in the words of Mr Mercer, "can compete with anybody. And when I say anybody," said Mr Mercer, "that includes the Koreans",' Goldsmith stated.

'So it was a general benefit and I am proud of what I did.'

Physically over this period, Goldsmith had changed visibly. Ever since he was a boy he had always looked older than his age, but now his remaining hair was grizzled, and those who hadn't seen him in a couple of years reckoned he had aged ten years. He was 53, but looked 63. He had been to clinics and specialists without finding any relief from his mysterious malaise.

Back in London, Annabel found him slumped so badly one morning that she summoned her own local doctor, Matthew Gardiner, who immediately came around. Gardiner heard his symptoms, poked and prodded him for about ten minutes, and then pronounced: 'You've got diabetes.'

He was right. Goldsmith had probably been suffering from it, in a very mild form, for several years. He was tested, went on to new treatment, and instantly felt better. Yet in this period he had changed in ways which those who had known him for many years remarked on. In some ways he had become more placid, no longer roused to the same degree of anger which had burned so fiercely during the *Private Eye* affair. Yet in other ways he had a shorter fuse, which could be easily ignited. Put some white bread in front of Goldsmith and he will sweep it from the table. 'If something small goes wrong he goes berserk,' says an aide. 'And everyone in the office knows it.'

Goldsmith identified the opposite tendency in himself. 'I feel that I have mellowed to the point of degeneration,' he complained, only half ironically. He had always taken his energy for granted, believing he could drive himself indefinitely at a pace which would have killed others. But suddenly it was if he had intimations of mortality; he began to lose his interest in running big companies, in taking on huge bureaucracies – and even in making more money. Time was beginning to run out, and there were better things to do with what remained. Although he had not quite finished with the world of business, after Goodyear he was in the twilight of his industrial career. He still had some big bids left in him, and at least one coup of breathtaking proportions and timing. But Goldsmith's days as a great raider of corporate America were over.

28

The Crash of October 1987

On 16 November 1987 *Time* magazine carried Goldsmith's picture on the cover, with the heading, 'The Lucky Gambler', and the caption, 'Sir James Goldsmith, having beaten the markets, ponders his next move.' In the year since the end of the Goodyear battle, Goldsmith had undergone a change of direction as radical as anything in his life. As the *Time* cover story recorded, he had also become an American folk-hero for something other than buying companies or being rich: he was now the man who had not only anticipated the great stock market crash of 19 October 1987, but had actually done something about it. He had sold everything he possibly could, down to his house on 80th Street, just before the bottom fell out.

In much the same way as he had quit England in the latter half of the 1970s, and France a few years later, Jimmy Goldsmith had now quit America. *Time* put him on the cover, not because he had made the biggest takeover yet, but because he had done precisely the reverse: he had timed the sale of his assets with such exquisite precision that he was now the most talked-of person in the business community. He was seen as the man who, almost alone, had anticipated a crash which many (particularly Jimmy) assumed would be at least as great as 1929. *Time* compared him with Joseph P. Kennedy, father of President John. F. Kennedy, who liked to tell the story of how, in October 1929, a shoeshine boy on Wall Street began telling him about how he was picking stocks. Kennedy instantly decided that if shoeshine boys were gambling on this market, it was time to be out. 'With much the same prescience, Sir James Goldsmith saved his fortune from the crash of '87.'

The wave of selling that hit the world financial markets that week had all the hallmarks of a crash of historic proportions – at least for a few weeks. Wall Street, which had been headed toward the 3,000 mark on the Dow Jones averages, lost 500 points in a single day, and the chairman of the New York Stock Exchange borrowed a nuclear disaster phrase to talk about the danger of 'financial meltdown'. Some of the cleverest and richest financiers in the world were wiped out, including the Australian Robert Holmes à Court; Rupert Murdoch's fortune dropped by $700m in one day (most of it in a single hour), as Australian markets suffered the worst damage. The Hong Kong market, unable to face a second tidal wave in 48 hours as the crash rolled around the world from east to west, closed its doors, and in every market, from Frankfurt and London to the American West Coast and on out to Japan, the panic grew by the hour.

Goldsmith watched it with all the glee of a man who had foreseen it, got his money out, and told every friend who would listen to do the same. 'A lot of financial managers in the US and Europe must now be wishing their name was Sir James Goldsmith,' one London broker was quoted as saying. He had not just sold out his shares and other investments, but everything he could get rid of: his house had gone right at the top of the market; his office under Roland Franklin had been run down to just a few caretaker staff; in late July he had astonished the business world by selling all but 5 per cent of his French flagship company, Générale Occidentale, including the Grand Union supermarket chain on which he had laboured so hard (he backed the management in buying it from Générale Occidentale); in September he and John Aspinall had sold the London casino to Brent Walker for £90m, Goldsmith's share realising £34m in return for an original investment of less than £800,000. Even L'Express, which Goldsmith had reshaped the previous year into a whip to use on the 'wets' inside the new French conservative majority, and the publishing group, Les Presses de la Cité, which he bought during the Goodyear bid, had gone.

As the rumours of what he was up to spread through the community, there were many who watched in astonishment. Share prices and asset values everywhere in the world were rising; there was an economic boom and political stability, with market economics on the rise everywhere; socialism was in retreat. There was scarcely a cloud on the horizon. '[Goldsmith] appeared to have lost his sense of financial balance,' commented *Time*.

Goldsmith, however, had been seeing something else. The same finely adjusted antennae, which had allowed him to read correctly the market boom of 1971–2, then the financial crash of the mid-1970s, and the boom again of the early 1980s, were again telling him there was a major crash on the way. 'It wasn't any one sign,' he said afterwards. 'Everything was pointing to it. Prices were much too high, and the bills coming out of the US Congress were as bad as anything produced by the socialists in Britain in the early 1970s.' The leaders in the industrialised countries, he argued, had failed to take the necessary economic measures to tackle the US trade deficit when they met in Venice that summer, and Goldsmith had become convinced that the deteriorating American trade figures would push down the dollar, while rising interest rates everywhere would hit both bond and stock prices. There were 'rude shocks' ahead, he told his friends.

On Wall Street that summer a few others were getting the same feeling of foreboding, but they were remarkably few. Donald Trump would later claim to have got out of the market early, but as his empire crumbled in the property crash that was about to begin on the Eastern seaboard of the US, his precautions looked pathetically inadequate. Laurence Tisch, the head of CBS, made the same boast with more justification. Almost all the great raiders were caught, including Carl Icahn, the man with the hair-trigger market reactions, who was left with the bankrupt TWA airline on his hands, the penalty of a raid too far. Ron Perelman would be forced to divest himself of Revlon to pay back borrowings.

Goldsmith however was sitting on the best part of a billion dollars in cash, mostly held through the Brunneria Foundation, his family-owned holding company which was based in Liechtenstein, which in turn controlled two Panama-registered companies. These companies in turn controlled 90 per cent of General Oriental, registered in the Cayman Islands, which owned 1.5m acres of forests, which were valued in the balance sheet at $1.6 billion (and which Goldsmith later sold for $1.3 billion, net of tax), plus oil and gas leases. In Britain, he had no investment interests at all (although Annabel kept Ormeley Lodge), in France he owned only half the house in rue Monsieur (the other half is Ginette's) and the Laurent restaurant. Except for his trees, his wealth was in cash, held short-term in a variety of currencies. Goldsmith was now preparing himself for a financial Armageddon, something far worse than 1929, a financial crash so great that no bank could be trusted, where no one currency would be safe, and where even major governments could fail (he would not even trust long-term American Treasury bonds).

Goldsmith's swings in mood were not always as rational as he would like to pretend. Undoubtedly he has an instinct, his gambler's instinct if you like, for markets and trends, which is not always right but which in his lifetime has certainly been right more often than not. He also believes, like any good gambler, in shortening the odds, and has, from his earliest days, been a keen reader of economic columns, of newspapers and magazines, but more particularly, of raw economic data. He studies American, British, and French economic statistics with much the same attention as he studies balance sheets – and with a skill which would have earned him a place as an economic forecaster in any of the Wall Street or London investment houses. He had learned the importance of this when he was building his grocery business, first in Britain, later in America, and over the years became increasingly adept at building, and relying on, his own forecasts. He also assiduously sought opinions from those with a track record, phoning a group of friends and contacts on a regular basis to test his own hypotheses.

But there is something else too: from boyhood his moods had swung wildly, from unqualified optimism and well-being to darkest depression. As he grew older, his personal swings of mood tended to echo his views on the economic cycle, and when he was in these moods, the world was black or white – it was either boom or bust, with little in between. Although there was a long-term philosophical line running through his corporate activities, Goldsmith's direction was also determined to a large extent by his own personal view of life. He could later explain that he left Britain because the country was falling apart at the time, and was no good for business any more, but the truth is if he had stayed for a few years more he would have participated in the Thatcher era, with a climate positively sympathetic to his style of entrepreneurship (as James Hanson, who did stay, was to find). The real reason he left was that, emotionally and psychologically, he was finished with Britain at that time; the same, to a lesser extent, was true of his departure from France. Now his anticipation of a crash and his move into cash was dictated by a complex web of factors, only one of which was the economic climate.

The Goodyear experience had scarred him, convincing hin that there could be no more Diamond-style deals, for him in particular but other raiders in general. The arrest of Boesky marked the beginning of the end of Drexel and the junk-bond era, although as 1987 opened that was still only dimly perceived by a few observers. For Goldsmith, 1987 began to look all too like 1973 in Britain.

He had also been shaken by the deterioration in his own health. Although immensely relieved to discover that all he had was mild diabetes, he had suddenly become aware of the passing years. He had worked, without much of a respite, for more than 30 years, and with

Laure pregnant again, he suddenly liked the idea of a pause in which to think about the way ahead.

There may have been another factor too: there was AIDS, which Goldsmith from the beginning took far more seriously than most. This, he insists, was never because he feared he himself had it or would get it – although given his active sex life that must have seemed a real possibility – but because for some time he had persuaded himself (and been persuaded by his brother Teddy) that the combination of world population growth, urban slums, mobility as a result of modern travel, and growing resistance to antibiotics and modern drugs all meant that humanity had never been more exposed to major epidemics. Teddy had been preaching it for years, forecasting as far back as 1970 that there would be a new epidemic which would defy modern medicines, and which would destroy a large part of the world population. To Goldsmith AIDS seemed to be just that.

In between his takeover bids, he took time off to study it – and became more depressed still. 'The fact that it was complex – turning our own defence mechanisms against ourselves – and evolving and slow acting, made it particularly dangerous.' In the way that Teddy could make his listener feel that all life was worthless because the world was already doomed, so Jimmy would terrify his friends with his views on AIDS. Jim Slater, the most orthodox of men in his private life, emerged shaken after a dinner in Aspinall's at which Jimmy relentlessly quoted to him the most blood-curdling statistics on the disease. It was, he insisted, a pandemic that would wipe out much of the human species, and argued that the superpowers must pool their resources in a massive research effort to counter it.

Goldsmith encouraged and paid for research, and read and absorbed every word. He would talk earnestly about the different strains of HIV which were evolving, some more benign, but some more efficient in methods of transfer – via saliva, sweat and, he would say chillingly, 'some researchers fear, in due course, after further mutation, mosquitos.' Of course, he would add, as his listener paled, 'this is still hypothetical'.

He tried to persuade the editors of *L'Express* to publish the results of some of his studies, but they were far from convinced. Their checks with AIDS experts suggested a far less apocalyptic view than Goldsmith's, and he in turn accused them of surrendering to the voice of the medical establishment. When the drug AZT came along, Goldsmith dismissed it as only adding to the problem – it simply meant a longer period for the disease to spread, and created a false impression that its development had slowed. The figures emerging from Africa, where the virus was different to the western virus, confirmed his growing sense of doom: up to 40 per cent infection in some regions and still growing. 'Nature has always responded to overpopulation in all living things by epidemics,' he argued. He read histories on the spread of previous plagues and concluded that once again Nature was demonstrating her power. 'Alternatively, man might demonstrate his ingenuity and postpone the day. But it will be close.'

In this gloomy frame of mind, he began to look again at his whole retailing policy. Was his concept of fresh food going to survive the AIDS era? It seemed to him that the scare was going to frighten people away from products prepared by hand. Grand Union's formula was based on service, with its in-store kitchens, its delicatessens, its fresh sandwiches, salads and so forth. Now it seemed to him that its customers were going to fear sweat, dirty hands, cooks cutting themselves, saliva and all the rest. They would want products prepared in sterile and controlled conditions.

One advantage of being a diabetic was the regular blood tests he was forced to take. He was clear. But what about future generations?

Again influenced by Teddy, he had become, at the same time, more and more gloomy about the dangers of nuclear energy. This strengthened when the Chernobyl accident occurred, and in May 1987 he wrote an article for *L'Express* attacking the 'arrogance' and the 'megalomaniac folly' of the French nuclear programme, and followed it up in September with another, denouncing the way in which civilian nuclear power was being developed in Europe. In France, as he was keenly aware, that message was pure heresy: 'It's like spitting in the face of the Madonna,' he remarked afterwards.

And yet, even as he planned his sales, so opportunities, too tempting to turn away easily, cropped up. That summer Drexel came back into his life briefly with a proposition: would he be interested in taking over the struggling airline Pan Am? They were, Drexel explained, not representing the airline, but the airline unions, who actually saw Goldsmith as their best hope. 'Jimmy was amused that someone would actually seek him out,' says Al Dunlap, still running the timber interests. Goldsmith was even more amused that it should be the unions, rather than the management, which sought his help. But he was intrigued. Again, the mood on Wall Street was swinging back from the anti-raider hysteria at the time of Goodyear, and several more thoughtful articles had appeared arguing that the Goldsmith analysis had been correct. 'What interested Jimmy was his belief that America should have a flagship airline,' says Dunlap.

Diamond and Crown Zellerbach had been 100-year-old companies with good assets undervalued in the balance sheet. Pan Am was an old company too, but it had sold off many of its choice assets to keep itself afloat. The Pan Am building in New York had gone, as had the Intercontinental Hotel chain, the Pacific routes had been sold, and many of the aircraft were operated on sale and leaseback arrangements. Between them the sales had raised $1.6 billion, but instead of pumping the proceeds into the core airline business, the money had been used to subsidise continued loss-making domestic routes. 'Management used the money to buy time,' Goldsmith bluntly told Dunlap, as they pored over the airline's accounts. The management had committed other sins in the Goldsmith book: they had developed fringe operations, including the Shuttle and Express services out of New York, anything other than concentrate on what they were good at.

Curiously, even though his mood about the general economy was apocalyptic, he was reluctant to let Pam Am slip by. Dunlap recreated his team to analyse every department and category of business, looked at all the profit-making opportunities, and spent weeks adding up the off-balance sheet – or basically 'hidden' – liabilities. The exercise was being done with the approval of the Pan Am management, under Fred Acker, who could see bankruptcy steadily getting closer. The more the Dunlap team looked at it, the worse it got. The union's rule book, when it was delivered to them, was enormous and completely incomprehensible. 'Even the lawyers don't understand it,' someone commented. There were restrictive practices and inefficiencies which the Goldsmith team reckoned were 'grotesque'. Dunlap drew up a plan for cutting the workforce by 7,800 people, 1,200 of them from management (a 38 per cent cut), and the other 6,600 from the unions (a reduction of one-third). Pan Am, he reckoned, could still be saved if it chopped out its domestic routes (with another 1,850 people to go) and concentrated all its resources on the transatlantic and Latin American routes. His plan proposed some other drastic measures: a 20 per cent pay cut, the end of all restrictive practices, vacating the Pan Am building and a move to cheaper premises at Kennedy Airport.

The Dunlap analysis, produced for Goldsmith in August, concluded that Pan Am had a negative net worth of $68m. But by then the team had discovered another, even bigger, potential problem: the pension fund was drastically under-funded. If Goldsmith were to take the company on, he could, Dunlap advised, find he had an unfunded pension liability of $610m, plus another $500m for post-retirement medical aid. On that basis the negative net worth of Pan Am was a potential $1.2 billion, for an airline which had not invested in modern computer systems or refurbishment of its aircraft (a 'catch-up' programme, to bring computers and aircraft up to date, would cost another $400m).

At the end of August 1987, Goldsmith wrote to Acker politely thanking him for his help in preparing the study, and setting out some of the conclusions he had come to. Pan Am, he indicated, might still be saved, but only with the most drastic of action, and he saw no sign of either the sense of reality or the willpower to carry it through. He was withdrawing. It was his last potential target in the US. Now he sat and waited for the crash, which as autumn approached, seemed to him ever nearer. He spent much of the summer of 1987 in Europe, working with Gilberte Beaux on the sale of Générale Occidentale and the remaining assets. In late August he was in the house in Spain with Annabel and the children and Johnny Pigozzi went to see him there. Before he went, Goldsmith asked him to bring down all the information he could find on Robert Holmes à Court, now reckoned to be the richest man in Australia, who was moving rapidly up the order of the world's wealthy too. 'The man's a genius,' said Goldsmith admiringly. 'All these deals he does, nobody understands what he's doing, and then about a year later you see how clever he is.' Pigozzi gathered together all the reports on Holmes à Court's Bell Corporation, and they had dinner in Marbella. Over breakfast the next morning, Goldsmith's view of the Australian had totally changed. 'If the markets turn, this man will go down,' he exclaimed, as he browsed through the reports. Why? asked Pigozzi, who had bought shares in his companies. 'Because he has big positions in companies, but no controlling interest. He has borrowed the money and the only way to survive is if the market continues to boom. But if there's a turn in the market, he's going to be screwed because he won't have enough to pay the banks.' Goldsmith tossed the reports aside.

As the markets continued to boom through September, Goldsmith became even more convinced of his own analysis. Al Dunlap remembers getting a call a month before the crash. 'This thing is going in the shitter, Al,' he recalls Goldsmith saying. 'If you own any publicly traded shares, sell now. This thing is going to collapse.' When Dunlap made to protest, he cut him off. 'You do what you want, but I'm calling all my friends and telling them this is not going to last.'

On Thursday, 15 October, Wall Street suddenly began to crack, and on Friday the first signs of real panic appeared. Goldsmith was in Paris, but decided to fly back to New York where he could observe the phenomenon at first hand. That day Pigozzi rang him, and Goldsmith said: 'You should come with me to New York, it's all going to break this week-end.' Pigozzi had a date with a new girlfriend, and said he would join Goldsmith in New York on Wednesday. On Friday evening from a Paris restaurant he called his New York office. The market he learned was over 100 points off. He instantly rang Goldsmith to say he would go with him the next day. He then talked to several of his investment advisers, who urged him not to panic. Goldsmith, they said, 'was crazy'. What was happening was nothing more than a hiccup.

Goldsmith flew first to London where he planned a lunch party at Ormeley on the Sunday, and he and Pigozzi arrived to a scene of devastation. The greatest hurricane the south of England had known for well over a century had struck the day before, and many of the great trees in Richmond Park were knocked flat. Annabel's garden was wrecked, an apt precursor for what was about to hit the markets. On Sunday they were joined by Jim Slater, and Goldsmith's old backgammon opponent Joe Dwek (now working for Kerry Packer). Over lunch Goldsmith forecast the Dow could fall 500 points over the next few weeks. 'Now, how are you all going to take advantage of it?' he demanded. 'Each of you should have a strategy.' His guests were not all persuaded: Slater was convinced it was only a market reaction, but Dwek phoned a broker in Singapore and went short of the Japanese market, which would be first to open the next day. After lunch, Goldsmith and Pigozzi boarded Goldsmith's private plane and flew to New York, on the way making a list of 30 shares which had risen by 40 per cent during 1987. They intended to sell them short on Monday morning – provided they were no more than 10 per cent down (of the 30, only one share qualified the next day). They arrived in New York on Sunday evening, and the next morning Pigozzi woke early and switched on the television.

'And the thing was just going down and down. I spent the entire day in front of the TV and calling Jimmy every ten minutes. He was laughing because he was completely out, and I was crying. It was horrible. And he kept saying there had been every sign – the prices of yachts were at their highest, the prices of planes were sky high, the junk bond thing was going to come tumbling down.'

Goldsmith, however, was taking only limited pleasure in being proved right. The speed of the collapse, even to him, was awesome. 'I believed there was a risk of a meltdown of the financial system. Obviously, I was relieved to be out of it. But it was like winning a rubber of bridge in the card room of the Titanic.'

In the week that followed, the worst week on the financial markets for nearly 60 years, rumours of Goldsmith's coup spread. There were enough people who had been told by him in advance for the story to be believed – and a month after the crash *Time* asked for an interview. The US, he told the magazine, had become the 'king of the soft options'. If the economy was going badly, the government devalued. 'If an industry can't complete, you protect it. If management can't make it in the marketplace, you enshrine it by making takeovers difficult.' On the other hand, the fear engendered by the crash could stimulate the authorities to do the right thing, he added – although it was clear he didn't believe they would.

Goldsmith, *Time* concluded, had saved his fortune by selling early – 'but what now?'

Unknown to *Time*, or to anyone other than a handful of friends, the 'what now' was already assuming a visible physical presence as far away as Goldsmith could get from AIDS, from financial meltdown, political instability and the 'corpocracy' now running the world's business.

For the next two years Goldsmith's 'what now' was not another deal, but a project as absorbing as anything he had ever done. He was building himself a home, in virgin jungle on the west coast of Mexico. It would not, however, be just another home – he had three already – but his dream home, the first which would entirely reflect his own interests and personality, which would be built from scratch and which would have all the room his restless nature craved. Unlike the great English and French barons who built their houses in their own countries, Goldsmith, as the most international (the most fashionable word is 'global') of international businessmen, could choose anywhere in the world within reasonable range of his private jet. He chose Mexico because of the climate, the wildness, and the extraordinary beauty of the land on the coast.

In a sense it was the same instinct which had caused his cousins the Rothschilds to build Mentmore and their other grand houses in England, Germany and France more than a century before. But there were many differences too. When he built Mentmore, Mayer Rothschild hired Joseph Paxton, architect of the Crystal Palace, to build him a symbol of power and influence. Furnished with exquisite French antiques, paintings and Sèvres porcelain, Mentmore created the required effect of great opulence and magnificence. Goldsmith in 1987 was as rich as any Rothschild in the nineteenth century, and prepared to commit whatever money was needed to fulfill his dream. But his concept for his modern-day Mentmore was more personal, designed and built for an age when satellite telephones and television make every part of the world equally accessible and where the private jet brings the world's biggest cities as close as, say, Paris was to Mayer Rothschild in 1850.

His friends jokingly called it his Xanadu, but it had as little in common with Citizen Kane as it did with Mentmore. He did not have to impress anyone in Mexico with his power and influence – indeed, although he would have large parties there, he much preferred that only his friends ever saw it, and became irritated when American magazines began sending planes in to photograph it. He wanted a house, or more accurately, several houses, in which he would be entirely comfortable, in which every room and every view pleased him, built in a place where the sun could be relied on to shine (at least in the correct season), and where he could make his own personal contribution to the world's disintegrating ecological balance. Above all, he wanted space.

And so in the summer of 1987, even as he was negotiating with the Pan Am unions for the takeover of the ailing airline, he was flying in his Grumman G2 jet to the town of Manzanillo and traipsing off into the jungle with Laure to settle on the ideal site. He knew the area well, having often holidayed in Acapulco (200 miles further down the coast) and negotiated for several pieces of land before getting exactly what he wanted. Even then, gaining title from the hundreds of small landowners who had some claim to it was a major task.

For the site of the main house he chose a hill which rose steeply off the beach and commanded a view inland over a mature coconut plantation, one of the few bits of cultivation in the area, and of swampland just beneath, the little islands of which were filled at nightfall with thousands of pelicans, white egrets, herons and other seabirds coming in to roost. The river which drained the swamps contained crocodiles, hunted almost to extinction elsewhere in Mexico, and in the hills beyond were even rarer animals – jaguars, ocelots and pumas. Giant leatherback turtles dragged themselves up the beach to lay their eggs in a little cove near the river mouth, and out to sea, whales, on their migratory way along the coast, were often visible. For Goldsmith it was the nearest place on earth to paradise.

For his latter-day Paxton, he chose a man who was not an architect at all, but a designer, in fact a French designer who had never built anything bigger than a 15,000 sq. ft. house for Dino De Laurentiis on the coast of North Carolina and the Paris restaurant La Coupole. Robert Couturier was born in Paris 32 years before, scion of a cash-poor aristocratic family, studied design at the Ecole Camando, and arrived in New York in 1978 when he was 23. He worked for the designer Adam Tihany whose work includes some of the chic-er restaurants in Manhattan, including La Bice (a branch of the famous Milan restaurant) and the Metro. He and Goldsmith first met in 1982, introduced by Laure, when Jimmy decided to have his own townhouse in New York. Couturier's proposal to 'open the house' on 80th Street with its inner courtyard and atrium had impressed him, and Goldsmith and Laure let him do it, and were delighted with the result. Now Goldsmith invited him to work on a project which would undoubtedly make Couturier one of the best-known and most sought-after designers in the world. His directions to the Frenchman were simple enough: he wanted something 'comfortable, but not too grand'; it had to be 'impressive, but not overwhelming'; above all, it had to have 'space'.

Couturier instantly fell in love with the land at Cuixmala, straddling the states of Jalisco and Colima. At first sight, he says, he found it 'unbelievably beautiful, breathtaking. It was so stunning, so wild. When you're down there, there is a peace you don't find anywhere else in the world.'

That summer over 2,000 Mexican workers began digging the foundations for the main house, the guest houses and the support village. Hundreds more turned the swamps at the foot of the hill into deep lagunas, while others laboured on roads, stables and the airstrip. They arrived in school buses and trucks every morning from villages more than an hour away, and left the same way at nightfall. In the winter Goldsmith's friends turned up to inspect the land – Jim Slater, Jacob Rothschild, Henry Keswick, 'taipan' (head of the house) of Jardine Matheson, John Aspinall and the historian Hugh Thomas arrived on the airstrip to jettison their city suits, and watch the work. Rothschild later presented his host with a photo album, showing some of the world's leading businessmen, clad in shorts or jeans, helping mark out the lines of another Goldsmith building. Long before the place was finished, they too had fallen in love with it.

There were plenty of natural skills around, but Couturier's design was, initially at least, beyond the competence of the average Mexican carpenter or bricklayer. More intricate plaster work and columns had to be done again and again, and if Goldsmith wasn't entirely happy with a finished result, it was torn down and rebuilt. The basic structure was poured concrete reinforced with steel, the walls several feet thick both for coolness and for solidity, embedded deep into the hill. One of the engineers brought in to help Couturier remarked that a nuclear bomb could go off nearby but Goldsmith's house wouldn't move. The Palace of Goldsmith will still be there centuries after its creator has shuffled off this mortal coil. Who would live there, if anybody, he was not sure. His gloomy thoughts on AIDS, on what was happening to the world environment, and on the survival of western civilisation had dramatically shortened his horizons. 'I don't really have much confidence in future generations,' he says gloomily. 'People think that is important to me, but unfortunately I don't have much confidence in stability. I wish I did.' But if future generations of Goldsmiths could survive anywhere, they could survive here.

The house emerged as a combination of styles: Arabic, Mexican, Moorish and French, with even some Indian thrown in – the lattice-work screens, or *moucharabiehs*, which cover the otherwise open windows were made in India, and Goldsmith ordered so many for his hundreds of windows that he set up a whole new industry. It is capped by a dome, finished in Mexican-style blue and yellow ceramic tiles in zig-zag lines; the rest of the 60,000 sq. ft. structure was built on a single level, except for the basement kitchens and servants' quarters (and a room to house Goldsmith's office equipment under his own study). Couturier designed it in the shape of a long fat-bodied Y, the dome sitting on the notch, the two arms embracing a wide flight of stairs that leads to the huge lattice-work front door. The outside is painted a soft pastel pink, contrasting sharply with the green of the jungle, the blue of the sea, and the mass of colours from the gardens which seemed to spring up overnight. Almost the first sight to hit the visitor is one familiar from John Aspinall's zoos in Kent: an enormous bronze of Aspinall's old silverback gorilla, Dzoum, playing with one of his tiny offspring, sited to the side of the entrance overlooking the Pacific (Aspinall had six copies made, of which Goldsmith has two, the other being in the garden at Ormeley Lodge). On the other side, standing equally dramatically against the lagunas, jungle and hills, is another Aspinall favourite: a black rhinoceros.

They are among the few sculptures or decoration in the house. The style inside is essentially minimalist, walls, floors and ceilings painted the same cool white, broken only by white latticed windows and white doors. The many windows are glassless behind their screens, each main Spanish-style window capped by two or three matching little ones, letting the cool ocean air run through the house. Goldsmith hates air-conditioning and will only allow it at Cuixmala in the library and the kitchens. 'What would you do, Jimmy, if you were put in an air-conditioned room?' someone asks him. 'I'd smash a window,' retorts Goldsmith grimly. Here there was no need – the house is pleasantly cool, bright and airy. Every room opens out onto its own terrace, mostly with a sea view. But if Goldsmith hates air conditioning, he loves couches – huge, sprawling affairs, with immense cushions covered in a material Goldsmith and Laure bought on an expedition to India.

At the bottom of the Y, with a sweeping view of sea, beach, lagoons and jungle, are two eight-columned open-sided turrets with thatched roofs – the Mexican palapa, which Goldsmith loves. This is the area where Goldsmith likes to drape his long body across one of the huge couches and survey from his cool shaded terrace the jungle stretching to the horizon. The land, most of it owned by the Cuixmala Ecological Foundation, which is funded by his Goldsmith Foundation, stretches inland to the hills only just visible in the heat haze. To the south his land goes as far as a river, the line of which can also only just be seen; to the north it is bounded by another line of hills.

To north, east and south Goldsmith is the master of all he surveys. The fourth boundary of his fastness can not only be seen but heard: he sleeps, eats and works overlooking the Pacific Ocean, which rolls ceaselessly on to a wide endless beach at the bottom of the cliff below the terrace. He owns the beach too, at least as far as the distant headlands in either direction. Only the sea itself is not his.

He built other houses on a hill across a series of lagoons and a small fertile plain – small dots seen from his own terrace, but on closer inspection elegant Italianate or Spanish-style villas, all different, all commanding views equal to Goldsmith's own. He even built a village, tucked carefully into the fold of the hills where it perfectly complemented the landscape. His friends and family came to stay in the houses; his senior staff – full-time doctor, biologist, estate manager, pilots, his personal (French) secretary – lived here too, all of them in individually designed houses built in a three-year burst of concentrated work.

This is now Jimmy Goldsmith's personal paradise, an 18,000-acre corner of wildest Mexico, where he can winter under cloudless skies among his friends, family, 320 staff (plus another 100 on his coffee plantation 150 miles away) and the teeming wild-life which he encourages to inhabit his ecologically balanced world. Spring and autumn find him in Paris or London, and summer on his large estate in Burgundy, which Couturier and Laure have also transformed.

Even in paradise however there are flaws. Part of his dream when he went to Mexico was that he could have all the women in his life around him. The big house of course was Laure's – she had helped design it, and rules over it. For Ginette, Couturier excelled himself with perhaps the most beautiful of all the houses on the property, a series of round rooms on different levels, grouped around a little bay, suggesting an ancient Italian monastery at the bottom of Goldsmith's hill. Ginette loved it, and spends more time there than anyone other then her son Manes (who also had his own house). Goldsmith wanted to do even better for Annabel, build her whatever she wanted, on any part of the huge property, but Annabel would not go, and neither, out of loyalty to her, would any of her children – at least not yet. For her it was Laure's territory, and she told Jimmy, coolly but firmly, that she would not set foot on it, just as she did not expect Laure to set foot on hers.

There are also some dangers: Wall Street almost lost its finest when John Gutfreund, the legendary head of Salomon Brothers in New York and model for the chief executive officer of Pierce & Pierce in Tom Wolfe's *Bonfire of the Vanities*, ventured out too far to sea when he was a Goldsmith guest, and very nearly didn't make it back.

There are other hazards too: 'bandits and scorpions', says Goldsmith. The former are kept at bay by more than 50 guards and gamekeepers, all of them armed, who suddenly appear from bushes and follow their proprietor around the estate at a discreet distance. But occasionally the bandits, who used to regard the land at Cuixmala as their own, exact their toll by hijacking one of the trucks bringing in supplies, leaving only the driver tied up on the side of the road.

Scorpions are almost as serious. Goldsmith had had scorpion traps – tiled trenches out of which a scorpion cannot crawl – built in front of every outer doorway. Every evening a 'scorpion patrol' goes around the outside of the houses. But the system had its gaps: little Jethro Goldsmith, his 18-month-old son by Laure, stepped on a scorpion near the swimming pool. Fortunately, Goldsmith had set up a whole system to cope; Laure immediately plunged the boy's foot into ice and the resident estate doctor was summoned from his well-equipped medical centre with his special serums. Even so it was a close thing – although seldom fatal to adults, a scorpion bite can often kill small children.

Dress style in the Mexican House of Goldsmith is as casual as the decor. The proprietor himself ambles around in a T-shirt, casual trousers and rope-soled shoes – never anything else, apart from a white straw hat when he steps into the sun.

'Everything we eat here comes from the estate,' says Goldsmith proudly.

He wants to make it a 'live' estate, capable in financial terms of making a contribution to its own upkeep, not because he needs the money but because he likes it that way. If the rest of the world breaks down in disorder, Goldsmith and those close to him can survive here. All the meat comes from his own animals; huge oysters, lobsters and other shellfish are pulled from the rocks down the coast; the sea, lagunas and river swarm with fish; fresh vegetables, fruit – particularly pineapples – eggs, yoghurt, milk and honey come from the farmland. And high up in the mountains, on an entirely separate estate, Goldsmith has a coffee plantation.

He had old Aztec canals dug out and soon the waterways swarmed with crocodiles, 200 of them in one laguna alone, that nearest the house, some of them more than four metres long. 'The parrots are coming back too,' he says, more in hope than anything else. Only a few have been seen so far; they too had been hunted almost to extinction and the few that remained were driven away by the building work. The resident biologist is one of the few to have seen the pair of jaguars, but Goldsmith keeps a hopeful eye out. He once spotted a puma crossing the road. Aspinall persuaded him to add more exotic creatures: giraffes, deer and zebras now roam the jungle.

The land and the house on the coast however are only half the Goldsmith establishment in Mexico. The other half is El Jabali, 5,000 feet up and situated at the foot of a stunning volcano. It was originally built as a coffee plantation by a German called Vogel a century ago, and bought by Señor Don Antenor Patino, Jimmy Goldsmith's first father-in-law, who planned to turn it into a hotel and holiday resort for the very rich. In later years Goldsmith became close to the old man, who turned to him more and more for advice and help as his financial affairs went wrong. Under the Code Napoleon in France, Jimmy was entitled to half of his first wife's estate, but he never touched it, leaving it intact for his own daughter Isabel, who also inherited from her grandfather Patino a third of El Jabali.

Isabel in fact probably knew Mexico better than Jimmy did. She had spent Christmases with her grandfather at a large house he built in the early 1970s, the housewarming party for which was organised by her husband Arnaud de Rosnay. But when Jimmy began renting a house in Correas, on the Mexican coast, each winter, she was not invited.

The house in Mexico brought Jimmy and Isabel closer, both in physical terms – she lived there – and emotionally as well. The complex, lonely Isabel had matured into an even more complex and still lonely – or at least lone – woman, who still found relationships difficult. Her marriage to de Rosnay lasted only two years, and she didn't enjoy it. 'At the time I was only eighteen and suddenly I found myself thrown into a world where everyone was much older and I was treated as an equal,' she told *Tatler* in 1991. 'I don't like feeling old now and I certainly didn't like feeling old then. I hate being able to take someone for granted just as much as I hate being taken for granted. I like a bit of suspense in a relationship. I'm an ideal mistress.' (In 1984 de Rosnay disappeared without trace on a windsurfing passage across the Formosa Straits in the South China Sea.)

Life as a divorcée was no easier for Isabel. She took a small flat on her own in Paris, but she had only the same allowance she had had before she was married, and it was not what she had been used to. She resented the fact that Jimmy looked after everyone else so well, so one day she packed up and moved back into the rue Monsieur. Goldsmith was delighted to see her back, but this was the mid-1970s, and he was spending most of his time in London and New York. He took Annabel and her children on holidays and Ginette and the children on holidays – and Isabel fitted in with neither party. If she mentioned it, he would immediately say, 'Come along', but she found herself forced to ask his secretary what his plans were. New Year, when Jimmy always took Ginette, Manes and Alix away, was perhaps the worst time for Isabel. She returned to the house in Paris just after Christmas one year to find everything locked up, except the kitchen and her bedroom. They had gone, and she didn't know where. 'My father likes to have everybody in little packages,' she complained to friends. 'He puts labels on them and he puts them in boxes and they all come out to be fed. He rents a house for Annabel, he rents a house for Ginette, he goes on holiday with Laure. The wives are taken care of, fine, end of story. Isabel is over eighteen, she copes on her own, never included. Everyone flown out on private planes, not even a ticket or a forwarding address left for me.'

When she was 28, Don Antenor Patino died and she inherited a large fortune, but she remained introspective and essentially lonely. She did not lack boyfriends, but few lasted long. 'I don't think people are quite sure about me when they meet me,' she told *Tatler*. 'And as for men they're in a complete panic. I can't think why I have to spend my time reassuring them. I've had very little success as you can see.' She was, she added, 'fascinated with death and life after death. I suppose it's because I have never come to terms with not knowing my mother.'

She had never liked the Patino property of El Jabali which Jimmy bought in 1986. To get there was either a long car journey, or a bumpy plane ride, and she invariably felt sick when she arrived – and then didn't know what to do there. 'Everyone loves it, and it's spectacularly beautiful,' she says. 'But it's not my cup of tea.'

Isabel had inherited the El Jabali volcano property along with two of her aunts, and when Jimmy offered to buy it, all three willingly accepted. Isabel then bought out her aunts' share in another Patino property on the coast, Las Alamandas, which was, by coincidence, only 45 minutes drive from where Jimmy began building his mansion at Cuixmala. She also bought an apartment in Los Angeles and a house in Tregunter Road, in London, where Jimmy had lived briefly.

Las Alamandas she converted into a sort of hotel, a retreat, as *Tatler* called it, 'for rich hippies, an expensive hideaway where you can be assured of organic fruit, drinkable water, and utter peace and quiet to stimulate the creative juices.' She ran it like a home, but charged her guests (unless she invited them).

In 1987 she spent New Year with Jimmy, the first New Year she had been with him, she pointed out, since they went to Gstaad when she was 20.

Goldsmith now had two properties in Mexico, perfectly complementing each other.

El Jabali is high and dry, with enormous trees – on the coast all the trees are shrunken and bent – cascading waterfalls, and hidden valleys with babbling brooks which open out into deep, tranquil lakes which mirror the volcano. It is enormously verdant, with great herds of Goldsmith cattle standing chest-high in the lush grass.

It was at Cuixmala in January 1989 that Jacob Rothschild first raised the subject of Jimmy Goldsmith's return to the takeover scene. The crash of October 1987 had not turned into the full-scale depression that both Goldsmith and Rothschild, who was almost as gloomy, feared. There were opportunities passing them by. The takeover scene was rolling again, bigger than ever. He produced a list of potential targets, high on which was a company which Goldsmith had nearly taken over 16 years before: the giant British-American Tobacco Company, now known as BAT Industries. Goldsmith was not entirely finished with the takeover world.

29

Battle for BATs

Given the atmosphere which surrounded his departure from Britain a decade before, Sir James Goldsmith could scarcely have anticipated the reception that greeted the announcement that he was back. Britain had changed a great deal in those ten years, and Goldsmith, busy in America and still nursing his resentment, had not fully appreciated it. Jacob Rothschild, Gordon White and other friends, including Rupert Murdoch (who had also moved on from Britain to America in the 1970s but had retained major operations in London), told him that ten years of Thatcherism had done much to end the stifling effects of self-perpetuating vested interests. But Goldsmith still felt tentative.

Goldsmith very firmly ruled out making a bid in the US. The takeover business there had passed out of the hands of the raiders who could no longer compete against the mass of institutional money assembled by the professional transaction experts. 'It's no longer private money: it's fee-driven money,' Goldsmith argued. His point was this: a new type of takeover animal had appeared, epitomised by the specialist takeover house, Kohlberg Kravis and Roberts, or KKR. In much the same way as Drexel had been able to assemble huge rafts of junk bonds, KKR and others had available even larger sums of pension fund and insurance company money. With this money they could bid for any company in America regardless of size, as indeed KKR did for RJR-Nabisco, for which it offered the enormous sum of $23 billion. KKR seldom put up much of its own money – it made its profits in fees, and by awarding itself a stake in the target company. In early 1989, Goldsmith reckoned there was a pool of well over $20 billion immediately available to the leveraged buy-out specialists, and more even behind that. 'I can't envisage where I'd be top bidder in the US,' he said.

447

Al Dunlap and his finance director Russ Kersh had now finished reorganising Crown Zellerbach, and were underemployed, awaiting a new challenge, and Goldsmith, despite his trepidations about the market, was tempted to give it to them. But he could see no way he could venture into the US while the fee-driven money was against him. He needed a good financial crash to scare that money away before it would be his kind of market again. Goldsmith never liked to buy in the same shop as everyone else, and the American shop that year was over-crowded.

He had explained this to Rothschild many times over the past year, and Jacob, every bit Goldsmith's equal in his ability to analyse financial trends, agreed. Were there other markets to go for? Goldsmith thought fleetingly about the Far East, but he didn't understand the markets there – he had never been to Japan although he was fascinated by the place – and they seemed to be pretty well picked over by the Hong Kong Chinese, notably Li Ka-Shing and Sir Y. K. Pao. Goldsmith had been to Hong Kong several times and concluded that there were more entrepreneurs per square inch there then anywhere else in the world. 'I'm too old to learn about those markets,' he remarked that winter.

So if the Far East was out, and America was out, what was left? The French and German markets were not easily raidable, because of their more closed stock markets and tighter relationships with the banks. That left Britain. Over breakfast in Mexico, sitting out under the palapas overlooking the Pacific on one side and the lagunas on the other, Rothschild began to kindle his interest in a list of potential targets he had brought with him. They included Britain's General Electric Company (no relation to the American GE), which at that stage was proposing to take over its smaller rival, Plessey. Goldsmith was not keen – for one thing GEC's boss, Lord Weinstock, was an old friend and a fearsome adversary. But he was interested in its value relative to its market price. When they found later that the fundamental value was less than the market price, it caused both Goldsmith and Rothschild to become more cautious still about the general level of the market.

The prime target on the list was thus BAT Industries. Jimmy told Rothschild of the time, towards the end of the Heath government in 1973, when BAT had almost been in his grasp. Goldsmith had just bought Allied Suppliers and was on a roll. The tobacco giant, one of the largest and most establishment companies in Britain, had for many years been controlled by Imperial Tobacco, which still held a 28 per cent stake. In much the same way as he had persuaded Unilever to part with its key shareholding in Allied Suppliers, in 1973 Goldsmith reckoned he could persuade Imperial to part with its 28 per cent stake in BAT.

With great secrecy he put together a plan under the code name 'Project Grand Slam', and prepared to make a bid which would, at a stroke, have made Cavenham one of the largest companies of its kind in the world, a version of Philip Morris which used its worldwide marketing skills to combine tobacco and food with considerable success. Imperial had decided to reduce its dependence on tobacco, and was not averse to unloading the BAT stake.

Goldsmith rang the Imperial chairman, Sir John Partridge, and asked for a meeting. Would he agree to sell the stake? Partridge agreed he would, and over the next few weeks the terms were worked out: Cavenham would buy 15 per cent of BAT for cash and the rest of the Imperial stake in loan stock. Goldsmith was elated: he was on the edge of creating a company the same size as Unilever, which he planned to 'twin' between France and Britain, in much the same way as Unilever and Shell were 'twinned' between Britain and the Netherlands. It would also give him the presence in America he wanted.

They were about to make a public announcement when Partridge suddenly got cold feet. Britain was moving towards an election, and the position of the Heath government was shaky. A major contested takeover bid, led by a man who had a reputation as an asset-stripper, was just what the government would probably hate at that moment. Partridge decided he must inform Edward Heath personally about it, and went to Downing Street to outline his agreement with Goldsmith. What, Heath asked, would BAT's reaction be? When Partridge indicated – as Heath must have suspected – that the BAT board would almost certainly fight to the last man, Heath said he did not want a major public takeover battle raging at that time. But if BAT could be persuaded to accept, he had no objection.

Goldsmith was deeply disappointed when Partridge told him that he was only prepared to go ahead with the deal if Goldsmith could reach agreement with the BAT board. Both men knew that it was pointless trying to persuade BAT to surrender without a fight. But Goldsmith went through the motions, arranging to see the BAT chairman, Sir Richard Dobson, who was civil but firm. He did not want to be taken over, and Jimmy bought Grand Union instead.

In the years since, BAT had grown into a bigger, more attractive target. Partly as a result of the scare Goldsmith had given them, it embarked on a major diversification policy, buying Saks Fifth Avenue, Marshall Fields, and other non-tobacco interests. In 1989 it had just completed the $5.2 billion takeover of the Farmers Group, a Los Angeles-based motor insurance company, making it a significant financial services company – it already owned Eagle Star, bought for £1 billion, and Allied Dunbar (for £664m). In the US, it ranked third behind Philip Morris and RJR in the tobacco market with its Kool brand, and dominated some of the third-world markets such as Brazil. It bought the Argos chain in Britain. It was, in short, a prime candidate to be trimmed back to its 'core' operation.

Yet Goldsmith remained cautious, less enthusiastic, certainly at the beginning, than Rothschild. The bid would be enormous – over $20 billion minimum and, before it was through, probably even bigger than RJR-Nabisco. The next biggest bid ever made was Chevron's $13.2 billion takeover of Gulf Oil. Warner's takeover of *Time*, the biggest ever in the media world, was half the size.

Goldsmith and Rothschild decided to assemble a team of backers, and Kerry Packer soon flew down. He landed on the airstrip within sight of Goldsmith's palapas, the King Air clipping a tree on the way in. The huge Australian, now easily the richest man in Australia, emerged to be greeted by Jimmy with the news they were going to make their biggest bid yet.

A few weeks later Goldsmith flew to New York to start the process. He wanted his own team in London to handle it, and on one of the first seasonable days of 1989 he and Al Dunlap went for a long walk, as they often did, in Central Park.

'I know you're bored and there is not much we can do right now,' he told Dunlap. 'The problem is that everyone has raised these huge amounts of funds, and it's other people's money. The deals are absolutely fee-driven – the more money they pay, the higher the fees, and they don't care if the companies run well afterwards because they get their money up front.'

Goldsmith continued, 'With us, we invest our own money, there's no fee taken and we have to get the company right in the end. These leveraged buy-outs have gone crazy, they make no sense. People are playing with other people's money and have nothing personally at risk. So for the time being we are out of business over here. But there will be a time when this whole thing will have collapsed and we will be able to come back.' There was however, he told Dunlap, a deal they could do in London. 'Would you go over there?'

The bid for BAT would need an elaborate structure, and a detailed plan. In March 1989, the first part of it was put into place when Goldsmith bought a 37.4 per cent stake in a minor leasing company,

Anglo Leasing, from J. Rothschild Holdings, Jacob's company. Dunlap and Kersh moved in, and Anglo now became the vehicle through which the bid would be controlled. Although it was a fairly low-key event, it still made headlines, as the two friends put out a statement saying Anglo would be used as a vehicle 'for identifying and acquiring one or more publicly-quoted UK companies whose business can benefit from greater focus and improvement in operating efficiency.' It was Goldsmith's first public move since he had quit the markets before the October 1987 crash, so caused a stir for that reason. It caused even more of a stir because it marked, however mutedly at this point, his return to the British investment scene.

Goldsmith was back in Mexico when news of his reception arrived. 'The trumpets were out in force yesterday heralding the return of Sir James Goldsmith,' said the *Independent*, a paper which had not even been around when Goldsmith left. 'Goldsmith's back!' greeted the *Daily Mail*. 'It sounds like electrifying news . . .' In *The Times*, Kenneth Fleet wrote that he was 'intrigued' by the return of a 'man of deep intelligence, powerful intellect, the instincts and courage of a great gambler, wide financial horizons and narrow obsessions.' The London Stock Market had its best days for months, causing the *Financial Times* to comment, 'Few individuals can move an entire stock market. But Sir James Goldsmith . . . seemed to achieve just that this week.' There was much talk about the 'frisson of excitement' which had run through the stock-markets, and the 'authentic chill in the nation's boardrooms'.

Maybe, Goldsmith mused, Britain had changed after all. *Private Eye*, which once led the British press in the attack on him, could only now mumble ineffectually about the 'unquestioning adulation' which suddenly attached to him – before recycling the same old anti-Goldsmith material which had appeared on its pages several times before.

It had been a duller world without Goldsmith around, and the City, the press and the government seemed to be remarkably pleased to see him back.

When he arrived in London a few weeks later, he appeared a very different Goldsmith from the man who had left in such a fury ten years before. He was relaxed, genial and expansive, the great anger gone from him, the old combative glint in his eye cooled to a more quizzical and amused appraisal. There was nothing to fight any more, which suited Goldsmith because there was little fight left in him. There were still newspaper groups available – it was suggested once again that he buy the *Express* group – but he no longer had any interest. He had, he said, got that out of his system. A decade of Mrs Thatcher had done the job for him. In the 1970s, socialism and the left were on the rise everywhere he looked; now they were in retreat. The unions had been beaten in Britain, and were a spent force. The press was run by strong proprietors who had also tamed their workforces. The entrepreneurial spirit was on the rise.

At the Bank of England in March he took part in a debate about hostile takeovers where, for once, public opinion seemed to be with him rather than against. His message was familiar enough to those who had listened to him over the years, put across with academic references and a persuasive argument that takeovers were good for the economy and for improving badly managed companies. Where once he might have been hissed, or at least listened to in stony silence, now he was cheered.

Behind the scenes the Dunlap team were working on their BAT analysis. Dunlap and Kersh were at their desks in Anglo, and other deals were being considered. One of the first was an odd one: Saatchi & Saatchi, the advertising agency which had become the biggest in the world through a series of over-ambitious takeover bids, was crumbling, and the brothers Charles and Maurice wanted to do a management buy-out. They were willing to pledge all they owned to bid for it at 250p a share, against a high point of 700p. Goldsmith's team rejected it: there were no assets, huge debts and major problems ahead. The shares later collapsed to just 10p.

In May, however, there was a more attractive proposition: Ranks Hovis McDougall was a food group which Goldsmith knew a great deal about, since he had followed it from the days of Cavenham when it was in and out of his target group all the time. This was a purely opportunist move, a distraction from the bigger task of BAT, but one which caught Goldsmith's fancy. Nine months before, the Australian food company, Goodman Fielder, Wattie, had made a bid for RHM and gained 29.9 per cent before the matter was referred to the Monopolies Commission. Goodman backed away and offered its stake for sale, and RHM, concerned that it would remain a perpetual bid stock, decided to eliminate the threat. So RHM made a bid for Goodman Fielder. It was a mistake, almost a fatal one. RHM's shares abruptly fell from the 465p which the Australian group had offered to a low of 341p, valuing RHM itself at £450m less than Goodman had offered.

Goldsmith could not resist. The Dunlap team created a new vehicle called Sunningdale which quickly bought Goodman Fielder's 29.9 per cent stake at £4 a share. A startled RHM suddenly awoke to the fact that it faced a much more serious threat, as its shares rose rapidly to 450p and the City analysts talked about a break-up value of anything between £5 and £7 a share. Within 24 hours of their purchase, the Goldsmith team was showing a paper profit of £94m on an investment of £415m.

Goldsmith was now beginning to fire in the way he once had in the old Cavenham days, his mind running rapidly through the possibilities. He actually quite admired RHM and its managing director Stanley Metcalfe. His purchase, he explained that week, had been purely a reaction to the situation created by RHM's strategic error in bidding for Goodman.

Having acquired the stake in this spontaneous and unconsidered way, Goldsmith now had Dunlap work out a plan which he prepared to put to Metcalfe and the RHM management. He would not, he decided, mount a full-scale bid, but rather encourage RHM into doing what he would do if he did take it over. It was classical Goldsmith stuff, the same theme he had now been advocating for over 20 years: the company must 'focus' by trimming back to its core business of milling, baking and cakes. It should sell its business in the US where RHM, in Goldsmith's view, was simply following the current British fashion of having a presence there. He had much to say about the quality of the RHM products. Bread consumption in Britain, he pointed out, was the lowest per capita of any European country, and there was a good reason for it: the British loaf was 'unhealthy and poor tasting', whereas if RHM and others could produce 'healthful' bread – healthful as opposed to the faddish health foods – which would be both 'delicious tasting' and economic, the bread market could begin to grow again.

He had more elaborate plans than that, however. As the weeks rolled on, he conceived a grander scheme: RHM, he decided, should be persuaded to acquire a key shareholding in Cadbury Schweppes, another of Britain's major food companies, then owned by the American group General Cinema. It should then bid for the whole of the company, sell off the Schweppes soft drinks side (he even lined up a potential buyer), and create a new company which would concentrate on milling, baking, cakes and confectionery – the type of company he had originally sought to create with Cavenham in the early 1960s. Goldsmith and his partners would remain as major shareholders, represented on the board.

That spring Goldsmith spent more time in London than he had done for years. Jacob Rothschild inherited a fortune of over £90m when his aunt Dollie died, including her house in St James's Place, directly opposite the Stafford Hotel in the same little square where Jacob's own offices were. Jimmy gratefully borrowed it on a verbal agreement that he could use it for three years for meetings, for entertaining, and simply to rest, rather than return to Ormeley Lodge. RHM was no more than a distraction from the main target, which still remained BAT, and by July the large team of bankers, accountants and brokers working with Dunlap were in position. Just as Anglo had created a new company, Sunningdale, to take the stake in RHM, so they now created another, Bermuda-based company, Hoylake, to bid for BAT.

The announcement of the bid on 11 July 1989, was one of the biggest media events of the year. Goldsmith, Rothschild and Packer posed for a vast battery of cameras and television crews before going back into the offices of Hambros Bank, opposite the Tower of London, to hold a press conference that had standing room only.

If the bid was enormous by American standards, by British it was astronomical. Worth £13 billion, it was only a whisker short of the RJR-Nabisco bid. It caused the value of BAT to rise by £3.7 billion in three hours – which was greater then the entire value of the country's previous biggest takeover (Hanson's £3.5 billion acquisition of Consolidated Gold Fields).

That day Goldsmith introduced a new word into the language: instead of 'demerging' or 'breaking-up' (or, if you will, 'asset-stripping'), he and his partners, Jacob and Kerry Packer, intended to 'unbundle' BAT. 'You have a major conglomerate where the parts would be worth more outside than in,' he told the press conference. 'Tobacco is an industry with a great deal of cash flow and profits. That cash is better with the shareholders than in other businesses.' BAT, he added, had spent £7 billion on acquisitions in the past ten years. 'But its market value at the end of last year was' – he paused for maximum effect – '£7 billion.'

If he got control of BAT, Goldsmith said, he would sell the American insurance subsidiary, Farmers, before anything else, but later the stores in America would go as well. Although he did not announce it that day, Goldsmith had devised a plan for getting round what his team had identified as the single biggest hurdle in the bid: the US state insurance regulators, who controlled the insurance business in the nine states in which Farmers did business. It had taken BAT over a year to fight its way through the thicket of controls and regulations which America has built around its insurance business, arguing its case individually in each of these states. BAT won, against ferocious opposition from the Farmers management, basically because it had money and time. However this had been a wearing and irritating process. Every argument from foreign ownership to the conflict between selling insurance and tobacco was thrown at it. The battle left a nasty taste, not least among some of the regulators who had first strongly opposed BAT, then reversed themselves.

Goldsmith knew something about the insurance regulators in America. When he made his run on Continental, which had a large insurance business, he had worked his way through the process successfully, and believed this time it would be easier. BAT, he believed, had only won because it had increased its offer for Farmer to the point where the management had recommended the bid, and dropped its opposition. Goldsmith's plan was to bring in a big insurance company which would agree to buy Farmers in advance – to which, he believed, the insurance regulators could have no objection. 'We and our army of advisers had underestimated the changes that occurred in the US since that time,' he says ruefully.

'We knew there would be a problem with Farmers,' says Dunlap, 'because BAT had problems when it bought it. But the way we analysed it, here were two British companies, Hoylake and BAT, fighting each other, so why should the American regulators object? And we thought we wouldn't get caught in the craziness that was going on in America, because there wasn't anyone there big enough to bid against us.'

At that stage he had not yet lined up a bidder, but in Paris Gilberte Beaux was working on this: Axa-Midi, an ambitious and fast growing group, the eighth-largest in Europe, run by a man who was determined to launch his company into America, Claude Bebéar. In the battle ahead, Bebéar would become a key player.

Unlike the BAT bid for Farmers, the Goldsmith offer for BAT was going to be a highly leveraged one, made mostly on borrowed money – he had engaged Drexel Burnham to play a lead part in organising a large tranche of the money. The partners and their supporters would put up some £800m, and the other £12 billion-odd would be borrowed, at least at the outset. That week-end, Robert Harris, the left-wing columnist, writing in the *Sunday Times* complained that the trio of Goldsmith, Rothschild and Packer were greeted as 'heroes' and 'wizards' and mourned that 'not a squeak of protest is heard'. On the other hand the *Independent* considered they were to be 'welcomed': 'They will shake up managers who deserve to be shaken up.'

The reaction in the press and the City owed more to excitement than to reason. The London market climbed 56 points on the day, reflecting the view that no company was now safe, whatever its size. The injection of some £13 billion, from whatever source, would inevitably cause prices to rise. But Goldsmith, at least for a week or two, managed to ignite the interest of the investing public who in these early days were on his side.

BAT's chairman, Patrick Sheehy, a tough veteran of many a takeover battle himself, dismissed the trio as 'an *ad hoc* troupe of financiers', who simply intended to 'remove value' from existing shareholders. Goldsmith that week, however, held the intellectual high ground, easily anticipating the first stages of the defence that BAT was assembling.

Behind all the euphoria the financial establishment was not taking the bid too seriously. The professionals were as aware as Goldsmith of the obstacles, which probably made BAT bid-proof. At the outset Goldsmith estimated the odds at no better then evens, but reckoned that the potential gains were worth the risk. Rothschild, although he had initially proposed the bid, was more gloomy. Jacob is by nature a pessimist, without Goldsmith's balancing periods of euphoria. That week-end he calculated the odds at about four to one against.

To win, the Goldsmith team had to steer its way through a minefield of regulations and conventions in Britain and America. BAT rushed to the courts in half a dozen different countries where it did business, from Britain to Indonesia, to plant further little booby-traps. As a further line of defence, BAT also asked for a reference to the Monopolies and Mergers Commission (it was later turned down). Even if the Goldsmith team could get over those hurdles, they still had to raise the money. Then they had to persuade more than 50 per cent of BAT shareholders to accept their offer.

By now Goldsmith and Jacob Rothschild were lining up other backers to spread the risk and add further prestige: they brought in the Banque Paribas, the Italian Agnelli family, Lord Weinstock of GEC and others. There was much talk about how Goldsmith would use junk bonds, but Goldsmith had never used junk bonds and would not use them as his major source of finance now. As he had done for Crown and Diamond, he reckoned he could raise most of what he needed from the banks, and by pre-selling assets such as Farmers. His bid, Goldsmith insisted, would not be leveraged in the sense that it would leave the company saddled with a burden of debt for years to come. 'We are proposing a temporary situation whereby we "unbundle" BAT and repay the debt with the proceeds of the asset sales. We end up with a major company, with a classical balance sheet, totally focused on tobacco. We would expect the process to be finished within twelve months of completing the takeover.'

Summer that year in London was almost as hot and sticky as it had been for the *Private Eye* trial in 1976, but Goldsmith stayed put. Tongue in cheek, Jacob Rothschild interpreted the motivation that drove Jimmy and him to stick it out: 'You can describe Jimmy and myself as the joint chairmen of the Society of Catalysts, rather then predators and pirates.' Jacob was at pains to keep the tone calm and gentlemanly, avoiding personal remarks about Sheehy and his board. Jimmy, he pointed out, could always go somewhere else if the atmosphere soured, but Rothschild lived in England and had a position in society he must keep up. Besides his money from the French side of the Rothschild family – to which he was only distantly related – he would soon inherit the English title, becoming Lord Rothschild when his father died.

For his part, Goldsmith was happy to conform to the new spirit of courtesy that had been shown to him. The two men toured the big BAT investors, with a round of lunches, dinners and meetings. 'There is scarcely a fund manager who does not at least express grudging admiration for Sir James Goldsmith's personal charm and capacity to flatter an audience,' commented the *Financial Times*. 'The thoroughness with which he appears to have prepared his case and presents his arguments also wins plaudits.' One investment chief was quoted that week as commenting: 'I'd never met him before, and, yes, I was impressed. He's nobody's fool, it's a well-put case and it has a certain logic.' There were many who questioned the broad anti-conglomerate argument of course, but few who could out-argue Goldsmith head to head.

The most pressing problem was time. In July the Goldsmith camp had merely announced its intention to bid. But from that moment, the clock was running. A formal bid had to be made within 30 days, and after that the Takeover Panel in London allows a company 60 days to complete its bid. By the early days of August, the state insurance commissioners in America had not even begun their hearings, and the Goldsmith bid was conditional on their agreeing to the transfer of ownership of Farmers.

It was soon obvious there was no chance of the US regulators completing on time. Angry and frustrated, the Goldsmith team launched a series of court actions to hurry them up. It was a mistake: BAT announced it would intervene in the actions, ensuring further delays. The bid was beginning to go wrong, pushed in the direction Goldsmith had sought to avoid: into the hands of the US regulators who he instinctively felt would kill it.

The bid now highlighted a direct conflict between the two sets of regulations in Britain and America. Goldsmith had fought year-long bids before in the US, and this now promised to be a long haul. But the British under the City's Takeover Panel, which unlike the American Securities and Exchange Commission is a non-statutory body, insisted there had to be a conclusion 90 days after the bid announcement.

The Goldsmith bid was dead, unless they persuaded the Takeover Panel to extend its deadline, on the grounds that the biggest bid ever made in London was being determined, not by the BAT shareholders, or by the City authorities, but by a group of minor bureaucrats in state capitals of America.

On 2 August Roxani Gillespie, insurance commissioner for the state of California, wrote to the National Association of Insurance Commissioners suggesting joint action to block the Goldsmith challenge in the courts. Hoylake was getting bogged down in litigation, and Goldsmith's enthusiasm was beginning to wane. But he was far from giving up. On 7 August 1989, he announced the formal offer to a packed audience, looking more like a professor then the famed raider, hunched at the rostrum and peering over the half-glasses he had recently taken to wearing. Occasionally he used a long white stick to point to a figure on a chart, as he plunged into a lengthy, almost academic, analysis of his subject. He talked about corporate governance, about the nature of debt instruments, the technicalities of the American Constitution, and much else. It was more of a seminar than a press conference, although there were flashes of the old-style Goldsmith, as when Jacob, in more lugubrious style, complained about the excesses of some of the BAT entertainment habits, particularly at its client entertainment centre in Brazil.

'Some of us have a certain puritanical streak to us,' said Jacob.

'I'm looking forward to seeing it,' flashed Goldsmith. 'Unlike Jacob, I'm not puritanical.'

The documents showed that Goldsmith himself was prepared to invest £250m of his own money in the bid, as were both Rothschild and Packer. The other backers were impressive: the Duke of Beaufort, a friend of Rothschild, was putting up £10m, Bankers Trust was in for £20m, Banque Paribas for £60m, and William Simon, the former US Treasury secretary, was in for £1m.

Meanwhile, BAT had hired an American firm of detectives, Kroll Associates, to inquire into Goldsmith's past. There was much talk of dirty tricks and elaborate public relations strategies. In Washington a group of 200 Congressmen voiced fears about jobs and security laws if the bid went through – BAT employed 55,000 people in the US and had gone to great trouble to present itself as a local company. Goldsmith responded with a rare flash of anger. 'This is yet another tribute to the tentacular lobbying power of a sprawling tobacco-based conglomerate.' Two senators, Wendell Ford and Mitch McConnell, both from the tobacco state of Kentucky, accused him of being 'a break-up artist' and an asset-stripper. 'We say it would be good for Goldsmith's wallet but disastrous for BAT businesses, employees, stockholders and communities,' they said.

'It's really quite simple,' continued Senator McConnell. 'American interests are at risk. Our constituents' jobs are at risk. The financial vitality of American companies and the economic health of our communities are at risk.' Given the fact that BAT was a actually a dyed-in-the-wool British company, this was an odd defence. Goldsmith could only stand back and admire the astonishingly successful campaign BAT had mounted against him in the US. BAT, Goldsmith calculated, had employed 17 legal firms, eleven lobbying firms, six public relations firms and at least one detective agency. If he won, he added, he would have to pay for it all.

In mid-September, Goldsmith regained some of the initiative, by persuading the Takeover Panel to give him an unlimited extension to the bid timetable while he tried to clear the regulatory hurdles in the US. It was an unprecedented decision. Goldsmith issued a quick, enthusiastic press release in London, then boarded a plane for the US where the battle proper was being fought – exactly what he had hoped to avoid by bidding for a British company.

Events were moving against him, as they had at Goodyear. On 26 September BAT unveiled a major profits rise and a higher dividend, hinting also that it might do its own unbundling. And when, some weeks later, Sheehy announced a radical plan to slim BAT down to two divisions, tobacco and financial services, a major plank in Goldsmith's strategy was gone. This was a major about-turn for a company which had been steadily buying into new businesses for 20 years. Goldsmith's advisers prepared a statement attacking the move, but instead he announced it gave him a 'warm feeling'. Secretly, he could not help feeling deeply disappointed. There were some consolations however: BAT shares rose on the news, and *The Times* commented 'many a glass' would be raised to Goldsmith's name for forcing BAT to unlock its latent shareholder value. Sheehy argued that he was only bringing forward something BAT had intended all along, but the City viewed the statement with some scepticism.

By now the battle had passed from Goldsmith's hands to those of Claude Bebéar and Axa-Midi which was now officially aboard, and which had the irksome task of persuading the US state commissioners that it was acceptable as an owner of Farmers. Goldsmith left it to Bebéar and in December went to Mexico, by now bored with the whole issue. The house at Cuixmala was finished, the gardens were beginning to look established, and Laure and the children were there. Goldsmith was learning Spanish, slowly and painfully, and watched world events on his huge screen which brought in the financial news via satellite.

If he could have recaptured the hunger that had driven him to risk everything over the Diamond bid, or to drive his way through the Crown Zellerbach poison-pill defence, then BAT might have fallen. But Goldsmith no longer had the stomach, nor the interest, for a prolonged fight. Nevertheless, it had been worth returning to England to lay the ghosts which had haunted him from the 1970s, and to establish the thesis, which greatly mattered to him, that big conglomerate companies were often better broken up into their component parts.

In the United States that winter, the campaign almost ground to a halt. The state of Illinois, the first of the nine states where Axa-Midi had to win, only resumed its hearing on 24 January 1990. Four of the states had not even set dates for their hearings. BAT meanwhile was busily selling off both Saks and Marshall Fields, hiving off its Argos chain in Britain, and floating off its paper interests. There would still be something to unbundle, but it was growing less by the month.

In February there was another blow. Drexel, which had been one of Goldsmith's lead bankers in the bid, collapsed, and the whole junk bond market went into a dive. Goldsmith hadn't intended to use any junk – he had lined up buyers for virtually all the unwanted pieces, so the debt, he says, would have been extinguished immediately – but the Drexel crash added to the financial climate, which was increasingly against all leveraged bids, however they were financed.

In April Roxani delivered the knock-out blow: the California state regulators did not find Axa-Midi acceptable. From Paris Gilberte Beaux insisted that Hoylake would fight on, but both Goldsmith and Rothschild knew they were beaten. So did Al Dunlap.

We thought we could deal with it by presenting Farmers to Axa-Midi for $4.5 billion [says Dunlap]. And we reasoned, here's Axa Midi, with a better credit rating than Farmers, been in business 200 years, the directors are impeccable – who could object to this? We thought it would be great for Farmers, they will be associated with a superior management, they will gain an international reputation, and contacts, and I really thought it would work. I was plenty naive, I'll confess.

The night of the ruling, we saw that even if you wore sandals and came from Bethlehem, you couldn't win this fight. We had been run from state to state through nine states, and had spent huge sums of money. We kept saying, look at the results of the Goldsmith groups, and look at the results of BAT. But I will always believe BAT got its influence through the tobacco lobby in America which worked on the various states, and we never stood a chance.

Goldsmith called Dunlap over to Paris to tell him he was going to drop out, and Dunlap told him he was about to advise the same thing. A few days later, on the morning of Sunday, 22 April 1990, Jacob (now Lord) Rothschild rang Goldsmith in Paris. 'Enough is enough,' he said.

'So what do we do?' he asked.

'It's pretty obvious, isn't it,' Rothschild replied.

Withdrawing was not quite so easy, however. Claude Bebéar still believed he could overcome the problems, and was determined to press on, test a few more states and then perhaps persuade Roxani Gillespie in California to change her mind. Farmers was Bebéar's chance of entry into the US market, and he wanted it badly. The financial climate in Paris at the time was far more bullish than it was either in America or Britain. That day Goldsmith went around to see Bebéar and broke the news. He did it gently, and at some length. BAT was now unbundling so fast there was little left for them to go for, he said. In America the climate was completely against them. The *Wall Street Journal* had that week said the bid was another 'victim of a monumental change in official and public attitudes towards hostile and leveraged bids – particularly by foreigners in the US'.

Even then Bebéar was anxious to continue, and Goldsmith and Rothschild had agreed that if he persisted in going on, they must too. Bebéar asked to sleep on it. The next morning Goldsmith rang Jacob: Bebéar had agreed to pull out.

It was another 24 hours before the news reached Patrick Sheehy at the BAT headquarters in Victoria Street. The press began ringing to say there were rumours a statement was imminent. Did BAT know anything about it? They didn't at the time, but learned what it was a few hours later when the official statement appeared. Apart from a modest Goldsmith quip, the official statement was brief and to the point:

'Hoylake announces that it will not renew its offer for BAT. The directors of Hoylake wish BAT and its unbundled offspring great success within their new structures.'

*

So ended what was (almost) the biggest takeover battle in corporate history – and the postmortems began.

The *Financial Times* believed there was a 'central flaw in [Hoylake's] much touted philosophy of management'. The 'flaw' was Goldsmith's assumption that bureaucratic conglomerates like BAT could not change, whereas Sheehy and his team had shown 'remarkable speed and flexibility'. A former Goldsmith aide had a similar analysis: 'He was like a man pushing at a jammed door to open it. The greater the push, the greater the door jam.'

At BAT, Sheehy had a different explanation. 'I never felt he would get through the regulators either here or in the US with such a leveraged bid.' And perhaps he knew more about that than Goldsmith did; Sheehy, it should be pointed out, had been through exactly the same regulatory authorities only a year before. He had also fooled Goldsmith into under-estimating him.

There was another reason, too, which Sheehy cited with a triumphant smile. 'When he launched his bid, we were looking for £2 billion profits for 1989 on top of strong growth the previous year. We couldn't tell people that until we had put out our statement about the reshaping [Sheehy's word for unbundling]. The truth is, he picked the wrong year.'

For his part, Goldsmith, too, had a battery of explanations. 'We hadn't fully appreciated the degree of agency capture which had taken place in America,' he said, returning to a familiar theme of his: the regulatory agencies, particularly at state level, he argues, had become the tools of the industries they regulate – the regulators have been taken over by the regulated. 'Jimmy can be pretty high on something, or pretty low,' says Al Dunlap. 'He really can't accept things that happen for the wrong reasons, but he's a gambler after all, and he knows that sometimes you lose and that's that. But to have the cards, as it were, and still to lose because someone else is playing by other rules – he can't accept that easily.' Yet he was gracious enough in defeat, casting no aspersions or blame, except on the bureaucrats.

Rothschild and Packer would each take a loss of about £40m on the deal (and another £100m split between the three of them when they eventually sold their RHM shares at a loss of £1 a share), and Dunlap quietly folded his tent and went back to America to pursue his own career.

Goldsmith took off in his Grumman G2 with Laure and a small group of friends, en route to the Middle East, where he stopped in Cairo, before going on to India, Peking and Mongolia. He had been planning the trip for months, poring over maps in Mexico, questioning his pilot on the range of the plane, asking friends for interesting places to visit. It was a complete holiday, Goldsmith-style: Richard Nixon and other friends had opened doors for him in China and he was received as a visiting head of state, asked to appear on television, and given special banquets, before going on to Mongolia where he linked up with John Aspinall. Aspinall had another purpose there: he was releasing back into the wild a breed of Mongolian pony, extinct anywhere other than in captivity, from his Kent zoos. From there Goldsmith flew on to Japan, his first visit, and back to Mexico and the United States. He didn't brood on BAT, but he used the time to think deeply about what he should do with the rest of his life.

30

The Jolly Green Giant

From the earliest moment he could remember Jimmy Goldsmith had nurtured one particular ambition: to be rich, to be a millionaire. One of Teddy's earliest memories of his younger brother is of his father telling him he had to go to school because he had to learn to read. 'No, I don't,' retorted Jimmy. 'When I'm old, I'll be rich enough to pay somebody to read for me.' Goldsmith was now in the 'can't count' category, in the Jean Paul Getty sense – it was Getty who said that no one is seriously rich if they still count their money. Goldsmith was a billionaire, and not just a paper one – his money was in cash and trees, and there was too much of it to count. He was giving it away, some towards right-wing pressure and study groups but mostly for environmental causes. For some years the word had spread among the green groups that Goldsmith was a soft touch, particularly if Teddy approved. And Teddy often did, although he himself was careful not to exploit his brother's generosity. The environment was the theme, almost the *raison d'être*, of Cuixmala – Goldsmith had little interest in just building a comfortable house, but wanted it to be something more. An article in *The Times* accused him of having 'Ozymandian tendencies', adding that his 'huge environmental reserve in Mexico, devoted to organic farming and the collection of rare animals, can be regarded as an attempt to leave a monument that time will not wither', and there was some truth in that. Goldsmith was not setting himself up as 'king of kings' in the Shelley sense of 'Look on my works, ye Mighty, and despair!', but at the same time Cuixmala was built sturdily out of the strongest, most durable materials. Goldsmith might say he had little hope for future generations, but he could still dream that his Mexican palace would avoid the fate of the palaces built by Ozymandias, 'Nothing beside remains. Round the decay/Of that colossal wreck, boundless and bare/ The lone and level sands stretch far away.'

Posterity and tradition, which once meant a great deal to Goldsmith, meant less as he grew older, basically because in his more melancholic moods he did not believe posterity would have much time. In Mexico in the winter of 1990 there were days, sometimes weeks, when he was alone with Laure and the children, the visitors gone, the BAT bid bogged down in the courts of California, and less to do than he had ever experienced in his hectic life. He read, he went for rides, he walked, swam and played with little Charlotte and Jethro. It was his third year of it – the first one of recuperation, the second one of waiting for the crash to come, and the third – the third was beginning to drag.

Cuixmala was really Laure's house; she had worked with Robert Couturier on every detail, watched over the building much more closely than Jimmy had, and she was the woman who lived with him there. Annabel still would not go, nor would her children. Ginette lived in her side of the house in the rue Monsieur, but now Laure lived with Goldsmith in the other half. Laure was already at work with Couturier restoring Goldsmith's huge house in Burgundy, Montjeu, and Goldsmith became as involved as he had been in the building of Cuixmala.

Montjeu is in many ways the exact opposite of Cuixmala. It is really three houses, two seventeenth-century châteaux flanking an enormous third. The gardens were the work of France's greatest designer, André Le Notre, who undertook the gardens of Versailles for Louis XIV, after successes at Vaux and Chantilly. Le Notre reigned for 50 years, producing, with the help of many sculptors, St Germain, Fontainebleau, St Cloud – and Montjeu. At Montjeu, Le Notre designed a château garden on a grand scale – large open parterres, the view extending along *allées*, with a succession of vistas and fountains. The gardens and houses were run down when Goldsmith bought them, but their restoration was fun. The original wall, much restored by Goldsmith, runs around 3,000 hectares of forest full of wild boar and deer. Goldsmith wanted to add wolves, because that would have created an ecological balance, but the annual autumn boar hunt is such an integral part of the local life that he thought better of it. It would be ready in time for the wedding of his second daughter, Alix, at the end of July 1991, when Jimmy's eight children were all together for the first time.

In these last few years he had become closer to Laure, who occupied a central place in his life. Of all the women in his life, she was probably the most cerebral. He bought a magazine in Paris, *Point de Vue – Images du*

Monde, which wrote about leading French families in much the same way as *Hello!*, and she ran it. But she usually found time to accompany him on his long trips, was mistress of Cuixmala, and it was with her more than anyone else that he discussed his longer-term plans. She and Ginette were friends – or at least friendly – Ginette often joining the Goldsmith party for dinner in Mexico or in the house in rue Monsieur, or taking the role of an aunt with Charlotte and little Jimmy (Jethro). For her part, Annabel, from the time Jimmy moved to New York in 1980, simply set about building her own life, which included Jimmy when he was there but which revolved mainly around her children.

Instead of the three wives that the world still believed he had, and for which he was greatly envied, Goldsmith was coming closer to having one: Laure. He continued to see all three of the women in his life, still treated them as he always had, but in middle age, he was becoming more monogamous.

He was also losing interest in the business world. He forced himself into pitting his wits against the markets, playing the commodity, currency, stock and bond markets, but it was a discipline to keep his mind active and his hand in, rather than any great desire to make money. Ostensibly this was his waiting time, when he would consolidate his cash and his plans, ready for spectacular re-entry into the takeover market just when everyone else was in trouble. The world recession he had been forecasting was late in coming but as 1990 wore on, it was finally arriving – never quite as bad as he predicted, but steep enough for all that. Yet still Goldsmith hesitated. Did he really want to plunge back into business? He didn't need the money; he was already giving it away. The thought of running a large organisation again bored him. Even the game of taking over companies, fighting the battles against serried ranks of lawyers and dug-in managers, brought no surge of excitement. Was he burnt out? He wondered about that too. The early days of his business life, when he had lived on the very brink of bankruptcy, had probably taken more of a toll than he realised at the time. In his late fifties he looked older, and there were times when he felt it too. The discovery that he was diabetic came as a profound shock to him, and was one of the main reasons for his retreat in 1987 in the Goodyear battle. 'I'm conscious of a lack of vigour,' he remarked in Mexico in the spring of 1990. For some years severe allergies had seized him, rendering him almost helpless with watering nose and eyes; in the spring of 1990 he saw a specialist in the American Hospital in Paris who discovered that for some years he had had several polyps high in his nose. Nose drops cured it, and Goldsmith declared he hadn't felt better in years. He became more careful about what he ate; he had never been a drinker, other than an odd glass of wine, but he had been a voracious eater, burning off the calories with his ceaseless pacing and great bursts of energy. His weight had remained stable most of his life.

People remarked on how like his father he had become: patrician, easy-going, relaxed, tolerant, endlessly courteous. Occasionally he would flash, but less and less often.

Over dinner with a group of friends, including Aspinall, one evening in the autumn of 1990, Jim Slater teased him. 'Instead of working to become worth $5 billion, Jimmy, why don't you become worth $2 billion instead and spend the rest keeping us all alive?'

Goldsmith took it lightheartedly: 'I think I'll take the $5 billion.'

But he was thinking seriously along those lines. He had more money than he needed, even with the Mexican houses, Burgundy, Spain, Paris and all the rest; his extended family had more than they could ever use. He had proved himself in the business world (although he would always be criticised for moving on from one business – and country – to the next), pitted himself against the best entrepreneurs in three countries, and had little interest in doing it again. He had done it all.

Meanwhile Teddy worked on him endlessly to take up the environment as his principal interest. The elder brother knew from old he had to watch his step with Jimmy. In full flow Teddy Goldsmith could be as apocalyptic about the eco-system as Jimmy could be about the financial scene. He had a habit of rubbing his beard, fixing his listener with his blue eyes, and presenting his arguments in an unbroken and numbing flow, very much as a challenge to his audience. The human species, according to Teddy, was headed for extinction and it was already too late to do anything about it. If you believed or even half believed him, then all human effort in the field of commerce, politics, the arts was pointless – the world was doomed because of the enormous damage man had already inflicted on the environment. Hearing him at his own dinner table, Jimmy, in one of his more morose moods, would find his spirits sinking. When he argued back, it became something of a shouting match, with Teddy going off in a huff. Teddy's politics were very different to Jimmy's. He hated what Mrs Thatcher stood for, regarded Ronald Reagan as a disaster, and scoffed at his brother's support for them.

Jimmy banned all talk of the environment when Teddy was around. 'I know all that, you've told me all that,' he would snap. 'You're boring me with all that.' Several times he left the table and there were months, even years, when he and Teddy barely spoke.

Teddy regarded his younger brother with a degree of awe. Their lives had diverged 30 years before, with Jimmy devoting himself to making money and Teddy to the search for an alternative, undestructive way of life which he pursued with much the same demonic energy as Jimmy devoted to business. As the rich member of the family, Jimmy had systematically taken on responsibility for cousins, aunts, his parents – even his eccentric brother. His early friends and his relatives on his mother's side were not rich, and he had paid debts, guaranteed overdrafts and provided regular allowances, the cumulative total running into millions. He was wryly amused one day in 1990 when his first cousin in France (who was 80) rang to ask how he was. When Goldsmith answered, 'rather poorly', she exclaimed: 'You cannot possibly die on us. Who would pay for the family funerals?'

By a curious coincidence, two television programmes broadcast in the same week in Britain in February 1990 pointed up the difference in vision of the two brothers. A programme called *Fragile Earth* on Channel Four had Teddy campaigning against the destruction of the globe in the name of profit, while Jimmy, interviewed by Anthony Sampson for *The Midas Touch* on BBC2 extolled the virtues of active investment. Whereas Teddy was arguing the case for the simple life, Jimmy told Sampson he found nothing offensive about conspicuous wealth.

> People are upset by vulgarity [he said], but vulgarity is to some degree a sign of vigour. It means that new people, coming from nowhere, are making it. It's the old American dream – anybody can become a millionaire. If we don't want vulgarity, what is the alternative? Either generalised wealth, which I don't think anyone is seeking, or the protection of privilege which means there is no change. If we want change, we're going to have to have vulgarity. It's one of the things which irritate which are necessary.

His image of the natural world was one in which predators were necessary in order to keep animals from becoming what he called 'degenerate' – very much as expounded to him over many years by Aspinall, and very much the way he believed the corporate world had to be run.

Both programmes used a leitmotif of New York skyscrapers rising out of a wasteland, with Teddy making a rather different point: the fact that seven million cars a year are junked in America, and that New York alone dumps 22,000 tons of rubbish each day confirmed his belief that 'there is no development without destruction.' The natural world, he insisted, was dying. 'This may sound dramatic but I think it's a perfectly realistic statement to make, and I'm not the only person who makes it. And it's dying fast, so fast that if current trends continue much of it will cease to be able to support complex beings like humans within decades.'

Despite their differences, Teddy's passion had long convinced his brother of the importance of environmental issues. Teddy, according to his younger brother, was 'more conventional than I was' for the first 28 years of his life. He became, he said, 'intellectually independent' at 28 when he found a subject that was to dominate the rest of his life. 'Teddy was the first person, in my view, to realise that we were destroying the world – that humans had gone mad and were destroying the very environment in which they lived.' At the time he was dismissed as a crank, because, as his younger brother remarked wryly, 'the only way in which the conventional majority can handle somebody who sees things they can't see is by calling them a crank. Some of his early disciples were John Aspinall and myself.'

In 1952 Teddy started gathering material for a work entitled 'The Theory of Unified Science', which was to remain unpublished, but which 20 years later had acquired a glossary of over 200 words unknown to anybody but Teddy. He was, he told friends, inventing a new language that would enable scientists to communicate with each other. 'Scientists,' he would say, 'are constantly barking up a gum tree because they cannot understand each other. They are looking at little bits of reality – that is why they can't perceive the whole. They are victims of their own specialised disciplines.'

In 1962, while still living in Paris, he began to gut anthropological, cybernetic and ecological works for what he intended as a gigantic seminal work which would shock the world. He studied deep into the night, reading and making notes, until he was almost buried by his material. At one stage, in all innocence, he advertised in the European edition of the New York *Herald Tribune* for a secretary 'for nocturnal services', and actually received hundreds of replies from girls who were astonished to discover that what he had in mind was taking dictation of his summaries of the great anthropological works of the past hundred years, working between the hours of 6 pm and midnight. Impressed by the response, a friend of his placed the same ad in the *Tribune* and married the secretary he chose. The story became one of Teddy's little jokes. 'It would be a morality tale but unfortunately they got divorced soon after – in Chicago, I believe.'

This was very much a private study by Teddy, a curiously lonely pursuit of a subject which others, including his brother, would find infinitely depressing in its conclusions, and which brought him much personal ridicule. Economic and industrial growth was the theme of the day, and Teddy seemed hopelessly out of step. But he ploughed on. By the late 1960s the investment in his brother's business had made him rich enough to return to Britain and buy a farm in Cornwall where he continued his studies. Then in 1970, his great work still unpublished, he set up the *Ecologist* magazine, backed by Jimmy, Aspinall, and a couple of other friends including Lord Londonderry and Richard King, chairman of the Pan Australian unit trust group. Teddy put up £20,000 of his own money. The first issue in July 1970 received considerable publicity, but interestingly none of the press reports referred to Teddy as 'the brother of Jimmy Goldsmith' as they invariably would a few years later. Teddy at that time was as well known as his brother, whose fame as the runaway playboy was now a yellowing pile of cuttings in newspaper vaults. The *Ecologist* received a fair amount of publicity, some of the reports poking a little gentle fun at Teddy who, looking like a bearded prophet of doom, was an easy enough target. But there was a serious undercurrent to much of the comment, a feeling of unease that he might just be right, although 20 years ago the environment was not the fashionable cause it is today. The magazine cover depicted a man struggling for life in a cesspool of his own waste, and it contained some dire warnings: the dangers of over-population in the Third World which would lead to untold pollution and starvation, unchecked urban development, and Teddy's belief, sharper today than it was then, that 'in food supplies and natural resources we are living off our capital'.

There was one particularly prescient warning in that first issue: an article which warned that if a nuclear reactor blew up it would produce a radioactive cloud several hundred times more lethal than those over Hiroshima and Nagasaki. In an interview with the *Sunday Times* Teddy talked frankly of the propaganda reasons for starting the magazine. 'I don't suppose I can get at the man in the street, but I think I might be able to get at the opinion makers – academic, communications, people in Parliament, people who read the *New Scientist*, the *New Statesman*, the *Spectator* and the *Sunday Times*.' The conclusion of the journalist gives a flavour of Teddy at the time:

'He's a bit of a dynamo is Goldsmith, a non-stop and non-stoppable talker. He might just rouse us out of our apathy about the dreadful things we are doing to the world we live in.'

In the 1960s and 1970s Jimmy financed various reports, including an Ecological Foundation report written by Hugh Montefiore, later Bishop of Kingston. He watched admiringly as Teddy's campaign gathered momentum. In 1971 Teddy published a book called *Can Britain Survive?*, which predicted an anarchical and feudal society as governments did everything they could to combat unemployment and inflation by increasing economic growth, while he argued that the only answer was to decentralise society into small, self-regulating groups. It has not turned out that way, but Teddy's fans would argue that he is simply ahead of his time, and that the underlying message still stands.

A year later he came out with his blueprint for survival, which he printed in the now struggling *Ecologist*, and was roundly condemned by, among others, *Nature*, for attempting 'to fan public anxiety about problems that have either been exaggerated or which are non-existent.' Influenced by Aspinall, he held a rally in the Royal Albert Hall to declare a state of emergency for world wildlife, calling for bans on whaling and on the import of skins of animals such as the clouded leopard, the tiger and snow leopard. He moved the magazine and his headquarters to his 300-acre farm in Cornwall which he ran as an ecological unit and in 1974 launched his own ecological party. Aspinall, in a jocular moment, promised to find him two camels which could be festooned with posters and ridden by Arabs to publicise it. Unfortunately Aspinall didn't have his own camels, and, as Teddy lamented, 'nobody seems anxious to lend us any'. The idea of having Arabs ride them, he added, was because 'Arabs are the only people who can afford to live here now'.

The influence of his brother and his best friend affected Jimmy Goldsmith in different ways through the 1970s and 1980s. For example, he gave £80,000 to help finance a film, later shown on BBC, about a tribe of Colombian Indians called the Kogi which had survived untouched and unscathed by the outside world, high in the mountains. When Goldsmith heard they had invited a camera crew in he was intrigued: the Indians wanted to send a message to their 'younger brothers' in the rest of the world, warning of what they were doing to themselves. Goldsmith thought it was wonderful.

He was also proud of a speech he made at a conference in Wolfson College, Cambridge, in 1976 on the subject of poison in food. He was one of the biggest food retailers in the world at the time, but the speech was an attack on the food industry, in particular on intensive farming. It was a technical speech, pointing out that animals laid down two kinds of fat: adipose storage fat, mainly consisting of non-essential saturated fats, and structural fats, rich in essential longchain polyunsaturated fatty acids. 'In free-ranging animals, there appears to be roughly one part of adipose fat to three parts of structural fat. In intensively reared animals, these figures seem to be reversed.' Yet adipose fat was associated with degeneration while structural fats contained 'high proportions of phospholipids, which are essential in the production of nerve tissue'. The brains and nerve structure of children fed on intensively farmed meat might not develop properly. No one knew what damage hormones fed to cattle did but 'autopsies on intensively bred animals make grisly reading'.

When, in 1977, Teddy told him about the dangers of a new oxide reprocessing plant to be built at the Windscale nuclear power station in Cumbria, in the north of England, Goldsmith was appalled. Teddy had achieved notoriety of a sort by that stage, and insisted on having his voice heard at the inquiry. His brother financed a campaign by the environment group Friends of the Earth, although their views on most issues were politically opposite to his. Teddy appeared at the inquiry into British Nuclear Fuel's proposal, to tell the inspector, Mr Justice Parker, that this would help 'the inevitable and fast approaching collapse of industrial society'. In seeking to reprocess Japanese nuclear waste, he argued with habitual vehemence, Britain had joined 'the ranks of the banana republics, whose political leaders are prepared to do dangerous, biologically destructive and socially destructive things for other, richer countries in order to earn quick money'. Pollution, he added, might add to the conditions in which industrial society would become no longer feasible. Damage was cumulative and exceeded the rate of natural recovery. Warming to what was already a familiar theme to readers of the *Ecologist*, he added that pollution was annihilating fish, stunting plant growth, contributing to the development of new diseases and affecting weather. He hadn't quite arrived at the 'greenhouse effect' stage but he was getting there.

By May 1977 brother Jimmy had had just about enough of his elder brother. As Teddy expounded on his new theory, 'De-Industrialising Society', which argued that the wages and productivity spiral should be ended by removing consumer durables from our lives (he also at the same press conference said he did not believe in Women's Lib), he was asked what Jimmy thought of all this. 'He respects my views,' he said. 'But he finds them depressing. He prefers jollier company to mine.' Later he would add, even more dolefully, 'I suppose he probably thinks we go too far.'

For all of that, 'Teddy was a huge influence on me – probably more than even he realises – because he opened my mind to the whole concept of the destruction of the environment,' says Jimmy. 'At the same time Aspinall started on his mission in life – to protect species of animals endangered by the destructive capacity of man. So on the one hand there was Aspinall protecting animals from man and on the other there was Teddy committed to exposing the destructive capacity of man in the environment in general.'

They could agree on a number of issues: they had an equal contempt for the ability of governments to do anything about the problems because their time horizon was too short. They also shared the view that in most countries politicians were both superficial and dishonest. 'Teddy and I also agree that the solution can't be provided by bureaucracies or corporate bureaucracies, because their principal task is to ensure the survival of their bureaucracy, not the survival of anything else,' says Jimmy. But there the level of their agreement ended. 'Basically he looks backwards and believes that the solution is to go back to more primitive societies,' says Jimmy. 'Whereas I'm absolutely convinced that you must go forward because you have no choice. And that going forwards is going towards a post-industrial society. In a post-industrial society it is just perhaps possible – I would put it no higher than that – that humans will start to learn that they have to live within nature and not abuse her.' Teddy was equally forthright about where they differed. 'The idea that it is by maximising one's personal short-term economic advantage that one can best contribute to the welfare and prosperity of our society is to me preposterous.'

And so they argued, fell out, came back together again, only to argue once more. During the 1970s, when *Private Eye* was pursuing him and he was at his most unpopular in the press, Jimmy's interest in environmental issues was barely acknowledged, and he made no fuss about it. Yet the clues were there, as for instance over the issue of nuclear power, supported strongly by the right, strongly opposed by both Goldsmiths. Teddy's argument that there would be a major accident with devastating effects for millions had persuaded Jimmy at an early stage. 'Teddy and Aspinall made me aware of the incredible folly of man, who received a world which was superb and wonderful – the result of millions of years of natural selection – and had then come to believe that it was no more than his plaything,' said Jimmy in an interview for the *Sunday Times* in 1989. 'The things I hate, like nuclear energy and genetic engineering, are simply symptoms of the hubris of man. They made me realise that this incredible arrogance would probably lead to disaster, that ultimately man was going to destroy the world.'

The problem with listening to Teddy was that if you allowed yourself to be persuaded, then you accepted there was not much future for anyone, and Goldsmith was too busy in the 1980s with his major deals to dwell too closely on that idea. Teddy had now sold his farm in Cornwall and moved to a house at the top of Richmond Hill from whence he ran *Ecology*, operating with a tiny staff of dedicated enthusiasts from the basement. He had married again, to a tall, willowy New Zealander and fellow-ecologist, Katherine James, only three years older than his daughter Dido. Typically for a Goldsmith, she had borne him a child before he was able to get his divorce and marry her. His daughter Clio had become, like her mother, a model and then an actress. Teddy travelled the world to speak at seminars, staged sit-ins at the United Nations over the rainforests, appeared on endless television shows to be interviewed in either English or French.

In 1986 three of Teddy's forecasts came true: AIDS arrived on the public scene in a dramatic way, the nuclear power station at Chernobyl blew up, and a hole was discovered in the ozone layer. 'He'd been predicting things like that for 30 years and they all happened in a single year,' said Aspinall with some awe. Jimmy was equally impressed, looking on his brother with a new respect.

The crash of 1987 drew Jimmy to Mexico and gave him the chance to create his own Teddy-style community which could survive, near the site of some of the most ancient civilisations, in the event of a holocaust, well away from nuclear fall-out and from AIDS. But those three years passed, and life was slipping away. 'The secret is to create new ambitions all the time,' he often said. But what new ambitions were there?

Early in October 1990, Jimmy Goldsmith was in New York when he read in the *Wall Street Journal* that his friend Rupert Murdoch was having problems. The markets around the world at that point had turned sharply against companies with high levels of debt, and at $10.6 billion, Murdoch's debt was greater than that of many third-world countries. Murdoch had assets too, and his profits still more than covered his interest payments, but recession in the United States, where he had expanded rapidly, and in Britain, where he had launched Sky Television and spent £650m on new printing presses in Wapping, Liverpool and Glasgow, left him very exposed.

Goldsmith watched with a detached interest the fall in the price of News Corporation shares, and its various debt issues. The whole world was entering recession and stock markets everywhere were falling, led by the mighty Japan which had already fallen 40 per cent in 1990 alone, 15 per cent in a single week in October. One of the companies most affected was News Corporation. From time to time Goldsmith had invested in the News Corp Swiss Franc convertibles, yielding 25 per cent, a level which recorded the market's pessimistic view of Murdoch's survival chances. The two men ran across each other occasionally, in the Concorde lounge, or at dinners, and at the lavish birthday party the American publisher Malcolm Forbes threw in Morocco for his seventieth birthday. But Goldsmith was not now looking for a re-entry into British publishing, and his interest in Murdoch's affairs, at least up until October, was that of a disinterested observer. The methods of the two men in running their companies were not dissimilar: both had, for different reasons, been keen to avoid dilution of their equity, both believed in borrowing to buy under-valued assets (Murdoch to a greater degree than Goldsmith) and then trusting to their own skills to prove themselves right, both were natural gamblers, instant and instinctive decision-makers, and they had been talked about in the same breath as leading predators for years. Their paths had crossed and re-crossed – in the bidding for *New York* magazine, the battle for Beaverbrook, the takeover of St Regis and much else. Over the years they had become friends, Goldsmith impressed with 'Rupert's courage' in his bold business decisions, Murdoch impressed by Goldsmith's ability to see the wider picture.

When Goldsmith left the market in the summer of 1987, Murdoch accelerated his takeover spree. On top of his $2.5 billion acquisition of the Metromedia television business from John Kluge, he had rushed on with a $3 billion takeover of Triangle, owners of TV Guide in America, bought from the former American ambassador to Britain, Walter Annenberg. He then added the business once run by his father, the *Melbourne Herald* and *Weekly Times* Ltd. in Australia, for another $2 billion. As if that were not enough, in the spring of 1989 he launched Sky Television in Britain, a hugely adventurous gamble that was soon losing him over £2m a week. At the same time, he re-equipped his print works around the world, and expanded the production of feature films from Twentieth Century Fox from six a year to 21. Most of it was paid for with borrowings, and, very seriously for Murdoch, he miscalculated the interest rate trends through 1990, believing they would come down in the early summer. The autumn of 1990 caught him with over $2.5 billion of short-term debt, with no hope of repaying it out of profits. And to crown it all, recession in the English-speaking markets, where almost all of Murdoch's newspapers and other interests were based, squeezed profits. Where once he used to pay back the banks by dispossing of assets, that autumn there were no buyers about, at least not at the prices Murdoch wanted.

In an article in the *Independent* (29 October 1990), the former *Times* editor (and no friend of Murdoch's) William Rees-Mogg summed up his position neatly: 'Every entrepreneur earns profit by being exposed to risk. If he is betting on red and black comes up three times running he ought, of couse, to be able to stand it; six times is more than he will expect; 12 times may be fatal even for the most prudent. Rupert Murdoch is living in a world in which black has already come up six times.'

Similar thoughts were running through Goldsmith's mind in New York as he read of yet another setback for Murdoch. The Australian-cum-American media baron owned, through family trusts, 44 per cent of News Corporation, and had consistently and fiercely refused to dilute it through the issue of new equity capital. Equally consistently the banks asked for it, arguing that his small equity base could not support such a huge debt structure. Now Murdoch came up with a new proposal: he would issue non-voting stock, in the same way that several of the big American publishing houses had done. This was equity capital in every sense of the word except for voting rights. Murdoch's ownership would be reduced but his voting power would not.

But when he proposed it there was an immediate uproar from the Australian Stock Exchange, from big shareholders in News Corporation and from the Australian press. The Australian Stock Exchange said it would not quote the shares and Murdoch retorted in that case he would de-list his company and keep his quotes in London and New York, thereby depriving the Australian stock market of probably its best-known company and one of its most actively traded stocks. There was nothing in the rules, Murdoch pointed out, against non-voting shares – it was just that there hadn't been any issued. The row would boil on for several weeks, until Murdoch got his way. But by that stage his share price had more than halved, and his problems were front-page news two weeks running in the *Wall Street Journal* and every other major paper around the world.

Murdoch was still fighting the Australian Stock Exchange when Goldsmith put a call through to him in London. An idea had gripped him and, without properly investigating the ramifications, he acted on the spur of the moment. For some time Goldsmith had been working on a plan for getting out of his forest interests without incurring too high a tax charge. One way was to swap his shares in the company that owned them for something else, such as a large slug of News Corporation shares.

Goldsmith no longer cared whether he had voting shares or not – he was almost unique in that sense. With this factor in his favour, he reasoned that Murdoch would give him a higher price than anyone else would and there would be no tax. In Murdoch's shoes he would leap at it: in a single move Murdoch would expand his capital base by $1.6 billion, alter all his debt-to-equity ratios without disturbing his own voting control, and bring in some solid assets into a business which largely consisted of intangibles. It would also have added $100m a year of profits to the Murdoch empire without raising the debt.

As events were to unravel, when Goldsmith called, Murdoch was in a meeting with bankers and his financial staff. If Goldsmith had said the matter was urgent, Murdoch, as is his wont, would have come instantly to the phone, but he didn't, and Murdoch's secretary suggested that Goldsmith should call again in a couple of hours at which stage Murdoch would be at his penthouse apartment in St James's Place, almost next door to Goldsmith's London house.

Punctiliously, Goldsmith rang back, as usual dialling the number himself. Murdoch's butler answered. Mr Murdoch, he said, was dining with a small group but had left instructions to be interrupted so he could take Sir James' call. He would go and fetch him. For no reason other than his natural politeness, Goldsmith demurred. No, he said, don't spoil his dinner. He would ring back again later in the week, there was nothing urgent.

He had not thought through the proposed deal beyond the point where he trusted Murdoch, believed that if anyone could pull through he could, and that this was the ideal time to acquire shares in News Corporation when they were flat on their backs. If Murdoch survived, the shares would double or treble, in which case, voting or non-voting, he would have transformed the book asset value of his forests into something between $3 and $5 billion. That would be the coup to end all coups. But what if Murdoch didn't survive?

That thought nagged at him as he got out the News Corporation accounts. There in graphic detail was the story of Murdoch's enormous burst of takeover activity written in debt terms. Short-term borrowing had risen from $600m to $2.8 billion in a year. The more he looked at it, the more horrified Goldsmith became. The debts were so large, he decided, that Murdoch was actually out of the danger zone – the banks dare not foreclose, in the same way they could not foreclose on, say, Brazil, because they could not afford the write-offs. It was Keynes' old adage that if you owe the bank £100, the bank controls you; but if you owe the bank a million pounds, you control the bank. If Murdoch's debts were half or one-third of their size, that would be real trouble for him. But as it stood, the banks would recognise that the best hope they had for getting their money back was to give Murdoch time to manage his way out of trouble. They would, of course, tie him down to ensure he made no further acquisitions, force him into more disposals, and basically reduce him to the point where he was working for the banks rather than for himself. But they would not force him into receivership, which technically they had the power to do, because of his inability to repay his short-term debt on time. As he read on, Goldsmith came to another abrupt conclusion: if Murdoch did buy the forests it would certainly help his balance sheet, but it would create an even more serious problem for him. By itself, the acquisition of the forest company would not be enough to save him, but it would improve his financial ratios to the point where the banks could risk closing him down. In other words, Goldsmith would be propelling him into the danger zone. Not only would Murdoch be finished, but Goldsmith would lose a large share of his personal fortune.

'If I had talked to Rupert that night,' said Goldsmith later, 'I believe he would have agreed to do the deal there and then, and I would have gone through with it.'

Deciding they had both had a narrow escape, in the following days he decided against calling Murdoch, and considered another plan. Lord Hanson and Sir Gordon (now Lord) White were having problems, although more of a technical hiccup than Murdoch-sized difficulties. In 1989 they paid over £3 billion for Consolidated Gold Fields, Britain's second-largest mining finance house. With it they acquired a 49 per cent stake in Newmont Mining, the largest gold-mining company in the United States. They had reshuffled and reshaped their acquisition in their usual deft manner, getting more than half their money back through disposals, leaving the rest in very cheaply. The Hanson duo had completed a complex financial operation revolving around Newmont, whereby they had bought its stake in one of America's biggest coal-mining companies, Peabody, to give them full control of that company. But their minority interest in Newmont remained, returning them $20m a year in dividend payments in a stake valued in the stock market at around $1.5 billion. It made no sense to bid for the rest of Newmont, since it would have diluted Hanson's earnings per share, and they found it impossible to reduce the holding through sales in the market – the gold share market is a narrow one and any large lines of stock would severely depress the share price. The Denver-based Newmont had itself been through considerable upheaval. It was heavily criticised for taking on debts of nearly $2 billion in an effort to fight off the unwelcome attentions of T. Boone Pickens, the Texas corporate raider, although it was able to repay them by concentrating the business on gold. Hanson had no wish to buy any more of Newmont, and in any case Newmont had first option to buy Hanson's 49 per cent stake – but no means of exercising it.

In September White thought he had found an elegant solution: the price of gold had risen sharply following Saddam Hussein's invasion of Kuwait, and seemed certain to rise higher. To White that was a time to sell rather than to buy, so he got his financial advisers to put together an offer of the entire Newmont stake which he would float on the stock market. It was by no means a risk-free exercise – the last Hanson flotation, in July 1989, had been the Smith-Corona typewriter business which, hit by Asian competition and a slump in the US typewriter market, had promptly slumped, leaving a sour taste, and the Newmont flotation was viewed with a degree of suspicion.

Luck was not on White's side. The crisis in the Gulf subsided in the first weeks of October, the oil price fell, and with it the price of gold. Newmont shares slid sharply lower, and White began to think about calling it off.

Then Goldsmith called. They had talked from time to time about Hanson buying Cavenham Forest Industries for several years, but at that stage it had been a straight sale, Hanson cash for Goldsmith trees. White had sent a team to carry out the usual thorough due diligence investigations, and had in his files a detailed report. But Goldsmith had, he reckoned, wanted too much for them. The Hanson speciality was to buy assets that others spurned, in unfashionable, low technology industries, and with a combination of disposals and better management, increase the return substantially. Goldsmith had done all that with the forests, acquired with both Diamond and Crown Zellerbach, and was not now a forced seller. So there had been no deal.

Now Goldsmith's proposal was a variation on his Murdoch thoughts: a swap of his forest company, not for cash, but for Newmont shares. The figures, he pointed out, were roughly in line. Cavenham Forests made a profit of $97m a year, five times what Hanson was getting out of Newmont, there was cash in the balance sheet rather than debt, and trees fitted well both into Hanson's business philosophy but also into its mix which included industries supplying the building industry. White went for it, as Goldsmith thought he would.

The next day White arrived in his office on Fifth Avenue, called off the Newmont flotation, and put his lawyers and bankers to work over the week-end. By Tuesday, 17 October 1990, they were able to announce a deal: Goldsmith would swap his 85 per cent stake in Cavenham Forest Industries for 41 per cent of Newmont; Jacob Rothschild, who controlled 15 per cent of Cavenham Forests, automatically received 15 per cent of the sale proceeds, giving him 7 per cent of the Newmont stake. The deal was worth $1.3 billion – and would be Goldsmith's last.

'I can't tell you what a joy it is to be out of business,' boomed Goldsmith that week-end. He was in Deauville, where he had gone, alone, to think about the deal and about what came next. Deauville, one of his childhood stamping grounds, was empty and out of season. Once he made up his mind, he had begun telephoning, first White in New York, then his advisers and finally the financial press. 'I've found a new virginity!' He was, he said, retiring from business. From now on he was devoting himself entirely to a new activity: saving the environment.

This announcement was greeted with blank disbelief in the City of London, along Wall Street and in the boardrooms of the hundreds of companies which had once so feared him. The headline writers had some fun with it: 'Mister Goldfinger turns green', or 'Sir Jimmy Greensmith'. There were, of course, many sceptics: 'But will the predator really change his spots?' asked Anthony Sampson in the *Independent*, while *The Times* expressed a different worry. Was capitalism compatible with greenery? it wondered. 'The natural reaction, as with all prophets, is to write this off as an act of mild dottiness,' it said, before going on to express the concern that too many other entrepreneurs might follow. 'In the scale of virtue, saving rainforests beats driving powerboats or swilling champagne with models in an effort to recapture one's vanished youth. The money is his, made fairly according to the rules of the game. If he chooses to spend it in this way, why not? At the same time, it is to be hoped that Sir James' career will not be followed by all of his ilk.' Otherwise who would create the wealth?

Goldsmith had once again made headlines around the world. Most commentators considered the switch from arch-capitalist to conservationist was an act of some eccentricity, but harmless enough; maybe it would do some good, it would certainly not do any harm. Only Teddy, perhaps, and Jimmy himself, his mind already whirring with plans of what he might do, were aware of how seriously Jimmy was taking his new role.

By a coincidence that week in October also saw publication of Teddy's latest work on the environment, a glossy book called *5000 Days to Save the Planet*, which was as gloomy as anything he had ever produced. His theme was this: 50 years ago the world's environment was still in balance, the rainforests and the ozone layer still intact. The world was vast, beautiful and powerful, seemingly beyond damage by man. Today, destruction and pollution could be seen everywhere, 'brought about by the heedless rush towards consumerism and commercial gain'. There was now a hole in the ozone layer, global warming and acid rain, getting worse by the day and by the hour. Yet governments were doing nothing to stop it, and unless concerted action was taken immediately, within 15 years it would be too late for mankind. As a species, man, like the many other species disappearing daily from the forests, was doomed to certain extinction. Teddy had not altered with age, even if his brother had.

The book, co-authored with three other ecologists, quoted Teddy's very first editorial in his *Ecologist* magazine written 20 years before: the termination of our industrial society within the lifetime of someone born in 1970 'is inevitable – unless it continues to be sustained by an entrenched minority at the cost of imposing great suffering on the rest of mankind.'

Without knowing what Jimmy was about to announce, Teddy that week held forth on the dangers of what lay ahead: the incidence of cancer was rising so rapidly that within a generation it would affect 100 per cent of the population. Water was becoming so precious that it would be dearer than champagne. Fertilisers and chemicals put in the soil were 'criminal' – they gave off gases which poisoned the atmosphere, destroyed the soil they were put on, and leaked into the rivers and lakes, destroying them too. In Teddy's view, the makers of nitrates and other fertilisers should be prosecuted – or worse. His day was now coming.

Back in Paris that week-end, Goldsmith was still bubbling with his new career. 'I'm back at work, which I haven't been for the past three years,' he said. He had, he added, been able to give himself the luxury to choose in a relatively relaxed frame of mind after three years of semi-retirement. But it was not something he was going to do casually. It would, he said, be full-time, active work. Everything he had done so far had been small. But not any more.

Jimmy Goldsmith had found what he had been searching for: a new ambition.

Epilogue

'The last hundred years have seen the greatest disaster this world has ever seen,' says Sir James Goldsmith. 'We have destroyed the environment and today everything is unimportant compared to the protection of the planet. All the struggles internally are relevant only if the planet itself survives. We have destroyed our seas, our air, our forests – and we will ultimately destroy ourselves. We are going to live in a world in which the only animals that survive are those that adapt to the horrors which we will have created.'

This gloomy message from one of the world's richest men explains better than anything his reasons for abandoning the world of business. What shall it profit a man if he shall gain the whole world, but can't breathe the air or drink the water? These thoughts were not of course new to him, but in late middle age, the more reflective Goldsmith could no longer see much point in building new businesses, or creating extra wealth for himself. His old friends – and enemies – would still ask: does he mean it? And he would answer with an emphatic 'yes' – followed by an earnest explanation for his change of direction. 'If we have any wisdom – which we haven't yet shown – we have the possibility of moving towards a post-industrial age, of creating a posterity and working circumstances which will allow us to try to put some of the things right that have gone wrong because of our shared responsibility.' Did that mean he was renouncing capitalism, too? No, the environmental damage done in the totalitarian regimes, he retorts, is even worse than that done in free enterprise countries. And there is a reason for that. 'It's not because one system is evil and the other is good. Where you have private enterprise and a free political system you have decentralisation, so when you have bad eggs they can only do a limited amount of damage because they only have a limited amount of power. But in a highly centralised totalitarian bureaucratic regime, the power at the centre is so great that the damage the same individual can do, if he is placed in the centre, is infinitely greater.'

This, he argues, particularly applies to nuclear energy, 'which in my view is one of the greatest dangers – it's Satan's energy. When people say, 'Ah, more people die in the coalfields than in nuclear plants,' that is perfectly true. And it's tragic that they should die in the coalfields, but they are individual, localised tragedies, whereas when the Chernobyls of tomorrow take place, they will be world tragedies.'

But if his commitment to the environment is genuine enough, there remains the question: what can he – or anyone – do about it? Goldsmith is probably the first modern entrepreneur to devote his energies and his fortune (which is probably of the order of $2 billion), to environmental causes. Given his record in the industrial world, his commitment has to be good news for all of us. In many ways, Goldsmith sees his new career as an extension of the old. 'I am convinced that despite some conflict, private industry and environmentalists are condemned to be allies because, with current levels of population, prosperity is necessary to heal the environmental and social wounds of the past as well as to plan for the future.'

When he retired from business, he had only a vague idea of how he would best apply himself. Even now, a year later, he says his ideas are only 'half-baked'. But his role is slowly emerging in his mind. 'When one grows older, one mustn't rely on energy, one mustn't rely on being a militant, or an activist, but on the other hand, certain skills that you lose are replaced by other things. It is not a blind alley.'

He knows about organisation, about the power of publicity, of the effect of well-placed articles and speeches – and how to harness the energy and goodwill he sees in the disparate and badly organised environmental lobby. He also has access to virtually unlimited funds – his own. He will not, he insists, hijack the environmental lobby, or steer it in directions environmentalists do not want. But he can focus it on a few select but important causes where something might be achieved, before going on to the bigger, more intractable issues, such as nuclear power and the rainforests.

He spent the spring and summer of 1991 closing down the remnants of his business empire, and preparing the way for his new role. Goldsmith has always been almost obsessive about tidying up as he has moved on. When he left Britain at the end of the 1970s, he kept no business interests other than his (passive) investment in Aspinall's club; similarly in France when he moved out of food, he did so completely. When he sold out of America before the 1987 crash, there were no half measures – everything, except his forests, went. Then when he retired, even the forests had to go. His investment in Newmont Mining was always an expedient for organising the sale of his trees, and within a few months he was in negotiation to swop his Newmont shares into the bigger gold mining company, American Carrick (it fell through). He spent months closing his various offices, retiring his staff and withdrawing from all active involvement in the world that had once fascinated him. He would still back people who interested him, but his role as an investor would be strictly 'passive'.

His industrial career had given him a degree of knowledge of the food and the chemical industry, and he now prepared to turn this against those industries which he felt were particularly destructive of the environment. He began with agriculture, where Teddy had for years been preaching the virtues of small farms. In a speech to the world Economic Forum in Davos on 5 February Goldsmith set out his objections to European agricultural policies, which he claimed were adding to the world's problems: large mechanised farms, encouraged in Europe by the Common Agricultural Policy and national government subsidies, had altered the balance and character of society, he said. 'To maximise production, you assemble larger farms, and reduce crop diversity to a minimum – monocultures are easier to mechanise. You intensify production using greater amounts of pesticides, chemical fertilisers, hormones and other devices and you create surpluses, the famous lakes and mountains, the storage and disposal of which, including export subsidies, account for about half of the European Community's agricultural budget and which, when dumped on other nations, do terrible damage to their rural and social traditions.'

But that was not all. Agricultural policies were driving more people off the land and into urban slums, destabilising the countryside and creating an alienated underclass in the cities. Goldsmith demanded that the funds should be redeployed from the big farms to the smaller, family units.

'When I look to the Third World, I shudder,' he said. The current GATT proposals on agriculture would stop the poor nations limiting the amount of food they imported, with the result that local agriculture and fisheries would be 'devastated by "cheap" imports from industrialised countries' which would be massively subsidised. 'Whole populations would be uprooted from their traditional communities and chased into urban slums.'

If Goldsmith had his way, the world's food would be produced entirely organically, from small, family farms. He was aware that was impractical.

But at least, he argued, the present trend could be arrested before it was too late.

The speech was reported, but not widely, and Goldsmith was finding entry into the environmental world far from easy. At one stage he decided on a bold course: something could be achieved quickly on the ozone layer. The big manufacturers of CFC gases had already acknowledged their products were harmful by agreeing to phase them out, but Goldsmith argued they were doing it too slowly. If the environmental groups got together and threatened to sue the companies and their individual directors, the process could be speeded up. Teddy got the environmental groups, including Friends of the Earth, to form a rough alliance, and Goldsmith outlined his proposal for major legal actions around the world. His plan was received with grave suspicion. How were they to know, asked one of his audience, that he was not just trying to knock the shares of Du Pont or ICI so that he could buy them cheaply? Goldsmith replied patiently that he had retired from business, and had no such intention. But, said another questioner, he was the major shareholder in Newmont Mining which was one of the biggest strip-miners of coal in America. How could he resolve that with his environmental crusade? Goldsmith tried to explain that Newmont had actually sold all its coal interests to Hanson, and in any case he was only a passive investor, but the audience was sceptical. When the same questions arose at the next meeting a few weeks later, he began to back away. Friends of the Earth were interested in his campaign, but told him they would prefer it if he were not associated with them. On the other hand, they needed his money, and would be grateful for a donation of $250,000. Goldsmith, by now nettled, pointed out that if his association was seen as an embarrassment, he would not further embarrass the organisation by giving it money.

On the agricultural front, he reckoned he was making some progress – although this was not easy either. In May 1991, he took a group representing most of the environmental groups to see the British Minister of Agriculture, John Selwyn Gummer, to tell him he was totally wrong in opposing European (actually Irish) proposals for switching the emphasis of support from the big efficient farms to the small inefficient ones. Gummer was not impressed, and the meeting ended stormily. But a few months later, Goldsmith was back again, armed with more facts, figures and argument. He formed a similar alliance of the various lobby groups in France, and began tentatively to contribute funds towards alliances in other countries. 'I think it will be an overwhelming lobby group for politicians, because there are millions of people in every country who feel strongly about the way agricultural policies are destroying the environment. And it will be a huge influence on national governments.' Goldsmith funded half the cost of setting up secretariats in Britain and France to run the agricultural campaigns, but the cost was tiny – this was an area where he found people worked out of conviction, and his role was to organise and focus them. In France, he got many of the mayors involved in his organisation. 'I really think it will be difficult for governments to take these situations on. I would fund a major campaign at election time, and they know that too.'

In the meantime he was pursuing more modest environmental goals. Cuixmala was part of his personal contribution – the protection of a sizeable part of what remained of Mexico's depleted dry tropical forest. In Burgundy, he created a centre for crafts near Montjeu, designed to bring skilled workers, dying out in France as everywhere else, back to the region. He planned a couple of organic farms 'just to see whether the figures work out', which he could use as a platform to argue the wider case for traditional-style farming.

All of this was done at a pace which by Goldsmith's former standards was positively leisurely. He seemed to become more patrician by the day, slow to rouse even to irritation, let alone anger. He was as sociable as ever, entertaining his friends in Mexico, Richmond, Burgundy or Paris, spending time with his children and with Annabel. He no longer cared what *Private Eye* and the newspapers said about him, realising, too late, that if he didn't care about them, they would soon stop caring about him. He moved through the salesrooms in Paris, London and New York, buying paintings and furniture for Montjeu whose enormous rooms – an almost uncountable number of them – required large quantities of furnishings. He also began something he had planned for years: the creation of a large library. Originally, he thought Mexico would be the place for this, but the climate there is hostile to wood, let alone books, even with air conditioning. Now he would build it in Montjeu.

At the debate on takeovers in the Bank of England the previous year, Sir John Harvey-Jones, the former chairman of ICI, had turned to him and asked, 'What monument will you leave, Sir James?' Goldsmith replied that he didn't believe in businesses as monuments: 'Businesses have to be alive, not dead like monuments.' Building a monument to yourself, he went on, was an ego trip, and an extraordinary definition of a business. 'I am absolutely convinced that you can be useful to a company for a limited period, and then no longer,' he said later. 'Take Grand Union, for example. There was a period of incredible innovation, and then bit by bit my contribution diminished as innovation came to an end. I used to go to meetings in the beginning and there would be thirty-seven points to be followed up. Later, I would make one point while summing up. Anyone who stays with a company all his life is in fact staying out of fear, because their image, their position in life, is linked to that company.'

These thoughts made him more philosophical still as he built his library. Posterity would not have much interest, he reckoned, in Sir James Goldsmith, whatever he did or said. Any biography of him would, in a few years time, be just another book in his library. 'It takes between forty and fifty thousand books. In my whole life I have assembled, in all my houses, about 7,000 books, and I always thought that was a lot of books. To get together 40–50,000 books is a huge task, which I am doing and rather enjoying. Dealers in France send me lists, and I see this plethora of biographies of people who were no doubt significant in some way, and have now faded into complete obscurity. I don't expect to do anything else.'

Does that matter to him? 'Matter or not, it is a fact.' Would he like to have done something different with his life? Goldsmith hates retrospection, but does have one regret. 'Suppose I had been born without an appetite for riches, or with sufficient riches so as not to have to worry about it, I would have gone into politics. I would have gone into politics in any case, if there hadn't been a war and I had not been uprooted from France during a period which was extremely formative, between the ages of six and twelve. I was biologically unacceptable to the political world in the UK – I would never have been able to behave as the British public like their politicians to behave. On the other hand I could have gone into politics in France. But when I got back to France after the war I was a foreigner forever, as I was in Britain when I arrived. Even though I'm bilingual, I hate making speeches in French, although I can do it when the adrenalin is running. English is my mother tongue.'

He would have been, he says, a 'conviction politician', doing things he believed in. 'I need to believe in something in order to do it. I have to work myself into a feeling that what I'm doing is for a wider cause, even if I'm doing it for financial reasons. Even the takeovers, I believed that what I was doing was right, and I still do.'

At the end of July 1991, Goldsmith presided over one of the happier events of his life: the wedding of his second daughter, Alix. Goldsmith gave a grand reception at his château in Burgundy, where the restoration work was almost finished. For the first time, it was a full family occasion: Ginette, the mother of the bride, was there with her son Manes. Isabel had helped her half-sister choose her dress, and was now in attendance. Laure was in residence at the Montjeu château, with her two children, Charlotte and Jethro. And Annabel ventured into Laure's domain, bringing her children with her.

Goldsmith's original objective of restoring the family fortune had long been accomplished. Here, at Montjeu, he had a house worthy of any nineteenth-century Rothschild. There were plenty of younger Goldsmiths to carry on the dynasty. Goldsmith should have been as content on that day as he had ever been. But is anyone ever content for long? 'I have great pleasure in what I have done,' he says. 'But I've only been successful in a very limited way. Any normal person should be dissatisfied with what they have achieved, no matter what they have done. The greatest critic should be yourself.'

Bibliography

Aspinall, John. *The Best of Friends*. Macmillan, London, 1976.

Bruck, Connie. *The Predators Ball*. Simon and Schuster, New York, 1988.

Callaghan, James. *Time and Chance*. Collins, London, 1987.

Chester, Lewis and Fenby, Jonathan. *The Fall of the House of Beaverbrook*. André Deutsch, 1972.

Clutterbuck, David and Devine, Marion. *Clore*. Weidenfeld & Nicolson, 1987.

Cowles, Virginia. *The Rothschilds*. Weidenfeld & Nicolson, 1973.

Davis, Richard. *The English Rothschilds*. Collins, London, 1983.

Evans, Harold. *Good Times, Bad Times*. Weidenfeld & Nicolson, 1983.

Fallon, Ivan, and Srodes, James. *Takeovers*. Hamish Hamilton, London, 1987.

Frantz, Douglas. *Mr Diamond*. Bloomsbury, London, 1987.

Goldsmith, James. *Counter Culture*. Privately published in Great Britain, 1985. Distributed by W. H. Allen & Co.

—*Counter Culture* Volume 2. Privately published in France, 1988.

—*Counter Culture* Volume 3. Privately published in Great Britain, 1990.

—*Counter Culture* Volume 4. Privately published in Great Britain, 1991.

Gordon, Charles. *The Two Tycoons*. Hamish Hamilton, London, 1984.

Iacocca, Lee. *Talking Straight*. Bantam Books, New York, 1988.

Ingrams, Richard. *Goldenballs*. Private Eye Productions, Londo[n, 1979.]

Jay, Douglas. *Sterling*. Sidgwick & Jackson, London, 1985.

Jenkins, Simon. *The Market for Glory*. Faber and Faber, L[ondon, 1986.]

Johnston, Moira. *Takeover: The New Wall Street Warrio[rs. Arbor House,] 1986.

Kessler, Ronald. *The Richest Man in the World; The Story of Adnan Khashoggi*. Warner Books, New York, 1986.

Masters, Brian. *The Passion of John Aspinall*. Jonathan Cape, London, 1988.

Michel, Allen and Shaked, Israel. *Takeover Madness*. John Wiley & Sons, New York, 1986.

Munster, George. *Rupert Murdoch: A Paper Prince*. Viking, 1985.

Pincher, Chapman. *Their Trade is Treachery*. Sidgwick & Jackson, London, 1981.

Sampson, Anthony. *Anatomy of Britain*. Hodder & Stoughton, London, 1962.

The Midas Touch. Hodder & Stoughton, London, 1989.

The Changing Anatomy of Britain. Hodder & Stoughton, London, 1982.

Slater, Jim. *Return to Go*. Weidenfeld & Nicolson, London, 1977.

Stern, Fritz. *Gold and Iron*. Allen & Unwin Ltd., London, 1977.

Tolchin, Martin and Susan. *Buying into America*. Times Books, New York, 1988.

Wansell, Geoffrey. *Tycoon: The Life of James Goldsmith*. Grafton, 1986.

Wilson, Derek. *Rothschild: A Story of Wealth and Power*. André Deutsch, London, 1988.

Wesker, Arnold. *Journey into Journalism*. Writers and Readers Publishing Cooperative, London, 1977.

Whitcomb, Noel. *A Particular Kind of Fool*. Quartet Books Ltd, London, 1990.

Index